Life along the Inner Coast

Life along

THE UNIVERSITY OF NORTH CAROLINA PRESS

CHAPEL HILL

ROBERT L. LIPPSON ✤ ALICE JANE LIPPSON

the Inner Coast

A Naturalist's Guide to the Sounds, Inlets, Rivers, and Intracoastal Waterway from Norfolk to Key West

This book was published with the assistance of Progress Energy.

The paper in this book meets the guidelines for
permanence and durability of the Committee on
Production Guidelines for Book Longevity of the
Council on Library Resources.

The University of North Carolina Press has been a
member of the Green Press Initiative since 2003.

Library of Congress Cataloging-in-Publication Data
Lippson, Robert L.

Life along the inner coast : a naturalist's guide to
the sounds, inlets, rivers, and intracoastal waterway
from Norfolk to Key West / Robert L. Lippson and
Alice Jane Lippson.

p. cm.

Includes bibliographical references and index.

ISBN 978-0-8078-3303-2 (cloth : alk. paper)

1. Natural history—Atlantic Coast (U.S.) 2. Intracoastal waterways—Atlantic Coast (U.S.) 3. Coastal
ecology—Atlantic Coast (U.S.) 4. Mangrove ecology—
Atlantic Coast (U.S.) 5. Barrier island ecology–Atlantic
Coast (U.S.) 6. Atlantic Coast (U.S.)—Environmental
conditions. I. Lippson, Alice Jane. II. Title.

QH104.5.A84L57 2009

578.75'10916348--dc22   2009016645

13 12 11 10 09   5 4 3 2 1

We dedicate this book to our mentors
and cherished friends who have inspired us
throughout our lives:

T. Wayne Porter
Michigan State University

Ranice Crosby
Johns Hopkins University

Romeo J. Mansueti
Chesapeake Biological Laboratory
(former husband of Alice Jane Lippson
who died at age forty in 1963)

L. Eugene Cronin
Chesapeake Biological Laboratory

William Hargis Jr.
Virginia Institute of Marine Science

Contents

Preface

A little over 100 years after Captain John Smith and his fellow crew members settled along the marshy shores of the James River, colonists began planning canals that would link the Chesapeake Bay with Albemarle Sound to the south. In fact, in the early 1760s, a company called the Dismal Swamp Adventurers, which was owned by George Washington and a few associates, dug the first canal, the "Washington Ditch," to transport cypress and juniper logs from the heart of the Dismal Swamp. By 1805 a shallow draft canal had been dug that linked Deep Creek near Norfolk with the Pasquotank River, which flowed into Albemarle Sound. Then in 1859, a rival group completed the Albemarle and Chesapeake Canal, which connected Hampton Roads through the North Landing River into Currituck Sound and then into the Albemarle. But the two competing companies suffered financial woes and as a result had difficulty improving their facilities.

In 1912 the federal government purchased the Albemarle and Chesapeake Canal and in 1925 purchased the badly silted Dismal Swamp Canal and began the costly process of upgrading both canal systems. Canals were widened and deepened and weary bridges were replaced, and boat traffic then began increasing in the toll-free Intracoastal Waterway. Tugs and barges carrying lumber and other commodities shared the waterway with passenger steamers on their routes from Norfolk to the southern ports of Elizabeth City and Beaufort, North Carolina, and by the mid-1900s, increasing numbers of private sailboats and motor yachts began cruising south to Florida in the fall and north in the spring.

The Inner Coast between Norfolk and Key West in the 1900s up until about the 1970s was sparsely settled; oh, to be sure, there were the ports of Norfolk, Beaufort, Charleston, Savannah, and Miami, but there were few towns in between, and most of those towns were sleepy little watermen's communities where boats tied up at the shrimp docks. Hilton Head Island was only just being developed, and heavily wooded Daufuskie Island, lying just south of Hilton Head, was a land from another time, with only a small community of homes, most owned by Gullah people.

This was about the same time that more and more people were being attracted to the coasts: the Pacific, the Gulf of Mexico, and the Atlantic. Some moved permanently into developing communities; others lived part-time in condominiums; and many others were seasonal visitors in resorts, hotels, and other rental properties. The migratory trend of humans has not diminished, and some studies indicate that more than 60 percent of the U.S. population now lives within 50 miles of our coasts. They come for the warmer climate, for fishing, boating, and golfing. Because their friends and families have already moved to the coast, they are beckoned to "come on down."

There are fewer and fewer sleepy villages along the Inner Coast; now there are gated communities and "look at me" houses nestled on the edges of wetlands and in some cases on former wetlands. Islands in the Lowcountry of South Carolina and Georgia are being recast as the perfect places for retirement, replete with shopping centers, golf courses, and marinas. The profusion of homes and shopping malls and schools and recreational areas and the new roads to connect them has resulted in a sprawling "coastalopolis." Millions have relocated to the coast because they love it, and now our coast is being loved to death. There are few among us who really want to destroy our environment; we just want to improve it, and those improvements have resulted in a tyranny of small decisions. All of the habitats and the plants and animals that live in and along the Inner Coast are at peril, and so we have written this book so that others will learn about the wonders of these waters and perhaps begin to forge a fierce resolve to maintain this wonderful place and the plants and animals that make it so special. We too love this region; we have lived in Chesapeake Bay for many years, and one of us was raised in south Florida, so we are quite aware of why so many want to live along the Inner Coast.

A book such as this one, which covers so many species of plants and animals and the habitats in which they live along the Inner Coast from Norfolk, Virginia, to Key West, Florida, is built on the work of many others. It gives us great pleasure to publicly thank our friends and colleagues who have been so helpful on this very long cruise through the Inner Coast.

Jack G. Goellner, director emeritus of the Johns Hopkins University Press, has always been closely involved with our publications at the Hopkins Press, and when the time came to seek a publisher for *Life along the Inner Coast*, Jack stepped forward and encouraged us, made contacts, and provided the introductions to the wonderful folks at the University of North Carolina Press. Jack, we are forever grateful for your wise counsel and warm friendship. As one

of his successors proclaimed, "Jack thinks outside the dust jacket."

Yates and Mavis Barber are two very dear North Carolinians who have opened their home to us in Elizabeth City and their fish camp in Maple on Currituck Sound. Yates has accompanied us through the inky waters of the Dismal Swamp and the Pasquotank River aboard our trawler *Odyssey*, regaling us with nonstop facts and lore about his beloved North Carolina. Yates knows what he is talking about, as he is a very good environmental biologist. Lloyd Culp, former refuge manager of the Great Dismal Swamp National Wildlife Refuge, was kind enough to take us up Washington Ditch in his skiff to the heart of the Great Dismal: cypress-lined Lake Drummond. He was most helpful, as was a fellow U.S. Fish and Wildlife Service biologist stationed at Alligator River National Wildlife Refuge, just south of Albemarle Sound.

The National Marine Fisheries Service laboratory on Pivers Island in Beaufort, North Carolina, has been our homeport on many occasions. The director, Dr. Ford "Bud" Cross (now retired), and his staff were very helpful, from allowing us to dock our trawler at the pier and providing a small boat and other equipment so that we could collect specimens on Shackleford Banks and Carrot Island to inviting us to their homes: Joe Smith, a menhaden expert, showed us where the cobias were, and Ann Manooch spent an inordinate amount of time helping us in the lab library. Our very good friends Carolyn and Dr. Hoss (also a former director of the Beaufort lab) gave us a great deal of their time and help, including leading some expeditions into the field to bird and to photograph plants. Dr. Doug Wolfe and his wife Nancy made us feel at home while Doug helped us with the identification of some mollusks with the aid of his impressive collection. Dr. John and Nancy Merriner, Dr. Gordon Thayer, and others of the Beaufort laboratory staff were remarkably cooperative, and we very much appreciate their help and friendship.

Gloria Hillenburg, the "Turtle Lady of Ocean Isle Beach, North Carolina," is the coordinator of the Sea Turtle Watch Program on Ocean Isle Beach. Gloria is an exuberant woman with a passion for sea turtles and sharing information about them.

Our good friend and longtime colleague Dr. Fred Holland, director of the National Oceanic and Atmospheric Administration Hollings Marine Laboratory and former director of the South Carolina Department of Natural Resources laboratory in Charleston, was amazingly patient and helpful to us, and we are appreciative for his help and the friendship of both Fred and his wife Helen. We thank George Riekerk, Drs. Elizabeth and Charles Wenner, and many others on the staff who answered our pesky questions and always pointed us in the right direction.

Our visit to the University of Georgia Marine Institute at Sapelo Island was short but fruitful. Short because there was a hurricane heading for the area and many of those on the island were about to leave for the mainland as we arrived, and fruitful because we had the opportunity to meet with Mary Price and the lab librarian, who were immensely helpful even though they were a bit harried about the gathering storm.

We thank Dr. R. Grant Gilmore, a world expert on the fishes of the Indian River Lagoon, formerly with Harbor Branch Oceanographic Institute. Grant, along with Dr. Mary Rice, former director of the Smithsonian lab, visited us on our boat that was tied up to the Smithsonian Marine Station pier. We thank them both for their kindness and hospitality; they were helpful, just as all the other scientists and local experts were whom we visited along the Inner Coast.

The beautiful village of Islamorada, located on Upper Matacumbe Key, not only is surrounded by gin-clear, turquoise water, coral reef patches, mangroves, and seagrass meadows but also has a small but very well stocked library and a warm and helpful staff whom we are very pleased to thank for their help and interest.

Dr. Richard Snider of Michigan State University advised us on the little-known seashore springtail and held forth many a time on invertebrates in general.

Our good friend, Cap'n Ed "Snoozer" Watson, has been so very helpful on this long journey. He has boated us through the mangroves in Marathon in search of periwinkles and tunicates with infinite patience and good humor, and he has provided us with an assortment of underwater pictures, one of which introduces the chapter on weed beds and seagrass meadows.

We love the poetry of the "Bard of the Chesapeake," Tom Wisner, and that of Russell Flynn Jr., which is evocative of the Inner Coast. We are pleased that they allowed us to share their words and observations.

We are very pleased to acknowledge with our deepest thanks the efforts and patience of David Perry, assistant director and editor in chief of the University of North Carolina Press; Zachary Read, assistant to David Perry; Paula Wald, associate managing editor; Heidi Perov, design and production manager; and Dino Battista, senior director of marketing. We thank Anna Laura Bennett for her wonderful job of editing our manuscript.

Finally, we take great pleasure in introducing a brilliant new illustrator, our granddaughter, Anna Radcliffe Mansueti, who drew the wonderful illustration of the manatees.

Life along the Inner Coast

Introduction

This is a guidebook to the plants and animals of the watery realm that extends from the temperate climes of southeast Virginia to subtropical Key West, Florida. We call this beautiful, ever-changing system of sounds and rivers and wetlands the Inner Coast. We use the term "Inner Coast" to depict a very special area, a beautiful and varied country that can best be appreciated by spending some time along its meandering shores, boating, fishing, birding, or just enjoying. The Inner Coast, with all of its rivers, backwaters, sounds, and inlets, is a place of discovery. In many areas there is an overwhelming feeling of remoteness, and yet it is very close to many major cities.

This is a diverse region 1,243 miles long, bounded on the east by barrier islands and on the west by sounds, bays, lagoons, and vast wetlands up to the head of tidal freshwater. The 1,243 miles is a linear measure, as the gull flies, of the coast from Norfolk, Virginia, to Key West, Florida. But that only begins to suggest the actual shoreline of the Inner Coast. Consider the tidal shorelines of the many rivers and hundreds of creeks, bays, sounds, and lagoons within the Inner Coast, and it becomes apparent that the borders along the various bodies of water measure in the thousands of miles.

Stretching from the Chesapeake Bay to the Florida Keys, the Inner Coast is a giant mixing bowl of freshwater and saltwater containing a rich broth of nutrients and organisms that, perhaps, is one of the most productive regions, anywhere.

Embedded in this great watery realm is the Atlantic Intracoastal Waterway, the AICW, more commonly known as the ICW or the Inland Waterway, and by some as the Ditch. The Ditch provides a convenient way to explore many parts of the Inner Coast and a physical link among its many distinct regions and river systems. The ICW starts at mile marker 0 at the foot of West Main Street in Norfolk or, more precisely, at nun buoy 36 in the Southern Branch of the Elizabeth River, and ends at Key West, Florida.

The Atlantic coast of the United States from the mouth of the Chesapeake Bay to Key Biscayne, Florida, is low and sandy compared to the rockbound coast of New England. Beyond Cape Florida, at the southern tip of Key Biscayne, near Miami, the coast breaks up into a group of islands known as the Florida Keys, a 134-mile chain of sand, shell, and coral islands and mangrove islets.

The gradual gradation from cooler to warmer temperatures, going from north to south, greatly affects the distribution of plants and animals. Oysters give way to other hard-bottom, or live-bottom, communities, such as sabellid worm rocks and coral reef assemblages, and mangroves begin to dominate the shorelines as salt marshes decline.

But then there are plants and animals that are widely distributed and tolerate various salinities and temperatures, as well as soil types and other factors. Some species, such as the blue crab, thrive throughout the Inner Coast region; the live oak and saw grass can be found from Virginia to Florida as well. Birds,

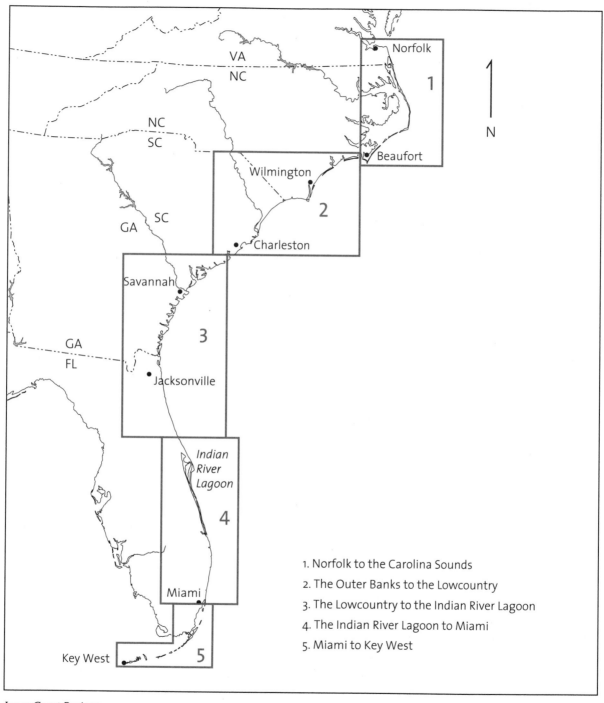

Inner Coast Regions

1. Norfolk to the Carolina Sounds
2. The Outer Banks to the Lowcountry
3. The Lowcountry to the Indian River Lagoon
4. The Indian River Lagoon to Miami
5. Miami to Key West

however, have adapted a different strategy: they migrate. Oh, to be sure, there are many bird species that do not travel immense distances. The brown pelican comes to mind. During the summer months, this familiar bird can range along the Atlantic coast, from New Jersey south, but as the summer wanes, it retreats southward to winter in the Carolinas and down along the coast to Florida and the Gulf of Mexico.

Some species of plants and animals are adapted to certain combinations of salinity (salt content) and temperature, and some to water depths or bottom types.

One of the most important factors in understanding the ecology of the rivers, estuaries, and sounds of the Inner Coast is the distribution of salinity throughout the system. Unlike the offshore waters of the ocean, where salinity varies little over a broad area, the Inner Coast is a vast, interconnected chain of estuaries and lagoons, large and small, that range from freshwater to high-salinity water. In fact, that is the very essence of an estuary: a bay, or sound, where a river meets the sea, with resultant gradations of salinity from very salty water to freshwater. Scientists often describe the type of estuary along the Atlantic coast as somewhat restricted embayments in which the flow of freshwater mixes with high-salinity ocean water. Salinity is a measure of a complex of salts present in the water and is expressed as parts per thousand (ppt). The salinity of offshore water is approximately 35 ppt, or 35 parts of salt to 1,000 parts of water.

The coastal plain from Virginia through Georgia extends from the shoreline westward to where the land rises at the fall line, and to where the rivers become estuaries as they flow toward their destiny, the Atlantic Ocean. Florida does not have appreciable elevations and is almost entirely within the coastal plain. Consequently, tidal excursions in rivers in Florida, such as the Saint Johns River, extend to a point in the river where the tide diminishes, turns, and begins to ebb. In the states north of Florida, the tides extend up the rivers to the geological fall line, where the waters are fresh and yet tidal influence is still apparent. Salinity increases downstream as freshwater mixes with the saltwater flowing through the inlets from the sea.

Deeper waters may be somewhat saltier at the bottom than at the surface. A number of physical and geographic factors contribute to this phenomenon, the most significant being that saltier ocean water is heavier, or denser, than freshwater and sinks and lies along the bottom, under the lighter, freshwater lens. In addition, the Coriolis force, a product of the earth's rotation, spins the water to the east, which results in somewhat saltier water on the eastern side of some of the larger estuaries. Also in some larger estuaries, high discharges of freshwater from mainland rivers can result in fresher waters along the western shores and somewhat saltier waters along the eastern margins of the sounds and bays.

Varying salinities in Inner Coast waters create a wide range of suitable habitats for both freshwater species and many ocean species. The upper reaches of most estuaries are fresh to brackish and provide habitat for many freshwater species as well as estuarine species of fishes and invertebrates, whereas ocean species are commonly found in lower estuaries near the inlets to the sea. Those species with the greatest tolerance for salinity changes, called euryhaline species, can be widely distributed in an estuary. Thus certain euryhaline freshwater species, such as the yellow perch and the brightly colored pumpkinseed sunfish, may be found well downstream in salinities as great as 10 ppt, and euryhaline marine species, such as the spot and the Atlantic croaker, may be found in upstream waters that are nearly fresh. No matter what the habitat—a beach, a marsh, an intertidal mudflat—salinity determines, to a large extent, the kinds of species that live there.

> The day is brisk
> The air is sweet
> The miles they pass
> Beneath my feet
> Slipper shells
> And angel wings
> In an empty whelk
> The ocean sings.
> —From "The Walk to False Cape"
> by Russell F. Flynn Jr.

Exploring the Inner Coast

We have divided the Inner Coast into five regions that reflect the differing characteristics of the coast, including the transition from the Temperate Zone to the Subtropical Zone. The regions are as follows: region 1, Norfolk, Virginia, to Beaufort, North Carolina; region 2, Beaufort, North Carolina, to Charleston, South Carolina; region 3, Charleston, South Carolina, to Indian River Lagoon, Florida; region 4, Indian River Lagoon, Florida, to Miami, Florida; and region 5, Miami, Florida, to Key West, Florida.

From Norfolk, Virginia, to the Carolina Sounds

Wandering down the Inner Coast, whether by boat down the ICW or by car down the old coastal highway U.S. 17, there is water and there are wooded shorelines everywhere. Below Norfolk, the boater heading south has a choice of routes: the Albemarle and Chesapeake Canal, usually called the Cut, or the Dismal Swamp Canal. Here the river is lined with thick stands of trees and fringing marshes and old tugs, barges, and menhaden clippers left to molder in little backwater pockets. Marsh hibiscuses nod their white and pink heads along the edge of the river, and small stands of thin red maples, interspersed by tulip poplars and black gums, grow on the small rises above the marshlands. Here and there, cypress trees stand sentinel, often bearing rough, twiggy nests of young ospreys.

The majority of boats, both recreational and commercial, use the Virginia Cut route, as the channel is deeper and wider than the Dismal Swamp Canal. But for sheer beauty and closeness to natural surroundings, the Dismal Swamp is the preferable route. The Great Dismal Swamp is a place of undeniable beauty; its dark, placid, mirrorlike waters reflect the surrounding dense forest bordering the canal and the banks of the Pasquotank River. The shorelines of the Dismal Swamp and the many rivers that dissect these low-lying lands are not generally distinct—there are few beaches or bluffs—but the shorelines are marked by a vanguard of bald cypress, tupelos, red maple, and other water-tolerant species. Inky water swirls around the swollen bases of the trees and disappears into the interior of the swamp, where at some point a slight elevation in land occurs, and other plant species, such as Atlantic white cedar, sweet gum, water oak, sweet bay magnolia, and pond pine, take hold.

The U.S. Fish and Wildlife Service manages 106,000 acres of the swamp, which is accessible by road as well as by boat. There are contiguous swamplands that are not officially included in the Great Dismal Swamp National Wildlife Refuge but are important components of the swamp ecosystem. Lake Drummond lies almost in the center of the swamp and is the liquid, amber-colored heart of the Dismal Swamp system. There are lush growths of devil's walking stick and titi and entanglements of grapevines and poison ivy everywhere along the banks of the Dismal Swamp Canal and the Pasquotank River. Turtles, basking in the sun, line up on half-submerged

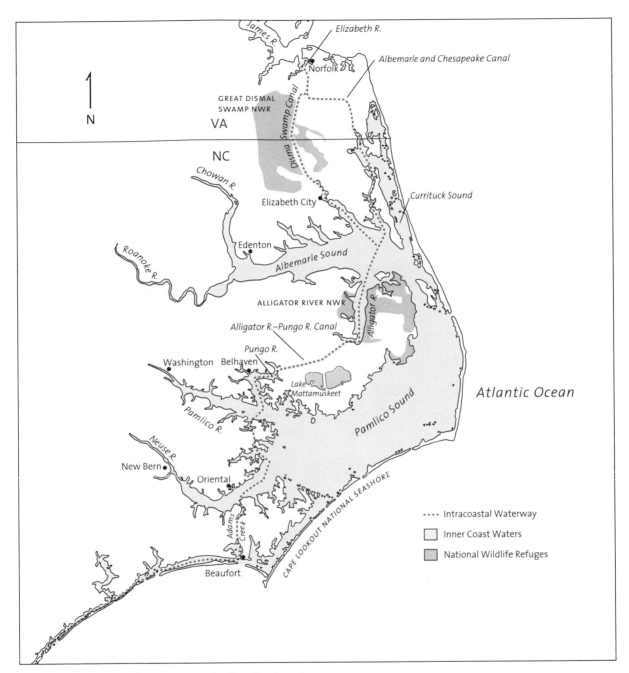

Coastal Region 1: Norfolk, Virginia, to the Carolina Sounds

trees; pileated woodpeckers "thunk" on tree trunks deep in the woods; and little, sunny yellow prothonotary warblers flit along the edges of the swamp. There are snakes aplenty, from canebrake rattlers, cottonmouths, and copperheads to small, harmless worm snakes, twenty-one species in all. And there are bears. Approximately 300 to 400 black bears call the Great Dismal Swamp home.

The Dismal Swamp route continues through the dark-stained, forest-lined Pasquotank River to Elizabeth City, North Carolina, and beyond into Albemarle Sound. Bald cypress, black gum, red maple, sycamore, and river birch are some of the trees along the shorelines of the Dismal Swamp, the Pasquotank and Chowan rivers, and the Alligator River–Pungo River Canal. These trees also line the edges of the North Landing River in Virginia and the shorelines of Currituck Sound and Albemarle Sound, as well as the rivers that flow along the western margins of the Inner Coast, such as the Chowan, Perquimans, Pasquotank, and Neuse rivers, to name but a few. There are many smaller tributaries as well that connect to the southern shores of Albemarle, including the Scuppernong River, near Columbia, North Carolina, and the Roanoke River, just west of the Scuppernong. Rockyhock Creek, Queen Anne Creek at Edenton, and Little River are some of the tributaries that flow into Albemarle Sound from the north; all of these streams, some entirely freshwater and some brackish, are lined with bald cypress, magnolias, and loblolly bay and are populated by many species of amphibians and reptiles.

The Great Dismal Swamp and the Alligator River National Wildlife Refuge are notable, but there are several more areas that contain a variety of freshwater and saltwater habitats, wooded swamps, open savannas, and piney woods and pocosins. The Northwest River Marsh, a freshwater area that drains into the North Landing River and Currituck Sound, is only one of many areas that is a wonderful combination of wet woods, marsh, swamp, and standing or tidal waters. Saw grass, the same species that typifies the Florida Everglades, grows here and is colorfully punctuated by pink and white marsh hibiscuses with a backdrop of wild rice and big cordgrass. Redwinged blackbirds love to nest and sing in these open areas; tree swallows streak after insects over the water and over marshes along the edge of the woods. Nearby, herons and egrets stalk along the shallows slowly, carefully, craftily moving and searching for fishes and frogs for dinner.

Lake Mattamuskeet, a large lake just to the west of Pamlico Sound, has a profusion of hooded pitcher plants growing in the canals and wet ditches along its perimeter. The lake has a large population of nonnative, but here to stay, mute swans, and beneath their large webbed feet swim crappie and other members of the sunfish family, white perch, and striped bass introduced from nearby sounds such as the Pamlico. There are many wildlife management areas in the coastal plain of North Carolina; some are state owned and managed, and others are under the jurisdiction of the U.S. Fish and Wildlife Service.

From the Outer Banks to the Lowcountry

The ICW route leaves the broad sounds of North Carolina behind and now follows a series of dredged channels and small sounds through shallow waters and by a number of ocean inlets. Narrow barrier islands with sandy beaches on the ocean side and salt marshes on the bay side shelter the Inner Coast. The mainland side along Bogue Sound is lined with loblolly pines and live oaks and many, many homes. Bogue Banks, lying along the ocean, is lined with homes and vacation resorts and interspersed with sculptured maritime forests shaped by the forces of wind, sand, and salt.

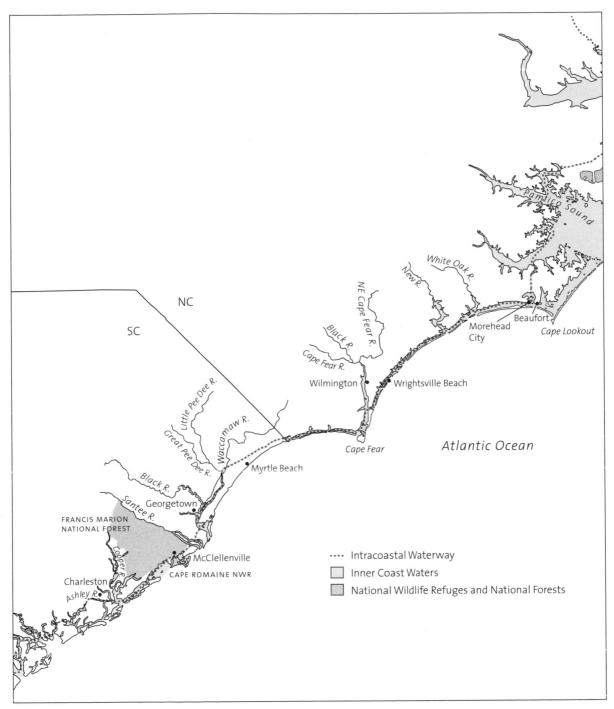

Coastal Region 2: The Outer Banks to the Lowcountry

NC

SC

White Oak R.

New R.

NE Cape Fear R.

Black R.

Cape Fear R.

Wilmington

Wrightsville Beach

Little Pee Dee R.

Great Pee Dee R.

Waccamaw R.

Cape Fear

Atlantic Ocean

Pamlico Sound

Beaufort

Morehead City

Cape Lookout

Black R.

Santee R.

Georgetown

Myrtle Beach

FRANCIS MARION NATIONAL FOREST

Cooper R.

McClellenville

Charleston

Ashley R.

CAPE ROMAINE NWR

•••• Intracoastal Waterway

◻ Inner Coast Waters

◼ National Wildlife Refuges and National Forests

A few miles up the White Oak River above Swansboro, where the tidal waters become fresh, cypresses and black gums stand along the shore on fluted and flared trunks. Longleaf and loblolly pines stand back from the water and grow in moist, open savannas, in association with many wildflowers, toothache grass, and the fascinating insectivorous sundew plant.

There are large salt marshes with hammocks of trees and shrubs behind Hammocks Beach State Park, west of Swansboro, and farther south lies Camp Lejeune, the huge marine base that sprawls from the ocean north to Jacksonville, North Carolina, and is bounded on the east by U.S. 17. The 5-mile cut through the military reservation flows by marshes and high-tide shrubs and upland pine forests and then empties into the New River, where the ICW and the New River Inlet meet.

Some of the herbaceous plants, shrubs, and trees that are commonly seen in this area, as well as in many other areas of the Inner Coast, grow at the upper edges of marshes, on small islands of higher ground, and on the sandy soils of barrier islands.

The tides begin building in this area, and the currents run fast. The Inner Coast is narrow here, and the ocean is constantly ducking in and out of view; divided and subdivided salt marshes fill the waterway from the barrier islands to the uplands. The Inner Coast is lined with homes and marinas, and there are boats everywhere. Myrtle Grove Sound, just below Wrightsville Beach, is less than 10 miles from Wilmington on the Cape Fear River.

The Cape Fear River is a maze of small islands that are the bounty of dredged spoil deposition. Shrubs and trees have taken root on these islands, and thousands of colonial wading birds—white ibises, blue herons, great egrets, and brown pelicans—roost and breed there. The Cape Fear River arises in central North Carolina at the confluence of the Haw and Deep rivers and flows southeastward for about 200 miles, past Wilmington and Southport, by Bald Head Light, and over Frying Pan Shoals into the Atlantic.

The ICW continues southward by highly developed Oak Island, past Holden Beach, where cabbage palmettos may be seen at their most northern point. Ibises roost in shrubs; ospreys carry fish to their nests; northern harriers glide across the marshes in search of prey; an occasional flight of wood storks wings by; and ruddy turnstones patter along the shore, searching for small crustaceans and other tasty morsels to feed on.

A few miles southward, the shallow, marsh-lined Shallotte River flows out the sandbar-guarded inlet to the sea. The tidal amplitude is much greater as we approach the Lowcountry, and when the tide is low, mounds of oysters, locally called coon oysters, can be seen growing in hillocks along the shore.

Calabash Creek meets the Little River Inlet at the South Carolina state line. Live oaks grow so thickly in the little seafood community of Calabash that they dampen the sound, and their massive, spreading branches certainly screen the sun. Little River flows through a long, 26-mile-high banked cut that parallels Myrtle Beach, which is named for the fragrant wax myrtle, a close relative of the northern bayberry.

The scenery begins to change; the shoreline is lush with bald cypress, live oak, cabbage palmetto, and towering loblolly and longleaf pines. Lily pads and tiny duckweeds float on the quiet backwaters, and the water is darkly stained with tannins. The beautiful Waccamaw River is just ahead.

Black willow, red bay, water ash, black oak, red maple, marsh fern, and swamp rose grow in profusion in this great tidal freshwater swamp. And there are alligators. Prince Creek, a small, curved waterway that flows around Longwood Island, not far from U.S. 17, is lined with the tall, thorny branches of the swamp rose. Clumps of rice cutgrass, torn from the land's edge, are carried by the tidal currents like small, green, floating islands.

The maritime and bay edge forests now take on a different appearance. Live oaks, draped with Spanish moss, and cabbage palmettos grow in beautiful groves along with southern magnolia and an understory of dwarf palmetto, red cedar, Carolina laurel cherry, and holly. Typically, cabbage palmettos group together in stands, whether backing up a marsh or lining a river bank.

Extensive mud banks and sand spits appear as the tide rushes to the sea and the marshes widen and stretch to the horizon. The ICW pours into Charleston Harbor, where the Ashley and Cooper rivers bathe Charleston's peninsula before flowing through the wide inlet to the Atlantic.

The secretive yellow-crowned night-heron is not so secretive in the spring in Charleston. Walk through White Point Gardens in the famed Battery in Charleston in May and search the treetops, and you will be rewarded with a view of several nests of yellow-crowned night-herons. Later in the spring and early summer, the immature birds can often be spotted along the marshes and shallows of the Cooper River.

From the Lowcountry to the Indian River Lagoon

South of Charleston, we are in the Lowcountry. The rivers wind and turn on themselves, and then the loops and turns straighten out in a patchwork of marshes and islands such as Wadmalaw, Edisto, and Otter. The lovely town of Beaufort, South Carolina, fronts the Beaufort River. A confusion of islands lies to the east: Ladys, Morgan, Coosaw, Fripp, and Hunting islands, to name a few. The land is low and the tides are high, bringing an intimate relationship between land and sea. Cabbage palmettos and loblolly and longleaf pines grow in association with live oaks on these islands, and where these maritime forests face the sea, as, for example, on Hunting Island State Park, that intimate relationship is starkly confirmed. The seas, energized by storms, have churned into the soft sands and have uprooted and cast aside live oaks, cabbage palmettos, and pines, carrying away the sand and leaving a tangle of dead trees.

The ICW continues southward, past Hilton Head and Daufuskie islands to the Savannah River, which forms the border between South Carolina and Georgia. The Savannah River begins at the Hartwell Reservoir, some 300 miles above Savannah, in "Dueling Banjo" country, where it merges with the confluence of the Tugaloo and Seneca rivers. The Savannah River has been dammed in several areas along its course north of Augusta, and, consequently, the natural shorelines have been modified. There are fewer bottomland forests and swamps in the upper reaches of the river. However, below Augusta, the Savannah River flows naturally through the coastal plain, and this stretch of the river is lined with bottomland forests. Some of the typical species in these wet woods are canopy trees such as bald cypress, water tupelo, and water hickory. Dogwoods, Carolina laurel cherry, magnolias, and dwarf palmetto are some of the understory plants that grow in these forests. There are also a variety of turtles and snakes living in the moist areas along the river, including the eastern cottonmouth, the southern copperhead, and rattlesnakes.

Just 5 miles upstream of the port city of Savannah, on the South Carolina side of the river, the Savannah National Wildlife Refuge sprawls over 25,000 acres of tidal streams, bottomland hardwoods, estuarine and freshwater wetlands, and the remnants of old rice plantations. U.S. 17 runs through the middle of the refuge, where there is a large variety of wildlife, depending on the season, including many species of

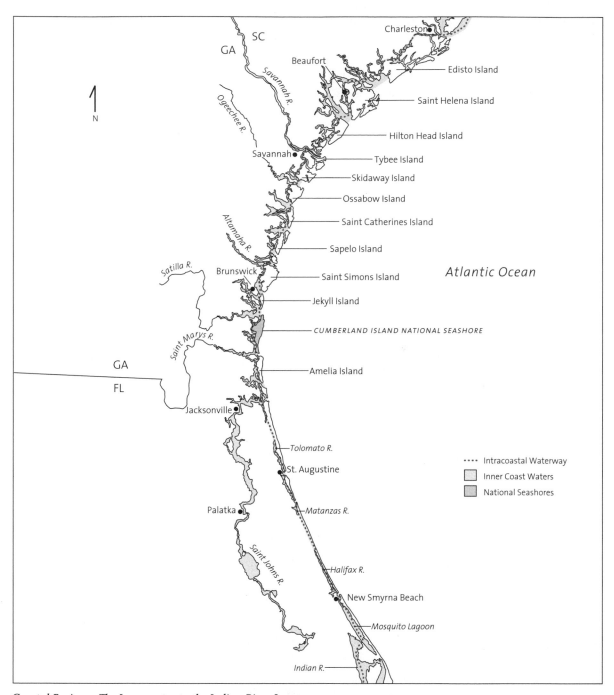

Coastal Region 3: The Lowcountry to the Indian River Lagoon

ducks, wading birds and shorebirds, alligators, and even an occasional manatee. Interstate 95 lies less than 5 miles to the west.

Approximately 16 miles downstream of Savannah is another refuge, the Tybee National Wildlife Refuge. This small refuge, part of a complex of seven refuges that spans 100 miles of South Carolina and Georgia coastline, is located in Jasper County, South Carolina. Tybee Island, Georgia, the northernmost barrier island on the Georgia coastline, lies on the south side of the Savannah River. The coastline south of the Savannah River is a maze of salt marshes dissected by countless creeks, rivers, and inlets. The barrier islands are dense with pines, live oaks, and cabbage palmettos. The mainland to the west is also dense with trees, including extensive slash pine plantations. The Ogeechee, Altamaha, Satilla, and Saint Marys rivers flow into the Lowcountry estuaries and sounds of Georgia, delivering silt, freshwater, and rich detritus to the coastal waters.

The Inner Coast is rather narrow below the Saint Johns River, but it eventually broadens into a long series of coastal lagoons just south of St. Augustine. The old city of St. Augustine gives way to marshes on the bay side of Anastasia Island and to freshwater swamps on the mainland. There are vast swamps in this area that sweep to the west. Interstate 95 and U.S. 1 daily convey thousands of cars and trucks through the wet mazes of freshwater swamps, prairies, and wetland hardwood hammocks. Interstate 95 crosses over Pellicer Creek and close to Faver-Dykes State Park, a 1,450-acre park that looks like the Florida of many years ago. The live oaks are adorned with resurrection ferns and green-fly orchids, an epiphyte that has small, yellowish green, very fragrant flowers. There are beautiful plants, some that are quite rare, growing under the canopy of live oaks, including Indian pipe; spring coralroot, an orchid with reddish

stems and white flowers spattered with magenta; and coontie, a small, palmlike shrub that belongs to the cycads, an ancient family of plants.

Pellicer Creek Aquatic Preserve is adjacent to Faver-Dykes State Park and about 16 miles south of St. Augustine. It is situated in the poorly drained coastal lands that are designated lowlands. The plant communities within the preserve include freshwater and saltwater marshes, wet hardwood forests, longleaf pine woods, dry oak woods, mixed upland hardwood forests, and wet prairies. There are a number of other swamps in this low coastal area—Fish Swamp, Big Cypress Swamp, and Graham Swamp—all surrounding Interstate 95 and just minutes away from the retirement community of Palm Coast City.

The busy Florida east coast towns of Ormond Beach, Daytona Beach, and New Smyrna Beach surround the long, narrow Halifax River Lagoon. Near the southern end of the lagoon and close to the Ponce de Leon Inlet, a number of marshy islands, overgrown with shrubs and small trees, crowd the waterway. Over to the west, beyond the shores lined with homes, are countless acres of swamps, ponds sloughs, and lakes. This enormous, watery wilderness is where the north-flowing Saint Johns River arises, but this spongy, soggy land also sends its water to the south, where it ultimately fills the huge, shallow Lake Okeechobee basin. The sheetflood of water in this basin continues ever southward, where it becomes a low-lying plain of saw grass, wet prairies, cabbage palmettos, hummocks of isolated hardwoods, slash pine flatlands, and cypress swamps. This is the "River of Grass" . . . the Everglades.

From the Indian River Lagoon to Miami

Mosquito Lagoon lies below New Smyrna Beach, bounded on the east by a narrow barrier island and

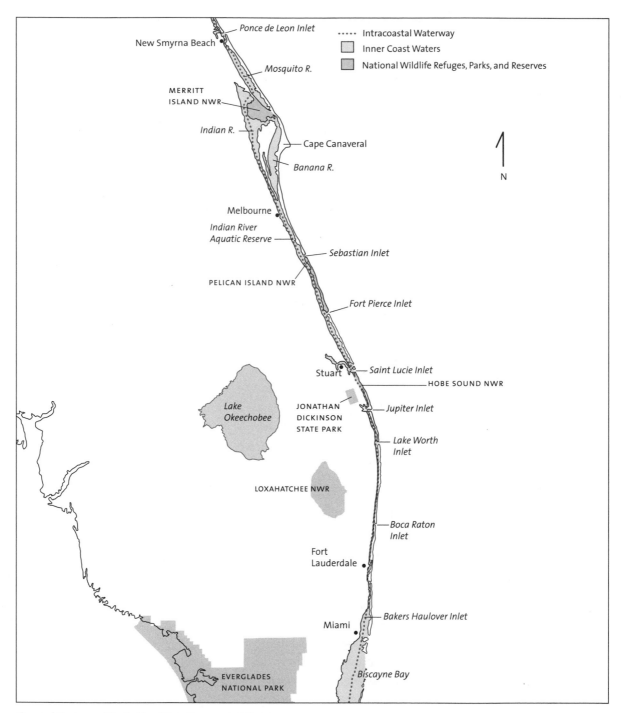

Coastal Region 4: The Indian River Lagoon to Miami

on the west by Turnbull Hummock and the wet hinterlands. Mosquito Lagoon is a shallow body of water dotted with myriad shrub-clad islands. Part of the Cape Canaveral National Seashore, it joins the Banana River and the Indian River Lagoon to form a biologically diverse transitional system. The Indian River Lagoon system extends 157 miles, about one-third of Florida's east coast, from the Ponce de Leon Inlet at the northern end to Jupiter Inlet at the southern end. The lagoon has an exceptionally rich floral and faunal population; in fact, scientists have reported that no other estuary in North America contains such a large number of species of plants and animals. In addition, it may well have the most diverse bird populations in the United States.

This is an important transitional system because of its unique geographic position. Cape Canaveral is considered the point where the temperate biogeographic Carolinian Province merges with the subtropical Caribbean and Antillean provinces. The northward-flowing, warm oceanic current, the Gulf Stream, or the Florida Current, not only greatly influences the climate of the Florida coast but is also a liquid highway that transports adult and larval fishes and many other pelagic organisms. As a result, a rich mix of temperate and subtropical flora and fauna overlap in this area, and the focal point appears to be the Indian River Lagoon system. There is a shift of wetland vegetation in the lagoon: the familiar marsh vegetation of the Temperate Zone of the Lowcountry, North Carolina and Virginia, begins to give way to a more tropical wetland system. The northerly portions of the Indian River Lagoon system consist of various salt marsh species such as salt grass, salt meadow hay, and cordgrasses, the same grasses that are abundant and common all along the Atlantic coast. Then, about 30 miles south of Cape Canaveral, at latitude 28° north, red mangroves become so dominant along the shoreline that they form forests. The

shift has actually been subtly occurring along the Inner Coast from about St. Augustine south. There are little pockets of black mangroves, white mangroves, and buttonwoods growing here and there. They are quite evident at the top of the Halifax River Lagoon, near Tomoka State Park, and there are patches of red mangroves widely distributed throughout Mosquito Lagoon. Mangroves become more abundant, and the familiar grassy salt marsh species became less so, south of the Indian River Lagoon. Mangroves and associated species here, in fact, play the vital role that salt marshes do in the north. The mangrove wetlands contribute leaves, stems, and seeds that are ultimately reduced to organic detritus, which is in turn fed on by many species of small crustaceans and fishes, as well as other organisms. The roots of mangroves trap silt and retard erosion, and they provide a place of attachment and foraging for a variety of organisms, including oysters, barnacles, tunicates, sponges, and crabs. In addition, there are many species of birds that nest and roost in the branches of mangroves.

From Miami to Key West

The shores of Biscayne Bay are crowded with houses, apartment buildings, and a multitude of business establishments, as well as tropical vegetation. Graceful, curved coconut palms sway in the breeze; Norfolk Island pines, with their dark green branches whorled around their trunks, are randomly scattered throughout the area; majestic royal palms, with their concretelike trunks, mark the entrances to hotels and line the streets; and dark green, feathery Australian pines grow along the causeways. Only one of these trees, the royal palm, is native to Florida. All of the others have been introduced from the tropical Pacific.

Coconut Grove, south of downtown Miami, and

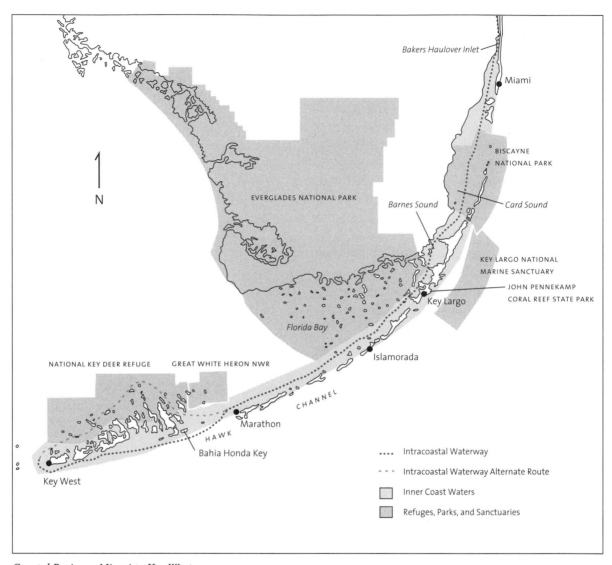

Coastal Region 5: Miami to Key West

Matheson Hammock were once tropical hardwood hammocks, and even though these areas are now highly developed, the tropical vegetation persists. Mangroves fringe the shoreline and form small islets of trees; mahogany and gumbo limbo trees grow large and shade the streets; strangler figs and poisonwood trees crowd vacant lots, along with a bevy of introduced tropical vegetation from herbaceous plants and shrubs to mango and avocado trees.

Biscayne National Park is the largest marine park in the nation, with approximately 95 percent of its 173,000 acres covered by water. The keys to the east, Elliott Key and Old Rhodes Key, are fringed by entanglements of red mangroves, and the keys to the west, the Arsenicker Keys, are islets of red mangroves. Elliott Key, a 7-mile-long island that separates Biscayne Bay from the Atlantic, is a state park with trees such as gumbo limbo, mahogany, fish poison tree, and strangler fig growing in the tropical hardwood hammock. There are plenty of raccoons on these islands as well.

Below Miami and Homestead, the small town of Florida City serves as a hub from which roads to the west go through Everglades National Park and those to the south go toward the Florida Keys. U.S. 1, the main road through the Keys, travels through the saw grass and other vegetation of the Everglades, crosses Barnes and Blackwater sounds, and intersects Key Largo. There is, however, a second route out of Florida City, Card Sound Road, which places the traveler right in the midst of the red mangroves. The road spans Barnes Sound and then is immediately enveloped in creeks that intertwine and bathe the tangled green forest. Egrets and herons roost in the treetops; white ibises work the mudflats; and busy fiddler crabs scurry about. The road joins the north end of Key Largo and then turns south, where it connects with U.S. 1, which links the Keys as they arc to the southwest, and Key West.

❧

Habitats of the Inner Coast

The habitats along the edges and within the waters of the Inner Coast, and the plants and animals that dwell within those habitats, are the main focus of this book. The habitats are described starting from the bordering upland areas and progressing down the slope to the aquatic habitats. Thus we begin by describing forested wetlands, maritime and bay edge forests, and marshes and then, sequentially, shoreline habitats such as beaches, intertidal flats, piers, pilings, and rubble structures. Finally, we describe life in the subtidal habitats of the shallows, the seagrass meadows and weed beds, and live bottoms—oyster reef and coral patch reef communities and worm rocks.

Forested Wetlands, Wooded Shorelines, and Swamps

Forested wetlands and swamps are part of a large and complex wetland system. Swamps are low-lying areas that retain water throughout the year. Experts in the field sometimes refer to them as hydric forests. Forested wetlands thrive in periodically flooded or saturated soils. Both forested wetlands and swamps are often overlooked as parts of the estuarine system, let alone as areas of natural beauty, and are not always considered as vital habitats. These somber and mysterious places are not particularly inviting to the casual visitor: they are wet during the spring, often muddy and strewn with fallen trees, and nicely populated with mosquitoes and biting flies—and festooned with a confusion of poison ivy, grapevines, and green briar.

Maritime and bay edge forest communities grow on drier soils along shorelines of rivers, on dune ridges, and on elevated hillocks in marshes. These forest communities comprise various species of trees

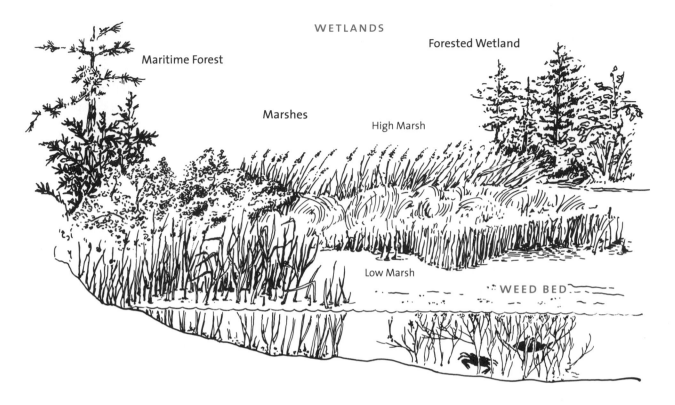

WETLANDS

Maritime Forest

Forested Wetland

Marshes

High Marsh

Low Marsh

WEED BED

and shrubs that can withstand salt-laden soils, constant winds, and salt spray.

Marshes and Mangrove Swamps

Marshes and mangrove swamps are wetland habitats of the Inner Coast that form important transitional zones between shallow-water habitats and upland vegetation such as maritime and bay edge forests. There are millions of acres of diverse wetlands in the Inner Coast system that extend from the tidal freshwater and forested wetlands of the upper rivers to the broad reaches of the lower estuaries and sounds. There are several types of wetlands throughout the Inner Coast: forested wetlands, mangrove swamps, freshwater marshes, and high and low saltwater marshes, all of which depend on water-soaked soil for their existence.

Wetlands are shoreward extensions of estuaries, sounds, and rivers. They supply an abundance of food and provide critical habitats that enable the plants and animals of the Inner Coast to flourish. They also bring beauty and peace and a sense of constancy throughout the Inner Coast.

Beaches

Sand beaches form extensive habitats along the Atlantic seacoast, but in the sounds and rivers in the Inner Coast, they are found only where conditions are suitable for maintaining this type of shoreline. Waves, currents, sediments, and the slope of the shore all influence the composition of a shoreline. A true sand beach slopes gently toward the water and is composed of sand grains or, sometimes, pebbles or coral rubble. In some areas of south Florida and the

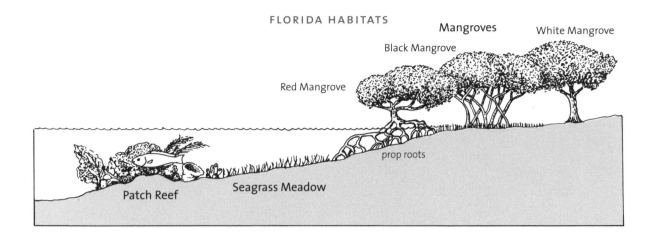

Mangroves

Black Mangrove

White Mangrove

Red Mangrove

prop roots

Patch Reef

Seagrass Meadow

Keys, small pocket beaches are composed of coral rubble or, in Florida Bay, of limy muds.

A beach is usually located in an area exposed to high winds and waves that endlessly sort and re-sort the sand grains. Offshore, the prevailing currents must be strong enough to move and deposit sand particles toward the area to maintain the beach.

Beaches are contiguous with and adjacent to many other habitats. Often, as a beach slopes toward the water, the grains of sand become finer and combine with accumulated organic material, gradually changing the beach into a sand-mud flat. A beach may be bordered by a marsh; rocks or jetties may jut out from the beach; or a pier may cross over a beach and extend to the water. These variations in beach structures are special habitats that allow plant and animal communities to develop and maintain themselves in what would be, normally, a very harsh environment.

Intertidal Flats

The intertidal flat, like a beach, is a rigorous environment for marine, estuarine, and tidal freshwater plants and animals, as intertidal flats are intermittently exposed to the heat of the sun with each tidal cycle and to the drying action of air and wind. Dis-

tinct intertidal zones exist on tidal flats as they do on beaches. The high-tide zone is often occupied by semiterrestrial crustaceans that can remain out of water for extended periods. The variety and number of intertidal plants and animals gradually increase toward the lowest intertidal zone, which is exposed only during the lowest tides. The type of flat is dependent on the kinds of sediments that are deposited there: soft-bottom flats contain a high percentage of very fine silt and clay particles, whereas hard-bottom flats are composed mostly of sand particles or, in some areas of the subtropical coast, of coral rubble.

The intertidal mud, sand, or coral rubble flat habitat is contiguous with many other habitats. Landward, it may be bordered by a beach, a marsh, a bulkhead, or a stretch of riprap. Beyond the water's edge, there may be a rich stand of aquatic plants, an oyster bar, or a coral reef patch.

Places to Settle: Pilings, Floating Docks, Rubble Structures, and Mangrove Prop Roots

Almost any hard surface along the shoreline presents an opportunity for sessile organisms to attach themselves. Sessile animals are a group of unrelated species that must fasten themselves to a hard

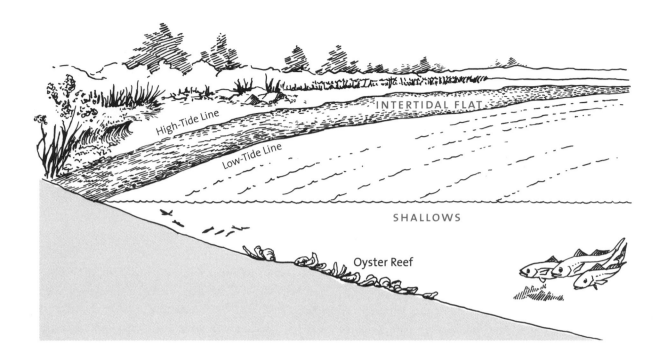

High-Tide Line

Low-Tide Line

INTERTIDAL FLAT

SHALLOWS

Oyster Reef

substrate in order to survive, feed, and reproduce. Most species cannot exist on a soft or shifting substrate; hence attached life is found on just about any submerged object or structure—bulkheads, pilings, floating docks, mangrove prop roots, crab pots, beer cans, and even ropes dangling in the water.

Sessile organisms are quick to colonize and flourish. They are a diverse group from many phyla comprising hundreds of species that have certain characteristics in common. Most of the species produce planktonic larvae that float about in the currents for a time. Some species are planktonic for only a few hours or days; others remain planktonic for weeks. In any event the larvae must find a suitable substrate and attach, or they will perish. Another characteristic of sessile species is that most reproduce asexually, ensuring even greater chances for their survival.

Just as the sand beach and the intertidal flats have

various intertidal zones, pilings, breakwaters, and mangrove prop roots have vertical intertidal zones.

The Shallows

It is difficult to set a rigid border between a shallow and a deepwater habitat because they form a continuum. We subjectively consider shallow waters to be no more than 20 feet because beyond that depth the penetration of sunlight diminishes and the water column often stratifies into layers of differing temperatures and salinities.

The shallows are a fairly rigorous place to live, perhaps not as harsh as the intertidal zone, but nonetheless plants and animals are exposed to extreme environmental changes of both short and long duration. The sun can superheat the water to the bottom with little moderation from incoming tides. In winter, in the Temperate Zone, the shoreward por-

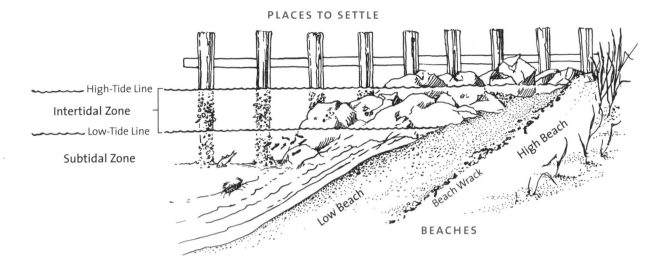

High-Tide Line

Intertidal Zone

Low-Tide Line

Subtidal Zone

Low Beach

Beach Wrack

High Beach

BEACHES

tion of the shallows may be covered with ice. The shallow waters then become colder than the deeper offshore waters, where surface air temperatures exert less influence. Winds and storms severely impact the shallow shore zone, churning the water down to the bottom and suspending great clouds of sediment. Torrential rains may wash tons of soil off the land, turning the waters into thick, brown soup, and rainstorms can abruptly lower salinities and flood the shallows with freshwater. Most estuarine species are adapted to these sudden, short-term changes, but higher-salinity marine species that have moved into an Inner Coast river mouth or sound have difficulty with the sudden physiological changes imposed on them by drastic changes in salinity.

Weed Beds and Seagrass Meadows

Large stands of rooted aquatic plants grow lushly in shallow-water shoreline areas throughout the Inner Coast, in tidal freshwater rivers as well as in bays and sounds. These aquatic plants are similar to our familiar land plants, with green leaves, buds, flowers, seeds, and roots firmly anchored in the sand and mud of the bottom. In south Florida waters, grasses,

such as turtle grass, form extensive meadows in the soft sediments. Several species of algae mingle with the grasses, and here and there small corals grow among the vegetation.

Stands of aquatic vegetation create special habitats quite different from unvegetated shallows. The plants grow rapidly and provide food and shelter for many animals. Submerged aquatic plants are directly fed on by only a few aquatic organisms; more important, they serve as an indirect food source by generating great amounts of organic detritus, which is formed as the leaves die and decompose. Plant leaves provide a base for a lush covering of microorganisms, algae, and a variety of small invertebrates, which are, in turn, grazed on by larger animals. The root systems of the plants stabilize bottom sediments, and the plants themselves dampen the effect of waves, creating a more stable environment.

Live Bottoms: Oyster Reefs, Patch Reefs, and Worm Rocks

Live-bottom communities along the Inner Coast are generally oyster bars in the temperate regions and coral reefs in the subtropical waters of Florida. Live bottoms are communities of associated organisms attracted to the area because of the opportunity for attachment. Larvae of various types of organisms attach themselves to the host substrate much as they would to a rock, a piling, or an old tire. The host substrates are usually oysters or corals. Fishes move in to feed, lay eggs, and secrete themselves in the crevices provided by a cluster of oysters or a coral head.

Oyster bars are found all along the Inner Coast. Where the tidal amplitude is not great, as in the North Carolina sounds, oysters live subtidally, mostly in water depths between 5 and 25 feet. In the more southerly regions, as in South Carolina and Georgia, where tides can exceed 9 feet, the oysters are intertidal, meaning that dense clusters of oysters are exposed when the tides ebb and then are covered once again as the flood tides rush in.

Oyster bars are rich communities where sessile organisms thrive and where mobile epifaunal animals such as worms and snails come to feed and reproduce. Most of the attached colonial animals of the piling community are equally at home on the hard substrate of an oyster shell. Hydroids, distant relatives of corals, grow in profusion on oyster shells, as do bryozoans, anemones, and sea squirts. Worms are plentiful in an oyster bar community. Oyster flatworms crawl over shells, preying on attached barnacles and oyster spat, the young of oysters. Errant worms, or wandering worms, such as clamworms, thread worms, and paddle worms, crawl over the shells in search of food. Oyster mudworms and whip mudworms build mud tubes; the oyster mudworm builds its tubes just inside the shell of an oyster. Small mud crabs abound in the oyster community, and snails of various kinds, from algal and detrital feeders to predators, glide over the abundant attached mussels and oysters.

There are many fishes that live within the community. The oyster toadfish is a common denizen of the oyster bar community, where it feeds and where the females attach their very large eggs. Gobies, blennies, and skilletfish are small fishes of the oyster bar community that are abundant but reclusive and solitary in habit.

The coral patch reef ecosystem functions in much the same way as the oyster bar community. The basic building block of the coral reef is the coral polyp. These anemonelike individuals secrete hard skeletons of calcium carbonate derived from the surrounding high-salinity seawater. They grow and divide continuously, and over time they form coral colonies, which become part of the coral patch reef complex. Corals are slow growing; it takes hundreds of years for a coral reef to develop to a substantial size.

There are several types of coral reefs, but the inshore coral patch reef is the only reef habitat that we cover in *Life along the Inner Coast*. These patch reefs are small, scattered reefs, usually composed of various species of boulder corals, with colorful sponges and soft corals attached to the boulder corals or to the sea bottom. Seagrass meadows often grow adjacent to patch reefs. Soft corals appear to be plants rather than corals; they may be bushy or fanlike, or they may have long, thin, whiplike branches. These plantlike organisms are, in fact, corals, but they do not produce coral rock communities, and they certainly do appear to be plants swaying in the ocean currents. Inshore patch reefs are usually surrounded by seagrasses where long-spined black sea urchins feed at night and where stingrays fan the sandy bottom searching for mollusks. Gray snappers and white grunts move across the grass beds and feed and rest around the patch reefs.

Oyster bars and coral reefs are islands of intense biological activity; the many diverse organisms that constitute the reef community live in close association with one another. The intermingling and interdependence of the many residents reflects the complex physiological and behavioral relationships that have developed over the eons.

Worm rocks are another type of live-bottom community that is seen along the Inner Coast only from near Cape Canaveral to about Miami. Small worms construct extraordinary reefs in the high-energy swash zone that consist of sand tubes often embedded with bits of shell. These reefs often protect the beach from erosion and provide an unusual habitat for fish and invertebrates that ordinarily would not exist in such an inhospitable environment.

❧ Classification of Plants and Animals

To some, the biologist's favorite preoccupation seems to be one of categorizing organisms and labeling them with obscure scientific names, much to the consternation of the layman. This process, called taxonomy, the science of plant and animal relationships and classification, is important because it provides some order and logic for understanding the relationships among the various groups and species of organisms. Furthermore, it gives every described species a name that is understood by scientists throughout the world, no matter what language they speak. The most widely accepted system of classification is the Linnaean system, a hierarchy of categories. It proceeds from kingdom to phylum, class, order, family, genus, and species. Most scientific names are two words of Latin origin. The first word of the scientific name of a specific organism is the genus; the second is the species. The name *Callinectes sapidus*, the blue crab, for example, translated from the Latin, is "beautiful savory swimmer." Most of the species distributed throughout the Inner Coast also have common names, some of which are regionalized and therefore differ from one area to another. We give the scientific name of the organism when we

fully describe it; thereafter in the text we refer to it by its common name.

The characteristics of the major phyla that we include are briefly described below. However, it is often difficult for a novice to determine even the phylum of a particular organism, especially some of the many wormlike creatures that are found in abundance throughout the waters of the Inner Coast. The descriptions of some classes, the major subgroups within a phylum, are also discussed under some of the larger phyla.

Plants

PHYLUM CHLOROPHYTA: GREEN ALGAE

These are typically green plants ranging from apple green to grassy green to blackish green. They may be attached as single plants or grow in colonies. They can be gelatinous, fleshy, or filamentous, or they may have a calcareous texture. Green algae, also called seaweeds, grow in many wonderful variations, from soft fans and knobby, brushlike growths to velvety tufts, feathers, and even underwater pansies. They can be erect, or they can form a tangled mass of green filaments on mangrove roots. Some species sprawl across rocks and look like patches of shelled green peas, and some species occur as single, large cells that resemble translucent marbles. Green algae are widely distributed in freshwater habitats, estuaries, and the ocean.

PHYLUM PHAEOPHYTA: BROWN ALGAE

Brown algae are not as widely distributed as green algae. They are almost always found in marine habitats, and particularly in cold waters, as are the kelps that grow in New England and California waters. There are a few brown algal species that are quite common and abundant, such as sargassum, or gulf-

Green Algae

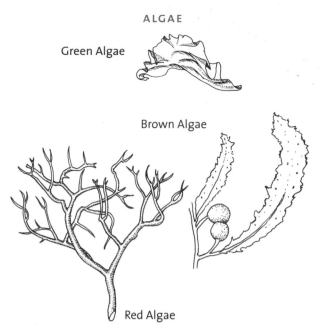

Brown Algae

Red Algae

weed, most often found stranded on beaches. Some sargassum weed species are pelagic and drift in patches as large as several acres on the surface of the ocean; other species attach to the bottom or to pier pilings. There are several species of brown algae that flourish in the warm waters of Florida and the Caribbean. Almost all of these species of brown algae are attached to rocks, stones, and coral fragments. Some grow in sheltered, quiet backwaters, and others are adapted to wave-swept, high-energy habitats.

PHYLUM RHODOPHYTA: RED ALGAE

Red algae are the most highly varied and abundant group of algal plants by far. There are thousands of species, particularly in tropical and subtropical waters. Their characteristic color is, of course, red, but they range from pale gray and white, through tans and gold, to light blues and lavenders, and an array of reds. They can be calcified, leathery, flat bladed, shrubby, rubbery, or hard and brittle. Red algae, similar to brown algae, are almost entirely marine. A few species, however, are estuarine.

DIVISION POLYPODIOPHYTA: FERNS

The complexity and difficulty of the classification of ferns is matched by no other group of plants. Some specialists place ferns in the division or phylum Pteridophyta, or Pteridopsida; others place ferns in the division Polypodiophyta; and still other experts classify ferns in the divisions Lycopodiophyta, Equisetophyta, Filicopsida, and Psilotophyta. The classification of ferns is a work in progress. We use division Polypodiophyta with the realization that further research may well change fern classification in the future.

Ferns are an ancient group of non-seed-bearing plants with vascular systems, specialized tissues for conducting food and water within plants. Ferns have large pinnate (featherlike) leaves, often called fronds. They typically have a horizontal stem, or rhizome, that stores food for the plant. Sporangia are borne on

FERN

HIGHER PLANT

the leaves or on separate, specialized spore-bearing leaflets. Spores, the reproductive bodies of ferns, are contained within the sporangial sac. There are about 12,000 species of ferns in the world, most of which live in the tropics.

PHYLUM SPERMATOPHYTA: HIGHER PLANTS

Spermatophytes have true roots, vascular stems, and flowers or other structures that produce seeds. Most of the conspicuous plants are spermatophytes. Typically spermatophytes are divided into two large groups: Angiosperms, those flowering plants that bear seeds enclosed in a vessel, or carpel, and Gymnosperms, nonflowering plants that produce seeds that are not enclosed in a carpel and are termed "naked" seeds. Gymnosperms include conifers, pines, cedars, firs, and redwoods. Conifers have simple, reduced leaves that are generally evergreen. The reproductive structures are borne in the male and female cones.

Angiosperms are classified into more than 300 families largely on the basis of the reproductive organ, the flower. The vascular tissue of flowering plants is more specialized than that in conifers. The carpel, unique to flowering plants, aids in the dispersal of seeds, and only angiosperms produce fruit. The diversity within the angiosperms is staggering: they occupy an amazing variety of habitats; they flourish in freshwater and saltwater; they grow in the deserts of the world and atop the rain forest canopy; and they attach to rocks in the inhospitable alpine regions.

Animals

PHYLUM PORIFERA: SPONGES

Sponges are the simplest forms of multicelled animals, with no organs or differentiated tissues. A simple skeletal structure of tiny glassy or calcareous spicules or spongin fibers provides a framework for the living cells. Water carries food and oxygen to the living cells through tiny pores on the surface of the sponge, passes through a network of canals and chambers, and then exits through larger pores. Sponges throughout most of the Inner Coast are low, encrusting forms that grow over rocks, stones, or pilings or are irregularly shaped masses with knobbed, fingerlike projections. Often broken pieces of sponge are washed up on shore. There are, however, sponges that grow in the Florida Keys that are more varied and often quite large. In fact, some types have been

SPONGES

Fingerlike Sponge

Encrusting Sponge

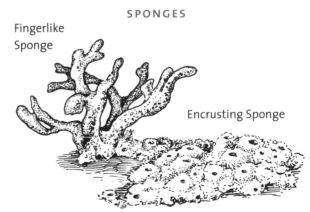

harvested for use as commercial bath and car wash sponges.

Sponge identification is usually based on microscopic examination of spicule types that form the mineral skeleton. Most collectors, consequently, will be able to identify sponges only as belonging to a general type. However, a few species are easily recognized, such as the redbeard sponge, with its bright red to orange color and intertwining fingers, and the large, charcoal-colored loggerhead sponge that grows on the turtle grass flats of the Florida Keys. Sponges have so many growth forms and colors that they may be confused with other encrusting growths, such as bryozoans and hydroids.

PHYLUM CNIDARIA: HYDROIDS, JELLYFISHES, SEA ANEMONES, AND CORALS

Cnidaria includes a number of varied classes of marine invertebrates that share certain characteristics. Cnidarians are more advanced than sponges. They are composed of two specialized layers of cells separated by a gelatinous noncellular layer, the mesoglea. They have one opening, a mouth, which is connected to the gastrointestinal cavity. Radial symmetry, in which the body parts are arranged around a central axis, is characteristic of this phylum. Cnidarians are unique in the animal world in possessing stinging cells, or nematocysts. The Greek word *knidē* means "stinging nettle." Another interesting characteristic of the phylum is the development of two life forms: a sessile polyp stage and a free-floating medusa stage. Some species alternate between stages, whereas others have only a polyp or a medusa stage. Three classes of cnidarians occur in the Inner Coast.

Class Hydrozoa: Hydroids. Hydroids are abundant in the estuaries and rivers of the Inner Coast but often go unnoticed because they appear simply as thin,

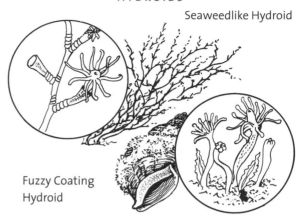

HYDROIDS

Seaweedlike Hydroid

Fuzzy Coating Hydroid

fuzzy coatings on piers, rocks, or shells or as waving fronds that can be mistaken for seaweeds. On the coral reefs and grass beds of Florida, hydroids are also abundant and often go unnoticed. Of the many types of hydroids that occur along the coast, some species form both polyps and hydromedusae (tiny, floating jellyfishes), and others occur only as polyps. Most hydroids are colonial; that is, they are a collection of individual animals called zooids, each with a mouth and tentacles, but with interconnected digestive cavities. Hydroid colonies attach to the substrate by means of a horizontal root system. In some hydroids the zooids arise directly from this base; in others the zooids emerge from branching stems that are supported by a chitinous envelope around the soft tissues.

Class Scyphozoa: True Jellyfishes. The medusa stage dominates among Scyphozoans. The medusa bell is far larger and more noticeable than that of the hydromedusae, and the mesoglea is thick and gelatinous. Most jellyfishes have tentacles equipped with many stinging cells extending from the rim of the medusa bell; the mouth is edged with oral folds. The polyp

TRUE JELLYFISH

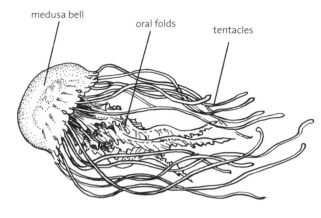

medusa bell

oral folds

tentacles

stage is a tiny, inconspicuous form whose primary function is to produce new medusae.

Class Anthozoa: Sea Anemones and Corals. Anthozoans do not have medusae, only a polyp stage. Anthozoan polyps differ from hydroid polyps in that the gastrointestinal cavity is divided into radiating compartments by thin, membranous partitions called longitudinal septa. Nematocysts are found on the feeding tentacles surrounding the mouth and the internal septa as well.

Sea anemones are solitary, soft-bodied polyps, topped with a ring of tentacles surrounding a slitlike mouth. Some anemones are attached to firm substrates; others bury themselves in the bottom muds. There are many species of sea anemones. Many are small, inconspicuous, and pale colored, particularly in the temperate region of the Inner Coast. In the Florida Keys, however, many of the tropical forms are large and brilliantly colored.

Hard corals are closely related to sea anemones, but rather than being solitary polyps, they are a colony of polyps, each connected to the other over the surface of their skeletal base. The distinct indenta-

tions of coral skeleton, or cups, mark the location of individual polyps.

Soft corals are similar to sea anemones and hard corals but are distinguished by having eight pinnate tentacles, whereas hard corals are characterized by having tentacles in multiples of six. A soft coral is a colony of small polyps supported by a skeletal mass of calcareous spicules, or horny material. A network of gastrodermal extensions that perforate the skeleton connects the polyps. Unlike the living tissues of hard corals, which grow completely above the skeletal base, the living tissues of soft corals lie within the skeleton. A few corals, such as star corals and sea whip, are common in the Temperate Zone. The diversity and abundance of corals increases dramatically in the warmer and clearer waters to the south.

PHYLUM CTENOPHORA: COMB JELLIES

Ctenophores are similar to jellyfishes, with radial symmetry and a jellylike body tissue similar to mesoglea. However, they have no nematocysts, and their bodies are divided internally by eight ciliated bands edged with fused cilia or combs: "ctenophore" means

SEA ANEMONES AND CORALS

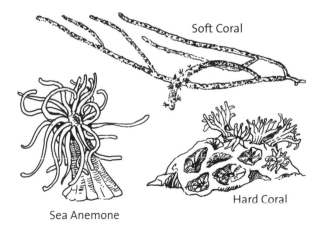

Soft Coral

Hard Coral

Sea Anemone

COMB JELLY

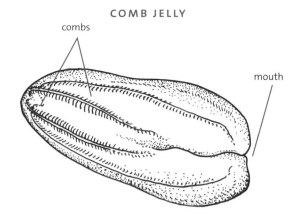

"comb bearer." The combs beat rhythmically, propelling the animal through the water, a swimming method that differs from that of jellyfish, which propel themselves by pulsating the medusa bell.

PHYLUM BRYOZOA: BRYOZOANS

Bryozoans, or moss animals, are colonial, sessile animals, similar to hydroids, but with individual zooids that are not connected to each other, as they are in hydroids, and with lophophore (horseshoe-shaped) tentacles. Bryozoans are more evolutionarily advanced than hydroids. Because details of their body shapes and structures are not easily discerned without the aid of a microscope, most bryozoans are difficult, if not impossible, for the nonspecialist to identify. Bryozoans grow in many shapes, structures, and sizes; some are microscopic and grow along a creeping stolon, or horizontal runner. Some are flat, hard, lacy-looking crusts growing on stones, shells, and vegetation; some are erect and appear like branched seaweeds or hydroids; and some are rubbery, lumpy masses very similar to certain sponges.

PHYLUM PLATYHELMINTHES: FLATWORMS

There are many different "worms" and wormlike creatures abounding in the waters of the Inner Coast. It is important to be able to determine which general group or phylum a specimen belongs to if one wishes to identify the species. Each phylum has distinctive characteristics that allow most laymen to identify the type of "worm" they have in hand. Platyhelminthes is a very primitive group of worms that includes parasitic tapeworms and flukes as well as the free-living turbellaria. Turbellarian flatworms are common but are often overlooked in Inner Coast waters. Most are very small and are hidden in the bottom sediments, but a number are large enough to be easily visible. Almost anyone who has picked up a small shell or stone from the water has probably unknowingly seen a flatworm that appeared as only a flat, gelatinous form. Flatworms are very thin, somewhat leaf shaped, soft, and unsegmented. They are one of the earliest groups of animals to develop bilateral symmetry, a mouth (but no anus), and a digestive cavity, which in the larger, free-living forms is highly branched. They are often distinctly marked with tiny eyespots or other color patterns. We have included only one type of flatworm belonging to the genus *Stylochus*, as it is common on oysters and is easily recognized.

BRYOZOANS

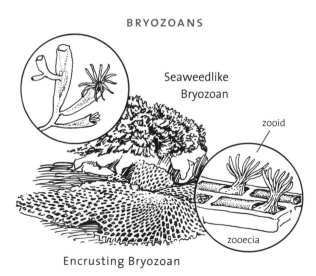

Seaweedlike Bryozoan

zooid

zooecia

Encrusting Bryozoan

FLATWORM

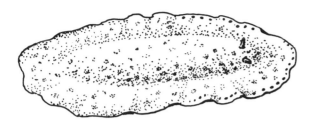

PHYLUM RHYNCHOCOELA: RIBBON (NEMERTEAN) WORMS

As their name implies, ribbon worms are elongated, unsegmented, and often flattened worms without appendages. They are soft bodied and break into fragments when handled. Ribbon worms are contractile; they lengthen and shorten as they squirm and sometimes twist into a tangle. Ribbon worms are also known as proboscis worms because of a unique whiplike appendage that projects from their heads. The proboscis is used for defense and capture of prey and may actually be longer than the worm's body. The proboscis retracts through a pore into a fluid-filled cavity surrounded by muscle. There are many ribbon worms in these waters buried in the mud, hiding under stones or among seaweeds, or fouling growths on piers and jetties. Some are symbiotic and live in close association in hard clams, other mollusks, and blue crabs. We describe one, the large and distinctive milky ribbon worm that can attain a dramatic length of 4 feet.

RIBBON WORM

PHYLUM ANNELIDA: POLYCHAETE WORMS

Annelid worms are one of the most diverse and abundant groups of invertebrates in the Inner Coast. The well-known terrestrial earthworm belongs to this phylum. Annelids are far beyond flatworms and ribbon worms in evolutionary development. They have a mouth and an anus, a specialized head region with a brain, specialized organs for grabbing and tearing prey, and body cavities with organs analogous to our own. Some are extremely resistant to pollution and occur in contaminated sediments where little else lives. Most of the marine annelids belong to the class Polychaeta, meaning "many hairs," referring to the number of bristles arising from special appendages called parapodia. The parapodia extend from the sides of the body, one pair to each body segment. The parapodia are of diverse form and shape: they may be lobed, jointed, feathery, stalked, or paddlelike.

SEGMENTED WORM

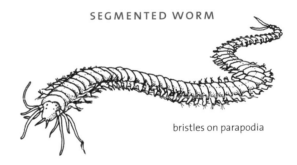

bristles on parapodia

The head regions of polychaetes are also quite varied and are equipped with structures such as specialized tentacles, intricately feathered extensions, and beaklike jaws. Species identification is often based on minute differences in parapodia or head structures. Polychaetes of many types are found in almost every habitat in the Inner Coast. There are burrowers, tube builders, crawlers, and swimmers.

Clams, oysters, and snails are easily recognizable representatives of this diverse and important phylum. Of the eight classes of mollusks within the phylum, five occur within the Inner Coast: gastropods (snails), with a single shell; pelecypods (clams and oysters), with two valves or shells; polyplacophors (chitons), with eight shell plates; cephalopods (squids and octopuses), with an internal vestigial shell; and scaphopods (tusk shells), with a shell in the form of a tapered tube. The three classes of mollusks that we do not discuss are Caudofoveata, which are wormlike, shell-less mollusks that live on the deep-sea floor; Aplacophora, which are also wormlike, shell-less mollusks that live on the deep-sea bottom; and Monoplacophora, limpetlike mollusks known only from fossils until 1952, when the first live specimen was collected at a considerable depth.

Class Gastropoda: Snails. The class Gastropoda contains the largest number of mollusk species. Representatives of this large and diverse group include periwinkles, whelks, slipper snails, cone snails, cowries, and nudibranchs, as well as land snails and land slugs. The distinctive shapes and colors make identification relatively easy and enjoyable for the amateur. Many gastropods have well-developed heads with tentacles and eyes, and a large muscular foot adapted for gliding over almost any surface.

Class Pelycypoda: Bivalves. The bivalves are also well represented throughout the Inner Coast and include not only oysters and many species of clams, but also mussels and arks. Pelecypods differ from gastropods in that most of the species have two valves, or shells, and a wedge-shaped foot adapted for burrowing into soft sediments rather than for gliding over surfaces. Some live individually in the bottom, or along the surf line; others are attached by byssal threads or

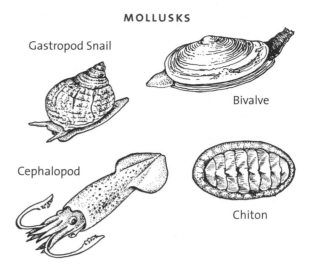

MOLLUSKS

Gastropod Snail

Bivalve

Cephalopod

Chiton

are cemented to one another. They have two basic modes of feeding: suspension feeding, in which food particles are filtered from the water, and deposit feeding, in which the bivalve sucks up organic material from the soft muds by means of long, flexible inhalant siphons.

Class Polyplacophora: Chitons. These unusual mollusks, the chitons, are elliptical-shaped animals with eight connected shell plates on top of their body and a flat, suckerlike foot on their lower, or ventral, surface. This strong foot enables the chiton to cling tightly to rocks, shells, and other hard surfaces, from which they are difficult to dislodge. Their distinctive body structure makes it almost impossible to mistake chitons for any other animal. Chitons graze like gastropods, moving slowly over rocks and shells and scraping off the algal film with small, rasping teeth.

Class Cephalopoda: Cephalopods. Squids, octopuses, and other members of the class Cephalopoda bear little resemblance to snails and clams, and yet they are, indeed, related. Cephalopods are the most highly

ANATOMY OF PELYCYPODS

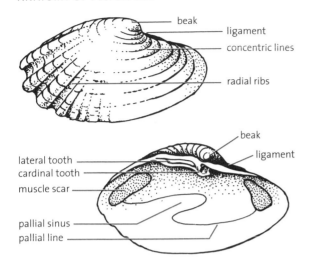

beak
ligament
concentric lines
radial ribs

beak
ligament
lateral tooth
cardinal tooth
muscle scar
pallial sinus
pallial line

ANATOMY OF GASTROPODS

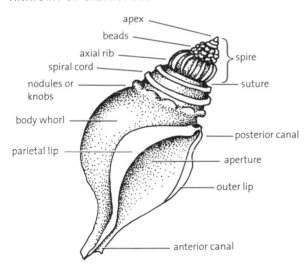

apex
beads
axial rib
spiral cord
nodules or knobs
body whorl
parietal lip
spire
suture
posterior canal
aperture
outer lip
anterior canal

developed of all mollusks, with large heads and eyes and a crown of tentacles homologous to the foot of other mollusks. The chambered nautilus is a cephalopod with an external shell; the squid and the cuttlefish have only a remnant of an internal shell; and the octopus has no shell. There are several spe-

cies of squids and octopuses that occur in the Inner Coast.

Class Scaphopoda: Tusk Shells. Scaphopods are small mollusks that live in slightly curved, tapered shells that are open at both ends. They burrow in the bottom sands or muds with the larger-diameter-end down and the slender end elevated just above the bottom. They have paired clusters of contractile tentacles that aid in the capture and manipulation of prey. Various species of tusk shells live in shallow and moderate to deep depths.

PHYLUM ARTHROPODA: JOINTED-LEGGED ANIMALS

Phylum Arthropoda contains more species and more individuals than any other animal group in the world and accounts for approximately 80 percent of the known animal species, largely because of the thousands of insect species that belong to this phylum. Arthropods have an external skeletal framework rather than an internal one, as do human beings and many other animals. Their bodies are covered with a hard, chitinous shell, or exoskeleton, to which their musculature is attached. Articulated joints allow movement of each body segment and appendage. In order to grow, arthropods must molt, leaving the old shell behind and forming a new, larger shell.

There are three major types of arthropods characterized by the kinds of anterior appendages and by certain other features. All three groups of arthropods are represented in the Inner Coast. Class Chelicerata, the first major group, includes horseshoe crabs, mites, spiders, scorpions, and ticks. In other words, the horseshoe crab is more closely related to the common spider than to a blue crab, although, superficially, it does not resemble either one.

The second major group, subphylum Crustacea, includes crabs, lobsters, shrimps, and barnacles in

Horseshoe Crab

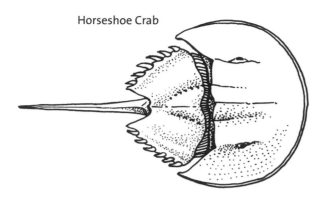

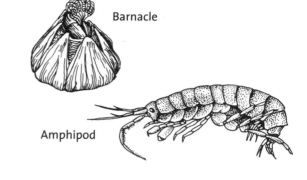

Barnacle

Amphipod

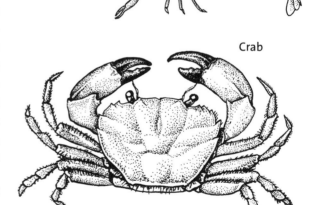

Isopod

Shrimp

Crab

addition to innumerable microscopic animals of the zooplankton community, such as copepods. Some crustaceans are quite familiar and are immediately recognized as crustaceans, such as crabs and shrimps. A number of distinct kinds of shrimps inhabit Inner Coast waters, including the tiny, translucent mysid shrimp, penaeids (the shrimp we love to eat), mantis shrimp, snapping shrimp, glass shrimp, and arrow shrimp. Lobsters and crabs range from the familiar Maine lobster to spiny lobsters and the odd slipper lobster. Crabs come in a multitude of colors and patterns, and they range in size from the tiny oyster pea crab that lives within an oyster's shell to very large land crabs. Some species live on sandy beaches; others skulk along the bottom; some often swim on the water's surface. There are semiterrestrial crabs that scamper over the rocks and live in the spray zone, and some that spend most of their lives in mangrove trees.

Barnacles are also crustaceans, though highly modified crustaceans. They were once thought to be mollusks because of the calcareous shells they construct and occupy. The animal within the shell, however, is jointed legged, and its early stages of development are typical of other crustaceans. They are usually attached to a hard substrate and are sessile except in the larval stage. There are approximately

1,000 species, and, similar to crabs and other arthropods, they have evolved into many forms and have adapted differing modes of feeding. Some are parasites and radiate throughout a crab's body; some are burrowers in coral sands and mollusk shells; some

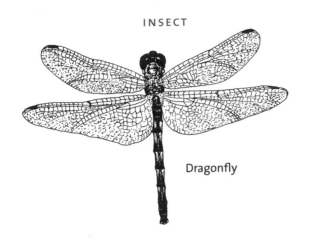

Dragonfly

think resemble tiny praying mantises, are transparent in some species and deeply colored in others.

The third major group, class Insecta, is a huge group that has adapted to almost every habitat that exists. They live in the sea, in briny salt ponds, and in sulfur seeps. They abound in the marshes and other wetlands and even in mangrove swamps. There are over a million species of insects known and undoubtedly some that are not yet known. Insects are primarily terrestrial, although several species live in tidal freshwater and the saltier waters of the Inner Coast.

PHYLUM ECHINODERMATA: SPINY-SKINNED ANIMALS

This group of exclusively marine animals (they live only in saltwater) includes the familiar sea stars, sea urchins, and sand dollars. "Echinoderm" means "spiny skinned," referring to the prickly internal calcareous skeleton that protrudes through the skin. The echinoderm body is divided into five parts around a central axis, a structure that is termed pentamerous radial symmetry. This five-sided symmetry is obvious if one looks at a sea star or the surface of a

attach themselves to crabs; and some are found only on whales and sea turtles.

Two groups of small crustaceans, isopods and amphipods, are not familiar to most casual observers, but they are abundant and ubiquitous species of the Inner Coast and, once noticed, will become familiar to any collector. Many common species are large enough to be identified rather easily. Isopods are buglike creatures with bodies flattened top to bottom; amphipods are more shrimplike in appearance, with bodies flattened from side to side. The terrestrial pill bug, or sow bug, that lives under rocks or pieces of wood is a very common and well known isopod. Isopods live on land, in freshwater, and in the ocean. Most species of isopods are free living; some are parasitic in or on fishes; and some, like the gribble, are destructive wood borers.

Amphipods are quite common along beaches. Some live under beach wrack above the surf line; some live where the waves break and the sand churns; and some live at sea, hitching rides on jellyfish. There are also several species that live in freshwater. The curious little skeleton shrimps are often abundant on crab traps and buoys and on trailing ropes rich with sessile organisms. These little shrimps, which some

ECHINODERMS

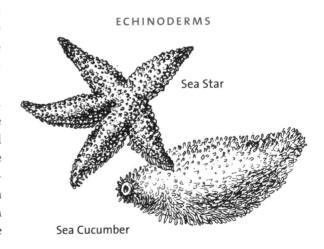

Sea Star

Sea Cucumber

sand dollar. Echinoderms are considerably more advanced evolutionarily than other radially symmetrical animals such as jellyfish and sea anemones. Their unique method of locomotion is accomplished by the progressive suctional grasping and releasing of their hundreds of tiny tube feet. Sea stars, or starfish, are particularly adept at opening clams and oysters by exerting a powerful, unrelenting suction with their tube feet. Many echinoderm species are distributed throughout Inner Coast waters.

PHYLUM CHORDATA:
NERVE CORD ANIMALS

Chordata is a very large phylum that includes two subphyla of invertebrates. They have a notochord, a flexible, rodlike structure considered to be a primitive backbone. A third subphylum, Vertebrata, comprises the vertebrates of the world: fishes, amphibians, reptiles, birds, and mammals—and thus humans.

Subphylum Hemichordata: Acorn Worms. Hemichordata is a small phylum or subphylum of wormlike marine creatures that are interesting to scientists because their larvae have characteristics of both invertebrate larvae and fish larvae. Some zoologists believe the subphylum Hemichordata to be a transitional one between invertebrates and vertebrates. However, this advanced status is not apparent as one studies the adult acorn worm. Acorn worms live in U-shaped burrows in intertidal mudflats and sandy and muddy bottoms of shallow waters. There are only a few species of acorn worms in Inner Coast waters.

Subphylum Urochordata: Tunicates. Tunicates show chordate characteristics, for example, the primitive notochord that occurs only in their larval stages. Tunicates of the Inner Coast, as adults, are ses-

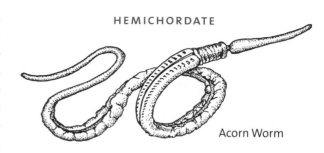

HEMICHORDATE

Acorn Worm

sile animals with a tough outer skin, or tunic. The ubiquitous sea squirt and the sea pork are tunicates. It is hard to believe, but these undistinguished, gelatinous growths covered by leathery skin may be precursors of the whole spectrum of higher animals with backbones.

Subphylum Vertebrata: Vertebrates. Vertebrates are animals with a backbone and a braincase, or cranium. The backbone is made up of a series of separate segments called vertebrae. The central cord of the nervous system runs through the backbone, which supports and protects it. Six classes of vertebrates are included in this book: cartilaginous fishes, bony fishes, amphibians, reptiles, birds, and mammals.

Fishes are classified as those with cartilaginous skeletons, such as sharks, rays, and skates, and those with calcified skeletons, the true bony fishes. The limbs of fishes, analogous to our arms and legs, are

TUNICATES

Sea Squirts

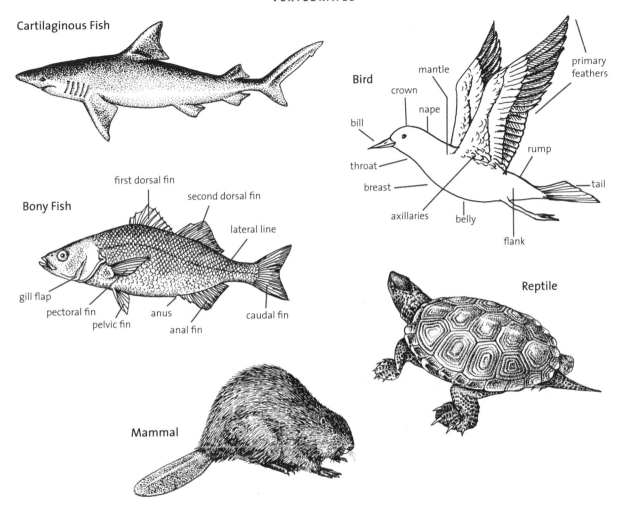

Cartilaginous Fish

Bird

mantle

crown

nape

bill

primary feathers

throat

rump

breast

tail

axillaries

belly

flank

Bony Fish

first dorsal fin

second dorsal fin

lateral line

gill flap

pectoral fin

pelvic fin

anus

anal fin

caudal fin

Reptile

Mammal

the paired pectoral fins, extending from each side, and the paired pelvic fins, extending from the belly. Most fishes have several simple fins, including one or more dorsal, or back, fins; a caudal, or tail, fin; and an anal fin. The coelacanth is considered to be the missing link between fishes and the earliest four-legged animals: the tetrapods, or amphibians. The only living species of this ancient group, the coelacanth, often called a living fossil, was only discovered in 1938 off the coast of Madagascar. Evolutionary biologists generally agree that amphibians evolved from early coelacanthlike Crossopterygian (tassel-finned) fishes.

Amphibians probably evolved during the Devonian period, about 350 million years ago. Amphibians spend some time in water as well as on land in moist situations. Most amphibians lay their eggs in freshwater or in moist soil. The eggs develop into aquatic larvae. There are three groups of amphibians: The wormlike caecilians are known only from the moist tropics. Some caecilian species have fishlike scales embedded in their skin. Order Caudata contains the tailed amphibians, salamanders. The third group, the order Anura, includes the tailless species, frogs and toads. Amphibians and reptiles are collectively called herpetofauna. Amphibians are ectotherms; that is, they generally have body temperatures close to the temperature of their environment.

Reptiles include turtles, alligators and crocodiles, and lizards and snakes. Reptiles have a dry skin covered with scales, or scutes. Most reptiles, including turtles, alligators, and most lizards, have two pairs of limbs; however, snakes, as well as a few species of lizards, are legless. Reptiles are fertilized internally, and most lay large, well protected eggs that have an abundant yolk supply. They are air breathers and are equipped with lungs rather than gills.

In many ways, birds are similar to reptiles, from which they are believed to have evolved. They breathe by the use of lungs; their feathers, unique in the animal world, were derived from reptilian scales; and they are egg layers, as are reptiles. The four limbs of birds have been modified into a pair of wings and a pair of legs. Their bones are hollow or very light, and they have replaced the heavy-toothed jaws of reptiles with lighter beaks and bills—all modifications that enable them to fly.

Mammals are warm-blooded vertebrates with several more highly evolved skeletal structures than are found in other vertebrates. They have hair and generally have two pairs of limbs, although the hind legs have been lost or greatly modified in some species, such as dolphins. Mammals give birth to live young and nurse them. Mammals are quite diversified in their appearance, behavior, feeding, and habitat requirements. They range from birdlike bats to armor-plated armadillos to plankton-feeding great whales.

How to Use This Book

This guidebook is organized according to the major habitats of the Inner Coast waterways. The diversity of habitats along the waters of the Inner Coast engenders, as one might expect, a large number of species of plant and animal life, which we describe in the following chapters. We have made some subjective decisions regarding the inclusion of the species described in this book. Some species that are included are representative of similar species in the group; other species are so uncommon that we felt it best to use the available space to discuss the more abundant and the more widely ranging species. We have also made an effort to include only those species that can be identified without the aid of a microscope. We appreciate and understand that some of our readers will wish to delve more deeply into a particular species, a species that, for the reasons stated above, has unfortunately not been included. Therefore, we have included a selected list of publications that will be of help in the further study of particular groups of organisms and habitats.

Many of these plants and animals have a wide range, and some may be found all along the Atlantic coast. Others have a restricted or more limited range. Climate, of course, plays a significant role in the distribution of a species, but available and suitable habitat also is a key factor in whether a certain organism is present and, if so, abundant. We have had to decide in which chapter to place each particular species, be it plant or animal, recognizing full well that there may be other chapters in which one could choose to describe and discuss the organism. We have made our decisions to place an organism in one habitat over another based on research, both in the field and in the literature, on our personal observations, and on the interest of a balanced presentation. Take the blue crab, for example, which is a wide-ranging species that is distributed from Long Island Sound (and sometimes farther north) all the way to Brazil. It could obviously be described in the chapter on salt marshes or the chapter on seagrass meadows. We elected to introduce the blue crab in the chapter that describes the shallows. The shallows teem with life: oyster spat settle on older oysters, ribbed mussels and sea squirts find places of attachment, worms crawl about, and fishes lay eggs and hide in crevices. Blue crabs prey on many of these organisms, and they, too, have places to lurk and hide. The same rationale holds for, say, the herring gull, which we placed in the chapter on beaches. These raucous, ever-hungry birds may be seen wheeling in the sky high over a town dump or following a tractor through a newly plowed field. They strut along the beach searching for tasty morsels, roost on pilings, and sun themselves in parking lots and on rooftops, and they concentrate at fishing piers and float in the shallows.

When we discuss a species, we provide key characteristics to aid in its identification, and we frequently indicate its range throughout the Inner Coast. In addition, we discuss ecological relationships, feeding behaviors, growth patterns, and reproductive activities. Most species are delineated with original pen-and-ink illustrations by Alice Jane Lippson. The species have been thoroughly researched to ensure that the illustrations are accurate. We have also included a phylogenetic table of species, from the most primitive to the most advanced, that graphically portrays the range of plants and animals included in this book.

1

Forested Wetlands, Wooded Shorelines, and Swamps

Wooded shorelines are dominant features throughout the Inner Coast. Mysterious and foreboding wet woods line the river banks and shallow sounds from salty estuaries to tidal freshwater. Cypress trees merge into indistinguishable curtains of feathery branches, and, here and there, an old, mature, flat-topped bald cypress towers above the smaller trees below. Tupelos, sycamores, and tall, furrowed tulip trees, often overgrown with tangles of grapevines and poison ivy, thrive in the rich bottomlands and moist soils of the Inner Coast. Heavy-limbed live oaks draped with Spanish moss arch over fan-shaped palmettos in the more southern regions. Thickets of evergreen magnolias, red cedars, oaks and maples, and smaller shrubs and ferns form almost impenetrable forests along the waterways.

Great meadows of waving salt marsh cordgrass are interrupted in places by rises, or hammocks, that furnish just the right habitat for a mixture of palmettos, cedars, shrubby marsh elders, and prickly pear cactus. Mangrove swamps along the subtropical Inner Coast are the home of red mangroves, with their distinctive arched prop roots, and black mangroves that send up spiky aerial roots. Mahoes, Australian pines, and cabbage palmettos grow along ridges just high enough above the water-soaked soils to allow them to flourish.

🌿

Forested Wetlands and Swamps

There are thousands of miles of shoreline along the waters of the convoluted and dissected Inner Coast. Where the shoreline elevation is low, forested wetlands and wooded swamps appear; where the shoreline is sufficiently elevated above high tide, there is usually a maritime or bay edge forest. Because forested wetlands occur in floodplains that form vital transitional zones between aquatic ecosystems and terrestrial uplands, they are often difficult to classify or even to recognize. Forested wetlands are sometimes classified as seasonally flooded basins or flats, mixed bottomland hardwoods, or, more specifically, tupelo-cypress swamps or oak-gum-cypress associations. There are millions of acres of diverse wooded wetlands in the Inner Coast system. Forested wetlands, also known as flooded woodlands, are flooded usually only during seasonal times of high water. As the river waters flood over the low floodplains and naturally occurring levees and spill onto the forest floor, shallow, temporary vernal ponds are often created. In some areas where the natural drainage is poor, pocosins, literally "swamps on a hill," form special habitats within the forested wetlands.

Wooded swamps are similar to the temporary vernal ponds, but swamps are more permanent bodies of water, often receding during dry seasons and times of drought and increasing during times of high water and rainy seasons. However, there is always some standing water in a wooded swamp. Tidal freshwater swamps may be found in the upper reaches of many Inner Coast rivers with diverse flora and fauna usually dependent on the latitude and, therefore, the climatic zone. Some tidal freshwater swamps are dominated by bald cypress and tupelo, red maples, and black willow and interspersed with tulip poplar, sycamore, and Atlantic white cedar. Farther south, water ash, tupelos, and bald cypress grow in association with loblolly pine and saw palmetto. In central Florida and down to the Florida Keys, yet another type of swamp appears: the mangrove swamp, a complex of halophytes, plants that can tolerate and thrive in a saline environment.

Wet woods are not sharply separated from adjoining upland forests; they are, in fact, a continuation of the uplands. As the land slopes to sea level, certain

A forested wetland scene.

woody and herbaceous plants, commonly considered species of drier habitats, take hold in the wetter, more poorly drained soils. Many shrubs and trees usually referred to as pioneer species, such as willows, buttonbush, river birch, red maple, and gums and oaks, can establish rather quickly in moist bottomlands.

Forested wetlands and swamps, along with vast acres of freshwater and saltwater marshes, floating weed beds, rooted aquatic vegetation, and minute floating plants called phytoplankton, provide a perpetual energy source—the engine—that forms the basis for the immense annual production of life in the Inner Coast. Lunar- and wind-driven tides and seasonal rainfall periodically flood wooded wetlands and marshes. Nutrients and minerals transported to these areas by the ebb and flow of the tides provide for the maintenance and continued existence of these essential wetlands. But the tides and heavy rainfall runoff carry more than nourishment; they also transport the myriad larvae of crustaceans, insects, mollusks, fishes, and other organisms to the rich organic habitat of the forested wetlands. The muddy floors of these

dank habitats, along with the roots, stems, and leaves of the plants, provide a fertile diet for bacteria that constantly break down the plant material into soupy, organic ooze, called detritus. The detrital material, along with its rich complement of bacteria and algae, becomes food for countless animals. These areas literally pulsate with life. Snails feed on the leaf litter and on detritus and algae; monstrous-looking dragonfly larvae in permanent ponds feed on beetle larvae and small fishes; and fiddler crabs in the mangroves extract sustenance from the rich muds. The young of both freshwater and saltwater fishes seek the shallow waters of the wetland channels and pools, where their food is concentrated, and where they have greater protection from predators. Plants and animals live and die in close relationships, continuously renewing and recycling nutrients.

Forested wetlands and swamps have an abundance of snakes and turtles, as well as breeding songbirds, such as warblers, thrushes, vireos, and woodpeckers, because the lush growth provides nesting cover, protection from predators, and an ample food supply.

Owls and hawks lurk in these woods and feed on the songbirds and on rodents and other small mammals that are everywhere on the forest floor.

❧ Maritime and Bay Edge Forests

Maritime and bay edge forests flourish where the shoreline is elevated along the Inner Coast. These forests are associations of shrubs and trees that may be found along the edge of a beach in the dune ridges, along the shore of a river, or even as an isolated outpost on a rise in the middle of a broad marsh. Maritime forests are nothing more than groups of adaptable trees and shrubs that can endure salt-laden soils, pummeling wind-driven sand, and salt spray. Cedars, pines, oaks, and bayberry trees are shaped and sheared by onshore winds. Sands shift and cover shrubs, and the soil may be wet for extended periods. The species of shrubs and trees that are found in a maritime forest have adapted to the severe conditions along the coast. The live oaks growing in the salt spray community can be molded into a rolling thicket, often taking the form of the back dunes that they are growing on. The maritime forests growing in areas exposed to ocean winds are examples of forests that have been shaped by the relentless wind. The vulnerable terminal buds of live oaks and other trees such as dogwood, red maple, black cherry, red cedar, and loblolly pine are killed by the salt spray concentration, resulting in abundant lateral branching and a dense canopy of stunted trees.

In contrast, live oaks growing back from the beaches, in more protected areas, have great, sinewy branches and the large trunks of typical, majestic live oaks. The maritime forest protected from the ravages of salt and wind becomes a place of serene beauty. Maritime forests usually do not contain a large number of species. Pines or live oaks and perhaps cabbage palmettos form a canopy over smaller trees and shrubs, such as laurel cherry, holly, and red bay. The forest is often draped with tangles of poison ivy and fox grape vines.

"Bay edge forests" is our term for maritimelike forests that grow along river courses and on the upper edges of marshes and in general do not experience the severe conditions that species of shrubs and trees endure in a true maritime forest setting. A typical bay edge forest in North Carolina or Georgia may include loblolly pines or slash and longleaf pines, cedars, live oaks, and hollies. Farther south, in coastal Florida, bay edge forests are likely to include buttonwood and white mangrove, cabbage palmetto, and an understory of saw palmetto. Maritime and bay edge forests are actually habitats of the upland margins and are not truly part of the aquatic system of the Inner Coast. However, because they are so obvious throughout the Inner Coast, we have included them in this chapter on wooded shorelines.

Vegetation of Wooded Shorelines

Plants respond to habitat variables, for example, sandy soils, organic moist soils, standing water, salinity, and, in a broader sense, climatic conditions. There is a process called ecological succession in which a community of plants becomes established, such as in an area that has recently been modified by the construction of a dam upriver. Plants that can accommodate to disturbed wet soil begin to take root, such as reed grass and other grasses, dog fennel, black willow, and red maple. A plant community of this type is often referred to as a pioneer community. The establishment of the pioneer community is the beginning of ecological succession; the pioneer community begins to modify the very habitat that originally made the community possible. Soils become stabilized as the pioneer community lays down leaf litter and fallen branches decay and become mineralized by bacterial and fungal communities. The soils become deeper and more organic in content. Trees grow larger and shade out the grasses; vines wind upward around the trees to seek the light; and many fruits and seeds are produced.

The process continues: pioneer communities of insects, snakes and turtles, birds, and other animals respond to the changes in the plant communities, and so the faunal community changes as well. Take, for example, the bird population in a newly established pioneer community where most of the plant species are grasses, asters, goldenrods, and small shrubs. The bird species will be few and somewhat predictable: a species or two of sparrows, an occasional warbler, a stalking blue heron, a red-winged blackbird, and not much more. The habitat does not support nesting or roosting, only foraging. Over time, the pioneer community is modified into what ecologists call a seral stage, part of an orderly process that changes the plant community and animal community to a stable, mature, relatively unchanging community, often called the climax community. The slow, inexorable process of ecological succession takes place in all types of environments, whether it be a grassland savanna, a rocky coastline, or a pine forest.

These perfectly natural and logical changes take place within the various climatic zones. In the area we define as the Inner Coast, we are speaking of the Temperate Zone and the Subtropical Zone. The Temperate Zone occupies a broad area of the Atlantic coastline from the Maritimes of Canada to central Florida. The composition of the plant communities changes from north to south. As we proceed south from Virginia, certain species of plants that flourish in the colder climes begin to drop out, and other, more southern species take their place. In South Carolina, even though the area is still within the Temperate Zone, the climatic succession is trending toward the subtropical, as cabbage palmettos and longleaf pines become more dominant. From central Florida down through the Florida Keys, the plant species become more and more tropical in nature, reflecting the proximity to the Caribbean and the Tropical Zone.

TREES

Bald cypress, *Taxodium distichum*, is found everywhere in the Great Dismal Swamp and in rivers of the region, such as the Chowan, Pasquotank, and Perquimans. Bald cypress is a relative of redwood and sequoia trees. It is tall and straight, and where it grows in water, the trunk is often swollen and buttressed. Bald cypress develops peculiar extensions of the root system called knees; some believe that cypress knees aid in oxygenation of the tree, and others hold that the knees help support the tree in the soft, waterlogged soils. Bald cypress trees have soft, feathery, needlelike leaves that turn brown in the winter and drop to the ground. They produce small, gray, ball-shaped cones, with one or two at the end of a twig. As bald cypress trees mature, they lose their conical shape and develop a distinctive, flattened crown. There is a closely related species, pond cypress, *Taxodium ascendens*, that some authorities consider to be a variety of the bald cypress that grows sporadically throughout the Inner Coast. The pond cypress does not have a feathery appearance like the bald cypress because it has short, nearly scalelike needles that grow closely pressed against the stems.

Black gum, *Nyssa sylvatica*, also known as black tupelo, swamp gum, or sour gum, is a tree of the bottomlands. These trees grow in forested wetlands and tidal freshwater swamps, but they can grow in dry upland soils as well. They are tall, straight trees with brown to gray, deeply furrowed bark. The dark

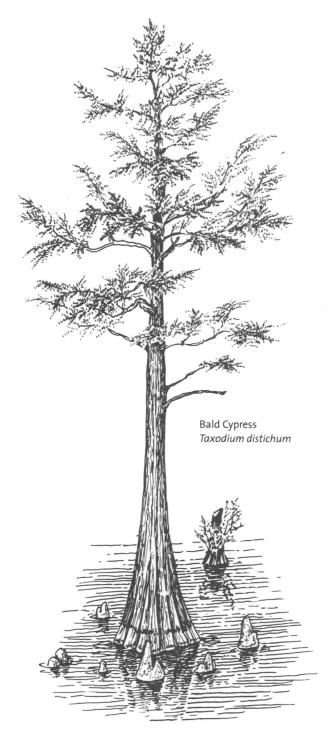

Bald Cypress
Taxodium distichum

blue fleshy fruit, a drupe, has bitter-tasting flesh surrounding a stony seed. Black gums range the entire coast down to central Florida.

Red maple, *Acer rubrum*, also known as swamp maple, is a highly adaptive species that grows almost anywhere; it is one of the most common and widely distributed tree species in eastern North America. These trees can grow in almost any type of soil and forest type; they do well along the edges of swamps and river bottoms as well as on dry upland sites. They often grow in pure stands where conditions allow. Red maples are medium to tall trees that sometimes attain a height of 90 feet, but often they are quite spindly and much smaller. They have oppositely arranged three-pointed, or lobed, leaves that turn red in the fall. The flowers develop in early spring, sometimes weeks before the leaves appear. The winged fruits, called samaras, hang on slender stalks. The red maple is found all along the Inner Coast and beyond, from Nova Scotia into Florida.

The American sycamore, *Platanus occidentalis*, is a large deciduous hardwood tree that is common in eastern North America in the bottomlands and moist soils of forested wetlands. It is closely related to the plane tree of Europe. Sycamores grow rapidly and can grow to a height of 175 feet and a diameter of 12 feet; however, they are generally smaller. They are a distinctive and beautiful tree of the forest and are easily recognized by their mottled gray, green, brown, white, and yellow scaly bark. The leaves are maplelike, lobed and coarsely toothed, and alternately arranged along the stems. The sycamore develops drooping, globelike fruits that produce hundreds of seeds that are scattered by the wind where they germinate on the wet soils.

The river birch, *Betula nigra*, is another quite beautiful tree that has become a favorite ornamental species throughout the Inner Coast region down to north Florida. It is often found growing in asso-

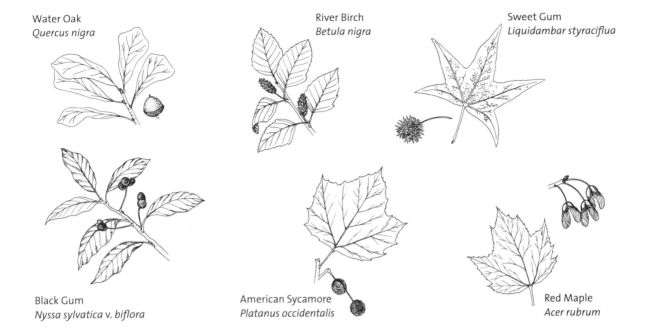

Water Oak
Quercus nigra

River Birch
Betula nigra

Sweet Gum
Liquidambar styraciflua

Black Gum
Nyssa sylvatica v. *biflora*

American Sycamore
Platanus occidentalis

Red Maple
Acer rubrum

ciation with the American sycamore. The river birch can be recognized by its distinctive peeling bark that is pinkish to reddish brown in younger trees and darker, fissured, and shaggier in larger, more mature trees. The alternately arranged leaves are somewhat arrow shaped and sawtooth. The inconspicuous flowers develop winged nutlets that quickly take hold in the rich, moist bottomlands. The river birch is the most southerly distributed birch species and ranges from southern New England to northern Florida.

There are many other trees that grow in the moist soils of forested wetlands, where they furnish habitat and food for a number of animal species. Atlantic white cedar, *Chamaecyparis thyoides*, called juniper in some areas, has long been valued in shipbuilding and for siding houses. Atlantic white cedars are restricted to freshwater swamps and bogs along the Atlantic coast. They commonly grow with red maple, black gum, sweet bay, and one or more pine species, such as loblolly or pitch pine. However, white

cedars often grow in pure stands, crowding out other species except where the open canopy allows shrubs and vines a place to flourish. White cedars are graceful, symmetrical, cone-bearing (coniferous) trees, usually with a straight trunk and with a tapered or conical crown. The leaves take the form of small, flat, overlapping scales that look very much like those of the eastern red cedar. The twigs of the white cedar, however, are somewhat flattened in cross section and differ from the angled or square twigs of the red cedar.

Sweet gum, with the melodious scientific name *Liquidambar styraciflua*, is a deciduous tree of rich, moist bottomlands, although it sometimes grows in upland habitats. Sweet gums range from southern New England to Central America. These are large trees ranging up to 150 feet in height and 5 feet in diameter. The leaves are arranged alternately along the twigs and are star shaped, with five- to seven-pointed lobes that somewhat resemble maple leaves.

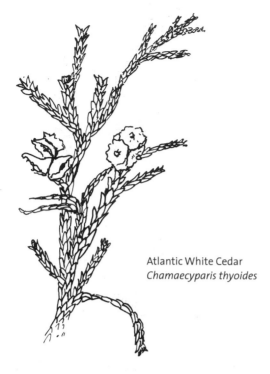

Atlantic White Cedar
Chamaecyparis thyoides

The leaves are dark green in the summer and turn a beautiful scarlet in the fall. The tree is quite resinous and aromatic; in fact, the scientific name of the sweet gum refers to its resinous qualities. This tree of the witch hazel family develops small, greenish flower clusters in the spring and an abundance of round, persistent, prickly, wooden fruits in the autumn.

Water oak, *Quercus nigra*, is one of the many oaks that grow in close association with sweet gums along the wooded shores of the Inner Coast. This tree typically has a rounded or conical crown and is a medium-size tree that grows to a height of 75–100 feet and a diameter of perhaps 2–3 feet. The leaves of the water oak are not the typical oak leaf shape; they are quite variable in form and are usually spatulate or wedge shaped, and sometimes they are slightly three lobed. The acorn is almost round, with a shallow cup that just covers the base of the acorn.

Along the wooded shores of the Inner Coast, there are a group of trees or large shrubs that superficially resemble one another. Most have evergreen leaves, although some are deciduous in their northern range. Some, but not all, have showy aromatic flowers, and they all thrive in the warm, moist soils of the lowland areas of the Inner Coast. These are the magnolias, the red bay, and the loblolly bay. They even have similar common names: sweet bay, bull bay, red bay, and loblolly bay. However, these plants are representatives of three separate families: the magnolia family, the laurel family, and the tea family.

There are several native magnolias in North America, including the cucumber magnolia, the umbrella magnolia, and the bigleaf magnolia. However, the southern magnolia (often called the bull bay) and the sweet bay (or swamp magnolia) are the most common and abundant magnolia species along the Inner Coast. These trees range along the river edges and wooded shorelines from the mid-Atlantic to Florida.

The southern magnolia, *Magnolia grandiflora*, is the handsome evergreen tree with leathery leaves and showy, fragrant flowers that so symbolizes the South. Southern magnolias grow in lowland areas, usually never above 500 feet. They can attain a height of up to 100 feet, particularly in rich, moist, well-drained soil. The leaves are large, broadest at the middle, and up to 8 inches long; they are smooth, dark, and shiny green on the top surface and are often covered with rust-colored hairs on the lower surface. The saucer-size flowers are produced in the spring and are very fragrant. They bear conelike fruits with scarlet seeds that are eaten by some birds. Turkey and quail often feed on the seed-laden fruit that drop to the ground. Southern magnolia is found down to central Florida.

Sweet bay, *Magnolia virginiana*, a close relative

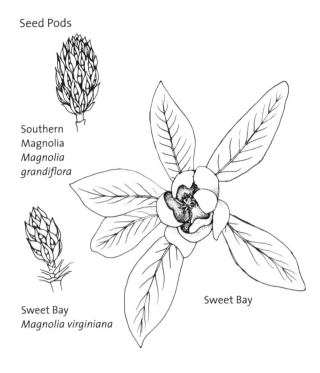

Seed Pods

Southern
Magnolia
*Magnolia
grandiflora*

Sweet Bay
Magnolia virginiana

Sweet Bay

members of the laurel family, and when the leaves and twigs are crushed, they emit an aromatic odor characteristic of the laurel family. Red bay is common in shallow depressions between sand dunes and along wooded shorelines and is found south to the Florida Keys. The bark of the red bay is somewhat furrowed and is reddish brown to brownish purple. The evergreen leaves are lance shaped and 2–8 inches long. The undersides of the leaves are sparsely hairy to smooth. The flowers are small and inconspicuous. Some botanists consider the swamp bay, *Persea palustris*, to be a variety of the red bay and not a distinct species. The species are quite similar in appearance, with only an apparent difference in the arrangement and number of hairs on the undersides of the leaves. The swamp bay tends to grow in wetter soils than does the red bay.

The loblolly bay, *Gordonia lasianthus*, a member of the tea family, is a small to medium-size tree, or shrub, with alternate, leathery evergreen leaves. This

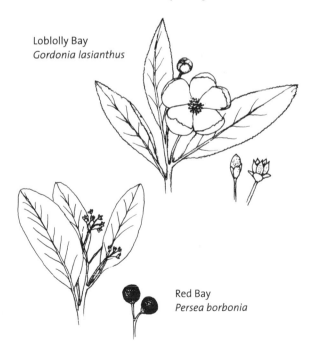

Loblolly Bay
Gordonia lasianthus

Red Bay
Persea borbonia

of the southern magnolia, also flowers in the spring and grows in association with holly, red maple, and red bay. This magnolia is shrubby and deciduous in its northern range and larger and evergreen in the southern part of its range. The sweet bay is smaller than its cousin the southern magnolia. The leaves are also smaller, and the lower surface is covered with silvery hairs rather than the rust-colored hairs found on the southern magnolia. The flowers are showy and fragrant and are about 5 inches wide. The cone-shaped fruits with dark red seeds are smaller and more rounded than those of the southern magnolia. Sweet bay ranges into southern Florida, but not to the Florida Keys.

Red bay, *Persea borbonia*, is closely related to the avocado. Red bays are medium-size trees or large shrubs with alternately arranged evergreen leaves. The red bay and its close relative the swamp bay are

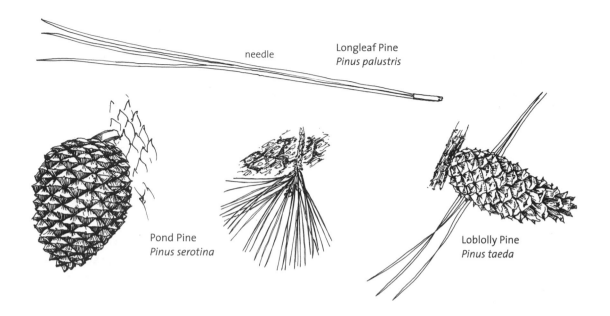

needle

Longleaf Pine
Pinus palustris

Pond Pine
Pinus serotina

Loblolly Pine
Pinus taeda

species is sometimes confused with red bay, but the leaves and twigs of the loblolly bay are not aromatic when crushed. The showy flowers, however, are wonderfully fragrant, and long before you catch a glimpse of a loblolly bay, the perfume of its white blooms wafting across the quiet waters in late spring and early summer make you keenly aware of its presence. The loblolly bay is a tree of the coastal plains and ranges from North Carolina to central Florida. It grows in similar habitats along with the magnolias and swamp bay.

There are a number of pine species along the Atlantic coast that grow from the water's edge to the rolling sandy hills of the Piedmont region. Three of the most common species are the longleaf or southern pine, *Pinus palustris*; the loblolly pine, *Pinus taeda*; and the pond or pocosin pine, *Pinus serotina*. The longleaf pine grows on sand hills and scrub lands and is often associated with loblolly and slash pines. This is a tall, straight species of pine ranging up to 130 feet tall. The needles, 8–18 inches long, are bunched in threes toward the ends of the twigs and give the tree a rather fluffy or tufted appearance. The cones are tapered and 6–10 inches long. The longleaf pine is a valuable commercial species grown for its lumber, turpentine, and resins. Longleaf pines grow from southeast Virginia to central Florida.

The loblolly pine is another important commercial species harvested for its lumber. This a fast-growing tree, often maturing in ten to twelve years. The loblolly is a very adaptable species common in the Inner Coast and may be found in maritime forests, where the soil is often moist and salt laden, and in drier bay edge forests. It often associates with sweet gum, water oak, and sweet bay, and it is quite common on old, abandoned, exhausted fields. Loblolly pines tend to be self pruning, and as a consequence the older trees lack branches on their lower two-thirds. As the tree matures, the bark develops irregularly shaped, thin plates that resemble the hide of an alligator. Its light green, 6- to 9-inch-long needles are usually bundled in threes. They are stiff and may be slightly twisted. The 2- to 6-inch cones are oblong and tapered to a tip. The light brown to reddish scales of the cones are armed with a straight or slightly curved spine.

The pond pine generally grows in low, wet depressions and in peaty swamps and bogs. It grows very well in soils with a high water table and tolerates wide fluctuations in water table levels. It is a medium-size tree and grows to a height of perhaps 75 feet. The 4- to 8-inch needles are slender and flexible, usually three to a bundle, or occasionally four. The light brown cones are somewhat globe shaped and usually persist on the tree for one to two years before shedding their seeds. The pond pine has little commercial importance. It ranges from southern New Jersey to central Florida along the Inner Coast.

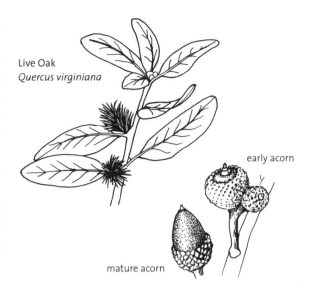

Live Oak
Quercus virginiana

early acorn

mature acorn

Typical Southern Trees. The live oak, *Quercus virginiana*, is *the* southern tree. No other tree is so evocative of the Lowcountry. It has a short, thick trunk and pendulous, sinewy branches arching to the ground. The live oak's deeply furrowed bark is often clad with a leafy carpet of resurrection ferns and draped with Spanish moss.

The live oak is, surprisingly, a fairly fast-growing tree of the Inner Coast. This large, spreading tree grows in sandy coastal soils but also occurs in moist, rich woods and along stream banks. It typifies the coastal maritime forests of South Carolina and Georgia and usually grows in association with laurel oak, sweet gum, southern magnolia, American holly, cabbage palmetto, and dwarf palmetto. In more open areas, yaupon holly, red cedar, and wax myrtle thrive where the sunlight penetrates through the dense canopy.

Live oaks are called "live" because they are evergreen. The small, leathery leaves are persistent and do not drop off at the same time; the oak is never bare. New leaves appear during the spring, and the older leaves drop throughout the year. The leaves are 2–5 inches long and rather thick, stiff, and leathery.

They do not resemble typical oak leaves. They are generally oblong, entire, or slightly toothed and are dark green on the upper surface and somewhat hairy and grayish green on the undersurface. They produce prodigious amounts of shiny, dark brown acorns that provide a rich source of food for wild turkeys, wood ducks, jays, quail, raccoons, deer, and squirrels.

The wood of the live oak is very dense and heavy and was highly valued as a shipbuilding lumber during the early days of sailing ships. The U.S. Navy acquired entire forests of live oaks for use in building ships. The massive, curved limbs were shaped into knees and ribs for the hulls.

The live oak ranges all along the Inner Coast, from Virginia Beach, Virginia, through the Florida Keys.

Southern trees are often bedecked with plants that cling to the deeply fissured bark of live oaks and pines. Long skeins of gray, twisted threads hang down from branches and drape over electric power lines; the scraggly tendrils attach to almost anything. This is Spanish moss, *Tillandsia usneoides*, but it is neither Spanish nor a moss; it is a plant that belongs to the pineapple family, the bromeliads. A truly epiphytic plant, literally, a plant that grows on another, Spanish moss clings to its host and absorbs water and nutrients through its minute, hairlike scales. It takes nothing from the host tree except space. However, the wiry gray skeins can grow into large masses that can block needed sunlight from reaching the tree. Great groves of live oaks draped with Spanish moss and resurrection fern, with an understory of palmetto, are natural parks that simply cannot be improved on. The yellowish green flower of the Spanish moss is tiny and inconspicuous. Seminole bats roost and rear their young in clumps of Spanish moss, and some warblers and flycatchers build their nests from its wispy threads.

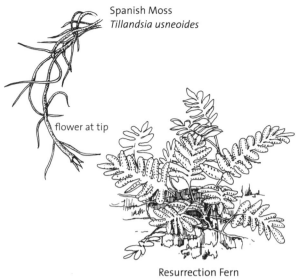

Spanish Moss
Tillandsia usneoides

flower at tip

Resurrection Fern
Polypodium polypodioides

Another air plant, for that is what an epiphyte is, is the resurrection fern, *Polypodium polypodioides*. This fern attaches to the rough bark of tree limbs, particularly on live oaks, magnolias, and cypresses. The plant takes hold with spreading, creeping rhizomes and sprawls over tree branches and sometimes over rocks. Like Spanish moss, it becomes a nonpaying tenant of its host. The leathery evergreen leaves are very sensitive to moisture, and, as a conservation measure, when there has been a lack of rain, the leaves curl up and turn a deathlike brown, only to quickly be "resurrected" when it rains.

The cabbage palmetto, or sabal palm, *Sabal palmetto*, is the state tree of both South Carolina and Florida. This slender, straight palm grows to 75–80 feet, with a tightly rounded crown of fan-shaped leaves. The unbranched trunk is grayish tan and marked with leaf scars. The trunk often has a crisscross network of "boot jacks," the woody remnants of the leaf stalks that have not yet dropped. The leaf stalk, called a petiole, of the fan is smooth and continues into the fan as an arching midrib. The fruit, blue-black drupes, are attached to stalks that hang in pendulous clusters, as do the fragrant, creamy white

flowers. The cabbage palmetto is a species of the coastal plain and usually does not grow farther than 75 miles from the coast. If the live oak signifies the South, the cabbage palmetto signals the approach of the subtropics. From the first few that grow just north of the South Carolina state line, they begin to increase and become backdrops to the marshes; they line the sandy shores of barrier islands; they grow in groves mixed with red cedars, hollies, loblolly pines, and live oaks; and they grow in small, oasislike hammocks out in the salt marshes.

Cabbage palms are considered a wind-adapted species; that is, they can endure the heavy winds of hurricanes and nor'easters because their trunks bend and sway, and their tight crowns of tough fans offer little resistance to the onslaught. However, there is a limit to their endurance, as they have a small, balled root system that is frequently washed out by rough surf generated by heavy storms.

The cabbage palmetto is one of only six or seven native palms in Florida. Silver palms, thatch palms, and the Paurotis palm all have fan-shaped leaves and

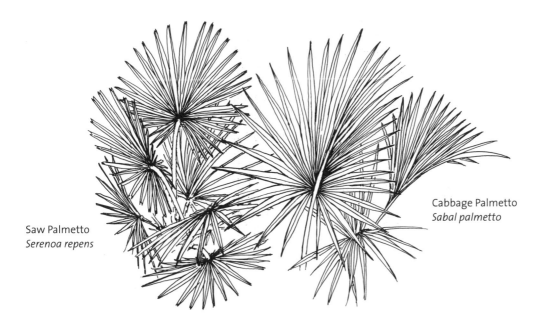

Saw Palmetto
Serenoa repens

Cabbage Palmetto
Sabal palmetto

are somewhat similar to the cabbage palmetto. The graceful symbol of south Florida, the coconut palm, in fact is an introduced species, as are most of the dozens of species of other palms growing in Florida. The cabbage palmetto ranges from North Carolina through Florida.

Tropical Trees. Below Jacksonville, near St. Augustine, the influence of the subtropics is quite pronounced, and it becomes more so the farther south one goes in Florida. There are three quite dissimilar, rather attractive plants that appear along the Inner Coast of Florida that we have dubbed the "trio of undesirables." These three are nonnative, or exotic, invasive, and undesirable introduced plants.

The Australian pine, *Casuarina equisetifolia*, is really not a pine at all; in fact it is not a conifer, or cone bearer. Three similar-appearing species of the same genus have been introduced to south Florida. They have dark green, feathery, scalelike leaves that appear to be needles but are actually jointed branchlets that give them a somewhat piney look.

This Australian native tree grows from about Fort Pierce southward through the Keys. It is an invasive tree that grows quite well along the upper edges of beaches and along canals, and it outcompetes native trees, including sea grape and bay cedar. It is quite nice to walk under the shade of these beautiful trees because hardly any vegetation grows under them. Apparently the soft carpets of needlelike branchlets that drop from the tree exude a chemical that stifles the growth of other plants.

The Brazilian pepper tree, *Schinus terebinthifolius*, is a sprawling evergreen shrub or small tree that grows to a height of about 25 feet. Brazilian pepper—a member of the cashew family, which also includes poison ivy, mango, and poison oak—bears small white flowers in clusters usually in the spring. It produces abundant bright red berries, drupes, on the female plant from late fall through winter; the fruit is persistent, so that there are usually some red berries present year-round. The leaves are aromatic when crushed and smell like turpentine. Some people are allergic to the plant and suffer skin irritations

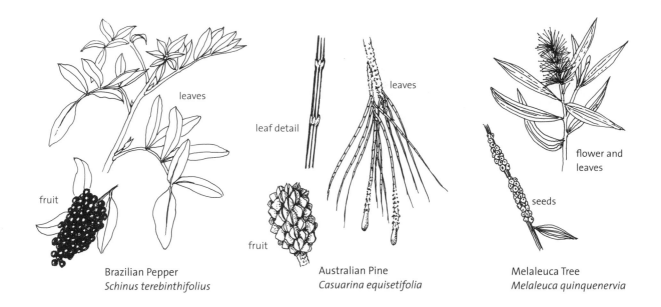

leaves

leaf detail

leaves

fruit

flower and
leaves

fruit

seeds

Brazilian Pepper
Schinus terebinthifolius

Australian Pine
Casuarina equisetifolia

Melaleuca Tree
Melaleuca quinquenervia

or respiratory complications. This highly invasive pest plant has adapted to a variety of habitats from central and southern Florida to the Keys.

The third plant in this trio of undesirable exotics is the melaleuca tree, *Melaleuca quinquenervia*, or cajeput tree. *Cajeput* is a combination of the Malaysian words for "tree" and "white bark." The melaleuca tree is an introduced Australian species that was originally intended as an ornamental to be used in various ways in parks and yards. The climate and the wet habitats of Florida suited the melaleuca tree, and it has become well established throughout south Florida wherever there are wet or moist conditions. It will take over an area and grow in thick groves, entirely displacing native plants. Melaleuca grows from the Indian River southward.

There are some shrubs or small trees with heart-shaped leaves that tend to grow in sprawling, dense thickets along the waterways in south Florida and the Keys. They belong to the mallow family, a large family of plants comprising over 900 species. Some

of the plants are quite familiar to most of us, including the beautiful ornamental hibiscus, okra, and rose of Sharon. Then there is cotton, as well as some twenty species that have growth forms that range from herbaceous plants and shrubs to small trees. All of these plants have the familiar hibiscuslike blossom, whether it is herbaceous, like the hibiscus's, or woody, like the rose of Sharon's.

Two of the many plants of the mallow family that grow in south Florida and the Keys are the sea hibiscus, *Hibiscus tiliaceus*, and the seaside mahoe, or Portia tree, *Thespesia populnea*. These shrubs or small trees are native to Asia and were introduced for their beautiful ornamental flowers. They are found throughout the Caribbean and south Florida.

The sea hibiscus is an evergreen shrub or small tree with a broad, rounded crown and a short trunk. The 4 1/2-inch-long heart-shaped leaves are alternately arranged with margins that may be smooth or slightly toothed. The underside has fine white hairs. The familiar hibiscuslike blossom has five overlap-

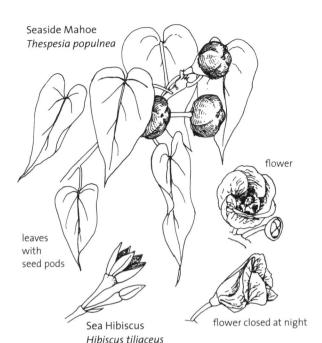

Seaside Mahoe
Thespesia populnea

leaves
with
seed pods

flower

Sea Hibiscus
Hibiscus tiliaceus
seed pod

flower closed at night

ping lemon or light yellow petals with a red spot at the base of each petal. The flower, about 5 inches across, never opens fully; rather, it is cup shaped. The flowers fade to a dull red or purple at day's end.

Seaside mahoe grows widely in coastal woods, in hammocks, and along the water's edge in south Florida and the Keys. It typically grows as a spreading shrub with low branches but can grow to a tree about 30 feet tall. Its glossy leaves are alternately arranged and are similar to those of the sea hibiscus except that they are only 2–5 inches long, and they lack hairs on the underside. The flowers are almost identical to those of the sea hibiscus, with pale yellow petals that fade to a dull pink or rose by dusk. To distinguish between the two species, check the leaves and fruit: seaside mahoe has leathery, globe-shaped capsules; sea hibiscus has smaller seeds with pointed tips.

Beneath the tall trees of wooded shorelines, there are also many shrubs, small trees, tangles of vines, and ferns that form the understory. Just what is a shrub? Our definition of a shrub is a small, woody plant that usually has multiple trunks, but may have a single trunk, and does not exceed 15 feet in height. Some shrubs may be described by others as trees, and vice versa. The lush vegetation of the understory offers food, nesting areas, and protection for many birds, reptiles, and mammals. Some of the species of smaller trees and shrubs that are found throughout the Inner Coast are the devil's walking stick, American holly, yaupon holly, winterberry, titi, northern bayberry, and wax myrtle.

The devil's walking stick, *Aralia spinosa*, is a delicate and attractive member of the ginseng family. Its common name undoubtedly refers to the many stout prickles, or thorns, that arm the trunk and the wide-spreading branches. The leaves are large, alternate, and featherlike. The small, whitish flowers grow in dense clusters and produce black, fleshy berries on reddish stalks. The devil's walking stick ranges from Nova Scotia to north Florida.

Hollies are a common component of acidic bottomland soils, where they often grow in association with dogwoods, sweet gum, red maple, and southern magnolia. They also grow among pines in sandy soils. Hollies flower in the spring, and the female trees typically produce red berries in the fall. Most holly species are small to medium-size trees or shrubs with alternate leaves that are usually leathery and evergreen. The flowers are generally quite small and aromatic; the fruits are red, yellow, or black berries.

American holly, *Ilex opaca*, is perhaps the best-known holly of the many holly species that grow throughout North America. It is the shrub or me-

Passage through the Great Dismal Swamp, with sweet gum entangled with muscadine grape vines in the foreground on the left and titi in front of a devil's walking stick on the right.

dium-size tree that is frequently depicted on Christmas cards. Its familiar deep green, leathery leaves and typical wavy margins armed with spines and red berries are a Christmas icon. American holly grows throughout the Atlantic coast, down to about central Florida. The American holly can grow to a height of about 50 feet and develops a pyramidal crown and a straight trunk. The fruits of most hollies are eaten by a large number of songbirds and game birds; they eat the fruit and distribute seeds throughout the forests. It is common to see hollies growing under the spreading branches of a sweet gum or a southern red oak.

Yaupon holly, *Ilex vomitoria*, a more southern species than American holly, ranges from Virginia to central Florida and farther south along Florida's west coast. The yaupon is a small tree or shrub that tends to form thickets. The shiny green leaves are alternately arranged and slightly wavy, or crenate. The twigs bear an abundance of red berries that tend to persist throughout the winter. Indians brewed a tea from the leaves of the yaupon for various religious and purification rites. Yaupon holly is very rich in caffeine, and it apparently caused the imbiber to retch the contents of his stomach, hence the name *vomitoria*.

Winterberry, *Ilex verticillata*, is a deciduous holly that grows as a shrub or small tree in swamps and moist areas. Winterberry is widely distributed, ranging from the Maritimes to northern Florida. Typical of most hollies, the winterberry is slow growing. The leaves are leathery, egg shaped, and coarsely toothed. This holly produces bright red berries that persist throughout the winter, as they do not appear to be a favored food of wildlife.

Titi, *Cyrilla racemiflora*, is a small tree or shrub that typically grows in thickets. Titi (pronounced "tie-tie") is a reluctantly deciduous plant that appears

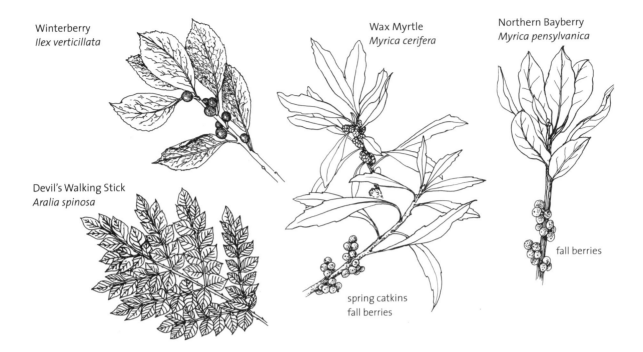

Winterberry
Ilex verticillata

Devil's Walking Stick
Aralia spinosa

Wax Myrtle
Myrica cerifera

spring catkins
fall berries

Northern Bayberry
Myrica pensylvanica

fall berries

to be evergreen; leaves, however, drop throughout the winter, and some remain until new foliage appears in the spring. Abundant flowers are borne in clusters at the ends of twigs; the nectar of these flowers is a favorite of bees. Titi grows along the edges of forested wetlands, swamps, and pinelands and is common throughout the Inner Coast to north Florida.

Northern bayberry, *Myrica pensylvanica*, and wax myrtle, *Myrica cerifera*, are two shrubs commonly seen growing along the upper edges of marshes, on small patches of high ground and maritime and bay edge woods, and on sandy, sun-baked soils of barrier islands.

Northern bayberry has a gray trunk with small, dark blue, hard berries that adhere closely to the stem. The northern bayberry is a reluctantly deciduous shrub that does not shed all of its leaves at the same time. It is a stiff-branched shrub that grows to a height of 10 feet or more. The round-tipped leaves

may be entire—that is, smooth bordered—or they may be finely toothed. The leaves are dark green on the upper surface with yellow resinous spots on the underside. The northern bayberry thrives in acidic soils along with pines, cedars, dogwoods, and hollies. They are tolerant of some salinity in the soil and varying soil moisture. The northern bayberry grows in maritime and bay edge woods, between dunes, and at the upper edges of marshes. It ranges from the Maritimes to North Carolina, where it dwindles and is replaced by the more southerly distributed wax myrtle.

Wax myrtle, also called southern bayberry or candleberry, is a shrub or small tree that can grow to a height of about 25 feet. They have deep green, alternately arranged leaves that tend to cluster at the ends of twigs. The leaf is often twisted near the center of the blade. The leaves and the small, grayish blue to purple berries that grow close to the stem are laden

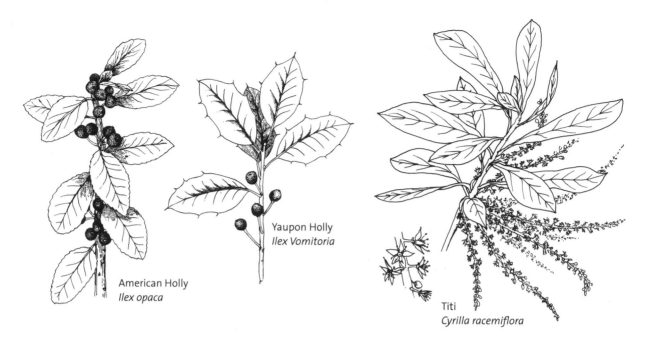

American Holly
Ilex opaca

Yaupon Holly
Ilex Vomitoria

Titi
Cyrilla racemiflora

with waxy, aromatic granules. The leaves are fragrant when crushed. The berries were once boiled to extract the fragrant wax for candle making. The wax myrtle ranges from southern New Jersey to Florida. It is widespread throughout Florida, including the Keys.

There are fan palms that sprawl and carpet the floor of piney woods and groves of live oak. They closely resemble cabbage palmettos and, in fact, appear to be young cabbage palmettos. But they are different species that do not grow into tall trees but remain as shrubby bushes or small, branched trees. These are the saw palmetto and the dwarf palmetto.

The saw palmetto, *Serenoa repens*, is a creeping palm (*repens* means "creeping" or "crawling") with horizontal buried stems that sometimes are upright and treelike. The saw palmetto has three-edged spiny petioles, or leaf stalks. Palmetto thickets can be quite dense; the plants grow close together and can reach a height of about 4–8 feet. The sharp, sawtoothlike

spines curve downward and present a formidable armament for any person or animal attempting to pass through palmetto scrub. The fan-shaped leaves are quite similar to those of the cabbage palmetto except that the leaf stalk does not continue as an arching midrib; rather, the leaflets of the fan are attached to the end of the leaf stalk. The fragrant flowers are creamy to pale yellow and hang in clusters from elongated, branched stalks. The fruits are bluish black drupes. Saw palmettos are common in piney flatlands and under the canopy of live oaks, particularly where there is some light penetrating the canopy. They sometimes grow at the upper edges of salt marshes and on isolated hammocks, but they prefer drier soils. The saw palmetto is found in South Carolina only in Jasper and Beaufort counties, the two most southern counties, and is quite abundant and common throughout Florida and Georgia.

Dwarf palmetto, or bluestem palmetto, *Sabal minor*, is quite similar to the saw palmetto; however, its leaf stalks are not armed with spines. The fan-shaped leaves may be green to bluish green, and, as in the saw palmetto, the leaflets are attached to the end of the leaf stalk. The stems are usually buried with just the leaf stalks and fan-shaped leaves aboveground. The flowers and fruit are similar to those of the saw palmetto. The saw palmetto and dwarf palmetto may be found growing in the same locale; however, the dwarf palmetto grows quite well in wetter soils. It is more tolerant of cooler temperatures than the saw palmetto and ranges from Dare County, North Carolina (the county bordered by the Alligator River), throughout the Inner Coast, down through Georgia and Florida. The fruits of the palmettos, including the cabbage palmettos, are fed on by robins, crows, mockingbirds, and raccoons. Extracts of the fruit are used in the treatment of prostate disorders.

HERBACEOUS PLANTS, WOODY VINES, FERNS, AND SUCCULENTS

We have included several plants from different groups that grow along the forested shorelines. There are many flowering plants that punctuate the shoreline, with colorful names such as lizard's tail, swamp azalea, spider lily, and jewelweed. Woody vines are everywhere intertwined among the trees, including yellow jessamine and the lovely coral honeysuckle vine, prickly greenbrier, and poison ivy. Ferns carpet the moist soils in wet woods and along the shorelines.

Little yellow sundrops accent the green foliage of the dense forest. Sundrops, *Oenothera fruticosa*, are particularly abundant along the Dismal Swamp Canal. They are members of the evening primrose family, but unlike most members of the family, sundrops bloom during the day. Look for yellow flowers with four petals on erect, hairy stems 2 to 4 feet long.

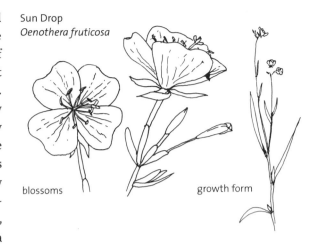

Sun Drop
Oenothera fruticosa

blossoms   growth form

The swamp rose, *Rosa palustris*, grows upright to almost 10 feet tall. Its thorns are somewhat decurved; that is, they point downward. The 2-inch, pale pink, five-petaled showy flowers with yellow centers are short lived. The flowers tend to grow in clusters. The fruit is a hip, the typical fleshy or leathery fruit of roses that matures in the fall. The swamp rose is a plant of the coastal plain that grows in tidal freshwater marshes, water courses, and forested swamps. It ranges from New England to central Florida.

Grapevines, thorny and wiry tendrils of greenbrier, and poison ivy literally cover shrubs and small trees and climb the trunks of larger trees to reach the sun. It is often difficult to see the host shrub under the heavy growth of vines. Along the shorelines of wetland forests, there are three species of wild grapes: the summer grape, or pigeon grape; the fox grape; and the muscadine grape, or scuppernong grape, that grows in a tangled profusion on shrubs and trees.

Summer grape, *Vitis aestivalis*, grows up into the trees. The leaves are heart shaped with 3–5 lobes; the tendrils are divided; and the fruit is dusted with a whitish cast. The leaves of the fox grape, *Vitis labrusca*, are similar to those of the summer grape;

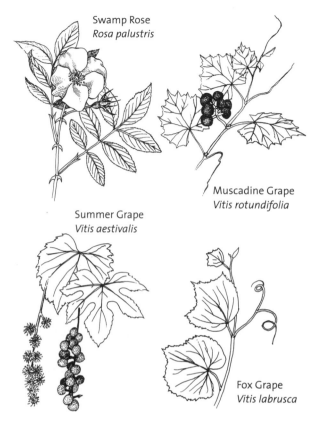

Swamp Rose
Rosa palustris

Muscadine Grape
Vitis rotundifolia

Summer Grape
Vitis aestivalis

Fox Grape
Vitis labrusca

momea. The royal fern is a tall, feathery fern that grows in clumps or tussocks in moist bottomlands, swamps, and freshwater marshes. It has spore-bearing leaflets at the ends of stalks that look like clusters of rust-brown flowers. The royal fern is distributed throughout the world except for Australia. The cinnamon fern is also a tall-growing fern, up to about 5 feet tall, that has leaflike fronds that may be 12 inches wide. The compound leaflets of the sterile frond are usually alternately arranged, sometimes almost oppositely arranged. The fertile fronds are what give the cinnamon fern its name. The compound leaflets of the fertile fronds bear sporangia that are at first greenish and then ripen into a cinnamon-brown. Cinnamon ferns grow in piney woods, swampy areas, and most bottomlands. The cinnamon fern ranges from the Maritimes to Florida.

Prickly pear cactus, *Opuntia humifusa*, grows on dry, sandy soils, in open woods and often on small hummocks along with a few red cedars or southern red cedars, pines, wax myrtles, and occasionally Spanish bayonets. The prickly pear ranges widely from Massachusetts to Florida and throughout the Caribbean, where it is frequently called tuna. It often

however, the undersurfaces of fox grape leaves are overgrown with tan to reddish hairs. The grapes are deep, dark red to almost purple-black. The muscadine grape, *Vitis rotundifolia*, has heart-shaped leaves with toothed margins. The fruit is purple to black, and sometimes the grapes are amber green and are known as scuppernongs. Carolinians make scuppernong wine from the grapes and wreaths from the woody vines.

Ferns of many species, depending on soil types and moisture and light levels, carpet the forest floors. Two of the more common ferns that grow in this region of the Inner Coast are the royal fern, *Osmunda regalis*, and the cinnamon fern, *Osmunda cinna-*

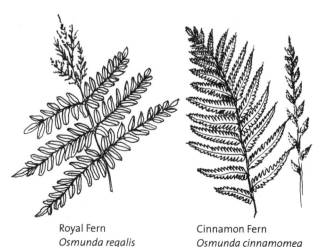

Royal Fern
Osmunda regalis

Cinnamon Fern
Osmunda cinnamomea

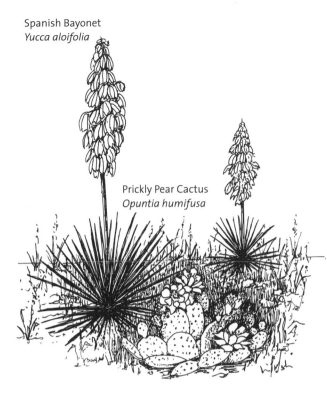

Spanish Bayonet
Yucca aloifolia

Prickly Pear Cactus
Opuntia humifusa

grows erect to about 15 inches, but it also sprawls in dense mats. The succulent, green, fleshy pads of the cactus are variously armed with nodes bearing tufts of reddish brown bristles and round, needle-sharp spines. They bear lovely, 3-inch yellow flowers in late spring and summer and edible, fleshy red to purplish fruit in late summer and fall.

Spanish bayonet, *Yucca aloifolia*, is a plant of the lily family that grows to 10 feet high or more. This succulent has a 3- to 5-inch erect trunk that is equipped with 2-foot-long, straplike leaves edged with spines and a very sharp, pointed tip. As the leaves age, they turn brown and droop around the base of the plant like a hula skirt. Creamy white, densely clustered flowers are borne on spikes that may be as long as 2 feet. Spanish bayonets form thickets as new buds, or offshoots, grow from the base of the trunk. They grow along the shores of the Inner Coast on washed-up oyster shells, or shell mounds, along the back margins of marshes, on hummocks, and on sand dunes. The Spanish bayonet ranges along the southeast coast from Virginia through Florida.

Animals of Wooded Shorelines

INSECTS

The wet floors of forested wetlands and swamps provide breeding grounds for myriad insects that dart through the luxuriant growth, fly in cloudy swarms, and skitter across the surface of practically any body of standing water. There are millions of mosquitoes and biting flies, gnats and no-see-ums, predacious diving beetles, sculling water boatmen, gliding dragonflies, and lacy-winged dobsonflies that are beautiful as adults and grotesque as larvae. All of these are widely distributed along the Inner Coast from Virginia to Florida. Although many of these species are found in forested wetlands, we will discuss them in other, more specific habitats, such as marshes, beaches, and shallow waters.

AMPHIBIANS AND REPTILES

Amphibians and reptiles, collectively called herpetofauna, or "herps" for short, abound in areas where there are decayed logs, piles of brush and leaves, lush growths of intertwining vines, wet soil, standing water, flowing streams, and sunny slopes. The Inner Coast provides just such habitats for many herps, including frogs, snakes, turtles, and alligators.

Frogs. There are many different frogs in North America: cricket frogs, tree frogs, chorus frogs, true (or pond) frogs, and the closely related toads. Typical toads generally have warty skin and short legs for

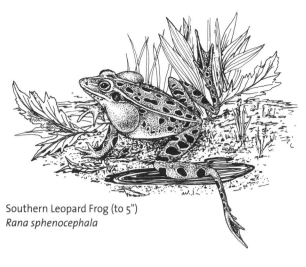

Southern Leopard Frog (to 5")
Rana sphenocephala

hopping and for short jumps. Frogs usually have smooth skin and long, muscular legs for leaping and swimming.

The southern leopard frog, *Rana sphenocephala*, belongs to a tangled complex, or assemblage, consisting of many subtle differences in form, color, pattern, and size. The confusion of slight differences has resulted in frequent changes in the taxonomy, or classification, of frogs. The southern leopard frog's species name, *sphenocephala*, from the Greek meaning "wedge head," quite nicely describes the shape of its head, which is more pointed than that of its close relative the northern leopard frog. Southern leopard frogs average 2 to 3 1/2 inches in length, and in some localized areas, such as the lower Florida Keys, they may reach 5 inches. They may be green or brown or sometimes a combination; they have a variety of dark spots or splotches on their backs and sides; and their bellies are white. They also have a light-colored line along the upper jaw and light-colored dorsal lateral ridges running along the back. The tympanum, a circular membrane located behind the eye and considered to be the frog's eardrum, is characterized by a white spot in the center. Southern leopard frogs

are often hunted for their delectable legs. They are not easy to catch, as many a youngster has learned: the frog sitting on the edge of a canal usually quickly escapes by springing into the water and, at the same time, turning instantly to the right or left, leaving the hunter perplexed as to where the frog has gone.

The call of the leopard frog is a short, guttural trill of ten to twelve per second, and they also make a "chuckling" call. The female lays a firm mass of eggs on aquatic vegetation, and the eggs hatch into tadpoles in about two weeks; three months later, the tadpoles begin their metamorphosis into frogs. There is a Florida form of the southern leopard frog, considered by some to be a subspecies and by others to be just a minor variant of the same species. The southern leopard frog is abundant and widely distributed throughout the Inner Coast and the mid-central United States.

Snakes. The eastern diamondback rattlesnake, *Crotalus adamenteus*, is one of the largest, most feared venomous snakes in North America. Its scientific name means "one that makes a rattling noise and is both stubborn and unyielding," a most appropriate description. Rattlesnakes, as well as copperhead and cottonmouth snakes, belong to the pit viper family, or Viperidae. They all share certain characteristics: most are stout bodied, with vertical pupils; they have heat-sensing pits on both sides of their broad, triangular heads; and they form internal eggs. The young are born alive as small and venomous copies of the adult.

The eastern diamondback rattlesnake can grow to over 6 feet long. This fearsome snake is easily recognized by its dark brown or black diamond markings bordered by white, cream, or yellow edges. The rattling apparatus at the tip of the tail is formed of horny interlocking segments made of keratin, similar to the composition of our fingernails. The num-

Eastern Diamondback Rattlesnake (to 96")
Crotalus adamenteus

head

body pattern

tail

Eastern Cottonmouth (to 74")
Agkistrodon piscivorus

head

body pattern

tail

ber of segments in the rattle is not a good indication of a snake's age, as some people believe, because as many as four rattle buttons can be added in a year, and, to further confuse the issue, some rattles may be lost because of injury. Nevertheless, the rattling of an eastern diamondback rattlesnake, whether it has four rattle segments or ten, can cause an instantaneous flow of adrenaline in the unwary intruder, producing a skin-tingling, hair-raising sensation . . . and an immediate realization that a rattlesnake is nearby. Eastern diamondback rattlesnakes sound their rattle by vibrating their tail, which produces a dry, buzzing sound. Sometimes, when disturbed, they will quickly slither away, but often they will coil in a distinctive "S" posture, with the forward part of their body raised vertically, and stand their ground. Diamondback rattlers feed on rabbits and other small mammals. Eastern diamondback rattlers inhabit the coastal plain of southeast North Carolina, South Carolina, and south to the Florida Keys, where they commonly take to the saltwater and swim to isolated mangrove islands. They lurk in the cavities of tree stumps, under piles of brush, and in the burrows of small mammals.

There are three other rattlesnakes that occur along the Inner Coast: the canebrake rattlesnake, or timber rattlesnake, and two pigmy rattlesnakes, the Carolina pigmy rattlesnake and the dusky pigmy rattlesnake. The canebrake rattlesnake is found in southeastern Virginia, particularly in the Great Dismal Swamp and in the mountains of western Virginia, and the Carolinas. It is not as distinctively marked as the eastern diamondback and is probably not as aggressive. Canebrake rattlesnakes are marked with brown to black zigzag splotches or chevrons. They are found sunning on rocky outcrops, in swamps and pocosins, and canebrakes. The two pigmy rattlesnakes, as their name implies, are smaller than the eastern diamondback and canebrake rattlesnakes: they usually are less than 2 feet long. The rattling sound of a pigmy rattlesnake has been likened to the distinct buzz of a cicada. Both species of pigmy rattlesnakes live in the piney flatwoods of the coastal plain and around marshes and lakes. The Carolina pigmy rattlesnake ranges from eastern North Carolina down through Georgia and westward to Alabama. The dusky pigmy rattlesnake is found throughout Florida.

Southern
Copperhead (to 53")
Agkistrodon contortrix

Almost every snake that is seen in the water is immediately labeled as a poisonous water moccasin or cottonmouth, when, in fact, all snakes can and do swim. There is a large group of water snakes, including the northern water snake, gulf salt marsh snake, mangrove salt marsh snake, and Atlantic salt marsh water snake, that are at home in the water, as well as on land. These snakes are nonpoisonous, but they are often aggressive and will readily strike when provoked. The northern water snake, as well as some of the other, more southern water snakes, is frequently confused with cottonmouth snakes of the poisonous pit viper family.

The eastern cottonmouth, *Agkistrodon piscivorus*, of the Southeast is a heavy-bodied snake that can reach a length of about 6 feet. It has a dark body and a lighter-colored belly. Young cottonmouths are well marked with cross bands and yellow tails; older cottonmouths are often indistinctly marked and may be completely dark brown or black. When agitated, a cottonmouth will often defend itself by standing its ground, coiling its body, and vibrating its tail. On occasion, it will also throw its wide head back and open its mouth wide to expose the whitish interior, hence the name cottonmouth. The Florida cottonmouth, a close relative of the eastern cottonmouth, is similar in behavior and size, but the cheek stripes on its head are bold and apparent even in older and darker individuals. Both cottonmouths are denizens of wet woodlands, swamps, rice fields, rivers, streams, and ponds. They feed on fishes, baby alligators, snakes, young turtles, and frogs and other amphibians. The eastern cottonmouth ranges along the coastal plain from southeastern Virginia to Georgia, and the Florida cottonmouth is distributed throughout Florida.

Another member of the pit viper family is the southern copperhead, *Agkistrodon contortrix*. This poisonous snake reaches a length of over 4 feet. It has the typical stout body and wide, triangular head of most pit vipers. The southern copperhead intergrades with the northern copperhead in higher elevations. The southern copperhead is a handsome snake with a tan or pinkish body marked with a brown narrow-waisted hourglass pattern. It is primarily a snake of the lowlands near swamps and cypress-lined bodies of water, where it feeds on small rodents, lizards, frogs, and large insects such as cicadas. The southern copperhead ranges from the coastal plain of Virginia to extreme northern Florida.

Turtles. Turtles have expanded ribs that form part of the carapace, the upper shell, and a horny beak that lacks teeth but can inflict a painful bite. Turtles, similar to other reptiles and amphibians, cannot control their temperatures internally and are often referred to as cold blooded, or poikilothermic. Their body temperatures vary with environmental temperatures, and, consequently, turtles and snakes

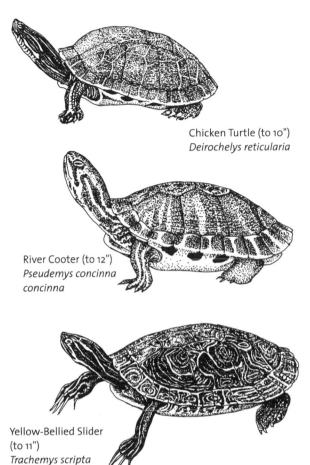

Chicken Turtle (to 10")
Deirochelys reticularia

River Cooter (to 12")
*Pseudemys concinna
concinna*

Yellow-Bellied Slider
(to 11")
Trachemys scripta

low and greenish gray stripes, and the thighs of the back legs are vertically striped, sometimes comically, called "striped pants." The closely related Florida chicken turtle, *Deirochelys reticularia chrysea*, is more boldly colored and patterned.

Chicken turtles, so called for their once highly favored meat, are great walkers and roam extensively overland. They avoid rivers, favoring still, calm, weedy ponds and lakes, ditches and sloughs, and cypress-lined ponds. Chicken turtles change their diet as they mature, being carnivorous when young and almost exclusively vegetarian as they age. In turn, they are preyed on by raccoons, otters, herons, and alligators. The chicken turtle ranges from Virginia Beach near Back Bay, where it was reportedly introduced, throughout the coastal plain of North Carolina, South Carolina, and Georgia. It inhabits the northern portion of Florida, where it merges with the Florida chicken turtle, which is distributed throughout central and southern Florida, except the Keys.

Cooters and sliders love to bask in the sun, and they often line up on logs or stack one on another on a tree snag or rock or other favorite haul-out. These are large turtles, about a foot in length. The term "cooter" is used throughout the South and is probably derived from the African word *kuta*, which means "turtle" in some Niger-Congo regional dialects.

The river cooter, *Pseudemys concinna concinna*, has a dark rough or crinkly carapace marked with cream to yellow concentric rings. River cooters are gregarious creatures, often associating not only with other river cooters but also with yellow-bellied sliders and Florida redbelly turtles. River cooters prefer rivers with a moderate flow of current, and consequently, they are found in upper coastal rivers and the piedmont, where the rivers flow faster than down along the lower coastal plain. The river cooter ranges along the Inner Coast from Virginia through the

are quiescent when the external temperature is cold and active when the external temperature is warm. Turtles love to bask in the sun, sometimes floating at the surface or lined up on logs or tree snags and along the edges of shorelines.

The chicken turtle, *Deirochelys reticularia*, is a common turtle throughout its range. The species name, *reticularia*, refers to the netted, finely wrinkled carapace. The carapace is long and narrow, widest over the hind legs. The bottom shell, or plastron, is yellow and usually unmarked. The yellow-striped neck is very long when fully extended, almost as long as the shell. Its forelegs are marked with wide, yel-

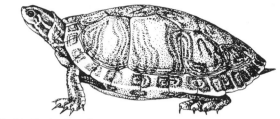
Florida Cooter (to 15")
Pseudemys floridana floridana

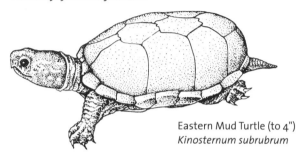
Eastern Mud Turtle (to 4")
Kinosternum subrubrum

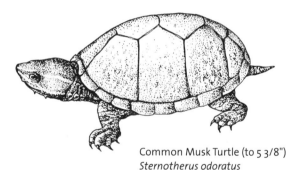
Common Musk Turtle (to 5 3/8")
Sternotherus odoratus

Carolinas and into northeastern Georgia. There are two other species of cooters that prefer slower-moving streams, boggy areas, and calm backwaters and sloughs: the Florida cooter and the peninsula cooter. The Florida cooter, *Pseudemys floridana floridana*, belies its name, ranging from Virginia through the Carolinas and Georgia to northern Florida. The Florida cooter is a large turtle measuring to 15 inches in length. Its textured carapace is patterned with irregularly branched yellow markings. In contrast to the river cooter, the Florida cooter prefers the quiet

waters of places like the Great Dismal Swamp and slow-moving rivers rank with vegetation.

The peninsula cooter, *Pseudemys floridana peninsularis,* ranges from north central Florida, where it mixes with the Florida cooter, down to Key Largo. Its extended head and neck are characteristically marked with long, yellow narrow loops, or hairpins. It is the only cooter marked in that manner. The peninsular cooter is a conspicuous and common turtle in canals and sluggish streams.

The yellow-bellied slider, *Trachemys scripta*, is another sun lover. It is a smaller version of the larger cooters, measuring some 11 inches. It generally has a dark carapace with light yellow or transverse bars, more easily seen in young turtles and females, particularly when their shells are wet and glistening. The yellow-bellied slider, as the name implies, has a yellow plastron marked by a few blackish blotches. It is also marked with distinctive patches of yellow just behind both eyes, which taper into two yellow stripes extending down the neck. Its legs are striped with yellow, but the stripes are narrow compared with those of the chicken turtle. Like the chicken turtle, it has posterior thighs marked with yellow stripes, or "striped pants." The yellow-bellied slider and its close relative the red-eared turtle were once familiar as the turtles that were sold as pets in dime stores. The yellow-bellied slider ranges from southeast Virginia to northern Florida.

Musk and mud turtles are small, drab turtles with the nasty habit of protecting themselves by exuding a foul-smelling discharge from glands located at the sides of their carapaces. They are also quite willing to bite; small they may be, but defenseless they are not. They are predominantly aquatic and crawl along soft-bottomed, shallow bodies of water.

The eastern mud turtle, *Kinosternum subrubrum,* also aptly known as the stinkpot, is 3 to 4 inches long with a relatively smooth, olive to dark brown carapace. They have a large, double-hinged, or articulated, yellow to brown plastron. There are few distinctive marks on the head; it may be slightly spotted, all dark, or faintly streaked with light yellow, irregular lines. The mud turtle is the exception to most mud and musk turtles in that it often wanders overland. It tolerates brackish water more than do the other members of this group and may often be found along the margins of tidal marshes. It is found where waters are slow moving, such as the backwaters of meandering rivers and streams, and also is quite common in ditches, ponds, and lakes.

The eastern mud turtle is primarily a nocturnal animal feeding underwater at night on insects, small clams, snails, worms, and vegetation. These turtles often nest or rest during the day in muskrat and beaver lodges and alligator nests. They range throughout the Inner Coast down to north Florida, where they merge with the closely related Florida mud turtle, which is distributed throughout Florida as far south as Key Largo.

The common musk turtle, *Sternotherus odoratus*, also known as a stinkpot, or stinking Jim, is an abundant but infrequently observed little turtle. It is strongly aquatic and seldom leaves the moving shallow waters that it favors. The musk turtle has the peculiar habit of sometimes climbing and basking on small tree limbs that overhang the water, and when alarmed, they have been known to drop in on canoes and other craft. Musk turtles have two light yellow stripes on their heads and very small plastrons compared to those of mud turtles. The musk turtle is abundant throughout the Inner Coast from Virginia and throughout Florida, except the Keys. The loggerhead musk turtle, characterized by an enlarged head in older males, is found in north Florida and along the east coast to about Cape Canaveral.

BIRDS

Not everyone is a bird watcher, but birds are so conspicuous that it is difficult to avoid seeing and hearing them anywhere one goes. They soar high overhead; they perch on power lines and tree limbs; they flit through the woods; they hop and strut over stream banks and golf courses; they dive and dabble in the water; and they make themselves heard by singing, calling, and tapping on trees.

Heavily wooded shorelines provide excellent habitats for feeding, nesting, and roosting for a variety of birds. Hawks perch, sentinel-like, on tree limbs; vultures festoon dead trees almost as in cartoons; and here and there is a lyrical, almost liquid, call of the wood thrush.

Then, with a "zweet, zweet, zweet," the prothonotary warbler, *Protonotaria citrea*, announces itself where it is perched on a branch overhanging a stream bank. This beautiful yellow warbler is found in river-bottom forests, swamps, cypress-lined ponds, and wooded areas where the water is slow moving or stagnant. The male prothonotary warbler has a bright orange-yellow head and breast, gray wings, and a short gray tail. The female is also yellow and gray but is not as brilliantly colored. The unusual name "prothonotary" refers to court officers and church scribes who, at one time, wore yellow hoods or bright yellow robes. Prothonotary warblers typically nest in cavities of sweet gums, red maples, river birches, and ash trees. They are common along the Inner Coast from Virginia to central Florida.

The hooded merganser, *Lophodytes cucullatus* (which in Latin and Greek refers to the crest or hood of this member of the merganser family) is most often found in wooded wetland ponds and swamps and sometimes in the brackish waters of the Intracoastal Waterway and tributaries. The hooded merganser, never very abundant, has a characteristic

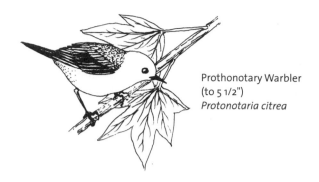
Prothonotary Warbler
(to 5 1/2")
Protonotaria citrea

puffy, black and white hood in the male; the female has a brownish hood. They are great divers, and their forcepslike, narrow bill is beautifully designed to grasp fishes, frogs, and insects. They nest in tree cavities in wooded wetlands, much like wood ducks. Hooded mergansers are found throughout the Inner Coast, particularly during the fall and winter.

The wood duck, *Aix sponsa*, is a startlingly beautiful duck with a wonderful scientific name that means "waterfowl in a bridal dress." The male is vividly marked with a striped face and a head dressed in iridescent greens and purples, with a smooth, swept-back crest, a white throat, and a chestnut-colored breast. The female is mottled brown with a white teardrop-shaped eye patch and a short, dark crest. The sharp bill is marked with red or orange in the male and a duller brown in the female. The wood duck's feet are equipped with sharp claws that enable it to climb and perch in trees.

The wood duck was close to extinction in the late 1800s because of heavy market hunting for its plumage, meat, and eggs. In addition, logging in the early 1900s laid waste to the wood duck's essential habitat, the wooded wetlands of the Inner Coast. Hunting restrictions placed on the wood duck (and other waterfowl) have helped the population rebuild, and their nesting potential has been greatly improved by hunting and conservation groups' placing nesting boxes in their bottomland nesting areas. Wood ducks typically nest in tree cavities lined with down. Ducklings, as young as two days old, can climb up to the cavity of the tree to the opening of the nest by using needle-sharp claws and the hook at the end of the bill. The ducklings jump from the nest to the ground when the mother calls and are soon swimming in woodland ponds of the bottomlands. Wood ducks are widespread throughout the Inner Coast.

Bald eagles, *Haliaeetus leucocephalus*, are a common sight these days along the Inner Coast. They are often spotted perched high in a tree near the water's edge, patiently waiting for a small mammal to reveal itself or a duck to swim into range, but they more usually feed on fishes. Surprisingly, this fierce-looking predator often feeds on carrion, particularly dead fish along the shore.

Bald eagles, the symbol of this country, are also a symbol of what humans have done to the environment, as well as what we have done to right some of those wrongs. Perhaps the bald eagle was the only living creature in America that could have provided the rallying point around which society could take a

Wood Duck (to 18 1/2")
Aix sponsa

Hooded Merganser (to 18")
Lophodytes cucullatus

Bald Eagle (to 37")
Haliaeetus leucocephalus

stand. The stand was a success, and now bald eagles are again flourishing.

The bald eagle is one of the ten species of the sea eagle group throughout the world. Adult bald eagles are instantly recognized by their massive white heads and tails; large, hooked yellow beaks; and yellow feet and eyes. They do not attain that familiar plumage until their seventh year; the young are entirely brown, without white heads or tails. An adult eagle's wingspread may exceed 7 feet. They soar with flattened wings, as contrasted to vultures, which soar with wings cocked at the midline in a shallow V or, as some call it, a dihedral.

Eagles nest high in the trees. Some of the older nests, which are rebuilt from year to year, are massive; they may weigh hundreds of pounds. Eagles, like ospreys, build their nests of branches, sticks, and leaves, and then they become creative, collecting an odd assortment of embellishments to decorate their lifelong abodes. They may weave in old fishing rods, tractor caps, shoes, or gloves found along the shore to finish the project.

Vultures are expert soaring birds that expend little effort climbing, circling, and gliding. Sometimes vultures are called buzzards, but buzzards are Old World birds more closely related to hawks. The vultures in North America apparently are more closely related to storks. Even though all vultures seem to resemble each other, New World vultures and condors differ internally from Old World species in the structure of their skulls and in the proportion and arrangement of their toes. American vultures, including the California condor and the Andean condor, are among the largest birds alive today. All American vultures have naked heads, which makes them perfectly suited for sticking their heads into the cavities of dead animals. They lack a voice and can make only a menacing hissing sound. Their talons are weak and not useful for grasping and carrying off prey, as other raptors, such as eagles and hawks, do. The turkey vulture, *Cathartes aura*, is the most widely distributed vulture in North America, and it is abundant year-round along the Inner Coast. Turkey vultures, as well as other vultures and condors, primarily feed on carrion, although they sometimes feed on insects and hapless fishes stranded in shallow ponds. The turkey vulture has a wingspread of 6 feet and a bare red head, and the trailing halves of the wings are silvery gray. Vultures are social birds and are often seen wheeling in great circles by the dozens or on the ground feeding on the carcass of roadkill. They roost communally in large trees and on buildings.

The black vulture, *Coragyps atratus*, is only slightly smaller than the turkey vulture. Its head is naked, gray, and wrinkled, and its primaries (the fingerlike feathers at the end of the wing) are silvery gray. It flies somewhat differently than the turkey vulture: it periodically flaps its flatter wings and does not teeter or rock, as does the turkey vulture. The black vulture is a more aggressive bird than the turkey vulture,

Black vultures scavenging on the shore.

and when feeding together, the black vulture usually wins the larger chunks of meat. The black vulture is a more southern bird, although it is expanding its range in the Northeast.

Travel along a back road or a waterway anywhere along the Inner Coast, and chances are that you will spot a lone bird quietly standing upright on a tree branch. It may have a buff-colored breast streaked with red or dark brown markings, a belly band, and a strongly hooked beak; there is no question that it is a hawk, and odds are that it is a red-tailed hawk, *Buteo jamaicensis*. The red-tailed hawk is the most widely distributed hawk in North America; it ranges from the Atlantic coast to the Pacific, and from Canada to the Gulf of Mexico. These are bulky and broad-winged hawks that soar like vultures, effortlessly, some say "pinned to the sky." They hunt for small mammals, reptiles, and birds from their lofty perches or as they wheel in never-ending circles. The red-tailed hawk has a bright rusty red tail that is quite visible when the bird is in flight, a sure indication that it is a red-tailed hawk.

Where there is water, there will generally be a belted kingfisher, *Ceryle alcyon*, perched on an overhead power line or in a tree or shrub near the water's edge. The belted kingfisher at first glance seems to resemble a blue jay or a squat, stubby woodpecker with a shaggy crest. But the raucous, woody, rattling call signals that this is a perky, feisty, belted kingfisher. Belted kingfishers live along the edges of ponds and lakes and along estuarine shorelines and rivers. They range throughout much of North America. There are two other species that are found only in southern Texas, usually in the Rio Grande valley.

Belted kingfishers feed primarily on fishes, although they sometimes feed on small snakes, aquatic insects, tadpoles, crayfish, and young birds. They are crow size and stocky, with large heads, large bills,

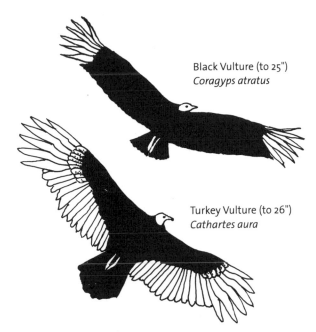

Black Vulture (to 25")
Coragyps atratus

Turkey Vulture (to 26")
Cathartes aura

The length of the tail and the light underwing pattern separate the two vultures.

leaves into which the female deposits about six white eggs. When the young have left the nest and are just beginning to fly, the parents drop food into the water to tempt them to drop off their perches and catch their meal. Kingfishers are very wary of humans and, when alarmed, will dash from cover and fly parallel over the water with their heads slightly raised. They fly with rapid, halting wing beats, uttering their rattling, staccato call that, once heard, will not be easily forgotten. Although they will not tolerate other belted kingfishers in their territory, they commonly share hunting grounds with herons, egrets, and other wading and diving birds, such as cormorants and swans and, farther south, roseate spoonbills.

Wet woods and swamps are favorite haunts of the yellow-crowned night-heron, *Nyctanassa violacea.* The yellow-crowned night-heron is a medium-size heron with a blue-gray body, a black head with a distinctive white to creamy cap, and stark white cheek patches. It is slightly smaller than its close relative the black-crowned night-heron. Its bill is shorter but

and short necks. Both sexes have a ragged crest, a white neck, and a gray-blue breast band; the female has a reddish brown belly band. A kingfisher habitually hunts from a few favored perches in its small territory; it darts to where it has spotted a fish or other prey, hovers over the spot, and plunges into the water. It then returns to its favorite perch, usually with a fish grasped in its bill. Kingfishers are normally solitary birds, except during breeding season, and will not share their small territory with other kingfishers. During breeding season, the male and female construct an unusual nest, a horizontal burrow dug in a sandy bank along the water. Their strong bills and legs are well adapted for digging and removing sand and debris from the excavation. The tunnel into the bank side can be 3 or more feet long. They line the end of the burrow with grasses and

Red-Tailed Hawk (to 22")
Buteo jamaicensis

Belted Kingfisher (to 13")
Ceryle alcyon

stouter, and its legs are longer, so that, in flight, they extend well beyond its tail. Yellow-crowned night-herons have orange eyes, a black bill with a yellowish patch at the base, and yellow to orange legs. The sexes are similar in coloration and pattern; the immature birds are brownish. They stand straighter than do black-crowned night-herons. These birds are called night herons because they usually forage during times of low light . . . but not always; they often actively hunt during the day, when the tides are low and the water is shallow. They are generally solitary feeders—in fact, they are generally secretive loners—but they will often share a mudflat or a shallow stretch of water with another yellow-crowned night-heron. They specialize in catching land crabs, fiddler crabs, and crayfish with their stout bills, but they also feed on fishes, insects, and mussels. They typically stand or slowly stalk the shallows, and when they see a quarry, they lunge and stab their prey.

Yellow-crowned night-herons are denizens of cypress and mangrove swamps, shallow tidal waters, and river bottoms. Sometimes they nest with other colonial waterbirds, and sometimes they nest as a single pair. Typically, they build rather substantial twig nests in trees about 30–40 feet above the ground, but they also nest in mangroves and shrubby thick-

ets. They range all along the Inner Coast from Virginia to the Florida Keys.

The black-crowned night-heron, *Nycticorax nycticorax*, is a stocky gray and white heron with a black crown and back. It has two or three white plumes trailing from the back of its neck. The slightly downcurved bill is relatively short for a heron. The legs and neck are also short compared to those of the blue heron and other "day-herons." The stocky appearance of this bird is further enhanced by its habit of hunching its neck into its body. Black-crowned night-herons roost in trees and await the dark to track their prey, which consists mostly of fishes and other aquatic organisms and occasional snakes, frogs, and rodents. They begin breeding as early as February, but most egg laying occurs between mid-March and late April. Their fragile nests are placed on shrubs, in dense undergrowth, and in cattail marshes. They live year-round in the Inner Coast.

The white-crowned pigeon, *Columba leucocephala*, is a rather large pigeon, about 13 1/2 inches long, with a gleaming white crown, or cap, setting off a

Yellow-Crowned
Night-Heron (to 24")
Nyctanassa violacea

Black-Crowned Night-Heron (to 25")
Nycticorax nycticorax

when they return from underwater excursions, they are often seen on tree stumps or low branches with their wings outspread; they are drying their plumage so they will be able to fly more efficiently, and they are also absorbing heat from the sun to regulate their internal temperature. Anhingas also share a characteristic of grebes: they can regulate the amount of air in their bodies so that they can either float high on the water or sink below the surface.

Anhingas are long, thin-necked birds with a small, snakelike head and a stiff, fanned tail. They have an interesting darting way of swimming. The male anhinga is black with a glossy green iridescence with silvery streaks on its wings and back. The female's neck and breast are tawny-tan or buff colored with a darker body. The immature birds are brownish. They nest with wading birds in small groups, mostly on willow clumps and other low shrubs.

These birds of the southern swamps—for they favor freshwater ponds and cypress swamps but are also found in the saltwater shallows and in the mangrove swamps—fish in a most unusual way. They swim underwater, and when they spot their prey, they quickly lunge with their powerful necks and impale the fish on their long bills. Then they rise to

slate gray body that appears almost black. Females and juveniles have a grayish crown. Like all pigeons, they have small, round heads and rather straight bills. The white-crowned pigeon's bill is somewhat yellow with a red base. This unmistakable pigeon is found only in south Florida, in the Keys and the Everglades, particularly along the back roads on No Name Key and Big Pine Key, and when they come in to roost on the red mangroves in Islamorada. They are also quite commonly seen on power lines along U.S. 1.

Anhinga, *Anhinga anhinga*, an interesting bird of the southern swamps, has various descriptive names: snakebird, water turkey, and darter. Anhinga (which means "water turkey" in a native South American language) is closely related to the cormorants. The anhinga, however, does not have a hooked bill like the cormorant but instead has a stiletto-shaped bill, beautifully adapted for impaling fishes and other prey. It shares another characteristic with the cormorants: the lack of oil glands. There is a tradeoff in lacking oil glands: diving birds, such as the cormorant and the anhinga, do not have to struggle with buoyancy; they glide through the water and use their energy to capture their prey. However, there is a price to pay:

White-Crowned Pigeon (to 13 1/2")
Columba leucocephala

With wings typically raised, one anhinga rests on a branch while another, swimming with its small head raised, shows why they are often called "snakebirds."

the surface, flip the fish off their bills, and catch and swallow it almost in a single, fluid motion. The anhinga ranges from the Carolinas through Florida.

MAMMALS

There are many bats that flit and glide, almost swimming through the air, at dusk and through the night. Most of North America's bats are insectivorous; they feast on flies, mosquitoes, small moths, flying ants, caddis flies, and other tasty flying morsels. Bats are the only mammals capable of true flight. They fly with a to-and-fro motion of their wings, as if they are swimming or rowing through the air. These flying shrews do not see well—the old saying "as blind as a bat" is not too far from the truth—but they can hear, and they hear in a most extraordinary manner. They emit high-pitched squeaks that are beyond the range of human hearing, and they send these squeaks out, while on the fly, in a barrage of rapid emissions. These high-pitched sound missiles bounce off potential prey and other objects, and the echo returns almost instantly to the bat's remarkable and complex hearing apparatus. The object is analyzed, and all the while a constant stream of new squeaks and echoes pass back and forth as the bat catches its prey and goes on to another and another. Dolphins and porpoises use echolocation, or sonar, to find their prey in a similar way.

One of the smallest bats in eastern North America is the eastern pipistrelle, *Pipistrellus subflavus*. This tiny bat is about 3 1/2 inches long and weighs less than 1/2 ounce. The scientific name means "little, pale yellow bat"; however, they range in color from a light yellowish brown to a reddish brown. The pipistrelle is one of the first bats to appear in the evening, and sometimes they are aloft during the day. They alight from maritime woods and bay edge forests and, with their characteristic jerky, erratic flight, skim over the surface of the water, sometimes in the company of tree swallows and swifts, who are all wheeling, gliding, and veering for a tasty morsel.

Eastern Pipistrelle
(to 3 1/2")
Pipistrellus subflavus

Seminole Bat (to 4 1/2")
Lasiurus seminolus

Pipistrelles are not generally gregarious; they roost singly or in small groups. They have two mating periods a year: they mate in the fall, and the sperm is stored while the female is in hibernation; and then they mate a second time, in the spring. The young are born during late spring and early summer, and the usual litter of two begins flying about three weeks after they are born. Pipistrelles roost near the water in clumps of Spanish moss, in rock crevices, in buildings, and sometimes in mines and caves. They range from the Maritimes to Florida.

The Seminole bat, *Lasiurus seminolus*, is one of the hairy-tailed bats. They are brick red to mahogany brown, and the tips of their hair may be frosted white. They are abundant along the southeast Atlantic coast from North Carolina to Florida. They hang in clumps of Spanish moss about 3 to 5 feet above the ground and leave their mossy abodes in the evening to forage for insects. They usually feed about 20 to 50 feet above the ground, utilizing their exceptional echolocation apparatus. Seminole bats produce unusually large litters, with as many as four young born at a time. They roost, solitarily, in wooded areas wherever there is Spanish moss.

The sandy soils of the piney flat lands, the dense growth beneath bay edge and maritime forests, stream banks, and bottomland woods are favorite habitats of raccoons and opossums. The raccoon, *Procyon lotor*, is a cunning, bushy-tailed bandit. Raccoons' tails have alternating black to brownish rings. They have black masks, edged in white, over their eyes, making them look like an old-time comic strip's version of second-story thieves. They are certainly nimble and deft; they are capable of gaining entrance to a shed by turning an unlocked doorknob or lifting the cover off a garbage can. They have a rather hump-backed, shuffling or lumbering gait, and they are normally nocturnal. However, raccoons seem to be frequently afflicted with rabies in certain areas of the country, and then they become disoriented and wander, almost aimlessly, during the day. They normally feed on mollusks, amphibians, birds' eggs and their nestlings, crayfish, large insects, farmers' corn, and the fruits of greenbrier and palmettos. In turn, they are preyed on extensively by alligators. Their species name, *lotor*, means "to wash," and they do seem to wash their food, particularly when they are near water, but in fact they are tearing or shredding their food with their agile fingers. Raccoons are good climbers and

Raccoon (to 32")
Procyon lotor

Opossum (to 40")
Didelphus virginiana

Cotton Mouse (to 7")
Peromyscus gossypinus

Beaver (to 46")
Castor canadensis

often nest in the cavities of trees, as well as in underground burrows. There seems to be a great variation in the size, color, skull shape, teeth, and pattern in raccoons throughout their range. Some experts have determined that there is more than one species, or subspecies, of raccoons based on morphological and DNA analyses, but we will leave those arguments and future determinations to mammalian specialists. Raccoons are rather gregarious and remain in family groups. They are most abundant in the Southeast but range along the Atlantic coast from southern Canada through Florida.

The opossum, *Didelphus virginiana*, is the size of a heavy house cat and appears to many like a very large rat. Its fur, or pelage, is long and grizzled gray or sometimes brownish. It has a pointed white face with paper-thin black ears and a long, bare, prehensile tail. It belongs to a primitive order of mammals, the marsupials, that includes the kangaroo, wombat, and bandicoot. The opossum is the only North American representative of the marsupial group. It is a common, widespread species, and it favors moist woodlands, shrubby swamps, and thicket-lined streams, as well as dry, upland forests. Opossums are usually nocturnal and solitary, and they spend their days in the cavities of trees, under piles of brush, and in rocky crevices. They forage for food at night and, being omnivorous, will feed on almost anything, from insects and palmetto fruits to the overripe flesh of dead animals. They particularly favor carrion on roads and, in turn, frequently become carrion themselves.

The female gives birth to tiny, almost embryonic young after an incredibly short gestation period of only twelve to thirteen days. The young are so small that the entire litter can fit in a teaspoon. The young, as many as fourteen, fasten themselves to a nipple in the mother's pouch, the marsupium, and remain attached, while suckling, for about two months.

The beaver, *Castor canadensis*, is North America's

largest rodent. It weighs 30 to 60 pounds, and sometimes more. It has huge, chestnut-colored, rodent-like teeth; a 10-inch-long, 6-inch-wide, scaly, horizontally wide tail; and webbed hind feet. Combine that equipment with an unusually dense coat and the ability, when submerged, to seal off its nostrils and ears with valves and to remain submerged for up to fifteen minutes, and a picture of an extremely well-adapted semiaquatic mammal appears.

A "thwack" sharply reporting across a still pond is a sure sign of a beaver. This strange mammal is truly a busy creature of forested wetlands. Beavers, sometimes referred to as the engineers of the animal kingdom, rearrange wooded habitat and streams to suit their needs; a still pond where they can float logs and build a lodge to raise their young is essential. They construct dams by blocking streams with logs and saplings and plastering the upstream surface with mud and sticks; the downstream side is mostly an open framework of saplings. Dams and lodges are built by the family: parents, yearlings, and kits, or cubs. Beavers can fell a small maple or alder in a matter of minutes. They float the logs down the stream to constantly rebuild and improve their watery abode. Their building supplies are also their food. They also like aquatic plants, particularly the tender shoots of water lilies. Beavers are generally nocturnal, but they may begin their work in the afternoon. Averages of two to four kits are born between April and July. They are well furred at birth and weigh about 1 pound, and they are out in the water, swimming, in about a week.

It seems that beavers and humans have always had an interesting relationship. When North America was being explored by Europeans, it was probably the beaver, more than any other animal, that contributed to the development of Canada and the United States. The value of the beavers' pelts and the demand for them in Europe stimulated trappers and settlements to open up the West. Feuds and Indian wars were fought over trapping rights and territories. By the early 1900s, the beaver populations had plummeted, and they were scattered. Later, measures were taken to reintroduce the beaver to many parts of Canada and the United States. The beaver returned to its former habitat, and now there is a new tension zone between beavers and humans. Humans have moved into the beaver's territory in many places, and a felled prized ornamental tree is a matter of serious contention between suburbanites and beavers. However, beavers do some beneficial engineering: the ponds that beavers create collect silt and sediment from runoff that has largely originated from expanded housing developments, and the ponds help to stem the flow of eroded materials into the downstream estuaries and sounds. The beaver ponds also create valuable waterfowl and fish habitats wherever they occur. Beavers range across North America and down to the edge of northern Florida.

The cotton mouse, *Peromyscus gossypinus*, is a relative of the very common and widespread white-footed deer mouse. The cotton mouse is the darkest mouse in the southeast coastal states. This little rodent is about 7 inches long from its nose to the tip of its tail. It is reddish to dark brown on the top and whitish below. It is a creature of bottomland forests and swamps, where it forages at night on berries, seeds, insects, and spiders. Cotton mice have about four litters a year, with an average of three or four young per litter. The gestation period is twenty-three days, and the young reach adult size in about two months. These little mice manage to do a lot of eating and reproducing in a short time, for they live no more than about four or five months. The cotton mouse ranges from Virginia down through the coastal Carolinas, Georgia, and Florida. There is a subspecies of the cotton mouse, *Peromyscus gossypinus allapaticola*, the Key Largo deer mouse, that is confined to the northern part of Key Largo, where it lives in mature tropical hardwood hammocks. The Key Largo cotton mouse is a protected endangered species, particularly because of the alteration and destruction of its critical habit.

The Key deer, a browser on red mangroves, the smallest of the twenty-eight subspecies of the Virginia white-tailed deer, is a protected and endangered species that is often seen on Big Pine Key and No Name Key. The National Key Deer Refuge, located about 100 miles southwest of Miami and 30 miles northeast of Key West, manages about 8,500 acres of pineland for the protection of these little deer. Buck Key deer average about 75 pounds, though the does are a little smaller. There are approximately 800 of these small deer within the refuge. Big Pine Key and No Name Key are also excellent spots to see the white-crowned pigeon.

2

Marshes and Mangrove Swamps

Marshes are habitats that lie between terrestrial uplands and shallow water. They are dominated by herbaceous, erect, rooted plants, generally classified as hydrophytes, that is, plants that grow in water or wet soil and normally remain standing until the next growing season. Wetlands specialists classify marshes into several types, including persistent emergent wetlands; palustrine emergent wetlands; and shrub-scrub wetlands, including broad-leaved deciduous wetlands and needle-leaved deciduous wetlands. These habitats are sometimes referred to as swamps, forested wetlands, and tidal marshes. Here, we also distinguish between low, regularly flooded tidal marshes and high, irregularly flooded tidal marshes.

Persistent emergent wetlands are the familiar marshes that grow along the southeast Atlantic coast. These are the marshes that so characterize the Inner Coast. Plants such as salt marsh cordgrass, salt meadow hay, big cordgrass, and black needlerush are typical of tidal estuarine marshes. Palustrine emergent wetlands, in part, are freshwater or slightly brackish wetlands that grow in tidal estuarine rivers. Some of the plants that are found in freshwater marshes are the familiar cattails and other grasslike plants, such as saw grass, bulrushes, sedges, and the common reed; there are also a number of flowering plants, including flags, smartweeds, and pickerelweed.

Shrub-scrub wetlands are somewhat intermediate wetlands that often link marshes to forested wetlands and to upland forests as well. The shrubs and young trees that compose this habitat are all woody and are usually less than 20 feet tall. Shrub-scrub wetlands are further divided into broad-leaved deciduous wetlands, characterized in salt marshes by groundsel trees and marsh elders and in freshwater marshes by willows and red maples. Needle-leaved deciduous wetlands are another type of shrub-scrub habitat,

and along the Inner Coast, the bald cypress is the most representative species growing in this habitat. Wetlands are fragile and vulnerable to natural and human forces. Storms lash the coast and erode the marsh banks, but humankind has had the greatest effect on marshes and other wetlands. Thousands of acres along the Inner Coast have been altered to provide sites for homes and golf courses along the waterfront. In the past there was little understanding or appreciation of the critical ecological role wetlands play in providing vital habitats for fisheries, as well as for birds and wildlife. A healthy marsh also provides effective erosion control and functions as a living filter system for removing pollutants and utilizing excess organic materials, that is, the nitrogen and phosphorous in fertilizers so copiously used by homeowners, golf course managers, and farmers.

Wetlands are the pulsating heartbeat of the estuaries along the Atlantic coast from the Chesapeake Bay to the Gulf of Mexico. These pocket marshes, fringes of grasses, and great meadowlands of green- and gold-bladed and flowering plants and shrubs are highly productive. They also provide important habitats for small fishes, grazing snails, crabs, burrowing mollusks, and many species of birds. Some of the meadowlands are so vast that they seem to stretch, almost uninterrupted, to the horizon.

Wetland plants grow lush and thick during the warmer months, and as the summer wanes, they begin to turn brown and bend with the wintry winds. Choppy seas and occasional storm-lashed waves flood the marshes during the winter, herding dead blades of grass and stems into long, sinuous windrows of brown and gray remnants of last year's greenery. But the dead plant remains to contribute greatly to next year's rich profusion of estuarine animals.

The windrows of dead plants begin to decay—bacteria and molds hasten the process—and as the waters warm, the plant remains break down into detritus. This material is literally "the stuff of life," for minute organisms feed on the rich populations of bacteria growing in the detrital stew, and larval shrimps and fishes and a multitude of other species in turn feed on the grazing microcrustaceans. The complex food web is beginning to form. The vast network of marshes, swamps, wooded wetlands, and mangroves contributes the initial food, organic detritus, to the tidal rivers and estuaries of the Inner Coast. However, there is some controversy among researchers about the value of detritus as a food for invertebrates.

Tidal Saltwater Marshes

Low, Regularly Flooded Saltwater Marshes

Saltwater marshes along the Inner Coast signify the very essence of an estuary. The communities of plants and animals that exist in these estuarine salt marshes are present because of the combination of saltwater and freshwater that constantly washes over these low-lying habitats. Marshes are shaped and reshaped in response to storms, adjacent water depths, soil types, and erosion. Maturing shrubs and trees frequently shade out certain sun-loving plant species. In addition, siltation from upland runoff can change the contours and elevation of a marsh, also allowing different plants to establish themselves.

Natural and human-induced changes often cause erosion at one location and accretion at another. Marshes along the Inner Coast are constantly being changed by these dynamic forces: they may form broad meadows, grow in dense pockets in a cove, or endure as thin and vulnerable fringes along a shoreline. Marshes, particularly meadows, are frequently penetrated by sinuous streams and ditches that interlace the broad marsh, transporting tidal water over the lower elevations and often into the higher elevations of the marsh. As the tides flood the marshes, the meanders and depressions in the marsh literally throb with life. Small fishes congregate in great numbers to feed on bits of plants, detritus, and larvae of snails and insects. Not only is their food concentrated in these watery havens, but they are also somewhat protected here from larger predatory fishes. They may be safe from below, but from above, stealthy herons, egrets, and rails stalk their prey and gorge themselves on the small fishes, fiddler crabs, and snails as well.

Low, or regularly flooded, salt marshes, are flooded on each high tide and are typically dominated by salt marsh cordgrass. Salt marsh cordgrass, *Spartina alterniflora*, also known as smooth cordgrass, is considered by many to be the most valuable and productive plant species in the marsh. It may grow as a narrow fringe seaward of the high marsh or as dense, lush stands, referred to as pocket marshes, and in coves or at the heads of tidal creeks. However, salt marsh cordgrass attains its most spectacular growth when it occurs in low-lying meadows that seem to have no end, and it is in these broad marshes that small tidal creeks carry rivulets of tidal water deep into the marshy pastures.

Salt marsh cordgrass com-

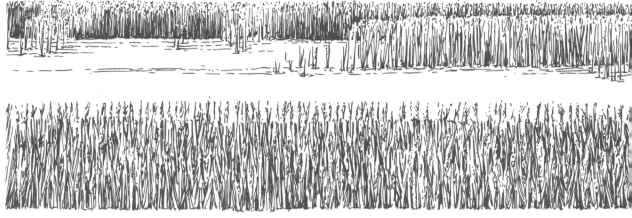

Great expanses of salt marsh cordgrass are dominant in many regularly flooded low marshes.

monly appears in two forms: the tall form and the short form. The tall form is bathed by daily tides in the lower elevations and along the edges of tidal rivulets and ditches, and it responds by growing to heights of 7 feet or more. The short form of salt marsh cordgrass occupies the drier, higher elevations of the marsh and grows to only about 2 or 3 feet in height. Most salt marsh plant species cannot tolerate as wet a habitat as salt marsh cordgrass, so they grow in slightly higher elevations.

Much has been written about salt marsh cordgrass. In fact, the plant is familiarly known even to many who are not ecologists or botanists as simply spartina. Salt marsh cordgrass is the ideal plant to live in such a rigorous environment as the low marsh, a place where storm-lashed waves batter the land and gouge and erode chunks of soil from the shoreline. Few plants can endure inundation twice daily by saltwater that in some areas is almost as salty as the ocean. Salt marsh cordgrass is one of those pioneer species that is able to establish itself in a seemingly hostile environment. Seeds or rhizomes of salt marsh grass float in with the tide and are able to take root where nothing else is growing. Salt marsh cordgrass propagates primarily by rhizomatous growth that creates a tangled, interlocking network of strong horizontal roots that not only promotes the growth of a vigorous stand of plants but also inhibits erosion. Those who have waterfront property are indeed fortunate if they have a protective fringe of salt marsh cordgrass between their upland lawns and the water. Salt marsh cordgrass also has the ability to withstand being bathed in saltwater by regulating the salt content within its stems by exuding salt through salt glands. You can actually feel and see the salt crystals that have been deposited on the leaves.

Salt marsh cordgrass is a perennial grass that blooms from midsummer to early fall. The bloom, or inflorescence, properly termed a panicle, is a long spike of flat, greenish white flowers. Salt marsh cordgrass is emerald green in the spring as new shoots arise from the nodes of the rhizomes. Vast green meadows of salt marsh cordgrass are commonly seen along the Inner Coast, particularly along Pamlico Sound in North Carolina and in the Low-country of South Carolina and Georgia. As the sum-

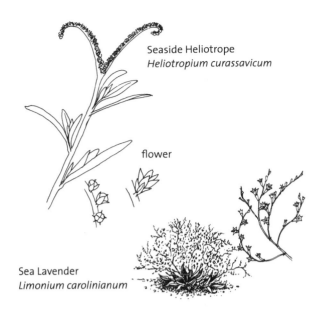

Seaside Heliotrope
Heliotropium curassavicum

flower

Sea Lavender
Limonium carolinianum

very tiny, perhaps only 1/8 inch wide, but when there are a number of sea lavender plants blooming at the same time, they produce a hazy, almost ethereal mist of lavender.

Seaside heliotrope, *Heliotropium curassavicum*, is another flowering species that occasionally punctuates the greenery of the low marsh with touches of white or bluish flowers. Seaside heliotrope is a perennial with succulent, fleshy, almost veinless leaves that are linear and blunt at the tips. The small, whitish, tubular flowers may be tinged with blue or purple and are borne on terminal curled spikes, or racemes. Seaside heliotrope is also found in high marshes and, sometimes, along the edges of mangrove swamps.

High, Irregularly Flooded Saltwater Marshes

High marshes, or irregularly flooded saltwater marshes, are marshes that are inundated not on every daily high tide but only during exceptionally high tides, such as spring tides, and by wind-driven flooding. Exceptionally high tides, or spring tides, occur every two weeks, at about the times of the new and full moons. They derive their name from the Old English *springan*, "to jump."

As the elevation of the marshes subtly increases, plant species that require drier soils begin to appear in the higher elevations, and plants that require almost constant immersion begin to disappear. High marshes are generally, but not always, a continuation of low marshes. Occasionally the uplands slope toward the water and terminate as embankments somewhat above sea level, where only a high marsh will develop. Consequently, there is a marked and visible zonation, demarcated by the various species of plants, in most marshes. If you could look at a cross section of a salt marsh from the water's edge to the terrestrial uplands, you would see that salt marsh cordgrass occupies the lower elevation and edges of

mer wanes and fall approaches, salt marsh cordgrass turns golden brown. Nowhere is it more evident than in the marshes of Glynn near Saint Simons and Jekyll islands in Georgia. Salt marsh cordgrass ranges from the Maritimes to Florida and along the Gulf of Mexico to Texas.

Although salt marsh cordgrass is the dominant species found in low tidal saltwater marshes, there are some other species that are able to exploit microhabitats within the dense stands of salt marsh cordgrass. Where there are subtle changes in the marsh floor—a depression, a sandy panne, or a slight rise—other species take hold, such as sea lavender, or marsh rosemary, *Limonium carolinianum*. Sea lavender is a perennial herb that often grows along the upper edges of low marshes and is sometimes interspersed in the low marsh. It is a small to medium-size plant that grows to 3 feet tall in some situations and is characterized by a basal rosette of leathery, fleshy leaves that may be 2–10 inches long. The tiny lavender or bluish flowers bloom from midsummer through early autumn. The individual flowers are

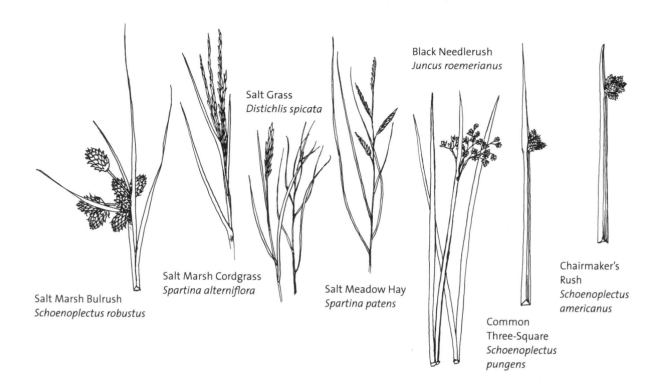

Black Needlerush
Juncus roemerianus

Salt Grass
Distichlis spicata

Salt Marsh Cordgrass
Spartina alterniflora

Salt Meadow Hay
Spartina patens

Salt Marsh Bulrush
Schoenoplectus robustus

Chairmaker's
Rush
*Schoenoplectus
americanus*

Common
Three-Square
*Schoenoplectus
pungens*

marsh streams. Here and there within the zone of salt marsh cordgrass, there are often small hillocks or slight elevations that allow plants such as black needlerush to grow. As the marsh rises, the tall form of salt marsh cordgrass gives way to the short form and to salt meadow hay, black needlerush, and many species of sedges and lovely flowering plants such as sea oxeye, salt marsh fleabane, and salt marsh asters. The highest edges of the marsh are occupied by groundsel trees and marsh elders, often referred to as high-tide bushes.

Whereas the low marsh is often an uninterrupted stand of a single species—salt marsh cordgrass—the high marsh is a mosaic of textures and colors. Grassy plants grow in association with sprawling succulents, and flowering herbs grow among the woody shrubs along the upland margins of high marshes. The high marsh habitat is less rigorous than the low marsh. The soil is drier, less salt is deposited, and the topog-

raphy and the soils of the high marsh floor can be quite variable. These factors allow for a high diversity of plant species in the high marsh.

Islands of black needlerush and three-square grow in dense stands of uniform heights within meadows of the short form of salt marsh cordgrass. Swirling salt meadow hay and stiff sprigs of salt grass often grow intermixed with other species or in pure stands where the conditions are favorable. Interspersed among the slate gray, brown, and green of black needlerush and three-square are dashes of pink and lavender and blue and white, sure evidence that salt marsh fleabane and salt marsh aster are in bloom.

Black needlerush, *Juncus roemerianus*, is easily distinguished, even at a distance, from most other marsh species because of its dark color, which appears as brown or gray-black. This is a sharp-tipped, round-stemmed, stiff rush that bears small clusters of greenish to brown flowers above the middle of the stem. This plant is very common in the Lowcountry and northern Florida marshes.

The sedge family has about 600 species worldwide, with approximately 90 known in North America. Most sedges have triangular stems in cross section, giving rise to the mnemonic "Sedges have edges." However, as is usual among things biological, there are exceptions. As an example, the soft-stem bulrush, a member of the sedge family Cyperaceae, does not have edges but, rather, is round in cross section. There are a number of sedge species called three-squares, and there is an equal amount of confusion among experts as to the classification, particularly regarding the scientific names of some of the species. Three-squares are called three-squares because of their distinctive triangular stems. They are all somewhat similar in that they arise from rhizomes and are grasslike, three-sided herbs with seed heads that grow somewhere near the tips of the stems. The fruits of sedges are golden brown nutlets that are quite large when compared to the small, grainy seeds of grasses. Sedges, as a group, are quite adaptive to many habitats and range from moist swales and ditches to swamps, freshwater marshes, and tidal saltwater marshes.

Chairmaker's rush, or Olney's three-square, *Schoenoplectus americanus*, formerly known as *Scirpus olneyi*, grows in brackish salt marshes and sometimes in regularly flooded (low) salt marshes but more often in irregularly flooded (high) salt marshes. This sedge often grows in great stands that, in some marshes, rivals the growth of salt marsh cordgrass. It can grow to about 7 feet tall. The stems are sharply three sided, or triangular in cross section, and the sides are deeply concave. The inconspicuous flowers are attached within 2 inches from the tip of the stem and develop dark gray to almost black nutlets. This three-square and a closely related species, the common three-square, *Schoenoplectus pungens*, formerly called *Scirpus americanus*, were once used to weave backs and seats for chairs. The common three-square is quite similar to chairmaker's rush, except its stem is not as concave and its seed clusters do not grow as close to the tip of the stem. Both species are wide ranging.

Another related species, the salt marsh bulrush, or leafy bulrush, *Schoenoplectus robustus*, also has triangular stems like chairmaker's rush and the common three-square. But unlike the other two species, salt marsh bulrush has several thin, tapering leaves growing from the middle portion of the stem, giving the plant a very leafy look. This species of three-square grows in the same habitats as the other two species.

In the higher elevations of the marsh, salt meadow hay and salt grass begin to dominate the marsh. These grasses are short and wiry and form dense marsh patches that often grow in an unrestrained or unruly way; they may grow erect or prostrate, but they typically do not grow in uniform stands as do black needlerush, the three-squares, and salt marsh cordgrass.

Salt meadow hay, salt meadow cordgrass, and marsh hay are all names for *Spartina patens*, a fine, wiry grass that grows in the upper marsh, between dune swales, and often as a carpet under marsh elder and red cedar at the edge of a marsh. Salt meadow hay has long, tapering leaves that tend to roll inward and give the leaves the appearance of being round. The stems are weak at the base, and, consequently, when the plants are buffeted by winds and occasional flooding tides, they bend and swirl and intertwine with other plants and form a characteristic cowlick pattern within the marsh meadowland. Salt meadow hay ranges from the Maritimes along the Atlantic coast to Florida and westward along the Gulf of Mexico.

Salt grass, or spike grass, *Distichlis spicata*, is an-

A high marsh typically has "cowlick" waves of salt meadow hay intermixed with salt grass. Dark stands of black needlerush and common three-square line the lower marsh, while marsh elder, on the left, thrives on higher ground.

other grass that often grows in association with salt meadow hay and other plants of the upper marsh. Salt grass is able to adapt to both wet and dry conditions. It can tolerate somewhat wetter conditions than salt meadow hay can, but it also grows well in habitats, such as salt pannes, that are frequently sandy, dry, and hypersaline. In the Lowcountry, it grows very well on sand dunes. Salt grass is a perennial grass that grows 6–18 inches tall. It arises from wiry, matted rhizomes and may either grow low and prostrate or erect. The salt grass stem is stiff and round, and its wiry leaves are about 2–4 inches long. The plant overall is a pale green compared to the brighter green of salt meadow hay.

There are a number of interesting plants in the high marsh that are not important components of the marsh in terms of productivity or dominance. Many of these minor and diverse plant species have unusual growth forms, such as glassworts, and others, such as salt asters and goldenrod, punctuate the marshes with a wash of color.

Water hemp, *Amaranthus cannabinus*, has a scientific name that suggests that it is related to the marijuana plant, *Cannabis*, but it is not. *Cannabinus* is derived from Greek and means "slender" or "thin as a rod," which perfectly describes the growth form of water hemp. Water hemp has narrow, willowlike leaves attached by long stalks, or petioles, to an erect, slender stem that can grow to 8 feet tall. The leaves may be up to 6 inches long and are alternately arranged. The small green or yellow flowers grow on spikes that originate in the leaf axil. In the early summer, water hemp is often obscured by other plants; however, in the late summer, water hemp seems to suddenly emerge as a large, red-stem, treelike plant. The small, yellowish green flowers often turn red in the fall. Water hemp generally grows as a single plant dotted here and there in the high marsh and sometimes in tidal freshwater marshes as well.

Marsh orach, or spearscale, *Atriplex patula*, is a sprawling, fleshy member of the goosefoot family. This family of plants contains a number of shrubs

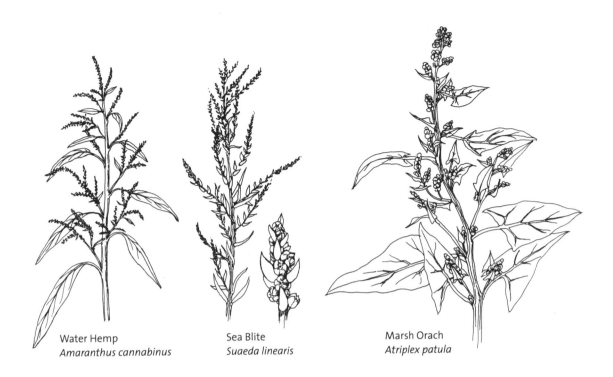

Water Hemp
Amaranthus cannabinus

Sea Blite
Suaeda linearis

Marsh Orach
Atriplex patula

and fleshy succulents, including beets and spinach. The species name, *patula*, means "spreading" or "sprawling," and marsh orach commonly grows in a prostrate or vinelike manner, although it also grows erectly. Its stems are grooved, and its light green, arrowhead-shaped leaves are usually alternately arranged, although the lower leaves may be oppositely arranged. It bears small green clusters of flowers. Marsh orach is not confined to the high marsh and may be found on the edges of sand dunes and inland saline soils.

Sea blite, *Suaeda linearis*, is another member of the goosefoot family. This erect, fleshy annual grows in the high marsh and along the edges of mangrove swamps. It usually grows as a single plant or in small clumps or patches. Sea blite grows to about 3 feet tall. Its stems are grooved and sometimes tinged with red. Its alternately arranged, linear leaves are

dark green and fleshy. It bears small green flowers in the upper leaf axils and blooms from late summer into fall.

Glassworts are also members of the goosefoot family. Three species of glassworts commonly grow along the Inner Coast: the dwarf glasswort, *Salicornia bigelovii*; the common glasswort, *Salicornia europaea*; and the perennial glasswort, or woody glasswort, *Sarcocornia perennis*. These succulent plants are almost leafless; the leaves are reduced to scales, and the flowers are tiny and inconspicuous. They have fleshy, jointed stalks and grow in clumps, particularly on salt flats and sandy pannes. Late in the season, as autumn approaches, the stems of glassworts turn pinkish red. The dwarf glasswort, similar to other glassworts, has jade green stalks during the summer months and grows to about 4 to 18 inches tall. The common glasswort is quite similar

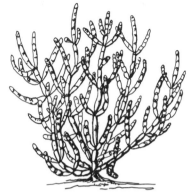

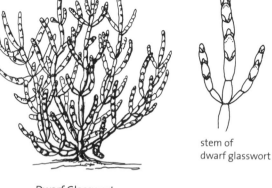

stem of
dwarf glasswort

Common Glasswort
Salicornia europaea

Perennial Glasswort
Sarcocornia perennis

Dwarf Glasswort
Salicornia bigelovii

to the dwarf glasswort; however, it has creeping lower branches that differentiate it from the dwarf glasswort. The perennial glasswort is a low-growing, fleshy plant with woody, creeping stems that run along the ground and form a carpet, or mat, of plants.

The aster family, Compositae, is well represented in the high marsh by shrubby, thick-leafed sea oxeye, tiny asters of various hues, and the purplish blossoms of the salt marsh fleabane.

Sea oxeye is a distinctive shrubby plant that arises from rhizomes and tends to grow in dense colonies, on salt flats, on the upper edges of salt marshes just seaward of the maritime forest, and sometimes even in the lower marsh. The plant is grayish green because the stems and leaves are covered with a down of grayish white hairs. Sea oxeyes generally grow to about 2 feet, but they may reach a height of 4 feet. The fleshy, succulent, oppositely arranged leaves are

sessile—that is, they lack a petiole—and are attached directly to the stem. The sharp-tipped leaves may have smooth, or entire, margins, and some may be toothed as well. The sunflowerlike blooms of the sea oxeye are unmistakable in the marsh: they are bright yellow and are borne on the terminal tip of the stem. They bloom from midsummer through November. There is also a closely related species, the bay marigold, that occurs in the estuarine and mangrove areas of south Florida. It is similar in appearance to the sea oxeye; however, it does not grow in dense clumps and may stand somewhat taller.

The salt marsh aster, or perennial salt marsh aster, *Aster tenuifolius*, is one of approximately twenty-three species of asters that grow in the marshes all along the Inner Coast. This little white to magenta daisy is a perennial with long, narrow, gray-green, alternately arranged leaves. It arises from creeping rhizomes and may reach a height of 2 feet. It grows

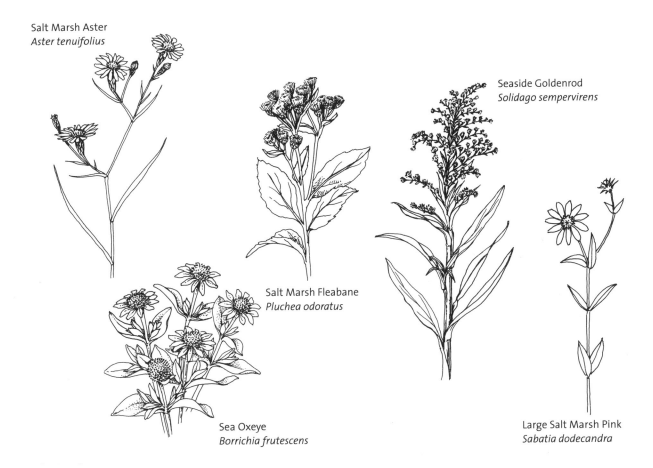

Salt Marsh Aster
Aster tenuifolius

Seaside Goldenrod
Solidago sempervirens

Salt Marsh Fleabane
Pluchea odoratus

Sea Oxeye
Borrichia frutescens

Large Salt Marsh Pink
Sabatia dodecandra

intermixed with other plants in the high, irregularly flooded salt marsh and is only conspicuous when it blooms from August through November.

Salt marsh fleabane, *Pluchea odoratus*, is also called camphorweed for the aromatic odor that emanates from its crushed leaves. The fleabane grows to about 3 feet tall. Its long, oval-shaped leaves are fleshy, sharply toothed, and alternately arranged. The entire plant, and especially the leaves, is covered with fine hairs. The individual pink to purplish flowers are small, but they are tightly crowded into flat-topped clusters or heads that make them quite visible along the edge of the high marsh. They also grow

in swales and ditches and bloom from midsummer to early fall.

The common salt marsh pink, *Sabatia stellaris*, and the large salt marsh pink, *Sabatia dodecandra*, sprinkle the high marsh with their nodding heads of pink and yellow. The common salt marsh pink, or sea pink, is usually less than 2 feet tall and has narrow, elongated leaves. The leaves are oppositely arranged and are attached directly to the main stem. The pink flowers have five petals and a yellow, star-shaped center accented with reddish edges. Common salt marsh pinks are also found along the margins of rivers and ditches, in brackish swales between dunes,

Common Salt Marsh Pink
Sabatia stellaris

seaside goldenrod, marsh hibiscus, seashore mallow, and various grasses.

Seaside goldenrod, *Solidago sempervirens*, can grow 5 to 6 feet tall; its dark green leaves are fleshy and entire and are attached directly to the stem. The showy yellow blossoms of the seaside goldenrod paint a golden accent on the upper marsh. They bloom from late summer and linger to the October frost. There are many species of goldenrods, and apparently some species hybridize, making identification difficult. Seaside goldenrod, however, is a common species that inhabits the upper edges of irregularly flooded, high marshes, as well as the upper zones of freshwater marshes, beaches, and dunes.

Marsh hibiscus, *Hibiscus moscheutos*, and seashore mallow, *Kosteletzkya virginica*, are two of the loveliest flowers of the marshes. The flowers of both are typical hibiscus blossoms, with five petals surrounding a bright yellow, pollen-laden stamen, some-

and infrequently in tidal freshwater marshes. The flowering period is unusually long: they bloom from mid-June into early October.

The large salt marsh pink, or perennial pink, arises from rhizomes and may reach 3 feet or more in height. The leaves are sessile and oppositely arranged. The pink, rarely white, flowers are composed of seven to thirteen petals with yellow centers outlined in red. In southern New England, the large salt marsh pink grows in high marsh habitats, but in its more southern range, through the Carolinas to Florida, it is more often found growing in wet pinelands and around bogs.

On the edge of the high marsh—where only the highest spring and storm tides reach and where the wrack line is strewn with last season's dried, gray cordgrass stems, crab pot floats, caps, and an assortment of plastic containers—is where the shrub line defines the edge of the marsh and the uplands. Groves of groundsel trees and marsh elders intermingle with red cedars and wax myrtles, and beneath them grow

Marsh Hibiscus
Hibiscus moscheutos

times referred to as a brush. The marsh hibiscus, or rose mallow, has large, showy flowers up to 6 inches in diameter; the petals may be white or pink, and they usually have red to pink centers. The seashore mallow, or pink mallow, has numerous blossoms, smaller than those of the marsh hibiscus: the pink blossoms of the seashore mallow are about 1 to 2 inches in diameter. Both species have grayish green leaves that are generally, but not always, three-lobed. They grow in profusion along the edges of irregularly flooded high marshes, freshwater marshes, nontidal marshes, and ditches. The marsh hibiscus usually begins blooming first, late July through September, and the seashore mallow follows, from August into October.

There are a number of plant species generally referred to as smartweeds that grow in the upper edges

of freshwater marshes and sometimes in brackish marshes; some species grow in standing water, and others grow in moist ditches. Almost all homeowners have had to contend with smartweeds in their gardens. Smartweeds share a key characteristic: they all have swollen nodes along their stems that are covered with a whitish membrane. The pink or white flowers of most smartweeds typically grow in small clusters on short spikes. The halberd-leaf tearthumb, *Polygonum arifolium*, and water smartweed, also known as dotted smartweed, *Polygonum punctatum*, grow along the edges of tidal freshwater and slightly brackish areas as well as swamps and wet meadows.

The halberd-leaf tearthumb was probably named by the first person who grasped the stems of this plant armed with prickly, recurved spines and suffered the fate that most of us have: sliced and raked skin! The tearthumb has arrowhead-shaped leaves, and when the plant is young, the weak stems stand erect and grow to about 4 feet. As it matures, the plant reclines and intertwines with other vegetation, such as the seashore mallow.

Water smartweeds grow to about 3 feet; they have smooth, narrow or linear leaves that taper at both ends. They have small greenish or greenish white flowers borne on erect spikes. They are often known as dotted smartweed because their sepals, the outermost parts of a flower, are dotted with white glandular spots. Both species are widely distributed throughout the United States.

Clumps of switchgrass, *Panicum virgatum*, sometimes as tall as 6 feet, grow along the margins of the

The beautiful pink hibiscuslike blossoms of the seashore mallow, Kosteletzkya virginica, *brighten the high marsh, along with the small pink flower clusters of creeping prickly halberd-leaf tearthumb,* Polygonum arifolium, *and the pink to greenish white flower spikes of water smartweed,* Polygonum punctatum.

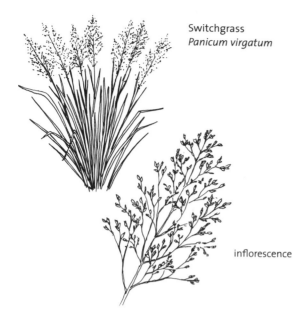

Switchgrass
Panicum virgatum

inflorescence

The band of small shrubs lining the edge of the marsh defines the zone between the extreme high tide and the upland. There are two shrubs that are widely distributed along the upper margins of the high marsh throughout the Inner Coast that particularly define this transition zone: the groundsel tree, *Baccharis halimifolia*, also known as saltbush or sea myrtle, and the marsh elder, *Iva frutescens*, also known as high-tide bush. There is also a third shrub, the seashore elder, that is usually found growing on dunes rather than along the marsh (see chapter 3). The groundsel tree and the marsh elder are shrubs or small trees that grow on high spots in the marsh and along the margins. The marsh elder is some-

upper marsh, on dunes, and in open woods. There are about forty-five or fifty species of *Panicum* growing along the Inner Coast, and most of them are difficult to differentiate. They arise from coarse rhizomes and develop arching, long, tapered leaves and feathery seed heads. The seeds of switchgrass and related species are an important food source for songbirds, game birds, muskrat, and marsh rabbits.

Common reed, *Phragmites australis*, a species that is found almost worldwide, often grows in thick, almost impenetrable stands that can grow to a height of 10 feet or more. The stems of common reeds are round and hollow and arise from a network of rhizomes. They grow rapidly and have long, tapering leaves that may be 2 feet in length. The flower spray, or inflorescence, matures into a showy, feathery seed head that is at first purplish brown and then turns fluffy white as it ages. This is a very invasive plant that grows in freshwater, saltwater, and even roadside ditches. It outcompetes some of the more valuable wetland plants and is particularly successful where the ground has been disturbed.

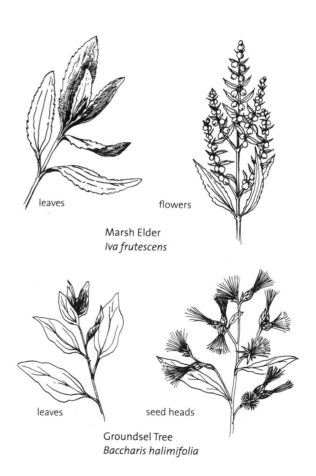

leaves   flowers

Marsh Elder
Iva frutescens

leaves   seed heads

Groundsel Tree
Baccharis halimifolia

what more tolerant of standing saltwater than is the groundsel tree, which grows somewhat above the extent of tidal water. The two shrubs are similar in appearance, but their leaves are arranged differently. The marsh elder has fleshy leaves arranged in an opposite pattern, whereas the leaves of the groundsel tree are thinner and are alternately arranged. These shrubs flower in late summer through fall; the groundsel is particularly showy at that time. The groundsel produces small, white, dense blooms that clothe the bush in cottony tufts late into October.

🌿

Tidal Freshwater Marshes

Tidal freshwater marshes, like tidal saltwater marshes, may be regularly flooded low marshes or irregularly flooded high marshes, with a transitional zone of shrub-scrub that merges into the uplands. They also, typically, have a belt of rooted emergent plants in the shallow water where the bottom rises to meet the regularly flooded marsh. Tidal freshwater marshes grow inland from the sea and up the coastal rivers and sounds where the waters are fresh or only slightly brackish. They are influenced by lunar tides but are dominated by freshwater from rivers and precipitation. As the salt content of the water decreases, the plant and animal diversity greatly increases. There are many more types of plants and animals found in tidal freshwater marshes than in saltwater marshes.

The upper reaches of rivers along the Inner Coast are lined with narrow fringes of marsh, dense pockets of marshes at the heads of creeks and embayments, and great meadows of greenery accented with the colors of many varieties of flowering plants. The emergent vegetation in the shallows in front of the marsh sometimes stands erect during an ebbing tide and seems to float on waxy, green leaves during high water. There is color everywhere: blue and yellow flags grow in the shallows and along the shore; spatterdocks bear bright yellow globular flowers; and the aggressive, channel-choking water hyacinth veils its destructive habits by carpeting the water with a mosaic of deep green foliage and lavender flowers. The golden nutlets of sedges and the brown, sausage-like heads of cattails vie with the dazzling white of swamp lily blossoms and the nodding heads of marsh hibiscus.

Where there is a diversity of habitats, such as in tidal freshwater marshes and saltwater marshes, there will be many species of animals: Small fishes come into the marsh streams on a flood tide, then hide and feed on insects and other small invertebrates in the vegetation along the edges of the marsh. Marsh rabbits feed on the rushes and, in turn, become food for alligators and snakes. Overhead, swallows, bats, and dragonflies wheel and hawk for mosquitoes, and closer to the marsh floor, northern harriers glide, almost at grass-top level, searching for small, unwary rodents. Secretive rails and bitterns, often heard but seldom seen, slip with ease through the dense, reedy grasses, where they feed on seeds, snails, crayfish, and frogs.

Tidal freshwater marshes form an extensive maze of habitats throughout the Inner Coast. In Virginia, the Great Dismal Swamp and the shores of the North Landing River are lined with cattails, rushes, saw grass, and a multitude of lovely flowering plants. In North Carolina, the Currituck and Albemarle sounds, the Alligator River system, and the vast upper portions of the Chowan, Pasquotank, Pamlico, Neuse, and White Oak rivers are bordered by lush growths of tidal freshwater marshes. The Low-country of South Carolina also has extensive tidal freshwater marshes in the Ashepoo, Combahee, and Edisto rivers, collectively known as the ACE Basin. The dark-stained Great Pee Dee and Waccamaw rivers and side streams are heavily vegetated by giant

Feathery tufts of common reed, Phragmites australis, *bend in the breeze over cattails and the showy blooms of marsh hibiscus at the edge of a tidal freshwater marsh. Out in the water, the yellow cups of spatterdock rise above their flat, rounded leaves. The emergent leaves of arrow arum and pickerelweed are just beyond. Stands of big cordgrass and three-squares line the other shore.*

cut-grass and the lovely swamp rose. Georgia also has a great many acres of tidal freshwater marshes along the upper portions of the Savannah, Ogeechee, Altamaha, and Satilla rivers. The Saint Marys River, the southernmost river in Georgia, forms the boundary between Georgia and Florida along its lower course. It originates in the Okefenokee Swamp and eventually flows easterly, where cypresses and water tupelos tower above the pickerelweed, bladderworts, and duck potato.

Florida, of course, has its share of valuable and beautiful tidal freshwater marshes; much of the Saint Johns River below Jacksonville has pockets and meadows of freshwater marsh vegetation. To the south, arrow arum, swamp lily, sedges, and various soft-stem rushes grow along the shores of the Saint Lucie and Loxahatchee rivers. Farther south, near Fort Lauderdale and Miami, there is an extensively engineered system of canals that was designed to regulate the flow of water from the Everglades; some of the canals are tidal and actually form the backyards of many residential communities. These canals have small pockets of freshwater marshes and a number of species of emergent aquatic plants, along with alligators and purple gallinules swimming among them.

Yellow spatterdock blossoms float on the surface on platterlike green leaves, and in the still freshwaters of the Inner Coast, the fragrant starburst blossoms of white water lilies accent the dark water. Spatterdock, *Nuphar lutea*, also known as the yellow pond-lily or cow-lily, grows throughout the range of the Inner Coast in ponds, slow-moving freshwater streams, and tidal freshwaters. Spatterdocks are quite evident in Dismal Swamp waters, and they are almost unmistakable, with rounded, tight, yellow blossoms poised on large green leaves that sometimes float on the surface of the water and are sometimes totally immersed. The leaf usually has a triangular slit, or

Spatterdock
Nuphar lutea

sinus, where the leaf stem and blade meet. The leaves are highly variable and can be oval, wide, long, or even heart shaped.

The white water lily, or fragrant water lily, *Nymphaea odorata*, is a plant of slow-flowing tidal freshwaters, ponds, ditches, and shallow lakes. The white water lily has large round leaves up to 10 inches across and a showy white flower with a yellow center.

Alligator weed, *Alternanthera philoxeroides*, is an introduced aquatic plant from South America and is a member of the amaranth family. Its rooted, dark green, floating leaves, which are sometimes emergent, can form tangled masses and extensive mats in tidal freshwaters and slightly brackish waters. The growth of alligator weed in some waterways can be so thick that it reduces the flow of water. The lance-shaped leaves are oppositely arranged and are usually attached directly to its vertically lined, smooth stems. Small, fragrant flowers that bloom from early spring into October are borne in heads or clusters on 3-foot-long stalks.

White Water Lily
Nymphaea odorata

that are triggered by small microcrustaceans and insect larvae. The bladder immediately expands and sucks in the hapless victim. Digestive enzymes and bacteria within the bladder make quick work of the meal and efficiently reduce the prey to a nutrient-rich cocktail. Bladderworts bloom in June and July.

Pickerelweed, *Pontederia cordata*, also called tuckahoe, is related to water hyacinth and can grow aggressively in thick stands in tidal freshwater marshes and slightly brackish marshes, in the shallows of ponds and lakes, and in swales and ditches. The leaves of the pickerelweed are heart shaped or, occasionally, lance shaped. The spires of bright blue to violet tubular flowers are borne on a fleshy, 3- to 4-inch-long spike. Numerous species of dragonflies and damselflies are often seen darting over the

Water hyacinth, *Eichornia crassipes*, is another tropical aquatic plant, introduced into Florida in the 1880s, that congests waterways if its growth is not controlled. The growth of this aggressive plant can block the flow of water and shade and crowd out other, native aquatic plants. It flourishes in slightly brackish water and freshwater canals, rivers, ditches, and ponds. This member of the pickerelweed family has cuplike, fleshy, leathery, oval to round leaves that are borne on unusual inflated or bulbous stalks that are almost 1 foot long and keep the plant afloat. A stalk that may be as much as 15 inches long bears bluish to lavender, six-petal flowers with a yellow center in the uppermost petal. Water hyacinths bloom from early spring to September.

Bladderworts, *Utricularia* spp., are strange little plants with yellow snapdragonlike flowers that float in the shallow, quiet backwaters of freshwater rivers and ponds. They are rootless and grow in great numbers in some areas. These attractive, innocent-appearing plants are said to be North America's only carnivorous aquatic plant. They are equipped with ingenious pear-shaped bladders that some think aid in the floatation of the plant. But the bladders have another sinister purpose—they vacuum in small, unsuspecting prey. The bladders have sensitive hairs

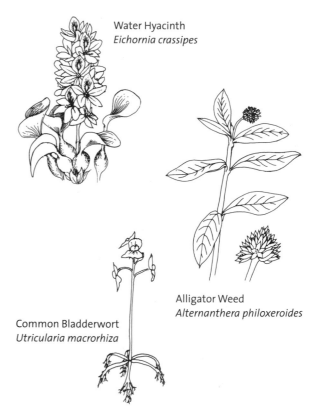

Water Hyacinth
Eichornia crassipes

Alligator Weed
Alternanthera philoxeroides

Common Bladderwort
Utricularia macrorhiza

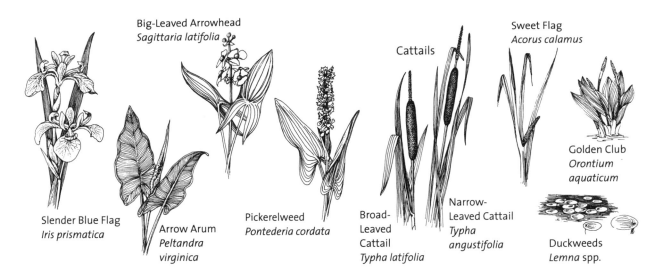

Big-Leaved Arrowhead
Sagittaria latifolia

Cattails

Sweet Flag
Acorus calamus

Golden Club
Orontium aquaticum

Slender Blue Flag
Iris prismatica

Arrow Arum
Peltandra virginica

Pickerelweed
Pontederia cordata

Broad-Leaved Cattail
Typha latifolia

Narrow-Leaved Cattail
Typha angustifolia

Duckweeds
Lemna spp.

plants, busily hawking mosquitoes and other insects. Pickerelweeds bloom from March to November.

Pickerelweed often grows in association with two similar-appearing emergent aquatic plants: big-leaved arrowhead and arrow arum. Big-leaved arrowhead, *Sagittaria latifolia*, also known as duck potato or wapato, has arrowhead-shaped leaves (*Sagittaria* means "arrow shaped"), and the leaves of the arrowhead may be more than 1 foot wide, or they may be quite slender. The leaves arise from a basal clump. The entire plant can reach a height of 4 feet. It has white three-petal flowers with yellow centers that are attached to an elongated stalk. The underground rhizomes produce starchy bulbs, known as duck potatoes, that are often eaten by waterfowl. Arrowheads grow in shallow tidal freshwaters, nontidal marshes, and along the edges of stream, lakes, and ponds. A closely related species, the lance-leaved arrowhead, has lance-shaped leaves.

Arrow arum, *Peltandra virginica*, also known (along with pickerelweed) as tuckahoe, has glossy, broad, triangle-shaped leaves that arise from a basal clump, similarly to the big-leaved arrowhead's. The leaves may grow to 3 feet long, and the plant may attain a height of 4 feet. Arrow arum is related to jack-in-the-pulpit and skunk cabbage; one of the family characteristics of this group is the development of a spadix, a fleshy spike that arises from the root and bears small, inconspicuous yellow flowers. Later, a fruit pod develops, and in late summer and early fall, the pod decays and releases small, fleshy seeds onto the marsh mud. Arrow arum grows in shallow tidal freshwaters, slightly brackish marshes, and along the muddy edges of lakes and ponds.

Pickerelweed, big-leaved arrowhead, and arrow arum are all somewhat similar in appearance. They grow in similar habitats, often in association with each other. How does one distinguish one species from another? First, closely look at the venation of the leaves: If the leaves have a number of parallel veins and no branching of the veins, it is a pickerelweed. If the leaves, whether they are arrow shaped or triangular, lobed or not, have three major veins arising from the attachment of the leaf to the stalk and several minor veins, it is arrow arum. If the leaves have veins that originate from the point of attachment with the stalk and follow the outline of the leaves, it is an arrowhead.

The golden club, *Orontium aquaticum*, is a member of the arum family and is related to arrow arum. Superficially, however, it does not resemble the other members of the group. Its leaves are fleshy, oblong or egg shaped, and parallel veined. The leaves of the golden club are attached to long rhizomes, allowing the leaves to float on the water or to project above the surface. The plant is named for its unusual and lovely flowers. A tubular, brilliant white stalk, the spadix, arises from the base of the plant and bears numerous golden yellow flowers along its top third. The combination of the dark green leaves and the snowy white spadix crowned with golden flowers allows one to identify this attractive plant at a glance. It blooms from early spring into May. Golden club grows in the mud along the shores of regularly flooded marshes and ponds and lakes.

Often in the quiet backwaters, interspersed among the aquatic emergent plants there may be literally millions of minute plants floating on the surface of the water. They float at the mercy of the winds and currents; they may coat the surface of the water in a small cove one day and string out in cloudy green tendrils the next. These are duckweeds. Structurally, they are the simplest of all the flowering plants, and one genus, *Wolffia*, known as watermeal, is the smallest of all the flowering plants. Duckweeds can be so numerous that they coat the surface so that no water can be seen; they adhere to floating branches and coat the tops of turtle shells. Some species are rootless, and others have one to several threadlike roots dangling from the underside of the plant. The genera are usually easily distinguished from one another, but the species are much more difficult to determine. *Spirodela* has several tiny roots and is red on the underside; *Lemna* has one root and is green beneath; *Wolffia* looks like a tiny grain of meal and does not have roots; *Wolffiella* consists of strap-shaped bodies without roots and may occur as a single body or may radiate out from a single point as several "straps." Typically, several intermixed species grow in the same habitat. Duckweeds are found in sluggishly moving water, in ponds, swamps, drainage ditches, and the backwaters of streams and rivers. These sticky little plants are easily transported from one habitat to another by wading and dabbling birds.

In tidal freshwater marshes where alligator weed, mallows, pickerelweed, and blue flags grow is often where lovely white swamp lilies and spider lilies accent the marsh with their brilliant white blossoms. The swamp lily and the spider lily are not true lilies; they actually belong to the amaryllis family, which includes daffodils and amaryllises. A distinguishing difference between members of the amaryllis family and members of the lily family is in the place of attachment of the flower parts: the flower parts of the amaryllis group are attached above the ovary, and the flower parts of the lily group are attached below the ovary.

The swamp lily, or string lily, *Crinum americanum*, is a fragrant plant with an onionlike bulb and fleshy, straplike leaves that can grow to 5 feet long and 3 inches wide. The very large, showy white blossoms, which are sometimes tinged with pink, are borne in terminal clusters. Swamp lilies grow in tidal and nontidal freshwater marshes and in wet woods and swamps. They bloom from May through November and range from Georgia to Florida and west to Texas.

The spider lily, *Hymenocallis crassifolia*, is even grander than the swamp lily. It grows to about 2 feet tall from a large underground bulb. The leaves are linear and about 1/2 inch wide, with tubular bases where they join the bulb. The large white flowers are quite distinctive; the center of the flower is a funnel-

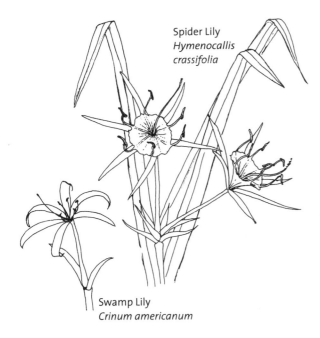

Spider Lily
Hymenocallis crassifolia

Swamp Lily
Crinum americanum

like disk that has six spidery petals growing from the perimeter of the disk. It blooms from the middle of May through June. The spider lily grows in somewhat the same habitats as the swamp lily and is also found in mangrove swamps. It ranges from North Carolina to Florida and along the Gulf of Mexico.

Close to the marsh, where the water is muddy and the mud is watery, grow several species that have a similar appearance; they grow rather tall, some as high as 10 feet; they are grasslike in that they have narrow, bladelike leaves; and they often grow in dense stands. These are the sweet flags, the blue flag, and cattails.

The sweet flag, *Acorus calamus*, also called calamus, which means "reed," has erect bladelike or irislike leaves and a long, yellowish spadix that appears to protrude from the side of the stem. Sweet flag belongs to the arum family, which includes the calla lily and the familiar tropical houseplants dieffenbachia and philodendron. The clublike spadix of the sweet

flag bears diamond-shaped patterns of minute, yellowish green florets. There are many common names for the sweet flag, including sweet grass, sweet root, sweet cinnamon, and sweet rush, all alluding to the fragrant odor of all parts of the plant when crushed or bruised, including the gingery rhizomes. Many cultures have used parts of the sweet flag for various ailments. Root tea has been used as aromatic bitters for fever, cold, cough, and stomachache. Some have made a gingerlike candy from the roots, and others have used it as an insecticide or as a spicy room freshener.

Sweet flag often grows in dense colonies, sometimes as tall as 5 feet, but usually shorter. It grows in freshwater marshes, at the edges of swamps and ponds, in shallow waters, and in wet ditches, where it blooms from May through August.

There are several species of flags, including *Iris prismatica, Iris virginica, Iris versicolor,* and *Iris pseudacorus,* that grow along the Inner Coast. These wild irises closely resemble the familiar horticultural varieties so abundantly planted everywhere. *Iris prismatica,* the slender blue flag, is quite widespread throughout the region and is, perhaps, the smallest of the irises, reaching a height of about 2 feet. It has narrow leaves and beautiful bluish violet flowers. The slender blue flag usually grows in brackish or saltwater marshes, but seldom in freshwater.

Iris virginica, the southern blue flag, grows to over 3 feet high. It bears a showy bluish violet blossom. The sepals, the largest blades of the iris flower, are splotched with yellow, and the long, swordlike leaves are clasped at the base, where they arise from thick, poisonous rhizomes. Unlike the slender blue flag, the southern blue flag generally grows in freshwater rather than saltwater. It also may be found around the margins of swamps, wet pinelands, and savannahs. The southern blue flag blooms from April through June. *Iris versicolor,* the northern blue flag, is quite similar to the southern blue flag but ranges from Virginia northward to the Maritimes. *Iris pseuda corus*, the yellow flag, is an introduced species from Eurasia. It is widely distributed and blooms from June through August.

Flags are sometimes intermixed with cattails, wild rice, giant cut-grass, saw grass, and big cordgrass. All of these species grow in wet soils or in the muds of freshwater and brackish shallows.

Cattails, with their sausagelike flower heads and long green leaves shaped like straps, are immediately recognized by even casual observers. The flowering heads, or spikes, bear both male and female flowers; the male component is above and the female is below. Cattails grow from creeping rhizomes that can create dense thickets, or "forests," and they also produce prodigious amounts of downy, airborne seeds. Stands of cattails are sometimes so dense that they shade and crowd out other plant species. The starchy rootstocks of cattails supply food for muskrats and Canada and snow geese, and the tall plants also furnish cover and nesting sites for marsh wrens, red-winged blackbirds, and swamp sparrows. Rails, grebes, least bitterns, mute swans, and American coots use dead cattail stems and leaves to construct nests.

Typha angustifolia, the narrow-leaved cattail, grows to about 6 feet; its elongated basal leaves are about 6 inches wide. The male spike on the flowering stalk is separated from the female sausagelike cylinder by a space that may vary from 1/2 inch to 4 inches. Narrow-leaved cattails grow in brackish and freshwater habitats, including ditches and wet areas near saltwater. They bloom from May through July.

The southern cattail, *Typha domingensis*, is similar to the narrow-leaved cattail but grows somewhat taller, from 8 to 13 feet. It also has a space between the male and female flowering heads.

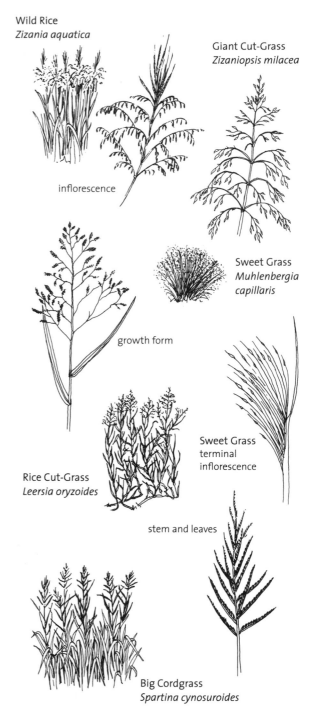

Wild Rice
Zizania aquatica

Giant Cut-Grass
Zizaniopsis milacea

inflorescence

growth form

Sweet Grass
Muhlenbergia capillaris

Sweet Grass
terminal inflorescence

Rice Cut-Grass
Leersia oryzoides

stem and leaves

Big Cordgrass
Spartina cynosuroides

The broad-leaved cattail, or common cattail, *Typha latifolia*, grows to a height of 10 feet, and the leaves are about 1 inch wide. There is no separation between the male and female flowering spikes. The broad-leaved cattail tends to grow in freshwater rather than brackish water or saltwater and is typically found in freshwater marshes, both tidal and nontidal, swales, and ditches and in the shallows of ponds and lakes. It blooms from May through July.

Wild rice, *Zizania aquatica*, is a tall grass that can reach 10 feet. It arises in soft mud and shallow water on stems that are thickened at the base. The large, tapered leaves may be 4 feet long. The flower cluster, the panicle, is divided into two parts: the male flowers are below and the female flowers are above. The feathery heads bear the seeds that are highly valued as food for humans and waterfowl alike. Wild rice grows in freshwater, both tidal and nontidal, and in slightly brackish water. It flowers from May through October.

Giant cut-grass, *Zizaniopsis milacea*, also known as southern wild rice, forms extensive and very dense colonies. The smooth, 10-foot stems arise from scaly rhizomes. The leaf blades are about 3 feet long, and the edges are armed with fine, sharp teeth. The inflorescence, the panicle, has male and female flowers on the same branches. The female flowers are at the tips and the male flowers are near the base of the stem and are not divided into two ranks, as in wild rice. Giant cut-grass is an unfriendly native plant that is quite invasive and grows in almost impenetrable stands in shallow freshwater and brackish water marshes, sloughs, ditches, and along the shores of pond, lakes, and streams. It flowers from May to July.

Rice cut-grass, *Leersia oryzoides*, is a widespread native grass that grows 2–5 feet tall. The alternately arranged leaves of rice cut-grass are about 8 inches long and are yellowish to dull green. The upper and lower surfaces are covered with stiff hairs, but the edges of the leaves and leaf sheaths are what give this plant its name, for they are furnished with sharp saw teeth, much like saw grass, and can quickly slice through skin and draw blood. The terminal inflorescence, or panicle, typical of grasses may have spikelets up to 8 inches long. Rice cut-grass often grows in dense thickets or colonies in tidal freshwater marshes and infrequently in brackish marshes; in swamps, ditches, and wet swales; and along muddy shores.

Saw grass, *Cladium jamaicense*, the symbolic grass of the Everglades, is a member of the sedge family and is not a true grass. It is tall, about 10 feet, and is coarse and grasslike. The hollow stems grow from rhizomes; the 3-foot-long or longer leaves are armed with formidable, sharp saw teeth along the underside of the midrib and the margins. The large flower-

Saw Grass
Cladium jamaicense

inflorescence

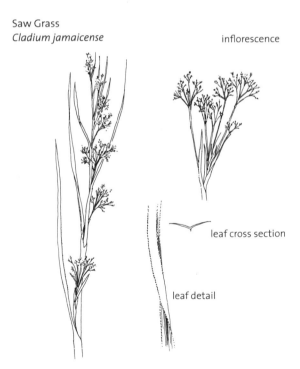

leaf cross section

leaf detail

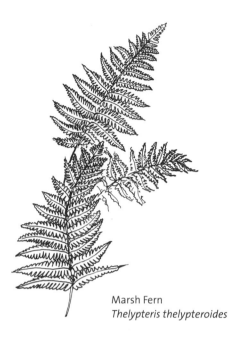

Marsh Fern
Thelypteris thelypteroides

it has approximately twelve lancelike leaflets. This common sun-loving fern grows in wet meadows, shrubby swamps, ditches, and forested wetlands, and sometimes along the upper margins of salt and brackish marshes.

Sweet grass, *Muhlenbergia capillaris*, also known as muhly, is a grass that grows in clumps that may be 3 feet across and 3 feet or more high. It may grow in isolated clumps along a sandy edge, or it may carpet a wet flatwoods. In early summer, the clumps produce long, narrow green blades, but in late summer and early autumn, sweet grass develop light purplish to pink flower heads, or inflorescences, that wreathe the plant in a wispy haze that may persist for almost two months. Descendants of slaves from West Africa in the Charleston and Mount Pleasant areas weave sweet grass, cabbage palmetto leaves, and black needlerush stems to create the famous and valuable sweet grass baskets of South Carolina.

Mangrove Swamps

Just as forest wetlands and marshes are a transition zone between an estuary or a river and the uplands, so it is with mangroves, also known as mangrove swamps; they are the zone between the shallows and the uplands. Mangroves are tropical shrubs or trees that grow along the Florida coast in or near the water. There are four species that are generally considered mangroves; they are listed here to indicate their usual habitat, from shallow water to rich mud to slightly higher elevations: red mangrove, black mangrove, white mangrove, and buttonwood. Mangroves are halophytes, which is another way of saying that they are salt-tolerant plants to various degrees. In general, mangroves range from about St. Augustine to the Keys, where they find their fullest expression.

ing head bears drooping branches of reddish brown spikelets that bloom from July through October. It grows in tidal and nontidal freshwater and slightly brackish marshes.

The tallest member of the spartina group, big cordgrass, or giant cordgrass, *Spartina cynosuroides*, is a plant of tidal freshwater and brackish marshes. It can grow to 12 feet tall and is easily recognized by its chevron-shaped green to tan flowering head that extends above the leaves. It forms thick stands in tidal freshwater and brackish marshes. Its leaves are armed with sharp, tiny teeth. Big cordgrass may stand well back from the high tide line and often forms a towering backdrop to the lower marsh community.

Marsh ferns and clumps of sweet grass grow along the edges of freshwater marshes. However, they also grow in other habitats. The marsh fern, *Thelypteris thelypteroides*, is an erect fern that can grow to 28 inches. Its rhizomes are black and branched, and

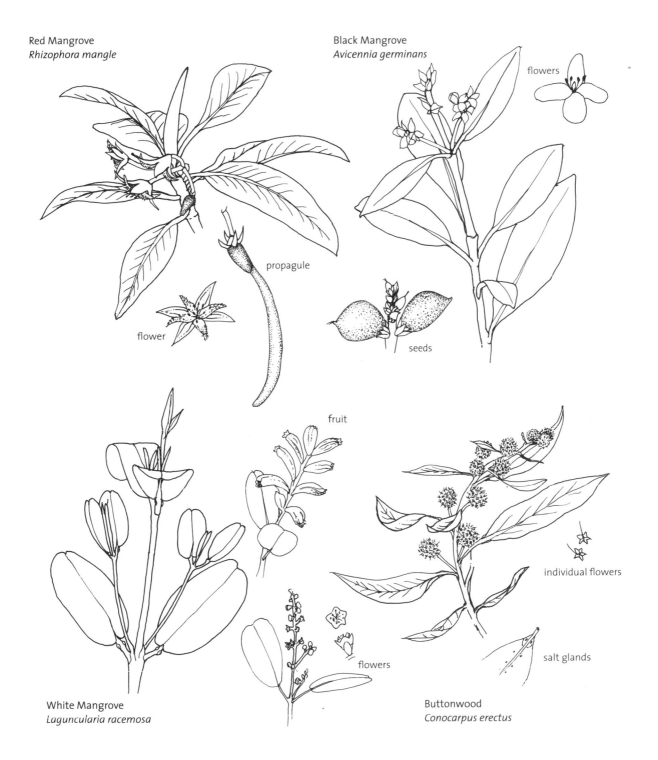

Red Mangrove
Rhizophora mangle

Black Mangrove
Avicennia germinans

flowers

propagule

flower

seeds

fruit

individual flowers

salt glands

flowers

White Mangrove
Laguncularia racemosa

Buttonwood
Conocarpus erectus

Red mangrove, *Rhizophora mangle*, grows throughout the Keys and south Florida. Sometimes red mangroves fringe the shorelines, and sometimes they form islands. They grow as small, scattered, single, almost tentative little arch-rooted bushes on silt-laden, shallow shoals when they begin life. They also grow into islands of luxuriant forests in shallow waters where the wave energy is low and the deposition of marl muds or calcareous sands is high. They are the pioneer species of the mangrove group because as they grow and entangle with one another, they trap coral muds and silt that begins building land, wet and mucky though it may be; it becomes the successional habitat for the next mangrove species, the black mangrove. Red mangrove forest islands are overwashed by the daily tides and occasional storms; other species of mangroves are often present, but red mangroves predominate. Red mangroves may reach as much as 80 feet in height, but typically they are somewhat shorter. Gray bark conceals the dark red wood beneath. The leaves are a shiny green above and a paler green below. The most notable characteristic of a red mangrove is its arching, woody prop roots that arise from the trunk and branches.

Pencil-shaped propagules—long, green bean–shaped embryonic seedlings—are attached to the parent plant. The waxy propagules develop roots, drop off the trees, and are carried by the currents to new locations, where they send out roots into the soft, muddy bottom and begin a new mangrove community. Red mangroves are salt excluders; they can adjust to fluctuations in the salinity of seawater by filtering seawater at the root surface by a process known as reverse osmosis.

Black mangrove, *Avicennia germinans*, grows landward of the red mangrove, often in sediments so mucky, salt laden, and rich with organic material that little or no oxygen can penetrate to its roots.

Red mangroves cope with anaerobic conditions by absorbing oxygen through pores, or lenticels, in the stiltlike roots that arch above the bottom. Black mangrove trees do not have arching prop roots, but they have adapted to the anoxic muds by developing air roots. Some call them pencil-like, or quills, or woody spikes, or pegs; botanists call them pneumatophores. In some areas where black mangroves thrive, the pneumatophores protrude from the wet soil in dense thickets under the tree canopy. At low tide, air is conducted through the pneumatophores and into the tissue system of the tree. The black mangrove has oppositely arranged, long, narrow leaves that are dark green on the upper surface and covered with down on the undersurface. It may grow to a height of 30 feet. The fragrant flowers are pale yellow or white, and the seeds resemble leathery lima beans. The black mangrove is the most cold-tolerant mangrove species and is the most widely distributed of all the mangroves, ranging from north Florida to the Keys, Louisiana, and the Caribbean. The red mangrove–black mangrove zone constantly builds soil from the accumulating organic material trapped by the trees' roots. As the land almost imperceptibly rises, the white mangrove and buttonwood replace the red and black mangroves. The soils are looser, and, consequently, the roots of the white mangrove and buttonwood are oxygenated and usually have no need for specialized root adaptations.

The white mangrove, *Laguncularia racemosa*, has dark green, thick, leathery, oppositely arranged, oval-shaped leaves. It has small, white, bell-shaped flowers and ribbed, leathery fruit about 1/2 inch long. The leaf stalk, or petiole, has two salt glands at the base of the leaf that excrete excess salt. White mangroves grow as shrubs or small trees to about 40 feet tall. They range from about Daytona Beach, Florida, to the Florida Keys and throughout the Caribbean.

The buttonwood, *Conocarpus erectus*, typically grows landward of the white mangrove. It usually grows at the highest elevation of the marsh or swamp, and it can be found in hammocks, as well as along the shore. It is the least salt tolerant of the mangrove group. This species has alternately arranged leaves; the other three species have their leaves arranged in an opposite pattern. The leathery, dark green leaves are long and pointed at both ends, with two salt glands at the base. The tiny green flowers of the buttonwood are formed in dense, rounded flower heads. The fruits are purplish, leathery balls. The buttonwood ranges from south Florida and the Keys and throughout the Caribbean to South America.

Many organisms, such as crabs, snails, insects, and birds, are just as intrinsically parts of the mangrove community as are oysters, algae, and sponges. Some are sessile, or attached, and some are free to flit, clamber, glide, and roost; mangroves are their home.

There is a busy world in and around the shallow waters of a red mangrove community. Juvenile fishes, spiny rock lobsters, and small shrimps swim around the arching prop roots, foraging on algae, bits of organic material, and small organisms. They also use the extensive root system to hide from marauding predators. Prop roots are also home to many mobile organisms that climb, slither, and glide, such as worms, isopods, amphipods, snails, and a number of crabs. These organisms wander around the mangrove root system beneath the surface of the water. They also graze on the rich organic muds and algae covering the exposed prop roots. Some crabs even feed in the tree canopy. Several species of barnacles live on the roots of the mangroves or glued forever to the shells of oysters.

Insects of Marshes and Mangrove Swamps

Insects: those pesky, flying, climbing, swimming, biting creatures that almost everyone likes to swat and spray because they cause torment and destroy our prized ornamentals. Some in fact do, but many insects pollinate the very ornamentals and wildflowers that we prize. Some, like dragonflies, prey on mosquitoes; others become food for fishes. Certain insects selectively control other, plant-damaging insects. And then there are the lovely butterflies and electric blue damselflies.

Insects are probably the most successful and numerous group of animals on earth because they have been able to adapt to almost every habitat on the planet. They live in the ground and in the tissues of plants; some are parasitic on other plants and animals; they fly; they burrow; they live in freshwater and saltwater; and they have developed simple to complex life cycles. There are approximately 90,000 species of insects in the continental United States and Canada and many more thousands throughout the world. We cover only a few species of insects in this book; most are aquatic, some are semiaquatic, and some flutter and flit near the water.

Dragonflies and damselflies are, perhaps, the most distinctive of all the insects. Their larvae, called naiads or nymphs, are totally aquatic. Some species may persist as naiads for as long as four years. Dragonflies and damselflies undergo incomplete metamorphosis: The egg hatches into a naiad, and the naiad molts into the adult. The pupation stage, which occurs in butterflies and moths, is skipped. The terrestrial adults range from slight and slender, as in some damselflies, to large and robust dragonflies. The adults are elongated and often very colorful insects, with large, membranous wings that are held outspread or vertically but never folded against the body. They have extremely large eyes, making their heads appear quite wide, and they come in an assortment of colors, from shocking pink and crimson to green, electric blue, yellow, and bronze to dull brown and black. Dragonflies have captured the imagination and fancy of amateurs and professionals throughout the world who have given them common names that rival those of butterflies and birds. There are petaltails and darners and cruisers and skimmers, and within those groups are phantom darners, cobra clubtails, common sanddragons, royal river cruisers, shadowdragons, and yellow-legged meadowhawks, to name just a few of the hundreds of species that range throughout North America.

Dragonflies and damselflies often mate in tandem as they fly over the water or meadow. When the female is ready to lay her eggs, she may broadcast them directly into the water, attach them to a stick or the underside of a floating leaf, or insert them into the soft tissues of an aquatic plant. The naiads that hatch from the eggs develop into some of the most bizarre and fascinating creatures in the animal world. These hideous, predacious larvae are equipped with a specialized lower lip, the labrum, that springs out with lighting speed to capture insect larvae, tadpoles, and, occasionally, small fishes. These grotesque larvae, depending on the species, may be stout or elongated, are usually dull colored, and may be adorned with spines or covered with algae and organic debris. Damselfly naiads have three leaflike gills projecting from the tip of the abdomen, and dragonfly naiads have internal rectal gills.

There are many species of dragonflies and damselflies throughout the Inner Coast; however, we have space in this book to mention only a few.

The seaside dragonlet, *Erythrodiplax berenice*, is a small, slender dragonfly. Mature males are usually

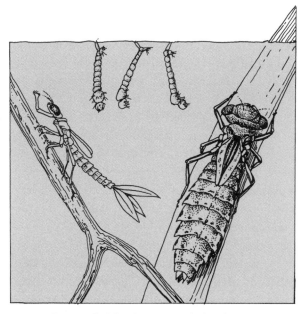

Aquatic larvae of wetland insects include a large dragonfly naiad, a predacious damselfly naiad with leaflike gills at the tip of its body and lower labrum extended to catch its prey, and small mosquito wrigglers at the surface.

all black; the females are more variable in coloration and pattern and may have orange and yellow stripes before eventually turning black. This species is the only dragonfly that can breed in full-strength seawater. The male and female fly in tandem over the water as the female lays her eggs in floating algal mats. They inhabit salt marshes and mangrove swamps. The mangrove darner is another dragonfly found around mangroves. This dragonfly grows to about 3 1/2 inches long, somewhat larger than the seaside dragonlet; both sexes are usually green. They are confined to extreme southern Florida and the Keys.

The green darner, *Anax junius*, is a large, fastflying dragonfly that can exceed 3 inches in length. Adult males have blue abdomens, and the females and young have reddish abdomens. They are called darners because their abdomens are long and slender

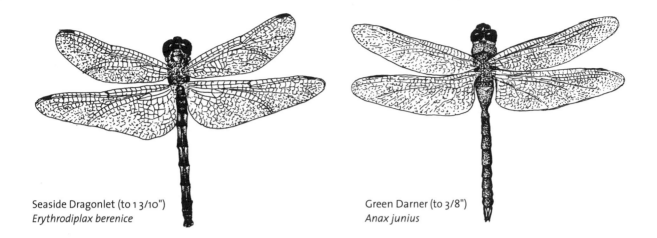

Seaside Dragonlet (to 1 3/10")
Erythrodiplax berenice

Green Darner (to 3/8")
Anax junius

and shaped like a darning needle. The green darner is the most common and widespread darner in the United States. They are active throughout the day and often perch on weed tips. They often gather in large swarms and hawk for insects just as swallows often do. They lay their eggs in still, marshy waters that may be slightly brackish and in freshwater temporary ponds.

The twelve-spotted skimmer, *Libellula pulchella*, is another widespread dragonfly. The males are handsomely marked with flashy, alternating black and white wing spots. These are denizens of tidal freshwater marshes, slow streams, lakes, and ponds. They typically forage for insects from tall weeds in open fields. They range along the Inner Coast to southern Georgia. There are several other skimmers that are found in Florida, such as the golden-winged skimmer, Needham's skimmer, the purple skimmer, and the blue corporal.

Damselflies are usually much smaller than dragonflies, and, when at rest, they hold their wings together vertically over their bodies.

Dancers, *Argia* spp., are usually less than 2 inches long and are often blue or purple, or brown and yellow with black markings. The violet dancer is a widespread damselfly that is found along slow-flowing streams, in the quiet backwaters of large rivers, and over shallow lakes. The male has a violet body and a black head, and the female is dark brown to black. These damselflies often fly in tandem over the water. When the female is ready to lay her eggs, the male grasps her from above, and she then dips the tip of her abdomen under a submerged leaf, where she deposits her eggs.

Doubleday's bluet, *Enallagma doubledayii*, is a striking damselfly that has an electric blue abdomen with black markings. Its head and thorax are also brightly colored blue and yellow and marked with black. The female, while being grasped by the male, inserts her eggs into the soft tissue of aquatic plants.

Where there are wetlands—marshes, streams, moist bottomlands, swamps, and swales—there will be vicious horseflies and deerflies that inflict painful bites. The females are the biters; the males feed on the pollen and nectar of flowers. Horseflies and deerflies have large heads with bulging eyes and wedge-shaped wings. Horseflies are larger than deerflies; they are heavy bodied and may be as much as 1 inch long. Houseflies are slightly larger than deerflies.

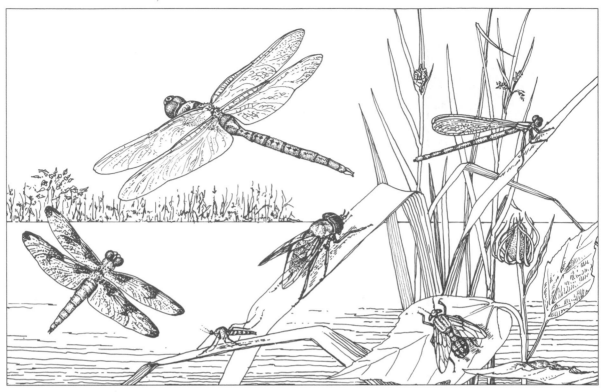

Common insects of wetlands. The larger of two dragonflies, a green darter, hovers over a twelve-spotted skimmer, Libellula pulchella (to 2 1/4"), and a damselfly with wings typically raised rests on a blade of three-square. Flies and mosquitoes abound in a marsh: a large American horsefly, Tabanus americanus (to 1 1/8"), and a salt marsh mosquito, Aedes solicitans (to 1/4"), alight on three-square blades, and a deerfly, Chrysops sp. (to 5/8"), rests on a marsh hibiscus leaf.

Deerflies are mostly yellow and black, with dark stripes on the abdomen, and they have brilliant green or golden eyes.

Both flies lay their egg masses on vegetation over-hanging the water. When the larvae hatch, they drop into the water and feed on other aquatic insects and worms and are, in turn, fed on by fishes and dragonfly naiads. The larval stage can last from a few months to a year, depending on the species. The larvae then pupate. Deerfly pupae tend to remain in the water, and horsefly pupae are found in drier soils. The adult fly emerges from the pupa and mates, and the cycle begins anew.

Mosquitoes belong to the same group as flies, the order Diptera, and, like flies, have only two apparent wings. The second pair are reduced to stabilizing flight organs, the halteres. This is a large group that includes not only the many species of flies and mosquitoes but also crane flies, midges, gnats, and a host of others. Mosquitoes, from the Spanish word meaning "little fly," are some of the planet's most dangerous animals. Lions, bears, poisonous snakes, and sharks are some of the animals that we instinctively fear, but not the pesky mosquito. However, it is the mosquito that carries many diseases deadly to horses, cattle, and humans throughout the world.

Mangrove Skipper (to 2 3/4")
Phocides pigmalion

Mangrove Buckeye (to 2")
Junonia evarete

West Nile fever, malaria, dengue fever, encephalitis, and dog heartworm are just some of the lethal diseases spread by the bite of mosquitoes. *Culex pipiens*, the common house mosquito, carries the West Nile virus. Most female mosquitoes require a blood meal in preparation for laying eggs; the males feed on pollen and nectar. There are about 2,500 species of mosquitoes distributed throughout the world, with about 200 species in the United States and 77 of those species in Florida.

The salt marsh mosquito, *Aedes solicitans*, is a typical mosquito of the Inner Coast. It breeds in brackish and saltwater marshes, where the female deposits her eggs on floating vegetation or sticks or on the bare mud of the marsh floor during low tides.

The eggs require a period of drying before they are ready to hatch. They hatch two weeks later, in synchrony with the next spring tide. The resultant larvae, called wrigglers, feed on algal cells and single-celled organisms. Golden brown adult salt marsh mosquitoes eventually emerge from their pupae and swarm around brackish and salt marshes.

Butterflies and moths are a diverse group that both decorate and pollinate. Some are very small and drab; some are large and showy, such as the green luna moth; most are short-lived; and some, like the monarch, migrate thousands of miles to spend the winter in the South. There is also a little skipper that feeds primarily on the nectar of the red mangrove blossom.

The mangrove skipper, *Phocides pigmalion*, is a small butterfly that has many characteristics similar to those of moths. Skippers are considered to be a primitive group of butterflies that have thick, stout bodies, large heads, and relatively short wings. Some species hold their wings in a somewhat vertical position, as do most butterflies, but other species of skippers, when at rest, hold their wings horizontally. Skippers, rather than soaring and fluttering as do most butterflies, rapidly dart here and there among the mangroves. The mangrove skipper is dark brown to black with iridescent blue streaks on the wings. The caterpillar is powdery white with a brown head marked with two large orange to yellow spots; it feeds on red mangrove leaves. The mangrove skipper ranges through south Florida and the Keys wherever there are red mangroves.

The mangrove buckeye, *Junonia evarete*, is another butterfly that frequents mangrove forests. Buckeyes are mostly tropical and cannot survive freezing temperatures. The mangrove buckeye belongs to a large and diverse group known as brush-foots. The front pair of legs is reduced and hairy and is kept folded against the thorax. The mangrove buckeye is a brownish-winged butterfly with a wingspan of about 2 inches. The wings are ornamented with one eyespot on the fore wing and two eye spots on the hind wing. The largest eyespot, closest to the front of the wing, is ringed with an orange band, and the underside of the wing is brown and has a single eyespot ringed with orange. Buckeye caterpillars are black and dusted with white flecks and have two rows of orange spots along the sides. The adult mangrove buckeye feeds on the flower nectar of black mangroves, and the caterpillars feed on the leaves of black mangroves, in contrast to the mangrove skipper, which feeds only on red mangroves. Mangrove buckeyes are found along tidal flats and black mangrove swamps in extreme south Florida, south Texas, Mexico, and the West Indies.

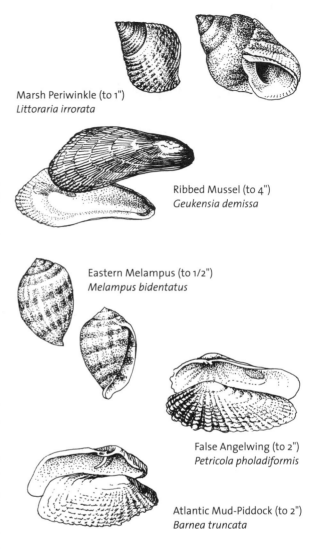

Marsh Periwinkle (to 1")
Littoraria irrorata

Ribbed Mussel (to 4")
Geukensia demissa

Eastern Melampus (to 1/2")
Melampus bidentatus

False Angelwing (to 2")
Petricola pholadiformis

Atlantic Mud-Piddock (to 2")
Barnea truncata

🌿 Mollusks of Marshes and Mangrove Swamps

Regularly flooded, or low, saltwater marshes are rich environments for many species of invertebrates and fishes. The tidal fingers that connect to shallow depressions within the marsh provide feeding areas and protection from predators. The intertidal zone of the salt marsh is home to several species of mollusks, as well as fiddler crabs, marsh crabs, and shrimps.

Look closely at the stems and leaves of salt marsh cordgrass, and what appear to be gray fruiting bodies associated with plants are actually marsh periwinkles. The marsh periwinkle, *Littoraria irrorata*, has a heavy, thick shell about 1 inch long. The whorls of the shell are separated by shallow grooves. The shell is usually grayish white to yellowish tan, with small dashes of reddish brown on the spiral ridges. The opening of the shell can be sealed by the brown, leathery operculum, common in marine snails, that protects the snail from desiccation.

The marsh periwinkle is an abundant and conspicuous snail and is particularly abundant on salt marsh cordgrass. Periwinkles tend to synchronize their movements up and down the stems of the cordgrass with the ebb and flow of the tides. The omnipresent blue crab is a particular marauder of periwinkles; as the tide floods the low-lying marshes, the blue crab moves in to feed on the snails. The marsh periwinkles ascend the grass stems to escape the rapacious appetite of the blue crabs, and when the tide ebbs and the crabs are gone, the periwinkles descend from their perches and spread across the marsh floor, where they feed on organic detritus, algae, and the leaves of salt marsh cordgrass. Two other species of periwinkles, the mangrove periwinkle and the zebra periwinkle, are quite common and plentiful in southern Florida and the Keys.

There is a secretive little snail that lives under moist litter at the upper edge of the salt marsh. This small, herbivorous gastropod, only about 1/2 inch long, is the eastern melampus, *Melampus bidentatus*. The eastern melampus is ovate and is creamy brown to an almost coffee bean color. This is an intriguing little snail because it employs a strategy to deal with the dilemma of being an adult air breather and a larval form that can extract oxygen only from the water. It has developed a mechanism that brings into play the place where it lives as an adult and a precise synchrony with the twice-monthly spring tides. The adult lives among the stems of salt meadow hay and under stones and litter, and there it lays hundreds of gelatinous-covered eggs. As the spring tides roll in on the marsh, water washes over the egg masses, keeping them moist. The eggs are timed to hatch in about thirteen days, with the arrival of the next spring tide. When the eggs hatch, enormous numbers of larvae, called veligers, are released into the estuary and become part of the teeming plankton soup. The larvae spend about two weeks as plankton and then, again synchronized with the spring tide, are washed back up into a marsh, where they develop into air-breathing adults. The coffee melampus, a close relative of the eastern melampus, lives in the muddy flats around black mangroves, where it feeds on the embryonic seedlings of the mangrove.

The ribbed mussel, *Geukensia demissa*, lies almost entirely buried in the spongy floor of the lower

Eastern melampus are often found under flotsam at the upper edge of a marsh.

marsh, with only its anterior end protruding above the surface. The ribbed mussel is about 2 to 4 inches long, blackish brown in color, and ornamented with rough radial ribs. The interiors of the shells, or valves, are bluish white, and the posterior ends of the inner shells are tinged with purple or purplish red. Ribbed mussels are often found in small clumps of several individuals where they are attached to the roots of cordgrass by leathery, elastic byssal threads. They occupy the intertidal zone and are well adapted to withstand dry periods and fluctuations in temperature. The ribbed mussel is a filter feeder and feeds on detritus, algae, and zooplankton that are carried in by the rising tides. This little mussel plays an important role in cycling nutrients through the estuarine system.

False angelwings, *Petricola pholadiformis*, are boring clams that do not bore into hard surfaces; rather, they burrow into stiff clay, heavy mud, and peat.

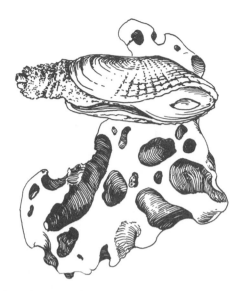

The Atlantic mud-piddock leaves distinctive borings in clumps of hard peat. The shell has wide gapes at both ends.

They resemble the true angelwings that do bore into pilings, but they are placed in separate families and are not closely related. False angelwings are about 2 inches long with thin, elongated valves marked with growth lines and robust, radiating ribs. They are most often found burrowed into the muddy banks of salt marshes all along the Inner Coast to Florida and the Gulf of Mexico.

The Atlantic mud-piddock, *Barnea truncata*, also belongs to a group of clams that are capable of boring into rocks, wood, coral, and stiff, dense clay. They have thin, brittle white shells that are elongated and gape at both ends. The anterior ends of a piddock clam are sharply sculptured for boring into hard substrates. The Atlantic mud-piddock (sometimes known as a fallen angel wing) is chalky white and about 2 inches long.

The angelwing, *Cyrtopleura costata*, is a mollusk that burrows into stiff clay and mud, peat, and sand in the banks of marshes and mudflats and in the sandy and muddy bottoms of the shallows. The valves of this mollusk form separate grinding plates. These are large shells that can be up to 8 inches long, but they are too small to totally encase the bivalve's soft body parts. The angelwing's shell has well-developed ribs that are sharp and angular, which aids in burrowing as the animal rocks itself back and forth into the substrate as much as 3 feet deep. The shell is white and covered with a thin yellow to tan periostracum. Angelwing shells are usually washed up on beaches or stranded along marshes; they are avidly sought by shell collectors, but unfortunately, because the shells are thin and brittle and the musculature is weak, the shells are usually not intact. Angelwing clams are quite common throughout the Inner Coast and are sometimes plentiful in certain areas, such as the Indian River Lagoon in Florida.

Crustaceans of Marshes and Mangrove Swamps

Grazing and foraging crabs abound along marshes and mangroves. Most of the crabs are semiterrestrial: they spend some of their time hiding in burrows full of seawater and other times scurrying across the sand-mud flats or hiding under debris. They are fed on by a number of predators, including raccoons, blue crabs, rails, and herons. There are four species of small, square-back crabs common in the marshes along the Inner Coast. These are the square-back

Angelwing (to 8")
Cyrtopleura costata

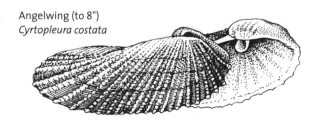

marsh crab, the heavy marsh crab, the humic marsh crab (see chapter 5), and the mangrove marsh crab (see chapter 5). All of these species have square or almost square carapaces with stalked eyes that are positioned in the corners of the carapace, where the front of the carapace meets the sides. Though never found in great numbers, they are widely distributed and quite common throughout the area.

Sesarma cinereum, the square-back marsh crab, is also called the friendly wharf crab for its habits of scampering into boats and suddenly appearing on piers. These crabs actively crawl about on stone jetties and wharves or rest in shallow burrows along the edges of marshes. This little crab has a brown to olive back. It tolerates brackish water, almost fresh, to high-salinity saltwater. Square-back marsh crabs are relatively resistant to desiccation and can remain out of the water for some time.

The heavy marsh crab, or purple marsh crab, *Sesarma reticulatum*, has a thick carapace that is slightly wider than it is long; its claws, or chelipeds, are heavier than those of the square-back marsh crab. This species tends to inhabit the lower, muddy areas of marshes and usually remains below the high-tide line in the wetter areas of the marsh. Its carapace is variably colored and may be purple to dark brown, dark olive, or nearly black, and its claws are usually yellow with white tips. Heavy marsh crabs dig burrows that often have multiple openings and are usually surrounded by a mud chimney. They often live within fiddler crab colonies and will feed on them if they can catch them, but they are chiefly herbivorous and feed on salt meadow cordgrass and salt marsh hay. They are usually found in mid-estuarine salinities, and they range from Massachusetts to central Florida.

Fiddler crabs, the prairie dogs of the salt marshes, are wary and quick like their furry counterparts out west. Fiddler crabs have eyes at the tips of elongated

Mangrove Tree Crab (to 1")
Aratus pisonii

Heavy Marsh Crab (to 1 1/8")
Sesarma reticulatum

Squareback Marsh Crab (to 1")
Sesarma cinereum

stalks. They are ever watchful, and when alarmed, they will vanish down any available nearby burrow. On a marshy flat, hundreds or thousands of little crabs may be visible feeding, digging, and waving their large claws in ritualized combat when suddenly they become startled by a shadow or a predator, and then they instantly disappear. They will often move as a herd, retreating from the water's edge en masse to hide in the marsh.

These semiterrestrial crabs—they are behaviorally terrestrial but physiologically aquatic—are unmistakable in appearance. For example, the male has one enormous claw and one very small claw, or cheliped, and their bodies are almost square. The females have two very small claws that are quite useful for feeding but not for courtship display or threatening behavior, as in the male. The large claw of the male is virtually useless for feeding, which gives the female an advantage in processing the stew of algae, bacteria, and detritus. The crabs extract their food from the mud and sand and return the sediment in the form of little, round pellets strewn over the flats.

Four species of fiddler crabs are common along the Inner Coast: the red-jointed fiddler, the Atlantic sand fiddler, the Atlantic marsh fiddler, and the mudflat fiddler. Two other burrowing species, the swamp ghost crab and the blue land crab, are found in Florida.

The red-jointed fiddler, *Uca minax*, is perhaps the most widely distributed fiddler because of its tolerance of a range of salinities. It is sometimes called the brackish water fiddler because it can be very abundant in low- to mid-salinity waters. The joints of its legs are decorated with red patches that look like red bands. The outer surface of the ivory-white hand of the male's claw has large nodules, or tubercles, that grade into granules. The red-jointed fiddler is usually found in muddy and sandy areas, particularly around salt marsh cordgrass and black needlerush that are tidally flooded by brackish water or freshwater. It ranges from Massachusetts to north Florida.

The Atlantic sand fiddler, *Uca pugilator*, also known as the china-back fiddler in some locales, usually has a yellowish white carapace. When the male displays, in seemingly unending courtship activities, the cardiac region in the center of the carapace, which is normally brown, takes on a fleeting violet to purplish patch of color (the china back). The outside of the male's creamy white, large hand is smooth. The Atlantic sand fiddler is abundant on sandy and muddy flats that border marshes and along tidal creeks, where it often intermingles with the Atlantic marsh fiddler in the wetter zones.

Uca pugnax, the Atlantic marsh fiddler, has a carapace that is usually brown but may shade to pale gray or almost white. The large cheliped of the male is rough and granulated. The Atlantic marsh fiddler

The red-jointed fiddler crab raises his "fiddler claw" to court a female. Species of fiddler crabs may be identified by examining the fiddler claws of the males.

lives in very wet areas along the edges of salt marshes and on intertidal flats that are protected from rough seas. It ranges from Cape Cod, Massachusetts, to about Daytona Beach, Florida.

Uca rapax, the mudflat fiddler, is also known as the mangrove fiddler. The carapace and the large claw of the male are light tan. This is a crab of sheltered mudflats and the muddy floors of mangrove swamps. It ranges from central Florida to South America.

The swamp ghost crab, or mangrove land crab,

Red-Jointed Fiddler Crab (carapace to 1 1/2")
Uca minax

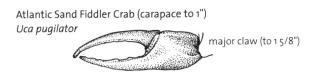

major claw (to 2")

Atlantic Sand Fiddler Crab (carapace to 1")
Uca pugilator

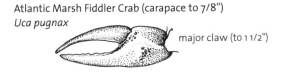

major claw (to 1 5/8")

Atlantic Marsh Fiddler Crab (carapace to 7/8")
Uca pugnax

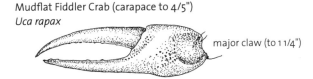

major claw (to 1 1/2")

Mudflat Fiddler Crab (carapace to 4/5")
Uca rapax

major claw (to 1 1/4")

large claw has slender, gaping, untoothed fingers. Blue land crabs often stray 2 to 3 miles inland because they are able to survive for a few days without wetting their gills. They frequently migrate in large numbers crossing roads, sometimes to the consternation of motorists and homeowners. Sometimes only females migrate, and at other times males and females migrate. Their route takes them from the red mangrove zone, across roads, and along irrigation ditches. These are very abundant crabs in some areas: as many as several thousand burrows per acre may be present, particularly under trees, where they feed on fallen leaves, blossoms, and fruit. The blue land crab is a favored food of some people living in the Caribbean and Central and South America. It ranges from central Florida, near Vero Beach, to the Florida Keys and along the Gulf Coast to Texas, as well as the West Indies, Bermuda, and Brazil.

Ucides cordatus, has an oval carapace with an overall purplish appearance, but may be blue gray with purple and reddish splotches. Its walking legs are long and hairy and the male has an enlarged toothed cheliped, similar to fiddler crabs. The swamp ghost crab digs wide burrows in the mud usually under red mangroves where it often intermixes with fiddler crabs. It feeds on the leaves of the red mangrove. This is a commercially important crab in Puerto Rico, Trinidad, Tobago, and Brazil. The swamp ghost crab is distributed in south Florida, and throughout the West Indies to Brazil.

Cardisoma guanhumi, the blue land crab, or the great land crab, somewhat resembles fiddler crabs in its general shape, the position of its stalked eyes, and the male's enlarged claw, but blue land crabs are much larger than fiddler crabs. Adults are pale, bluish gray, and the young are blue to violet or sandy colored. The males have unequally sized claws; the

Blue Land Crab (to 4")
Cardisoma guanhumi

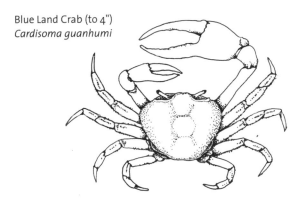

Swamp Ghost Crab (to 3 1/2")
Ucides cordatus

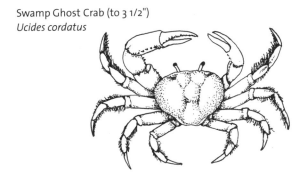

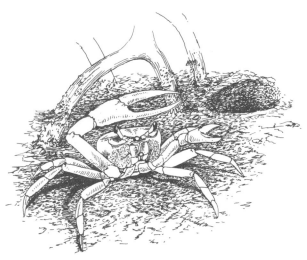

A blue land crab leaves its burrow dug at the base of mangrove roots.

The mangrove tree crab, *Aratus pisonii*, is a crab that moves freely through the mangrove canopy. These little crabs have small tufts of hairs on the outer surfaces of their claws. They are brown or mottled green with brownish red legs. Their eyes are widely spaced and set at the corners of the carapace. They have sharp-pointed legs that aid them in climbing through the trees, where they feed on mangrove leaves, caterpillars, beetles, and other insects.

Even though this little crab is semiterrestrial, like other crabs it has an aquatic larval stage. The female lowers her body into the water and releases the eggs, which quickly develop into tiny larvae called zoeae. The weak-swimming zoeae become part of the planktonic assemblage in the shallow coastal waters and feed on algal cells and, in turn, are fed on by many species of fishes. The greatest peril that the young face is when they are in the planktonic larval stage. When they emerge from the water as small but recognizable crabs, they become quite adept at eluding predators by scurrying from one side of the tree to the other; they even drop into the water if they

must. Predation on the adult crabs is much lower than that on the zoeae; however, birds, such as white ibises and herons, and raccoons and other mangrove crabs feed on these little crabs when they can catch them.

❧

Great Reptiles of Marshes and Mangrove Swamps

Alligators and crocodiles are the largest of all the reptiles in North America. They have survived for 200 million years—they date back to the age of dinosaurs. These behemoths react to temperatures just as their relatives snakes and turtles do: they are slow to move when the temperature is cool and bask in the warming sun for hours. They are stealthy predators that freeze until their prey moves in range of their powerful jaws.

The American crocodile, *Crocodylus acutus*, is at its most northern distribution in extreme south Florida and has never been abundant in North America. Most experts believe there are about 500 to 1,200 crocodiles along the southern mainland of Florida and in the Florida Keys. The crocodile has a long, tapering snout, in contrast to the American alligator's broadly rounded, shovel-like snout. The crocodile has a prominent tooth, the fourth, in the lower jaw that protrudes when its mouth is closed.

American crocodiles are shy and reclusive animals that are rarely seen. They live where the saw grass and ocean meet: in estuarine swamps, shallow salty embayments, coastal lagoons, and mangrove swamps. They range through Central and South America and Mexico. In the United States, they are found only in a few places in south Florida: along the remote, mangrove-lined edges of Little Madeira Bay and Joe Bay and along the northern edge of Florida Bay, which is within Everglades National Park. They

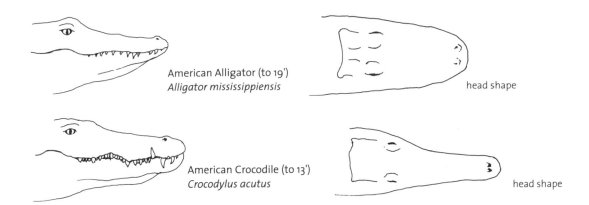

American Alligator (to 19')
Alligator mississippiensis

head shape

American Crocodile (to 13')
Crocodylus acutus

head shape

also inhabit an area on the northern tip of Key Largo and a most unlikely site, the cooling canals of Turkey Point Nuclear Power Plant in southern Biscayne Bay, a scant 25 miles from bustling downtown Miami.

Adult crocodiles are slate gray to dark greenish gray; the young have narrow black crossbands on the body and tail. Crocodiles nest on marl banks and on secluded sand and shell beaches. They also nest on the banks of canal levees close to mangrove swamps in northern Key Largo. The female buries about forty to fifty eggs in the marl or sand, and they hatch in about eighty-five days. Raccoons are the primary predators of the eggs and hatchlings. The crocodile feeds on almost anything within its habitat, including coots, moorhens, marsh rabbits, crabs, diamondback terrapins, and mullets.

The American alligator, *Alligator mississippiensis*, is the largest reptile in North America. The longest alligator on record measured a little over 19 feet; however, most gators do not exceed 16 feet. "Alligator" comes from the Spanish *el lagarto*, "the lizard." By the 1970s, alligators were declining throughout their range because of poaching, overhunting, and habitat destruction. They were placed under the protection of the Endangered Species Act of 1973, and they have since made a remarkable recovery. Even though it is no longer biologically endangered, the alligator is

classified as threatened to help ensure the conservation of the similar-appearing crocodile, which is endangered.

Alligators are inhabitants of freshwater swamps and marshes, slow-moving rivers, ponds, and ditches. They are sometimes found in brackish water and can tolerate moderate levels of salinity; however, their preferred habitat is freshwater. In some areas, particularly in the Florida Everglades, where the water levels fluctuate, alligators plow out depressions in the muck and create "alligator holes" so that they can survive drying conditions. These alligator holes attract herons and egrets and other water birds and also concentrate local populations of fishes, such as gars and catfish, and turtles. The alligator hole offers protection for many aquatic species and a dining room for the gator.

Adult alligators, both male and female, are slate gray or black with white to creamy yellow throats. They are often covered with a sticky layer of green duckweed, as it is their habit to float quietly like logs with only part of their backs, heads, and snouts visible at the surface. The juveniles are brightly colored with a pattern of yellow crossbands on a black background. They feed on a varied diet of insects, small fishes, crayfish, and frogs. The adults eat almost anything that comes near their ready jaws, including fishes, turtles, small mammals, birds, and small alligators.

Alligators have hundreds of pimplelike bumps covering their faces and jaws; recent research has demonstrated that these bumps are very sensitive pressure receptors that accurately locate disturbances, even ripples, in the water. Alligators are able to locate their prey and immediately turn toward their meal with the aid of these nerve-packed receptors.

Alligators, both males and females, often bellow and emit low-frequency vibrations that travel considerable distances in the water. They also slap the surface of the water with their heads, transmitting aural and visual cues for communication and courtship. The males produce musk as an olfactory cue that is also part of the complex courtship in alligators. After mating, the female builds a nest of vegetation and mud on a shore bank or on floating vegetation above the water. She will lay an average of about forty to fifty eggs in a conical depression in the top of the nest and then remain near the nest during the incubation period of about two months. The sex of the alligators is determined by the temperatures within the nest. Cooler temperatures favor the development of females, and warmer temperatures produce males. The sexes of crocodiles and many turtles are also determined by the heat in the nest. The hatchlings alert the mother waiting nearby with their high-pitched grunting. She gathers several of the 9-inch, needle-toothed hatchlings in her powerful mouth and carries them to the water. She repeats the trip until all the little ones are deposited in the water, where they remain as a group, called a pod, for the next year.

Florida and Louisiana, for many people, is where the gators are, and, in fact, those two states have the largest populations of alligators in the United States. But alligators range from North Carolina, in the aptly named Alligator River National Wildlife Refuge, down into the swamps and rivers of South Carolina and Georgia, and westward to the lower Rio Grande valley.

Birds of Marshes and Mangrove Swamps

Many of the bird species around tidal marshes and mangrove swamps are showy and prominent, such as the herons, egrets, ibises, and wood storks. Ducks and geese and their brethren, though sometimes not easily identifiable, are obvious as they bob up and down in the shallows or fly by like jet-powered footballs. There are also little brown or black birds that range from the size of a sparrow to the size of a robin or a crow. These birds are somewhat more difficult to identify than the larger birds unless you know the way they perch or the way they fly or their particular call. For example, the yellow-rumped warbler is a small, sparrow-size warbler that seldom comes to rest in the open. These little grayish birds, sometimes known as butter butts, flit endlessly in and out of the branches of shrubs such as marsh elders and bayberries, flashing their yellow rumps, busily calling out "check-check-check," and then disappearing in the foliage. Their color pattern, their call, their flying behavior, and their habitat usually furnish enough clues to identify this bird. Are the legs of that storklike bird extended beyond its tail? Is the neck crooked or held straight? Are the wing beats slow and deep? What unseen bird deep in the marsh is uttering staccatolike "kek-kek-kek"? Is that small bird hopping like a robin or striding about like a grackle? These visual and aural cues, behavioral traits, and habitat preferences are an immense help in identifying birds throughout the Inner Coast.

The red-winged blackbird, *Agelaius phoeniceus*, is a common and abundant bird throughout much of North America. This songbird is very much at

Red-Winged Blackbird (to 8 3/4")
Agelaius phoeniceus

male

female

The generic name of the red-winged blackbird, *Agelaius*, means "gregarious," or "living in large groups," and that is precisely what red-wings do. As fall approaches, they throng in enormous flocks mixed with grackles, starlings, and cowbirds. They fill the sky with great clouds and spirals like never-ending plumes of smoke. They twist and turn and suddenly descend into a meadow or a grove of trees, where they may stay for several days or more, noisily twittering and whitening the roosts with droppings until an unknown signal spurs the flock to move on.

The tree swallow, *Tachycineta bicolor*, is a small, sleek, and agile flier that is found over the water and open fields not far from woods. Its iridescent bluish green back and white underbelly easily separate this species from other swallows along the Inner Coast. Tree swallows are gregarious and feed in flocks and hawk for insects such as mosquitoes and flies. They also feed on berries, particularly bayberries, which allows them to overwinter along the coast when there are few insects available. They usually nest in isolated pairs and build their nests of grass and straw in tree cavities and also in bluebird nesting boxes.

When tree swallows are not performing aerobatics, they often line up in long rows, wing to wing, on power lines and tree branches. They nest and summer in the northern half of the United States and much of Canada, from the Pacific to the Atlantic coast, and they winter along the Inner Coast.

The fish crow, *Corvus ossifragus*, looks like the common American crow. It is a bit smaller, but size is not a good criterion for distinguishing it from the American crow. However, fish crows' call usually gives them away: listen for a short, almost begrudging, nasal "ah-ah" or "cah." Fish crows are very common along the Inner Coast and gather by the thousands in winter roosts. They are birds of the salt marshes, beaches, tidal flats, and river courses. Typical of most crow species, they are omnivores: they will eat

home in freshwater and brackish marshes, and it seldom nests far from the water. Male red-wings arrive in the marshes in early spring and claim their breeding territories on the tips and branches of reed grass and cattails. The males have distinctive red epaulets with buff or yellow borders that are often concealed on their shoulders. The female and the immature red-wings are brownish with bold brown streaks. The males announce their presence by singing their liquid call, "oka-leee," in the plume-topped reed grass meadows, and they flash their crimson shoulder patches both as a territorial display and as a courtship signal to females. The female builds a cup-shaped nest and lays three to six bluish green eggs that hatch in about ten days.

Tree Swallow (to 5 3/4")
Tachycineta bicolor

almost anything, including insects, crayfish, crabs, fishes, berries, nuts, seeds, bird and turtle eggs, carrion, and garbage. They will carry mollusks up in the air and drop them on the rocks below, just as gulls do, and then pick out the soft meat from the broken shells.

The boat-tailed grackle, *Quiscalus major,* is a crow-size bird that is found around the waterfront along the Inner Coast. This noisy, constantly vocal bird is a resident of marshes and beaches, but it is quite comfortable in parks and residential neighborhoods right in the midst of humans. Boat-tailed grackles chatter and utter a number of calls, including the familiar, buzzing "jeeb-jeeb-jeeb." They call from live oaks, from sidewalks, and on the wing.

Both male and female boat-tailed grackles have long, fanned-out tails. The males are larger and seem almost black, but in the right light they are actually iridescent blue-black. The females have brown backs and buff or tawny breasts. The males are frequently quite active when they display in front of females; they point their beaks skyward, ruffle their throat feathers, spread their wings, and chatter excitedly. Both males and females scavenge for food along the waterfront and seem to be perfectly at ease with humans, as many on Saint Simons Island, Georgia, will

attest. They feed on fiddler crabs, mole crabs, various aquatic invertebrates, worms, insects, bird eggs, seeds, and fruit.

There are some birds that live deep in the marshes and are seldom seen but are sometimes heard. These are the rails and bitterns. They are not at all related: the rail family includes the ducklike coots and gallinules, and the bitterns are members of the heron family. But both rails and bitterns are secretive and often solitary, in contrast to most members of their respective families.

The least bittern, *Ixobrychus exilis,* is the Inner Coast's smallest heron. It is brown and streaked with white, and its wings, head, and neck are tan. Its chest and throat are white, and it has a greenish black–capped head. This little heron, similar to the reclusive rails, lives deep in dense freshwater or brackish marshes where the cattails and sedges grow thick and lush. It is also sometimes spotted in mangrove swamps. It most frequently lives a solitary existence but sometimes associates in small, loose groups. It seldom wades but climbs over roots and stems of plants, sometimes in a hunched or crouched posture, with its neck extended and its bill nearly touching the water, as it hunts for small frogs, insects, killifish, and sometimes a small shrew or mouse. When alarmed, this little heron furtively slinks away or assumes a characteristic reedlike pose—it elongates its neck, contracts its body, and points its beak skyward—and remains frozen in that posture, sometimes swaying slowly side to side, to mimic the movement of the marsh plants. If it is further alarmed, it reluctantly and awkwardly springs into the air and, with legs dangling, flies a short distance away, drops into the marsh, and disappears. Sometimes, usually early in the morning, least bitterns show themselves along the muddy shore of a marsh. We have seen them on gray, overcast days when the mist is beginning to arise along the Intracoastal Waterway south of

Boat-Tailed Grackle (male to 18")
Quiscalus major

Fish Crow (to 15")
Corvus ossifragus

Georgetown, South Carolina, where the Santee River flows through the marshes. Merritt Island, Florida, near Kennedy Space Center is another good place to find the least bittern. Their call is a soft, whistling series of "kuk" or "coo-co-coo."

The American bittern, *Botaurus lentiginosus*, is a chunky, short-legged heron that, like the least bittern, is solitary, retiring, and secretive and is certainly less conspicuous than most herons. It is buff-brown and streaked with white and brown on its throat, neck, and breast. The American bittern shares some of the traits of its smaller relative the least bittern: it lives deep in the marshes and, when alarmed, prefers to freeze among the marsh plants rather than fly. This secretive heron has a peculiar call that announces its presence. Its call has been variously described as "oonk-a-lunk" and "goonk-glunk-a-lunk" and has been likened to the sound of a pitcher pump or the hollow whooshing of an Appalachian mountain jug band. This peculiar pumping sound is frequently heard at dusk around places like Lake Mattamuskeet, near the shores of Pamlico Sound, North Carolina. It feeds on catfishes, eels, snakes, frogs, and small mammals, which are all dispatched with a lightning stab of its sharp bill.

"As thin as a rail." Just where did that old saw come from? It pertains to certain members of the rail family, which also includes the coots and galli-nules. Rails have thin, compressed bodies that enable them to thread their way through the marsh thickets and disappear in the maze of stems and branches. Coots are more ducklike; they are divers and excellent swimmers that use their lobed toes and rear-positioned legs to great advantage for diving and swimming. The gallinules, the common moorhen and the purple gallinule, are good swimmers, but they also have long toes that allow them to walk over floating vegetation.

The clapper rail, *Rallus longirostris*, often called a marsh hen, is a chicken-size bird that lives in salt marshes and mangrove swamps. The clapper rail has a long, slightly curved bill and is grayish brown with lighter underparts. Their sides are barred with white and grayish brown stripes. Clapper rails are typically active at night; they are secretive birds and are usually not seen unless there are very high tides that force them off the reedy floor of the marsh. It is then that they are frequently seen along the edge of the marsh or even along nearby roads. Even though they are in the open, they act as though they are still in the marsh and walk about with little concern for their safety. They are reluctant fliers, and when flushed, they take off on a brief flight with their legs dangling and then drop into the marsh and disap-pear, similarly to the bitterns. Rails, however, are ca-pable of making long migratory flights. The best way

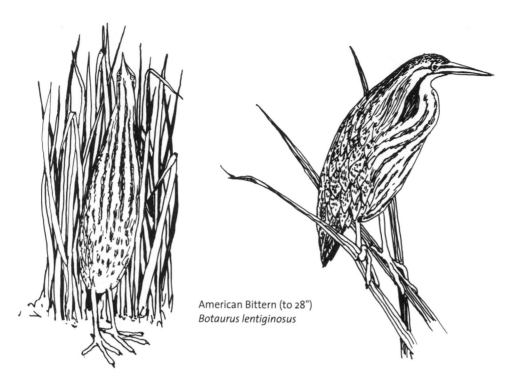

American Bittern (to 28")
Botaurus lentiginosus

to "see" a rail is with your ears; listen for the clattering "kek-kek-kek," especially at dawn and dusk.

The Virginia rail, *Rallus limicola*, is smaller than the clapper rail and is reddish-brown with a red bill. This rail is widely distributed in the United States from the Pacific to the Atlantic and from Canada to Mexico. It usually lives in freshwater and brackish marshes and sometimes spends the winter in coastal salt marshes. It has many of the same habits as the clapper rail and lives in the dense marshes where it feeds on aquatic insects, small fishes and crayfish, and snails.

The king rail, *Rallus elegans*, is a large bird, almost chicken size, and similar in coloration to but larger than the Virginia rail. The king rail is mainly a bird of freshwater marshes and may be found in swamps and abandoned rice fields in the Carolinas. Similar to the other rails, the king rail is infrequently seen, but sometimes the loud grunting and cackling notes and "chit-chit-chit" in a freshwater marsh reveal the unseen presence of the king rail. This rail is distributed from southern New England to Florida.

Gallinules are members of the rail family, and although they are chicken size and have extremely long toes like most rails, they have short, stout, cone-shaped bills rather than the long bills of the Virginia, clapper, and king rails. They also share some traits of the related American coot: they have a patch of naked colored skin called a frontal shield, and they constantly bob their heads and flick their short tails while swimming.

The common moorhen, *Gallinula chloropus*, sometimes known as the Florida moorhen or common gallinule, is a sooty to slate gray ducklike bird with a cone-shaped red bill tipped with yellow. It has a red frontal shield on its forehead, white edges on its wings, and a white patch under its tail. It utters a number of squeaks and harsh, grating calls. It clam-

Clapper Rail (to 16")
Rallus longirostris

bers about on vegetation and feeds on seeds, snails, and small fishes. Common moorhens live in freshwater marshes and backwaters with dense vegetation and can often be seen swimming and bobbing their heads in little open areas; then, just as quickly, rail-like, they disappear into the reeds and cattails. Common moorhens build their nests in clumps of sedges and reeds or in low shrubs in freshwater ponds, backwaters, and old rice fields. They are year-round residents along the Inner Coast from the Carolinas and westward to Texas.

The purple gallinule, *Porphyrula martinica*, is a vibrantly colored bird that is about the size of a clapper rail, but rather than being clothed with the somber grays and browns of the clapper, the purple gallinule is decorated with a vivid assortment of hues. It has an iridescent green and peacock-blue back and neck, a stout conical bill blazed with red and yellow, a pale blue frontal shield, a white tail patch, and yellowish green legs. The young have dark backs and buff under-

parts. Typical of gallinules and coots, the purple gallinule jerks and bobs its head as it swims about in freshwater marshes and dense swamps. It scampers about on lily pads and other floating vegetation and feeds on plant leaves, seeds, fruit, aquatic insects, frogs, and small fishes. It has the typical assortment of rail-like calls, including harsh clucks that sound like "cuk-cuk-cuk-kik." The purple gallinule ranges along the Inner Coast from the Carolinas and along the Gulf Coast to Texas.

The marshes and mangrove swamps are havens for herons and egrets. These stealthy birds stalk their prey by searching the shallows or lurking along the edges, waiting for an unwary fish or frog to come within a stab's length of their sharp bills. Some of these birds set up feeding territories, which they visit usually on a daily basis. Great blue herons and great egrets seem to tolerate humans to a degree and will often allow boaters and birders to approach, but only so close. It seems that each species, or individual bird, establishes an invisible boundary that allows it to pursue one of its most vital activities, searching for food, while existing in a tension zone rich with prey while not becoming prey itself.

Egrets, herons, and bitterns belong to the same family and in general resemble each other, as most have long bills and necks and long legs for wading in the shallows. Herons and egrets have the ability to change their shape and appearance: Sometimes they hunch up by tucking their long necks into their breasts, and they appear much shorter than they really are. At other times they extend their necks and seem to become much taller and slenderer birds.

The great blue heron, *Ardea herodias*, frequently changes its shape and posture in this way. This familiar heron, which is widespread throughout most of the United States, may appear huddled and hunched on a piling at one moment and then suddenly unfold to its full stature, squawk, and fly off with slow,

Purple Gallinule (to 13")
Porphyrula martinica

Common Moorhen (to 14")
Gallinula chloropus

deep wing beats, with its head and neck folded back to its breast and its legs trailing behind. The great blue heron is the largest heron along the Inner Coast. Its head is mostly white, with a black stripe extending from the eye and terminating in a feathery crest; its long neck is streaked with black; and its back and wings are usually a grayish blue. Breeding great blues have yellowish bills and plumes on the breasts and backs. There is an all-white form, sometimes known as a great white heron, found in southern Florida, particularly in the Florida Keys.

Great blue herons, similar to many other wading birds, are colonial nesters; they may nest with many other species all along the Inner Coast. Though great blue herons are gregarious during nesting season, they are usually solitary as adults. Like most herons and egrets, they are shallow water stalkers that hunt by taking slow, deliberate strides, sometimes stopping and then moving on. Sometimes a great blue heron will spread its wings to shade the sun and make its prey more visible, and then suddenly it will thrust its long bill into the water and seize one of the many fishes it will eat that day. Great blue herons also plunge into the water from piers to go after food, and they are occasionally seen floating like gulls or ducks

in deeper water. Great blue herons hunt along the edges of marshes, rivers, ponds, and lakes and feed on an assortment of food, including frogs, snakes, crabs, and sometimes small mammals.

Just past the wane of the moon of popping trees
great blue herons return to Nanjemoy.
I go through a mess of emotions
when I see one of those birds!
You should see one settling in,
looking like a goose flying backwards.
Nothing but a bushel of feathers
and a whole gang of legs hanging,
as it sails down all wobbly
into the face of a sporadic wind.
A gangly young Ichabod clown landing
perched high on bright yellow stilts.
—From "Toward the Full Blue
    Heron Moon" by Tom Wisner

The great egret, *Casmerodius albus*, is a large white heron with a long, heavy yellow bill and black legs and feet. The great egret is smaller and appears slenderer than the great blue heron; however, it is the second-largest heron along the Inner Coast. A breeding great egret is a magnificent bird with feath-

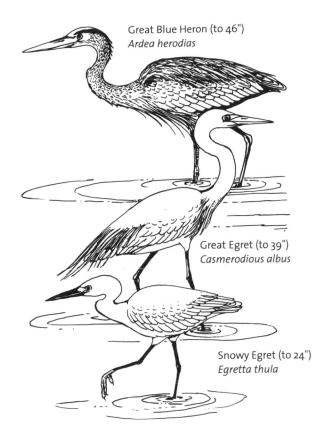

Great Blue Heron (to 46")
Ardea herodias

Great Egret (to 39")
Casmerodious albus

Snowy Egret (to 24")
Egretta thula

ery plumes, called aigrettes, trailing from its neck, back, and tail, and green lores, the area between each eye and the base of the bill. This stately bird hunts very much as the great blue heron does—slowly, methodically, and deliberately. Great egrets feed on a variety of food, including fishes, crabs, snakes, insects, and frogs. They are wherever there is water along the Inner Coast: in freshwater and saltwater marshes; at the edges of creeks, rivers, and lakes; and on tidal flats. They are found all along the Atlantic coast, the Gulf Coast, up into the Mississippi valley, and in some areas along the Pacific coast.

The snowy egret, *Egretta thula*, is a small, delicate white heron that is sometimes confused with the great egret, particularly when the great egret has pulled in its neck and the snowy egret has its neck

extended. The snowy egret, however, has a slender black bill, black legs, and yellow feet—a dead giveaway! Great egrets and great blue herons fly in a similar way, with slow and ponderous wing beats; snowy egrets have much more rapid wing beats. The snowy egret is also much busier in its quest for a meal than is the great egret, which is methodical and patient. The little snowy egret dashes here and there, using its strikingly colored feet to stir up the bottom, and then it stabs repeatedly for fishes and aquatic invertebrates. It nests in colonies with other waders, usually in shrubs, small trees, and mangroves. Snowy egrets are widespread in many aquatic habitats and may be found along river flats, in freshwater and saltwater marshes, and in mangrove swamps. They range along the Inner Coast to the Florida Keys and along the Gulf Coast through Texas and farther west.

In the 1880s, birds and bird feathers of all kinds, but especially great and snowy egrets, were in demand to decorate the lavish women's hats of the Victorian age. Hats were adorned with native songbirds, including warblers and bluebirds, and even terns. Men were also caught up in the craze and selected hats with feathered trim. But the birds that were in most demand were the great and snowy egrets, for they had the most beautiful and extravagant breeding plumage of all. Plume hunters slaughtered egrets by the thousands in their breeding colonies to harvest the most valued feathers of all, the aigrettes, those lacy, wispy plumes that are available only when the egrets breed. Bird lovers and naturalists became alarmed by the butchering of so many birds in the cause of fashion, and they began to decry the extermination of so many beautiful birds. The National Audubon Society and other organizations campaigned against the practice of killing birds to decorate millinery, and by the early 1900s, hats adorned with birds and their feathers were no longer fashionable. The feathers were once again worn only by the birds.

The cattle egret, *Bubulcus ibis*, is another white heron. However, it is unlike the other species of white herons and egrets, as it has a shorter bill and a stockier neck, and it is primarily a bird of upland habitats. During the spring and summer breeding season, the adult bird has short, buff-colored plumes on its head, breast, and back. It is commonly seen in newly plowed fields and pastures where horses and cattle feed, and where it feeds on insects stirred up by livestock and the farmer's plow. Cattle egrets fly with rather rapid wing beats and are frequently seen flying in loose flocks as they return to their roosts in the evening. The cattle egret is native to Africa; in the 1800s it spread to South America. The bird was unknown in North America until the early 1950s, and yet today it ranges throughout much of the United States, from the Atlantic to the Pacific.

Cattle Egret (to 20")
Bubulcus ibis

The tricolored heron, *Egretta tricolor*, formerly well known as the Louisiana heron, is smaller than the great egret and slightly larger than the snowy egret. The tricolored heron has a slate gray to bluish neck and back, and its underparts are white. This usually solitary heron is a slender and graceful bird that inhabits sheltered estuaries, freshwater and saltwater marshes, the edges of rivers, and mangrove swamps, where it feeds primarily on fishes. The tricolored heron stalks its prey methodically, as do most herons, but it also runs through the shallows in headlong dashes and then abruptly stops, spreads its wings, and strikes a killifish or small mullet with its rapierlike bill. The tricolored heron ranges along the Atlantic coast from New England and westward along the Gulf of Mexico.

The little blue heron, *Egretta caerulea*, is only slightly smaller than the tricolored heron and about the same size as a snowy egret; however, it is slightly stockier than the more delicate-appearing snowy egret. Little blue heron adults are dark slate blue with a brownish maroon or purplish neck. The immature little blue herons are often confused with snowy egrets and cattle egrets because they are almost entirely white except for their black wing tips. As the juveniles mature, their plumage changes from all white to mostly white with mottled gray patches on their backs and tails. Little blue herons hunt by slowly walking through heavily vegetated shallows, where they often stop and seem to stare or peer, and then they resume their deliberate pace. They feed on fishes, amphibians, and insects in marshes, freshwater ditches, ponds, and along coastal shorelines. They range along the Atlantic and Gulf coasts and the Mississippi valley.

The green heron, *Butorides virescens*, is a small, stocky heron with brownish red sides, a bluish green back, and a dark green crown that is sometimes raised into a scraggly crest. Its legs are a dull yellow except during breeding season, when they turn a bright reddish orange. Immature green herons are brown above with brown- and white-streaked underparts. These small, retiring herons are quite

A tricolored heron, Egretta tricolor *(to 26"), leans forward as it wades; a little blue heron,* Egretta caerulea *(to 24"), stands below; a green heron,* Butorides virescens *(to 18"), peers into the water from its perch; and a least bittern,* Ixobrychus exilis *(to 13"), hides among the grasses.*

vocal and often reveal their presence by uttering a "kyow" or "skow." When a green heron is flushed from cover and flies off, it utters a piercing "skeow." It is not generally a wader; it usually stands motionless at the edge of the water, frozen in a horizontal or crouched stance, until a small killifish or frog nears, and then it quickly lunges for its dinner. Green herons also rake the bottom in shallow water to stir up fishes. But perhaps one of the most unusual methods of green herons or, indeed, of any bird is the use of lures to attract their prey. These clever little birds will drop twigs or leaves or a feather into the water where small minnows school. The minnows, always on the lookout for a meal, rise to the surface to investigate their next meal and, all too late, meet their dinner partner. Green herons inhabit wooded stream sides, vegetated areas around ponds and lakes, and edges of marshes. They range throughout the eastern United States and the Midwest and along the Gulf of Mexico and the Mississippi valley, and they are scattered throughout the western states to British Columbia.

Wood storks, ibises, spoonbills, and limpkins are all relatively large wading birds that generally resemble herons but are not at all related. Only ibises and roseate spoonbills are in the same family; wood storks and limpkins are in distinctly different groups. These birds share highly adapted feeding habits: the limpkin specializes in feeding on snails, and ibises, spoonbills, and wood storks usually probe in murky, muddy water in search of their meals.

The wood stork, *Mycteria americana,* also known as a wood ibis or flint head, is a large, long-legged bird with a massive, slightly down-curved bill. The adult wood stork has a naked blackish gray head with a dark bill, a dark gray neck, a white body, black flight feathers, and a black tail. Immature wood storks have grayish brown feathered heads and yellow bills.

Flight feathers are a group of feathers on the trail-

Feeding on the edge of the marsh are a wood stork and two white ibises, an all-white adult and a mottled young bird molting from its brown fledgling plumage.

ing edge of the wings, known as the primaries, secondaries, and tertiaries, that also includes the tail feathers. The distinctive flight feathers of the wood stork enable a birder, even a novice, to identify a wood stork overhead. Wood storks fly with their long neck and legs outstretched, showing their black flight feathers. White pelicans have a similar pattern—they have all-white bodies, and their flight feathers are also black—but the wood stork and the white pelican fly differently. Both white pelicans and wood storks soar exquisitely and gracefully. However, white pelicans fly in synchrony with one another: when one turns, the others do as well. Wood storks are more individual: they often fly in loose flocks, known as kettles, and soar in ever-increasing and rising circles; some flap their wings in slow, deliberate beats, and others glide away on motionless wings.

Wood storks are elegant and majestic in the air but decidedly awkward and hulking on land. They stand about in somber groups with their bodies hunched up and sometimes clatter their very large bills in a noisy exchange. We have also observed them near Sebastian Inlet, on Florida's Indian River Lagoon, where some were standing while others were comi-cally sitting on the grass with their legs bent at the knees and outstretched in front of them.

Wood storks inhabit cypress swamps, where they construct their twig nests in dense colonies; they also build nests in mangroves. They are found in wet meadows, coastal marshes, ponds, and swamps along the Inner Coast, where they have a wide and varied diet. Wood storks, similar to roseate spoonbills and black skimmers, have a triggerlike mechanism called a bill-snap reflex that immediately grasps a food item as soon as the bill comes in contact with it. Wood storks characteristically walk back and forth in shallow, murky water, dragging their great bills and cutting a swath through the muddy bottom, where they catch all manner of prey, including fishes, crayfish, baby alligators, aquatic insects, small turtles, and even berries and seeds in their "spring-loaded" bills. They are permanent residents in Florida and move north in the summer to Georgia and the Carolinas. They have been reported as far north as Virginia, and they also range along the rim of the Gulf of Mexico.

The white ibis, *Eudocimus albus*, is a white bird with black wing tips and a long, down-curved bill. Its bill, face skin, and legs are brilliant red during

In flight, the relative sizes and black wing patterns are clues to distinguish between the white ibis, Eudocimus albus *(to 25"), and the wood stork,* Mycteria americana *(to 40").*

breeding season and pink during the rest of the year. Immature ibises are brown above and white below, with brown bills and legs. As the young birds mature, they take on a piebald appearance and are splotched with brown and white markings. They fly with rapid wing beats over the marshes in large, loose flocks and sometimes in long, straggling lines. White ibises frequent tidal mudflats, saltwater and freshwater marshes, mangrove swamps, and sometimes even open pastures. They feed by touch, probing the muds on tidal flats and sweeping their long, curved bills from side to side to catch crabs and crayfish in shallow water. They also feed on snails, snakes, and insects.

White ibises roost in large colonies mixed with herons and egrets in mangroves and small trees and shrubs. We have often seen ibises roosting with herons and brown pelicans in the noonday sun on Battery Island and other dredge-spoil islands in the Cape Fear River near Southport, North Carolina. They are common and abundant from the Carolinas to Florida and westward along the Gulf of Mexico.

The roseate spoonbill, *Ajaia ajaja*, is a magnificent pink bird with a bizarre, spatulalike bill. The adult is pink with red-shouldered wings, a white neck, an orange tail, and a naked, green to buff-colored head. The young are a much paler pink, and their heads are covered with white feathers; their pink color intensifies with age. These beautiful birds were once hunted to near extinction by plume hunters in the late 1800s, who sold the wings as fans for ladies.

The roseate spoonbill feeds in the shallow waters of coastal saltwater and freshwater marshes, in mangrove swamps, on mudflats, and in lagoons where the bottom is muddy and the water is often murky. It swings its flat, wide bill to and fro through the water, and when the bill touches a shrimp or minnow, it immediately grasps the prey, and the bird is rewarded with another meal. Roseate spoonbills also feed on crayfish, snails, aquatic insects, and some plant material. They nest and roost in colonies, often intermixed with white ibises and herons. They build their stick nests on the horizontal limbs of small trees and red mangroves and occasionally on scrubby shrubs. They usually group in small flocks and are often seen in the Merritt Island National Wildlife Refuge near Cape Canaveral, Florida, and infrequently on tidal flats in North Carolina.

An adult roseate spoonbill, Ajaia ajaja *(to 32"), sifts through shallow waters with its spatulate bill while an all-white immature roseate spoonbill looks on.*

The limpkin, *Aramus guarauna*, resembles to some a rail, to others a crane, and to still others a heron. It does have similar characteristics, but the limpkin is in a family by itself. Limpkins are goose-size, dark brown birds speckled with white. They have long, slightly down-curved bills and long legs. Their call has been described as a loud, wild-sounding, anguished, and eerie banshee wail. The long "kar-r-ee-ow" pierces the night and has earned this brown swamp wader the name "crying bird."

This mostly solitary bird inhabits freshwater marshes, land along lakes and ponds, and sometimes wooded swamps. It feeds on a variety of aquatic animals, including freshwater mussels, worms, and frogs, but its preferred food is the apple snail. The Florida apple snail is the largest freshwater snail in America, and the limpkin is well equipped to feed on it: the bill of the limpkin is slightly curved to the right, which enables the limpkin to turn the snail out of its shell. The limpkin's bill also has a gap that allows it to grasp the very large apple snail and carry it to land. Apple snails are also the favored food of snail kites, white ibises, boat-tailed grackles, alligators,

and redear sunfish. Limpkins feed by slowly walking through shallow water, probing for snails on the bottom or plucking them off floating vegetation.

The limpkin ranges throughout Central and South America. In the United States, it is found only in Florida and in southern Georgia where the Okefenokee Swamp drains into the Suwannee River. There have been rare reports of limpkins in the Waccamaw River drainage in South Carolina.

Many birds of prey are seen over marshes and coastal lowlands. Ospreys hunt over the open waters around marshes; bald eagles and red-shouldered hawks occupy favorite perches and scan the marsh; red-tailed hawks wheel high above; American kestrels perch on power lines; and short-eared owls glide in on silent wings at dusk. All are looking for unwary prey.

The northern harrier, *Circus cyaneus*, however, is the premier hunter on Inner Coast marshes. Formerly known as the marsh hawk, this long-winged, long-tailed raptor sails low over marshes and fields, alternately flapping and gliding as it courses over the ground, back and forth, looking and listening for

Limpkin (to 26")
Aramus guarauna

prey. Its flight is slow and buoyant. It has an owl-like facial disc that apparently concentrates the sound of prey; coupled with the bird's keen eyesight, it puts mice and voles in constant jeopardy of becoming lunch. Northern harriers perch on low stumps close to the ground to consume their prey.

Male northern harriers are gray above and pale white below. The slightly larger female has a dark brown back streaked with tan, and its underwings are boldly barred. Both sexes have a conspicuous white rump patch that identifies them as northern harriers. Male northern harriers court females by diving in a series of spectacular loops and rolls. Northern harriers build their nests of sticks and grasses, lined with fine material, on the ground, in which the female lays three to nine bluish eggs.

There are many species of ducks along the Inner Coast. Some ducks prefer freshwater ponds and backwaters, and others favor open, saltier waters. Some, like the American black duck and the northern pin-

tail, are dabblers; others, like the canvasback and scaups, are divers. Some dabblers, or dippers or puddle ducks, as they are also known, can dive, and divers can dabble. Dabblers are ducks that characteristically stretch their heads down into the water and tip up their rumps to graze on submerged aquatic vegetation and aquatic organisms. They can dive to feed or to escape danger, but they usually feed from the surface by dabbling. Most dabblers have a white or colored wing patch on the trailing edge of each wing called a speculum. The speculum is a good field mark for identification. Sometimes the speculum is evident when the duck is loafing on the surface, but it is more apparent when the duck is on the wing. When alarmed, dabblers explode out of the water and rapidly fly off.

Divers usually dive for their food and to evade danger; they also sometimes dabble. Diving ducks have legs that are positioned far to the rear of their bodies, and they have very large feet; dabblers' legs are set farther forward, and their feet are smaller. Divers do not spring out of the water like dabblers, and they must patter, or walk, across the water for some distance before they gather altitude. Diving ducks are superbly adapted for diving and swimming underwater, but they are ungainly, at best, on land because of the rearward position of their legs. Dabblers, in contrast, are able to walk about on land and are perfectly at home grazing on seeds and grain without falling over on their breasts, as do some divers.

The mallard, *Anas platyrhynchos*, is a familiar dabbling duck widely distributed throughout North America. Mallards are found anywhere there is water: in freshwater and saltwater marshes, rivers, ponds, lakes, coastal estuaries, and city parks. The male mallard, or drake, is so commonly seen that we often overlook that it is one of the most strikingly beautiful of all of the ducks. The male has a metallic green

A female northern harrier, Circus cyaneus *(to 18"), flies low over a marsh, ready to strike, while a male soars in the background and a flock of tree swallows hawks for flying insects.*

head and neck set off with a white ring, a chestnut-colored breast, a yellow bill, and orange feet. The black feathers at the tip of the tail are curled. The female is mottled brown with an orange bill marked with brown or black. In both sexes, the speculum is purplish blue and bordered in white. After the breeding season, the males molt into an eclipse plumage that is dull and mottled, and they then resemble the females and the juveniles. The mallard apparently is capable of interbreeding with the domesticated white Pekin duck, the Muscovy duck, and the closely related American black duck. This interbreeding produces hybrids in an array of colors and patterns that can be confusing to the birder. The female mallard is very vocal and is the one that voices the familiar "quack-quack."

Mallards typically breed and nest in the Prairie Pothole region of the Dakotas and Canada, but many do not migrate but rather breed locally along the Inner Coast and in other parts of the country. The premating behavior of mallards is active and frenetic: Males surround the female and harass her until she flies off a short distance. The males immediately follow her and dash and lunge at her and pull her under the water. They stand on the water and flap their wings, and they chase her up onto land until she finally chooses a mate. The female lays eight to ten pale, greenish buff eggs in a shallow ground nest, usually located near the shore or in marsh grass. The eggs hatch in twenty-eight days, and almost immediately the precocial ducklings are in water and following their mother. The young ducklings actively seek

Two male and two female mallards, Anas platyrhynchos *(to 23"), rest on a marsh flat.*

aquatic insects and other small invertebrates along the shore and are able to fly about two months after leaving the nest.

The American black duck, *Anas rubripes*, is a dabbler that is closely related to the mallard. Both the male and female American black duck are a uniformly sooty, dark brown, though the male is darker, and both have slightly lighter heads and pale gray underwings. The male has a yellow bill and red to reddish orange feet. The female's legs are not as brightly colored, and the yellowish bill is mottled with brown. Typical of dabblers, they have bluish purple speculums bordered by black, and sometimes white. American black ducks are common in saltwater marshes and range throughout the Inner Coast down to northern Florida.

The northern pintail, *Anas acuta*, is a long-necked, slender-bodied duck. The male has a long, filamentous tail extending from its wedge-shaped rump, a chocolate brown head, a white neck and breast, and a finger of white extending up onto the head. The female has mottled brown plumage with a tan head, and the tail is shorter than the male's. Both sexes have a bronze to brown speculum. The male's call

is a soft or mellow whistle, and the female's call is a harsh "quack." Northern pintails are graceful birds that are very wary. They are swift, suspicious, and agile, and, as is characteristic of puddle ducks, they hurtle into the air and quickly disappear. Northern pintails are found in a variety of habitats, including freshwater and saltwater marshes, tidal mudflats, lakes, ponds, and flooded fields. They feed mostly on seeds and insects.

The gadwall, *Anas strepera*, is another dabbler that has few distinguishing characteristics. The male gadwall is grayish with a black rump and light brown head. Its bill is black, and it has a white speculum. The female resembles a female mallard, with a white belly, a white speculum, and a grayish bill edged with orange. Gadwalls fly in small, tight flocks and favor shallow waters with dense vegetation, where they prefer to pick snails, small invertebrates, and aquatic insects from the floating vegetation. They also eat some plant material, and occasionally they will dabble by tipping up and feeding below the surface of the water.

The northern shoveler, *Anas clypeata*, somewhat resembles a mallard with its green head, white breast,

Snow Goose (to 28")
Chen caerulescens

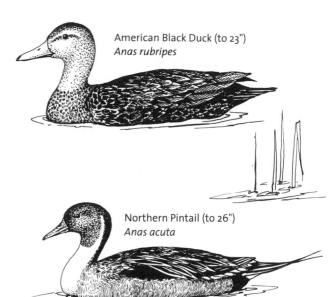

American Black Duck (to 23")
Anas rubripes

Northern Pintail (to 26")
Anas acuta

male

Northern Shoveler (to 19")
Anas clypeata

male

male

male

Blue-Winged Teal (to 15 1/2")
Anas discors

Gadwall (to 20")
Anas strepera

and reddish brown flanks. However, it has a large shovel- or spatula-shaped black to grayish bill that is longer than its head and is decidedly different from that of the mallard. The female is brown; its bill is grayish yellow and marked with orange edges. The distinctive, oversize bill of both sexes is equipped with a row of bristles or comblike structures, somewhat like a mustache attached to the inside of the upper bill. Shovelers, sometimes called spoonbills, use this bill to good advantage as they swim and feed in shallow water over muddy bottoms. They filter out the mud with their bill fringes and feed on the remaining small crustaceans, mollusks, seeds, and aquatic plants.

Northern shovelers are agile fliers. Similar to shorebirds, they often wheel and circle and then alight, only to take off again. They are recognizable in flight by their pale blue forewing patch and their green speculum. Northern shovelers arrive along the Inner Coast in early fall and are among the last ducks to depart for their nesting grounds in the spring. They range all along the Inner Coast and westward to Texas in saltwater and brackish marshes and in estuaries.

The American wigeon, *Anas americana*, often called the baldpate, is a saucy, ever-alert puddle duck that is seldom still and always quick to sound the alarm. The male American wigeon has iridescent commalike markings extending from around the eyes and down the side and back of the neck. The top of its head is crowned with a white stripe of feathers, giving it the appearance of a baldpate. The male's throat is streaked with gray, and its breast and back are brownish. The female has a grayish brown–streaked head and a russet-brown breast and back. Both sexes have a stubby blue bill tipped with black and a green speculum.

The American wigeon is a dabbler and not a proficient diver. Thus it has the habit of occasionally waiting for a deep diver, such as a canvasback or redhead, to bob to the surface with a succulent tidbit of vegetation, at which point it quickly filches the food. American wigeons also spend a considerable amount of time grazing on grass, seeds, and grain on land. Like all dabblers, they can spring vertically from the water, and then the flock acts as one, grouping close together, wheeling and veering much like a group of pigeons. They spend their winter along the Inner Coast and along the Gulf of Mexico on estuaries and freshwater and saltwater marshes.

The blue-winged teal, *Anas discors*, is a small, half-size, brownish dabbler with pale blue shoulder patches. The male has a gray head with a large white crescent in front of each eye. The female is a mottled brown with a lighter brown or tan head and has a brown stripe through each eye. Typical of many dabblers, they are agile fliers that fly in compact flocks, twisting and turning, revealing their blue wing patches. These are common and abundant little ducks that nest on the marshy prairies and potholes of the central United States and Canada. They arrive along the Inner Coast early in the fall and spend most of their time in freshwater and brackish marshes, where they feed on seeds, aquatic vegetation, grain, snails, and insects. They winter all along the Inner Coast from the mid-Atlantic to Florida, and westward along the Gulf of Mexico to Texas.

Many kinds of birds feed and loaf along the edge of a marsh. Some, such as snow geese, feed on grain and grass on the uplands and then, by the hundreds, turn to grazing in the shallows along a freshwater or tidal saltwater marsh.

The snow goose, *Chen caerulescens*, winters along the Inner Coast from the mid-Atlantic down to Florida. Where they occur, these very social birds are usually found in large flocks of several hundred or more. There are several variants within the species: the greater snow goose; the lesser snow goose, which

American Wigeon (to 19")
Anas americana

is a smaller form, or morph, than the greater; a cross between the Ross's goose and the snow goose, a more delicate-appearing bird with a rounder head and a smaller bill than the snow goose; and, of course, the blue goose, which is not really blue but usually gray-brown. There are many variations, or intergrades, of the blue goose. Some have completely dark bodies; others have dark backs and breasts; and still others have black backs and white necks, breasts, bellies, and wings. All are now considered variants of the white snow goose. The snow goose is characterized by partial or extensive white plumage, contrasted with dark flight feathers on the wing tips, and a pink-

ish orange bill marked with black, called a "grinning patch."

Snow geese move around on their wintering grounds along the Inner Coast. They may be found foraging in brackish or freshwater marshes that are vegetated with cordgrass, cattails, and sedges. They also feed and loaf in great numbers on upland grain fields, where they use their serrated bills to good advantage by grubbing out the rootstocks, rather than clipping the grasses as do Canada geese. Snow geese call with a shrill "la-uk" that has been likened to a dog's bark. The gabble is constantly repeated in resonant waves throughout the large flock.

🌿
Mammals of Marshes and Mangrove Swamps

There are many mammals that prowl and scurry through marshes and mangroves. Some climb the pines and mangroves, such as the cunning raccoon and the prehensile-tailed opossum, while white-tailed deer and the diminutive key deer nibble grass and leaves along the edges of marshes. River otters are sometimes seen along the edges of marshes or swimming close to shore. Armadillos snuffle about, rooting out grubs in the soil, and marsh rabbits and other small rodents nest and feed on the marshes and mangroves. Other mammals, such as muskrats and nutria, are at home in the marshes and shallow waters. Occasionally black bears are seen along the Inner Coast, particularly in the Great Dismal Swamp and coastal North Carolina.

The nine-banded armadillo, *Dasypus novemcinctus*, is a bizarre invention of nature that is closely related to South American sloths and anteaters. The armadillo is a cat-size, cylinder-shaped, armor-plated insect eater. The upper part of its body is encased in bony plates covered with a layer of horny skin and small hairs. The entire armored canister is composed of large shields on the shoulders and rump, with a total of nine bony bands between the shields. These industrious diggers are equipped with strongly clawed feet that enable them to dig multiple burrows and to probe for food. They dig in the soft soil for insects and also gather earthworms, millipedes, and spiders from under fallen logs with their sticky tongues. Their favorite food seems to be larval and adult scarab beetles, termites, and ants. They apparently do not see well. On several occasions we have walked up behind them as they were grubbing in the soil, and when they sensed that we were nearby, they jumped straight up into the air and then quickly shuffled off into the palmetto brush. They are often found near water and, in fact, can swim rather well for short distances. They usually feed and burrow in deep sandy soils in forested and open areas; however, we have seen them around the edges of marshes on Cumberland Island, Georgia, and in various parts of Florida.

The reproductive mode of nine-banded armadillos is as strange as their appearance. They mate in July and August, but the implantation of the fertilized egg is delayed until November; this delayed implantation results in a long period of arrested development of the embryo. In an unrelated phenomenon, the developing egg, now termed a blastocyst, divides and divides once again into four growth centers that are attached to the uterus by a common placenta. The development of the embryos then proceeds normally for about four months, and, usually by March, identical, same-sex quadruplets are born. The young mature rapidly. Within weeks they are snuffling along with their parents on foraging expeditions. They are sexually mature at about one year old and have a life span of about twenty years.

Nine-banded armadillos' actual life span is frequently less than twenty years, however, as they are often killed on the highway, particularly along major highways in north Florida. Very much like the similar-appearing opossum, they are unwary and are often hit by cars as they graze along the side of the road and then decide to cross over to graze on the median strip. In some parts of the country, they are called hillbilly speed bumps or possums on the half shell. These unusual mammals are native to South and Central America and apparently expanded their range into Texas in the 1880s. The Florida population is the result of the release of a few animals from a small zoo in 1924. The nine-banded armadillo now ranges from Texas and Oklahoma, through the lower Mississippi valley to Alabama, and into Florida to about Miami. It ranges northward along the Inner Coast to Georgia and perhaps into Jasper County, the southernmost tip of South Carolina.

The marsh rice rat, *Oryzomys palustris*, is grayish brown with buff-white underparts. Its head and body are about 6 inches long, and its tail also measures about 6 inches. Marsh rice rats are fond of rice; they eat great quantities where it is available to them. However, they are omnivorous; in addition to a variety of plant materials, including marsh grasses, they eat fiddler crabs, snails, clams, baby turtles, and fishes. Marsh rice rats inhabit marshy areas and almost any place where grasses and sedges are available for food and protective cover. They build runways and nests among the salt grasses and sedges, and they quite often travel in shallow water. The marsh rice rat is semiaquatic and will quickly swim or dive into the water to avoid becoming a meal for a hawk or an owl. They are also preyed on by mink, raccoons, foxes, and snakes.

Marsh rice rats mate almost continuously in the southern part of their range, and a female may produce as many as six litters per year, with an average litter size of four offspring. The young grow very quickly; they are weaned in less than two weeks and

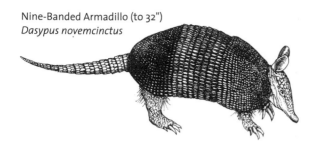

Nine-Banded Armadillo (to 32")
Dasypus novemcinctus

reach sexual maturity in about six weeks. Their life expectancy, typical of many rodents, is usually less than a year. The marsh rice rat ranges from New Jersey and all along the Inner Coast to Florida and westward to eastern Texas.

The endangered Key rice rat is considered by some authorities to be a distinct species; others consider it to be a geographical variety of the marsh rice rat. The Key rice rat is somewhat larger than the marsh rice rat and is silvery gray. It is restricted to the lower Florida Keys and prefers freshwater marshes and mangroves.

There are several other small rodents that live within the marshes and mangroves or along their margins. The very abundant and widely distributed hispid cotton rat lives in a variety of habitats and can be quite destructive to agricultural crops. The tiny least shrew, one of the smallest rodents, is quite secretive and often lives in the burrows of other small mammals. The nearly blind eastern mole burrows along the upper edges of marshes and grasslands and in forested lands.

The marsh rabbit, *Sylvilagus palustris*, is a somewhat smaller version of the familiar eastern cottontail. It is darker; its ears are shorter; and its tail is dingy gray. Its species name, *palustris*, is Latin for "marsh" or "swamp," and that is where this rabbit dwells. Marsh rabbits are found in coastal marshes, riverine bottomlands, and swamps. They are often seen around stands of saw grass, along canal banks, and in mangrove swamps. Unlike eastern cottontails, marsh rabbits readily take to the water, particularly when they are threatened. They are preyed on by dogs, cats, foxes, coyotes, bobcats, hawks, owls, snakes, and alligators. Marsh rabbits are nocturnal; they forage for food at night. They feed on emergent aquatic vegetation, marsh grasses, rushes, and the twigs and leaves of woody plants.

Marsh rabbits breed throughout the year in the more southern range of the Inner Coast. They average three to four young, born after a gestation period of about one month. The female prepares a nest of her soft underfur and dried grass in a shallow depression in the ground. The young rabbits are usually ready to breed by the time they are a year old. Marsh rabbits range from southeastern Virginia and all along the Inner Coast to the Florida Keys and westward to Alabama. The marsh rabbit is the only species of rabbit found in the Florida Keys.

The river otter, *Lutra canadensis*, is a sinuous, graceful, and powerful swimmer that belongs to a large family that includes minks, weasels, skunks, ferrets, and the ferocious and storied wolverine. River otters have sleek fur that is a lustrous dark brown with lighter underparts. Their elongated bodies, webbed feet, and muscular, furred tails propel them through the water. They almost seem liquid themselves as they twist, dive, and frolic as few other wild animals do. Otters are as comfortable on land as in the water. They often have "rolling places"—areas of flattened vegetation or bare spots where they playfully roll and tumble. They are quite vocal: they chatter and whistle and grunt and snort. Otters are energetic and busy animals, often sliding down muddy banks and into the water, but make no mistake; otters are efficient predators on fishes, small mammals, and crustaceans such as crayfish and crabs. In freshwater streams and swamps where otters and beavers coexist, the otters often prey on the beaver kits.

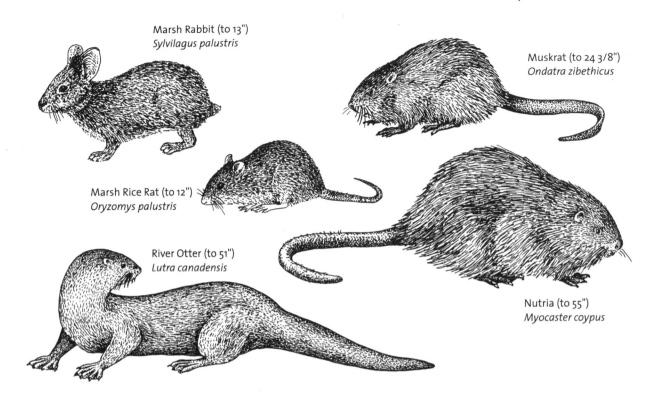

Marsh Rabbit (to 13")
Sylvilagus palustris

Muskrat (to 24 3/8")
Ondatra zibethicus

Marsh Rice Rat (to 12")
Oryzomys palustris

River Otter (to 51")
Lutra canadensis

Nutria (to 55")
Myocaster coypus

River otters inhabit saltwater and freshwater rivers along the Inner Coast, lakes, and wooded swamps, and sometimes they are found far from the water. We have seen them sliding down the muddy banks along the Intracoastal Waterway and prowling along the marshy shores, and we have seen these nimble and graceful hunters scampering between the large rocks flanking Fort Sumter in Charleston Harbor. River otters are widely distributed throughout Canada, Alaska, and the Northwest and along the East Coast down through Florida, but they do not live in the Florida Keys. They also range to the west into Texas.

The muskrat, *Ondatra zibethicus*, belongs to the largest family of mammals in North America. Muskrats are at home in freshwater, brackish, and saltwater marshes, as well as in ponds, lakes, and rivers. They are about the size of a small house cat. Their dense, glossy fur ranges from a light silvery brown to dark brown, or sometimes black. *Ondatra* is the Iroquois word for "muskrat," and *zibethicus* comes from the Latin for "musky odored." Muskrats deposit musk secretions on trails to mark their territorial boundaries.

Muskrats have long, scaly tails that are almost hairless and flattened from side to side, very much like the tails of most mice and rats. Their eyes and ears are small, and their hind feet are partially webbed. Muskrats, as well as beavers, have fur mouth flaps that seal their mouth openings behind their protruding incisor teeth, which permit them to gnaw below the surface without swallowing water. They are excellent swimmers and can travel long distances underwater, into the underside of their lodges. Muskrats' homes are usually dome shaped and are quite evident in winter marshes. The lodges are constructed of aquatic vegetation, particularly from three-squares and cattails. Female muskrats produce several litters a year with an average of four to seven young in a brood. The young grow rapidly and, within a month, are gone from the lodge and on their own.

Muskrats feed on sedges, cattails, black needle-rush, arrowhead, water lilies, saw grass, and other vegetation, as well as an occasional clam, crayfish, or frog. They are trapped for their fur pelts throughout their range, and in some areas, particularly in the Chesapeake Bay and in the Carolinas, they appear in homes and in some restaurants as "marsh rabbit."

Muskrats are widespread throughout North America and are common and locally abundant along the Inner Coast to southeast Georgia. They are absent from Florida except in the extreme western panhandle. The round-tailed muskrat, or water rat, is about half the size of a muskrat, and its tail is round rather than flattened from side to side. It is found in similar habitats as the muskrat and is distributed from southeast Georgia and throughout Florida, but it is absent from the Florida Keys.

Consider a 15- to 20-pound rat emerging from the water that at first glance resembles a beaver with large, protruding, orange-red incisors, and you have met the nutria, *Myocastor coypus*, known as coypu in South America and in many North American zoos. The generic name for the nutria, *Myocastor*, is from the Greek words for "mouse" and "beaver." To confound the story of this animal even more, the common name, nutria, means "otter" in Spanish.

Nutrias are well adapted for life in the water; their hind feet are webbed, and their eyes, ears, and nostrils are set high on their heads. Similar to beavers and river otters, nutrias have valves in their nos-trils and mouths that seal out water while they are swimming and feeding underwater, and they use their strong, laterally compressed tails as rudders. Nutrias are native to South America. They were introduced in the 1890s and then reintroduced in 1930 into Louisiana in an attempt to establish a fur farm industry. The fur farms did not fare well, as nutrias are hard to breed and rear in captivity, and fur prices declined. As a result, many nutrias were simply released to the wild, where they became well established and reproduced successfully and abundantly. The introduction of twenty nutrias into Louisiana in 1938 resulted in a staggering 20 million animals in just twenty years. Nutrias produce young throughout the year. The female's mammary glands are located high on her side to allow the young to suckle while in the water; the young reach sexual maturity at four to six months. The litters average four to five young each, with one female producing up to three litters a year.

Nutrias primarily feed on marsh plants, chairmaker's rush, salt meadow hay, and salt marsh cordgrass, as well as many other plants, including ornamentals. Nutria are very destructive to the habitat on which they depend. They use their large incisors and powerful forefeet to dig under the root mat, leaving the marsh pitted with holes and devoid of vegetation. These areas are called "eat outs." Consequently, wetland managers have taken steps to control nutrias in many states by bounty trapping and other means. The largest concentrations of nutrias are in the coastal areas of Louisiana, Texas, Mississippi, and Florida. They also occur in large numbers in Alabama, Georgia, North Carolina, Virginia, and Maryland.

3
Beaches

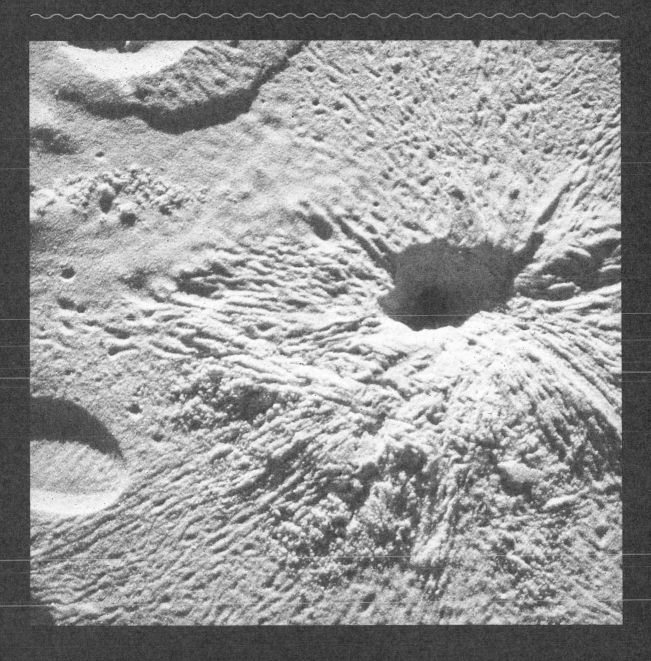

Sand beaches form the most visible natural feature of the Atlantic coast from Long Island, New York, to south Florida, but along the Inner Coast, inside the barrier islands, there are few classic sand beaches. Instead, the beaches are usually narrow flats composed of silty muds or very muddy strips just above the high tide line. There are also washed shell deposits of stranded bleached shells, particularly oyster shells, that form "beaches" along the sinuous, marsh-lined shore.

Generally, sand beaches slope gently toward the water and are composed of sand grains or sometimes pebbles and sand. Sand beaches are usually located in exposed areas that are vulnerable to winds and waves. Offshore, the prevailing currents move sand grains on and off the beach, depending on the season, prevailing wind direction, and storms. The sand grains are endlessly sorted and re-sorted, changing the shape of the beach and often accreting at one end and eroding at the other.

Along the Inner Coast, sand beaches are usually adjacent to inlets or near the ends of barrier islands. A good example is the extensive sand beach on the sound side of Core Bank at Cape Lookout, North Carolina. Sand continuously moving onshore into Onslow Bay has accreted behind Cape Lookout and along the Shackleford Banks. Other examples are the sand beaches that have formed inside the barrier islands along the Intracoastal Waterway near Little River Inlet in South Carolina.

In the Florida Keys, many of the beaches are quite different from those to the north. They are composed of a pavement of weathered, porous limestone, the remains of ancient coral reefs that are strewn with calcareous rubble: shells, coral bits, nuggets of encrusted coralline algae, and splashes of red color, usually found under limestone rocks, that are caused by a shelled amoeba called a foraminifer. This same foraminifer is so abundant in the waters off Bermuda

that the beaches are tinged with pink. Many of the beaches along the Florida Bay are soft and soupy marls, mixtures of calcium carbonate and clay.

These seemingly inhospitable beaches are, in fact, home to many species that burrow in the soft sands and muds, such as worms; mole crabs; zebra periwinkles, which cling to depressions in the limestone beaches in Florida; and beach hoppers, which thrive under the wave-tossed gulfweed wrack. Birds are often the only obvious signs of life on a beach: they forage on the beach because of the abundant life and remnants of life there for the picking. Beaches are repositories of shells that hint at the offshore beds of mollusks, shiny brown sea beans, wrenched from vines in South America and now stranded with pieces of candle sponge, sometimes wrapped in the gelatinous coat of a pink moon jellyfish. Remnants of a rubbery bryozoan with the hair-raising common name dead man's fingers beckon you to come closer, and when you do, you might see a half-buried sand dollar and the spiny legs of brittle stars strewn in the sand as well. Beaches are never-ending tapestries that constantly change in shape and texture.

Plants of the Beaches

On some beaches and islands along the Inner Coast that are exposed to ocean wind and spray, a number of plants grow that are sometimes grouped and known as the salt spray community. Grasses such as sea oats and certain herbaceous plants, such as Russian thistle, sea rocket, and saltwort, are tough plants that are quite resistant to salt spray and the abrasive action of blowing sand. Behind this grass and herbaceous zone, sometimes called the pioneer zone, is a middle scrub zone, usually protected by frontal sand dunes. The scrub zone is a mixture of very hardy herbaceous plants, woody shrubs, and small trees.

Gulfweed, Sargassum fluitans *(to 3'), which can be found in drifts on the beach, often carries along many other species, such as gulfweed hydroid,* Aglaophenia latecarinata; *gulfweed anemone,* Anemonia sargassensis; *encrusting bryozoans; and minute round snails,* Hydrobia *sp.*

Some of the plants commonly growing in the scrub zone are seaside goldenrod, pennywort, wax myrtle, bayberry, groundsel tree, marsh elder, and holly. Virginia creeper, muscadine grape vines, and trumpet creeper grow over the shrubs and, where they are not supported, may even creep over the sandy crests of the dunes. Plant life at the crest of the beach, where tide- and storm-driven waves strand flotsam and jetsam—the wrack zone—is where various species of seaweeds are frequently stranded.

Seaweeds

Gulfweeds, or sargassum weeds, are species of brown algae that almost everyone has seen along an Atlantic beach or on beaches of the Inner Coast near ocean inlets. There are several species of gulfweeds. Some are benthic; that is, they are attached to hard surfaces on the bottom or along sea walls, rocks, and pilings. However, the most abundant species of gulfweeds are pelagic; that is, they float in virtual prairies and are carried by the Gulf Stream and other oceanic currents in great rafts that may be strung out in miles-long lines. A highly complex community of animals (including hatchling sea turtles), fishes, and an amazing diversity of invertebrates lurk in the tangled mass of golden brown plants. The gulfweed hydroid, *Aglaophenia latecarinata*, related to corals and jellyfishes, lives its life attached to drifting gulfweeds and obtains its food by stinging tiny larvae and other members of the complex zooplankton community. Gulfweed hydroids resemble tiny, feathery, white to pinkish plumes and are also known as feather plumes or ostrich plume hydroids.

The gulfweed anemone, *Anemonia sargassensis*, is another hitchhiker that is related to the corals and jellyfishes. It is a delicate, flowerlike creature that has forty to fifty colored tentacles artfully arranged around its oral disk. As the gulfweed drifts along, the gulfweed anemone snares its prey by stinging it with specialized stinging cells embedded in its tentacles.

Two species of gulfweeds are common along the Inner Coast: gulfweed, *Sargassum fluitans*, and sargasso, *Sargassum natans*. Sargasso is named for the great tract of ocean lying to the east of the Caribbean islands. Gulfweed is a pelagic species that has rather short fronds with serrated margins analogous to the leaves of higher plants. Round or oval floats or bladders enable gulfweed to wander on the surface of the sea. Storms and currents often wash these pelagic plants up on beaches in heaps and sometimes in long windrows. Sargasso has long, wiry fronds armed with spiny teeth. This light brown alga is distinguished by spines projecting from the tips of its bladders.

Sea lettuce, *Ulva lactuca*, is a silky, green, cello-

Sea Lettuce
Ulva lactuca

phanelike alga with ruffled blades belonging to the green algae group. This ubiquitous species is attached to the sea bottom by inconspicuous holdfasts that often detach, allowing the seaweed to float free. The floating mats often congregate in quiet, shallow waters. Sea lettuce is tolerant of a wide range of salinities, from brackish estuaries to full-strength seawater. It grows in great abundance where the waters

have been enriched by moderate pollution and freshwater runoff. When it dies and begins to break down, it releases hydrogen sulfide, which smells like rotten eggs and is not only unpleasant but can discolor the white-painted sides of nearby houses.

In tropical regions, remnants of an interesting type of seaweed, calcified algae, are often deposited on the beaches. These species of seaweeds absorb calcium carbonate from the waters and incorporate it as part of their cell structure. Calcified green algae belonging to the genus *Halimeda* are a diverse group of plants that are all highly calcified. When species of *Halimeda* die and break down, they become part of the sediments surrounding the reef and seagrass meadows. The calcified remains of these algae are deposited on the beaches of south Florida and the Caribbean and form a major component of beach "sand." *Halimeda* algae species take on many growth forms, such as necklaces of calcified, pea-shaped beads, flat disks, or segmented rods. *Halimeda opuntia*, an abundant alga of seagrass meadows, grows in low, dense clumps or mounds. This species is one of the most important contributors of carbonate sands.

The white remains of calcified disc algae, Halimeda opuntia *(to 8' tall), and broken reddish sticks of fragile coralline alga,* Amphiroa fragilissima *(mats to 2 1/2" thick), are often found on the beaches of south Florida. The tests of sea urchins and sand dollars are found all along beaches from Virginia to the Keys.*

Its branches are formed of flat, irregularly shaped, disklike segments. You can often see fragments of the green calcified segments and the bleached carbonate skeletons on Florida beaches.

Coralline red algae are also heavily calcified plants that belong to the *Lithothamnion* genus of the red algae phylum, Rhodophyta. These algae are the most abundant and diversified plant species in the tropics. They take many forms, from branched and segmented twiglike plants to flat encrusting forms and bushlike growths. They are very important in the ecology of a reef because they serve as a hard substrate for the settlement of other organisms and form rocklike ridges that protect the corals. Many of the coralline red algae are so heavily calcified and encrusted that they do not resemble plants and are thought by many snorkelers and scuba divers to be some sort of coral. Some coralline red algae grow on coral reefs in water depths of 30 feet or more; other species grow in loose, brittle clumps in the seagrass shallows. You can find small, calcified, purplish red nodules or cylindrical, pink, brittle segments, particularly on Florida Keys beaches. These are fragments of various species of coralline red algae that have been wrenched from a reef or seagrass meadow and washed up on the beach.

Fragile coralline alga, *Amphiroa fragilissima*, is a common species that grows in dense clumps lightly attached to the sea bed in shallow seagrass meadows. The pinkish, branchlike segments of the fragile coralline alga are thin and brittle and are often seen on a beach after a storm.

Herbaceous Plants

Sea rocket, *Cakile edentula*, is a low-growing, sometimes creeping, fleshy-leaved member of the mustard family. It grows along the upper beach, among sand dunes, and at the edges of salt marshes. Typical of

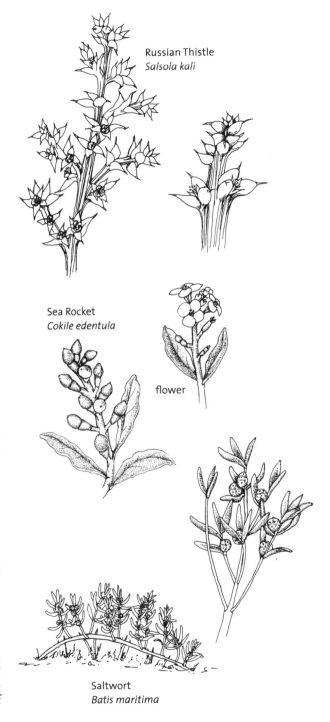

Russian Thistle
Salsola kali

Sea Rocket
Cokile edentula

flower

Saltwort
Batis maritima

Railroad vine, Ipomoea pes-caprae, *with pink petunialike blossoms, and sea purslane,* Sesuvium portulacastrum, *with pink star blossoms, creep out of a stand of beach grass. Bending panicle heads of the sea oat,* Uniola paniculata, *are in the background.*

plants of the mustard family, the small lavender to white flowers have four rounded petals. The fleshy, dark green leaves are alternately arranged and vary in shape from linear to smoothly lobed along the margins. Late in the summer, thick, fleshy seed pods develop along the flower spike. These distinctive fruits are divided into two segments; the upper section is bulbous, and the bottom section is narrower and cylindrical. Sea rockets grow down to central Florida and often are found where Russian thistle grows.

Russian thistle, also known as saltwort, *Salsola kali,* is a branched, fleshy-leafed plant armed with sharp spines. Its long leaves are alternately arranged, and its small greenish flowers are borne in twos and threes in the leaf axils. The stems are sometimes streaked with red to purplish lines, and as the plant matures, late in the season, the entire plant frequently turn reddish pink. Russian thistles are common along the upper beach in the wrack zone and along the edges of high marshes throughout the Inner Coast.

Saltwort, *Batis maritima,* is a yellowish green shrub with succulent, linear or narrow leaves. This evergreen plant sprawls over moist shorelines, on

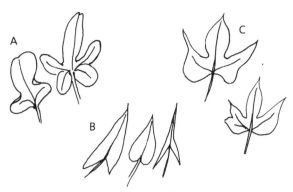

Leaves of other common morning glories.
A. *Beach morning glory,* Ipomoea stolonifera
B. *Salt marsh morning glory,* Ipomoea sagittata
C. *Coastal morning glory,* Ipomoea trichocarpa

the higher elevations of intertidal flats, among mangroves, and in salt marshes. It also occasionally grows upright to about 3 feet. Saltworts somewhat resemble perennial glassworts, which live in similar habitats. This fleshy-leaved plant is tolerant of high concentrations of salt because it is able to take up salt, store it within the cellular spaces of its leaves, and then shed the leaves. The leaves are oppositely arranged; the flowers are borne on short spikes. The male and female flowers arise on separate plants. Saltworts range from South Carolina down to the Florida Keys.

Sea purslane, *Sesuvium portulacastrum,* is a fleshy-leafed plant of the Inner Coast that sprawls over upper beaches, in dune swales, and along the edges of high marshes. They occasionally grow in mangrove swamps and sand flats in high marshes. The leaves are very fleshy and are oppositely arranged. They are usually dark green but are sometimes tinged or completely red. Lovely small but conspicuous pink flowers are borne on stalks arising from the leaf axils. The leaves of seaside purslane are succulent, salty, and edible.

Several morning glory species grow along beaches

and dunes, around the edges of brackish and freshwater marshes, and in sandy areas along railroad tracks and roadsides. Morning glory is an appropriate name, for they are in their glory in the early morn and usually fade before noon. Some morning glory species have been introduced, such as the red morning glory; however, many are native, including the beach morning glory, the salt marsh morning glory, and the railroad vine. The edible sweet potato is also a member of the morning glory family. Wild potato vine has been used by American Indians for rheumatism and a host of other maladies.

Railroad vine, *Ipomoea pes-caprae,* is a typical creeping morning glory vine with a five-petal, reddish pink, funnel-shaped flower. The bright green, fleshy leaves are alternately arranged. Railroad vines grow in coastal sand dunes and upper sand beaches and are common from coastal Georgia through Florida. The salt marsh morning glory, *Ipomoea sagittata,* has arrowhead-shaped leaves and a large, rose-colored flower. It is common along the edges of brackish and freshwater marshes and in dune swales from North Carolina southward to Florida.

Fire wheel, *Gaillardia pulchella,* also called showy gaillardia or Indian blanket, is aptly named. *Pulchella* means "beautiful," and the fire wheel is, indeed, a beautiful flowering plant. It is a plant of sunny, open sites. It has a showy and intensely hued daisylike blossom with petals radiating a blaze of color—light to deep red to purple with yellow tips, or sometimes all a brilliant yellow—offset by a deep reddish purple central disk. The flowers are 2 inches wide. The leaves, up to 3 inches long, are hairy or somewhat downy and may be entire or even feathery. The fire wheel may grow low along the ground or erect up to 2 feet or more. A common coastal plains species, it apparently was an escaped cultivated species that has naturalized widely and now decorates the dunes and beaches all along the Inner Coast.

Fire Wheel
Gaillardia puchella

The sea oat, *Uniola paniculata*, is a very important grass of the dunes, upper beaches, and loose sands. This tall, coarse grass with a panicle that resembles oats flourishes under the harsh conditions of wind, salt spray, drought, and blowing and shifting sands. In fact, salt spray stimulates growth; where it is strongest, such as along Bogue Banks, North Carolina, sea oats are the most dominant plant. They also grow rapidly when buried in shifting sand. Rhizomes of sea oats spread throughout the loose sands, sprouting buds off the rhizomes and increasing the plant's tenacious hold on its constantly changing environment.

Sea oats grow to about 6 feet tall with long, narrow leaves 8–16 inches long and less than 1/2 inch wide. In late summer, the seeds of the panicles turn an attractive bronze-yellow color. Sea oats were once a favorite plant collected in the fall for dried flower arrangements; however, they are now protected in most states because of their value in building and stabilizing dunes.

Trees and Shrubs

The trees and shrubs of the inner dunes and along the edges of the beaches in the temperate regions of the Inner Coast are essentially the same as those of the maritime forests and bay edges: live oaks, red cedars, magnolias, cabbage palmettos, and such. However, from the Indian River Lagoon southward through the Florida Keys, the upper beaches are lined with more tropical species, such as seaside mahoe, Australian pine, coconut and other palms, sea grape, and bay cedar.

Seashore elder, or beach elder, *Iva imbricata*, is a bushy-branched, 3-foot shrub that often grows in association with sea oats, panic grass, railroad vine, sea purslane, and sea rocket on beaches, dunes, and overwash areas. Its fleshy leaves can be smooth edged or toothed; the lowermost leaves are oppositely arranged, and the upper leaves are alternately arranged. The seashore elder is similar to a closely related species, the marsh elder, but its leaves and

Seashore Elder
Iva imbricata

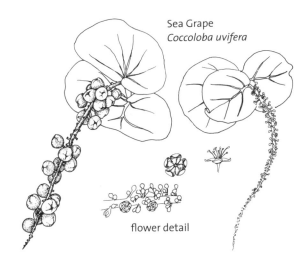

Sea Grape
Coccoloba uvifera

flower detail

stems are smooth in contrast to the hairy leaves and stems of the marsh elder. The small, greenish white flowers, borne on leafy spikes, bloom from late August to November. Seashore elder grows along the Inner Coast from Virginia through the Florida Keys.

Sea grape, *Coccoloba uvifera*, like the coconut palm and hibiscus blossom, is symbolic of the tropics. The sea grape is a small tree that is immediately recognizable by its distinctive thick, leathery, round to kidney-shaped leaves; the platterlike leaves frequently have red veins. Often the shallow roots can be seen protruding from the sand in twisted and plaited entanglements. Small, fragrant flowers on drooping stalks develop into clusters of purplish grapelike berries. The fruit is musty and sweet when ripe and can be eaten directly from the tree or made into jelly or wine. The tree can reach a height of about 50 feet, depending on where it is growing; however, it also grows as a low shrub along windy shores above the high-water mark. Sea grape thickets growing along exposed shores often exhibit the effects of "salt pruning." The thickets are molded into a wedge-shaped grove, with the taller shrubs on the inland side. Sea grapes are quite tolerant of harsh

conditions and grow well where the salt content is high and the soil poor. This native species of Florida grows in coastal hammocks, along the upper beach, and along the edges of waterways. It is often planted as a landscape ornamental and allowed to grow as a tree or even planted in a line and maintained as a hedge.

In sandy areas of south Florida, there are often thickets of an evergreen shrub, bay cedar, *Suriana maritima*, which is not at all related to true cedars. However, when the leaves of the bay cedar are crushed, they do emit a cedarlike fragrance. The long, grayish leaves have smooth margins and are alternately arranged. Small, rather inconspicuous yellow flowers are borne in small clusters or as solitary blooms. The fruits are woody, nutlike, and buoyant and, typical of the fruits of many tropical plants, such as red mangroves and coconut palms, may be carried by ocean currents to distant locations. Bay cedar, similar to seashore elder, is a pioneer species; it is one of the first shrubs to colonize beaches and dunes.

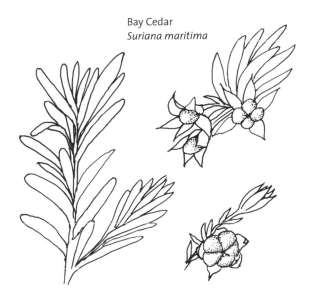

Bay Cedar
Suriana maritima

The egg cases of snails and skates are commonly found on the beaches of the Inner Coast. The sand collar of the shark eye snail, Neverita duplicata, *may be 5 to 6 inches in diameter. The flat-edged case of the knobbed whelk,* Busycon carica, *and the knife-edged case of the channeled whelk,* Busycotypus canaliculatus, *are 1 inch in diameter. It is rare to find an embryo of a clearnose skate,* Raja eglanteria, *still within its protective, leathery mermaid purse, 2 inches long.*

🌿 Signs of Life on the Beaches

The shells of mollusks are the most common and recognizable signs of life on Inner Coast beaches. Shell collecting is enjoyed by almost every beach stroller. Some pick up shells, glance at them casually, and then drop them or flip them over the waves; others are more deeply interested in shells' beauty and form or are curious and wish to identify them. Most of the shells found on the beaches are, of course, all that remains of once live creatures that dwelled within the protective coverings of calcium carbonate. There are other signs of mollusks besides shells scattered here and there along a beach, such as leathery egg cases of whelks and sand collars embedded with the eggs of shark eye snails.

Whelks construct strands of coin-shaped, rubbery

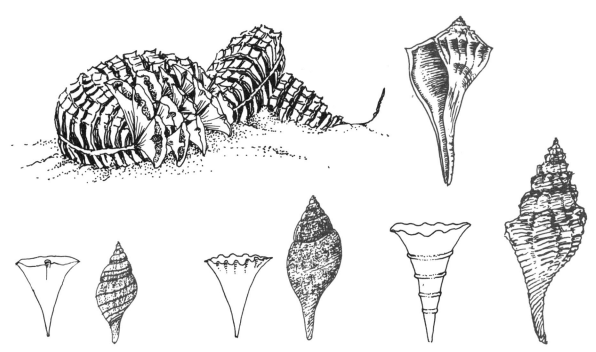

The egg cases of the lightning whelk, Busycon sinistrum, *are similar to those of the knobbed whelk but thinner. Other snails with distinctive egg cases are the banded tulip,* Fasciolaria lilium; *the true tulip,* Fasciolaria tulipa; *and the horse conch,* Pleuroploca gigantea.

capsules that were originally attached to rocks and shells on the ocean floor. The strands are often dislodged and drift ashore, where they are usually found along the wrack zone mixed with darkened masses of gulfweeds, pieces of rubbery pink sea pork, colonial tunicates, and various parts of horseshoe crabs. The egg cases are usually empty: the telltale hole near the edge of the capsule is evidence that the tiny snails have emerged. Sometimes, however, there may be a few snails left within the leathery chambers. Each species of whelk forms differently shaped capsules: the edges of the egg cases of the knobbed whelk and the lightning whelk are ridged and indented, and the egg cases of the channeled whelk are knife edged.

Sand collars, the egg cases of predacious shark eye snails, are cup-shaped collars, or rings, of sand held together by mucous with hundreds of tiny eggs inside. They are usually dry and fragile after exposure to the sun and are easily broken. You may find many other remnants of marine life on a beach, including fish skeletons, crab carcasses, dead coral rocks, and mounds of dying jellyfish. Skates, relatives of sting rays and sharks, are also represented on beaches by their strange little egg cases, known as mermaid purses. On south Florida beaches, it is common to find rose corals.

Mermaid purses are the dark brown to black, tough, and leathery egg cases of skates. Skates are similar to sting rays; however, they lack a stinger, and the tail is shorter and broader than a ray's. Moreover, a ray gives birth to live young, whereas a skate lays an egg enclosed in the curious mermaid purse, where

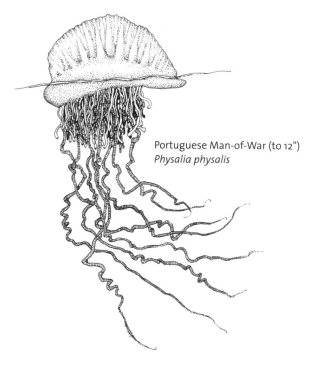

Portuguese Man-of-War (to 12")
Physalia physalis

it develops into a juvenile skate before emerging. Various species of skates produce different sizes and shapes of mermaid purses. They are all variations of a basic design: the 3- to 4-inch podlike cases have curved hooks and tendrils that anchor the egg cases to sea grasses. They are frequently washed ashore, usually as empty cases with splits along seams where the miniature skates have fluttered away. If the case is not split open, the embryonic skate may still be inside the egg case.

Many jellylike animals wash up on the beach after a storm. Jellies are sea drifters and are passive or weak swimmers at best. Jellies feed on small fishes, fish larvae, and plankton organisms. Some can inflict serious stings by discharging nematocysts tipped with neurotoxins. Others are relatively harmless: either they are not very venomous or they lack nematocysts.

The Portuguese man-of-war, *Physalia physalis*, has earned the reputation as one of the most venomous jellyfishes along the Atlantic coast. This is an organism with trailing tentacles as long as 40 feet, armed with a toxin that can stun fishes and cause serious stings to humans. The Portuguese man-of-war is a colony of highly modified individuals (polyps). Some are specialized for detecting and capturing prey, others for reproduction, and still others for feeding and digestion. The Portuguese man-of-war is equipped with a beautiful, brilliant blue to lavender gas-filled float and a crestlike structure that can be modified by muscular contraction to sail with the wind. These beautiful but fearsome jellyfishes are sometimes seen offshore in the Gulf Stream by the hundreds, and when the onshore winds are strong, they are frequently stranded on the beaches and washed into the inlets of the Inner Coast.

There is a curious little fish, the man-of-war fish, that nibbles the tentacles of the Portuguese man-of-war but appears to be immune to its stings. This little fish with dark blue blotches along its silvery sides is a member of the butterfish family and is related to the harvestfish, which swims with another venomous jellyfish, the sea nettle, that is so abundant in Inner Coast waters. Loggerhead turtles feed on the Portuguese-man-of-war. Beach walkers should be cautious when they come on a stranded Portuguese man-of-war, for they remain potent and dangerous for some time.

Life on the Beaches

There are two zones on the beach where there are noticeable populations of burrowing and scampering animals: the swash zone and the wrack zone. The swash zone is where the waves wash the beach; it is a high-energy area where the sands are tumbled, sorted, and re-sorted. Stones and coral rubble are

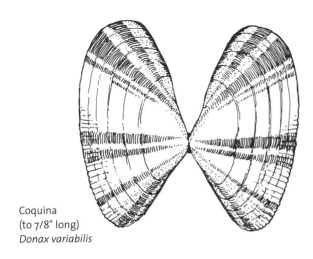

Coquina
(to 7/8" long)
Donax variabilis

constantly in motion in the swash zone, carried up the beach by strong surf and rolled back to the swash zone by the force of receding water. Animals in this zone constantly bury and rebury to maintain their position in this dynamic habitat. The wrack zone is a quieter place, a place of deposition, where high tides and storm-driven waves run up the crest of the beach to a point where the waves begin to recede and where the flotsam of the sea is stranded. The wrack zone is often separated by two well-defined wind-rows of seaweed, driftwood, shells, goose barnacles, and countless other items. The strand line closer to the surf defines the extent of the neap, or very low, tide; the strand line higher up the beach has been deposited by the spring, or very high, tide. Of course, storm events that bring strong onshore winds and heavy surf place their own strand line signatures on the beach. The animals that live in the wrack zone usually live under damp seaweed and other flotsam where there is sufficient moisture and protection from the drying sun and wind, and where they can hide from predators such as ghost crabs, tiger beetles, and shorebirds.

There is one mollusk, however, that not only leaves its shells on the beach but lives right in the swash zone—the very abundant coquina, *Donax variabilis*. This little, wedge-shaped clam, less than 1 inch long, is a favorite of beachcombers because of its brightly colored shells, or valves, which may be present in an assortment of pastel hues, from white and yellow to rose and lavender and purple and mauve, and are usually decorated with radiating or concentric bands of color, or both. The colors are more intense in the shells' interior. The colorful shells usually remain connected at the hinge line and look like beautiful beach butterflies. They are so abundant along certain beaches that they can be easily scooped up by the dozens in the swash zone and taken home for chowder.

Coquinas are constantly active, for life in the swash zone is perilous and ever changing. They move with the tides, swash riding: as the tide rises, they migrate shoreward; when the tide ebbs, they move seaward. As the waves flow up on the beach and then recede, coquinas burrow rapidly. When the next wave exposes them, they quickly dig back into the shifting sand. The coquina's shell is slender and knife edged. It has a well-developed foot that enables the clam to disappear into the wet sand in a matter of a second or two. Thousands of these beautiful little clams move up and down the beach in a rhythmic ballet timed to the motions of the waves and tides. Willets, dowitchers, and other shorebirds, as well as ghost crabs and silvery pompanos, which live in the surf, all feast on coquinas.

The swash zone is also home to the mole crab, *Emerita talpoida*, a busy, little, cylinder-shaped crab with a smooth carapace and a highly modified telson. The telson is the most posterior body segment that, together with the uropods, forms the tail fan that is particularly evident on shrimps and lobsters. Like coquinas, they move up the beach as the tide rises and retreat to the surf line as the tide wanes. Mole crabs are beautifully adapted to live within the

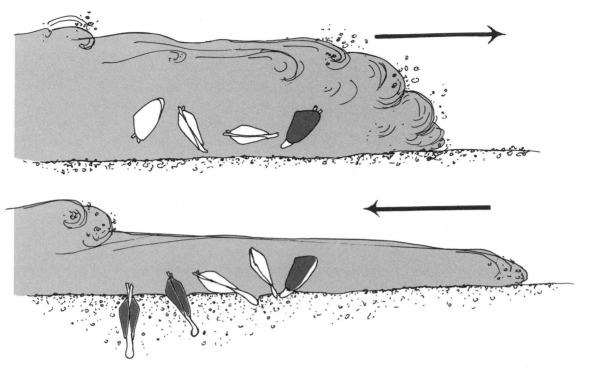

Coquinas ride the incoming waves. As the waves retreat, they extend their feet and quickly burrow into the bottom for protection.

churning environment of the swash zone; their egg-shaped bodies, robust digging legs, and shovel-like telsons allow them to almost instantaneously dig into the sand. A mole crab bears little resemblance to a typical crab. Its legs are small, and when it is not digging, which is often the case, it folds them close to its body. Mole crabs have no claws with which to bite, nip, or threaten. They are pale gray to light sand colored. Their dark eyes are poised on short stalks, and they have two pairs of antennae. The first pair extends from between the eyes and serves as breathing tubes; the second pair are long, feathery extensions that trap food particles from the roiling surf. When its antennal net is filled with pieces of food, the mole crab curls its antennae back to its mouth and extracts its food.

Mole crabs are easy to capture when they pop out

of the sand. Carefully watch the point where one has reburied itself; then quickly scoop the crab out with your hand. When you release it, you will marvel at the speed at which it disappears. If you search for mole crabs in spring or early summer, you may find three or four smaller crabs clinging tenaciously to a larger mole crab's carapace; the smaller crabs, about 1/3 inch long, are the males. In the winter, in the more northern region of the Inner Coast, mole crabs abandon the swash zone and retreat to deeper water offshore. Mole crabs are preyed on by birds, raccoons that wander the beach at night, ghost crabs, and fishermen who use mole crabs for bait.

The Atlantic ghost crab, *Ocypode quadrata*, scurries across the sand on the tips of its long legs, dashing and darting and then suddenly disappearing into a hole in the sand. The hole is the telltale entrance to

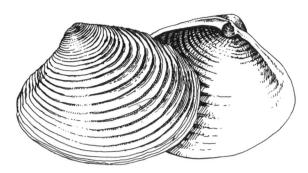

The shells of the channeled duck clam, Raeta plicatella *(to 3 1/4" long), are abundant on many beaches, a sign of populations offshore.*

a burrow that may be 3 or 4 feet deep. The burrows often have dead-end chambers branching off their main trunks and may even have two entrances.

Atlantic ghost crabs are nimble; in fact, their generic name, *Ocypode*, means "swift footed." Their common name is appropriate as well, for they may be seen at one moment and then, just like wraiths, instantly disappear. Not only are they fast on their sharply pointed feet, but they are perfectly camouflaged for life on a beach, particularly when they flatten their pale, sand-colored bodies close to the sand. Their two dark eyes at the ends of long stalks at times provide the only clue to their position. All the while ghost crabs scurry around, searching for food, engaging in mock combat with others of their species, and removing sand from their burrows, they leave distinctive crisscross tracks. Look for a fan-shaped scattering of sand around the opening of a burrow for a sure indication that ghost crabs are nearby.

Ghost crabs are semiterrestrial. They usually enter the water only to wet their gills and to release their hatching larvae. The larval crabs (zoeae) develop through several molts and finally metamorphose into tiny replicas of adults, at which stage they return to the beach to live out their adult lives. The more mature ghost crabs typically burrow highest up on the beach; younger ghost crabs, which are a mottled gray and brown and much darker than the adults, usually burrow closer to the water's edge. Ghost crabs are small to medium-size crabs; their distinctive, square-shaped carapaces are generally not over 3 inches wide and 1 3/4" long. When they hold themselves up high on their legs, however, they appear more imposing and menacing than their size warrants.

Ghost crabs are sometimes active during the day, but they are usually in their burrows when the sun is high. Late in the afternoon and during the early evening hours, large numbers of ghost crabs scuttle back and forth along the beach, searching for bits of food. Ghost crabs, like many other species of crabs, are opportunistic feeders; they prey on insects and bits of dead fishes and algae washed up on the beach. They are known to prey on eggs of least terns and piping plovers that have been laid in the sand in slight depressions or scrapes, and they are savage predators of newly hatched sea turtles.

Tiger beetles are also stealthy and agile predators of sandy areas, particularly beaches, and along the

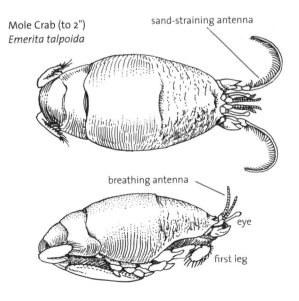

Mole Crab (to 2")
Emerita talpoida

sand-straining antenna

breathing antenna

eye

first leg

Atlantic ghost crabs, Ocypode quadrata *(carapace to 1 3/4" long), scurry from their burrows on the beach.*

sandy banks of rivers and the sandy edges of marshes. There are approximately 111 species of tiger beetles in North America and well over two dozen along the Atlantic coast. Tiger beetles are usually shiny, colored in metallic hues of green, bronze, or blue, and often decorated with yellow or white spots. Beach tiger beetles, as a group, are active scurriers and strong fliers. When another organism approaches the tiger beetle, the beetle will wait until some invisible line is broached, and it will then fly off in a flash and land some distance away, usually facing the interloper.

Some species of tiger beetles undergo incomplete metamorphosis from egg to larva to adult in one year; other species require two years for the life cycle to be completed. We have selected the highly endangered northeastern beach tiger beetle, *Cicindela dorsalis*, as an example of the typical natural history

of a beach tiger beetle. The northeastern beach tiger beetle is about 1/2 inch long, and it has white to tan wing covers, called elytra, that are sometimes embellished with fine, dark lines. Its head and thorax are a glossy bronze-green. Female northeastern beach tiger beetles deposit their eggs just below the surface of the sand and above the high-tide line. Highly predacious larvae hatch out in July. The larvae, referred to by entomologists as sit-and-wait predators, live in cylindrical, vertical burrows with their sand-colored heads bent at right angles to their bodies, poised to seize any hapless insect or amphipod that comes their way. The larva's fifth abdominal segment is equipped with two strongly curved hooks that are directed forward and firmly pressed into the sides of the burrow to prevent the larva from being jerked out of its underground retreat by larger and stronger

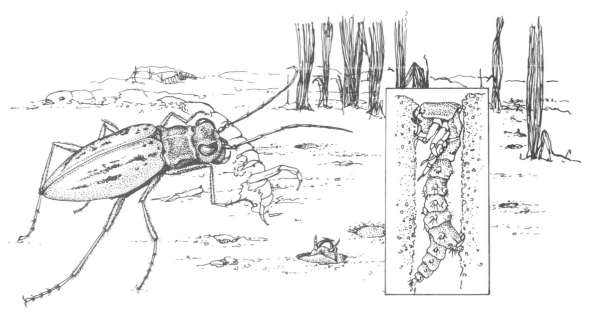

A northeastern beach tiger beetle, Cicindela dorsalis *(to 3/5"), feeds on a beach amphipod. Inset shows a tiger beetle larva fastened within a burrow with its head closing the entrance.*

insects and amphipods. The larvae may develop into adults the following year or persist in the larval form for two years.

Adult tiger beetles have few natural enemies other than grackles and an occasional marauding wolf spider; however, the larvae may be preyed on by an ant-like parasitic wasp. The wasp stings and paralyzes the larva and deposits an egg on its soft body. When the egg hatches, the larval wasp is supplied with an immediate meal.

There are other, smaller crustaceans that abound on different zones of the beach, such as amphipods, sometimes called scuds, beach fleas, beach hoppers, and side swimmers. Amphipods are small crustaceans, usually not more than 3/4 inch long, with shrimplike bodies with laterally compressed or flattened sides. There are many species of amphipods distributed throughout the world. Amphipods, typical of so many crustaceans and other members of

the phylum Arthropoda, have been able to adapt to a great variety of freshwater and saltwater habitats. They live in saltwater and freshwater marshes, along the margins of lakes and ponds, and in wet sand. Some scavenge on dead animals, and others are deposit feeders that subsist on organic detritus. Some species live in sponges, sea scallops, and worm tubes; others are part of the oceanic plankton; and still others are even parasitic on jellyfish.

We include three amphipod species as representative of the literally dozens of species that are common along the Inner Coast.

The sand-digger amphipod, *Neohaustorious schmitzi*, is found on the lower beach, where the sand is continually wet, and into the shallow, subtidal water. It is especially adapted for burrowing in loose sand. Sand-digger amphipods are equipped with large plates along the sides of their bodies that form a funnel. They burrow where the sand is water-

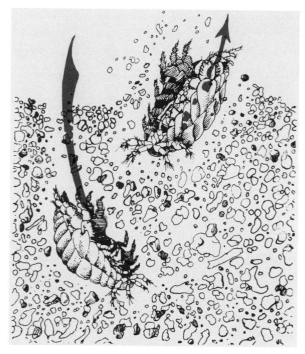

The sand-digger amphipod, Neohaustorius schmitzi *(to 1/5"), moves water currents in one direction to bury itself and in the opposite direction to feed.*

The beach hopper, *Talorchestia longicornis,* sometimes called the long-horned beach hopper, has long antennae that reach almost the length of its body. Beach hoppers are about twice the length of beach fleas and sandy colored, whereas beach fleas are dark olive to brown. Beach hoppers are also agile and unpredictable jumpers. They too are nocturnal. They tunnel into the sand during the day; at night, they emerge and move down to the water's edge in search of food. Juvenile beach hoppers live closer to the water than do the adults. During the day, juvenile beach hoppers may often be seen jumping and milling about in the damp sand. Amphipods are greedily fed on by sanderlings, ruddy turnstones, dunlins, and a variety of other shorebirds.

There are many species of insects that visit the beach. Some, such as mosquitoes and greenhead flies, are in search of a blood meal from humans. Dragonflies cruise by; midges swarm and hum; and on the upper beach, beautiful beach tiger beetles scurry about. One of the most unusual and smallest insects

logged, and as they excavate 1 or 2 inches into the sand, the funnel moves water and food particles to their mouth parts. At times, they emerge from their burrows and swim to the surface, but they almost immediately return and rebury. They range from Cape Cod to northeastern Florida and can live in brackish salinities and up to full-strength seawater.

Beach fleas and beach hoppers are active amphipods that jump like dog fleas; their vision is acute, and any slight disturbance springs them into a hopping frenzy. *Orchestia platensis* is one of many beach fleas that live along the Inner Coast. Typically, beach fleas live on the upper beach, where stranded seaweeds and other flotsam are strewn. They are usually nocturnal, but if you beach comb around the wrack for shells, they spring erratically in all directions.

A beach hopper, Talorchestia longicornis *(to 1"), jumps high over two beach fleas,* Orchestia platensis *(to 1/2").*

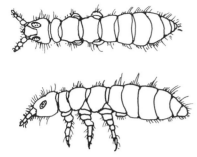

Seashore Springtail
(to 1/8" long)
Anurida maritima

along the waterfront is the seashore springtail, or oyster springtail, *Anurida maritima*. The seashore springtail is a collembola belonging to an order of primitive, wingless insects that occur throughout the world. The seashore springtail is tiny, usually less than 1/8 inch long. It is slate blue, has short antennae, and is clothed in an abundance of short hairs, or setae.

This little insect is strictly a marine species and occurs abundantly on the beach all along the Inner Coast. Although tiny, seashore springtails appear as a dark, milling mass when clustered together. At low tide, numbers of seashore springtails can be observed crawling about on rocks, oysters, seaweeds, and drift-

wood, where they graze on dead crustaceans, snails, and other mollusks. When the tide floods, these little insects crawl into crevices among the rocks, debris, and shells and are completely submerged until the tide ebbs. Many insects are able to breathe underwater with gills that extract oxygen, just as fishes do; other insects, such as mayfly naiads, depend on diffusion through their permeable cuticle; and still others have direct contact with the surface of the water or insert a specialized tube into plant stems and roots, where they obtain oxygen. The seashore springtail manages to survive underwater with the aid of a cushion of setae that traps air and allows the springtail to breathe underwater for several hours.

Birds of the Beaches

Birds are attracted to beaches by the abundance of food that lives buried in the sand or is momentarily revealed in the roiling swash zone. They pick over the remains of horseshoe crabs and the recent molts of lady crabs; they peck at amphipods living under seaweed in the wrack zone; and sometimes they simply rest on the beach. Shorebirds, which have short

Congregations of seashore springtails are often seen as dark patches on shells, peat clumps, and other surfaces on the beach.

tails and thin bills, such as ruddy turnstones, sander-lings, willets, and dunlins, usually congregate near the water's edge. Plovers have short bills and small, round heads. Most species of plovers live in open areas, usually along the shore. Gulls and terns are ever-present gleaners along the waterfront. They are vocal and active birds frequently seen picking through stranded seaweed or soaring overhead, searching for small fishes and shrimps. Often they loaf on the water in small groups, bobbing on the surface beyond the surf. Gulls and terns are similar in appearance, and yet there are distinct differences in their body shapes and in their behavior. Terns are generally more graceful and streamlined than gulls. Terns often fly with their bills pointed downward, whereas gulls tend to fly with their bills in a horizontal position. Terns typically have slender wings and bills, and most species have forked tails. Gulls are, as a group, larger, heavier, and blockier birds than terns, and they usually have squared or rounded tails. Terns usually plunge-dive headlong into the water after a fish. Gulls generally wheel and skim the water's surface searching for something to eat; however, they occasionally plunge-dive for their meal. Gulls and terns do share similarities in that their plumage varies with the season and their age.

Shorebirds

The ruddy turnstone, *Arenaria interpres*, is a medium-size, stocky wader with a short, slightly up-tilted, wedge-shaped bill. Ruddy turnstones have brown backs and reddish orange legs, with white on their heads and bellies, in what is sometimes referred to as a calico pattern. They are chunky, short-legged sandpipers that use their small, strong bills to adeptly turn over stones and debris in search of a meal. They eat a number of different food items, including insects, spiders, amphipods and other small crustaceans,

snails, and worms. These very abundant birds are usually seen in small flocks all along the Inner Coast during the fall and winter months. Look for them on the beaches along the surf line and on mudflats and rock jetties. A good place to see ruddy turnstones is on the rubble beach along the Charleston, South Carolina, Battery.

The sanderling, *Calidris alba*, is slightly smaller than the ruddy turnstone. Sanderlings are pale tan, about the color of a sandy beach. Their plumage is brown in the spring and light gray with white underparts in the winter. They display a prominent white stripe on the upper parts of their wings in flight. Their bills and legs are black. Sanderlings veer rapidly to the beach in small, tight flocks and dash to the surf just in front of receding waves. They probe the wet sand for worms, amphipods, and small mollusks and then scurry up the beach, like mechanical toys, barely ahead of the next advancing wave. Sanderlings nest in the Arctic tundra and spend the winter along the Atlantic, Pacific, and Gulf coasts.

The willet, *Catoptrophorus semipalmatus*, is a large sandpiper with long grayish legs and a straight bill. Its scientific name, in part, means "conspicuous feeder." Willets surely are conspicuous in flight when they flash their white and black patterned wings and announce their presence with a noisy, piercing "pil-will-willet." However, when they are feeding along the beach, their plumage is a nondescript, mottled gray-brown. Willets are nervous birds; they are often the first birds to sound the alarm when danger approaches. They nest in salt marshes among the salt marsh cordgrass and salt meadow hay from mid-May to late July. The nest is a grass-lined hollow on the floor of the marsh, where the males and females take turns incubating the four or five olive-colored eggs. After the eggs hatch, the female abandons the chicks while the male cares for them for about two more weeks.

Shorebirds along the beach in the fall. Ruddy turnstones, Arenaria interpres *(to 9 1/2"), poke among pebbles. A willet,* Catoptrophorus semipalmatus *(to 15"), stands alert while another takes flight, flashing its black and white wings. Sanderlings,* Calidris alba *(to 8"), probe at the water's edge, and a black-bellied plover,* Pluvialis squatarola *(to 11"), in winter plumage walks behind.*

Willets feed on a variety of organisms, including insects, worms, small snails, clams, sand-digger amphipods, fiddler crabs, mole crabs, and small fishes. They often wade into the water and feed by probing with their long bills. They are frequently seen resting and bobbing on the water during the day. Willets are found all along the Inner Coast and are often quite abundant particularly in and around salt marshes, where they nest in colonies.

Plovers are birds that live on the ground. Some inhabit coastal shores, while others, such as the familiar killdeer, favor meadows and plowed fields. Plovers as a group are somewhat robinlike but have longer legs. They characteristically dash a few steps in an almost mechanical way, halt suddenly, peck at a worm or an insect, and then burst into a short run, stop and peck, and run again. Plovers nest directly on the ground in dry fields and on sandy beaches above the highest tides.

The black-bellied plover, *Pluvialis squatarola*, is one of the largest plovers along the Inner Coast, where it is found on beaches, tidal mudflats, and salt marshes. It has a characteristic hunched stance and somewhat lethargic behavior that make it appear dejected. The black-bellied plover, when in its breeding plumage, has a black belly and sides and a speckled back. Typically, along the coast, the black-bellied plover is clad in its winter plumage of a grayish back and a lighter belly. The black wing pits, or axillaries, can be seen when the plover is in flight. They accentuate its white underwings, providing an immediate clue to the bird's identity. The black-bellied plover, known as the gray plover in Europe, is distributed throughout the world.

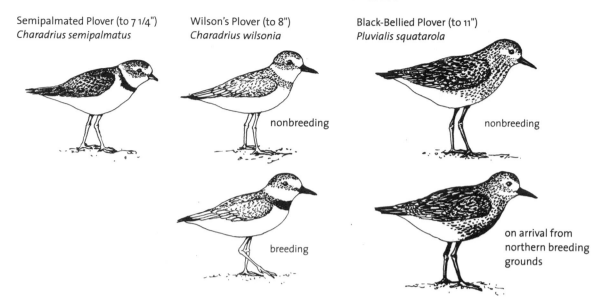

Semipalmated Plover (to 7 1/4")
Charadrius semipalmatus

Wilson's Plover (to 8")
Charadrius wilsonia

Black-Bellied Plover (to 11")
Pluvialis squatarola

nonbreeding

nonbreeding

breeding

on arrival from
northern breeding
grounds

Wilson's plover, *Charadrius wilsonia*, inhabits beaches, tidal mudflats, and washed-up shell beaches along the edges of salt marshes. This plover is smaller than the black-bellied plover and is distinguished by a dark neck ring and a stout black bill. Wilson's plover, like other plovers, runs along the beach in the characteristic stop-and-start patrol. This rather abundant bird is seen all along the Inner Coast and the rim of the Gulf of Mexico year-round.

The semipalmated plover, *Charadrius semipalmatus*, has a bold neck ring like Wilson's plover, but it can be distinguished by its black-tipped orange bill and its slightly smaller size. The semipalmated plover can be seen in the same habitats as Wilson's plover and the black-bellied plover. It ranges all along the Inner Coast and the Gulf of Mexico during the winter and nests in the Arctic tundra in the spring.

Gulls and Terns

The herring gull, *Larus argentatus*, is one of the largest gulls along the Inner Coast. Its plumage, as is

true of most gulls', gradually changes from an overall speckled brown in juveniles to the distinct plumage of breeding adults. Different species of gulls mature at different ages. The herring gull is a four-year gull—it requires that long to acquire its characteristic breeding plumage. Most other species of gulls require two or three years to attain sexual maturity and their breeding plumage.

The sexually mature herring gull has a pale gray body and a white head and belly. It has a yellow bill with a red spot near the tip of the lower bill, and it has pink legs and feet. Herring gull chicks peck at the red spot on the bill as a cue for the adult to regurgitate food into the wide-open bills of the ever-hungry chicks. Herring gulls are common along the Atlantic coast on piers and beaches and are frequently seen in great numbers wheeling and swarming over landfills. These large, raucous gulls are colonial nesters and lay an average of three olive to light blue eggs that hatch in twenty-four to twenty-eight days. Herring gulls are opportunistic feeders, as are most other

A first-year herring gull, Larus argentatus *(to 25"), calls raucously behind a mature adult in full breeding plumage.*
A third-year herring gull is at the water's edge. A Caspian tern, Sterna caspia *(to 23"), stands alert in the foreground.*

gulls. They feed on insects, scavenge small fish and crab remains, and even devour the eggs and young of other species of birds. They often drop clams and oysters from the air onto large rocks, parking lots, or piers to break the shells open so that they can feed on the succulent meats.

The Caspian tern, *Sterna caspia*, is the largest tern in North America and is larger than some gull species. This massive tern can measure 23 inches from the tip of its bill to the tip of its forked tail, making it only slightly smaller than the herring gull. It has a large red-orange bill marked with black near the tip and a black cap during breeding season. It can only be confused with the slightly smaller royal tern. The Caspian tern is widely distributed throughout most of the world. It breeds in small colonies along the Atlantic coast, where it constructs a simple nest in a scrape or depression or on mats of vegetation. The female lays two or three pinkish to buff eggs in the nest or sometimes in crevices between rocks. Caspian terns are the least gregarious of the tern spe-

cies and fiercely protect their young longer than any other terns, feeding them from five to seven months after they learn to fly. This large "sea swallow," similar to most other tern species, points its bill downward when searching for a meal. Caspian terns can often be found inland.

The royal tern, *Sterna maxima*, can sometimes be confused with the Caspian tern, but it can be distinguished from the Caspian by its shaggy black cap, more deeply forked tail, and lighter underwings. The royal tern is also slightly smaller and slimmer than the Caspian tern. Royal terns seldom leave the coastal waters. They breed all along the Inner Coast in large, crowded colonies on isolated sand beaches and sand bars and in sparsely vegetated areas. The female lays buff-white eggs in a simple scrape or depression in the sand. The young leave the nest and, within a few days of hatching, band together in what is termed a crèche. Amazingly, the parents are able to recognize their own young and feed only their own. Birds that live in large colonies, such as flamin-

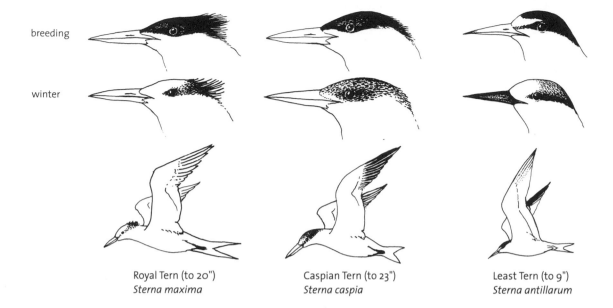

breeding

winter

Royal Tern (to 20")
Sterna maxima

Caspian Tern (to 23")
Sterna caspia

Least Tern (to 9")
Sterna antillarum

gos and penguins, often form crèches, as grouping reduces the risk of any single chick's being preyed on. This practice of grouping, whether it is called a flock, a school, a crèche, or a herd, reduces the risk to individuals because predators become confused by the constantly changing movements of individual prey.

The common tern, *Sterna hirundo* (its species name means "swallow"), and the similar-appearing Forster's tern, *Sterna forsteri*, are predominant terns along the Inner Coast. The species are approximately the same size, and both have black caps when they are in their breeding plumage. They have orange bills and are similarly colored. The differences are subtle but not impossible to discern. Generally, if the tern is a breeding adult, a Forster's tern will have silvery wingtips on the upper sides, whereas the common tern's upper wingtips will be gray. Forster's terns are widely distributed along the Inner Coast and along the shores of the Gulf of Mexico; common terns are found primarily from the Carolinas northward.

The nesting habits of the two species differ substantially. Forster's terns nest in salt marshes vegetated with salt marsh cordgrass and salt meadow hay. They build their nests on deposits of vegetation and other debris that provide elevated ridges to protect their nests from storm-washed tides. Common terns, on the other hand, nest in colonies on the sandy beaches of islands and on stony or gravelly areas, where they scrape small depressions in the sand or stony ground and line them with grass. Common terns are extremely aggressive on their nesting grounds and will attack intruders, including humans, by diving at them and inflicting wounds with their bills or feet. They are not reluctant to dive at an intruder and loose a mass of excrement as an added inducement to immediately depart.

The least tern, *Sterna antillarum*, is the Inner Coast's smallest tern. A breeding least tern, like other terns, has a gray back and wings, a black cap and nape, a white forehead, and a forked tail. The bill is pale yellow with a black tip. Least terns breed

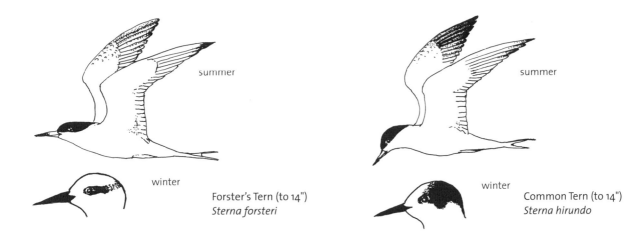

summer

winter

Forster's Tern (to 14")
Sterna forsteri

summer

winter

Common Tern (to 14")
Sterna hirundo

in their second year all along the Inner Coast. They typically lay one to three olive- to buff-colored eggs marked with brown splotches in shallow, unlined nests on sand bars or isolated beaches. Least terns often rest on pilings and navigation buoys. They fly with very swift wing beats and tend to hover longer than do other terns before plunge-diving into the water for small fishes or crustaceans. They also feed by skimming over the surface of the water and hawking insects, much as swallows do.

Intertidal flats, exposed at low tide and submerged at high tide, exist all along the sounds, marshlands, rivers, and channels of the Inner Coast. Intertidal flats, at first sight, seem bare and devoid of life, but on closer inspection you will find numerous signs of teeming life, especially in the muddier areas. Mudflats form where tide- and wind-induced energy is low. Fine sediments, composed of silts and clays, are suspended in the water in areas of high energy and then transported and deposited in sheltered areas of low turbulence, such as the meandering channels through a marsh. In areas of higher energy, particularly near ocean inlets and open beaches, the intertidal flats are composed of coarser sediments that consist of sand and heavily abraded shell fragments, pebbles, or, as in Florida, coral rubble. Intertidal mud and sand flats are often continuous with other habitats; they may be bordered on the landward side by a beach, a marsh, a bulkhead, or a stretch of riprap and on the seaward side by tidal channels, subtidal seagrass meadows, or broad open waters.

Intertidal flats, whether mud or sand, are brutally rigorous places for estuarine organisms to exist. Over the seasons, they are exposed to drying winds, summer heat, and winter cold. Exposure to the elements can cause desiccation and overheating or freezing when the tides are low and the flats are exposed. Various species have developed different methods to cope with the rise and ebb of the tides. Some animals, called infauna, live buried within the sand and mud. Other species live on the surface of the substrate and are called epibenthic species. Some epibenthic species, such as mussels and oysters, live forever attached to a hard surface and are known as sessile species. When the tide is high and the flats are submerged, small fishes, shrimps, crabs, and other species move in to feed on the worms, mollusks, and other creatures of the flats. As the tide ebbs, these grazers and scavengers usually cease feeding and fol-

low the receding waters into the shallows around the flats; however, there are some species, such as crabs, that can survive for extended periods out of the water and are able to feed on the flats during low tide. But perhaps, to most, the wading and probing shorebirds are the most conspicuous forms of life. Flocks of sand-colored shorebirds busily scurry over the rich feeding grounds; long-legged waders work the shallows around the flats; and long-billed shorebirds probe the muds for crustaceans and worms.

You may sometimes notice a green, dark brown, or black sheen over a flat, giving it an oily appearance. These sheens are caused by groups of organisms on the flats. Even when the glossy color areas are noticed, they are usually not recognized as forms of life. These colored, shiny patches are microbial and algal mats that are formed of bacteria and microalgae that thrive in the wet sands and muds of the flats. Bacteria break down the organic matter in wet soils and reduce it into mineral substances that then become available to benthic plants in shallow waters. Bacteria and, to some extent, fungi become an intermediary source of food between the relatively indigestible plants and detrital consumers. Some bacteria can live in the absence of oxygen and, in doing so, produce the characteristic, foul-smelling, sulfurous and iodide aromas so often noticed on a tidal flat or near a salt marsh at low tide. We do not cover bacteria and microalgae in this book, as they are difficult to distinguish without the aid of a microscope and special laboratory techniques. You should be aware, however, that bacteria and microalgae are essential components of intertidal flats ecology.

Vegetation of Intertidal Flats

Rooted aquatic vegetation is almost nonexistent on tidal flats because of the unstable nature of fine-grained sediments and the desiccation of plants at low tides, but occasionally there may be a sprig or two of salt marsh cordgrass or needlerush that has been transported from a nearby salt marsh and has taken root.

Numerous seaweeds (macroalgae), however, are commonly seen on intertidal flats. They may be attached to bits of stones or shells or grow luxuriantly on stranded hanks of rope. Many of the seaweed species found on beaches are also seen on tidal flats, such as sea lettuce, which can be seen in dense populations particularly where the sand flat or mudflat is located in quiet, protected water. Flats are often festooned with seaweeds wrenched from their underwater holdfasts and cast up in casually arrayed blades and threads of color, or in windrows and matted clumps of decaying vegetation. These same seaweeds also grow on rocks and piers or attached to the fronds and blades of widgeon grass or eel grass, or they may carpet the bottom with cellophanelike greenery. Almost any seaweed that grows in nearby shallow water areas may ultimately be seen on an intertidal flat, but we leave most descriptions of seaweeds to the habitats where they grow. Certain seaweeds, however, such as redweeds, green fleeces, and hollow-tubed seaweeds, are often stranded on the flats all along the Inner Coast from Virginia to the Florida Keys.

There are three species of redweeds, or red seaweeds, that at first glance look very much the same but on closer inspection may be easily discerned. They are all bushy, coarse seaweeds with fleshy branches. Tapered redweed, *Agardhiella tenera*, is a deep rose to dark red species with rounded branches that taper at the tips and at the bases, where the branches are joined to the stem. It lives in deeper waters attached to shells and stones.

Graceful redweed, *Gracilaria foliifera*, has flattened branches that range in color from deep green

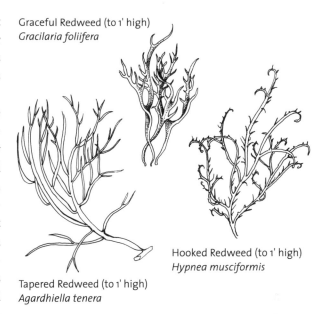

Graceful Redweed (to 1' high)
Gracilaria foliifera

Hooked Redweed (to 1' high)
Hypnea musciformis

Tapered Redweed (to 1' high)
Agardhiella tenera

to bright red. These plants grow in calm estuaries and bays, usually attached to small rocks and corals or growing in loose clumps.

Hooked redweed, or common red seaweed, *Hypnea musciformis*, is a bushy seaweed with cylindrical, almost cartilaginous branches that end in fishhooklike tendrils, which entangle the parent plant and attach secondarily to other seaweeds. These wiry plants can be deep green, orange red, or straw colored. Hooked redweed grows in sheltered coves and protected waters, where it entangles other algae or attaches by a holdfast to shells and stones or piers and pilings.

Green fleeces, dead man's fingers, sea staghorns, felty fingers, oyster thieves, and velvet sea fingers are all highly descriptive and common names of *Codium* spp., dark green mops of plants that grow attached to the sea bed or on jetties and piers. There are several species of *Codium* along the Inner Coast, as well as many species in European and Pacific areas. Green fleeces are easily recognized plants because

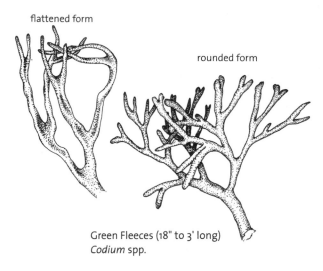

flattened form

rounded form

Green Fleeces (18" to 3' long)
Codium spp.

of their somewhat rubbery, ropelike, fuzzy, dark green branches. *Codium* species along the Atlantic coast are generally considered to be introduced and somewhat invasive species, as they compete with other, naturally occurring seaweeds and are thought by some to smother oysters. In some areas, green fleeces wash up in such abundance on the beach that they can become a serious nuisance as they rot and release the stench of rotten eggs.

Some of the most common seaweeds on the flats are the bright green hollow-tubed seaweeds, *Enteromorpha* spp. They are often attached to tiny shells or pebbles. The hollow strands of this seaweed may be curved, crinkled, tubular, or flattened, and often there are tiny, glistening air bubbles trapped within the strands. Hollow-tubed seaweeds are widely distributed and grow in shallow brackish and ocean waters throughout the world.

Animals of Intertidal Flats

Other than stranded seaweeds, an occasional shell, and ever-present birds, do any organisms actually live in or on the barren muds and sands of intertidal flats? Look closely on a mudflat to observe spiraling tracks running in all direction: a sure sign of eroded mud snails at work. Look even closer to find the dark, glistening snails that made those tracks. Other traces of life are small holes in the sand and mud surrounded by a keyhole-shape depression, made by a quahog. Little turbans of spiraled mud were made by acorn worms. Tubes with bits of algae and shells stuck to them are a sure indication that plumed worms dwell in the muds of the flat. A chimmneylike hole built of gray mud and sand is likely the lair of a snapping shrimp. Those little tracks with a straight line down the center were made by a hermit crab dragging its snail shell home.

Roamers over the Flats: Mobile Epifauna

Mobile epifauna are animals that glide and scoot over the surface muds and sands. Most species are crustaceans and snails that prey on the rich world of worms and clams, the infauna, which lie buried beneath the surfaces of intertidal flats. Many foragers, such as blue crabs, hermit crabs, small fishes, predacious whelks, and shrimps, come in with the tide to feed on organic detritus or to prey on intertidal burrowers. Several species of rays and skates may be present when the tides flood the flats; they flap their winglike pectoral fins and wash out clams, leaving extensive craters and pits behind. There are many smaller fishes—anchovies, silversides, mullets, and even a few sharks—that visit the submerged flats, as well as juveniles of several other fish species. Flatfishes, such as summer and southern flounders and tonguefish, are highly predatory species that arrive with the flooding tides and lurk in the sediments with only their eyes protruding, or they lie on the surface of the sediment and, like chameleons, almost instantaneously change their pattern and

Hollow-Tubed Seaweed (to 1' long)
Enteromorpha intestinalis

coloration to match the bottom. As the tide recedes, they leave the flats and return to their shallow-water communities.

Some mobile epibenthic species make forays at low tide from the landside out onto the flats, such as armies of scurrying fiddler crabs moving out of the marshes or several species of amphipods that graze on stranded bits of algae and, of course, the ever-present pestiferous biting deerflies and horseflies. Wading birds and shorebirds, as well as gulls and pelicans, are other groups that extensively use intertidal flats for feeding and resting. Who hasn't seen gulls and terns wheeling over a flat and then gliding down to join others looking for a scrap of food or settling down in small groups to rest on the sun-baked muds? When the tide is out, long-billed birds of many kinds are in. They probe and peck the muddy sands for worms and snails. Some are shallow probers and pickers, like the sandpipers and plovers that feed on amphipods and insects and the occasional unwary worm. Many wading birds are deep probers; for example, ibises, herons, egrets, and dowitchers wade along the flats and in the nearby shallows, piercing the sediments for worms and other infauna.

HERMIT CRABS

If you see a snail shell moving nimbly over the flats, you can be quite sure that the shell is occupied by a hermit crab. Hermit crabs, which carry their snail shell homes with them, are adapted to fitting their soft, coiled and unprotected abdomens into appropriated snail shells. Almost all snails have a right-handed spiral; that is, the snail's aperture is on the right when the apex is pointed up and the aperture faces the observer. Hermit crabs' odd-shaped abdomens are asymmetrical and turned to the right, so they are able to match the spirals of the snail shells and screw themselves tightly into the shells. It is almost impossible to remove a hermit crab from its snail shell house without tearing the soft-bodied crab apart.

Hermit crabs, similar to all other crabs, grow in steps. They molt and then increase in size and continue doing so until they reach a certain stage, when they undergo a final molt and grow no more. As hermit crabs grow, they need to find larger homes, and so they actively search out shells that will fit their new body proportions. They roll over empty snail shells looking for the perfect fit. Sometimes the shell is already occupied by another hermit crab, and then a tussle begins to determine which crab will occupy the shell.

Hermit crabs live their entire lives within shells except during their free-swimming larval stages. Most crabs, including hermit crabs, have a similar life cycle: The eggs hatch as tiny larvae called zoeae and then develop into secondary larvae called megalopses, which resemble tiny lobsters or freshwater crayfish. The megalops form then molts into a juvenile crab that continues to grow and molt into the recognizable adult crab.

Hermit crabs are opportunistic feeders; they will eat almost anything, including plants, organic detritus, dead fishes, dead mollusks, worms if they can catch them, and sometimes other hermit crabs. Hermit crabs are as much inhabitants of subtidal shallows as they are of the flats.

There are three very common species of hermit

Hermit crabs are often seen crawling over intertidal flats, home to the flat-claw hermit crab, Pagurus pollicaris *(to 4"),
here in a shark eye shell with a tricolor anemone,* Calliactus tricolor *(to 2' diameter), attached to it and a growth of snail
fur hydroid,* Hydractinia echinata; *the banded hermit crab,* Pagurus annulipes *(to 1"), in an oyster drill shell; and the long-
wrist hermit crab,* Pagurus longicarpus *(to 1 1/2"), in a marsh periwinkle shell.*

crabs that share the generic name *Pagurus*. Hermit
crabs in this group have claws, technically known as
chelipeds, that are unequal in size. The right claw is
typically larger than the left one. All three species
are common and abundant along the Inner Coast.

Pagurus annulipes, the banded hermit crab, is the
smallest of the group and can be recognized by the
brown banding around each jointed segment of its
walking legs and by its hairy claws. Banded hermits
live in small snail shells, such as those of greedy
dove snails, bruised nassas, and eastern mud snails.
Banded hermits are found on mudflats but they are
more common on shelly and sandy bottoms in shallow higher salinity waters.

The long-wrist hermit crab, also known as the
long-clawed hermit crab, *Pagurus longicarpus*, is
about the same size as the banded hermit. It has a
grayish to greenish body with long white claws that
are virtually hairless. These little crabs generally
occupy mud snail and periwinkle shells. Long-wrist
hermit crabs live in high-salinity to brackish waters
adjacent to intertidal flats. Their shells often have a
growth of a colonial hydroid called snail fur, *Hydractinia echinata*, which at times completely covers the
shell with a pink, furry texture.

Pagurus pollicaris, the flat-claw hermit crab, is
considerably larger than the two species described
above. It also tolerates reduced salinities and can be
found in shallow brackish water and full-strength
seawater near intertidal flats. The flat-claw hermit
crab has a heavy, flattened, and broad right claw and
is further distinguished by the tubercles, or wartlike
projections, on its wrist. It lives in shallow water on
sandy bottoms and on intertidal flats. This large spe-

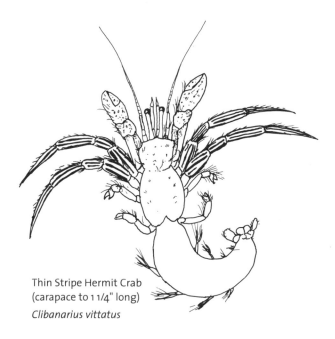

Thin Stripe Hermit Crab
(carapace to 1 1/4" long)
Clibanarius vittatus

cies occupies the large shells of shark eye snails and whelks.

Immerse the flat-claw hermit crab's shell in water and look for a small, colorful tricolor anemone, *Calliactus tricolor*, attached to it. The fuzzy tentacles of this little anemone are creamy brown; its muscular column varies in color from a light maroon to yellow and is often decorated with a splash of dark spots near its base. When the anemone is out of the water, it retracts its tentacles and appears as a small, gelatinous mound.

The thin-stripe hermit crab, *Clibanarius vittatus*, does not belong to the *Pagurus* family of hermit crabs. It has claws that are equal in size and are sparsely covered with hair. The hands of the claws are thick and about twice as long as broad. Its walking legs are decorated with longitudinal gray to white stripes. These rather large hermit crabs occupy shark eye snail shells, as well as whelk shells and scotch bonnet shells, and are found in brackish to high-salinity waters on muddy beaches, mudflats, and rock jetties.

The thin-stripe hermit crab is common in the Inner Coast. A close relative, the tricolor hermit crab, *Clibanarius tricolor*, has legs that are vibrantly colored with bands of white, orange-red, and blue.

CARNIVOROUS SNAILS AND OTHER GASTROPODS

Whelks are large snails, some of the largest along the Inner Coast, with massive shells that are familiar to even the most casual beachcomber. Who hasn't held an empty whelk shell or a conch to an ear to hear the murmuring of the sea? Whelks are aggressive carnivores that prey on other mollusks, particularly clams. There is a small fishery along the Atlantic coast for whelks that are primarily marketed in the Northeast. A popular Italian dish, scungilli marinara, is made from the rubbery feet of whelks. Three species of whelks are common along the Inner Coast: the knobbed whelk, the channeled whelk, and the lightning whelk.

The knobbed whelk, *Busycon carica*, is characterized by a series of rounded knobs on the shoulder of the body whorl. The inner lining, the nacre or mother-of-pearl, may be yellow-orange to brick red, and its large, fleshy body is gray.

The channeled whelk, *Busycotypus canaliculatus*, is slightly smaller than the knobbed whelk. The shell is pear shaped, with five or six whorls and a large body whorl that narrows down into a long, straight canal. The whorls are separated by sutures, or shallow grooves, and ringed with small knobs. The nacre within the aperture is yellowish to tan. Both the knobbed whelk and the channeled whelk feed on clams by forcing the edge of its foot between the valves of a clam to open it and then using its file-like radula to rasp away the soft body of the clam. The knobbed whelk and the channeled whelk are both right handed. To determine the handedness of

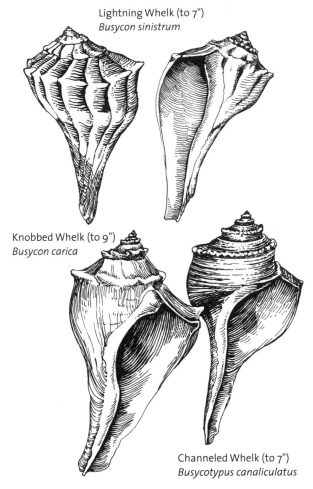

Lightning Whelk (to 7")
Busycon sinistrum

Knobbed Whelk (to 9")
Busycon carica

Channeled Whelk (to 7")
Busycotypus canaliculatus

purplish brown; hence the name lightning whelk. They have a row of small, triangular knobs on the shoulder of each whorl. As the lightning whelk ages, it loses the brilliant markings and turns a pale gray color. Lightning whelks are a more southern species that ranges from the Carolinas throughout Florida.

Slipper snails are cup-shaped snails that are often noticed cemented tightly to whelk shells and on the stranded remains of horseshoe crabs. Slipper snails are shallow-water snails. They vary from a somewhat flattened shape to an arching, dome-shaped form. The underside of a slipper snail is reinforced by a platform or a deck, and when the shell is empty, it does resemble a slipper. The surface of a slipper snail may be corrugated, ribbed, nodular, or smooth, depending on whether it has attached itself to a scallop shell, a bottle, or the interior of a whelk shell. In other words, slipper snails are highly plastic; their shape is influenced by their place of attachment.

Slipper snails have an unusual reproductive cycle in that they undergo sex changes: all the young are males, and when fully grown, they change to females. Generally a male glides into the vicinity of a female

a clam, hold the shell with the large opening facing you. If the opening is on the right, it is right handed. Both of these species range from around Cape Cod, Massachusetts, to central Florida.

The lightning whelk, *Busycon sinistrum*, is a left-handed spiraling whelk; its species name means "to the left." Because left-handed gastropod species are rare throughout the world, they typically pique the interest of shell collectors. Young lightning whelks are boldly marked with wavy streaks of mauve and

Atlantic slipper snails, Crepidula fornicata *(to 1 1/2"), pile one atop another in a communal stack over a shark eye shell. The smaller and younger slipper snails on top are males; the larger ones on the bottom are females. The males will eventually develop into females.*

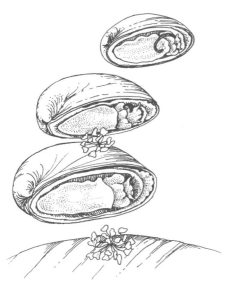

Female slipper snails lay bundles of egg-filled capsules attached by strands to the surface of the shell and then brood the eggs under their feet. The dark, curled penis of the male on top is slipped under the edge of the shell of the underlying female. During the period of transition from male to female, the snail retains a residual penis, as in the middle slipper snail.

Perhaps the most abundant and frequently seen snail on the flats is the eastern mud snail, *Ilyanassa obsoleta*. Sometimes there are swarms of these 1-inch, rather thick, oval snails strewn over the mudflats. The dark brown or sometimes almost black shells are often covered with mud and algae. Mud snail shells are crisscrossed with shallow grooves bearing small knobs or beads at the intersections of the grooves. Eastern mud snails feed primarily on muddy sediments rich with tiny algal forms such as diatoms. However, it is not uncommon to come upon hundreds of these small snails feeding on a dead clam, crab, or fish. They have a remarkable sense of smell and are quick to detect and move to a dead organism that has washed up on the flat. During the winter months, eastern mud snails aggregate in large numbers in eelgrass beds growing in the shallow water; in the spring, they return to the intertidal flats. If, however, you see an eastern mud snail slowly moving along and leaving a scratchy trail behind it, you can be sure that the snail shell is now occupied by a small long-wrist hermit crab.

The bruised nassa, *Nassarius vibex*, sometimes

and may even attach itself to the female. In fact, where there are soft bottoms with few hard objects on which to attach, slipper snails often attach to one another, forming a communal stack, with the older and larger females on the bottom and the newly arrived, smaller males glued to the top of the pile.

Slipper snails are quite abundant throughout the Inner Coast and can be found in large numbers washed up on beaches and intertidal flats. They are algae feeders and incorporate their food in mucus slime within their mantle. There are three common species in the region: the Atlantic slipper snail, *Crepidula fornicata*; the white slipper snail, *Crepidula plana*; and the convex slipper snail, *Crepidula convexa*. The convex slipper snail is often elongated and attached to eelgrass growing in shallow waters.

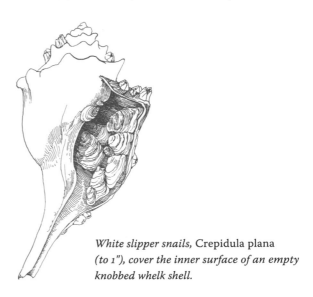

White slipper snails, Crepidula plana *(to 1"), cover the inner surface of an empty knobbed whelk shell.*

Eastern mud snails scavenge a dead blue crab on an intertidal flat.

known as a dog whelk, is a heavy-shelled snail slightly smaller than an eastern mud snail. The last whorl of the shell has about a dozen weak axial ribs that are coarsely beaded. Bruised nassas are highly variable from one population to another; they may be white to gray or brown and sometimes mottled or splotched with dark brown. The inner lip of the shell opening is flared out into a well-developed parietal shield. The bruised nassa, similar to the eastern mud snail, has a highly developed chemosensory ability that causes it to rapidly move toward a recently dead fish or crab or a polychaete worm egg mass.

The lettered olive, *Oliva sayana*, is a cylindrical, smooth, shiny, cream- or tan-colored shell that is almost 3 inches long. It has irregular, purplish brown, pyramidal markings on its glossy surface. The lettered olive is predacious. It has a strong muscular foot that it uses to burrow into the sand or to quickly capture prey. Lettered olives are quite abundant along the southeast Atlantic coast and have been designated the official state shell of South Carolina.

There are other snails, of course, that are often stranded on a flat as the tide recedes. Many of the snails live subtidally and are described under other habitats.

SPECIAL INTERTIDAL AREAS: BRACKISH ZONES AND WARM SEAS

Most visitors to the shore are familiar with and often walk along the sandy flats that lie along the coast, particularly near the mouths of rivers and close to ocean inlets. However, some places that are not so familiar or well visited are the intertidal flats that are common in the sounds of the Carolinas and Georgia and other Inner Coast bays and lagoons, where the tidal range is almost negligible and flats are revealed only when wind-blown tides occur. There are also extensive soft, muddy flats that lie along the many cuts and channels bordering the wide marshes—places that few wish to visit.

Intertidal flats also form in the upper zones of tidal rivers, where the water is fresher. These are

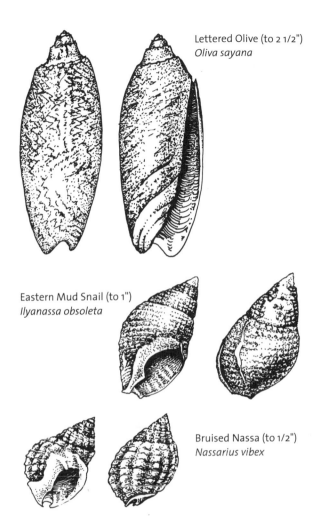

Lettered Olive (to 2 1/2")
Oliva sayana

Eastern Mud Snail (to 1")
Ilyanassa obsoleta

Bruised Nassa (to 1/2")
Nassarius vibex

the sandier flats that occur downstream. Then, too, the waters of the upper rivers are brackish as compared to the much saltier waters closer to the ocean. Where there are muddy, brackish water flats, there are dark false mussels, Carolina marsh clams, and a variety of freshwater snails.

Mytilopsis leucophaeata, the dark false mussel, is only about 3/4 inch long. It is dark brown to tan with a glossy periostracum. This is a very common bivalve that lives in brackish waters to almost freshwaters and attaches itself by its byssal threads to rocks, tree snags, and sticks on muddy intertidal flats and in the shallows. Sometimes dark false mussels undergo a sudden population explosion and increase in such numbers that they cling to pilings in clumps, smother the bottom, and even coat the bottoms of boats. They are very similar in appearance and behavior to their relative the introduced zebra mussel, which has caused so much havoc in the Great Lakes states.

The Carolina marsh clam, *Polymesoda caroliniana*, is a small, rather heavy-shelled clam that can be quite abundant in shallow brackish waters or even the freshwaters of muddy-bottom tidal creeks and rivers. The shell of the Carolina marsh clam is broadly rounded, and the exterior is glossy brown to olive green, but many of these little clams have lost some of their outer organic "skin," the periostracum, through erosion. The interior of the shell is white, but sometimes the nacre is tinged with violet or purple. In some areas of their range, Carolina marsh clams are so abundant that they are commercially harvested. They are rare in Virginia but are common and abundant in the Carolinas and Georgia and in rivers along the Gulf of Mexico.

Farther south, in the warmer waters of Florida, there are many subtropical snails, clams, and crabs that are closely related to and, indeed, resemble intertidal species found in more northern waters. Their

not usually high-energy areas as compared to downstream; the tides usually do not develop the strong currents evidenced closer to the ocean, and although the winds can blow mightily upriver as well as downriver, there are usually twists and turns and forested headlands that moderate the force of the wind. Because the winds and currents are typically weaker in the upper river sections, there is less energy available to move and sort the heavier sand particles, so the resultant flats are generally composed of fine silts and clays that create muddy substrates rather than

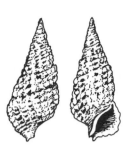

Ivory Cerith (to 1")
Cerithium eburneum

West Indian
False Cerith (to 1/2")
Batillaria minima

Carolina Marsh Clam (to 1 1/2")
Polymesoda caroliniana

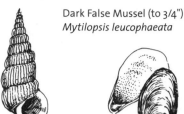

Dark False Mussel (to 3/4")
Mytilopsis leucophaeata

Ladder Horn Snail (to 1 1/4")
Cerithidea scalariformis

habitats are virtually the same, although the sands and muds of the flats are often intermixed with the remains of calcareous algae and offshore corals. On these flats, you will almost certainly encounter three small snails: the West Indian false cerith, the ivory cerith, and the ladder horn snail.

The West Indian false cerith, *Batillaria minima*, may be quite abundant, particularly on the mudflats of the brackish water Indian River Lagoon and in Florida Bay. These small, pointed, and elongated snails vary in color from black to gray and white, and they are often decorated with spiral lines of black or white. Their shells are adorned with fine nodules or knobs that spiral from the apex down to the last whorl. There are many snails that share a similar appearance to the West Indian false cerith, including true ceriths and horn snails, in that they are all slender and pointed and generally the same size. False ceriths are so called because they so closely resemble true ceriths; however, false ceriths have a concentrically spiraled operculum, the trapdoor of many snails. The operculum of a true cerith is not rounded and has fewer, usually incomplete spirals. There are other differences as well; for example, the siphonal canal, the groove in the lip of the snail, is short in the false ceriths and more pronounced and longer in the true ceriths.

The ivory cerith, *Cerithium eburneum*, is usually slightly larger than the West Indian false cerith. The pointed and elongated shell of the ivory cerith has a beaded appearance and may be white or splotched with reddish brown. These ceriths are abundant in the muds and sands of the intertidal zone, particularly in areas where sea grasses grow in the adjoining shallows.

The ladder horn snail, *Cerithidea scalariformis*, is another small, tapered snail that is similar in appearance to the West Indian false cerith and the ivory cerith. Ladder horn snails are about the same size as ivory ceriths. The shell opening, or aperture, is flared and horn shaped, and therefore these snails and their close relatives are known as horn snails. Ladder horn snails have russet or reddish brown shells with several deeply incised whitish bands and ten to thirteen rather inflated whorls that are sculpted with several coarse, spiral ribs. These little snails can be quite abundant on Inner Coast mudflats from South Carolina down to the Florida Keys, where they are commonly seen in the muddy bottoms around mangroves.

There are often some unusual crabs lurking in the intertidal waters, and you may come across the empty shells of recently molted crabs stranded on a flat. Along with the infrequent remains of spongy decorator crabs and nimble spray crabs, there will be an assortment of very common and abundant crabs from the surrounding shallows, including various species of swimming crabs and the massive-clawed stone crabs.

Animals That Live in the Mud and Sand of Intertidal Flats: Infauna

Benthic infauna includes many species of polychaete worms, acorn worms, bivalve and gastropod mollusks, anemones, and crustaceans. Some are suspension feeders that feed on particles in the water column; others are deposit feeders that obtain their food by ingesting sand and mud that contains bacteria, fungi, microalgae, and detrital particles; and still other species are predators or scavengers.

WORMS AND WORMLIKE BURROWERS

A number of worms and wormlike organisms live in the intertidal flats of the Inner Coast estuaries, from tidal freshwater to almost ocean-strength-salinity water near the inlets. There are approximately five unrelated groups of animals commonly referred to as worms: The simplest are the flatworms, such as those that live among oysters; this group also includes some serious parasites, such as tapeworms and liver flukes, that infest humans and many other animals. The second group is the roundworms, the nematodes, many of which are parasites and also cause enormous damage to crops. The third group of wormlike animals is the ribbon worms. Ribbon worms are unsegmented and are usually flattened dorsoventrally and are equipped with rapierlike lances concealed in the front ends of their bodies. The fourth group is the true segmented worms, the annelids, which includes leeches and earthworms and a large group of mostly marine species, the polychaetes. They are frequently known as bristle worms because of their bristly, paddle-shaped appendages extending from each segment; the Greek *polychaitēs* means "having many hairs." Each segment of a bristle worm has a pair of small, paddle-like appendages called parapodia that bear bundles of hairs, often referred to as setae. The fifth group of worms is the acorn worms, one of the strangest and least-known groups of animals that dwell on the flats. They belong to the phylum Hemichordata, which means "half a chord," referring to the notochord that scientists once thought they possessed. They do have gill slits and what appears to be a notochord but now is considered a stomochord, a rudimentary structure similar to a notochord.

Polychaetes are an amazingly diverse group of worms numbering several thousand species throughout the world. They range in size from less than 1/8 inch to well over 8 feet long and may be brilliantly colored, although most are pale sandy or dun colored. Polychaetes are usually placed into two groups: the errant polychaetes and the sedentary polychaetes. These categories are rather artificial; they simply refer to how and where these worms exist. Errant worms of the intertidal flats and adjacent shallows are mostly predators that wander over the surface of the sand and mud or burrow through the substrates in search of food. They can readily move through mud and sand by means of peristaltic contractions. Some errant, or wandering, worms construct tubes, whereas other species never build permanent "homes." Sedentary worms are tube and burrow builders that wait for their food to come to them. They typically have specialized structures, such as enlarged mouth parts or other appendages, to aid them in food gathering. Some tube builders are tiny and inconspicuous; others are quite large and easy to detect on intertidal flats. Sedentary tube-building worms often give away their hiding places under the surfaces of the tidal flats by depositing dollops of feces-laden sand and mud around openings of their burrows. There are many species of sedentary and errant worms living in other habitats as well—crawling among or attached to clusters of oysters or mussels on pilings or rocks or living on coral reefs or in mangrove swamps.

Sedentary Worms. The parchment worm, *Chaetopterus variopedatus*, so named for its parchment-like tube, burrows in the sediments of high-salinity tidal flats and adjacent eelgrass and shallow waters. It constructs a U-shaped burrow that may be 1 foot long or more, and each end projects above the surface about 1 inch. The whitish tubes are approximately 1 inch wide along most of its length but taper to narrow openings at each end. The worm inside is a very curious creature—pale, brightly luminescent in the dark, and oddly shaped with various appendages along different sections of its body. Paddle-shaped, winglike parapodia along the midsection of the worm maintain a current of water that washes through the burrow from one end to the other. Specialized appendages at the anterior end of the worm form a mucous bag that filters plankton from the constantly moving current. When the mucous bag is full, the pumping ceases, and the bag is detached and passed forward to the worm's shovel-like mouth. The parchment worm often, unwittingly, shares its burrow with the tiny parchment worm crab, *Pinnixa chaetopterana*. These tiny crabs, only about 1/2 inch long, are small enough to enter and exit the tapered ends of the worm tube. They feed on the stream of plankton passed through the parchment worm's tube. We have often seen hundreds of these papery, almost rubbery tubes stranded on the flats and beaches after a storm. The parchment worm ranges all along the Inner Coast in high-salinity water.

The lugworm, *Arenicola cristata*, is another intertidal worm that discloses its presence by depos-

iting "castings," sandy strings of feces held together with mucus, on the sediment near a funnel-shaped depression. This 10- to 12-inch worm lies deep below in a somewhat L-shaped burrow with the descending shaft below the hole at the posterior end of the worm and the anterior end at the other end of the tube, below the funnel-shaped depression. These burrows are often quite deep; they may extend 1 foot or more into the mud and sand near and in the shallows. The lugworm feeds by ingesting mud and organic matter, which creates the depression on the surface of the tidal flat. If you manage to extricate a lugworm from its burrow, you will find that it is a fat, blackish green worm with patches of reddish gills along the middle of its body.

The plumed worm, *Diopatra cuprea*, is another worm of the flats that lives in a tube, but its tube is exposed and easy to see. Walk on a tidal flat in a high-salinity area and look for 2- to 3-inch "chimneys" covered with bits of algae and shell; those are the homes of the plumed worm. Vacant tubes are frequently dislodged by storm-lashed waves and strewn about on beaches. The tubes are easily recognized, as they are soft, elastic, somewhat wrinkled, and garnished with bits of marine debris. Plumed worms are large; they may measure as long as 12 inches,

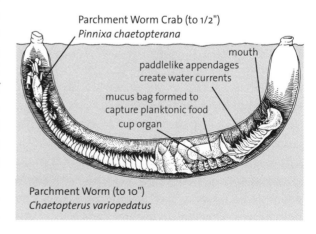

Parchment Worm Crab (to 1/2")
Pinnixa chaetopterana

mouth
paddlelike appendages create water currents
mucus bag formed to capture planktonic food
cup organ

Parchment Worm (to 10")
Chaetopterus variopedatus

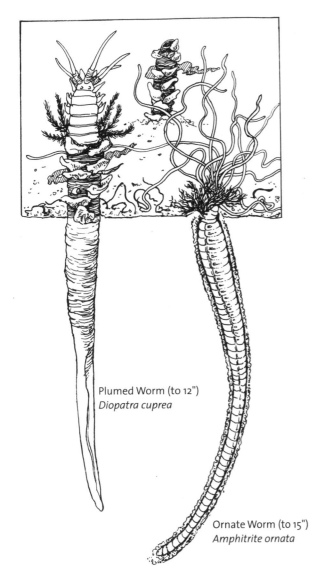

Plumed Worm (to 12")
Diopatra cuprea

Ornate Worm (to 15")
Amphitrite ornata

are other species within the plumed worm's family, Onuphidae. They have various common names: soda straw worm, shaggy parchment tube worm, and onuphis worm. They share some characteristics with the plumed worm: they are large worms with well-developed jaws and heads; they build tubes in the flats and shallows decorated with shells, stones, and algae; and they sometimes leave their tubes to snare unwary dinner victims.

The ornate worm, *Amphitrite ornata*, is another worm of the intertidal flats in shallow, high-salinity subtidal waters. It constructs firm, sand-encrusted tubes. It has bushy clumps of red gills at the end of its head, accompanied by a flowering spread of peach-colored tentacles. These long tentacles may be as long as the worm itself, which may grow to a length of 15 inches. The ornate worm is found throughout the Inner Coast.

The trumpet worm, or ice cream cone worm, *Pectinaria gouldii*, is a small worm that builds tubes of cemented sand grains that resemble ice cream cones. The trumpet worm lives buried with its head pointed downward at the water lines of intertidal flats and subtidally in the shallows and in deeper water as well. This small worm has a large, truncated head and a fan of glistening gold bristles used for digging burrows in the bottom. It also has a cluster of long, pale tentacles that extend out in search of food. The slightly curved trumpet shells so reminiscent of ice cream cones are common on brackish water intertidal flats and beaches all along the Inner Coast.

Another interesting tube builder at the low-tide line of intertidal flats is the common bamboo worm, *Clymenella torquata*. These worms build dense "fences" of 8- to 10-inch mud-encrusted tubes in quiet, protected sand-mud flats where the salinity of the water ranges from brackish to the salinity of seawater. The common bamboo worm's brick red, elongated body, up to 6 inches long, resembles sticks

and their tubes can extend as far as 3 feet below the surface. But plumed worms do not always remain in their dens, as they are active predators, somewhat unusual for tube dwellers. They move around, away from their tubular homes, in search of prey and scraps of food. Plumed worms have large jaws and can bite when handled, although the probability of catching a plumed worm is small indeed. There

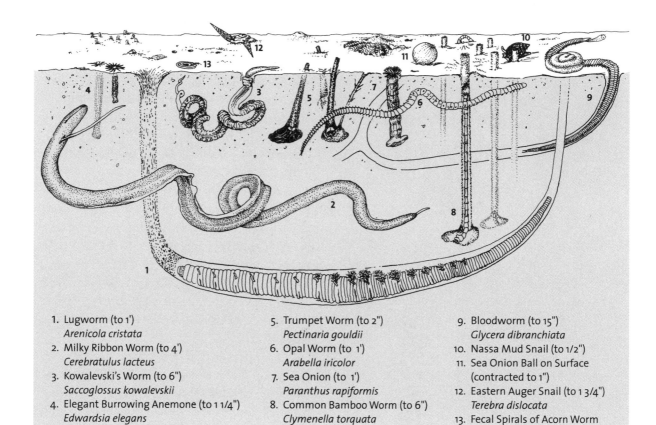

1. Lugworm (to 1')
   Arenicola cristata
2. Milky Ribbon Worm (to 4')
   Cerebratulus lacteus
3. Kowalevski's Worm (to 6")
   Saccoglossus kowalevskii
4. Elegant Burrowing Anemone (to 1 1/4")
   Edwardsia elegans
5. Trumpet Worm (to 2")
   Pectinaria gouldii
6. Opal Worm (to 1')
   Arabella iricolor
7. Sea Onion (to 1')
   Paranthus rapiformis
8. Common Bamboo Worm (to 6")
   Clymenella torquata
9. Bloodworm (to 15")
   Glycera dibranchiata
10. Nassa Mud Snail (to 1/2")
11. Sea Onion Ball on Surface
    (contracted to 1")
12. Eastern Auger Snail (to 1 3/4")
    Terebra dislocata
13. Fecal Spirals of Acorn Worm

of bamboo. It lives with its head down and the tip of its tail terminating in a funnel that can close off the top of the tube. Its blunt head, positioned at the bottom of the tube, is equipped with an eversible proboscis that can dig into the sediment deposits. Bamboo worm colonies often attract other animals, such as the bruised nassa and the tiny, spindle-shaped turret snail, where they scavenge for food. The tiny bamboo worm amphipod, just a fraction of an inch long, lives commensally with the bamboo worm. Parasitic snails common in seagrass meadows also inhabit bamboo worm tubes and feed on their hosts by inserting their long siphons into the worms' flesh.

There are also tiny little clams that occupy the space in the lower end of the worm tube.

Errant Worms. Burrowing wanderers, or errant worms, belong to various groups of worms, including thread worms, bloodworms, clamworms, red-lined worms, and paddle worms. Thread worms are long, slender, iridescent worms that burrow through sandy muds. They sometimes occur in very dense populations in brackish water and the saltier zones of Inner Coast estuaries, where they live in intricately intertwined burrows.

The opal worm, *Arabella iricolor,* is a bright green

to reddish brown or yellow, iridescent thread worm. It has no appendages on its conical head and very small parapodia. Opal worms burrow in sand and sandy mud in search of prey at the low-tide line and in the shallows. They range all along the Inner Coast.

The bloodworm, *Glycera dibranchiata*, has a creamy pink body with small, fleshy parapodia. It has a very large proboscis that can evert, or turn inside out, presenting a formidable, four-jawed poisonous apparatus that can kill or stun its prey and inflict a memorable sting on a worm digger or fisherman. These worms, also known as clam worms, or as "beak throwers" for their ability to evert their proboscis, are a valuable economic resource in Maine, where they are harvested on intertidal mudflats and sand flats for bait. A pound of bloodworms is more valuable than a pound of lobsters, so worm diggers in Maine, where bloodworms are quite abundant, avidly harvest these worms, which can reach a length of 15 inches. Bloodworms pull themselves through the mud by anchoring their muscular proboscis, or pharynx, in the sediment and springing their body forward, much like a sailor moving his boat through the shallows by throwing an anchor forward of the boat and then kedging, or hauling, the boat toward the anchor.

Ribbon worms, sometimes called proboscis worms or nemerteans by the experts, are quite abundant and widely distributed in many habitats throughout the world. They are unsegmented worms that are set apart from other worm groups by a remarkable, extensible prey-capturing proboscis. Some ribbon worms burrow deeply into soft sands and clays, and some may be discovered curled up under rocks and stones. There are about 900 species of ribbon worms. Most of them are carnivores or scavengers; however, some species live commensally within the shells of bivalve mollusks and tunicates. There are also several species that are parasitic on blue crabs and other species of swimming crabs. The parasitic ribbon worms usually infest female crabs that are carrying egg masses. They feed extensively on the developing eggs and can cause significant mortality in crabs.

The milky ribbon worm, *Cerebratulus lacteus*, is a large, flat, pale white to yellow or pink worm that may grow as long as an astounding 4 feet when fully extended. This long worm twists and turns on itself and knots itself into a convoluted mass when it is handled. It has a slitlike mouth on the underside of its grooved head and a pore at the tip of its head. The proboscis lies in a fluid-filled chamber within the worm's body and is hydraulically launched whenever a prey animal comes near. The proboscis is also equipped with a sticky secretion that quickly disables the prey. Milky ribbon worms feed on amphipods, polychaete worms, barnacles, and even soft clams. Breeding milky ribbon worms are a dark reddish color when they swim in the shallows in late spring and summer. It is quite startling to see a swarm of 3-foot worms writhing through the water on a moonlit night.

Acorn worms, long thought to be closely related to the chordates, are now believed by most scientists to be more closely related to echinoderm species such as sea stars, sea urchins, and sea cucumbers because of DNA-based studies on evolutionary relationships and the similarity of some hemichordate larvae to echinoderm larvae. There are approximately seventy species of acorn worms distributed throughout the world; they live in many habitat types, from the edges of beaches and mudflats to the oceanic depths.

The soft body of a typical acorn worm has three main parts: an anterior preoral lobe, or proboscis, that some think resembles an acorn; a collar situated just behind the preoral lobe; and a thin, sac-

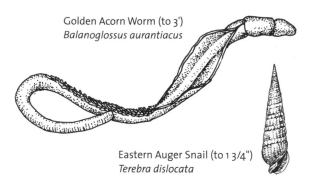

Golden Acorn Worm (to 3')
Balanoglossus aurantiacus

Eastern Auger Snail (to 1 3/4")
Terebra dislocata

like trunk. Acorn worms dig U-shaped, mucus-lined burrows in the soft sediments and constantly move through the sediments, ingesting organic material and excreting fecal material to the surface through the burrow hole.

The golden acorn worm, *Balanoglossus aurantiacus*, is infrequently seen but is easy to detect because of the ropy spirals of gray mud it deposits on the surface that smell like iodine. It has a white to yellowish acornlike proboscis and a reddish collar. Golden acorn worms are deposit feeders that ingest organic material from the sediment.

These worms, which have been reported to grow to a length of 3 feet, live in mucus-lined burrows with an opening to the surface at each end of the burrow. They extrude their coils of iodine-scented, sandy feces at one opening and feed on sediments at the other end of the burrow.

Look for the eastern auger snail, *Terebra dislocata*, lurking around the fecal coils of acorn worms. These screw-shaped snails prey on golden acorn worms, particularly during the night. There is often a depression in the surface of the mudflat because, as the acorn worm feeds, it causes the sediments to slump. The golden acorn worm is quite common on high-salinity mudflats and is distributed along the Inner Coast from North Carolina to Florida.

Kowalevski's worm, *Saccoglossus kowalevskii*, has

assumed the status of a laboratory mouse to many scientists interested in the genetic code of this worm and its relatives. In addition, biochemists are investigating the production of a rather odiferous compound of brominated phenols and other toxic compounds in these worms. The compounds emit the odor of iodine and are thought to be a chemical defense to avoid predators. Other scientists are studying the embryological and neurological relationships between this obscure group of worms and echinoderms and chordates. Kowalevski's worm has a helical coiled trunk and feeds in a different manner than does the golden acorn worm. It feeds by thrusting out its long proboscis and feeding on surface sediments. The telltale coils of feces that are deposited on the surface are smaller and not as tightly coiled as the golden acorn worm's deposits. Kowalevski's worm is a more northern species and is found as far south as the Carolinas.

Burrowing Anemones. Most anemones graze on the surfaces of sands, rocks, and coral beds, but there are a few species that have adapted to a burrowing existence. The elegant burrowing anemone, *Edwardsia elegans*, is a small, not very showy anemone that, when removed from the mud, resembles a small sea cucumber or worm rather than the flowery sea anemones that grow amid the corals. Though it may appear to be a worm, its longitudinal muscle ridges along its tubular body and its tentacle-encircled mouth are unlike those of any worm. However, when a few inches of water cover the flats, elegant burrowing anemones' tentacled "heads" begin to appear. When the tide ebbs, they retract their tentacles. They are typical estuarine species that live in mid- to high-salinity tidal flats and mud bottoms. The elegant burrowing anemone has a single row of fourteen to sixteen tentacles mounted on a collar followed by a deeply grooved muscular midsection that ends in a globular foot, called the physa, that is used for digging and anchoring in the bottom.

The sea onion, *Paranthus rapiformis*, is another small burrowing sea anemone that lives in high-salinity intertidal flats. It lives mostly in the soft bottoms of the subtidal shallows but can also be found on the flats at very low tide. The sea onion is a white anemone that anchors in the mud by means of an extended basal disk that holds the sea onion in the bottom like a mushroom anchor. Sea onions are larger than elegant burrowing anemones; they may extend about 1 foot into the sand. When they are washed out of their homes by strong waves and currents, they become round and look like buoyant, shiny pearl onions. The elegant burrowing anemone and the sea onion are found all along the Inner Coast.

Burrowing Mollusks. Traces of mollusks are evident on intertidal flats: empty shells and snail tracks are commonly seen on the flats, and small round holes on the surface are further clues to the unseen presence of mollusks below the surface. There are many species hidden below. Literally hundreds of individuals live in close-packed communities, vying for space and food with dense populations of worms and other infaunal animals. Some mollusks are miniscule and others are quite large; some species burrow deep into the mud and others lie just below the surface. A number of species, such as fan-shaped pen shells, scallops, and lucines, are primarily subtidal creatures that may also dwell in the flats.

Burrowing Razor Clams. Burrowing razor clams are some of the most abundant species that inhabit tidal flats. They usually have two characteristics in common: a fleshy, strong, and extensible foot used for quickly burrowing into the mud and sand, and a pair of siphons that can be extended above the surface of the mud and into the surrounding water. The incurrent siphon draws in oxygenated water and plankton or organic detritus, and the excurrent siphon expels waste products.

Razor clam shells are often strewn over the flats—a complete shell here and fragments there—indicate that somewhere in these muddy environs there are some razor clams. There are several species of razor clams (also known as jackknife clams) that live in the intertidal flats of the Inner Coast: the stout tagelus, the purplish tagelus, and the green, Atlantic, and minor jackknife clams. All five species occur along the Inner Coast from Virginia to the Florida Keys.

The stout tagelus, *Tagelus plebius*, has olive green to brownish yellow valves that are rounded and gaping at both ends. These deep-burying clams live in mucus-lined burrows in which the clam can ascend and descend by means of its robust but flexible foot.

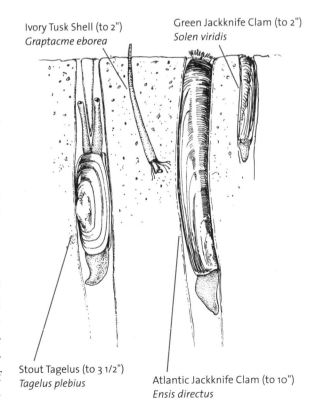

Ivory Tusk Shell (to 2")
Graptacme eborea

Green Jackknife Clam (to 2")
Solen viridis

Stout Tagelus (to 3 1/2")
Tagelus plebius

Atlantic Jackknife Clam (to 10")
Ensis directus

The stout razor clam's siphons are separate and are capable of elongating to 6 inches. The siphons have blunt tentacles that the clam uses to seal off the end of its burrow. Look for two small round holes on the surface about 1 to 3 inches apart. The stout tagelus is very abundant in some areas and is common in mid- to high-salinity waters.

The purplish tagelus, *Tagelus divisus*, is a smaller and more delicate version of the stout tagelus. It has rather thin, shiny, purplish shells that are often marked with reddish brown to purple streaks. The purplish tagelus lives in high-salinity waters in sandy mud.

The green jackknife clam, *Solen viridis*, belongs to the true razor clam family, Solenidae. The genus, *Solen*, is from the Greek for "pipe" or "channel," referring to the elongated shells of this group. A true razor clam looks very much like the case of an old-fashioned straight razor. Their shells are markedly elongated, about 4 times as long as wide, and usually gaped at both ends. The green jackknife clam is somewhat compressed and has a nearly straight hinge line. A live green jackknife clam has a glossy, almost varnishlike greenish to brownish periostracum. Green jackknife clams are found in rather high-salinity flats.

The Atlantic jackknife, *Ensis directus*, is a remarkably agile, razor clam. It can not only dig into wet sand with lightning speed but can also swim. The Atlantic jackknife clam is long and thin and slightly curved. Its shell is a shiny olive green that looks as if it has been varnished. These common, and sometimes quite abundant, razor clams normally lie deep below the surface in permanent burrows and are disclosed only by their keyhole-shaped siphon holes. When they feed, they lie close to the tops of their burrows, extend their very short siphons into the water, and pump in organic material and plankton suspended in the water. When they are disturbed by the ap-

proaching footfall of a collector or by a heron looking for a meal, they quickly contract their feet and vanish deep into their burrows. However, you may see a few Atlantic jackknife clams sticking up out of the mud. These clams seem to be attempting to pop up out of their burrows. This, apparently, sometimes happens when they are attacked from below by the predacious milky ribbon worm. *Ensis minor*, the minor jackknife clam, is a 3-inch-long, paler version of the Atlantic jackknife clam.

Tusk Shells. Scaphopods (literally, "shovel feet"), commonly called tusk shells, are a distinctive group of about 350 species of mollusks, all of which are marine. Most species of tusk shells live in the deepwater sediments of the world's oceans; there are a few species, however, that live in the shallows, and some that live in the intertidal zone. Tusk shells resemble miniature elephant tusks; they are slightly curved and tubular, with openings at both ends of the shell. The large end of the shell is embedded in the sediments by a cone-shaped foot while the tapered, narrow end extends above the bottom mud into the water. The strong burrowing foot can be extended into the bottom and serves to anchor the tusk shell. As the foot pulls the tusk shell through the sediment, long, sticky threads of tentacles, called ceptacula, borne

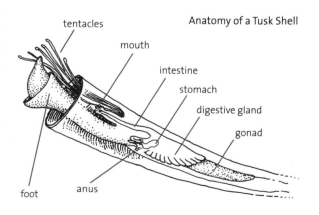

Anatomy of a Tusk Shell

tentacles
mouth
intestine
stomach
digestive gland
gonad
foot
anus

on the tusk shell's head snare small algal cells and other bits of food. The food is then transferred to the grinding radulae contained within the inconspicuous and reduced head of the tusk shell. The sexes are separate in tusk shells. When the female releases her eggs, they are externally fertilized by the males. The eggs hatch into the typical molluskan free-swimming larvae and a few days later develop into the final adult form and settle into the sediment. Indians of the northwest Pacific coast once strung necklaces of tusk shells and used them as wampum.

The ivory tusk shell, *Graptacme eborea*, is a shell of the shallows and the intertidal flats. The shell is a polished translucent white, sometimes tinged with pink and with a few fine scratches at the narrow end. Empty ivory tusk shells are often seen along the swash zone of beaches and scattered on the flats from North Carolina to Florida.

Burrowing Snails. Shark eye snails and white baby ear snails plow through the sediments in search of other mollusks; each snail has a large foot and an even larger appetite. Shallow furrows in the soft sediments are a sure sign that a shark eye or a white baby ear is on the move. These highly predacious hunters feed on the soft flesh of clams and snails by rasping away the shells of their victims, leaving characteristic holes that can be frequently seen near the beaks of dead clam shells. Snails in this family, Naticidae, build distinctive egg cases called sand collars, created from sand and copious amounts of mucus. Sand collars can reach 6 inches in diameter; they, or at least pieces of them, can be found on the flats and beaches.

The shark eye snail, often called moon snail, *Neverita duplicata*, is common on sandy intertidal flats and beaches throughout the Inner Coast. The large, globular, polished slate gray to tan shell is usually flattened and wider than high. Snails in this

Shark Eye Snail (to 4")
Neverita duplicata

White Baby Ear (to 1")
Sinum perspectivum

side view

family have very large apertures; the operculum that seals off the aperture is thin, brown, and horny.

The white baby ear, *Sinum perspectivum*, is a very flat, ear-shaped snail with an enormous aperture. The aperture is so wide and the shell is so flat that when you look into the empty shell, you can see the spire of the shell. The shells of live white baby ears, unlike the almost pure white shells collected on the surface, are dull gray covered with a brown periostracum. The large white mantle, a fleshy organ that regulates the growth of the shell in mollusks, almost entirely envelops the shell as the snail burrows through the sandy sediment. The white baby ear snail is difficult to confuse with any other species.

Burrowing Crustaceans. Snapping shrimps, sometimes called ghost shrimps, and mud shrimps are soft-bodied crustaceans that are more closely related

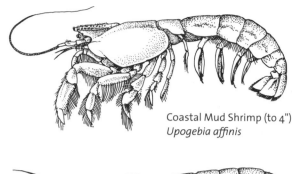

Coastal Mud Shrimp (to 4")
Upogebia affinis

Short-Browed Mud Shrimp (to 2 1/2")
Gilvossius setimanus

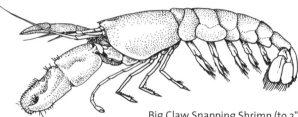

Big Claw Snapping Shrimp (to 2")
Alpheus heterochaelis

to hermit crabs than to shrimp. They look like pale, limp crayfish. Snapping shrimps have one claw that is much larger and longer than the other, and they also have a fringe of long hairs, called setae, on their second pair of legs. Some mud shrimps have claws that are equal in size. Their rostrum, the forward extension of their carapace, projects beyond their eyes. Typical of all decapod crustaceans, female snapping shrimps and mud shrimps carry their developing eggs under their abdomen, where they are attached to the hairy pleopods, sometimes called swimmerets. When the eggs hatch, tiny larvae, the zoeae, are released into the water, where they dance with the

plankton. After a few weeks, those that survive the onslaught of marauding fishes settle into the muds, where they develop into adults. Many snapping and mud shrimp species are burrowers that dig complex burrows that sometimes resemble tangles of tubular spaghetti. Other species simply wriggle under rocks and oyster shells; some may even be found in sponges. The soft-bodied burrowing shrimps rapidly eat their way through the sediments, feeding on microorganisms. Look for small holes about 1/4 inch in diameter near the low-tide line that are surrounded by fecal pellets deposited by the shrimps tunneling below. Mud shrimps often live communally with several others, each occupying one of the many branched chambers that are 2 or more feet deep. Snapping shrimps live in shallow depressions under shells on mudflats, and they sometimes announce their presence when they make a distinct snapping sound with their large claw.

The coastal mud shrimp, *Upogebia affinis*, is about 4 inches long and has a flat rostrum. The short-browed mud shrimp, *Gilvossius setimanus*, is smaller than the coastal mud shrimp and has a shorter, less obvious rostrum. The big-claw snapping shrimp, *Alpheus heterochaelis*, has a more robust body than the mud shrimps and boasts a large claw that creates the characteristic snapping sound.

Then there are the mantis shrimps. There are over 400 species that live in many regions of the sea, from deep waters to shallow subtropical and tropical habitats. They burrow into the mud or lie in wait in coral and rocky crevices. These highly predacious animals with the evocative common names spearers, smashers, and thumb splitters are only distantly related to shrimp. These raptorial carnivores feed on fishes, mollusks, crustaceans, and other mantis shrimps. *Squilla empusa* is the most common species of mantis shrimp along the Inner Coast. The species name means "ghost," but this is a ghost with bril-

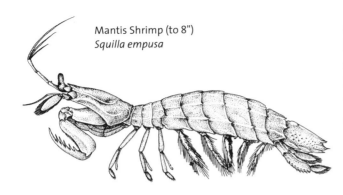

Mantis Shrimp (to 8")
Squilla empusa

liant green eyes and long, jackknife claws that lash out and snap tight like those of the better-known garden-variety praying mantis. These shrimps look like flattened lobsters with pale chartreuse bodies 8 to 10 inches long. Each segment of the abdomen is outlined in dark green and bright yellow. Few people have an opportunity to see these rather common creatures, as they are mostly nocturnal and lurk beneath the surface in chambered burrows. They live along the low intertidal zone of mudflats and in deeper waters as well.

Birds of Intertidal Flats

As the tides ebb and the intertidal flats emerge from the sea awash with seaweeds and alive with prowling crabs and industrious worms, the birds arrive. Rafts of gulls sun themselves in the shallows, and clouds of small sandpipers alight on the flats and begin foraging along the shore. Offshore, brown pelicans gracefully glide in unison and then wheel and land on the intertidal flats or in the shallows. Tiny brown sandpipers, "peeps," suddenly appear in compact flocks; they land on the flats, begin their pecking and probing of the sediments, and then suddenly vanish, only to reappear on another flat or farther down the beach.

The variously shaped bills of shorebirds and wad-

ers offer a clue as to how and what they feed on: long-billed, long-legged waders such as herons visually stalk their prey and spear it with a lightning thrust. Ibises sweep the murky water and the soft muds with their long, curved bills and reflexively snap their bills closed when they contact unseen prey. Shorebirds range in size from the tiny peeps, such as the least sandpiper, to the larger plovers. Small sandpipers and plovers have small bills and feed mostly by sight. The larger shorebirds, such as whimbrels and godwits, are equipped with long, sensitive bills and do most of their feeding by probing the sand and mud for hidden quarry.

The least sandpiper, *Calidris minutilla*, is the smallest member of the sandpiper family. This little bird, about the size of a sparrow, winters along the Inner Coast on mudflats in tidal creeks, along the edges of marshes, and on sand beaches. It is not only the smallest sandpiper but also the brownest. It has greenish yellow legs and a short, thin, dark bill. Least sandpipers are often in mixed flocks of other species of sandpipers. This little peep is somewhat approachable and frequently will not take wing until some invisible barrier is breached. Least sandpipers feed on marine worms, amphipods, small mollusks, insects, and occasionally seeds.

The western sandpiper, *Calidris mauri*, is the largest of the peeps, but using size in the field to identify

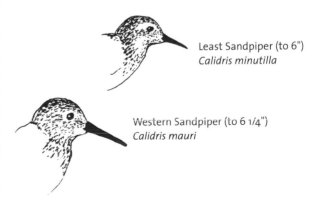

Least Sandpiper (to 6")
Calidris minutilla

Western Sandpiper (to 6 1/4")
Calidris mauri

Dunlins, Calidris alpina *(to 8 1/2"), and two short-billed dowitchers,* Limnodromus griseus *(to 11"), probe for food on an intertidal flat.*

peeps is difficult, for the difference among the three species of peeps—the least, the semipalmated, and the western sandpipers—is only a matter of 1/4 inch or so. The western sandpiper has darker legs than does the least sandpiper. It has a dumpier body shape, somewhat like that of a dunlin, than the least and semipalmated sandpipers. Western sandpipers seem to wade in deeper waters than the others, where they probe for amphipods, worms, and small mollusks. The western sandpiper commonly overwinters along the Inner Coast on intertidal flats.

Dowitchers are stocky and methodical birds with long bills and relatively short legs. There are two species in the area: the short-billed dowitcher, *Limnodromus griseus,* and the long-billed dowitcher, *Limnodromus scolopaceus.* The species name of the long-billed dowitcher means "pointed," and both species have long and pointed bills. Dowitchers have distinctive white or cream-colored eyebrows and are dull

gray above and white below during the winter, when we see them along the Inner Coast. The two species are quite similar in appearance, and the difference in the length of their bills is so subtle that it is difficult to distinguish between them. Some experts listen for the "tu-tu-tu" call of the short-billed dowitcher to separate it from the long-billed dowitcher's high, thin "keek." The two species also favor different habitats: short-billed dowitchers live on estuarine mudflats and sand beaches, whereas long-billed dowitchers prefer freshwater mudflats. Both species wade along the edges of the water, probing the muddy sediments with their long bills. Their rapid up-and-down feeding is quite amusing to watch and has been compared to the rhythmic motion of a sewing machine. Short-billed dowitchers feed extensively on bamboo worms, amphipods, and clams; long-billed dowitchers feed on a variety of insects, spiders, mollusks, and plant seeds.

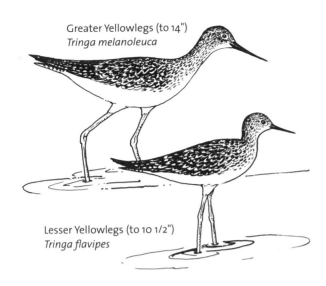

Greater Yellowlegs (to 14")
Tringa melanoleuca

Lesser Yellowlegs (to 10 1/2")
Tringa flavipes

The dunlin, *Calidris alpina*, is a small shorebird (peep), only slightly larger than sanderlings. Dunlins are often seen on intertidal flats and along beaches where the waves are receding. They have a hunched stance and appear to be neckless, and they are sometimes referred to as dumpy because of their shape. The dunlin has a black bill that is slightly drooped at the tip and black legs. In the summer, it is gray with a reddish brown back and a black belly patch; in the winter, it is predominantly gray. Dunlins are often seen in large numbers on Inner Coast mudflats and along estuarine shores. Like their close relatives the sanderlings, they peck and probe in a rapid series of forays, feeling for worms and small mollusks in the mud.

The lesser yellowlegs, *Tringa flavipes*, and the greater yellowlegs, *Tringa melanoleuca*, pose the same identification dilemma as the two dowitcher species. How do you tell one from another? The answer is that they are very difficult to differentiate unless they are seen together, which is usually not the case. The greater yellowlegs is slightly larger, about 14 inches long, as compared to about 10 inches for the lesser yellowlegs. The greater yellowlegs also has a longer bill that may be slightly upturned. The plumage of the two species is similar: brownish gray backs marked with white speckles, white bellies, and brownish gray streaks on their breasts and necks. The lesser yellowlegs, however, is not as strongly marked and is somewhat paler. Both have long yellow legs, sometimes tending to orange. These are very vocal birds and their calls are similar, "tew-tew-tew" with some slight variations. They are often seen on mudflats and in the shallows feeding on insect larvae, worms, snails, shrimps, and small fishes.

The spotted sandpiper, *Actitis macularia*, and the solitary sandpiper, *Tringa solitaria*, are larger than the least and western sandpipers. Spotted and solitary sandpipers bob and teeter almost as if they are unsure of their footing. The solitary sandpiper is larger than the spotted sandpiper and somewhat resembles its close relatives the greater and lesser

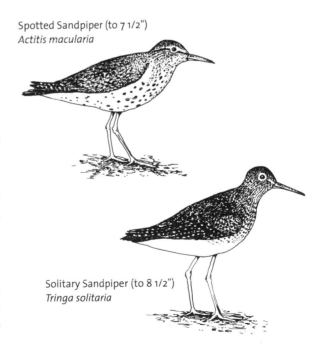

Spotted Sandpiper (to 7 1/2")
Actitis macularia

Solitary Sandpiper (to 8 1/2")
Tringa solitaria

yellowlegs. The adult solitary sandpiper in its summer plumage has a dark gray to brown back speckled with white, a white belly, and a characteristic white eye ring. Solitary sandpipers frequently bob their heads, but not as mechanically and constantly as do spotted sandpipers. The solitary sandpiper, true to its name, is seldom seen in the company of another one of its kind. It favors freshwater or brackish water mudflats, where it preys on insects, spiders, crayfish, and worms.

Spotted sandpipers are often called "spotties" or "teeter-tails" because they are boldly marked in the summer, with many round black spots scattered on their breasts and bellies, and because they seem to be in constant motion, teetering back and forth and

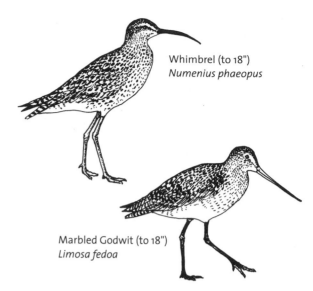

Whimbrel (to 18")
Numenius phaeopus

Marbled Godwit (to 18")
Limosa fedoa

Two American oystercatchers, Haematopus palliatus *(to 18 1/2"), feed on exposed oysters on a mudflat while a group of glossy ibises,* Plegadis falcinellus *(to 2'), search for worms and mollusks buried in the mud.*

Two black-necked stilts, Himantopus mexicanus *(to 14"), and an American avocet,* Recurvirostra americana *(to 18"), strut along a mud flat.*

bobbing their heads as they search for amphipods and other small crustaceans and worms on mudflats and along the edges of tidal creeks.

Godwits and whimbrels are very large sandpipers with the typical streaking and barring of the group; godwits have subtly upturned bills, whereas whimbrels have decurved, or down-curved, bills.

The marbled godwit, *Limosa fedoa*, has a long, slightly upturned bill that is brownish black at the tip and shades into pinkish orange at the base. It is a brownish bird overall—some experts call it cinnamon colored—with black mottling on its back. Flocks of marbled godwits winter along the Inner Coast on mudflats, salt meadows, beaches, and marshes, where

they feed on mollusks, crustaceans, and insects by probing in the mud with their long bills.

The whimbrel, *Numenius phaeopus*, is one of eight species of curlews, all of which have down-curved bills. It is a dusky, gray-brown bird with a brown bill, gray legs, and a dark brown or black eye stripe. Even though they have long bills, whimbrels pick rather than probe as they feed on crabs, amphipods, worms, and mollusks on tidal flats.

Of all the wading birds that are seen along the Inner Coast, the American oystercatcher, *Haematopus palliatus*, is one of the most obvious and easiest to identify. This boldly marked, stocky bird with its large orange bill, red eye ring, pink legs, and black

Reddish Egret (to 30")
Egretta rufescens

and white plumage looks like no other bird along the shore. It has a wonderfully specialized and powerful bill that is laterally flattened and adapted for feeding on oysters and other mollusks. It is adept at stealthily stalking oysters at low tide along the edges of tidal flats. A wading American oystercatcher plunges its bill between the slightly gaping oyster shells and severs the adductor muscle of the oyster to prevent it from closing. Sometimes, rather than stabbing its prey, the oystercatcher resorts to hammering the shell of the hapless mollusk with a rapid series of blows until the shell of the oyster, clam, or mussel is shattered and the soft body within can be grasped and eaten. These chunky, chicken-size birds often loaf and preen on the flats and beaches in pairs or in small groups. They will often allow you to approach before taking wing.

The American avocet, black-necked stilt, and glossy ibis are also birds that are easily identified.

These are long-legged waders with striking plumage and highly adapted bills.

The American avocet, *Recurvirostra americana*, has a thin and fine-drawn upturned bill, black and white wings, and a buff, almost cinnamon-colored head and neck in the summer; its winter plumage is grayish. This pigeon-size bird with long, grayish green legs wades in the shallows near brackish and freshwater mudflats and marshes. It sweeps its wispy upturned bill from side to side and feeds on small crustaceans and insects.

The black-necked stilt, *Himantopus mexicanus*, is placed in the same family as the American avocet. The birds have similar body shapes; however, the black-necked stilt has very long red legs, a glossy black back, and a long, straight, sharp-pointed black bill. The back of its neck is black, as is its head; it has a white patch above its eyes, and a white neck and belly. Black-necked stilts are noisy, gregarious, and excitable birds and are known in some parts of the Caribbean as crackpot soldiers. Black-necks frequently utter high-pitched "kik-kik-kik" calls. Black-necked stilts favor freshwater mudflats and marshes, where they feed by sight on a variety of insects, snails, shrimp, crayfish, and aquatic plant seeds. Both the avocet and black-necked stilt fly with their long legs extended well beyond their tails.

The glossy ibis, *Plegadis falcinellus*, has a distinctive, long, down-curved bill that its species name aptly describes as "sickle shaped." The glossy ibis is a dark bird that appears almost black in low light; however, in bright light, its wings are greenish marked with purple and pink, and its body is chestnut brown. Glossy ibises often feed on tidal flats, but they prefer marshes and moist meadows, where they feed in flocks by probing for insects, crayfish, crabs, and snails. They often fly in V formation and sometimes wheel and soar, similar to wood storks.

The reddish egret, *Egretta rufescens*, is a medium-size heron that stands about 30 inches tall. It is an active, almost erratic bird that runs, prances, spreads its wings in an arching canopy, stabs a crab or a fish, and then begins the dance once again. A breeding adult bears shaggy reddish plumes on its neck and head; its strong pink bill is tipped with black, and its back is slate gray. There is also another color form, or morph, that is pure white with blue-gray legs. The reddish egret is almost always near saltwater on tidal flats, salt pannes, and red mangrove swamps. Along the Atlantic coast, its range is limited to south Florida and particularly the Florida Keys.

5

Places to Settle
Pilings, Floating Docks, Rubble Structures, and Mangrove Prop Roots

Almost any hard surface along the shoreline and in the shallows is a haven for a multitude of seaweeds and sessile animals requiring a firm base on which to grow and reproduce. They may be attached to manmade structures, including bottles and flotsam, or to natural substrates, such as oyster shells, rooted aquatic plants, pebbles, and stones. They may be found on rare natural rocky areas along the Inner Coast and on mangrove prop roots in the warmer waters of Florida. These are wonderful places to observe some often unnoticed plants and animals up close. Lean over a floating pier to watch the rhythmic pumping of feeding barnacles and the swaying of delicate hydroids. Look down into the water around a piling to see tiny shrimps and crabs, lovely flower-like sea anemones, and curious organisms that may be animals . . . or are they plants?

A great proportion of hard surfaces in the Inner Coast are introduced manmade structures, such as rock jetties and groins that have been constructed to stabilize the transport of sediments. Some structures, such as seawalls, breakwaters, and bulkheads, have been built parallel to the shoreline to minimize or prevent erosion. Then there are the countless private piers, floating docks, marinas, and bridges that have been built all along the tidal shoreline of the Inner Coast. All of these manmade structures provide habitats for a wide variety of plants and animals.

Sessile animals and plants, organisms that attach to a hard substrate or to one another, are a diverse lot; they belong to many different and unrelated groups. However, they share some characteristics: They are quick to exploit available habitats, and most sessile animal species produce motile, planktonic larvae that allow the next generation to colonize a new habitat. Many sessile species can produce asexually as well, such as bryozoans. Their larvae can reproduce copies of themselves by budding, and then the buds asexually reproduce again and again, so that in a

matter of several days, there may be thousands of individuals forming a colony that began from just a few larvae. Sessile animals also mature rapidly, so that within a short time after settling, a new generation is released to colonize another piling or rock.

This chapter covers mostly manmade structures where tidal changes affect the distribution of flora

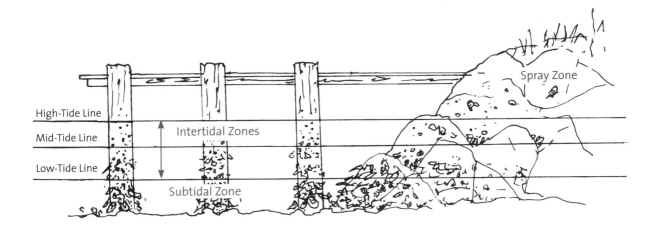

High-Tide Line

Mid-Tide Line — Intertidal Zones

Low-Tide Line

Subtidal Zone

Spray Zone

and fauna. Changes in tidal amplitude also affect the communities on and around red mangrove prop roots, which mimic in many ways those of pilings, docks, and other structures. Other chapters will discuss the colonization of sessile organisms and associated fauna in oyster communities, subtidal seagrass meadows, and coral patch reefs.

Pilings, floating docks, mangrove prop roots, and other manmade and natural structures, similar to sand beaches and intertidal flats, have vertical intertidal zones that are typically characterized by different forms of life. The changing tides generally create a pattern of zones or vertical banding, which is driven not only by the tidal range and salinity but by ecological interactions as well. The highest zone, the spray zone, and the other zones down through the subtidal levels generally have predictable assemblages of plants and animals. However, storms, diseases, population explosions, and predation often rearrange the communities so that a typical group of organisms usually found growing in a particular zone or band is obliterated or greatly changed.

Ecologists have given intertidal levels, or zones, various names: splash or spray fringe, high-tide level, mid-tide level, low-tide level, and subtidal level. Oth-

ers use supralittoral (splash zone), mid-littoral, and low-littoral. Still others separate the tidal zones into the splash and spray zone, high-tide zone, mid-tide zone, and low-tide zone. We use a combination of those terms. We refer to the highest tidal zone as the spray zone; below that is the high-tide zone; still lower is the mid-tide zone; and finally there are the low tide and subtidal zones. Where there are extensive tidal amplitudes, such as along the South Carolina and Georgia coasts, there may be differences between low tide and high tide of 8 feet or more. The zones with their characteristic groups of species are usually quite distinct. Where the tidal range is minimal, such as in some North Carolina sounds and the Indian River Lagoon in Florida, zonation is often obscure or absent.

The spray zone is where semiterrestrial crabs and sea roaches may be seen scurrying between limpets and chitons. Bluegreen algal species typically grow in the highest intertidal zone and appear as a dark band or stain on the surface of the structure. Green algae and some species of red algae are usually found below the bluegreens, and here the intermixed species grow in a profusion of shapes and colors. Some species have thin, flat fronds; some are tubular; some bear thin, green filaments. There are thick, dark green, jellylike seaweeds with branching fingers, and down deeper, there are wiry brown algal species that are equipped with tendrils for attachment and air bladders for flotation. There is great competition for a place to settle, and where there are no hard surfaces available for occupancy, many types of seaweeds simply attach to other species. Seaweeds that grow attached to other species are called epiphytes. But the confusion of sessile species doesn't stop with the seaweeds, as many animals require places for attachment as well.

On the highest intertidal zone of the structure, there is often a heavy encrustation of barnacles and, below them, other species of barnacles and clumps of mussels and oysters. At the low-tide line and below, the subtidal zone, where the structure—be it manmade or a mangrove prop root—is almost always submerged, the barnacles, oysters, and mussels are joined by an amazing diversity of invertebrates, including several species of sponges, hydroids, anemones, and soft corals. There are many bryozoan species and tunicates of many colors, textures, and shapes. Where there are sessile plants and animals, there are grazers and predators intermixed with tube-dwelling amphipods and sessile worms. There are also motile, grazing amphipods; slithering worms; predacious sea stars; a large number of crustaceans, including swimming and mud crabs; and many shrimp species. Small, secretive fishes dwell within the sessile community: secretive little gobies and blennies occupy empty oyster shells or lurk in small spaces between some tunicates and mussels. Other, usually somewhat larger fishes, including pinfish, black sea bass, gray snapper, and vividly marked porkfish, which often live on nearby oyster bars or other hard bottoms, make forays to rock jetties or pier pilings to feed on the rich assortment of plants and animals congregated on the hard surfaces.

Most of the species included here can be found throughout the Inner Coast. Tropical species, however, are more limited in their distribution along the Inner Coast and are discussed separately in the section of this chapter on mangrove prop roots, rocks, and manmade structures of south Florida.

Spray Zone and High-Tide Zone Communities

Plants and animals that occupy the spray zone are able to tolerate daily dry and wet conditions and heavy wave action that most other species cannot endure. They are able to thrive because other organisms that could be their competitors for space and food, as well as some predators, simply cannot tolerate the harsh conditions.

On the drier regions of piers and rocks, you can often catch sight of a small mottled crab, often called the wharf crab or friendly crab, scooting from one hiding place to another. Here too, marsh periwinkles climb high on the rocks and cluster in great numbers, just as they do on marsh grass stems.

Scurrying slate gray isopods, *Ligia exotica*, called sea roaches or, in Europe, sea slaters, are a common sight on pilings, jetties, and seawalls. These little isopods can be abundant, particularly in shady areas, and are often confused for cockroaches as they pick over organic debris. Sea roaches are related to a terrestrial group of isopods that have adapted to living near the sea. They graze above the water and only periodically do they move down to the water's surface to moisten their gills. They occupy an ecological niche that is similar to that of ghost crabs and fiddler crabs, but unlike those crustaceans, they do not release their larvae to the water. The female sea roach broods its young in an abdominal pouch and then releases them on land as tiny but fully formed sea

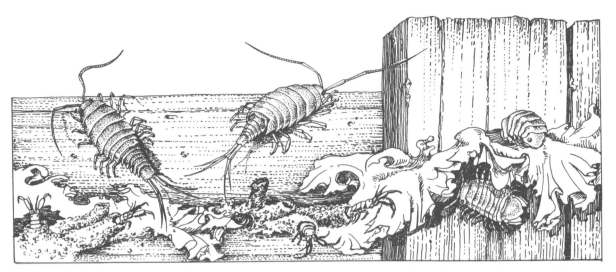

On the edge of a pier, there is a busy community. Sea roaches, Ligia exotica *(1 1/4"), quickly scatter about; sea pill bugs,* Sphaeroma quadridentatum *(3/8"), graze over a patch of sea lettuce; and slender tube-builder amphipods,* Corophium lacustre *(to 1/4"), pop in and out of their soft mud tubes.*

roaches that race about as quickly and furtively as the adults.

Barnacles and Other Crustaceans

Acorn barnacles are familiar to anyone who has been to the shore or scraped the bottom of a boat, but few would guess that they are crustacean relatives of crabs, not mollusks. Exposed barnacle shells are tightly closed and show no signs of life. However, if you place a barnacle in water, two "doors" will open, and a graceful fan of feathery appendages will slowly unfold and begin rhythmically sweeping the water. The tiny, feathery appendages are jointed and covered with a chitinous exoskeleton characteristic of crustaceans. The biologist Louis Agassiz described the barnacle as "nothing more than a little shrimplike animal standing on its head in a limestone house and kicking food into its mouth." Its conical limestone "house" is composed of six overlapping plates with an opening at the top covered by two valves (the

doors) and a flat-bottomed base secured to a hard surface by biological cement produced by the barnacle. Barnacles are often dislodged or die and leave only their circular, flat bases as evidence of their former presence.

Barnacles grow by adding calcium carbonate, derived from seawater, to the edges of each plate, which increases the diameter of the internal cavity. Meanwhile, the shrimplike organism within must also grow by molting its exoskeleton, just as blue crabs and other crustaceans do. Barnacles have both male and female organs and are, therefore, hermaphroditic; however, their eggs must be cross-fertilized by other individuals. Once cemented to a hard surface, barnacles, of course, cannot move, so fertilization is accomplished by a slender sperm tube that protrudes out of one barnacle and into the open valves of its neighbor. The fertilized eggs are incubated within the barnacle shell until they hatch into tiny larvae, which are then released to the water. In late spring and early summer, the waters swarm with barnacle

Sequential opening and closing of a barnacle.

larvae and larvae of other organisms as well. The larvae are so abundant that there may be thousands in a few gallons of seawater. The larvae are an important food source for young fishes and filter-feeding mollusks. They are consumed in such great numbers that relatively few survive to become adult barnacles.

The barnacle larva develops through two stages: nauplius and cypris. Nauplii are triangular-shaped creatures that persist for only a few days and then transform into cyprides, which resemble tiny, transparent seeds. Cypris larvae swim about for several days until they find suitable places to attach. Usually they attach in an area where other barnacles of the same species have previously settled; apparently, older barnacles release a chemical to the water that attracts the young barnacles to the same area. The cypris glues its head to the hard surface with cement produced by special antennal glands; industrial

chemists have tried to synthesize this cement, to no avail. The cypris soon begins to form the calcareous plates that will eventually encase its soft body.

Barnacles are prone to sudden die-offs even though they seem to be well protected by their hard, conical cases. Most species quickly succumb to prolonged drying, extremely cold weather, and harsh winds, but little gray and star barnacles manage to persist, particularly in the absence of competing organisms. Barnacles are also attacked by numerous predators and competing species that either feed on them or grow over them.

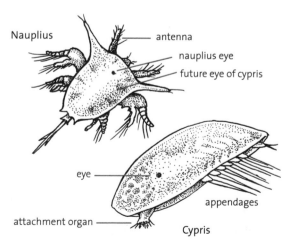

Microscopic stages of barnacle larvae. The nauplius has a single central eye, which is replaced in the cypris stage by two bilateral eyes.

Barnacle Anatomy

valve
jointed appendages
muscle to close valve

mouth
shell cavity
body plate
base

A cross section of a typical barnacle.

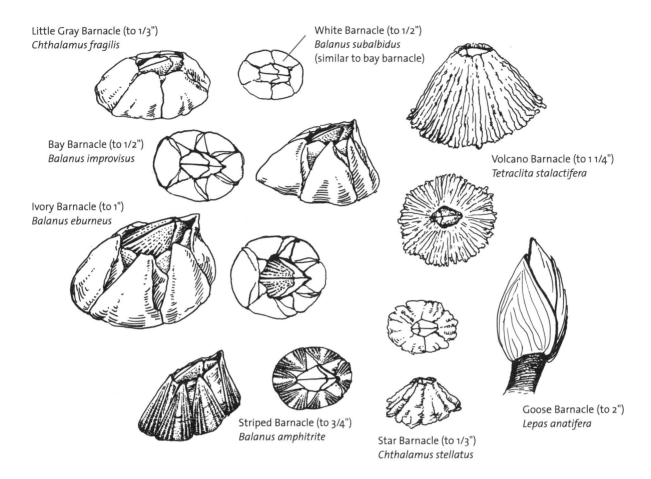

Little Gray Barnacle (to 1/3")
Chthalamus fragilis

White Barnacle (to 1/2")
Balanus subalbidus
(similar to bay barnacle)

Bay Barnacle (to 1/2")
Balanus improvisus

Volcano Barnacle (to 1 1/4")
Tetraclita stalactifera

Ivory Barnacle (to 1")
Balanus eburneus

Striped Barnacle (to 3/4")
Balanus amphitrite

Star Barnacle (to 1/3")
Chthalamus stellatus

Goose Barnacle (to 2")
Lepas anatifera

The little gray barnacle, *Chthalamus fragilis*, also called the fragile barnacle, is a very small barnacle that lives in dense clusters in the highest intertidal zone where it is exposed daily to the sun and the drying effects of wind over longer periods of time than are organisms that are attached in lower tidal zones. Its plates are smooth. Little gray barnacles are often so tightly crowded that they appear to be an uninterrupted, gray, crusty band.

The star barnacle, *Chthalamus stellatus*, lives in the same tidal zones as, and coexists with, the little gray barnacle in areas such as Florida's Indian River Lagoon and farther south. The star barnacle is as small as the little gray barnacle, but it can be distinguished from its close relative by its raggedy shell plates and star-shaped base; the base of the little gray barnacle is somewhat round and smooth. Little gray and star barnacles live on the stems of marsh grasses and on the upper intertidal zone of pilings, seawalls, and rocks, as well as on red mangrove prop roots.

Chitons and Limpets

The spray zone and high intertidal areas on rocks along the Inner Coast are frequently populated with unusual mollusks such as chitons and limpets, which

Many interesting creatures may be found on rocks within the intertidal zone: scorched mussels, Brachidontes exustus (to 1"), cluster in any crevice; cayenne keyhole limpets, Diodora cayenensis (to 1 1/2"), and eastern beaded chitons, Chaetopleura apiculata (3/4"), cling tenaciously; and an American warty anemone, Bunodosoma cavernata (to 3 1/2" tall), opens and feeds below the water but becomes only a jellied mass on the exposed rock.

thrive where turbulent waves cast spray over alga-coated rocks. Chitons are primitive mollusks; they are flattened oval creatures with shells that consist of eight segments, called valves, aligned in a row and surrounded by a fleshy girdle, the mantle. The eastern beaded chiton, *Chaetopleura apiculata*, is a common chiton found in rocky tidal pools and among the crevices in rock jetties from Virginia to north Florida. Eastern beaded chitons also live in relatively deep water, where they slowly glide over rocks, shells, and mounds of star coral, feeding on encrusting bryozoans and other small creatures. Chitons cling tenaciously with their broad, sole-shaped feet to spray-washed rocks; their feet create such strong suction that they are extremely difficult to dislodge. When they lose their grip or are pried loose, they curl up into balls, similar to the familiar pill bug found in gardens under rocks and rotting wood. Eastern beaded chitons are cream colored to brown.

The cayenne keyhole limpet, *Diodora cayenensis*, is usually seen on wave-washed surfaces along with barnacles, chitons, and periwinkles. These flattened, conical snails grip hard surfaces with the tenacity of chitons; they often grind shallow depressions in rocks to gain a better hold against the relentless surf. Like most limpets, the cayenne keyhole limpet resembles a tiny coolie hat with a dumbbell-shaped opening (the keyhole) placed slightly off-center from the shell's apex. The keyhole allows water and waste to exit. Cayenne keyhole limpets are whitish gray and sometimes pinkish; their radial ribs are rough, and every fourth rib is noticeably larger. These are common snails and are found all along the Inner Coast.

The striped false limpet, *Siphonaria pectinata*,

Striped False Limpet (to 1")
Siphonaria pectinata

Leafy Jewel Box (to 3")
Chama macrophylla

Atlantic Kitten Paw (to 1")
Plicatula gibbosa

has an oval to elliptical base that is slightly conical and also resembles a coolie hat. The background color of the shell is white, and it is striped with small, fine white ribs separated by shallow, reddish brown furrows. The interior of the shell is glossy and striped; the center is creamy brown. This species is known as a false limpet because it clearly resembles the true limpets, but it differs from them in that it is an air breather. The striped false limpet grazes on algae growing on rocks, cement pilings, and seawalls. It ranges from Florida to the West Indies and also may occur in Georgia.

🌱

Mid-Tide Zone to Subtidal Zone Communities

Moving below the highest tide zones to mid- and low-tide levels, the period of inundation is longer and the organisms that settle suffer less deleterious effects from the wind and the heat. Thus the diversity of species increases gradually with submergence. Many more species are found at the low-tide line and even more are found subtidally.

Seaweed Gardens

The mid- and low-tide zones are where several species of algae, usually referred to as seaweeds, are tolerant of exposure and wind and are able to grow in profusion. Many of the seaweeds that grow on pilings and other structures within the intertidal zones of the Inner Coast also grow in the shallows attached to shells, small stones, and seagrasses. Some of the most prominent and abundant green seaweeds that grow on intertidal structures and rocks are the same species commonly seen stranded on beaches and intertidal flats—sea lettuce, hollow-tubed seaweeds, redweeds, and green fleeces. Many other species grow luxuriously on hard intertidal surfaces. These species are also frequently wrenched away from their places of attachment and deposited by currents on beaches and flats. There are hundreds of species of red, green, and brown seaweeds growing in deep waters and the shallows; some of the more common and easily identified species of seaweeds are described below.

Green sea fern, *Bryopsis plumosa* (see chapter 7), has several common names, including moss seaweed, feather moss, sea down, and green hair. These names are quite descriptive of the green seaweed that is characterized by dark green to almost translucent tufts of feathery filaments. These soft green plants grow attached to rocks and pilings in sheltered locations where the wave energy is low.

There are many species of red seaweeds throughout the world; most of them are tropical, and some are important reef builders. Red seaweeds are extremely diverse in shape and color and, as with most seaweeds, are difficult to identify. Many species of *Porphyra*, a common red seaweed known as laver, grow from the highest intertidal zone down to the mid-tide zone and even deeper. The fronds of this reddish brown seaweed are often draped over rocks and mussels, stranded on seawalls and breakwaters, and growing on other seaweed species. Some species of laver are farmed in Japan and other countries and are widely marketed and consumed as nori, thin, dried sheets of seaweed used to wrap sushi.

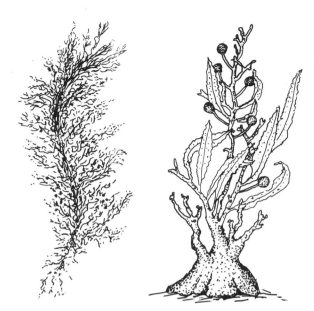

Brown Fuzz Seaweeds (to 2')
Ectocarpus spp.

Long-Leaf Gulfweed (to 2')
Sargassum filipendula

Brown algae are well represented by floating gulf-weeds that are often stranded on beaches and mud-flats. There is, however, a species of gulfweed, or sargassum, that grows attached to stones, shells, rock jetties, and pilings, and there are also smaller, fine-branched brown seaweeds that are related to the giant kelps found growing in colder waters.

Long-leaf gulfweed, *Sargassum filipendula*, grows in offshore shallow and deeper waters, but it also very commonly grows near the high-tide line on jetties and pilings. This wiry plant has rather long and narrow leaflike blades that are buoyed by their numerous spherical air bladders. Each blade has a distinct midrib and coarsely toothed edges. Extracts of this species of gulfweed are extensively used in cosmetic and skin preparations. Gulfweeds, as noted before, are havens for a diverse abundance of small shrimps, amphipods, and fishes.

There are a dozen or more species of brown fuzz seaweeds, collectively placed in the genus *Ectocar-pus* and other closely related genera. Brown fuzz sea-weeds flourish in cooler waters, so during the winter months, when most seaweeds have disappeared, the long, entangled strands of hairlike filaments of brown fuzz seaweeds become quite obvious. Often these brown seaweeds take the form of puffy, almost silky, yellow-brown or olive underwater masses.

Most species of seaweeds that occur on rocks and pilings also grow in shallow subtidal zones during various times of the year. Be aware that these plants are very adaptive and often are not tied to subtidal or intertidal habitats.

Animal Life in Profusion

Just as seaweeds are able to adapt to subtidal and intertidal habitats, many invertebrate species adapt as well. The mix of invertebrate organisms on a piling near the surface of the water is rich and confusing. Some organisms, such as barnacles, oysters, and mussels are usually easily recognized, but the presence of so many fouling organisms (those that settle down and attach to hard surfaces or other organisms) one on top of another is often perplexing.

MOLLUSKS

Oysters often grow in a well-defined band in the intertidal zone; they are quite evident growing on bulk-heads, pilings, and rocks along the Inner Coast, particularly in areas, such as Beaufort, South Carolina, where the tides range several feet between high and low stages.

The scorched mussel, *Brachidontes exustus*, usually grows in a band below oysters and barnacles. These small mussels attach to a hard substrate and to one another with characteristic byssal threads known to seafood lovers as the beard. They are elongated and are adorned with fine radial ribs. They are yellowish brown to coffee brown on the outside, and on the inside they are mottled purplish and creamy white. Scorched mussels sometimes aggregate in such large numbers that they form dense mats on carbonaceous beach pavement, particularly in the Florida Keys and the Caribbean islands.

Other mollusks commonly attached to piers and rocks included the leafy jewel box, *Chama macrophylla*. This small, irregularly rounded clam has leafy scales often referred to as foliations. The lower, deeply cupped, left valve is cemented to a hard surface such as a rock, piling, or seawall; within a coral crevice; or attached to a pen shell. The upper shell, or right valve, is flat and serves as the "lid" for the jewel box. Unfortunately, most leafy jewel boxes that tumble ashore have lost their distinctive leafy projections. The shells may be reddish purple, brown, purple, orange, or white. Leafy jewel boxes extend from the Carolinas to Florida and the West Indies and are more abundant in the southern part of their range.

The Atlantic kitten paw, *Plicatula gibbosa*, is a white to grayish, fan-shaped or cat's paw–shaped clam with five to seven coarse, heavy ribs. The ribs are lightly striped with a reddish brown hue. Unfortunately, when this little clam is tossed up on the beach, the colors quickly fade, and the shell takes on the light gray color of concrete. These are common clams found from the Carolinas to Florida and beyond to the West Indies.

MORE BARNACLES

The ivory barnacle, *Balanus eburneus*, is a common and obvious barnacle that thrives intertidally near the water line as well as subtidally. It is a medium-size to large barnacle that has a distinct conical shape and relatively smooth white plates. These are the barnacles typically found on eastern oysters and on frond and flat tree oysters in tropical waters. Red mangrove prop roots are often covered with ivory barnacles. Two smaller, related species, the bay barnacle, *Balanus improvisus*, and the white barnacle, *Balanus subalbidus*, are tolerant of lower-salinity waters and typically grow in the more brackish portions of Inner Coast estuaries. Another balanoid barnacle, the striped barnacle, *Balanus amphitrite*, is easily identified by its wide, vertical red bands.

The volcano barnacle, *Tetraclita stalactifera*, is a large barnacle found from Charleston, South Carolina, to Florida and southward throughout the tropics in high-salinity water. This distinctive barnacle is easy to identify by its large, creamy to grayish black shell that is conical or sometimes tubular. The shells are incised by fine ribbing, and the openings are often eroded.

There are other barnacles called goose barnacles that do not look like the typical acorn barnacles. Acorn barnacles attach directly to hard substrates and even to the backs of whales, crabs, and sea turtles. Goose barnacles, on the other hand, dangle on somewhat long, rubbery stalks that are cemented to hard surfaces. The shell encasing the animal within is made up of smooth, conical, ivory to cream-colored plates.

There are many legends and myths about the origin of the name "goose barnacle." Monks of the eleventh century claimed that the barnacle goose was an adult goose barnacle. Since barnacle geese were fish, not meat, eating a barnacle goose during Lent was permitted. Others postulate that goose barnacles got their name from their feathery feeding legs, called cirri, that to some resemble bird feathers.

Goose barnacles are creatures of the high seas, where they attach to anything that floats, including timbers, bottles, plastic coolers, and even tangled mats of gulfweeds. Gooseneck barnacles are often cast ashore as mementos of offshore storms. There are two common species of goose barnacles seen along the Inner Coast: the goose barnacle, *Lepas anatifera*, and the scaled goose barnacle, *Lepas pectinata*. The goose barnacle has smooth, almost translucent, bluish white calcareous plates. The scaled goose barnacle is somewhat smaller than the goose barnacle, and its plates are adorned with ridges and spines.

MORE BUGS ON THE PILINGS

A variety of small crustaceans, both amphipods and isopods, wander over barnacles and the damp, prostrate seaweeds that grow intertidally. Some are scuds, the same species that are found in the windrows of seaweed and debris heaped on the upper beaches and intertidal flats. Tube-building amphipods of the *Corophium* genus and other related species are abundant where mud and silt collect in the crevices between seaweeds, barnacles, and other sessile organisms. At times, these slender tube builders, which have mottled gray, flattened bodies similar to isopods, leave their mucus-lined tubes to graze on bits of food, but their usual mode of feeding is to stretch about halfway out of their tubes and strain bits of food out of the water with their large antennae. Slender tubebuilder amphipods are in turn heavily preyed on by fishes, hungry crabs, and nibbling ducks.

Skeleton shrimps, *Caprella* spp., are also curious little amphipods that live in the same area that tubebuilding amphipods do; they particularly like to

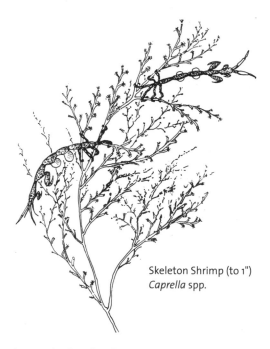

Skeleton Shrimp (to 1")
Caprella spp.

live in hydroid colonies, as well as among seaweeds and sponges. Sometimes there are so many of these shrimplike creatures within a hydroid colony that the hydroids seem to be writhing, but it is not the hydroids but the gangly skeleton shrimps attached to the hydroids by means of their hooked rear legs that are the cause of the rippling movements in the hairy hydroid colony. The sticklike bodies of the skeleton shrimps constantly dip and sway from side to side and back and forth. Their forward legs are free and folded as if in prayer, but they are actually poised to pounce on passing copepods, algal cells, or bits of detritus that come their way. Skeleton shrimps can hide among hydroids and seaweeds because of their peculiar shape and their ability to change color to match their background. They pitch and climb about the branches of hydroids like inchworms. The skeleton shrimp bends down and clasps a branch with its forelegs and then releases its hind legs and moves them forward to meet its forelegs, forming and re-

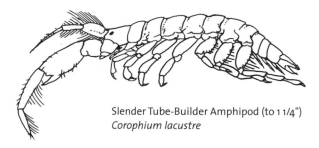

Slender Tube-Builder Amphipod (to 1 1/4")
Corophium lacustre

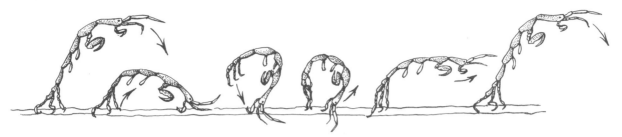

A skeleton shrimp sways up and down as it moves along like an inchworm.

forming a looping movement along the branch. Female skeleton shrimps carry their eggs in transparent abdominal pouches.

MYRIAD SMALL CREATURES

There are seemingly unidentifiable masses of organisms in the high-tide zone that pose perplexing questions, starting with, What are those things? Some of the masses look like small, lobed, grayish brown potatoes. Just beyond those are feathery structures nodding in the currents, and then there are almost transparent globes tinted with a lilac color. There are also some dingy, tan, grapelike structures with just a hint of what might be internal organs. There are red rubbery growths, inky black stains, and thin sheets of crusty, leathery pavement. All of these are the critters of the fouling community—sponges, hydroids, anemones, bryozoans, and tunicates. There are also a number of animals that are found in and around the sessile fouling community: the mobile epibenthos. This group includes slithering polychaetes, crabs and shrimps, and various echinoderms that slowly glide over the bottom and the sessile fouling community.

Sponges: Pore Bearers. Sponges are primitive animals in the phylum Porifera, which means "pore bearer" or "hole bearer," because they are networks of holes and channels that are lined with specialized cells equipped with tiny beating hairs. These cilia create currents and draw in particles of food and expel the waste material; other, amoebalike cells engulf and digest the food. Most sponges are marine or estuarine; however, there are a few species that live in freshwater inland lakes and streams throughout the world. These simple but very diverse animals grow in almost every type of habitat: in the shallows among corals and seagrasses; in very deep waters; and on pilings, rocks, shells, stones, and even the backs of certain crabs. They vary in color. Some form tiny, drab patches; others form brilliantly colored encrustations. They may be purple and red and yellow tubes or gigantic barrels that are large enough to sit in. Sponges grow at various levels on pilings, bulkheads, and rocks, and like most sponges everywhere, they are inhabited by hundreds of different invertebrates and small fishes. The common names of sponges, such as tube sponges, stovepipe sponges, rope sponges, stinker sponges, crumb-of-bread sponges, and boring sponges, to name just a few, rival the curious and descriptive common names of birds.

One of the most conspicuous fouling sponges on pilings and every other hard surface imaginable is the crumb-of-bread sponge, *Halichondria bowerbanki*. It often grows intertwined among seaweeds, hydroids, and worm tubes. The surface of this highly variable sponge has a breadcrumblike texture. This species

Eroded Sponge (colony to 3" wide)
Haliclona loosanoffi

Crumb-of-Bread Sponge (colony to 3' high, 12" wide)
Halichondria bowerbanki

Redbeard Sponge (colony to 8" high, 12" wide)
Microciona prolifera

forms encrusting masses and may be tan to yellowish or even cinnamon colored. The crumb-of-bread sponge is a typical estuarine species found in sounds and bays.

The redbeard sponge, *Microciona prolifera*, is a bright red sponge that is easily identified. These sponges can grow into heavy, rounded masses 1 foot or more in diameter, although smaller specimens are more common. The redbeard sponge is one of the few estuarine species that develops thick, tough, fleshy, intertwining fingers. Young redbeard sponges begin life as flat, bright red encrustations and then develop into the familiar vermillion clumps that attach to pilings and rocks and are often thrust up on beaches and sand bars after a storm.

The eroded sponge, *Haliclona loosanoffi*, and related species belonging to the genus *Haliclona* are usually fragile and delicate. Some form thin crusts, and others, such as the eroded sponge, develop chimneys 1 inch tall or taller bearing oscula for dispersing water and waste products. Eroded sponges are sometimes pink to purple but are more often creamy tan or yellowish gold, with a spongy texture. They are common on pilings, shells, and stones and attached to various seagrasses in the brackish waters of estuaries and sounds down through the Carolinas and perhaps farther south.

Hydroids: Feathery Animals. What appears to be a delicate seaweed frond is often one of the many species of hydroids that find places of attachment on almost any firm substrate. Some hydroids look like wispy, branching plumes; others resemble soft tufts; and still others form white, fuzzy encrustations sprawling over the substrate. Hydroids are closely related to sea anemones, corals, and jellyfishes, all of which belong to the phylum Cnidaria. Organisms within this phylum are characterized by specialized stinging cells, called nematocysts, embedded in their tentacles. In a sense, they are an aggregation of minute anemones that are usually encased in a chitinous covering called a sheath; the individuals are connected to each other within the sheath. Individual animals, or zooids, feed with small tentacles, technically termed hydranths, which are armed with nematocysts that stun their prey. The food then passes into the mouth and into the interconnecting branches of the colony. Some hydroids have elaborate branches with cuplike receptacles, called hydrothecas, that protect each feeding hydranth; other

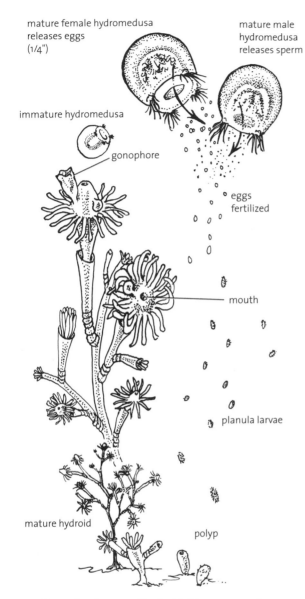

mature female hydromedusa
releases eggs
(1/4")

mature male
hydromedusa
releases sperm

immature hydromedusa

gonophore

eggs
fertilized

mouth

planula larvae

mature hydroid

polyp

The life cycle of a typical hydroid. Mature gonophores from the asexual hydroid stage release small hydromedusae, which eventually mature into male and female stages and which, in turn, release eggs and sperm. After fertilization the eggs develop into planulae. These larvae settle down, attach to a hard substrate, and form polyps that grow into hydroids. Hydroids can also reproduce asexually by dividing and growing.

hydroids have a much simpler architecture. Some hydroid colonies grow to be quite large, as much as 1 foot or more, but most species are just a few inches, and many are only a fraction of an inch tall.

Hydroids have complicated life cycles, as do most species in the phylum Cnidaria; they can, and often do, reproduce asexually and sexually at certain times of the year by budding off gonophores, structures that attach to the stems of adult hydroids. The gonophores produce miniature jellyfishes, hydromedusae, that, when mature, are released and float free in the water. There are many variations on this theme in the hydroid world. Some hydroids, such as the pink-mouth hydroid, produce markedly reduced hydromedusae that never become free swimming. The hydromedusae are the sexual forms of hydroids, which can also asexually reproduce by budding off new individuals. Hydromedusae are translucent and usually less than 1/4 inch in diameter, making them quite inconspicuous in the water. The eggs in female hydromedusae are fertilized by male hydromedusae to produce planulae, larvae that ultimately settle onto hard surfaces and begin to grow the necessary structures to attach and develop stolons, stalks, and hydranths. Eventually the individuals multiply asexually and form colonies of hydroids.

The pink-mouth hydroid, or pink-heart hydroid, *Ectopleura* (formerly *Tubularia*) *crocea*, forms dense tufts of long, sparsely branched and tangled stems. The stems of the pink-mouth hydroid attain a length of about four inches. The hydranths are quite noticeably pink and thus their common name. These conspicuous hydroids are common on pilings and rocks in high salinity waters. There is a closely related species of the pink-mouth, *Ectopleura dumortieri*, which grows in low salinity waters of the Inner Coast.

The bushy wineglass hydroid, *Obelia dichotoma*, is abundant and widely distributed. There are several species of wineglass hydroids, all somewhat

Bushy Wineglass Hydroid (to 4 3/4")
Obelia dichotoma

Garland Hydroid (to 9")
Sertularia cupressina

Stick Hydroids (to 4 3/4")

Eudendrium carneum

Eudendrium ramosum

Feather Hydroid (to 8")
Halocordyle disticha

Tubelarian Hydroids

Tube Hydroid (to 2")
Ectopleura dumortieri

Bushy Hydroid
Bougainvillia spp.

Snail Fur Hydroid (to 1/8")
Hydractinia echinata

Pink-Mouth Hydroid
(to 4" or more)
Ectopleura crocea

similar in appearance. Some species of *Obelia* have unbranched stems that grow in a zigzag fashion. The main stems of bushy wineglass hydroids arise from creeping stolons with short, rather delicate branches growing from the stems' internodes. The hydranths are wineglass shaped or sometimes bell shaped. Overall, bushy wineglass hydroid colonies are tinged a dirty white to tan.

Red stick hydroids, *Eudendrium carneum*, form orangish red–tinged colonies that grow to about 4 3/4 inches high in tangled, thicketlike masses. The hydranths in this species are flared or trumpet shaped, with annulated stems, and some lack tentacles. Stick hydroids typically do not have free-swimming hydromedusae. A similar species, *Eudendrium ramosum*, is white to pinkish green, and this species does have normal hydranths with tentacles.

The feather hydroid, or Christmas tree hydroid, *Halocordyle disticha*, is relatively easy to identify; it has alternately arranged branches mounted on single stems that bear prominent white polyps, "Christmas tree ornaments." The stems are blackish brown, and the hydranths are pink or white or, some say, silvery. They grow to about 7 or 8 inches tall. These graceful, feathery hydroids grow in high-salinity waters where there are strong currents and where they can sweep the water for food. The feather hydroid is apparently a tasty tidbit for foraging sea slugs, shell-less snails known as nudibranchs.

Garland hydroid, *Sertularia cupressina*, has a number of descriptive common names, including sea moss, sea fir, white weed, fern hydroid, and white hair. Watermen in the Chesapeake Bay refer to this species as white hair because, when they pull in their nets and other fishing gear in the winter and spring, their fishing equipment is often draped and wrapped with great quantities of this whitish hydroid. The growth form of garland hydroid is somewhat three dimensional; the main stem gives rise to side branches that then divide into two additional branches so that the colony resembles a salty fir tree. Plumes of this prolific hydroid extend to 9 inches. This is a cold-season species that attaches to almost any hard surface—oysters, mussels, rocks, pilings, bottles, slow-moving spider crabs, and worm cases. It dies out as the water warms, and consequently it is not evident on rocks and piers in the summer.

Bushy hydroids, *Bougainvillia* spp., form dense, scraggly gray to whitish colonies that are abundant during the summer and tend to die off in the colder months. *Bougainvillia* is a genus that has many nondescript, scraggly species that are a challenge to identify even for most experts.

Sea Anemones and Soft Corals. Sea anemones and soft corals, unlike hydroids and jellyfishes, have no medusa stage. Their mouths are surrounded by tentacles armed with stinging nematocysts typical of cnidarians. Anemones are usually solitary, sessile, single animals, whereas soft corals are colonial. Anemones are usually columnar or cylindrical when fully extended; they have a pedal disc that attaches to the substrate and a tentacled oral disc. When the tide has receded and anemones are stranded out of the water, they retract their tentacles and look like small globs of jelly. Place them back in the water, and soon their tentacles emerge and unfold, and they once again become beautiful flowers of the sea. Anemones can creep about the substrate manipulating their pedal disc somewhat in the manner of an inchworm, and some, such as the sea onion, are burrowers. Some species bury themselves in sand and muddy bottoms, with only their rows of neurotoxin-bearing tentacles exposed.

Soft corals are so called because they do not produce a stony skeleton of calcium carbonate like their relatives, the reef-building stony corals, but rather secrete a fleshy, elastic matrix that becomes

Ghost anemone (to 1 1/2")
Diadumene leucolena

the framework for the coral colonial community. The individual coral polyps are known as octocorals because they have eight feathery and retractile tentacles that surround their mouths.

Walk along a rock jetty and peer into a dark crevice where the tide has washed in, and perhaps you will be rewarded with the sight of the large American warty anemone, *Bunodosoma cavernata*. This greenish brown or olive anemone has forty vertical rows of pale blue, wartlike protrusions on its muscular column, or stalk. Its reddish groove of a mouth is surrounded by five rings of about 100 short tentacles. The tentacles are splotched with brown or olive green and are usually tinged with blue along one edge and red on the other edge. These 4-inch anemones creep along the substrate, particularly at night, when they are actively feeding and fully expanded. They are usually contracted during the day and look like reddish to black gelatinous blobs.

Look for American warty anemones on rocks, pilings, and the undersides of floating docks. They range from the Carolinas to the Florida Keys. There is another, closely related species, the red warty anemone, that may be found in Florida waters but is more common in the West Indies. There is considerable research on these species by scientists in-terested in the pharmacological properties of their neurotoxin. (See illustration on p. 200.)

The ghost anemone or white anemone, *Diadumene leucolena*, is a widely distributed anemone, particularly in lower-salinity waters. Ghost anemones are small, inconspicuous, pale, and almost transparent. Some individual ghost anemones are pale pink. These small anemones usually live on the shells of live oysters.

The striped anemone, *Haliplanella luciae*, is a little anemone with a big story. It has several other common names, including orange striped anemone, green striped anemone, and even orange striped green anemone. In addition, there has been some controversy over its valid scientific name; it has been designated as *Diadumene lineata*, *Haliplanella lineata*, and *Sagartia luciae*. Furthermore, the striped anemone is not indigenous to North America: research has shown that it was unintentionally introduced, perhaps as a fouling organism on ships' hulls or on introduced oysters from Asia, or as an organism released in the ballast water of ships. This little anemone is a native of Japan and China, but it has established itself from New England to Florida and all along the Pacific coast, and it was recently discovered in Hawaii.

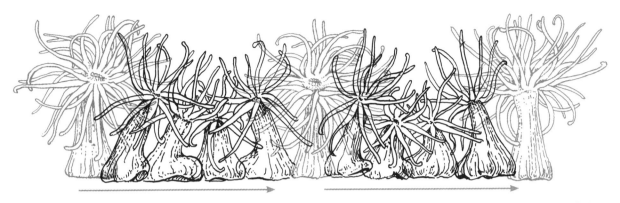

Many anemones are not permanently attached and are able to inch their way along by manipulating their bottom disks.

Striped anemones seem to prefer higher-salinity waters than do ghost anemones. They are dark green, almost black, with orange, red, yellow, or white vertical lines over their less than 1-inch bodies. They can be amazingly abundant, growing over ropes trailing in the water, on the sides of buoys, and on the undersides of floating docks.

Sea whip, or whip coral, *Leptogorgia virgulata*, is one of a group of soft coral animals that produce beautiful branching or single whiplike colonies that may be deep purple, violet, red, orange-yellow, or tan. These unmistakable corals are creatures of high-salinity regions of the Inner Coast, where they hang off bulkheads, pier pilings, and the undersides of floating docks, as well as deeper waters. The eight transparent, whitish tentacles of the individual polyps have somewhat sawtooth edges, and when the polyps emerge to feed, they look like white dots against the brightly colored skeletal rods of the whip coral. There is a small, beautiful snail associated with sea whips and sea fans, the one-tooth simnia, *Simnialena uniplicata*. It has a narrow, elongated shell with a deep furrow, the aperture, which extends the length of the shell. The shell is smooth and glossy and can be purple, yellow, white, or rosy red, but most often the shell closely matches the color of the sea whips and sea fans. The mantle of the snail completely covers the exterior of the shell, and it has whitish projections of uncertain use; they may mimic the appearance of the host, the sea whip, or they may be sensory organs.

The sea whip barnacle, *Conopea galeata*, is another interesting organism found only on sea whips.

Striped Anemone (to 3/4")
Haliplanella luciae

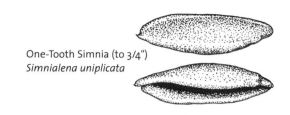

One-Tooth Simnia (to 3/4")
Simnialena uniplicata

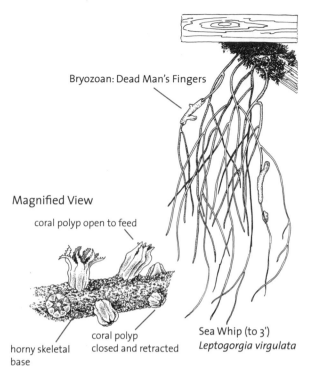

Bryozoan: Dead Man's Fingers

Magnified View

coral polyp open to feed

horny skeletal base

coral polyp closed and retracted

Sea Whip (to 3')
Leptogorgia virgulata

Sea whips are often covered with various other species, such as hydroids, encrusting bryozoans, and limy tube worms. The small sea whip barnacle, Conopea galeata *(to 1/2"), grows only on sea whips. The tissue of the sea whip often grows over the sea whip barnacle, obscuring its brown and white color pattern and leaving only its valves uncovered. One-tooth simnias frequently graze over the sea whips, eating the living polyps.*

They are obligatory commensals of sea whips, which means that they have evolved to the point that they can exist only on sea whips. The barnacle benefits by finding a place to settle, but there is no known value to the sea whip. The sea whip barnacle is small, perhaps 1/2 inch long, with a boat-shaped basal plate for attachment to the sea whip. These barnacles do have some brown and white markings, but they are usually obscured by the overgrowth of sea whip tissue, the coenchyme, which results in the barnacles' appearing to be the same color as their host: purple, yellow, orange, or white. Sea whips are not limited to the tropics; they range from lower Chesapeake Bay all throughout the high-salinity waters of the Inner Coast.

Bryozoans: Rubbery, Bushy, Mossy, and Encrusting Colonial Animals. Bryozoans are often referred to as moss animals, and certain species do resemble marine mosses, but bryozoans are a diverse group of colonial animals. Each individual animal, or zooid, is encased in a specially shaped and structured "house," or zooecium. At the tip of each zooid is a round or U-shaped crown of tentacles called the lophophore. The retractable lophophores bear cilia that create currents and sweep food to the zooid's mouth. Bryozoans are as varied in form as hydroids and sponges are, making identification exasperatingly difficult for the nonexpert. Most bryozoans, but certainly not all, occur in four basic forms: bushy, leafy, calcareous encrustations, and rubbery, gelatinous, finger-like growths.

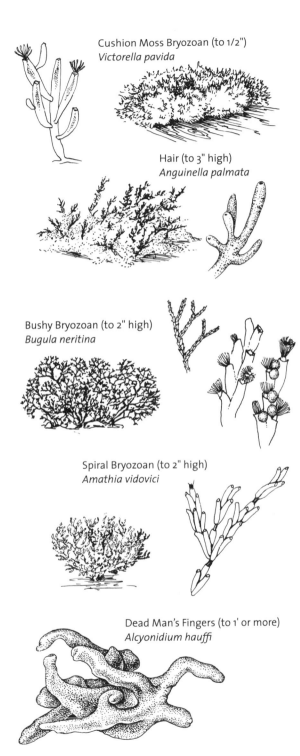

Cushion Moss Bryozoan (to 1/2")
Victorella pavida

Hair (to 3" high)
Anguinella palmata

Bushy Bryozoan (to 2" high)
Bugula neritina

Spiral Bryozoan (to 2" high)
Amathia vidovici

Dead Man's Fingers (to 1' or more)
Alcyonidium hauffi

Spiral bryozoans, sometimes called sheep's wool, *Amathia* spp., are typically soft, tufted, bushy growths with dark-colored zooecia that spiral around the stems. There are a number of *Amathia* species distributed throughout the world in low-salinity to high-salinity waters. Like all bryozoans, spiral bryozoans filter out tiny organisms suspended in the water. Spiral bryozoans are common and sometimes quite abundant. Look for them on seagrasses, pier pilings, floating docks, and rock jetties. They are also found on oyster shells and mangrove prop roots.

Hair, or muddy tuft bryozoan, *Anguinella palmata*, is a common species that forms colonies of branched, squishy, muddy tufts. Hair, as the watermen call it, is not the same species that they refer to as white hair, which is actually the garland hydroid. Hair thrives in high-salinity waters near inlets such as Sebastian Inlet, adjacent to the Indian River Lagoon, but this species also can be abundant in much lower-salinity water. It can be confused with brown seaweed because it is usually covered with brownish, soft silt that obscures the long, intertwining capsules of the zooecia.

Cushion moss bryozoan, *Victorella pavida*, forms soft, brown, matted, almost velvety coatings over pilings, stakes, crab pots, shells, and barnacles. A colony of cushion moss can grow so profusely that it completely obscures a barnacle community. The bottom of a boat can be covered with the cushiony growth of this bryozoan in a matter of a few weeks. Colonies of this species arise from a network of creeping basal stolons. Look for cushion moss bryozoa in the brackish waters of Pamlico Sound, North Carolina, and all along the Inner Coast where seawater has been diluted by freshwater rivers.

As confusing as the bushy group of bryozoans can be for the expert as well as for the amateur, encrusting bryozoans are unmistakable. Encrusting bryozoans are made up of individual, calcified boxes

Ivory barnacles may be completely covered with cushion moss bryozoans. Small marsh crabs are often seen scattering over barnacles, searching for food.

touch; they do not have the grainy and sandpapery texture of sponges. Dead man's fingers are encrusting organisms. When examined out of water, the bryozoan's surface is finely puckered, with each indentation marking the site of an inverted zooecium. However, when the same bryozoan is closely observed underwater, the tiny tentacled heads, the zooecia, can be seen as they emerge to feed. This particular species of dead man's fingers sometimes grows over whip corals, encrusting them in a gray, rubbery rind.

Lettuce bryozoans, *Thalamoporella floridana*, are calcareous, frilly bryozoans that look like creamy tan rosettes or small heads of lettuce. The first part of their scientific name, *Thalam*, is derived from the Greek for "inner room" or "chamber." Lettuce bryo-

within which zooids live. The lacy crust bryozoan, *Conopeum tenuissimum*, is a very abundant estuarine species. Its delicate colonies made up of countless little boxes coat just about any suitable substrate, pilings, rocks, shells, and even aquatic plants. It often completely covers oyster shells and prevents oyster spat from setting.

The coffin box bryozoan, *Membranipora tenuis*, is another common and very abundant encrusting bryozoan. This species can grow and expand so rapidly that it often overgrows lacy crust bryozoan colonies. Both species grow luxuriously, and when there is no longer any flat surface, they develop uplifted frills and curls. Barnacles and tunicates are often covered with coffin box bryozoans to the exclusion of lacy crust bryozoans.

An unusual bryozoan that occurs in the Inner Coast is a rubbery, gelatinous colony commonly called dead man's fingers, *Alcyonidium hauffi*. Dead man's fingers, as well as several other species of bryozoans, often resemble some sponge species because of their color and overall growth pattern. However, dead man's fingers are smooth and rubbery to the

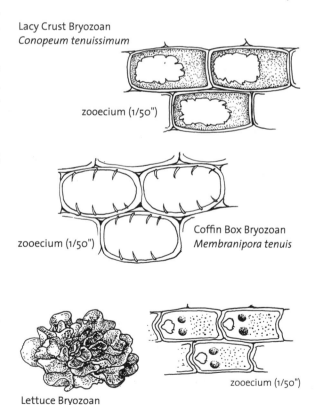

Lacy Crust Bryozoan
Conopeum tenuissimum

zooecium (1/50")

zooecium (1/50")

Coffin Box Bryozoan
Membranipora tenuis

zooecium (1/50")

Lettuce Bryozoan
Thalamoporella floridana

A lacy crust bryozoan spreads and grows over many other attached organisms, including sea squirts, barnacles, cushion moss bryozoans, whip mud worms, and slender tube-builder amphipods. Here, jellied coils of sea slug eggs are laid on the lacy crust as a clam worm burrows through.

zoans certainly do have a number of grooves, perforations, ruffles, fissures, and clefts. Typical of most bryozoans, lettuce bryozoans sprawl and grow over seagrasses, oysters, and mangrove roots, and sometimes they grow quite large on rocks and pilings. Lettuce bryozoans thrive in high-salinity waters from North Carolina to the Florida Keys.

Another warm-water bryozoan, the bushy bryozoan, *Bugula neritina*, grows in brownish or red tufts that are certain to be identified initially as some sort of seaweed, but these common and abundant bryozoans are branching colonies with typical U-shaped crowns of tentacles, the lophophores, at the tip of each zooid. The retractable lophophores bear cilia that create currents and sweep food to the zooid's mouth. This ordinary-appearing bryozoan species has created some excitement from scientists because it produces a chemical compound, bryostatin, that has potential as an anticancer drug.

Tunicates: The Vertebrate Connection. Tunicates are creatures that are diverse in shape and color, but all species have inhalent and exhalent siphons. Water enters through the inhalent siphon and is strained through a complex structure called the branchial basket, where tiny algal cells and bacteria are deposited on a mucus layer. Tunicates may be solitary or colonial animals. The bodies of solitary tunicates are generally sack shaped and covered with a matrix of tough, noncellular material similar to cellulose and referred to as a tunic, a coat that supports and protects the delicate animal within. Tunicates are called

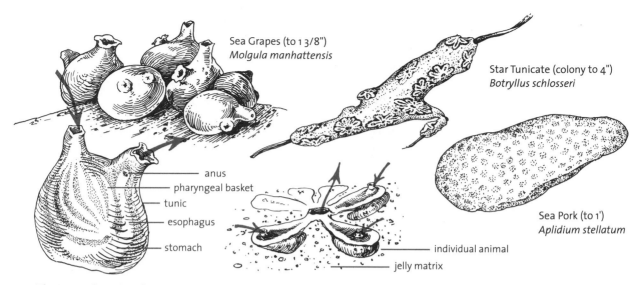

Sea Grapes (to 1 3/8")
Molgula manhattensis

Star Tunicate (colony to 4")
Botryllus schlosseri

anus
pharyngeal basket
tunic
esophagus
stomach

Sea Pork (to 1')
Aplidium stellatum

individual animal
jelly matrix

The internal organs of sea grapes can often be seen through the semitransparent tunic. The pharyngeal basket filters food particles from incoming currents. The arrows show the direction of water flow through the sea grapes and the individuals of a star tunicate.

sea squirts for their ability to shoot a jet of water from their exhalent siphons when squeezed or stepped on. Others seem like delicate and translucent prismatic lightbulbs that grow in long strings of individuals or in colorful colonial clusters. Some colonial tunicates look and feel like leathery or rubbery blobs; the individuals, or zooids, are embedded in the matrix. They may be easily confused with sponges, but sponges are very simple animals compared with tunicates. An easy way to distinguish sponges from tunicates is to touch them: sponges are usually rough and dry feeling; tunicates are often quite smooth and slippery.

Most tunicates are sessile; however, there are strangely shaped tunicates that are planktonic drifters and roam the open ocean propelled by cilia or muscular contractions and oceanic currents; these are the salps, larvaceans, and doliolids, which we do not cover in this book.

Tunicates are fascinating organisms because of their highly diverse forms and colors, but it is their larvae that are the most engrossing and remarkable features of tunicates. Most evolutionary biologists consider tunicates to be related to vertebrates: fishes, birds, and us! The free-swimming larvae of tunicates are called tadpole larvae. The "tadpoles" are, in fact, primitive chordates, as they possess notochords, rudimentary forms of vertebral columns. Like most marine and estuarine larvae, tunicate tadpoles are adapted for dispersal and settlement. In a matter of a day or two, the tadpole must find a place to land, or it will perish. The successful larva secretes a sticky substance and reabsorbs its tail and other structures, including the telltale notochord, and begins its life as an adult tunicate, a stage that gives no indication of its relationship to vertebrates.

Sea pork, *Aplidium stellatum*, is one of the leathery or rubbery tunicates that are frequently washed up on beaches after a storm. The thick and quite fleshy blobs bleach white after death, and then they look and feel like salt pork. Live colonies attach to rocks and pilings. They usually have cream or pinkish tunics with bright orange or red zooids arranged in circular or starlike groupings; the colony may grow to 1 foot in diameter. Beachcombers over the years have come upon lumps of sea pork along the Atlantic and Gulf coasts and have mistaken them for masses of whale ambergris, the pricey stuff of perfume, only to learn to their dismay that they are colonies of tunicates.

The star tunicate, *Botryllus schlosseri*, is a colonial tunicate that forms rubbery masses over pilings or envelops strands of seaweed and eelgrass. It thrives in shallow, sheltered areas. The colorful zooids are imbedded in the tunic in a star-shaped pattern. The color of the star tunicate is highly variable: sometimes the rubbery mass is golden yellow, with the zooids forming deep purple, starry formations speckled with white or gold, and other times colonies are purple or brown with lighter-colored zooids. The star tunicate is common in the summer, particularly in estuaries down to North Carolina.

Sea grapes, *Molgula manhattensis*, in contrast to sea pork and star tunicates, are solitary individuals. Sea grapes can grow in an astounding profusion; the rubbery globules with two prominent siphons can coat the sea bottom and obscure the outline of a piling, particularly at the piling's base. They can grow in such great numbers on the bottom of an idle boat that the boat can lose speed and maneuverability. Oysters brought to market along the Inner Coast are rarely without a few sea grapes attached to the shells. Sea grapes are widespread estuarine species. They grow in very low-salinity waters and even in the saltier water of ocean inlets. The tunics of sea grapes are tough, smooth, and translucent, though they are almost always covered with a coating of silt or mud and by encrusting bryozoans and hydroids.

The striped tunicate, or leathery tunicate, *Styela*

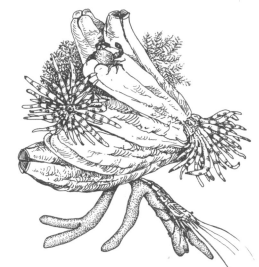

A cluster of striped tunicates, Styela plicata *(to 2" high), is a favored attachment site for other animals, including here the bushy bryozoan,* Bugula neritina; *feather hydroid,* Halocordyle disticha; *American warty anemone,* Bunodosoma cavernata; *and deadman's fingers,* Alcyonidium hauffi. *A peppermint shrimp,* Lysmata wurdemanni *(to 1 1/2"), finds a resting site.*

plicata, is also a solitary tunicate that often grows in clumps of individuals. It has a thick, wrinkled, and infolded tunic that is tough and gristly and is often overgrown with algae, bryozoans, hydroids, and other tunicates. The siphons are usually marked with pinkish or purplish stripes; the overall color of the tunic grades from a dirty white to tan. This is a common tunicate all along the Inner Coast. It grows on rocks, floating docks, pilings, and shells.

Two species of tunicates, the sandy lobed tunicate, *Eudistoma carolinense*, and the sea liver, *Eudistoma hepaticum*, although closely related, look nothing like each other. The sandy lobed tunicate has whorls that resemble a tortuous alpine highway; the coiled tunic is densely packed with sand grains, almost completely obscuring the zooids that make up the colony. Sea liver, on the other hand, grows as

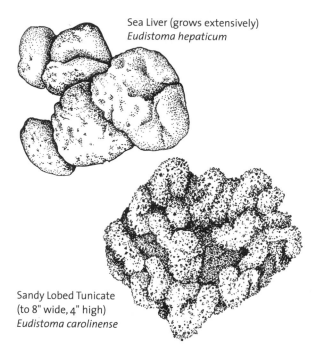

Sea Liver (grows extensively)
Eudistoma hepaticum

Sandy Lobed Tunicate
(to 8" wide, 4" high)
Eudistoma carolinense

region and bright red gills in the middle region of its body. It is also known as a rock worm for its habit of burrowing into stiff clay and muds. Look for this bristle worm in the muds between clumps of mussels, on a piling, in oyster bars and tunicates, and in eelgrass beds.

Mudworms, *Polydora* spp., are small, slender, abundant worms that thrive on muddy bottoms, particularly on oyster bars, where they build soft tubes from mud or sand. One species, *Polydora cornuta*, the whip mudworm, is often found on pilings and floating docks, where it builds soft, convoluted mud tubes that at times are so abundant that they smother other organisms growing on pilings, mud bottoms, and oysters. Most mudworms have two long, antennalike palps that may be seen waving as

soft, rubbery, shiny sheets of dark purple or brown masses that, indeed, look like liver (the species name also means "liver"). Sea liver is a species of high-salinity waters that can envelop sections of rocks and areas of floating docks. Look for sea liver near ocean inlets on floating docks and bulkheads.

Polychaetes: The Ever-Present Bristle Worms. **Many of the errant bristle worms of intertidal and shallow waters may be encountered wandering over the fouling growths on pier pilings or nestled among the plants and animals on the undersides of floating docks. Other burrowing worm species prefer the accumulated mud and silt on the hard substrates as places to feed and live.**

The red-gilled marphysa, *Marphysa sanguinea*, is a reddish iridescent worm that may reach a length of 12 inches or more. This blunt-headed worm has five slender sensory appendages arising from the head

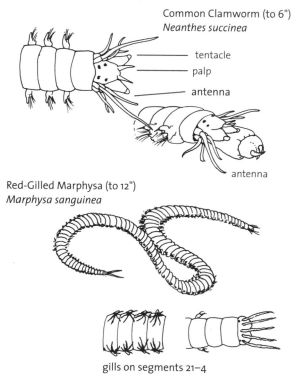

Common Clamworm (to 6")
Neanthes succinea

tentacle
palp
antenna

antenna

Red-Gilled Marphysa (to 12")
Marphysa sanguinea

gills on segments 21–4

Heteronereises, the spawning stage of the common clam worm, swarm to the surface on a moonless spring night.

are fairly large; some grow to 5 or 6 inches long, but smaller specimens are more common. The anterior portion of a clamworm's body is brownish bronze. The rest of its body is reddish with a prominent blood red streak along its back. There are four tiny eye spots, four pairs of tentacles, and a pair of fleshy protuberances called palps located on the head region. Don't be surprised if the clamworm you are examining suddenly ejects a large, club-shaped sac, the eversible pharynx, which is armed with two amber-colored hooks at the end. These worms are active and voracious feeders. The eversible pharynx is used to grasp any soft-bodied prey, such as other worms and bits of dead fish. As the pharynx retracts, the beak closes over the prey and draws it into the worm's mouth.

Common clamworms "swim" through the mud, and as they move through the bottom, they exude mucus, which hardens into a sheath; sand grains adhere to the outside of the sheath, creating a strong

they probe for bits of food. As they feed they collect tiny amounts of sediment that is ultimately excreted, and over time the mud will build up around the colony to a depth of several inches.

The common clamworm, *Neanthes succinea*, is another worm species that is wide ranging and very abundant. This worm is an inhabitant of estuarine waters and tolerates a wide range of salinity, from very brackish water to water almost as salty as the ocean. Common clamworms are found in the tidal freshwaters of rivers and near the salty ocean inlets, where they occupy intertidal and shallow subtidal habitats. They bury in the soft muds; crawl among the sessile communities of pilings, seawalls, and floating docks and across shells and bottom debris; and also graze over eelgrass blades. These worms

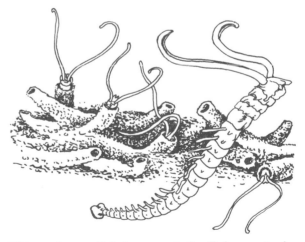

Whip mud worms, Polydora cornuta *(to 1"), form mats of soft mud tubes. The worm inside has a series of minute hooks and a suctionlike tail, which hold the worm inside its tube. The whiplike appendages are for feeding.*

but flexible tube. Clamworms move in and out of the tubes readily and often glide over the surface mud and become easy prey for fishes and crabs. During the breeding season, which is usually in May, clamworms metamorphose into an unusual sexual form called the heteronereis; this form has very large parapodia, the fleshy feet of polychaete worms, which enable the heteronereis to swim. During the dark of the moon, heteronereises swarm to the surface in a frenzy of mating. They are attracted to light; if you walk out on a pier and shine a flashlight on the water during spring or early summer, chances are you will be rewarded with the sight of hundreds of worms swimming rapidly in circles just below the surface of the water. They swarm for several nights in succession and finally they release their eggs and sperm and die. Tiny planktonic larvae develop from the fertilized eggs and eventually become recognizable clamworms. They then abandon their planktonic life, descend to the bottom, and assume the benthic existence of their parents.

Shrimps and Crabs. There are many different species of shrimp along the Atlantic coast, including the small but tasty northern shrimp found in the cold waters above Cape Cod; the arrow shrimp, a slender-bodied, rather elongated species that may be green, brown, purple, or translucent; and the excellent eating pink, white, and brown shrimps, the shrimps that most of us savor. These are the shrimps of shallow and deep waters, of grass beds and coral reefs. There are also several small shrimps that dwell in the shallows, often right under our feet: the grass and sand shrimps.

There are still other small shrimps, usually ranging in length from 1 to 3 inches, that are not necessarily closely related but are loosely grouped together as cleaning shrimps. Cleaning shrimps lurk near their home base, which is often a sponge or a crevice, and attract the attention of passing fishes by slowly waving their antennae or rhythmically rocking their bodies from side to side. Most cleaning shrimps are tropical and are associated with coral reefs. However, the peppermint shrimp, *Lysmata wurdemanni*, ranges along the Inner Coast from North Carolina down to the Florida Keys. The peppermint shrimp is about 3 inches long with a pinkish white body marked with fine, bright red stripes. Look for these colorful shrimps under floating docks and pier pilings among tube sponges and hydroids. If you are fortunate, you may see a peppermint shrimp or two picking parasites and dead skin off a fish.

Crabs abound in the Inner Coast. Some, such as the blue crab and the sargassum swimming crab, are very good swimmers because they have pairs of specialized paddlelike hind legs. Spider crabs, on the other hand, are slow and ponderous as they pick their way across the bottom. Many species of spider crabs have hooked barbs on their carapaces where sponges and hydroids have a place to attach. They then have a free ride to different feeding areas, and the spider crabs have a disguise. The sessile species and the crabs mutually benefit from the relationship.

The cryptic teardrop crab, *Pelia mutica*, is one of those slow-moving spider crabs. This little crab's red

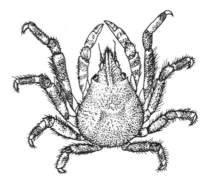

Cryptic Teardrop Crab (carapace to 1/2")
Pelia mutica

carapace is pear shaped, or teardrop shaped. Its legs are banded with red and white. Its rostrum, the spiny process projecting forward beyond the carapace, is deeply forked. Cryptic teardrop crabs, true to their name, are often unseen or unrecognizable because they are covered with sponges and hydroids. This little slow-moving crab lives in the lower intertidal zone on pilings, rocks, and shelly bottoms among sponges and hydroids from New England to Florida.

Echinoderms: Spiny-Skinned Animals. The phylum Echinodermata contains several groups of animals, such as sea stars, sand dollars, and sea urchins, that are quite familiar and fascinating to most people. Then there are echinoderms that are not as well known, including many slow-moving, soft bodied, and sedentary sea cucumbers; agile brittle stars; exquisite feather stars; and deep-dwelling sea lilies. Occasionally, after some rough seas, sand dollars, sea stars, and sea urchins end up on sand flats and beaches. Sometimes the whole animal is present, but more often there are only fragments of sand dollars, a leg or two of a sea star, or the calcite test (the "shell") of a sea urchin.

Sea urchins have various tubercles and knobs adorning the test that are attachments for their moveable spines. Live sea urchins have an immense number of tube feet, hydraulically manipulated "feet" that control the animals' slow, deliberate movement as they graze over algae and other food items. The test is also equipped with a number of stalked pincers, called pedicellariae, which aid in removing debris and fending off predators and fouling organisms. Sometimes the test of a dead sea urchin contains a small, bony structure within that is still attached to the test's inner wall by muscles and connective tissue; this structure is known as Aristotle's lantern, a complex organ designed for scraping and boring seaweeds, algae, corals, and even concrete. Sea

Purple Sea Urchin
(to 4" wide)
Arbacia punctulata

urchins produce relatively large eggs. Certain species throughout the world, including in the United States, are harvested to the point of overfishing for their roe, which are served in sushi restaurants as uni.

The purple sea urchin, *Arbacia punctulata*, is the most common sea urchin along the Atlantic coast. This easily recognized urchin is brown to purplish, sometimes almost black, with 1-inch, sharp-tipped spines. The test is usually the same color as the spines and is usually about 2 inches in diameter. The purple sea urchin favors jetties and pilings in the lower intertidal zone and is also quite common on seagrass beds and shelly bottoms. Most urchins are nocturnal feeders, and the purple sea urchin is no exception. It primarily feeds on red seaweeds and other seaweeds, but it also feeds on sponges, corals, and other encrusting organisms.

Sea stars, or starfishes, are perhaps the quintessential symbol of ocean shores; they are instantly recognized and treasured by meandering beachcombers. Dried and withered specimens, however, do not reveal the astonishingly complex system of rigid skeletal plates and soft tissues or the elaborate maze of hydraulic plumbing incorporated in a live sea star. The external surfaces of sea stars are similar in many ways to those of the pincushionlike sea urchins. Sea stars have various pimplelike papulae that aid in respiration; they also have tweezers-shaped pedicellariae used to clean debris and small fouling organisms from their rough skin. The lower surfaces of a sea star's arms are furrowed, technically called the ambulacral groove, where the many pairs of tube feet are situated. The madreporite is a perforated plate that is connected to a water vascular system that in turn operates the tube feet. The madreporite is located off center on the upper surface, the aboral surface, of the sea star. Sea stars are voracious feeders. Some use their tube feet to deliberately approach oysters, clams, crabs, worms, or even other echinoderms, whereas others are scavengers or mud feeders. Active predators stealthily stalk their prey, and upon contact, they wrap their arms about their dinner, applying inexorable pressure with their tube feet until the oyster or clam shell gapes. The sea star protrudes its stomach, located on its underside, called the oral surface, and makes quick work of its prey.

Brittle stars superficially resemble the familiar sea

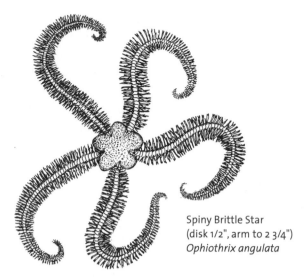

Spiny Brittle Star
(disk 1/2", arm to 2 3/4")
Ophiothrix angulata

stars; however, they are much more agile and quick moving. They are called brittle stars because they can voluntarily shed or break arms to escape the grasp of predators. Brittle stars can be very common and abundant burrowed under coral rubble or in seagrass beds, particularly in the Florida Keys, and some brittle star species may be found searching for food on a piling or in the crevices of rock and rubble structures.

The common sea star, *Asterias forbesi*, has thick, rather blunt arms. They typically have five arms; however, some have six or more. (Sea stars have the ability to regenerate their arms rather quickly, and sometimes they overcompensate and produce an extra arm or two.) The top surface of the common sea star is rough and strewn with tiny spines and bumps. The madreporite is bright orange. Common sea stars are variously colored, ranging from tan to yellowish orange or sometimes even purple; the underside, or oral surface, is paler. The common sea star can often be seen on rocks in the lower intertidal zone, particularly in high-salinity water near ocean inlets.

The spiny brittle star, *Ophiothrix angulata*, is only

Common Sea Star (to 5")
Asterias forbesi

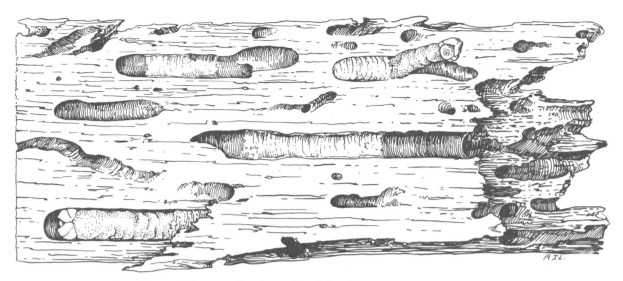

A shipworm-infested plank reveals the nacre-lined tunnels and live shipworms.

one of many species of brittle stars found along the Inner Coast, particularly in the Florida Keys. The prominent central disk of the spiny brittle star is usually less than 1/2 inch in diameter and has about 3-inch legs originating from it. This is a very spiny creature, with the longest spines near the disk. Some of the spines are minutely toothed, and others are smooth or flattened. The overall color of the spiny brittle can be pink to rose, orange, deep red to brown, gray, or green. Look for this common species with its writhing legs among mangroves in shallow water, on pilings, in coral rubble, and in seagrass beds.

SECRETS WITHIN

A sound-looking pier may suddenly collapse, its interior riddled from within by shipworms or gribbles, though its exterior showed no indication of the thriving and voracious community within.

Shipworms are very unusual organisms; they are not worms but wormlike mollusks. They are not filter feeders or predators, or detrital feeders like most marine invertebrates; rather, they digest cellulose from the wood fibers of boat hulls and pier pilings. Shipworms are truly the termites of the sea. Gould's shipworm, *Bankia gouldi*, is a mollusk closely related to angel wings and other boring clams that inhabit hard bottoms. A shipworm is a highly modified bivalve with two small shells, each about 1/3 inch long, located at the end of its long, soft, wormlike body. The forward edge of each shell has a series of sharply toothed ridges. Boring through a piling or other woody structure is done by rotating the toothed shells and rasping off tiny bits of wood. If you break open a piece of driftwood that shows signs of shipworm activity, you can often see a number of white limy tunnels, each about the diameter of a pencil. Some woody structures, such as the piece of driftwood you are examining, may be riddled with tunnels; however, the tunnels never intersect. Shipworms have incurrent and excurrent siphons, as do most clams. The siphons of the shipworm are positioned at the end of the soft body, which extends from the modified shells, or valves. The tunnel at the posterior end of the shipworm, where the siphons are located, is open to seawater through a very small hole. The two siphons extend through the hole, and when the shipworm is disturbed, the siphons are retracted and the hole is plugged by unusually shaped structures, the pallets.

Shipworms, like most mollusks, have planktonic veliger larvae, which remain in the water column for about two or three weeks before settling. If they are lucky, and most are not, they land on an untreated wood structure. The larva walks around by the means of a small foot, exploring the nooks and crannies, and eventually attaches itself by secreting a byssus. The larva then metamorphoses into an immature shipworm and tunnels into the wood, where it develops into an adult. The original, tiny entrance hole remains as its only connection with the outside world.

Like the shipworm, the gribble, *Limnoria tripunctata*, bores into wooden structures; however, it is not a mollusk but a crustacean and, more specifically, an isopod. Marine isopods are generally omnivores, but some are herbivores, some are true carnivores, some are parasitic, and some, like the gribble, are wood borers.

Gribbles are living augers; these little isopods, less than 1/4 inch long, drill their way into wood-hulled boats and wooden pilings, creating such weakened structures that they eventually collapse. There are fewer wooden boats today, and most pilings are chemically treated, so gribbles and shipworms are not of as much economic importance as they once

Gribble (to 3/16")
Limnoria tripunctata

were. However, as toxic boat-bottom paint ages and loses its effectiveness, and likewise with wooden pilings and other wooden structures in saltwater, these little gray gnawers answer the call. Gribbles live in the saltier parts of bays and sounds all along the Inner Coast and the West Indies.

FISHES

There are many kinds of fishes that are attracted to pilings, rubble structures, and mangrove prop roots. Some species have mouths that are equipped with heavy lips and sharp incisor teeth that are perfect for feeding on hard-shelled barnacles, oysters, and mussels. Other species do not have specialized mouth parts and feed on all sorts of food, from an occasional nip of algae to a hapless shrimp. Still others dash in and feed on smaller fishes and then return to deeper water. Piers, especially floating docks, mangrove prop roots, and rubble structures provide shelter, as well

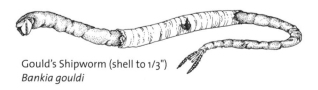

Gould's Shipworm (shell to 1/3")
Bankia gouldi

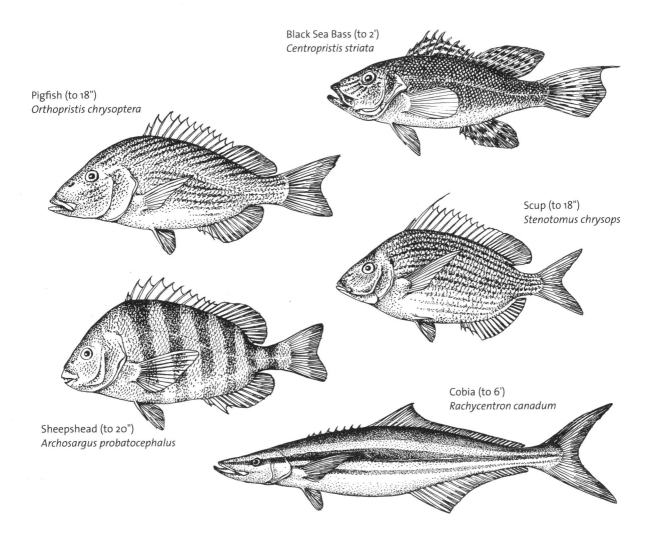

Black Sea Bass (to 2')
Centropristis striata

Pigfish (to 18")
Orthopristis chrysoptera

Scup (to 18")
Stenotomus chrysops

Sheepshead (to 20")
Archosargus probatocephalus

Cobia (to 6')
Rachycentron canadum

as food, for small fishes such as pinfish and the young of larger species such as lane snappers.

The sheepshead, *Archosargus probatocephalus*, is a small-mouthed fish with strong jaws and teeth, which it uses to handily crush the shells of crustaceans and mollusks. Sheepsheads are porgies, most of which are primarily tropical species, but there are a few more northern or temperate species of porgies, including scup and sheepshead. Most porgies congregate in small, loose schools; sheepsheads, how-

ever, are more solitary. Their bodies are heavy and bulky and are marked with black or brown stripes on a grayish to yellow background; the markings tend to fade with age. These are fishes of shallow coastal waters and estuaries from the Maritimes to Florida. They live around rocks and pilings, where they consume surprisingly large quantities of seaweed as well as barnacles, crabs, and mollusks.

The pinfish, *Lagodon rhomboides*, is perhaps the most abundant member of the porgy family along the Inner Coast. Pinfish are small fish with small mouths. Their silvery bodies are decorated with horizontal blue and gold stripes, and there is a distinctive black spot just behind the gill cover. They feed on almost anything, including seaweeds attached to pilings and rocks. They feed in loose schools around piers and rocks and are caught from New England to the Yucatan in the Gulf of Mexico. Pinfish are a favorite fish for children to catch because they readily bite on almost any bait. Recreational fishermen catch pinfish and keep them alive to use them as live bait for larger game fishes such as tarpons and cobias.

The scup, *Stenotomus chrysops*, is also a member of the porgy family, and this fish is often called a porgy. Scups congregate in the spring and summer in small schools in estuaries and sounds from Nova Scotia to South Carolina. They move over the shallows and around pilings and wrecks, where they nibble on barnacles, mussels, and small crabs on the bottom. Scups are bluish gray to silver and marked with dusky bars. The scup, pinfish, and sheepshead are similarly shaped fishes; they are deep bodied and slab sided, and their spiny- and soft-rayed dorsal fins are continuous.

The pigfish, *Orthopristis chrysoptera*, belongs to the grunt family. Most grunts inhabit tropical waters, but the pigfish can live in temperate waters as well, and it ranges from New England to the Gulf of Mexico. Pigfish have sharply sloping heads and deeply forked tails. These are colorful fish that vary considerably in color and pattern. Most authorities report that the pigfish is gray or sometimes bluish, with brassy or golden markings that form horizontally dashed lines. However, we have snorkeled over seagrass meadows and coral rubble bottoms and observed many pigfish that display rectangular, golden brown blocks running from just under their dorsal fins with another line of golden brown blocks running through their heads along the mid, or lateral,

line to their tails. These are very abundant fish that school in large numbers near rock jetties and over sand and mud bottoms. They are caught by commercial and recreational fishermen in coastal and estuarine waters. Pigfish are bottom feeders; they nose through the sand and mud, where they feed on almost any invertebrate, from worms to crabs.

The black sea bass, *Centropristis striata*, is another solitary fish that hovers around pilings, wrecks, and rock jetties. Black sea basses have long dorsal fins with fleshy tips at the ends of the spines and round caudal (tail) fins. In larger fish, the top half of the tail is extended into a long filament. Sea basses can grow to a length of about 2 feet and a top weight of 8 pounds, but they are generally smaller. Intense harvesting by commercial and recreational fishermen tends to select the larger fish, causing a decline in reproduction and a dwindling of stock along the Atlantic coast. These sought-after food fish have large mouths well armed with teeth. Their coloration immediately identifies them, as they are a deep blue-black with a vivid lighter blue color in the center of each black-bordered scale, which gives them an overall appearance of having bluish horizontal stripes. This same blue color is repeated below the eyes as well as on the dorsal fin. The blue color fades rapidly when black sea basses are removed from the water, and only a black body with some white markings remains. Black sea basses are found along the Atlantic coast from Maine to northeast Florida but are much more abundant from the mid-Atlantic northward. Black sea basses feed mainly on crustaceans and other fishes; older black sea basses consume significantly more fish.

The tautog, *Tautoga onitis*, also locally known as blackfish or tog, is a blocky and bulky fish with a long dorsal fin and a thick caudal peduncle, the tapered part of the body just before the tail. Males are dark olive to charcoal gray and may have a blotchy pattern

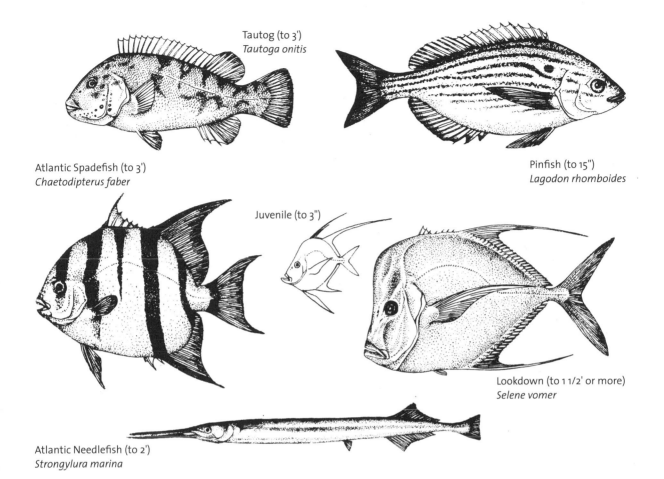

Tautog (to 3')
Tautoga onitis

Atlantic Spadefish (to 3')
Chaetodipterus faber

Pinfish (to 15")
Lagodon rhomboides

Juvenile (to 3")

Lookdown (to 1 1/2' or more)
Selene vomer

Atlantic Needlefish (to 2')
Strongylura marina

over the body. Females and the young are usually dark gray to almost black on a paler olive to brown or gray body; they are more heavily blotched and mottled than the males. Tautogs have been caught up to 3 feet long weighing about 20 pounds, but most landed tautogs weigh 2–5 pounds. Tautogs, similar to sheepsheads, feed on mollusks, especially mussels, and crustaceans around rock jetties, bridges, and pilings. Tautogs are slow growing and probably live for well over twenty years. They are quite territorial and maintain their space from other tautogs. They range from Nova Scotia to South Carolina and are much more abundant from North Carolina northward.

There are several members of the jack family, Carangidae, that are common and occasionally quite abundant along the middle region of the Inner Coast. The amberjack, Florida pompano, crevalle jack, and blue runner are just a few species of the jack family that, in some instances, occur from as far north as the Maritimes to as far south as the West Indies and the coast of South America. Most members of the jack family share certain characteristics: they are usually quite streamlined and silvery with few other markings; most have long pectoral fins and deeply forked tails; and many are highly predacious on other species of fishes.

The lookdown, *Selene vomer*, is an extremely deep-bodied fish and so laterally compressed that it is sometimes difficult to see it coming head on. The front of the head is so steep that it is almost vertical down to its large mouth. Its body is silvery and is often burnished with gold and bluish highlights; its scales are small and smooth. The fin rays of both the dorsal and anal fins are elongated, especially in juvenile lookdowns. Lookdowns gather in schools along the bottom, where they feed on small fishes and crustaceans, particularly shrimps. Lookdowns are attracted to lights shining from piers, and they actively roll on their sides, flashing their gleaming flanks as they feed on shrimps fatally attracted to the lights as well. Lookdowns range along the coast from Maine to Florida and into the Gulf of Mexico.

The Atlantic needlefish, *Strongylura marina*, another unusual-appearing fish, is also attracted to pier lights shining on the water. As its name implies, it is a long, narrow fish that can often be spotted patiently stalking killifishes and silversides in the shallows. Its jaws are extended into a long, slender beak lined with fine, pointed teeth. The upper jaw is not quite as long as the lower. The needlefish's body is light gray-green and rounded in cross section; its dorsal and anal fins are triangular and are positioned close to the squared tail. It has a broad silver stripe on each side. In early spring, Atlantic needlefish enter bays and sounds along the Inner Coast, where they spawn in late spring or early summer. Atlantic needlefish inhabit the coastal waters of the United States from Maine to Florida, the Gulf of Mexico rim, and the waters along the Atlantic coast of South America.

The Atlantic spadefish, *Chaetodipterus faber*, is a disk-shaped fish that resembles an angelfish but is placed in another family because of differences in the dorsal fins and the absence of a strong spine near the gill plate. Atlantic spadefish are laterally compressed, with triangular dorsal and anal fins positioned toward the tail. The deep body is striped with vertical black and white bars on a light gray to tan background. Juvenile spadefish are entirely black except for transparent fins. A large spadefish may weigh as much as 20 pounds; however, most spadefish weigh considerably less. Young spadefish in the Florida Keys have the interesting habit of drifting at an angle, sometimes almost on their sides, among the long black seed pods of red mangroves, perhaps as a way of avoiding predation. Atlantic spadefish are attracted to structures and often congregate in large, slowly drifting schools around coastal light towers and buoys. They are frequently found around rock jetties, where they feed on a wide variety of food that may include seaweeds, sea cucumbers, brittle stars, tunicates, worms, and sea anemones. Spadefish range from New England to Florida and the Caribbean Sea, but they are rare north of the Chesapeake Bay. Recreational fishermen, particularly in North and South Carolina, fish for these small-mouthed fish with small hooks baited with small chunks of rubbery cannonball jellyfish, which is abundant in the Carolinas.

The cobia, *Rachycentron canadum*, is distributed widely in warm seas throughout the world. Cobias roam the seas and are considered a pelagic species, but they also inhabit inshore bays, sounds, and mangroves and are usually around buoys, pier pilings, flotsam, and even moored boats. The cobia has a long body and a long head with a broad snout and small eyes. It has a series of small, separated dorsal spines running from just behind the gills to midbody; the second dorsal fin has an anterior elevated portion and runs from midbody to almost the base of the tail. Adult cobias have forked tails. The anal fin is shorter than the prominent dorsal fin but is essentially the same shape. Cobias are brownish silver and are marked with longitudinal dark bands running from the head to the base of the tail.

Cobias are large fish. Many are caught weighing 50 pounds or more; the record is 135 pounds. Cobia are highly predatory and feed on many species of fishes, including mullets, jacks, menhaden, pinfish, and a variety of snappers; they also prey on squids and crabs. Cobias are excellent game fish and are caught all along the Atlantic coast.

Birds: Aerial Gleaners

Birds, particularly the larger seabirds and shorebirds, are usually the most evident signs of animal life along the shoreline. Gulls and terns sometimes gather in large, mixed flocks; they probe and soar, searching for food. They sun and rest themselves on piers, bridge railings, and navigational structures, as well as on nearby roofs and parking lots, frequently preening their plumage to rearrange and oil their feathers, which are vital for flight and maintenance of body temperature. They devote most of their energy, however, in the constant quest for food for themselves and their nestlings. Some species, like gulls, will eat practically anything: insects, garbage, small mammals, bird eggs and hatchlings, berries, grains, fishes, and various invertebrates. Barn swallows eat great numbers of insects while on the wing, whereas other birds, such as brown pelicans and double-crested cormorants, are mostly fish eaters.

The barn swallow, *Hirundo rustica*, is a busy little bird that launches from piers and nearby trees to busily hawk for insects over the water and then returns and perches on the pier or a nearby branch, soon to begin the milling and darting through the air once again. Barn swallows are, perhaps, the best known of all the swallows. They have deeply forked tails and long, pointed wings. Their backs and wings are steely blue; their underparts are creamy buff; and their throats and foreheads are cinnamon or rust colored. Female barn swallows and juveniles

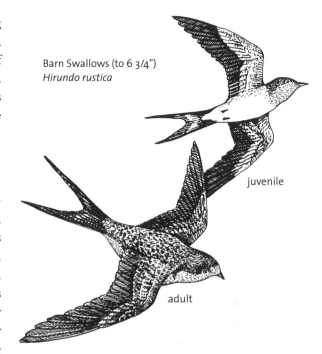

Barn Swallows (to 6 3/4")
Hirundo rustica

juvenile

adult

are similarly marked but paler. Barn swallows have large, gaping mouths that are well adapted for catching insects in midair. They are wonderfully agile and course through the air, swooping and veering in their quest for insects; when they sweep low over the water near a pier, you can hear their bubbly twittering and squeaking.

Barn swallows arrive along the Inner Coast in April after a long journey from their wintering grounds in the West Indies and South America. They build their nests of muddy pellets mixed with blades of grass and plant materials and line them with feathers. Swallows have very small, weak feet, so they carry mud in their capacious beaks. We have watched a male land on the soft mud, where it scoops up mud in its froglike beak and flies to a pier support, where the female takes the mud from the male. She works the mud and plant material into pellets, which she forms into a nest cemented to a pier timber, the underside of a bridge, or the side of a building. The female lays

Great Black-Backed Gull (to 30")
Larus marinus

Laughing Gull (to 16 1/2")
Larus atricilla

Ring-Billed Gull (to 17 1/2")
Larus delawarensis

juvenile

adult

Laughing Gull
in winter

an average of four brown spotted eggs. The eggs hatch in about three weeks, and three weeks later, the young begin their flying lessons.

Gulls and terns are typically found around seawalls, pilings, and jetties—in fact, on almost any structure that can be a place to rest and to preen their feathers. Bridges are favorite locations for gulls; they often hover, seemingly without effort, over them. Gulls use the rising thermals emanating from the heated pavement to give them lift and to maintain their positions, allowing them to conserve energy while searching for scraps of food.

The great black-backed gull, *Larus marinus*, is the Inner Coast's largest gull species. These birds have massive yellow bills and large wingspans that sometimes reach 5 feet. Like herring gulls, they require four years to reach sexual maturity. Great black-backed gulls' breeding plumage, however, is unlike that of any other gull along the Inner Coast. The upper parts of their wings are charcoal black; the underparts are white; and their legs are pink. The adult's yellow bill has a red spot, which its chicks peck to elicit regurgitated food. The call of a great black-backed gull is a deep "keeow."

Great black-backed gulls, like herring gulls and other gull species, drop clams and oysters on piers, parking lots, and bridges from aloft to crack open the hard shells. Broken shells littering the waterfront are evidence that gulls have been feeding on mudflats and along the shallows for the delectable mollusks. Great black-backed gulls are found all along the Atlantic coast.

The ring-billed gull, *Larus delawarensis*, is a three-year gull, meaning that it becomes sexually mature when it is three years old. Ring-billed gulls are the most abundant gulls in the winter all along the Inner Coast. They often intermingle with laughing gulls in the spring as they follow farm tractors turning over newly plowed soil, revealing insect grubs and worms. Ring-billed gulls resemble herring gulls because of their coloration and mewing call, but ring-billed gulls are smaller and are the only gulls with a black ring around the tips of their yellow beaks. Most ring-billed gulls leave the Inner Coast in the summer and head inland, where they become quite abundant around freshwater rivers and lakes.

The laughing gull, *Larus atricilla*, is named for its characteristic call, which sounds like a series of loud "ha-haahs." This is the most common gull along the Inner Coast in the summer. Laughing gulls be-

summer   winter

Bonaparte's Gull (to 13")
Larus philadelphia

Laughing Gull to (16 1/2")
Larus atricilla

come sexually mature in three years, and then they attain their unmistakable breeding plumage, which features a very black hood, white underparts, pale gray wings and back, black legs and feet, and a deep red bill. In the winter, they lose the vividly black hood and retain only pale gray remnants of the hood around the eyes and the back of the head.

The only other gull along the Inner Coast with a hooded head is Bonaparte's gull, *Larus philadelphia.* However, its hood is not as extensive as the laughing gull's; it ends behind the eye rather than covering the back of the neck, as it does on the laughing gull. In addition, this two-year gull is smaller and much more ternlike. Look for Bonaparte's gull in small, discrete groups bobbing on the water in the winter.

The double-crested cormorant, *Phalacrocorax auritus*, is a goose-size diving bird with a long neck and a distinctly hooked beak. The adults are charcoal gray to black with a greenish sheen that can be seen under certain lighting conditions. Young, immature birds have brownish backs and buff underparts. The double crests for which this bird is named are inconspicuous and generally not seen. The throat pouch, or gular membrane, is orange throughout the year. Cormorants, as well as some other birds, flutter

their throat pouches, which helps regulate their body temperatures; male cormorants also flutter their colorful throats to dazzle and attract females during their breeding season. The double-crested cormorant is the most common and abundant cormorant along the Inner Coast, particularly during the winter. Like Canada geese, these cormorants often fly in V-shaped formations, but unlike geese, they have distinctive kinked necks. Double-crested cormorants often stand upright on pilings and navigation aids and frequently hold their wings outstretched as they bask in the sun. When most birds preen their feathers, they are rearranging their plumage and, at the same time, oiling their feathers to make their plumage somewhat waterproof. Cormorants, however, lack oil glands; the lack of oil in their plumage allows them to sit low in the water and to dive without fighting the buoyancy that most diving birds experience because of their oiled plumage. The lack of buoyancy in cormorants allows them to be spectacular underwater swimmers as they hunt for fishes. Cormorants, like anhingas, must compensate for the lack of oil by sunning themselves with their wings outstretched to dry their feathers and also to regulate their body temperatures.

Cormorants are most often confused with loons, which are quite abundant in the winter along the Inner Coast. Cormorants rest on the water or swim with their hooked bills slightly tipped up. Loons also swim low in the water, but they hold their straight, thick bills parallel to the water's surface.

Like cormorants, the brown pelican, *Pelecanus occidentalis*, is a fish eater, but rather than the narrow, hooked bill of the cormorant, which can grasp only a single fish, the brown pelican has a massive bill with a capacious and elastic throat pouch that is capable of scooping up a quantity of small fish. A breeding adult brown pelican is marked with chestnut brown on the back of its white neck and yellow

soaring breeding adult
with darker neck

nonbreeding adult
with light-colored
head and neck

Brown Pelican (to 51")
Pelecanus occidentalis

Double-Crested
Cormorant (to 32")
Phalacrocorax auritus

on its forehead and at the base of its neck. Nonbreeding adults do not have brown on the neck, and juveniles are grayish brown all over. These short-legged, large, and rather ponderous birds have wingspreads of 6 feet or more and are very graceful flyers. They often fly in a V formation or in a long line just above the water, synchronizing their wing beats with one another: the lead bird flaps and glides, and then the second bird flaps and glides, and so on. When brown pelicans fly against the wind, they usually fly close to the surface of the water, with their wing tips almost touching the waves. Brown pelicans also soar gracefully high above the water with their heads tucked in close to their bodies, and then suddenly one or more will veer and plunge-dive into the water with their wings somewhat close to their bodies and their heads and necks retracted. These ungainly looking birds are quite buoyant and quickly bob to the surface after their power dive. They point their bills

downward and drain as much as 10 quarts of water from spaces between their bills. They then point their bills upward, gulp, and swallow their catch. They feed unceasingly, it seems, on schooling anchovies, silversides, and mullets. They often try to snare fish being reeled in by fishermen on piers, which sometimes results in both the fish and the flapping pelican being caught at the same time.

Brown pelicans, like bald eagles, ospreys, and other fish eaters, were at one time in serious decline and considered endangered in parts of their range because of the wide use of DDT. Pesticides like DDT became concentrated in fishes, and as the birds fed on the fishes, the pesticides were concentrated in their bodies, causing the production of very thin-shelled eggs, which the parents easily broke when they sat on them. Because of the research and writings of Rachel Carson and others, DDT was banned, and now brown pelicans, cormorants, eagles, and ospreys have significantly increased in numbers throughout their ranges. Brown pelicans, once considered a rarity north of Virginia Beach, Virginia, now nest successfully as far north as New Jersey and are quite common along the Delaware and Maryland coasts and in Chesapeake Bay. They range all along the Inner Coast and around the rim of the Gulf of Mexico.

The Subtropical Waters of Florida

Many of the sessile marine seaweeds and animals along the Inner Coast occur in the subtropical waters of Florida as well as in the more northern waters. As one moves southward, tropical species common to the Caribbean and the West Indies add to the diversity of communities on the hard substrates and mangrove roots of southern Florida. The tidal amplitude is relatively low in south Florida, so the distinct zonation evident in areas with a high tidal range is obscured in Florida. The spray zone on rocks and rubble structures hosts chitons, limpets, and scurrying crabs, but for the most part, life in south Florida is found near the water line and below.

Red mangroves make their first appearance in the vicinity of St. Augustine. There are just a few small, shrubby specimens growing near the larger, more cold-tolerant and low salinity–tolerant black and white mangroves. Farther down the coast, below New Smyrna Beach, in the shallow waters of Mosquito Lagoon, in sight of the Kennedy Space Center, islets of red mangroves with their arching prop roots become more evident, and ultimately, in the Florida Keys, the islets become islands of thick, lush mangrove forests. Red mangroves often grow in soft, silty bottoms where there are few places for animals to settle and permanently attach. There are also usually fewer piers and jetties where the mangroves grow, so the mangroves' spidery prop roots become "condominiums" for a host of warm-water sessile plants and animals.

Seaweeds

Most of the marine plants of the North—sea lettuce, redweeds, codium, and many others—are just as abundant in south Florida. Added to those plant communities is a vast variety of tropical species that typically live in shallow waters and around coral reefs but also attach to piers, floating docks, and mangrove roots.

Umbrella algae, sometimes called mermaid's wineglass, *Acetabularia* spp., are very small, just 2 or 3 inches tall, but so very distinctive that they can be easily identified, at least to genus. The umbrella alga's slender stalk is capped by a pale green to whitish, umbrella-shaped disk with twenty-two to thirty rays, which looks like the paper parasol stuck in a tropical drink. Small congregations of umbrella algae grow on submerged mangrove roots, mud adjacent to mangrove roots, floating docks, shell fragments, and other hard surfaces.

Petticoat alga and white scroll alga are species of

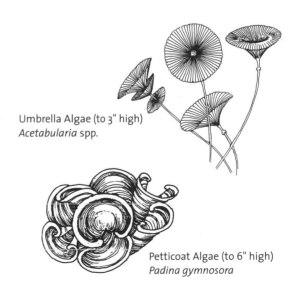

Umbrella Algae (to 3" high)
Acetabularia spp.

Petticoat Algae (to 6" high)
Padina gymnosora

brown seaweeds that can be readily identified to the genus, *Padina*. These unusual-appearing seaweeds have thick, ruffled blades that are rolled into rosette-like saucers. The leafy, fan-shaped blades are somewhat rounded and often banded in shades of chalky white, yellowish tan, or light brown. Look for these seaweeds in the shallows attached to rocks, shells, and mangrove roots. There are populations of these interesting seaweeds attached to rocks in the Saint Lucie Inlet near Stuart, Florida, as well as throughout south Florida and the Keys.

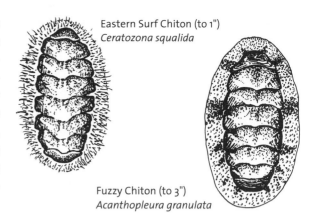

Eastern Surf Chiton (to 1")
Ceratozona squalida

Fuzzy Chiton (to 3")
Acanthopleura granulata

Mollusks

Two tropical chitons are commonly found along with the eastern beaded chiton of more temperate waters. The fuzzy chiton, *Acanthopleura granulata*, 2 to 3 inches long and usually so eroded that the typical brown coloration and granulations are not apparent. The girdle, the leathery rim surrounding the eight valves or plates of a chiton, is grayish white and matted with hairs. The undersides of the valves are light green.

The eastern surf chiton, *Ceratozona squalida*, has a brown, leathery girdle covered with a thick mat of brownish hairs. Like most chitons that live in the tumultuous surf, the valves are frequently eroded; however, you may find a specimen in good condition, in which case the whitish gray valves, or plates, will be roughly sculptured and mottled with bluish green.

The zebra periwinkle, *Nodilittorina ziczac*, is a 1/2-inch-high snail with a conical spire; its shell is thick and strong, and its aperture, the opening from which the snail's head and foot protrude, is purplish brown. The zebra periwinkle is marked with zigzags or wavy streaks of dark brown or purplish brown. Zebra periwinkles are quite common on rocks and rocky crevices close to the water.

The beaded periwinkle, *Tectarius muricatus*, is another very common and abundant periwinkle of south Florida and the West Indies. It is a rather heavy-shelled snail and may be bluish white, pale yellowish gray, or dirty white. The shell is adorned with rows of neatly spaced whitish beads, and the aperture is reddish brown. The beaded periwinkle is usually found on rocks well above the high-tide line, where it is moistened from time to time by salt spray.

The mangrove periwinkle, *Littoraria angulifera*, is a thin-shelled periwinkle with a pattern of dark blotches that form angular or oblique, rather indistinct stripes, somewhat similar to the pattern on the zebra periwinkle. The overall color of the cone-shaped, whorled shell is whitish yellow or orange to red-brown; the operculum is pale brown. As their name implies, mangrove periwinkles live on mangroves, where they glide up and down the prop roots, grazing on algae and organic material.

Nerite snails are another group that inhabits the same general areas as periwinkles. They are generally globular, with low spires, and some have toothed apertures. There are a number of species in the Inner Coast, and most are quite colorful and boldly marked.

The bleeding tooth, *Nerita peloronta*, may be

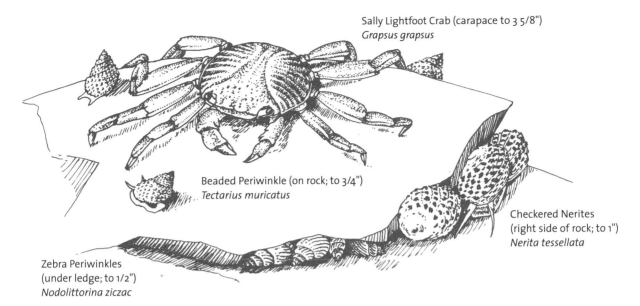

Sally Lightfoot Crab (carapace to 3 5/8")
Grapsus grapsus

Beaded Periwinkle (on rock; to 3/4")
Tectarius muricatus

Checkered Nerites
(right side of rock; to 1")
Nerita tessellata

Zebra Periwinkles
(under ledge; to 1/2")
Nodolittorina ziczac

grayish or yellowish tan with black, brown, or reddish zigzag markings. The inside of the inner lip, the parietal area, has one or two white teeth surrounded by an orange-red blotch. Found on rocks near the low-tide line, this attractive snail was very abundant at one time in south Florida, but over-collecting has reduced its numbers.

The four-tooth nerite, *Nerita versicolor*, is almost 1 inch high with a thick whitish shell decorated with zigzags and dashes of black and red. It has heavy white teeth within the inner lip and a finely beaded, brownish gray operculum. The four-tooth nerite is often found with the bleeding tooth on rocks close to the water.

The zebra nerite, *Puperita pupa*, is a smaller and thinner-shelled nerite than the bleeding tooth and the four-tooth nerite, but it makes up for its diminutive size by its arresting black and white markings. The shell is chalky white and marked with black stripes, reminiscent of a zebra's markings. The aperture and operculum are smooth and creamy to grayish yellow. Zebra nerites live in wave-washed pools

above the high-water mark and are found sporadically in south Florida.

The checkered nerite, *Nerita tessellata*, is about 1 inch long with two weak teeth within the inner lip. The shell is mottled with black and white in a random checkerboard pattern, and the black operculum is finely pebbled. Checkered nerites are usually found near the low-water line and may sometimes be seen in large numbers under rocks at low tide. They range as far north as central Florida.

The beautiful olive nerite, sometimes called the emerald nerite, *Neritina reclivata*, is a smooth, glossy, greenish yellow or sometimes brownish green snail. It has fine, black or brown or purplish spirally lines with a black or brownish operculum. The olive nerite lives on aquatic grasses in the brackish waters and freshwaters of Florida.

The flat tree oyster, *Isognomon alatus*, is an oyster with very flat, rough to flaky valves that is found attached to prop roots as well as to bulkheads, pilings, and other hard surfaces. It attaches itself by means of dark, cartilaginous or horny tufts of threads spun

Bleeding Tooth (to 1")
Nerita peloronta

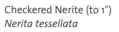
Checkered Nerite (to 1")
Nerita tessellata

Olive Nerite (to 1/2")
Neritina reclivata

color pattern of
four-tooth nerite

Four-Tooth Nerite (to 3/4")
Nerita versicolor

Zebra Nerite (to 1/3")
Puperita pupa

from a gland in the foot of the larva. The exterior of the flat tree oyster is gray to purplish, and the interior is somewhat pearly and may be stained or mottled with brown, black, or purple.

The Lister purse oyster, *Isognomon radiatus*, has rather irregularly shaped and sometimes elongated and twisted shells that are rough textured and corrugated. The shells are usually greenish brown to yellowish white with reddish brown rays. Lister purse oysters live in shallow water attached to rocks or the undersides of ledges and are sometimes found on shallow reefs, such as Molasses Reef off Key Largo and near Soldier Key in lower Biscayne Bay.

The frond oyster, *Dendostrea frons*, also known as the coon oyster or leaf oyster, is also found growing on mangrove prop roots. This is a somewhat smaller oyster than the flat tree oyster. It is thick shelled with variable sculptured ridges. Frond oysters tend to be somewhat rounded when attached to rocks or mangrove prop roots, but when they cling to sea whips, they develop fingerlike extensions on their shell edges that enable them to clasp the soft coral's thin, round stems. The valves, or shells, are reddish to purplish brown on the exterior and translucent white on the interior. At night, raccoons prowl the mangroves, where they feed on land crabs and particularly frond oysters.

Crabs

Some crabs are extremely nimble and quick, such as the Sally lightfoot crab, which is usually found along the edge of the water among rocks and rubble, spending more time out of the water than in it. The Florida stone crab and various species of mud crabs and marsh crabs, such as the humic and mangrove marsh crabs, sidle and slowly stalk their prey along the bottom; they tend to find shelter in oyster bars or among mangrove roots and leaf litter, or by burrowing in the soft bottom's sand and mud.

The Sally lightfoot crab, *Grapsus grapsus*, belongs to the Grapsid family of crabs, all of which have characteristic square or sometimes angled or slightly rounded carapaces; their eyes are spaced widely apart, almost at the front corners of their carapaces. Sally lightfoot crabs are colorful crabs usually dappled with splotches of red and green, though

Lister's Purse Oyster (to 2")
Isognomon radiatus

Flat Tree Oyster (to 3")
Isognomon alatus

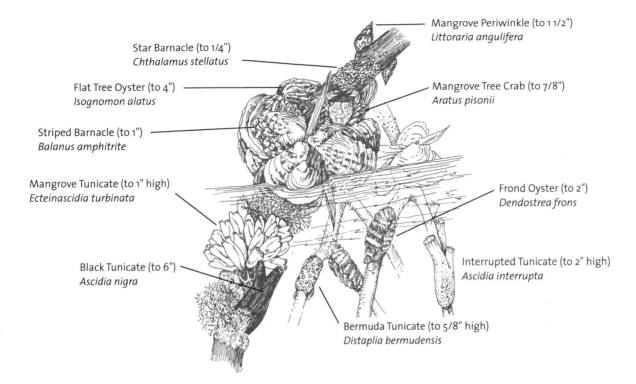

Mangrove Periwinkle (to 1 1/2")
Littoraria angulifera

Star Barnacle (to 1/4")
Chthalamus stellatus

Flat Tree Oyster (to 4")
Isognomon alatus

Mangrove Tree Crab (to 7/8")
Aratus pisonii

Striped Barnacle (to 1")
Balanus amphitrite

Mangrove Tunicate (to 1" high)
Ecteinascidia turbinata

Frond Oyster (to 2")
Dendostrea frons

Black Tunicate (to 6")
Ascidia nigra

Interrupted Tunicate (to 2" high)
Ascidia interrupta

Bermuda Tunicate (to 5/8" high)
Distaplia bermudensis

sometimes they are an overall dark red. These agile and swift crabs are almost completely terrestrial in their habits; they scramble from rock to rock, skittering here and there, and are usually moistened only by the breaking waves that splash on the rocks. Sally lightfoot crabs are the quickest crabs that you will ever see and never catch. Often the only sign of a Sally lightfoot is an occasional, brightly patterned molted exoskeleton left behind.

The mottled shore crab, *Pachygrapsus transversus*, is related to the Sally lightfoot crab; however, it is much smaller. The brownish black to olive carapace is sculpted with fine green to black stripes and is somewhat square. Typical of this group, the eyes are set close to the corners. The mottled shore crab is found around mangroves, rocks, pilings, and shore rubble, and it often feeds on the sand-builder worms that build extensive, moundlike reefs along the east

coast of Florida. Mottled shore crabs are found from North Carolina to Florida.

The nimble spray crab, *Percnon gibbesi*, has a thin, flat carapace that is longer (to 1 1/2 inches) than it is wide. The carapace and legs are usually mottled with brown, and the legs are often banded with pink, red, yellow, green, or light blue. These little crabs hide under rocks in the shallows or in the surf. They range from North Carolina down to the Florida Keys.

The Florida stone crab, *Menippe mercenaria*, is an important commercial and recreational species. Interestingly enough, only the massive claws are eaten. Usually only one claw is removed—though Florida regulations allow the harvest of both claws—and then the crab is set free, and in time another claw will regenerate. The stone crab's carapace is oval and dappled with tan, red, gray, and white spots. Juvenile

Nimble Spray Crab (carapace to 1 1/2" long)
Percnon gibbesi

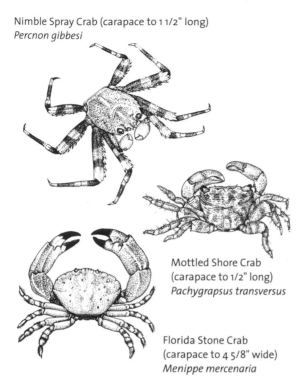

Mottled Shore Crab
(carapace to 1/2" long)
Pachygrapsus transversus

Florida Stone Crab
(carapace to 4 5/8" wide)
Menippe mercenaria

Mangrove Marsh Crab
(carapace to 3/5" long)
Sesarma curacaoense

Humic Marsh Crab
(carapace to 4/5" long)
Sesarma ricordi

bris. Humic marsh crabs range from south Florida to South America.

The mangrove marsh crab, or Curaçao marsh crab, *Sesarma curacaoense*, is smaller than the marbled marsh crab and has two spines behind each eye socket. The mangrove marsh crab is slow to move and is easily caught. It lives among the leaves and roots of mangroves and along the muddy banks of estuarine embayments. It ranges from south Florida to South America.

Sponges

Haliclona tubifera, the pink tube sponge, is best described as a pink, cushiony sponge with erect, spidery tubules. This sponge is found in the warm waters of Florida and the Caribbean, where it grows on mangrove roots, on pilings, in seagrass beds, and on shallow coral reefs.

The yellow tube sponge, *Aplysina fistularia*, is another species of warm tropical waters. These sponges are characterized by showy, soft-walled, yellow to orange tubes that usually grow in clusters like living pipe organs; the deeper the water, the longer the tubes. The tubes or barrels are thick walled and ridged. This species inhabits coral reefs but is frequently found growing on sea walls and other hard surfaces.

The chicken liver sponge, *Chondrilla nucula*, is a mottled gray or brown rubbery sponge of the tropics that, indeed, resembles a large, lobed mass of

stone crabs are purplish blue. The claws are unequal in size; the larger claw is usually a crusher, and the smaller one is a shearing claw. The fingers on both claws are black. Florida stone crabs dwell in the saltier areas of sounds and bays, where they dig shallow burrows in muddy bottoms, often at the bases of sea walls. They are also common around rock and rubble structures and on shelly bottoms. They too range from North Carolina to the Florida Keys.

The humic marsh crab, or marbled marsh crab, *Sesarma ricordi*, is orange or reddish yellow, or sometimes reddish brown. Its carapace is less than 1 inch wide. This little crab often has mottled, or marbled, brown and cream-colored legs. It lives above high water, sometimes in shallow burrows and often under driftwood, seaweed wrack, and mangrove de-

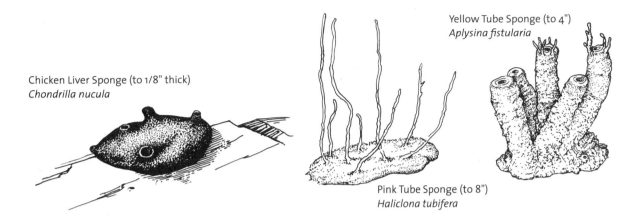

Chicken Liver Sponge (to 1/8" thick)
Chondrilla nucula

Yellow Tube Sponge (to 4")
Aplysina fistularia

Pink Tube Sponge (to 8")
Haliclona tubifera

chicken livers. Look for this slippery, slick sponge on rocks and pilings, in grass beds, and wrapped over red mangrove prop roots.

Tunicates

The Bermuda tunicate, *Distaplia bermudensis*, is a compound, or colonial, tunicate that grows in rounded, or sometimes flattened, mounds and crusts. The colonies are tough and slick to the touch and highly variable in color. The tunics are translucent, and the white-rimmed zooids, discernible through the tunic, may be red, pink, marbled chocolate brown, green, purple, or black and yellow. Bermuda tunicates grow from the Carolinas southward.

The painted tunicate, *Clavelina picta*, is a startlingly beautiful creature when it is viewed underwater. These delicate colonial organisms grow in a chain or clump attached to a shared stolon, or stem. The individual zooids may be almost 1 inch long. The tunic is pale white to yellowish or even purplish, and the siphons are rimmed with brilliant reds, purples, or lavenders. Painted tunicates often grow in clusters of fifty or more zooids attached to floating docks, rocks, ropes dangling in the water, and, of course, red mangrove prop roots. Painted tunicates are common in tropical and subtropical waters, but they grow in the offshore waters of the Carolinas and Georgia as well.

The light bulb tunicate, *Clavelina oblonga*, is a close relative of the painted tunicate. The zooids of lightbulb tunicates are somewhat larger than those of painted tunicates; their tunics are stiffer, and their siphons are outlined in luminescent white spots rather than the reds and purples that distinguish painted tunicates. Lightbulb tunicates, like their painted relatives, grow in large clusters on ropes, floating docks, jetties, and red mangrove prop roots. They too are common in subtropical and tropical waters, as well as in the offshore waters along the southeastern Atlantic coast. Both the painted tunicate and lightbulb tunicate grow extensively throughout the Indian River Lagoon, on the swimming floats at Elliott Key in Biscayne Bay, and throughout the Florida Keys.

The mangrove tunicate, *Ecteinascidia turbinata*, has club-shaped zooids similar to those of the painted and lightbulb tunicates. Its zooids are about the size of the painted tunicate's and range in color from a creamy yellow or gold to bright orange. Mangrove tunicates grow in clusters of hundreds of zooids, each of which is individually connected to a thin stolon. Medical researchers have isolated a new drug, ecteinascidin, from the mangrove tuni-

Painted Tunicate (individual zooids to 3/4" high)
Clavelina picta

Light Bulb Tunicate
(individual zooids to 1 1/2" high)
Clavelina oblonga

Bermuda Sea Squirt (colony to 5/8" high)
Distaplia bermudensis

Red Encrusting Tunicate (individual zooids to 3/8" high)
Symplegma rubra

cate that holds promise for treating breast and ovarian cancers. The mangrove tunicate is primarily tropical and is most often found attached to mangrove roots.

The red encrusting tunicate, *Symplegma rubra*, and the green encrusting tunicate, *Symplegma viride*, grow in brightly colored colonial patches. The zooids of both species are crowded in gelatinous, transparent tunics. The red encrusting tunicate has brightly colored, almost cherry red to orange, distinctly oval zooids. Look for red encrusting tunicates on the prop roots of red mangroves as well as on sea walls, floating docks, and rocks. Green encrusting

tunicates are quite similar to their close relatives the red encrusting tunicates; there are some slight differences between the species, but they are difficult to distinguish. Green encrusting tunicates tend to grow in a more loosely scattered fashion than do red encrusting tunicates, and they readily take the shape of the substrate on which they have settled. Green encrusting tunicates are not always green; they are commonly yellow-green but may also be orange, yellow, purple, or black. They grow on mangrove roots, but they also grow as encrustations on shells, bottles, rocks, and blades and bases of seagrasses.

The black tunicate, *Ascidia nigra*, is undoubtedly one of the easiest tunicates to identify along the Inner Coast. It is a solitary species that grows to 6 inches high, but is usually smaller; its tunic is thick, leathery, and black to blue-black. Black tunicates are very common on mangrove roots, sea walls, and floating docks. In some places, particularly in the Florida Keys, there may be fifty or more of these black, rubbery tunicates scattered on a bulkhead or among the prop roots of red mangroves.

The interrupted tunicate, sometimes called the translucent tunicate, *Ascidia interrupta*, is usually somewhat smaller than its relative, the black tunicate; it may grow to 2 inches high. It is a solitary species with a translucent tunic and green to greenish yellow siphons that are directed upward. Interrupted tunicates may be found in large aggregations in calm, shallow water, where they attach to shells, prop roots, and any other hard substrates that may be available.

Fishes

The sergeant major, *Abudefduf saxatilis*, is a colorful, deep-bodied, small fish that may attain a length of 9 inches but is usually much smaller. Sergeant majors are strikingly marked with five prominent verti-

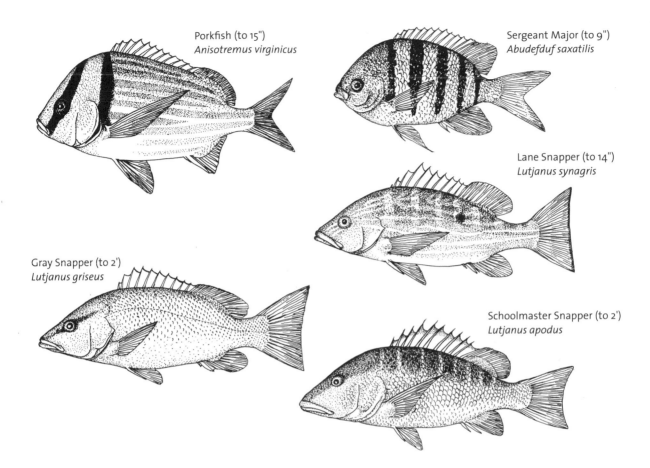

Porkfish (to 15")
Anisotremus virginicus

Sergeant Major (to 9")
Abudefduf saxatilis

Lane Snapper (to 14")
Lutjanus synagris

Gray Snapper (to 2')
Lutjanus griseus

Schoolmaster Snapper (to 2')
Lutjanus apodus

cal black bars; their bodies are a metallic greenish yellow above, shading to white on the belly. They are somewhat territorial and pugnacious fish, as is typical of their family, the damselfishes.

Sergeant majors tend to change hues depending on the environment. There seem to be two color phases: lighter when they are swimming above a coral rubble or sandy bottom and darker when they are lurking under a pier or hiding in a rocky crevice. The male sergeant major also becomes quite a bit darker, usually grayish blue, when guarding its nest of greenish eggs with red yolks.

Sergeant majors are nonspecialized feeders; their diet includes algae, planktonic organisms, small crabs and shrimps, various other invertebrates, and even small fishes. They are quite common over coral reefs, sometimes gathering in large concentrations in midwater; they are also common and abundant in shallow water around rocks, pilings, and bulkheads. Sergeant majors range as far north as North Carolina.

The night sergeant is closely related to the sergeant major, but it is heavier bodied and darker, with broader and darker vertical bars. The night sergeant is a more southern species; it is found only in southern Florida and in the Caribbean. Its range of habitats, as compared to that of the sergeant major, is rather limited; the night sergeant prefers living in surging shallow water near rocky and undercut limestone ledges.

The porkfish, *Anisotremus virginicus*, is another boldly marked and colorful small fish. It has an arched back, a sloping head, and a thick-lipped mouth. It is distinctly marked with a brilliant gold head, fins, and tail. It has two very bold black bars on its head; one bar crosses through the eyes, and the other bar crosses the body just behind the gill plate. Its silvery body is also marked with narrow yellow horizontal stripes. Porkfish belong to the grunt family, so named for their ability to make sounds by grinding their pharyngeal teeth; these teeth, located in the pharynx, are used to grind food as well as to emit grunts.

Juvenile porkfish have yellow heads and silvery bodies marked with two black stripes and a black splotch at the base of their tails. The juveniles, like many other juvenile species of fishes, are "cleaners," meaning they set up a symbiotic relationship with other species of fishes. Picking parasites and dead skin off their larger "client" fishes, the juvenile porkfish gain a dinner, and their client fishes become cleaner. Porkfish are common in southern Florida under floating piers and in rocky areas, where they feed on almost anything, including worms, various mollusks, brittle stars, crabs, and shrimps.

When you think of fishing or eating fish in Florida, snappers most often come to mind. Red snapper, mutton snapper, lane snapper, yellowtail snapper, and others of this group can be found offshore around coral reefs, on patch reefs close to shore, around mangrove prop roots and seagrass meadows, around rock jetties, and under floating docks. Snappers as a group share certain characteristics: Their dorsal fins are usually continuous. They may be slightly notched between the spiny-rayed sections of the dorsal fins and the soft-rayed sections, but they are never completely separated. Most snappers,

but not all, have sharp fangs protruding from their upper jaws, and most snappers have blocky tails that are only moderately forked. Finally, snappers are not confined to Florida. Of course, they are common in the Gulf of Mexico, but some species also range along the Atlantic coast as far as Chesapeake Bay or beyond.

The lane snapper, *Lutjanus synagris*, is a relatively small and colorful snapper. Lane snappers seldom grow to 5 pounds, and most weigh less than 1 pound. Lane snappers appear to have two color phases, a darker, deep-water intensity and a paler, shallow-water or resting phase coloration. They are pink to red with a faint greenish tinge on their upper sides and backs; their sides and bellies are silver and washed with a tinge of yellow. Their heads are marked with three or four diagonal orange-yellow stripes, and there are eight to ten yellow horizontal stripes on their sides, with a series of diagonal yellow lines running above the lateral line. They may also have several rather obscure reddish vertical bars running above the lateral line. Their fins are yellow or red, with a dark spot just below their soft-rayed dorsal fins. It's no wonder that the lane snapper is known as a candy striper or rainbow snapper in some locales.

Juvenile lane snappers are usually seen in shallow seagrass flats or drifting in small numbers under the cover of mangrove prop roots. Adult lane snappers are more often found in deeper waters, although they also occur in shallow water on hard, rocky or coral rubble bottoms. These little snappers eat a varied diet and are referred to as opportunistic feeders.

The schoolmaster snapper, *Lutjanus apodus*, is silvery gray tinged with yellow on its back. It also may have several vertical pale yellow bars running down its side. Its fins are pale yellow to orange, and it is often marked with vivid blue lines under the eyes. It has the typical canine fangs of snappers projecting from the upper jaw. A juvenile schoolmaster is marked with alternating vertical silver and bronze to yellow bars and a diagonal bronze streak extending from the tip of its mouth and across the eyes and head.

Schoolmaster snappers, true to their name, school in small groups and drift almost motionlessly under coral ledges and among mangrove prop roots. As is typical of most snappers, they feed nocturnally on invertebrates and fishes. Schoolmaster snappers occasionally wander as far north as New England, but they are more commonly seen in Florida and Caribbean waters.

The gray snapper, *Lutjanus griseus*, also commonly known as a mangrove snapper, is typically silvery gray with a bronze to brown streak running from the tip of its mouth and through the eyes. But these snappers can change rather quickly from pale gray to gray with reddish tinges; there may also be orange to rusty red dots on the scales, which form an overall pattern of spots. Gray snappers are generally larger than lane snappers and schoolmaster snappers; they may grow to about 20 pounds. They are important food fish and are caught by commercial and recreational fishermen. Gray snappers are common around pilings, rock jetties, and mangroves. Mangrove-lined creeks are important nursery areas for their young. Gray snappers range from North Carolina, where they are usually caught in offshore waters, and along the Atlantic coast, the Caribbean, and the Gulf of Mexico.

Shallow waters and the adjacent deep waters that lie offshore are essentially the same, but shallow waters, about 15–20 feet deep, lap the shoreline and connect to wetlands and forest bottomlands. Shallow waters cover intertidal flats at high tide; as the tides recede, the flats are once again exposed. Some large bodies of water along the Inner Coast, such as Currituck and Albemarle sounds, are almost entirely within the shallows. Shallows are the repository of run-off from farmlands and urban neighborhoods, but where the water is clear enough to allow sunlight to penetrate to the rooted aquatic vegetation below, one of nature's most profound processes takes place. The chlorophyll contained in the plant cells allows photosynthesis to do its magic: to convert sunlight and atmospheric carbon dioxide to chemical energy and to synthesize carbohydrates while releasing oxygen to the environment.

The twisted roots of cypresses and gums and the arching prop roots of mangroves provide places for sessile organisms to attach and for small fishes and crustaceans to feed and hide from predators. The shallows are where many species of fishes and invertebrates spawn. The shallows are also where wading birds probe for mollusks and hapless crabs and crayfish, where turtles bask, and raccoons take their evening meals.

The shallows are places that are rich in life, although some of the organisms are so small that they are rarely seen. Shallows are exposed to extreme environmental changes, ranging from superheated water in the summer and, in some areas of the Inner Coast, to icy edges in the winter. Winter winds and summer thunderstorms churn the shallow waters down to the muddy bottoms, suspending roiling clouds of sediments. Heavy rainstorms can wash tons of soil off the uplands, turning the waters into a muddy soup. These same torrential rains can quickly change the salinity of the water, forcing the flora and fauna to adjust or perish. Most estuarine species are adapted to abrupt salinity changes and turbid water and are able to endure the sudden changes that affect the shallows. That is not always the case with marine species that have wandered into Inner Coast shallows and are subjected to fluctuating salinity and quickly changing temperatures that challenge their physiological systems.

In shallow water environments, there are a variety of habitats, including manmade structures such as piers and rubble structures, and tidal flats. In fact, the whole world of the piling and jetty community is a shallow-water habitat at high tide, as are flooded marshes and low-lying shorelines.

We have separated the shallows into three major environmental regions: unvegetated shallows, vegetated bottoms, and tropical shallows. The chapters on beaches; marshes and mangrove swamps; intertidal flats; pilings, floating docks, and rubble structures; and live bottoms are essentially all about shallow-water habitats.

Unvegetated shallows have muddy or sandy bottoms that are often littered with shell hash or stones. The bottoms may be without vegetation for several reasons. The waters may be constantly roiled and murky, preventing the penetration of sunlight. The darkened waters are almost always caused by strong currents, windy conditions, recent rainstorms, or tannin-stained waters. And in some areas of South Carolina and Georgia where the tidal amplitude may reach 9 feet or more, there is little or no vegetation in the shallows because the swift tidal currents created by the rising and ebbing tides are quite substantial, resulting in heavy loads of silt constantly being carried up and down the waterways. The muddy water blocks the passage of life-giving sunlight and prevents the establishment and growth of plants. In addition, swift bottom currents carry loads of abrasive sediments that constantly scour the bottom. The

currents also constantly rearrange the soft muddy bottoms so that plant life cannot take hold.

But there are many areas along the Inner Coast where the shallows are relatively clear, so that sunlight penetrates to the bottom, though there are still few or no rooted aquatic plants growing there. These areas usually have sandy bottoms, and as the tides and winds roil the water, the relatively large sand grains are suspended in the water and then quickly settle to the bottom, creating unstable conditions that prevent the establishment of aquatic plant communities.

Many of the same species of worms, clams, snails, and other burrowers and wanderers of muddy and sandy intertidal flats also live in abundance in the subtidal shallows. Inhabiting the shallows is a diverse epifaunal community of barnacles, sea anemones, mussels, and bryozoans, as well as seaweeds that are attached to pieces of shells, sticks, and stones. The benthos is rich and plentiful in the shallows; however, there are other, often quite visible forms of life in the shallows—the floaters and swimmers. These are fishes, shrimps, swimming crabs, jellyfishes, comb jellies, and many other creatures.

Fishes along the Shore

There are many small and somewhat larger fishes that dwell in the shallows along the shore, including stubby little killifishes, silvery anchovies, silversides, schooling herrings, shad, menhadens, mullets, and odd creatures such as stargazers and flatfishes.

Killifishes: Bull Minnows

Killifishes, often called bull minnows, are minnows of sounds and estuaries; their name is derived from the Dutch word for "river," *kil*. Killifishes are stubby and chunky little fishes with rounded or squared tail fins and lower jaws that protrude beyond their upper jaws. They are generally greenish brown and usually tinted with a wash of gleaming silver, bronze, or brass. Some species have vertical stripes; others have horizontal stripes.

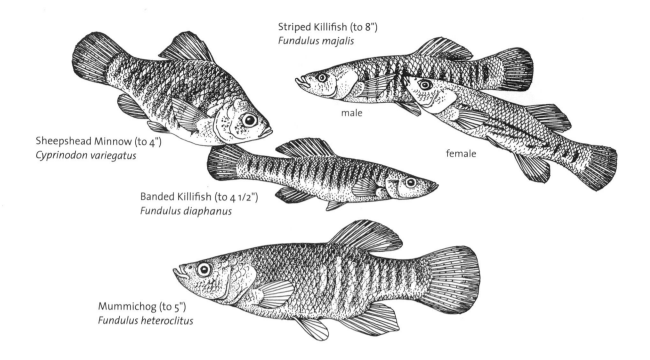

Striped Killifish (to 8")
Fundulus majalis

male

female

Sheepshead Minnow (to 4")
Cyprinodon variegatus

Banded Killifish (to 4 1/2")
Fundulus diaphanus

Mummichog (to 5")
Fundulus heteroclitus

Loose schools of killifishes are usually quite evident swimming in the shallows over sandy and muddy bottoms or through tangles of rooted aquatic vegetation. Their protruding lower jaws are nicely adapted for surface feeding, but killifishes also readily feed on the bottom and even in midwater; they are opportunistic feeders, and only the gapes of their mouths limit the size of their prey.

Schools of killifishes swimming over muddy shallows and particularly at the edges of marshes are most likely mummichogs, *Fundulus heteroclitus*. Mummichog is from the Narragansett *moamitteaúg*, "going in crowds." Mummichogs usually school close to shore; the school may include various age groups, from very small, immature fish to adults that are 4–5 inches long. Mummichogs are real homebodies; they do not range very far, only about 100 feet along the shoreline and perhaps 25 feet offshore. Mummichogs are stout-bodied little fish with blunt snouts and very

small mouths. Mature males and females differ in color as well as in the shapes of their fins. The males, when not in breeding season, have dark green or blue backs and sides marked with white and yellow spots; the sides are also marked with irregular silvery bars. The bellies of male mummichogs may be whitish gray, pale yellow, or orange, and their dorsal, anal, and caudal fins are typically dark green. The coloration of males at spawning time becomes intensified; their backs and upper sides become almost black, and their bellies become strikingly brilliant. Females are much paler; they lack the bold markings and coloration of the males. Mummichogs range all along the Inner Coast to northeast Florida.

The striped killifish, *Fundulus majalis*, is similar in general shape to the mummichog but is slenderer, and its snout is more pointed. The main differences between the species are their color and markings. Male striped killifishes, whether immature or adults, have seven to twenty dark vertical stripes, depending on the age of the fish. Adult females have two or three longitudinal stripes and two or three vertical stripes near the tail; females of less than 2 inches or so have vertical stripes similar to the males'. The striped killifish is also much paler than the mummichog. The males are usually olive green along the back with silvery sides; however, they are more colorful during the breeding season. The females are olive green above and whitish below. These abundant little fish are often found in close association with mummichogs all along the Atlantic coast.

The banded killifish, *Fundulus diaphanus*, is somewhat smaller than the mummichog and the striped killifish and is more streamlined. It has bright silverblue vertical bars, or bands, and a more pointed head than do the other two species. The banded killifish seems to tolerate fresher water than do the other two species; however, they are all often found together in brackish water. The banded killifish ranges from the Maritimes to South Carolina.

The sheepshead minnow, *Cyprinodon variegatus*, belongs to the same family as the killifishes, Cyprinodontidae. Sheepshead minnows are stubby, deep-bodied fish that grow to about 4 inches long. The males are brightly colored and are marked with iridescent blue during the spring and early spawning season; the females are olive or brassy colored. Sheepshead minnows are usually found over a sand bottom and can tolerate a broad range of salinities, from freshwater to very salty seawater, all along the Inner Coast.

Livebearers

There are some small, rather nondescript fishes that seem to be in every well-vegetated freshwater and brackish water canal and in the backwaters of rivers, ponds, and swamps. Most are members of the livebearer family (Poeciliidae). Many members of this group resemble the guppy, the best-known species in this family; the family also includes some other favorite aquarium fishes, such as swordtails and mollies. Livebearers are closely related to killifishes, but unlike egg-bearing killifishes, they give birth to live fish fry, just as guppies and mollies do in aquariums. Livebearers are stubby little fishes with single dorsal fins and rounded or squared tails.

If you see a small fish nibbling at the surface, chances are it is an eastern mosquito fish, *Gambusia holbrooki*, feeding on larval mosquitoes and other insects suspended just below the surface of the water. Eastern mosquito fish are often called topminnows because of their surface feeding habit. They are well adapted for this manner of feeding with their flattened heads, underslung lower jaws, and upward-opening mouths. They are small, grayish fish only about 2 inches long, with large eyes and a series of black spots on their dorsal and tail fins.

The male eastern mosquito fish guides sperm with the aid of its highly modified anal fin directly into the female at the "target," a dark spot near the female's urogenital opening. The eggs develop and hatch within the female, and the young, when born, are well developed and about 1 inch long.

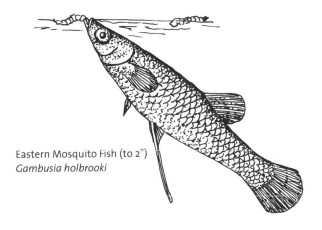

Eastern Mosquito Fish (to 2")
Gambusia holbrooki

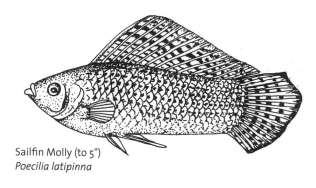

Sailfin Molly (to 5")
Poecilia latipinna

The natural range of the eastern mosquito fish is from Delaware along the Atlantic coast to Florida; however, it has been distributed worldwide to control mosquitoes. Unfortunately, when plants and animals are introduced, they often become serious pests. Eastern mosquito fish have been introduced to Australia, where they are called plague minnows, and to all other continents except Antarctica. They have been implicated as predators on native fishes, amphibians, and beneficial insects.

The sailfin molly, *Poecilia latipinna*, is a familiar and favorite species of aquarists. Sailfin mollies range from around Cape Fear, North Carolina, to Florida. They are very popular aquarium fish, but they are often discarded in favor of other species to rear, and so they have been poured into local waters everywhere. Consequently the distributional range of sailfin mol-

lies has extended well beyond their natural range. Sailfin mollies have large, billowing dorsal fins and rows of dark brown spots along their sides.

Livebearers are easy to rear and breed. As they reproduce, they bear a number of young that may be different colors from the parents or have odd-shaped fins. Some are maintained in the aquarium, others are traded or sold, and still others are released to the wild, and so it is not uncommon to collect wild sailfin mollies that are very different from their published descriptions.

Sailfin mollies feed on algae and organic detritus as well as mosquito larvae. They are very tolerant of wide swings in salinity and seem to do well in freshwater and brackish water. They are very common and abundant in Florida, where they intermingle with eastern mosquito fish under floating vegetation.

Anchovies and Silversides: Silvery Streakers

Anchovies and silversides are small, very abundant fishes that are favored prey for larger predatory fishes such as mackerel, bluefish, and striped bass. The anchovies along the Inner Coast are very similar to the salted and canned variety on grocery store shelves.

Anchovies and silversides are small fishes that are distinctly marked with bright silvery bands on

Bay Anchovy (to 3")
Anchoa mitchilli

Silversides (to 3")
Menidia spp.

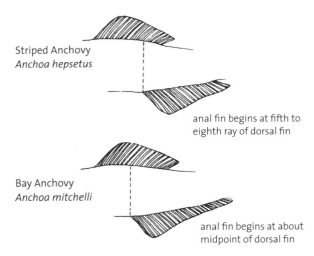

Striped Anchovy
Anchoa hepsetus

anal fin begins at fifth to
eighth ray of dorsal fin

Bay Anchovy
Anchoa mitchelli

anal fin begins at about
midpoint of dorsal fin

their sides. Silversides are slender and streamlined; anchovies are deeper bodied and stockier. Anchovies have very large eyes and mouths, and their rounded snouts overhang their mouths. Silversides have smaller mouths and eyes. Anchovies are soft and almost transparent; silversides are firm and opaque. In addition, anchovies have a single dorsal fin, and silversides have two dorsal fins. Silversides often form large schools close to the surface and are typically found in shallow waters over sand bottoms. Anchovies also form schools near the surface, but they are more widespread; the juveniles stay closer to shore, and the adults are found in deeper waters.

Anchovy and silverside species are difficult to identify to species; identification is best left to the experts. There are two species of anchovies on the Atlantic coast: the striped anchovy, *Anchoa hepsetus*, and the bay anchovy, *Anchoa mitchilli*. The bay anchovy is a smaller species. Its body is deeper and more compressed than that of the striped anchovy.

There are six species of silversides. The three most common are the inland silverside, *Menidia beryllina*; the Atlantic silverside, *Menidia menidia*; and the rough silverside, *Membras martinica*. All

three species range along the Inner Coast to Florida. The other three species—the hardhead silverside, the tidewater silverside, and the Key silverside—inhabit south Florida and the Caribbean.

🌿

Fishes That Come in from the Sea to Spawn

Fishes that spawn in estuaries, migrate to the sea, and then return to their natal streams to spawn are called anadromous, from the Greek word for "running upward." Salmon and striped bass are also anadromous fish species. Anadromous fishes almost certainly started life thousands of years ago as freshwater fishes and over time adapted to brackish water and then to saltwater habitats. However, their fragile and vulnerable early life stages, the eggs and larvae, are not adapted to anything but freshwater.

Innate behavioral stirrings bring ocean-run fishes back to their beginnings, where they spawn and complete the cycle of life. Most anadromous fishes return to the body of water in which they were originally spawned, the natal stream. Scientists believe that as the eggs, larvae, and juvenile fishes develop and swim through their natal waters, chemical and other cues are imprinted in their sensory systems, allowing them to return to their place of origin even after several years at sea.

Shad and Herrings

Herrings and shad are ocean-run schooling fishes that begin their lives in the freshwater and brackish water of estuaries and streams along the Atlantic coast. Some shad and herrings spawn in the open areas of large rivers; other species migrate beyond tidewater and fight their way through shallow riffles and torrential rapids to very small freshwater streams. After spawning, adult herrings and shads

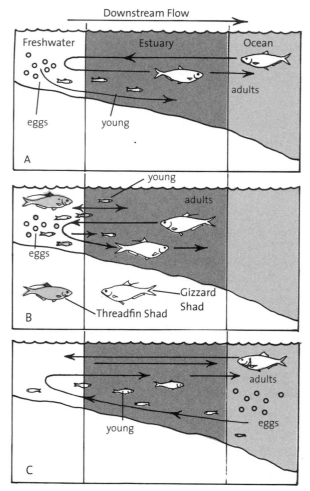

A. The anadromous species of the herring and shad family of fishes—the alewife, the blueback herring, and the American shad—move up from the ocean in spring to spawn in freshwater. The young move downstream into salty water, and as they mature, they eventually move into the ocean to join the adults.

B. Adult threadfin shad rarely move into the estuarine waters. Their young, however, are common visitors in low-salinity waters. Gizzard shad spend most of the year in the estuary but migrate upstream in spring to spawn in freshwater.

C. Menhadens spawn in the ocean, but both adults and young migrate into the estuary, moving well upstream, even into tidal freshwater areas.

descend the rills and rivers, and by summer most of them have returned to the sea. The young fishes, meanwhile, grow rapidly from larvae to juveniles, and as the season turns from spring to summer, the young fishes begin schooling and gradually migrate downstream, where they feed and grow in nourishing estuaries and sounds until autumn, when most of the young fishes swim out to sea. They range the Atlantic from Nova Scotia to the warm offshore waters of Florida for three to five years until they mature. Then, as winter turns to spring, the shad bushes along the shorelines burst forth with white blossoms and herald the arrival of herrings and shads, and once again the mysterious ritual of life begins anew.

Millions of adult shad and herrings ascend the countless rivers of the Atlantic from the Saint Johns River in Florida to the Maritimes, but many never reach the spawning grounds because the rivers are blocked by dams, or because of declines in water quality, or because they are caught in nets or by the hooks and lines of commercial and recreational anglers. This is an all too frequent commentary on the status of the world's fisheries.

Shad and herrings resemble each other so closely that only experienced fishermen and fishery biologists are likely to identify them with any accuracy. Shad and herrings as a group are thin, silvery fishes with a pearly opalescent glow along their sides; they have large, smooth, deciduous scales and sawtooth, thin-edged bellies.

There are four anadromous shad and herring species that inhabit the rivers and estuaries of the Inner Coast. Perhaps the best known is the American shad or white shad, *Alosa sapidissima*. The species name means "savory." The American shad is the largest—some weigh almost 10 pounds—and most delectable of the group. Shad roe are considered a delicacy by many throughout the mid-Atlantic.

The American shad has a dark bluish to greenish

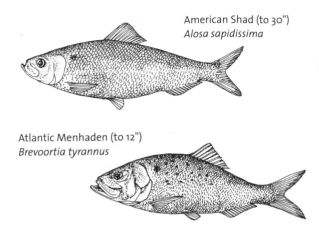

American Shad (to 30")
Alosa sapidissima

Atlantic Menhaden (to 12")
Brevoortia tyrannus

can be quite abundant in tidal freshwater and brackish water. The gizzard shad is usually not considered a good eating fish by humans, but it does serve as food for many predator fishes. Gizzard shad have deep bodies, small heads, and small mouths. The last ray of the dorsal fin is drawn out in a long, trailing filament. Gizzard shad live in the freshwaters of upper estuaries and sounds and in rivers, reservoirs, lakes, and ponds. They are widely distributed throughout the Inner Coast down to the Indian River Lagoon in mid-Florida.

The threadfin shad, *Dorosoma petenense*, resembles herrings rather than its deep-bodied cousin the

back with a dark spot on the side just behind the gills, followed by a series of four or five dusky spots above the lateral line. American shad are strong swimmers. Like almost all shad and herrings, the American shad has large, deciduous scales that are loosely fitted to its body so that it is not encased in an armored suit of scales. The loose scales, highly compressed body, and deeply forked tail make the American shad an agile and fleet fish that can ascend shallow rivers against rushing torrents of water moving toward the sea.

The hickory shad, *Alosa mediocris*, sometimes called the tailor shad, grows almost as large as the American shad and is quite similar in appearance except for its jutting lower jaw.

The two species of anadromous river herrings that inhabit this region are the alewife, also known as branch herring, *Alosa pseudoharengus*, and the blueback herring, *Alosa aestivalis*, also known as glut herring and, to add to the confusion, as alewife. The river herring is smaller than shad and not as deep bodied; it generally has a single spot on the shoulder rather than a series of spots.

Not all herrings and shad are anadromous. The gizzard shad, or mud shad, *Dorosoma cepedianum*,

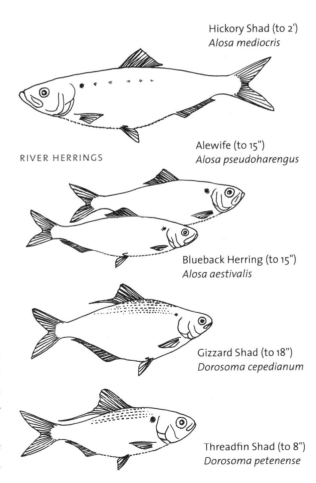

Hickory Shad (to 2')
Alosa mediocris

RIVER HERRINGS

Alewife (to 15")
Alosa pseudoharengus

Blueback Herring (to 15")
Alosa aestivalis

Gizzard Shad (to 18")
Dorosoma cepedianum

Threadfin Shad (to 8")
Dorosoma petenense

gizzard shad. It has a single dark spot just behind the head, a longer dorsal fin filament than the gizzard shad's, and fins that are usually washed with a yellow tint. Threadfin shad reach a maximum size of 8 inches. They are filter feeders that consume microscopic plants and animals.

Menhadens: Different and Most Abundant Herrings

The Atlantic menhaden, *Brevoortia tyrannus*, is a deep-bodied silvery herring with a distinctive black shoulder spot and a deeply forked tail. Unlike their relatives shad and herrings, which spawn in the upper reaches of estuaries, menhadens spawn in the inshore coastal waters of the Atlantic. Soon after hatching, the tiny menhaden larvae are swept into the estuaries, where they move upstream into low-salinity waters to feed and grow in the same nursery areas that nurture small herrings and shad. Juvenile menhadens tend to stay in the shallows close to shore, while the older ones cruise the deeper, open waters. In some years there are millions of menhadens packed in dense schools on the surface. It is mesmerizing to watch a school of menhadens swimming in close unison, following a single lead fish, with fins and tails just ruffling the surface. After a period of time, the leader turns and melds into the confusion of fish, and a new lead fish takes over the point. Menhadens swim rapidly through the water, straining hundreds of gallons of water through their open mouths and filtering out tiny planktonic organisms with their feathery gills.

Menhadens are among the least-known fishes, yet they support one of the oldest and largest fisheries along the Atlantic coast. Menhadens are so oily that they are almost inedible by humans, but this very quality makes them a rich source of protein meal, used as feed for chickens. Omega-3 oils, so important for promoting healthy hearts, are also important by-products of these little-known fish.

Menhadens are harvested along the Inner Coast in stationary nets called pound nets and in large numbers by menhaden "clippers," which often work in tandem with spotting airplanes that sight the schools and direct the menhaden boats to them. The menhaden boats deploy two stout, smaller, aluminum boats that are equipped with a large purse seine, which is in one continuous unit but is divided between the boats. The two boats depart the larger menhaden vessel and encircle the menhaden school: one boat, trailing its half of the net, goes to the right around the school, and the other boat, trailing its half of the net, steers to the left around the school. The boats meet and engage a special weight called a tom that purses the net from below, creating a floor. The net is set and the fish are trapped. The menhaden clipper moves in, and the fish are pumped out of the net into the hold of the ship. The hunt continues until it is time for the menhaden boat to return to its base and disgorge its oily treasure to the reduction plant. Years ago, there were many regional fisheries for menhadens from New England south; however, the number of plants and vessels has declined, and now there are only one or two active operations along the coast. The largest reduction plant with the largest fleet is located in Reedville, Virginia. Its boats fish the Virginia waters of Chesapeake Bay and nearby Atlantic coastal waters.

Menhadens are even more vital as food for many other species. In the late fall and winter and then again in the spring, migrating common loons feed on these oily fish by the thousands. Egrets, ospreys, gulls, and many other birds feed on menhadens from above, and bluefish and striped bass voraciously feed on them from below.

Atlantic menhadens range all along the Inner Coast. There are three other species of menhadens also found along the Atlantic coast: the gulf menhaden, which is an important commercial and prey species in the Gulf of Mexico, and yellowfin and finescale menhaden, which are considered minor species in terms of numbers and are not targeted as commercial species.

Striped Bass and White Perch: Temperate Basses

Temperate basses are medium-size to large fish that live in fresh, estuarine, and marine waters. They are separated from the sea bass family by the presence and number of opercular (gill cover) spines. The two dorsal fins are divided, or separate, rather than connected, as in the sunfish family, and the tail fin is forked.

The striped bass, *Morone saxatilis*, and the white perch, *Morone americana*, are both highly esteemed recreational and commercial species. The striped

White Perch (to 20")
Morone americana

Striped Bass (to 5' or more)
Morone saxatilis

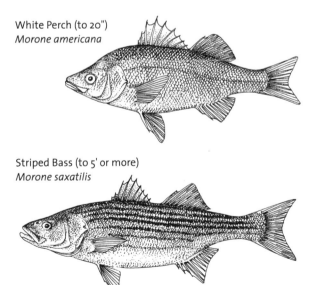

bass may be the most important recreational species all along the Atlantic coast, from the Maritimes to the Carolinas and beyond.

The striped bass is often called rockfish or just rock in the Chesapeake Bay area and linesider or striper elsewhere. It is an anadromous fish with some exceptions; striped basses have been widely introduced into reservoirs and large landlocked lakes, and if conditions are suitable for the survival of the eggs, normal reproduction occurs and the striped bass population is self-sustaining. Striped basses along the Atlantic coast and the Inner Coast migrate in from the sea and up rivers to where the water is almost fresh, but slightly salty. The females, often known as cow rocks, release their eggs into the water in the spring. The floating eggs are then fertilized by clouds of sperm from the smaller males. The eggs soon hatch and mingle with the herring and shad larvae that were spawned in the same regions of the estuary. As the larval fish mature, they migrate downstream and congregate in the shallows, where they spend the summer feeding and growing.

When the striped bass and white perch are only a few inches long, they are very similar in appearance. At this stage, both species have longitudinal stripes overlaying a series of vertical bars along their sides. Striped basses are voracious feeders and will attack schools of menhadens, silversides, and anchovies with a ferocious appetite, as any sport fisherman will confirm. Adult striped basses are silver with six to nine black stripes on their sides; their backs are olive green or bronze in Inner Coast waters and bluish when they have migrated out to sea. Sea-run striped basses can weigh 100 pounds or more but are smaller in the inshore coastal waters of the Inner Coast. They spawn in a number of estuaries, the most important ones being the Hudson River near West Point, New York; the Chesapeake Bay, particularly in Maryland waters; and far upstream in the Roanoke River in North Carolina. The striped bass ranges all along the coast to the Saint Johns River in Florida.

The white perch is truly an estuarine species; it is not found in the ocean. Inner Coast river systems apparently maintain their own discrete populations of white perches within individual river systems, in contrast to striped basses, which move throughout the estuaries. White perches are usually silvery, but as they grow older, they become dusky gray with touches of metallic green or blue, particularly on their backs. White perches are relatively deep-bodied fish, growing to about 4 pounds but usually smaller. They tend to school around bottom structure, and rocks and pilings in the shallows. They range down to the Saint Johns River in Florida.

Atlantic Sturgeon: Another Anadromous Fish

The huge, lumbering Atlantic sturgeon, *Acipenser oxyrhynchus*, used to be plentiful along the Atlantic Coast from Labrador to the Saint Johns River in northeast Florida. It is now seriously threatened throughout its range. The sturgeon fishery was important from colonial times to about the end of the nineteenth century, when the number of these primitive goliaths declined precipitously. Before the decline, sturgeons were harvested by the hundreds of thousands of pounds annually. The meat was smoked

and the roe were made into salty and savory caviar, much of which was exported to European markets. These large, sluggish fish were easily exploited. Their decline has been attributed to this overfishing, as well as to deteriorating water quality and, perhaps most of all, to the damming of rivers and streams, which prevented the fish from migrating upstream to the critical spawning areas. Occasionally, a huge sturgeon turns up in a fisherman's net, and because they are so rare these days, an article accompanied by a picture is usually published in the local newspaper about this rather strange-looking fish.

Sturgeons are prehistoric fishes with a geologic record dating to the Cretaceous period. There are seven species of sturgeons known from North America, and they all share certain characteristics: They are covered with five rows of bony plates, also called scutes or shields; one row along the center of the back, one row along each side, and two rows along the belly. These plates are sharp edged in young sturgeons but become blunted with age. The head is also covered with bony plates. Sturgeons have a soft, protractile, toothless mouth located on the underside of the long pointed snout, and four sensory barbels dangle in front of the mouth.

Sturgeons are bottom feeders. They prey on mollusks, worms, insect larvae, and other bottom organisms. They root in the mud and sand like aquatic pigs, nosing up worms and clams and sucking them up into their mouths.

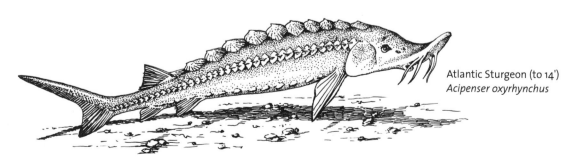

Atlantic Sturgeon (to 14')
Acipenser oxyrhynchus

Atlantic sturgeons can grow to a formidable size; the largest recorded specimen weighed 811 pounds and was 14 feet long, and there are still some Atlantic sturgeons that are 6 feet or more in Inner Coast waters.

The shortnose sturgeon is smaller than the Atlantic surgeon and differs little in appearance other than it has a shorter and broader snout and dorsal plates that are separated rather than overlapping. Shortnose sturgeons are very rare; they are officially classified as an endangered species.

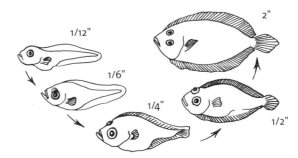

In the larval development of flatfishes, one eye gradually migrates from one side over the top of the head and is finally positioned close to the other eye.

Flatfishes: Lurkers in the Sand

Flatfishes are well adapted for living partially buried in sand and mud bottoms, as they have pancake-flat bodies with both eyes borne on the same side. They lurk half buried in the bottom sands and silts, dark side up, and always alert for passing prey. Most flatfishes can quickly change the colors and patterns of their dark upper sides to blend into the substrate.

There are about 600 species of these rather strange, oval, flattened, bony fishes found throughout the world, and almost 100 of those species live in North American waters. Flatfishes range in size from the 8-inch tonguefish that weighs just a few ounces to the monstrous Atlantic and Pacific halibuts that may grow as long as 7 feet and weigh more than 500 pounds. There are four families of flatfishes that include some commonly known fishes, such as flounders, soles, and halibuts, and some not so well known flatfishes, such as tonguefish, whiffs, and hogchoker. They all share certain characteristics: They are flat. They are able to quickly change their color. They start out life swimming like any proper larval fish, with one eye on each side of the head, but as they grow, one eye (whether it is the right eye or the left eye depends on the species) begins to migrate over

the top of the head until it reaches a position near the other eye. The little fishes also then begin swimming on their sides rather than in the usual upright manner of most fishes. They now have two eyes on the pigmented upper side and no eyes on the pale bottom side.

Flatfish families are separated into right-eyed and left-eyed species. To determine whether a flatfish is right or left eyed, simply hold or envision the fish like a typical fish by orienting the dorsal fin to the top; if the head points to the left, the fish is left eyed, and, of course, if the head points to the right, the fish is right eyed.

The hogchoker, *Trinectes maculatus*, is a right-eyed sole found in estuaries and sometimes even in tidal freshwaters. Hogchokers are quite common and ubiquitous fish throughout the Inner Coast. They are small, usually no more than 6 to 8 inches long, with a dusky brown upper side often adorned with several black bars, a white to sometimes slightly patterned blind side, and a very small mouth and eyes. Hogchokers are rather useless as human food because of their small size and bony frame; however, their flesh is quite tasty.

The winter flounder, *Pleuronectes americanus*, is another right-eyed flatfish that is common in shallow

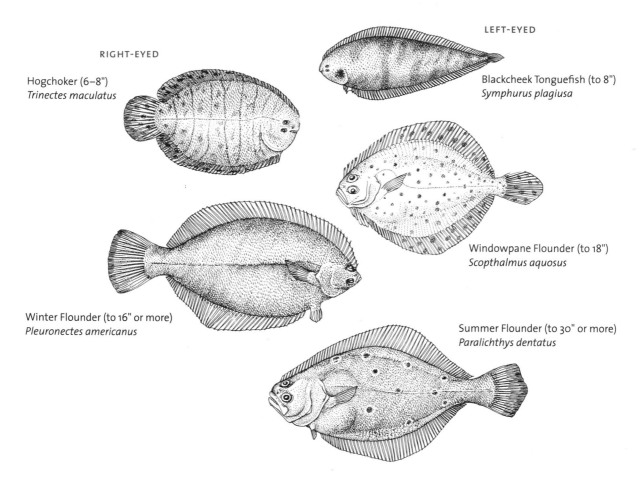

RIGHT-EYED

Hogchoker (6–8")
Trinectes maculatus

LEFT-EYED

Blackcheek Tonguefish (to 8")
Symphurus plagiusa

Windowpane Flounder (to 18")
Scopthalmus aquosus

Winter Flounder (to 16" or more)
Pleuronectes americanus

Summer Flounder (to 30" or more)
Paralichthys dentatus

waters, especially in the winter. (Its common name comes from its habit of living in deeper waters in the summer and appearing in shallow waters in the winter.) Winter flounders spawn in brackish waters of estuaries generally from North Carolina northward to Maine. They are usually a tawny to reddish brown and may be as dark as charcoal brown with a white eyeless side. They are very tasty fish and are sought by both recreational anglers and commercial fishermen.

The summer flounder, also called fluke and doormat, *Paralichthys dentatus*, is a large, left-eyed flounder that is avidly sought as a food fish. This floun-

der can reach a weight of 20 pounds or more, but smaller summer flounders of about 5–8 pounds are much more common. The eyed side is brownish tan and marked with several round dark spots. Summer flounders have large mouths equipped with sharp teeth. They lie on sandy bottoms, and as mummichog, squids, or shrimps happens by, these agile flounders leap off the bottom, swallow their dinner, and quickly settle back down to wait for the next meal. Summer flounders spawn offshore in deeper waters and enter estuaries and sounds in the summer months to north Florida.

The gulf flounder and the southern flounder are

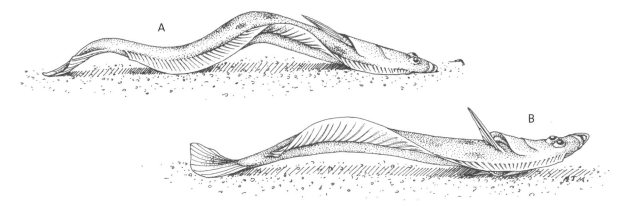

A summer flounder first sights its prey (A) and then quickly springs to engulf it (B).

closely related to the summer flounder; they are left eyed and are similar in appearance, though the gulf flounder is generally smaller than the summer flounder and the southern flounder. Gulf flounders are generally tan to brown on the eyed side and marked with numerous white blotches and three dark spots that form a triangle: one above and one below the lateral line, and one on the lateral line near the tail. Gulf flounders range from North Carolina down to the Florida Keys and the Gulf of Mexico. The southern flounder is a larger version of the gulf flounder but lacks the prominent dark eye spots seen on the other two species; the eyed side is usually brown and marked with a number of diffuse splotches. Southern flounders range from lower Chesapeake Bay down along the Inner Coast to Florida and the Gulf of Mexico.

The windowpane flounder, *Scopthalmus aquosus*, is a left-eyed flounder that is almost round in outline and has a very thin, compressed body. The eyed side is a pale, almost translucent olive green to tan adorned with numerous small spots. Windowpanes are found all along the Inner Coast but are more common to the north.

The blackcheek tonguefish, *Symphurus plagiusa*, is a strange little flatfish that is shaped like a tongue or a teardrop, with its tapered body narrowest at its tail. It is usually dark brown and marked with darker mottled bars and a dark spot on its gill cover, the opercle.

Fishes That Come in from the Sea to Feed

Hundreds of species of fishes live in the estuaries and tidal rivers of the Inner Coast. Probably half of those species are ocean fishes that enter the waters of the Inner Coast, usually in the spring and summer, to feed and then return to the sea in the autumn. Some ocean fishes wander into the sounds and coastal lagoons more or less accidentally—perhaps they were chasing some smaller fish, or perhaps a strong current steered them into the quieter backwaters of the Inner Coast. Others, such as sea trouts, bluefishes, and cownose rays, are predictable and regular seasonal visitors. Most marine fishes that are common in Inner Coast waters spawn in the ocean, but their larvae and juveniles are swept into the sounds and bays by winds and currents soon after their eggs hatch.

They grow rapidly in the estuaries nourished by the organically rich water swarming with planktonic organisms. First they feed on tiny floating algae, microcrustaceans such as copepods, and the spawn of millions of invertebrates, including barnacles, worms, and sea urchins. The small fishes grow rapidly in these waters, and as they increase in size, so do their appetites. They start feeding on larger invertebrates and small fishes such as anchovies and silversides. Adults of ocean fishes tend to remain in deeper waters, but the young favor shallow, inshore waters of bays and sounds.

Drums

Drums are a large family of fishes distributed in the world oceans and quite common in the Inner Coast. Drums as a group are somewhat elongated, but some are more perchlike in appearance. The dorsal fin is usually long and is separated by a deep notch between the spiny- or hard-rayed portion and the soft-rayed portion. Most species of drums are ocean and estuarine dwellers; however, there is a freshwater member of this group, the freshwater drum, that thrives in central North America. Most drums make rasping or loud, resonant drumming sounds that are produced by the contraction of abdominal muscles against their branched air bladders.

The spot, also known as Norfolk spot, *Leiostomus xanthurus*, is a very abundant little fish, particularly between Chesapeake Bay and Georgia. Schools of young spots can often be seen milling around pilings and jetties just 1 or 2 feet below the surface. Watch carefully to see them quickly turn and flash their distinctive shoulder spots. Menhadens have a similar shoulder spot, but they usually swim closer to the surface in tighter schools. The spot has a sloping head; an underslung mouth, properly called an inferior mouth; and a silvery body tinged with a

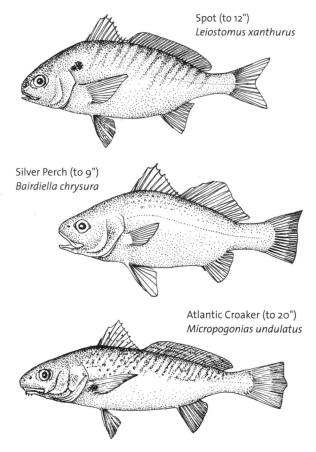

Spot (to 12")
Leiostomus xanthurus

Silver Perch (to 9")
Bairdiella chrysura

Atlantic Croaker (to 20")
Micropogonias undulatus

golden iridescence. The sides are marked with angled oblique dark lines that extend from the dorsal fin to just above the silvery belly. The tail is dusky and slightly forked; the dorsal fin is also dusky. The other fins are usually pale to darker yellow. Spots feed in the muddy-bottomed shallows on benthic invertebrates, particularly on tube-building worms and the siphons of clams.

The spot, even though it is a small fish, usually weighing only 1 pound or less, is a very popular sport fish, perhaps because it is usually so plentiful and delicious to eat. Many recreational fishermen also use spots as live bait for larger predatory fishes.

The Atlantic croaker, *Micropogonias undulatus*,

also called hardhead in some areas, makes the loudest and most resonant sounds of any of the drums. Small croakers, about 8 inches long, called pinheads in Chesapeake Bay, school close to shore in Inner Coast waters. Croakers are washed with a luminescent pinkish to a peach-colored glow when first taken from the water; brassy brown spots are arranged in angled wavy lines along their flanks, and the dorsal fin is also spotted. The domed head and inferior mouth are similar to those of a spot; however, the croaker has three to five pairs of barbels growing from its lower jaw. Croakers feed in the sandy and muddy shallows on crabs, shrimps, various mollusks, and fishes. They are quite abundant in Chesapeake Bay and the Carolinas and range as far south as mid-Florida to about Cape Canaveral. The average size of a croaker is about 2–3 pounds. The croaker is a favorite of fishermen using light spinning tackle. It is also a very important commercial species; hundreds of tons of these tasty fish are landed yearly.

The silver perch, *Bairdiella chrysura*, is not a true perch but a member of the drum family. As the name implies, it is a silvery fish, with a bluish to brassy-colored back and yellowish fins. The mouth is terminal. This is a rather small fish, usually no longer than 9 inches, and therefore is generally not esteemed as a food fish, although its flesh is very firm and tasty. Silver perches are abundant throughout the Inner Coast in shallow waters over sand, mud, and grassy bottoms. Small silver perches feed on an assortment of small crustaceans, including copepods, amphipods, isopods, and shrimps, as well as small fishes; larger silver perches feed on silversides, small herrings, and anchovies.

The red drum, also known as channel bass, redfish, or spottail bass, *Sciaenops ocellatus*, is silvery gray with a metallic reddish to copper cast. It is marked with one or two black eyespots, or ocelli, near the base of the tail. These are big fish; some may

reach a weight of 90–100 pounds and a length of 5 feet, but most weigh less than 20 pounds. Red drums inhabit Inner Coast estuaries until they are about four years old. When they attain a length of about 2 1/2 feet, they move offshore into deeper waters and join the spawning schools.

Large red drums are bottom feeders and prey on an assortment of crabs, mollusks, sand dollars, and several species of fishes, including the ubiquitous menhadens, pinfish, and pigfish, as well as other drums, such as spots and croakers, and even flatfishes. Red drums are rooters and can often be seen in shallow water with their heads down and their broad tails almost breaking the surface of the water, feeding on bottom organisms. The red drum is highly prized as both a game fish and an eating fish; this is the species first served as blackened redfish in New Orleans. Some of the largest red drums on record have been caught along the beaches of North Carolina's Outer Banks. The east coast of Florida, especially the Mosquito Lagoon, the Banana River, and the Indian River Lagoon, are also well known for red drums. Red drums are wide-ranging fish and are found throughout the Inner Coast and the Gulf of Mexico; they are most abundant in Florida and the Gulf states.

The black drum, *Pogonias cromis*, is the granddaddy of all the drums. This large, lumbering fish with an underslung mouth equipped with a beard of barbels on its lower jaw and a mouthful of clam-crushing teeth, weighs an average of 30–50 pounds. Those that live twenty-five or thirty years can weigh well over 100 pounds. The scientific name for this species is particularly appropriate: *Pogonias* means "bearded," and *cromis* means "to grunt" or "to croak." Black drum are not really black but silvery with a brassy sheen; their fins, however, are dark gray to black.

Black drums reach sexual maturity at the end of

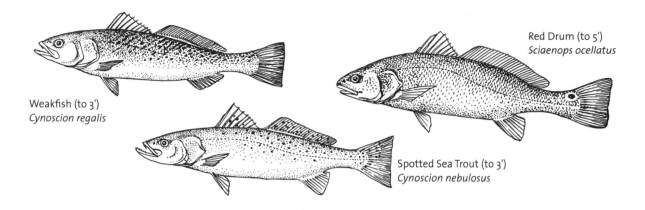

Weakfish (to 3')
Cynoscion regalis

Red Drum (to 5')
Sciaenops ocellatus

Spotted Sea Trout (to 3')
Cynoscion nebulosus

their second year and spawn in the ocean just off-shore bays and rivers, where the newly hatched fish move into the estuaries to feed and grow. Young black drums that weigh less than 8 pounds are called puppy drums and are marked with about six charcoal gray vertical bands extending from their dorsal fins to their silvery bellies.

Black drums range throughout the waters of the Inner Coast. In some areas, they are avidly sought by recreational fishermen, but in other areas, they are not a popular game or food fish.

Sea trouts are the most prized fish of the drum family because they provide great sport for the recreational angler and are wonderful to eat. Most of the fishes in the drum family are bottom feeders and have inferior mouths typical of bottom feeders. Some have barbels to sense their prey. Some, like the black drum, have grinding teeth that are beautifully adapted for crushing the shells of crabs and mollusks. Not so with the sea trouts: they are more streamlined fish that range the open waters; their upper jaws are equipped with a pair of sharp canine teeth, and they use them to good advantage, slashing into schools of menhadens, anchovies, and other small fishes.

The weakfish, also called gray sea trout or squeteague, *Cynoscion regalis*, is so named because its mouth is soft and fragile and easily torn when hooked. It is a silvery fish marked with an overall pattern of darker splotches; its fins are yellowish to dusky gray. Most weakfishes weigh between 1 and 3 pounds, but some of the older weakfishes exceed 15 pounds. Smaller weakfishes tend to graze in the water column and near the bottom, where they snare shrimps, crabs, and even small clams; the large fish are highly predatory and are voracious feeders on schooling fishes such as menhadens, butterfishes, and herrings.

The spotted sea trout, or speck, *Cynoscion nebulosus*, is dark gray to greenish above and tinged with blue; it is marked with a number of distinctive black dots along the upper half of the body, including the dorsal fins and tail. The spotted sea trout is similar to the weakfish; it is elongated and streamlined, and its mouth is large and armed with a pair of protruding fangs. Also like the weakfish, the spotted sea trout

Young Black Drum (adults to 5 1/2')
Pogonias cromis

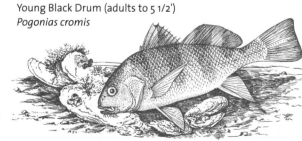

Striped Mullets (to 2')
Mugil cephalus

ranges the Inner Coast to Florida and into the Gulf of Mexico; however, the spotted sea trout is more abundant in the southern part of its range, from the Carolinas southward, whereas the weakfish is more abundant from the Carolinas northward.

Mullets: Silver Leapers

All through the Inner Coast, in the salty inlets, along marshy shores, and even up into freshwater, mullets are a-leapin'. They swirl in tight schools near the water's surface and are frequently grouped loosely together according to age and size. The smaller mullets, probably a year or so old, are known as finger mullets and are a favorite bait for all sorts of fishes, as well as a favorite food for all sorts of fishes and birds. The larger mullets, usually about two years old, range in size from about 1 to 2 feet long. Mullets are bottom grazers for the most part, feeding on organic material, algae, and an occasional worm or two.

Mullets are a favored food in some areas but are avoided as table food in other places along the Inner Coast because some people consider them muddy tasting. Mullets caught from the Indian River Lagoon, smoked, and sold along the road and in nearby restaurants are wonderful. So is the fried mullet served up in restaurants on Harkers Island and in Morehead City in North Carolina.

Most mullets are caught by commercial fishermen for the restaurant trade and, particularly, for bait. Mullets are important forage species for jacks, mackerels, bluefish, striped bass, and practically any other predatory fish. Chunks and fillets, as well as whole finger mullets, are the mainstays of recreational fishermen, whether they fish from the beach, from the many fishing piers jutting out into the water, or from boats. A favorite pastime of tourists from the Chesapeake Bay to the Florida Keys is watching brown pelicans crash-diving into schools of milling mullets. Pelicans also haunt fishing piers, watching for any fish that they can steal that is being reeled in by an angler. Pelicans also like to sit on the water, intently watching as fishing lines are being wound up, so that they can nab a chunk of mullet and fly off with it. There has been many a pelican that has had to endure the humiliation of being hauled up to the pier so that an entangled fishing line or hook can be removed and the pelican can be sent on its way by a disgruntled fisherman.

There are two common species of mullets along the Inner Coast and the inshore waters of the Atlantic Ocean: the striped mullet, *Mugil cephalus*, and the white mullet, *Mugil curema*. Both species of mullets spawn in the ocean when they are about two years old or older; the young hatchlings then move into the estuarine nursery areas. Several months later, they move into inshore coastal waters, often forming huge schools, which attract hungry fishes from below and hungry gulls and pelicans from above.

Both species of mullets are long, round-bodied, blunt-nosed fishes with small mouths and pectoral fins that are set unusually high on their sides. Both species are bluish gray or olive on their backs, shading to silver or white on their bellies. Striped mullets are marked with a series of spots that form longitudinal stripes, and white mullets are unmarked.

Eels

On dark early spring nights in dozens of rivers and inlets that open to the sea, glass eels, the immature form of the American eel, *Anguilla rostrata*, swarm close to the shore by the thousands in a timeless and mysterious drama that propels them upstream toward freshwater. They vanish during the day by burrowing into the muddy bottom or hiding under rocks or among the twisted roots of trees growing along the shore. Then, as darkness comes, the glass eels emerge from their nighttime refuges and resume their journey upstream. They are genetically programmed to reach freshwater and to complete their transformation from a one-year-old glass eel, so called because of their transparent bodies, to an elver, and then to an adult eel. They overcome many different obstacles as they migrate up rivers and then small streams and rivulets; they navigate through rapids and over falls; they sinuously wriggle over wet grass; and they burrow through moist sand, around spillways and dams, to reach ponds and headwaters where they have never swum before.

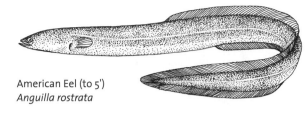

American Eel (to 5')
Anguilla rostrata

When they finally reach the freshwater destinations the transformation begins, the one-year-old glass eels develop pigmentation and they lose their transparency and become elvers and hungrily feed on crayfish, insects, and worms. They are now in their "yellow eel phase"; actually they are greenish brown to yellowish brown on their upper parts and grayish white on their bellies. They remain in the yellow phase for as long as twenty years; the females are larger than the males and may reach a length of 5 feet as compared to the 2-foot-long males. The females remain in the freshwater and the males are in the brackish waters of estuaries.

When sexually mature, American eels respond to some instinctive signal compelling the females to descend the freshwater rivers and move through the

LARVAL STAGES OF THE AMERICAN EEL

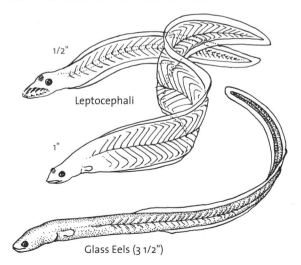

1/2"

Leptocephali

1"

Glass Eels (3 1/2")

salty estuaries, where the males are stirring as well, and all along the Inner Coast, they pour out of the coastal rivers and estuaries and move through the warm seas to an area south of Bermuda known as the Sargasso Sea, where they spawn and die. The newly hatched eels are bizarre, transparent, leaf-shaped creatures called leptocephali that were once thought to be a separate species of fish. Prevailing ocean currents and winds sweep the 1- to 2-inch larval eels toward the Atlantic coast of North America. It takes the eel larvae about one year to metamorphose into glass eels as they drift and ultimately enter rivers and estuaries to begin the cycle once again.

The conger eel, *Conger oceanicus*, apparently undergoes the same mysterious journey to an area of the Sargasso Sea. Conger eels spawn and apparently die there, leaving only their tiny leptocephali to repopulate the oceans and inshore waters with more conger eels. Scientists know much less about the life cycle of the conger than they do about that of the American eel. We do know that conger eels are much larger than American eels. American conger eels can reach a length of 6 feet or more and a weight of 70–80 pounds, but they are rather puny when compared to the European conger eels that have been caught weighing almost 200 pounds and stretching almost 12 feet long.

Conger eels resemble American eels; however there are some differences other than size. Conger eels are brownish gray to bluish gray above and white below, and their long dorsal and anal fins are edged with black. Conger and American eels also differ in the placement of the dorsal fins and the shapes of their jaws. The dorsal fin of the conger eel begins further forward than that of the American eel, almost to the pectoral fins, and the conger eel's upper jaw extends over the lower jaw, whereas the American eel's lower jaw is longer than the upper jaw.

Conger eels are more widely distributed than

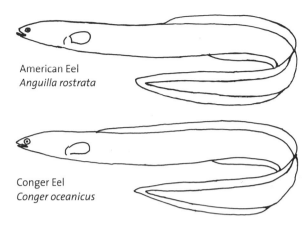

American Eel
Anguilla rostrata

Conger Eel
Conger oceanicus

American eels and live in a variety of habitats. They tend to hide in burrows and crevices in the bottom and have been found in waters over 1,000 feet deep as well as in the shallow waters of the Inner Coast, where they feed on an assortment of crustaceans, shrimps, and fishes.

❧

Finny Predators That Come in from the Sea

Many predatory fishes come into Inner Coast waters. Some come in on the rising tide to feed and then depart as the tide ebbs; others feed on the rich assortment of food in the river mouths, lagoons, and sounds during the warmer months; and still others make seasonal incursions, probably to spawn and certainly to feed.

Sharks, Rays, and Skates

Sharks, rays, and skates, collectively called elasmobranchs, are well represented in these waters. Elasmobranchs have cartilaginous rather than bony skeletons. They have five to seven gill slits, and they lack a swim bladder; however a large, oily liver, particularly in sharks, makes them quite buoyant. There

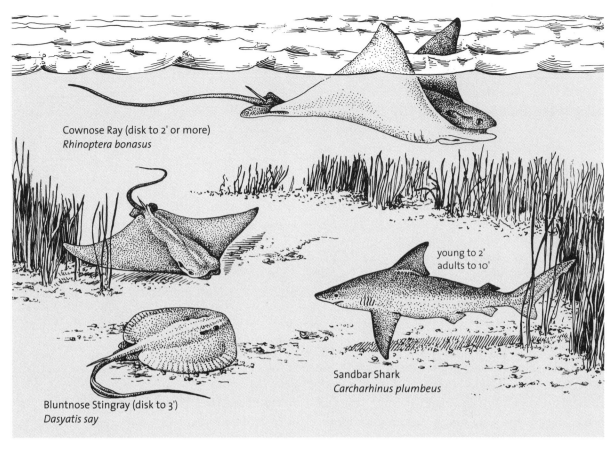

Cownose Ray (disk to 2' or more)
Rhinoptera bonasus

Bluntnose Stingray (disk to 3')
Dasyatis say

young to 2'
adults to 10'

Sandbar Shark
Carcharhinus plumbeus

are other characteristics that most of the species of elasmobranchs share, but it is safe to say that most people recognize sharks and rays.

Rays and skates are similar-looking elasmobranchs. They are flattened, and their large pectoral fins are attached to their heads like water "wings," allowing them to glide and "fly" through the water. Skates have pointed or diamond-shaped disks; rays may have diamond-shaped or rounded disks. Skates usually have thorny or roughened skin, and although rays may have skin as rough as sandpaper, it is relatively smooth when compared to that of skates. Most rays have venomous spines in their tails, which are formidable weapons. The lobed, fleshy tails of skates lack spines. Rays are ovoviviparous (livebearers),

whereas skates are oviparous and deposit curious leathery or horny egg cases, known as mermaid purses, which often wash ashore.

Rays and some sharks can wreak havoc in weed beds and sandy or muddy bottoms. Cownose rays, *Rhinoptera bonasus*, in particular, will sweep into the shallows, sometimes by the dozens or more, flap their winglike pectoral fins to blow the silt off a bed of clams, and then root them up with their cartilaginous snouts. After the rays expose the clams, they suck them in and crush them with their powerful grinding plates. The telltale pits and denuded areas in weed beds and seagrass meadows are often the work of cownose rays.

Cownose rays are also known as "double heads" in

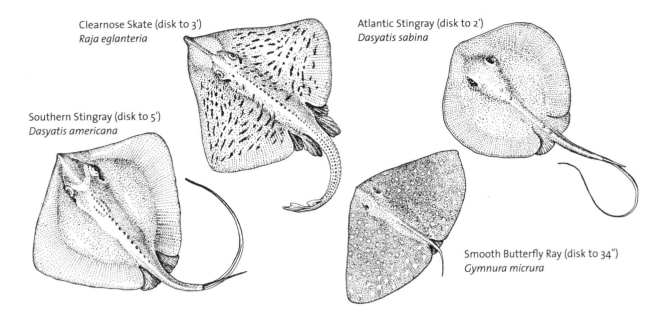

Clearnose Skate (disk to 3')
Raja eglanteria

Southern Stingray (disk to 5')
Dasyatis americana

Atlantic Stingray (disk to 2')
Dasyatis sabina

Smooth Butterfly Ray (disk to 34")
Gymnura micrura

some areas because of the indentations around their snouts, which give them the appearance of an upper and lower head. These rays are large and heavy with a wingspan of up to 3 feet. They have light to dark brown backs and are white or creamy yellow on their undersides. Their wing tips often break the surface like pairs of shark fins. They bear the young live in the sounds and bays of the Inner Coast. Cownose rays undertake long migrations in schools so large that there may be thousands in the group.

The cownose ray is armed with a long, poisonous spine located at the base of its whiplike tail, so take care if you hook one of these powerful fish. According to one story, Captain John Smith was wading in the shallows near the mouth of the Rappahannock River in Chesapeake Bay when he was stung severely by a cownose ray. He was in such great pain and became so ill that his crew despaired for his life. John Smith recovered, but the incident was memorialized by his crew, who named the place where he was attacked Stingray Point.

There are four other ray species that are quite common in Inner Coast shallows. Three of these rays—the southern stingray, *Dasyatis americana*; the Atlantic stingray, *Dasyatis sabina*; and the bluntnose stingray, *Dasyatis say*—have broadly diamond-shaped disks and long, slender tails, and as their common name implies, they are equipped with venomous spines. These rays are primarily bottom feeders, so they often lie partially buried in the sand with only their eyes and spiracles, respiratory valves for taking in water, projecting above the sand. The fourth ray, the smooth butterfly ray, also known as the sand skate, *Gymnura micrura*, has a very wide disk and a very short tail.

The southern stingray is light brown to grayish or olive green, and the ventral surface is white; the disk has rounded corners. The whiplike tail has a low ridge and, attached to the upper surface, a sharp-toothed stinger or spine. Southern stingrays feed on crabs, shrimps, spiny lobsters, clams, and small fishes. The southern stingray is the largest stingray in Inner Coast waters; its disk may be as wide as 5 feet.

The Atlantic stingray is the Inner Coast's smallest stingray, with no more than a 2-foot disk. The disk is yellowish brown on its upper side and whitish below; the disk is very rounded and smooth. Atlantic stingrays have been reported to feed on small crustaceans, worms, and other invertebrates. They are quite tolerant of freshwater and may be found far up some Inner Coast rivers.

The bluntnose stingray is a flat-nosed, round-shaped ray with a long tail; the disk can measure 3 feet across. It has one or sometimes two dangerous spines on the top of the tail; it also has characteristic finlike folds of skin on the top and bottom of the tail. It is brownish to greenish on top and whitish below. Bluntnose stingrays may be the most abundant ray in Inner Coast waters.

The smooth butterfly ray has a disk that is very broad and wider than long. Its disk is adorned with a lacy, mottled pattern colored with shades of brown to gray, light green, and often purplish overtones marked with many small light and dark spots or wavy lines. The smooth butterfly ray has no spine, venomous or otherwise, and is considered harmless. These graceful swimmers glide through the water often in great numbers as they enter the shallows on rising tides. Usually, however, they are secreted in the sand with only their spiracles and eyes uncovered. Smooth butterfly rays are quite common in Inner Coast sandy shallows, where they feed on small clams, crustaceans, and fishes.

The clearnose skate, also called the briar skate, *Raja eglanteria*, can be quickly identified by two, almost transparent patches on each side of its pointed nose. It has a typical skate tail: heavy and thorny. The clearnose skate's back is covered with prickles, and a line of sharp, short spines extends down the middle of the back and tail. There are two fins located at the end of the tail, which lacks a venomous spine. Its back is brown to gray with scattered dark spots and bars. Clearnose skates feed on crabs and other crustaceans, clams, squids, worms, and fishes. They are very abundant in Inner Coast waters.

The bull shark, *Carcharhinus leucas*, also known as the cub shark, is a big, heavy-bodied, sluggish shark that moves through the shallows and into the turbid waters of the Intracoastal Waterway and often travels considerable distances up rivers and into freshwater. Bull sharks can grow to about 11 feet long, though they are usually, but not always, half that size in Inner Coast waters. A research scientist working in Chesapeake Bay in the 1960s reported on two adult bull sharks caught in a commercial pound net. The larger of the two, a female, was 8 1/2 feet long and weighed in excess of 328 pounds; the smaller shark, a male, was over 7 feet long and weighed 202 pounds. The female's stomach was empty, but the male's stomach contained enough fish to stock a small seafood stand: seventy-four American eels, each 3 to 4 feet long; four white perches, and two croakers. Bull sharks feed on a veritable smorgasbord of coastal species, including stingrays, black-tipped sharks, shad, porpoise remains, sea turtles, crabs, mackerels, mullets, menhadens, and shrimps.

Bull sharks' snouts are blunt and rounded. Their first dorsal fin is broadly triangular and pointed; the second dorsal fin is set back closer to the tail and is much smaller. They have grayish backs shading to white on their bellies. The pectoral fins of bull sharks are large and broad, just the right design, it seems, to stabilize these big, slow-moving sharks.

Bull sharks enter Inner Coast waters not only to feed but also to give birth to their pups. A pregnant female can carry up to thirteen pups internally for ten to eleven months. The 24- to 32-inch pups swim away at birth. Coastal lagoons, such as Florida's Indian River Lagoon, and the sounds in the Carolinas and Georgia serve as nurseries for these big sharks.

Three species of sharks—the great white, the tiger

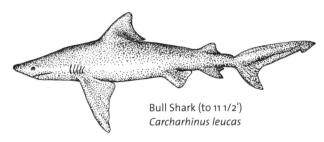

Bull Shark (to 11 1/2')
Carcharhinus leucas

shark, and the bull shark—seem to be responsible for most of the attacks on humans worldwide. Great whites and tiger sharks have been the subjects of a number of articles and movies involving attacks on humans, but the bull shark is relatively little known. Yet bull sharks' habit of swimming in shallow coastal waters brings them into close contact with humans. They may just be the most dangerous sharks of all because they swim where we swim.

The sandbar shark, *Carcharhinus plumbeus*, moves into Inner Coast shallows in the summer to bear its young, usually about eight to twelve pups. Sandbar sharks resemble bull sharks because of their sluggish, slow-moving habits, heavy bodies, broad snouts, and small eyes. The sandbar shark's first dorsal fin is very large and triangular, and the second dorsal fin is much smaller and located near the tail. The sandbar shark has a mid-dorsal ridge but the bull shark does not. Sandbar sharks are slate gray to brown above, shading to dingy gray on the sides and white on the belly. They may grow to 10 feet long, but most in shoal waters are 4 to 6 feet.

We have received information that commercial fishermen have targeted sandbar sharks as they move into estuaries to pup their young. Sandbar sharks' flesh and their large fins are tasty and of high quality. They are sold along the East Coast and are also shipped to markets in Asia, where shark fins are sold to make shark fin soup, which is considered a delicacy. State and federal fishery managers and biologists are concerned about the increased landings of these vulnerable sharks, which are considered an important species for a stable ecosystem.

Atlantic Cutlassfish

The Atlantic cutlassfish, or ribbonfish, *Trichiurus lepturus*, is a bizarre-looking fish that looks as if it comes from the profundal depths of the ocean. It is very compressed from side to side, with a body that tapers down to a filamentous point where its tail should be. It has a single, long, continuous dorsal fin. It looks like a snake, and in fact, it belongs to the snake mackerel family. The cutlassfish is a voracious predator, and this thin fish, which may grow 4 feet long, is well equipped to devour almost any prey. It has long jaws—the lower jaw projects beyond the upper jaw—with large fangs or lancelike teeth and very large eyes. Its silvery bluish body lacks scales and caudal and pelvic fins.

Cutlassfish at times enter bays and sounds in great numbers. They have been seen in great writhing balls that may be part of the spawning ritual. They are found in the shallows from spring through fall, when they migrate offshore in the ocean. Cutlassfish are closely related to the escolar and oilfish, which are oily but delicious. Cutlassfish are also quite edible, but few humans eat them.

Bluefish

The cutlassfish is a voracious predator, but perhaps the most rapacious fish of all is the bluefish, *Pomatomus saltatrix*. Bluefish are absolutely gluttonous,

Atlantic Cutlassfish (to 4')
Trichiurus lepturus

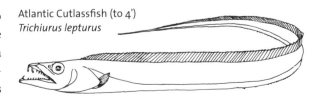

A school of menhadens is attacked from below by marauding bluefish, Pomatomus saltatrix *(to 3').*

and they will kill just for the sake of killing, even when they have had their fill. Those who have seen rampaging, or "blitzing," bluefish attack a school of croakers and spots along the shore will probably never forget the sight of bluefish trapping their prey in the shallows and taking great slashing bites from their bellies. They give no quarter, and as they drive the fish up on shore, the bluefish follow, skidding and snapping and flopping back into the water and then, in a frenzy, slashing more fish, until the school of croakers and spots or menhadens break up and disappear. A good look at the large, strong jaws and sharp, triangular teeth of a bluefish tells you that it is well equipped for its predatory life.

Bluefish are streamlined, powerful swimmers that tend to school by size, so when recreational fisher-men in Bogue Sound, North Carolina, begin hooking bluefish, most of the fish are similar in size. They could be younger bluefish, known as snapper blues or tailors, and weigh 1 pound or so, or they might be older bluefish and weigh between 10 and 15 pounds. These aggressive fish are greenish blue above and shade to silvery along their flanks and bellies. They have a dark splotch at the base of the pectoral fin. The first dorsal fin has seven or eight spines; the second dorsal fin and anal fin are both long; and the caudal fin or tail is deeply forked. Bluefish are migratory and generally move northward in the spring and summer and southward in the fall. They are quite abundant along the Inner Coast, particularly in the Carolinas, in the summer and plentiful in the winter along the Florida coast. The bluefish is an important recreational and commercial species, and in some years millions of pounds are caught by hook and line as well as by commercial fishing nets.

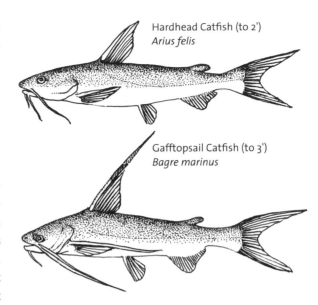

Hardhead Catfish (to 2')
Arius felis

Gafftopsail Catfish (to 3')
Bagre marinus

Unusual Fishes of the Shallows

Sea Catfishes

Sea catfishes are quite similar to the familiar freshwater catfishes and bullheads, with a couple of notable exceptions: Sea catfishes have four to six barbels; freshwater catfishes have eight barbels. But perhaps the greater difference is in the mode of reproduction. Freshwater catfishes generally create nests in the soft bottom by fanning their fins; the females deposit hundreds or thousands of eggs, depending on the species, in the nest, and then the males fertilize the eggs and stand guard until the eggs hatch. Sea catfishes have a decidedly different mode of reproduction: The females produce eggs the size of marbles, up to 1/2 inch in diameter—they may be among the largest of all bony fish eggs. The males then take the relatively small number of eggs into their mouths and brood them for seventy days or more.

There are two species of sea catfishes in the Inner Coast: the hardhead catfish, *Arius felis*, and the gafftopsail catfish, *Bagre marinus*. Both of these are common in shallow waters on sandy or muddy bottoms and often ascend rivers into fresher water. Hardhead catfishes are usually more plentiful than gafftopsail catfishes, and both are more common from Georgia southward through Florida, although a few are caught in the Carolinas. Both of these species find little favor with recreational and commercial fishermen, as they are not esteemed for eating quality. They also have strong, sharp pectoral and dorsal spines that can inflict serious and painful wounds, and when they are caught in commercial fishermen's nets, they snare the webbing with their erected spines and create a tangled mess.

The hardhead catfish is grayish green to brown above, grading to white or yellow on the belly. It has a pair of sensory barbels at the corners of its mouth and four barbels on its chin. The adipose fin, the fleshy, lobelike fin behind the dorsal fin, is black.

The gafftopsail catfish is named for its sail-like dorsal fin. This catfish is bluish above and silvery below. The pair of barbels at the corners of the mouth is somewhat flattened and long, sometimes reaching beyond the pectoral fin; it has two barbels on the chin. It also has long filaments on the dorsal and pectoral fins, and the fins harbor sharp, serrated, slime-covered spines.

Both species have hearty appetites and eat plants, worms, mollusks, shrimp, crabs, and, above all, the baited hooks of anglers.

Lizardfishes and Puffers

Lizardfishes are elongated fishes that are basically round but tapered at the head and tail. They have

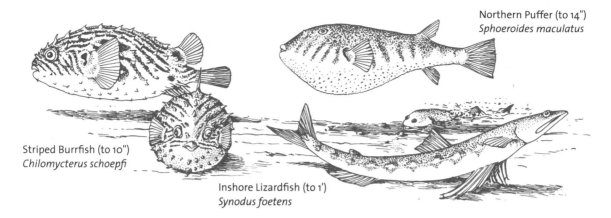

Northern Puffer (to 14")
Sphoeroides maculatus

Striped Burrfish (to 10")
Chilomycterus schoepfi

Inshore Lizardfish (to 1')
Synodus foetens

pointed reptilian heads and large mouths that open well beyond the eyes and are armed with small, very sharp teeth. They have a small, usually colorless adipose fin ahead of the forked tail. Lizardfishes are bottom feeders and are hard to spot on the bottom because they are usually sandy colored or grayish brown or olive. They can blend into the bottom by becoming very pale or dark, depending on the color of the background. Lizardfishes are patient predators, and snorkelers sometimes spot them perched on their strong pectoral fins or partially buried in the sand, waiting for a fish to pass by. Their eyes are positioned close together on top of their heads, so when they dig into the sand, they can still spot their quarry and quickly explode out of the sand, dart up, and engulf their dinner in one gulp. Fishermen are often puzzled when they catch a lizardfish because it doesn't look like any fish they have seen before. The inshore lizardfish, *Synodus foetens*, is marked with several diamond-shaped marks and a row of white spots on a sandy to brownish or olive body. It is a very common but little-known fish of Inner Coast waters and is found in sandy embayments, estuaries, and lagoons southward to Florida.

Puffers, or swellfishes, are curious creatures that can't help fascinating anyone who catches one, with their teeth like a chipmunk's and the ability to quickly swell into an inflated ball. Puffers can be quite common on sandy and grassy bottoms and over patches of coral. Puffers, as a group, are blunt-bodied fishes with large heads and jaws that are modified to form a beak of four heavy, chisel-like teeth. The gill openings are located at the base of the pectoral fins, and the rather large eyes are placed high on the head. They lack pelvic fins, and the rather small dorsal and anal fins are positioned close to the tail. Puffers do not have scales, but many species have numerous small, spiny prickles, and some have rather formidable spines.

Most species of puffers have mottled or variegated patterns of various colors on the upper sides with white or cream-yellow bellies. Their ability to suddenly inflate like a balloon may prevent them from being swallowed by a prospective predator. Puffers are not very strong swimmers; they glide along by fanning or sculling their small dorsal and anal fins. Some puffers have a toxin in their viscera, particularly in the liver, called tetrodotoxin; a small amount, when ingested, can be lethal. In Japan, the consumption of a puffer, known as fugu, is the gourmet diner's version of Russian roulette. Fugu is praised in Japan as both the most delicious of all fishes and the most feared, because improper preparation may cause the quick death of the diner.

Puffers are not usually eaten in our part of the world, except for one species, the northern puffer, *Sphoeroides maculatus*, also called sea squab or chicken of the sea. These small puffers are delicious and are not poisonous, although some scientists believe that there may be some toxin produced by these fish as well. There are small, localized commercial fisheries for this fish in Chesapeake Bay and the Carolinas, where they are sold in seafood markets from time to time.

The northern puffer, when in its usual, non-inflated state, is a small, club-shaped fish covered with prickles. It can quickly inflate with water or air for protection. An inflated fish, when thrown back into the water, floats upside down at the surface for a while and then deflates and disappears. Northern puffers are yellowish with deep greenish blue bars and small dark spots above and pure white on the belly. They are rather small fish, usually only about 10–12 inches long. They are found in the sandy and grassy shallows of the Inner Coast down to about Jacksonville, Florida.

The striped burrfish, *Chilomycterus schoepfi*, is another common puffer in the shallows from North Carolina southward. Striped burrfish have strong, thorny spines and short, rather rounded bodies. They are colorfully marked with dark brown or black wavy stripes and spots on a yellowish green body. Their spines are menacing when their bodies are inflated. Burrfish are weak swimmers, similar to northern puffers, but they are able to jet water out of their small gill openings and propel themselves along rather efficiently.

🌾

Freshwater Fishes of the Upper Estuaries

Many species of freshwater fishes can tolerate some brackish water of the upper estuaries and often mi-

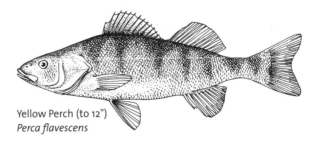

Yellow Perch (to 12")
Perca flavescens

grate downstream. They tend to congregate in shallow streams and the protected coves within the larger tidal rivers. As winter wanes, freshwater fishes move upstream, above tidewater, where they spawn in the spring and early summer.

Perches

One of the best-known freshwater fishes of the upper estuaries is the yellow perch, *Perca flavescens*. It has adapted to brackish water even though it is surely a freshwater species. It is a colorful fish that has a bright to yellow-gold body marked with six to eight dark vertical bands. The spawning males are even more brilliantly marked, with orange-red fins. Yellow perch is heavily fished throughout the northern parts of the United States and most of Canada; it is an excellent panfish, with firm, sweet, white flesh. It is typically a more northern species; however, it does range along the Inner Coast from Virginia to about mid–South Carolina.

Catfishes and Bullheads

Most catfishes and bullheads, similar to perches, often inhabit the brackish waters of tidal rivers and bays. These fishes are smooth skinned because they lack scales. They have wide mouths with eight cat-like "whiskers," or barbels. They use their barbels to sense food by touch and taste in the usually muddy waters where they reside. Catfishes have forked tails

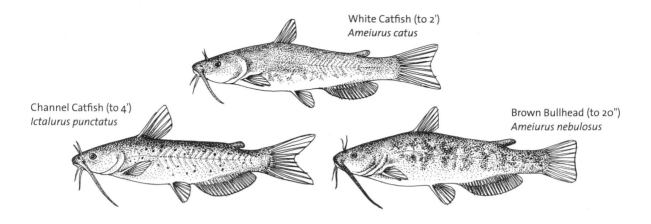

White Catfish (to 2')
Ameiurus catus

Channel Catfish (to 4')
Ictalurus punctatus

Brown Bullhead (to 20")
Ameiurus nebulosus

and bullheads have squared tails; all have pectoral fins armed with heavy, sharp spines. All also have an unusual, fleshy fin, called an adipose fin, located on their backs between the dorsal fin and the tail.

The channel catfish, *Ictalurus punctatus*, is a slender, somewhat streamlined catfish that has a deeply forked tail and brownish black spots scattered over its silvery tan body. Channel catfishes prefer medium to large rivers with sandy to rocky bottoms; however, they also thrive in ponds and lakes. Channel catfishes are omnivorous feeders and will eat plants, seeds, insect larvae, crayfishes, and other fishes. Channel cats can grow rather large, with some reaching 50 pounds. The channel catfish is a popular sport fish and is very good to eat; in fact, most catfishes that are served in restaurants and sold in supermarkets are channel catfishes that have been raised on fish farms. Channel catfishes live down to central Florida.

The white catfish, *Ameiurus catus*, is grayish brown with a white belly, no body markings, and a tail that is only slightly forked. This species is the smallest of the catfishes and seldom exceeds 3 or 4 pounds, although it can grow to about 15 pounds. White catfish are also found on muddy bottoms.

The brown bullhead, *Ameiurus nebulosus*, is mottled with brown or black and has a squared tail and dark chin barbels. Bullheads prefer slow-moving creeks and rivers with soft, muddy bottoms, and they are sometimes found in vegetated areas as well. They are usually smaller than their catfish relatives, but they are quite popular with fishermen and are sought after by many for food and sport.

The yellow bullhead, *Ameiurus natalis*, is similar in size and shape to the brown bullhead, but it has white to yellowish chin barbels and its body is yellow to olive colored. The brown bullhead and the yellow bullhead live in similar habitats, and both are found throughout most of the Inner Coast.

The Sunfish Family

The sunfish family is a homegrown family of fishes; it occurs naturally only in North American freshwaters. But members of this family, for example largemouth bass and bluegill, are so highly valued for food and for sport that they have been introduced into parts of North America where they did not originally occur. Indeed, they are now found in many parts of the world, including Africa and Europe. Sunfishes, whether they be bass, crappie, or pumpkinseed, share a similar characteristic, and that is the shape and structure of the dorsal fin: it has two parts, a spiny-rayed section and a soft-rayed section, that are joined as a single fin. Almost all species of the sunfish family build and actively guard their nests in the shallows, and it is usually the male that builds the nest and protects the young fry. Also, many members of the sunfish family, perhaps because of the similarities in their habitats, feeding modes, and spawning behaviors, easily hybridize and form new subspecies.

There are many species of sunfishes belonging to the genus *Lepomis* that occur in the waters of the Inner Coast, including the redear sunfish, the redbreast sunfish, the warmouth, and the spotted sunfish, but perhaps the most abundant and commonest of the sunfishes in Inner Coast waters are the bluegill, *Lepomis macrochirus*, and the pumpkinseed, *Lepomis gibbosus*.

If you mention sunfish, bluegill (or bream in the South) almost always comes to mind; it is widely distributed and widely caught in ponds, in shallow bays such as Currituck Sound in North Carolina, and in warm-water streams and rivers almost everywhere. Bluegills like vegetated areas, where they feed and hide from larger fishes and fishermen, but they usually move into sandy-bottomed shallows to feed in the morning and evening.

Bluegills can be identified by the black elongated flaps at the ends of the gill covers; no other sunfish has that distinguishing mark. They also have a dusky splotch on the soft-rayed portion of the dorsal fin. They are extremely variable in color; they can range from light orange to gold or even pink with several bluish to brown vertical stripes to a dusky, almost charcoal black body with darker vertical stripes. Bluegills probably originated in the central United States south to Georgia, but now they are found throughout Inner Coast waters.

Pumpkinseeds are scrappy and colorful fish and can be easily identified by the bright red or orange

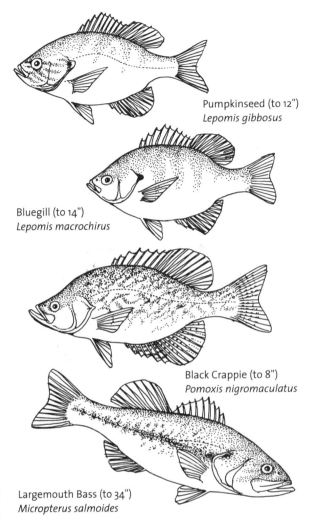

Pumpkinseed (to 12")
Lepomis gibbosus

Bluegill (to 14")
Lepomis macrochirus

Black Crappie (to 8")
Pomoxis nigromaculatus

Largemouth Bass (to 34")
Micropterus salmoides

spot, the pumpkinseed, on the gill cover flap. Pumpkinseeds are usually smaller than bluegills, but they are as bright and colorful as some tropical fishes. Their bodies are usually light olive to golden brown and sprinkled with olive or red and orange spots; sometimes they are adorned with wavy blue to emerald green horizontal stripes. Pumpkinseeds, similar to bluegills, inhabit vegetated soft bottoms and seem to prefer the shallows. They range along the Inner Coast down to about the Savannah River.

The two species of crappies, the white crappie, *Pomoxis annularis*, and the black crappie, *Pomoxis nigromaculatus*, sometimes known as calico bass, are favorite sport fishes of anglers throughout the country. They are good fighters, particularly on light tackle, and they are very good to eat. The white crappie probably originated in the Mississippi and Great Lakes drainage systems, but like most of the other sunfishes, it has been stocked all across the country.

White crappies have a compressed body when viewed head-on and are deep bodied when seen from the side; their mouths are large and their backs are arched. White crappies have olive to green backs and silvery sides flecked with dark spots that form about eight to ten vertical bars. White crappies prefer the dark, sluggish, warm waters of the rivers and streams from the lower Chesapeake Bay to northern Georgia.

The black crappie is a bit stockier than its close cousin, the white crappie. The black crappie usually does not show vertical bars but is flecked all over with dark spots; it also shows a metallic sheen on its olive to greenish back. But coloration and pattern in both species varies considerably, particularly because of the clarity of the waters that they inhabit. The surest method to determine whether you have caught a white or black crappie is to count the sharp dorsal fin spines; the black crappie has seven or eight spines, and the white crappie has five or six spines. Black crappies are usually found in the cooler, clear, but tannin-stained freshwaters of the Inner Coast.

There are a number of species of freshwater basses that belong to the genus *Micropterus*: the Suwannee bass, redeye bass, spotted bass, shoal bass, Guadalupe bass, smallmouth bass, and largemouth bass. But the largemouth bass is the only freshwater bass common in the waters of the Inner Coast. The largemouth bass is a prized game fish, perhaps the most important game fish in all of North America. There are highly organized tournaments held throughout the country devoted to catching the feisty largemouth bass, or "bucketmouth." Youngsters and oldsters as well fish for them with cane poles in ponds, along the shores of lakes, and in small boats in the quiet, weedy backwaters of warm-water rivers. And then there is the new breed of bass fishermen that takes to the tree stump–strewn waters of dammed-up lakes in flashy and fast fishing machines especially designed with casting platforms, electric trolling motors, and comfortable swivel seats.

The largemouth bass, *Micropterus salmoides*, is the largest of all the species in the sunfish family and may reach a weight of 15 pounds or more; the females are larger than the males. Largemouth basses are quite variable in color and pattern; their backs may be dark green to olive, and their sides and belly are usually light green to pale yellow or silvery white. The largemouth bass's upper jaw extends just beyond its eyes. Typical of sunfish, the male largemouth bass prepares a nest by fanning its fins over a gravel, muddy, or sandy bottom; the female, or sometimes several females, lays several thousand eggs in the nest, and then the male takes over and fertilizes the eggs and aggressively guards the nest and the young for about a month. Largemouth basses are top carnivores and will eat almost any live prey; they eat insects, crayfishes, frogs, fishes, and sometimes even snakes or small birds sitting on the water. Largemouth basses have been widely introduced and are found throughout the Inner Coast in rivers, ponds, and lakes and sometimes in brackish water.

Plankton Stew

Thousands of tiny plants and animals, collectively called plankton, float along with the currents or weakly propel themselves, sometimes up and down

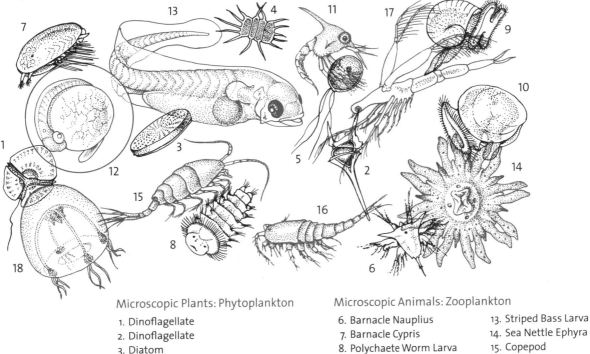

Microscopic Plants: Phytoplankton

1. Dinoflagellate
2. Dinoflagellate
3. Diatom
4. Green Alga
5. Golden Brown Alga

Microscopic Animals: Zooplankton

6. Barnacle Nauplius
7. Barnacle Cypris
8. Polychaete Worm Larva
9. Snail Larva
10. Oyster Larva
11. Crab Zoea
12. Herring Egg

13. Striped Bass Larva
14. Sea Nettle Ephyra
15. Copepod
16. Copepod
17. Giant Water Flea
18. Hydromedusa

in the water column but more often in a random fashion. The botanical portion of the plankton community is called phytoplankton, which means "green-celled wanderers." Phytoplankters are usually microscopic, single-celled algal plants. There are many groups of phytoplankters in the Inner Coast, such as bluegreen algae, a type of photosynthetic bacteria technically known as cyanobacteria, green algae, dinoflagellates, and diatoms. In tidal freshwater and in low-salinity water, bluegreen algae, under the right conditions, which usually include quiet and rather warm waters and high nutrient concentrations, can reproduce so rapidly that they form blooms, scum, or floating mats that are quite visible on the surface of the water. Bluegreen algae blooms range in color from viscous pea green to yellowish brown that can develop the consistency of paint that coats rocks and pilings as it dries. Bluegreen algae are a natural component in freshwater and low-salinity water; however, when the bluegreens begin to grow explosively and form their signature blooms, they produce chemicals that cause earthy or musty flavors, a concern when there are blooms in lakes and reservoirs that are used as municipal water supplies. Perhaps more important, bluegreen algae in high concentrations can produce endotoxins that can cause allergic reactions such as eye irritations and skin rashes. Some bluegreen algae also produce neurotoxins that affect the nervous system and can cause muscle tremors and breathing difficulties.

Dinoflagellates and diatoms are more common components of plankton, particularly in the higher-salinity waters of estuaries. Dinoflagellates have whip-like flagella that propel the tiny organisms in a vertical spirally path. Heavy blooms of certain dinoflagellates can color the water mahogany or sometimes red. "Mahogany tides" are quite common in certain areas of the Inner Coast when the water is warm and still. "Red tides" occur in high-salinity waters, particularly along the Gulf coast of Florida, and the species of dinoflagellate responsible for the obnoxious bloom produces toxins that can kill fishes and shellfishes and make life miserable for humans as well. Some species of dinoflagellates, including several forms that live in Inner Coast waters, are bioluminescent; that is, they produce a phosphorescent glow when the water is agitated by the passage of a boat or almost any disturbance at night.

Diatoms are some of the most beautiful creations found in nature; they look like crystalline pillboxes when viewed through a microscope. Diatoms are exquisite cells or groups of cells that are constructed of silica and tinted by golden brown chloroplasts, rather than the green chloroplasts usually found in plants. There are thousands of species of diatoms found throughout the world in freshwater and saltwater. They cling to aquatic plants; they grow on crabs, turtles, and whales; they grow on moist soils and Inner Coast sand bars—they are everywhere. Diatoms, together with dinoflagellates, fill the same role as grassy meadows and lush forests of the world's uplands: they convert sunlight and carbon dioxide into food and, in doing so, produce life-giving oxygen.

There are thousands of microscopic phytoplankton species in Inner Coast waters busily converting sunlight into living organic material. They are in turn consumed by tiny animals, zooplankton, which in turn are preyed on by larger animals, and so on in the march of life in Inner Coast waters. The greatest proportion of animals that feed on phytoplankton are miniscule forms themselves, including an indescribable number of planktonic invertebrate larvae. Most zooplankton species are so small that when a jar of water from a tidal river or sound is held up to the sunlight, the only animal life that can be seen is usually a bunch of dancing dots that are too small to discern.

One of the exceptions is the giant water flea, *Leptodora kindtii*, which belongs to a group of very small microcrustaceans called cladocerans. Most cladocerans live in freshwater and are typically found in rivers, lakes, and ponds, but some species, such as the predacious giant water flea, live in slightly brackish water. The giant water flea looks like an extraterrestrial visitor with a single eye, a transparent body, and two fringed "wings" flaring out from its back.

Copepods, another group of microscopic crustaceans, are said to be among the most abundant group of multicelled animals on earth. They are everywhere in Inner Coast waters, in the shallows as well as in open deep water. There are many species of copepods in these waters, but only an expert with a microscope can identify them to species. Fully grown copepods can be just barely seen in a jar of water from a river as they jerkily swim about. Some copepods feed on phytoplankton; others feed on detritus, bacteria, or protozoans (microscopic single-celled animals). Copepods, in turn, are a major food source for many larger invertebrates and fishes.

Jellies

There are many species of jellyfishes and comb jellies that live in Inner Coast waters and also in the adjacent Atlantic. Jellyfishes and comb jellies are the largest members of the floating plankton community. One of the most abundant species of jellyfishes in Inner Coast waters is the infamous stinging sea nettle, *Chrysaora quinquecirrha*. Populations of sea nettles during some years in certain places along the Inner Coast are so plentiful that merely entering the water, let alone swimming, wading, or water-skiing, is akin to undergoing a trial by fire. Sea nettles live in mid-salinity to high-salinity waters and do not survive in slightly brackish water or freshwater. Sea nettles, like most jellyfishes, are capable of some propulsion by rhythmically expanding and contracting their globe-shaped medusae. However, they are not strong swimmers and are passively carried by wind and currents, which transport them far and wide, often concentrating them in some areas and clearing them from other areas. Sea nettles are carnivorous opportunists and are equipped to entangle and snare almost any prey of the right size that comes their way. Their long tentacles, similar to those of their relatives anemones, hydroids, and corals, bristle with stinging cells called nematocysts. The prey is stunned by the stinging cells and then passed up through the long, ruffled mouth lappets to the mouth situated under the center of the medusa. It is quite common to see an undigested fish or shrimp within the globular medusa of the sea nettle.

Sea nettles, like most species of this group, are almost 90 percent water, yet many species of fishes, sea turtles, and crustaceans feed on them. Young fishes, such as the harvestfish, *Peprilus alepidotus*, and the butterfish, *Peprilus tricanthus*, seem to be immune to the poisonous stinging cells. They often live in close relation to the sea nettle and dart in and out of the mass of long, trailing, and deadly tentacles with impunity. Both the harvestfish and the butterfish are deep bodied and highly compressed from side to side. Their dorsal and anal fins are continuous

with their forked tails. Small spider crabs hitch rides on the medusa of the sea nettle and sometimes even hollow out a space in its gelatinous bell.

Some sounds and bays may swarm with sea nettles in July and August, but by fall they fragment and die. Sea nettles grow in size and maturity throughout the spring and summer, and by midsummer, their four-leaf-clover-shaped gonads ripen and can be clearly seen through the medusa bell. Male gonads are white or pink, and female gonads are olive to dusky gray. The males release their sperm into the water, and the females rhythmically contract their medusae and pump the sperm into their bells, where the eggs are fertilized. Each fertilized egg develops into a tiny, ciliated planktonic larva called a planula, which is smaller than a grain of sand. The planulae leave the female and become part of the plankton stew. The mature males and females eventually die after they spawn, but the planulae settle to the bottom and attach to hard substrates such as oyster and clam shells and tin cans. After the planula attaches, it begins to bulge out and develop into a flowerlike polyp that resembles a miniature sea anemone. The sea nettle polyps are able to asexually reproduce

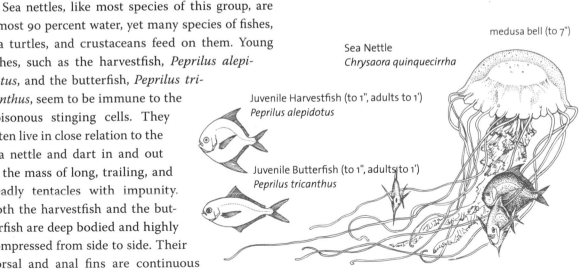

medusa bell (to 7")

Sea Nettle
Chrysaora quinquecirrha

Juvenile Harvestfish (to 1", adults to 1')
Peprilus alepidotus

Juvenile Butterfish (to 1", adults to 1')
Peprilus tricanthus

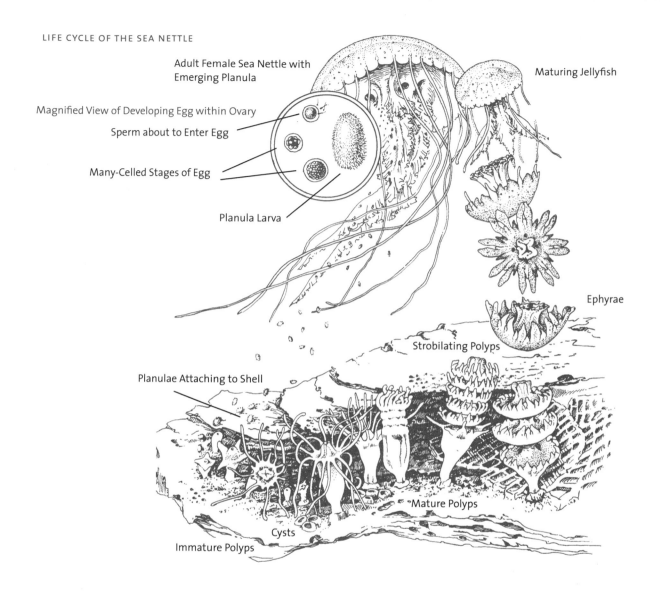

Adult Female Sea Nettle with Emerging Planula

Maturing Jellyfish

Magnified View of Developing Egg within Ovary

Sperm about to Enter Egg

Many-Celled Stages of Egg

Planula Larva

Ephyrae

Strobilating Polyps

Planulae Attaching to Shell

Mature Polyps

Cysts

Immature Polyps

many times over by budding off bits of tissue that grow into new polyps. Polyps can also endure periods of environmental stress, such as inappropriate temperatures and salinities, by encysting for months or years, until optimum environmental conditions return.

As the next summer approaches, the sea nettle polyps begin to produce tiny, floating, immature sea nettles by a process called strobilation. This occurs as the polyp forms a series of disks that resembles a stack of saucers. The disks are released and float free as a 1/16-inch medusae called ephyrae. The ephyrae grow rapidly and develop all the proper equipment of larger sea nettles; they grow tentacles and mouth lappets and become small copies of the adults. Sea nettles are troublesome all through the Inner Coast.

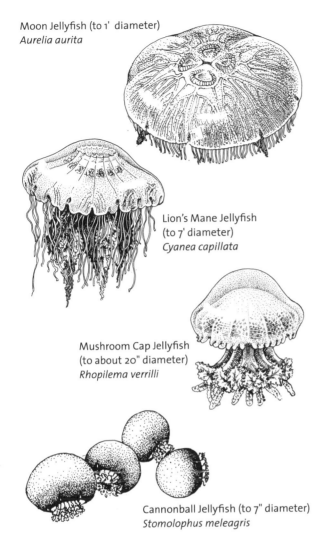

Moon Jellyfish (to 1' diameter)
Aurelia aurita

Lion's Mane Jellyfish
(to 7' diameter)
Cyanea capillata

Mushroom Cap Jellyfish
(to about 20" diameter)
Rhopilema verrilli

Cannonball Jellyfish (to 7" diameter)
Stomolophus meleagris

higher-salinity waters of lower rivers and estuaries. They feed mainly on fishes and moon jellyfishes, but like other jellyfishes, they are opportunists; they will feed on a multitude of invertebrate and fish larvae by spreading their tentacles as if casting a net and slowly sinking and stunning their unwary prey. Huge leatherback turtles that range up into Arctic waters avidly feed on lion's mane jellyfishes.

The cannonball jellyfish, *Stomolophus meleagris*, is also known as the cabbage head jellyfish and the jellyball. The milky white bell or dome is thick and rigid and is bordered with brown pigment on the lower edge. This jellyfish has no tentacles, but it has short oral arms hanging below the bell. Cannonball jellyfishes are not dangerous to humans. They are very abundant, particularly from South Carolina to Florida, and they are often washed up on the beaches by the hundreds after a storm. Immature longnose spider crabs and small grunts and trunkfish often ride within the bell, where they feed on plankton and find shelter. This species is a very important food for the massive leatherback turtle.

The mushroom cap jellyfish, *Rhopilema verrilli*, has a thick, deep bell that is deeply notched. It has a strong central structure, with oral arms hanging below the bell; this central structure is composed of a series of eight reddish brown arms that are fused under the bell. The bell, which can grow to a diameter of about 20 inches, is creamy white and is not considered venomous to humans. Mushroom cap jellyfishes often have small crabs attached to the underside of the bell. They prefer high-salinity waters.

The moon jellyfish, *Aurelia aurita*, is also a large jellyfish and can grow to about 1 foot in diameter. Its white bell is nearly flat, with a fringe of short tentacles around its margin. The pink horseshoe-shaped gonads are easily visible through the translucent gelatinous bell. Moon jellyfishes are very common and abundant in high-salinity waters. They feed on small

The lion's mane jellyfish, or winter jellyfish, *Cyanea capillata*, is another abundant jellyfish in the Inner Coast, but it occurs only in the winter and early spring. The lion's mane jellyfish, so called for its mass of long, thin, hairlike tentacles, is the Inner Coast's largest jellyfish, with a bell that can reach over 7 feet in diameter in Arctic waters. Lion's mane jellyfishes may be carried into lower-salinity waters by wind and current, but they reproduce only in the

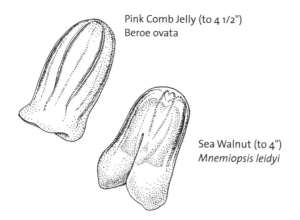

Pink Comb Jelly (to 4 1/2")
Beroe ovata

Sea Walnut (to 4")
Mnemiopsis leidyi

organisms such as fish eggs, invertebrate larvae, and copepods. Their sting is rather mild, particularly when compared to sea nettles'.

Ctenophores, commonly known as comb jellies, are amazingly abundant parts of the macrozooplankton along the Inner Coast. These saclike, transparent animals with rows of flickering cilia, or combs, not only are beautiful but also are ravenous predators that, depending on the species, feed on fishes and invertebrate larvae, copepods, and even each other. Their reproductive life cycle is much simpler than that of the jellyfishes; they have no asexual stage, no polyps, and no vegetative budding. The fertilized eggs develop into larvae that resemble the adults, and then they simply feed and grow. Comb jellies, because of their transparent bodies, are difficult to see during the day, but at night, if you disturb the water just slightly, they will put on a light show for you—they will emit a soft green luminescence. Comb jellies lack nematocysts and therefore do not sting; however, some species have long tentacles to entangle their prey, and others have smaller, internal tentacles to snare their food. Comb jellies may be the most efficient and voracious predators of fish larvae in the Inner Coast, and they consume prodigious numbers of copepods as well.

There are 100 or more species of comb jellies known throughout the world; the more common and most often seen species of the Inner Coast are the pink comb jelly, *Beroe ovata*, and the sea walnut, *Mnemiopsis leidyi*. The pink comb jelly is pale pink and shaped like a simple sac; its favorite prey is another common comb jelly, the sea walnut. Sea walnuts are shaped like colorless walnuts; they catch copepods, fish eggs, and invertebrate larvae by ensnaring them within their lobed sacs.

Crustaceans of the Shallows

Crustaceans come into their own in the shallows, where they are diverse and abundant. Many species of amphipods and isopods, shrimps and crabs occur in this habitat. Most small crustaceans of the intertidal flats are quiescent when the tide is out and the flats are exposed, but when the water returns and covers the flats, that habitat actually becomes the shallows, and the previously quiescent crustaceans become active: they hunt food, dig holes, fend off predators and competitors, and seek mates.

Isopods

The slender isopod, *Cyathura polita*, lives in muddy and sandy bottoms in burrows. It is a long, slender, semicylindrical isopod rather than being somewhat flattened from top to bottom, which is typical of most isopods. It is brownish, sometimes even green, and is about 1 inch long with a fanned-out "tail," more properly termed the telson. The slender isopod is adapted to a rather wide range of salinities but is usually found in the low-salinity waters of upper estuaries and tidal rivers. Slender isopods, similar to many species of isopods, burrow in muddy bottoms, feeding on organic detritus and constantly reworking the bottom as earthworms do in garden soil. They are fed on by fishes and crabs.

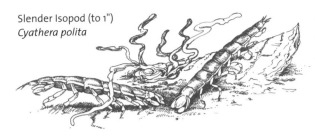
Slender Isopod (to 1")
Cyathera polita

Small fishes along the shore often have "bugs" that are attached to them just visible under their gill flaps. It is not uncommon to see striped bass, white perch, bluefish, and silver perch with just such unwanted visitors hanging on to their gills. The intruders are parasitic fish-gill isopods, *Lironeca ovalis*, which are rather large and specialized isopods that have an affinity for fish gill chambers. They are able to cling tenaciously to a fish's gill filaments with their many hooked legs. Fish-gill isopods apparently do not feed directly on the host fish but rather on bits of food that pass through the fish's mouth. There is also another rather common parasitic isopod known as the fish-mouth isopod, *Olencira praegustator*, which is usually found in the mouth cavities of menhadens. Both of these parasitic isopods are about 1 inch long.

Shrimps

Commercial shrimps, the kinds we eat, are found in the waters of the Inner Coast from about North Carolina south; they do occur north of the Carolinas, but only sporadically and usually not in sufficient numbers to be fished commercially. Shrimp boats moored in the ports of Beaufort and Morehead City, North Carolina; Charleston, South Carolina; and Brunswick, Georgia, attest to the importance of the pink, brown, and white shrimps in Inner Coast waters. These shrimps are harvested in the nearshore waters of the Atlantic and in the sounds and estuaries of the Inner Coast.

Pink, white, and brown shrimps spawn in the off-shore waters of the Atlantic, where the eggs hatch and develop through a series of larval stages. The juveniles enter Inner Coast waters in spring and swim into muddy-bottomed tidal creeks, and as fall approaches, they move into deeper estuarine waters and finally into the open ocean, where the spawning cycle is once again set in motion.

Penaeid shrimps—pink, white, and brown shrimps—are burrowers, to a greater or lesser extent, depending on the species. They grow rapidly and reach reproductive maturity in approximately one year. Most crustaceans, including shrimps, are opportunistic feeders and feed on small organisms, algae and bacteria scraped off seagrasses, and organic detritus.

Pink, white, and brown shrimps resemble one another; however, there are some differences that separate the species. The white shrimp, *Litopenaeus*

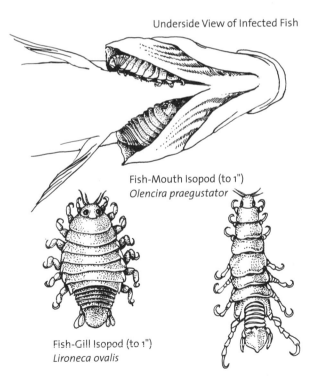

Underside View of Infected Fish

Fish-Mouth Isopod (to 1")
Olencira praegustator

Fish-Gill Isopod (to 1")
Lironeca ovalis

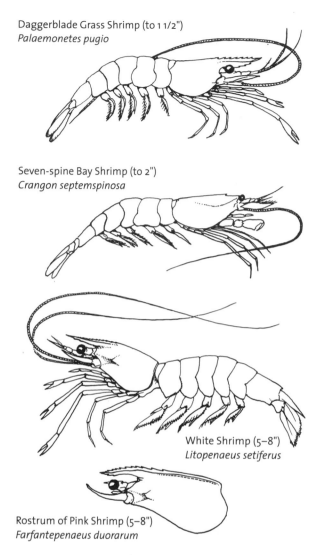

Daggerblade Grass Shrimp (to 1 1/2")
Palaemonetes pugio

Seven-spine Bay Shrimp (to 2")
Crangon septemspinosa

White Shrimp (5–8")
Litopenaeus setiferus

Rostrum of Pink Shrimp (5–8")
Farfantepenaeus duorarum

setiferus, has a rostrum, the toothed projection of the head, that extends about one-half the length of the carapace (the head segment); the rostrum has five to eleven closely spaced teeth. The body is a translucent bluish white, often marked with dusky bands and scattered tiny black spots. The sides and rostrum are tinted a light pink; the antennae are long and black. White shrimps are very abundant near marshes.

The brown shrimp, *Farfantepenaeus aztecus*, has

a grooved rostrum that extends the length of the carapace; the rostrum is armed with five to ten teeth. Its body is usually light or grayish brown with a few darker spots along the lower body. Brown shrimps favor muddy bottoms.

The pink shrimp, *Farfantepenaeus duorarum*, has a thin, shiny, almost translucent shell variably colored pinkish, blue-gray, or sometimes white. The rostrum is quite similar to that of the brown shrimp, with seven to ten teeth. Pink shrimps are usually found in Inner Coast waters on sand, shell-sand, and coral-mud bottoms.

Grass shrimps, *Palaemonetes* spp., in contrast to the penaeid shrimps, which have an obligatory oceanic phase, remain in estuaries, where they are quite common and abundant alongshore. The daggerblade grass shrimp, *Palaemonetes pugio*, generally known as the grass shrimp, is a delicate, almost transparent little shrimp with a strongly toothed rostrum extending beyond the eyes. The first pair of legs has distinct claws. This species is the most abundant of the several species of grass shrimps that occur in Inner Coast waters and is well adapted for living in low-salinity as well as high-salinity waters. When the female grass shrimp is gravid, the greenish to brown eggs can be clearly seen in the brood pouch within its transparent body. Females carry the eggs until they hatch into zoeae and swim away as part of the zooplankton. Grass shrimps are shallow water denizens and are very abundant, particularly in aquatic vegetation. It is not uncommon for some grass shrimps to be parasitized by a very small isopod, *Probopyrus pandalicola*, which forms an easily observed bulge in the gill region of the shrimp.

The seven-spine bay shrimp, also called the sand shrimp, *Crangon septemspinosa*, is another small shrimp of sounds and estuaries and nearby coastal waters. This little shrimp, about 2 inches long, is a rather thick-bodied shrimp when compared to grass

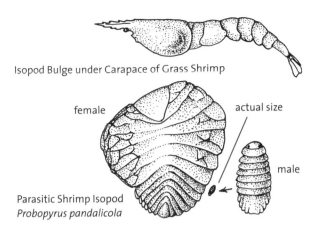

Isopod Bulge under Carapace of Grass Shrimp

female   actual size

male

Parasitic Shrimp Isopod
Probopyrus pandalicola

shrimps; it is somewhat transparent but is well camouflaged against the sandy bottoms and eelgrass beds where it is usually found. Sand shrimps, rather than being laterally compressed as are most shrimps, are slightly flattened from top to bottom. They are usually ashy gray or tan and are marked with star-shaped spots or flecked with brown and black and have a dusky tail fan.

Crabs

The blue crab, *Callinectes sapidus*, whose scientific name means "beautiful, savory swimmer," is an aggressive and pugnacious crab that is abundant and widely distributed throughout Inner Coast waters and beyond. Blue crabs are active and proficient swimmers because the terminal segments on their fifth pair of legs are modified into paddles. The muscles associated with the swimming paddles are the source of the succulent morsels of crabmeat known as lump meat or back fin.

Blue crabs are beautiful animals. The males have bright blue claws, and the mature female's claws are tipped in red; they both have olive to bluish green carapaces. Blue crabs have long, sharp spines at the widest part of their carapaces; the spines are reddish brown, and there is a series of heavy teeth along the front of the crab's shell. Blue crabs are the single most important commercial crab species on the Atlantic and Gulf coasts, and they are very popular among recreational fishermen as well. "Recreational fishermen" includes grandmas and grandpas, and big children and little kids. In some areas the favorite way to catch a blue crab is by tying a string to a chicken neck, dangling it in the water, and then landing the crab in a dip net. Others walk the shallows with a dip net, dipping crabs into a bushel basket lodged in the center of an inner tube. Still others fish for blue crab with small, collapsible crab traps. Each year, millions of pounds of blue crabs are caught by commercial fishermen and recreational fishermen from Chesapeake Bay to Florida and all along the Gulf Coast to Mexico.

Mating occurs from June through October. The males mate with females that have just undergone their final molt and are in the soft crab stage; soft crabs are considered a delicacy by many people. After the females develop their new, hard shells, they begin a directed migration in the early fall months toward the saltier waters of the lower estuaries and sounds of the Inner Coast. It is quite common in the waning months of summer to see many individual females making their way down the tidal rivers and upper estuaries by swimming along the surface of

Blue Crab (carapace to 9")
Callinectes sapidus

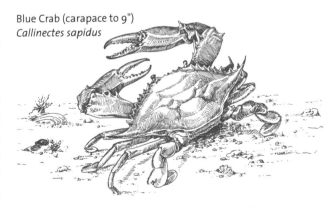

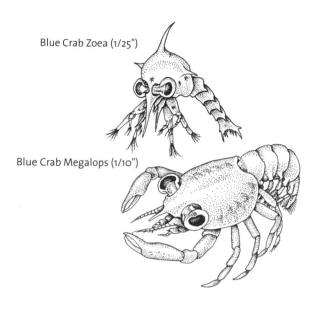

Blue Crab Zoea (1/25")

Blue Crab Megalops (1/10")

into second-stage larvae called megalopsae. Megalopsae measure about 1/10 inch long and closely resemble tiny lobsters or crayfish. They move along the bottom into the estuaries, where they molt into tiny but recognizable blue crabs. By the age of twelve to sixteen months, the crabs have molted several times and have grown to an average size of 5 inches across the widest part of their shell. By this time, most have reached sexual maturity. The empty shells, visible signs of recent molting, often wash up alongshore, vividly demonstrating the abundance of blue crabs in these waters.

Blue crabs, similar to most other crustaceans, are opportunistic feeders and feed on almost anything that they come upon, including vegetation, clams, worms, small fishes, helpless soft clams, and recently dead animals.

The lady crab, *Ovalipes ocellatus*, is also a swimming crab and is in the same family (Portunidae) as the blue crab. The lady crab is smaller than the blue crab, and its carapace is somewhat rounded and lacks the long, lateral spines found on the blue crab. The lady crab's carapace is yellowish gray and dotted with small, reddish purple spots. Lady crabs range along the Inner Coast at least as far south as Georgia.

The portly spider crab, *Libinia emarginata*, is most definitely not a swimming crab. It is a slow-moving, sluggish crab found on a variety of bottoms. It has a rounded, brown to yellowish tan carapace adorned with raised bumps and spines and a dense covering of short hairs. It has long legs; in fact, when they are stretched out, the crab can reach a spread of 1 foot. Portly spider crabs inhabit higher-salinity waters.

The longnose spider crab, *Libinia dubia*, greatly resembles its close relative the portly spider crab. However, its carapace is more triangular; its rostrum is longer and definitely forked; and the spines

the water on an ebbing tide to the higher-salinity waters near the mouths of rivers and ocean inlets. Most of the males remain behind in lower-salinity waters, where they overwinter in the deep, muddy-bottomed channels.

Blue crab females spend the winter in saltier waters, and as the waters warm in the spring, they begin to spawn. They carry an egg mass, often called a sponge; the eggs were internally fertilized when the males mated with the females the previous summer. The sponge adheres to the undersurface of the female's extended abdomen and may contain as many as 2 million eggs. The egg mass changes from golden to orange as the eggs mature and then to black when the eggs are ready to hatch. The eggs hatch, and small larvae called zoeae swim off and become part of the rich plankton stew of Inner Coast waters. Many of the zoeae are swept out into the ocean, where they mix with other blue crab larvae from other regions of the coast; eventually, onshore winds and longshore littoral currents entrain the crab larvae and sweep them into the hundreds of rivers and estuaries on a flood tide. After a series of molts, the zoeae transform

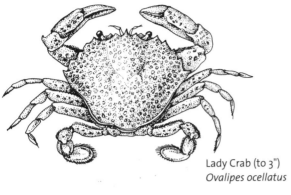

Lady Crab (to 3")
Ovalipes ocellatus

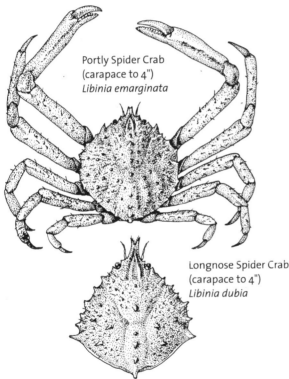

Portly Spider Crab
(carapace to 4")
Libinia emarginata

Longnose Spider Crab
(carapace to 4")
Libinia dubia

cies of jellyfishes, often in the space under the bell or even clinging to the oral feeding arms.

The spongy decorator crab, *Macrocoeloma trispinosum*, is an uncommon crab, not only in its low abundance but in its appearance as well. It is triangular in shape, with nodules and spines projecting from various points on its carapace. Decorator crabs are also spider crabs, and perhaps the best-known spider crab is the one frequently featured on restaurant menus and commonly known as the Alaska red king crab. The spongy decorator crab is a small crab, only about 2–3 inches in length, as compared to its distant cousin, which may approach a weight of 25 pounds and have a leg span of 5 feet. Spongy decorator crabs and other, related species also known as decorator crabs have dense, Velcrolike hairs to

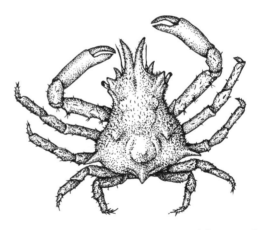

Spongy Decorator Crab (carapace to 1 1/2")
Macrocoeloma trispinosum

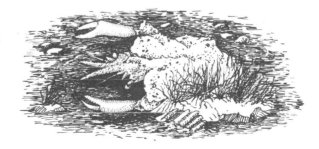

of its carapace are longer and sturdier than those of the portly spider crab. The two species are found in similar habitats. The juveniles of both species are often covered with a variety of sponges, hydroids, sea squirts, and limy worm tubes. Small spider crabs seem to have an affinity for living within several spe-

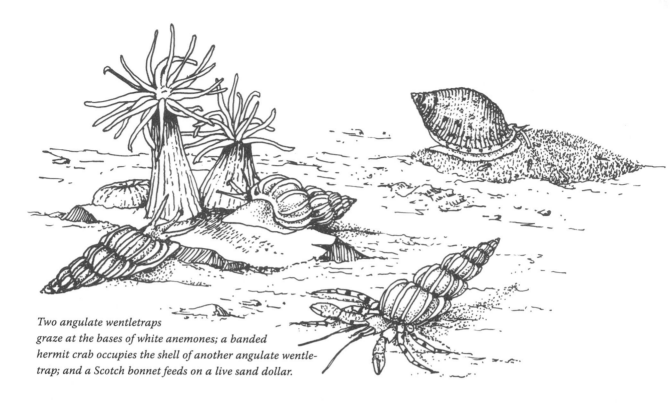

Two angulate wentletraps graze at the bases of white anemones; a banded hermit crab occupies the shell of another angulate wentletrap; and a Scotch bonnet feeds on a live sand dollar.

which the crab attaches all sorts of sponges, bits of shells, algae, and seagrasses. Spongy decorator crabs are often found, if you can see them, in beds of floating seaweeds, on mangrove roots, and on sandy-shell bottoms in shallow water.

❧ Mollusks of the Shallows

Most clams and snails that live in Inner Coast waters are well adapted for living out of water for periods of time, for example, during low-tide stages and during times of high pressure, when the strong winds blow out of the northwest and, as the locals say, "the dern water done blowed out of the sound." Some mollusks, however, are not so tolerant and rarely, if ever, inhabit areas where they might be exposed.

Snails

The angulate wentletrap, *Epitonium angulatum*, is an elegant little snail about 3/4 inch long. These beautiful snails with the odd name are glossy white and elongated, with eight to ten sculptured body whorls. The whorls are adorned with very prominent blade-like ribs that spiral around them up to the very tip, or apex, of the shell. Why the odd name of wentletrap? It's from the Dutch *wenteltrap*, "winding stair," and the name describes this snail perfectly. The angulate wentletrap, similar to other wentletraps, is carnivorous and is believed to feed on anemones living in the sandy bottom.

The Scotch bonnet, *Phalium granulatum*, belongs to the helmet snail family. These snails are carnivorous and prey on various echinoderms, such as

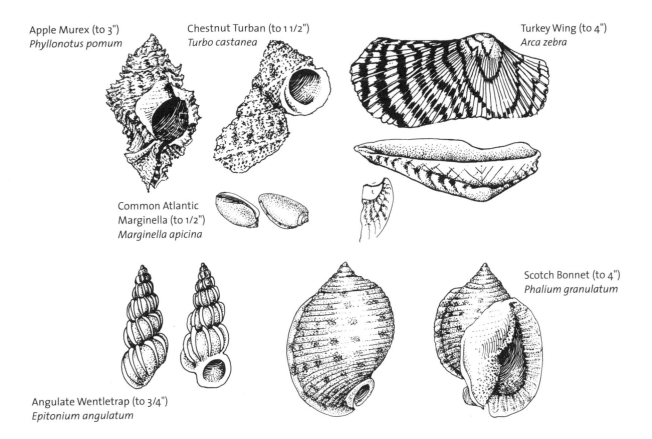

Apple Murex (to 3")
Phyllonotus pomum

Chestnut Turban (to 1 1/2")
Turbo castanea

Turkey Wing (to 4")
Arca zebra

Common Atlantic
Marginella (to 1/2")
Marginella apicina

Scotch Bonnet (to 4")
Phalium granulatum

Angulate Wentletrap (to 3/4")
Epitonium angulatum

sand dollars and sea urchins, as they prowl through the sand. Like other helmet snails, Scotch bonnets have large, inflated body whorls and short, conical spires. This snail grows to about 4 inches tall and has a white to creamy background highlighted with spiral bands of regularly spaced, reddish brown to yellowish brown squares. Scotch bonnet shells have a large aperture with a thickened outer lip and interior teeth. This snail is very common in the shallows and is often washed ashore in large numbers. The Scotch bonnet is the official state shell of North Carolina.

The apple murex, *Phyllonotus pomum*, belongs to a large family of carnivorous gastropods that are variously shaped, from elongated to oval or round. Depending on the species, they may be heavily ribbed, spirally sculptured, or short knobby shells, which may be smooth or equipped with long spines. Like most other members of the murex family, the apple murex preys on other mollusks and other invertebrates by rasping holes in their shells with its toothed organ, the radula, and then inserting its tubular proboscis and feeding on the soft bodies within. There are several close relatives of the apple murex that live in the waters of the Inner Coast, including the thicklip oyster drill, the Atlantic oyster drill, and the Florida rock snail, all of which prey on oysters and other mollusks and are similar in appearance.

The apple murex is a 2- to 3-inch-high snail with a

solid, roughly textured shell. It has a well-developed spire and a large body whorl decorated with nodules, ribs, and ridges. The shell is usually dark brown to yellowish tan, marked with irregular dark brown bands or, occasionally, marked only with spots or streaks of color. The aperture is almost round, and the interior is highly polished and ringed with pink, ivory, or orange.

The chestnut turban, *Turbo castanea*, has a solid, rugose, beaded shell with a fairly sharp apex. It grows to about 1 1/2 inches tall and not quite as wide in diameter. It can vary in color from grayish to brown, greenish, or yellowish orange; its aperture is round and white within. The chestnut turban is a herbivore and is usually found feeding on algae on rocks in the shallows.

The common Atlantic marginella, *Marginella apicina*, is a small, highly predacious snail that often grazes on organisms growing on pen shells. Atlantic marginellas are beautiful solid, polished, porcelainlike snails about 1/2 inch high with a large body whorl and a short spire. They are known as margin shells for the thickened ledges around the lips of their shells. Common Atlantic marginellas can vary in color from whitish to bright golden yellow or brownish orange. The aperture of the shell is long and narrow and about the length of the large body whorl. The inner lips have four ridges or pleats, and there are usually six or seven reddish brown spots along the edge of the margin. These snails are fairly abundant in the shallows on sandy and grassy bottoms.

Clams, Arks, and Other Bivalves

The turkey wing, *Arca zebra*, is a boldly striped ark with rectangular and inflated shells. The exterior of the shells is creamy white and is marked with reddish brown zigzag or wavy lines; the interior of the

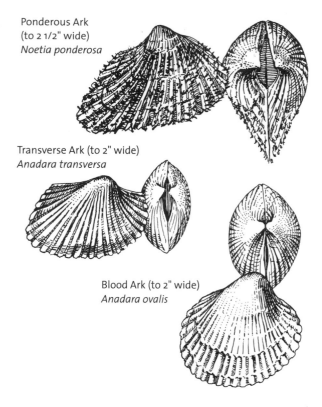

Ponderous Ark
(to 2 1/2" wide)
Noetia ponderosa

Transverse Ark (to 2" wide)
Anadara transversa

Blood Ark (to 2" wide)
Anadara ovalis

shells is whitish and sometimes tinged with lavender. There is a notch between the two shells to allow the strong byssal threads to emerge and fasten the ark to a rock. The periostracum of the live animal is brown and shaggy, and it may be encrusted with an assortment of fouling organisms.

Arks are heavy-shelled, boxlike clams that usually just protrude out of the bottom. However, the transverse ark, *Anadara transversa*, is not always a burrower; it may lie on the bottom sand among the seagrasses. The transverse ark is small, only 1 inch or so long, with an oblong shell. The white shell has about twelve radiating ribs. Transverse arks live in shallow salty waters all through the Inner Coast.

The blood ark, *Anadara ovalis*, is somewhat heart shaped or sometimes more rounded. The white shell has about thirty-five ribs and is covered with a thick,

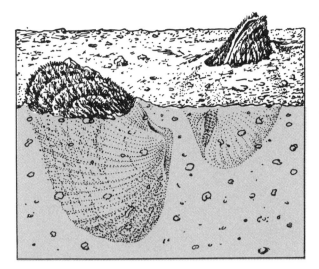

Ponderous arks lie half buried in bottom muds.

olive to brown periostracum on the lower part of the shell. The blood ark is named for its red blood, which is quite unusual, as most bivalves have clear, transparent blood. Blood arks grow in the same areas as do transverse arks.

The ponderous ark, *Noetia ponderosa*, is large and heavy, as the species name implies. It is heart shaped when viewed from the side. Ponderous arks are covered with a furry brown periostracum that is often eroded away from the beak.

The hard clam, *Mercenaria mercenaria*, is an important commercial species. This is the clam most often used in chowders and served on the half shell. Hard clams have hard, thick shells sculptured with closely spaced growth lines. The interior is pearly white but is often marked with a deep purple spot or stain. Hard clams are known by a number of colloquial and descriptive names, such as littlenecks, cherrystones, chowder clams, and quahogs. Littlenecks are young, small hard clams named for Little Neck, Long Island, New York, where they were originally harvested. Cherrystones are slightly larger hard

clams that are frequently served on the half shell; they derive their name from Cherrystone Creek, located on the lower Eastern Shore in Chesapeake Bay. Chowder clams are large, fully grown hard clams that are much too tough to eat raw on the half shell, so they are made into delicious chowders. "Quahog" is a modification of the Narragansett word for the clam. People often "tread" for hard clams along the Inner Coast by searching them out with their bare feet and then picking them up and dropping them into a floating basket. There is a small but intensive commercial fishery for these clams in the Indian River.

The dwarf surf clam, *Mulinia lateralis*, resembles very small hard clams except that its shell is smooth and flat and it is yellowish white. These small clams, sometimes known as coot clams, are frequently found in dense beds in the shallows, but at times they disappear from an area. These clams are a favorite food of waterfowl.

The Atlantic rangia, *Rangia cuneata*, also known as a wedge clam, is another clam that resembles the hard clam. Its shell is very thick and hard and is marked with concentric growth lines. The shell is gray to dark brown, usually mahogany brown. The umbones, the beaklike processes above the hinge line, are inflated, and the shell angles sharply to the posterior end. These clams can be very abundant in brackish water, muddy-bottom shallows.

The Baltic macoma, *Macoma balthica*, is also a small clam of the estuaries that ranges down to Georgia. Baltic macomas' chalky white shells are frequently found washed up on shore. Baltic macomas have long, thin, and flexible siphons, one of which is longer than the other; the siphons can be retracted into their shells. The longer, inhalent siphon slithers out of the gaping shell and sweeps across the soft bottom sediments to vacuum up organic detritus. Macomas also feed by siphoning water and extract-

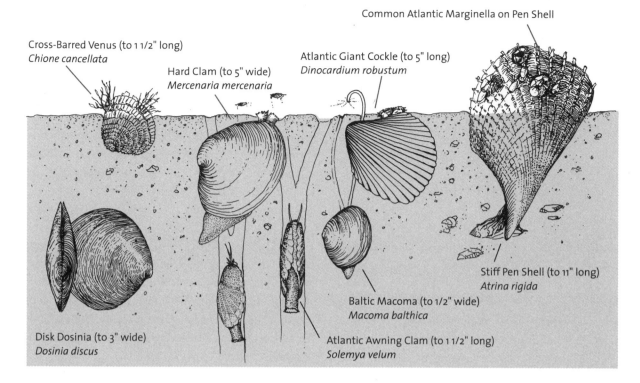

Cross-Barred Venus (to 1 1/2" long)
Chione cancellata

Hard Clam (to 5" wide)
Mercenaria mercenaria

Atlantic Giant Cockle (to 5" long)
Dinocardium robustum

Common Atlantic Marginella on Pen Shell

Stiff Pen Shell (to 11" long)
Atrina rigida

Baltic Macoma (to 1/2" wide)
Macoma balthica

Disk Dosinia (to 3" wide)
Dosinia discus

Atlantic Awning Clam (to 1 1/2" long)
Solemya velum

ing microplankton. Macoma clams are rapid and active burrowers and are able to quickly burrow to avoid predators.

Tellina clams usually have somewhat compressed shells with fine, concentric lines. They typically lie on their left sides beneath sandy or muddy bottoms with their long inhalent siphon extending into the surrounding water, similar to macoma clams. They feed on organic detrital deposits, and they also extract microplankton from the water.

The alternate tellin, *Tellina alternata*, is about 3 inches long. The shell is oblong and compressed with a narrowed and angular posterior end; the anterior end is rounded. The shell exterior is usually white but may be pale yellow or pink and sculptured with fine, concentric lines. The alternate tellin is a very common shell washed up on beaches.

The rose-petal tellin, *Tellina lineata*, is a smaller

version of the alternate tellin. It ranges in color from creamy yellow to rose. This beautiful clam ranges throughout Florida.

The Atlantic semele, *Semele proficua*, is a rounded or oval clam with relatively thin, compressed, dull whitish shells. The interior of the shell is glossy and usually yellowish and marked with pink or purple. Atlantic semeles dwell in sand or mud. They range from North Carolina southward.

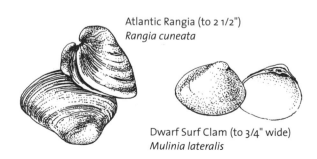

Atlantic Rangia (to 2 1/2")
Rangia cuneata

Dwarf Surf Clam (to 3/4" wide)
Mulinia lateralis

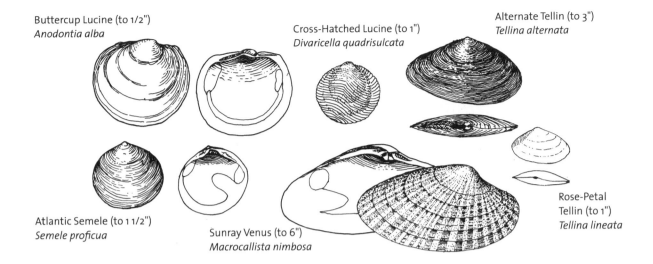

Buttercup Lucine (to 1/2")
Anodontia alba

Cross-Hatched Lucine (to 1")
Divaricella quadrisulcata

Alternate Tellin (to 3")
Tellina alternata

Atlantic Semele (to 1 1/2")
Semele proficua

Sunray Venus (to 6")
Macrocallista nimbosa

Rose-Petal
Tellin (to 1")
Tellina lineata

The Atlantic awning clam, *Solemya velum*, is a primitive clam that resembles a jackknife clam. Its shells are extremely fragile; they are oblong, and they gape at both ends. The surface of the shell is smooth and yellowish brown and often marked with yellowish brown, radiating bands. This clam has two interesting anatomical features: the live clam has a strong covering that overhangs the edges of the shell like a curtain, or awning, and it has a very strong foot that enables it to quickly burrow and to swim. These are rather small clams, only about 1 1/2 inches long. They range to north Florida in sandy and muddy bottoms.

Cockles are moderately heavy-shelled, heart-shaped clams. Some cockles are smooth, but many have spiny or rough exterior shells. Most cockles have short siphons, so they dig just slightly below the surface of the sand or mud bottom so that their siphons can extend into the water.

The yellow prickly cockle, *Trachycardium muricatum*, whose scientific name means "rough, spiny, and heart shaped," is a typical example of the cockle group. This very common clam grows to about 2 1/2 inches long. Its shell has thirty to forty prickly radiating ribs. Its exterior is creamy to light yellow and irregularly marked with flecks or splotches of brownish red, orange, or shades of yellow. The interior of the shell is white or sometimes yellowish. Yellow prickly cockles range Inner Coast waters from North Carolina to Florida and beyond. They are often found around inlets and in shallow bays on sand and mud bottoms.

The Florida prickly cockle, *Trachycardium egmontianum*, is similar in size and shape to the yellow prickly cockle, but it has stronger and more prominent spines.

The Atlantic strawberry cockle, *Americardia media*, is a strongly ribbed cockle with a yellowish white to tan shell marked with a series of buff, reddish brown, or purplish splotches. Strawberry cockles are about 1 to 2 inches long. They grow in the shallows, and like many other clams, they are often washed up on beaches after a storm. Atlantic strawberry cockles frequent Inner Coast waters from North Carolina to Florida.

The egg cockle, *Laevicardium laevigatum*, and the Morton egg cockle, *Laevicardium mortoni*, are very common cockles in shallow waters. Both are

Yellow Prickly Cockle (to 2 1/2")
Trachycardium muricatum

Egg Cockle (to 3")
Laevicardium laevigatum

Atlantic Strawberry
Cockle (to 2")
Americardia media

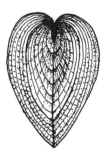

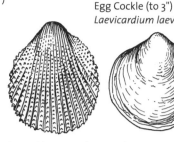

Atlantic Giant-Cockle (to 5 1/4")
Dinocardium robustum

Florida Prickly Cockle (to 2 3/4")
Trachycardium egmontianum

Morton Egg Cockle (to 1")
Laevicardium mortoni

typically heart shaped when viewed from their widest side. The egg cockle is larger than the Morton egg cockle; it may grow to as large as 3 inches, but is usually smaller. The shells of egg cockles are smooth, polished, and inflated. The shells are indistinctly ribbed and frequently tinged or marked with brown and purple or hues of pinkish rose or orange; often, however, they are bleached white after being stranded on the shore. Egg cockles have a strong foot and are reputed to be able to leap off the bottom and jump out of a collector's bucket.

The smaller Morton egg cockle has a rounder shell than that of the egg cockle and has finely beaded or pimply ridges marked with brownish zigzags.

The Atlantic giant cockle, *Dinocardium robustum*, is the largest cockle along the Atlantic coast. This cockle can reach a length of 5 inches, although it is usually smaller. The shell is large, inflated, and somewhat egg shaped, with thirty-two to thirty-six ribs. The exterior is whitish to straw-yellow, and the posterior slope of the shell is mahogany-red that shades to purple; the ribs are marked with reddish brown spots. The interior of the shell is rose to reddish brown with a white margin. These are common shells along the Inner Coast, particularly in the Carolinas and Georgia.

The buttercup lucine, *Anodontia alba*, is almost circular in shape with a chalky white exterior marked with weak, irregular growth lines. The interior of the shell is yellow to rusty orange. Buttercup lucines are a favorite shell of shell crafters because of their oval shape and colorful, concave interiors.

The cross-hatched lucine, *Divaricella quadrisulcata*, is a small bivalve, usually no larger than 1 inch. Its shell is almost perfectly round; the umbones are quite prominent; and the shell is glossy white. Its common name describes it rather well, because the shell is incised with a series of fine, curved lines, some of which form shallow Vs or a chevron pattern. This is a very abundant clam throughout the region.

The disk dosinia, *Dosinia discus*, and the elegant dosinia, *Dosinia elegans*, similar to the lucines, are almost circular. Both the disk dosinia and the elegant dosinia are flattened or compressed rather than inflated. The living shells are covered with a thin, varnishlike, yellowish tan periostracum. The chief difference between the two species is the pattern of concentric ridges and grooves: the disk dosinia has about fifty ridges per inch, separated by fine grooves, whereas the elegant dosinia has about twenty-five ridges per inch. These are truly clams of bays and sounds rather than the ocean side; they live in the shallows of the Inner Coast, where they burrow in sandy bottoms.

The sunray venus, *Macrocallista nimbosa*, has a smooth, colorful, elongated shell that is somewhat

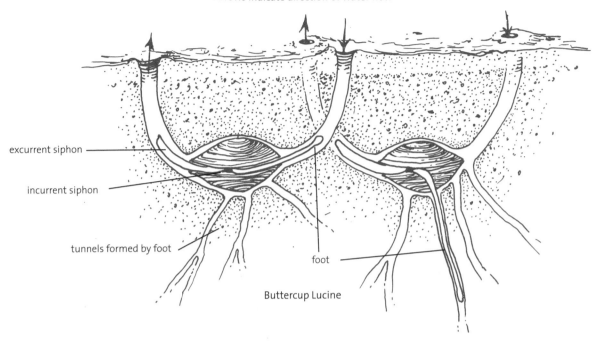

Arrows indicate direction of water flow

excurrent siphon

incurrent siphon

tunnels formed by foot

foot

Buttercup Lucine

compressed. The periostracum on live specimens is thin and varnishlike. The shells are tan or grayish lavender with darker, contrasting radial markings that resemble streaks of sunlight piercing the clouds after a rainfall. The interior of the sunray venus is white and sometimes tinged with a reddish blush in the middle portion of the shell. These showy clams can grow to 6 inches in length and are favored foods of gulls and terns. In some areas where they are abundant, they are savored by humans as well. Sunray venus clams are widespread throughout the region.

The cross-barred venus, *Chione cancellata*, is one of the most abundant shells washed up on beaches, particularly in Florida. This is a small clam, less than 1 1/2 inches long, with a heavy, solid shell that may be egg shaped or somewhat wedge shaped or triangular. The exterior of the shell is dirty white to yellowish and is frequently marked with brown rays. The

cross-barred venus has strong radial ribs intersected by leaflike or flakey concentric ridges. The interior is white and usually marked with blush or dark purple. This is a common clam in the sandy-bottomed shallows.

Pen shells are easily recognized fan-shaped shells that are commonly washed up on the shores. They are large and fragile shells of clams that live in sandy or muddy bottoms, where they lie deeply buried with their apex oriented downward and tethered by byssal threads to stones or shell fragments. The broad fan end of the shell projects 1 inch or so above the bottom. Pen shells are typically populated with commensal organisms that live freely within the mantle cavity, such as small shrimps and pea crabs, or with small communities of barnacles, oysters, or slipper snails that are forever attached to the exterior of their shells.

There are two pen shells that are often stranded

on the shoreline that are favorites of shell collectors and beach walkers: the stiff pen shell, *Atrina rigida*, and the sawtooth pen shell, *Atrina serrata*. The stiff pen shell is usually about 11 inches long, with fifteen to twenty-five radiating ribs that bear tubelike spines. The shell exterior is grayish tan to dark brown, and the interior is lined with iridescent nacre. The sawtooth pen shell is quite similar to the stiff pen shell, but it has many finer and sharper spines. Its shell is thinner and lighter in color than is the stiff pen shell's.

Scallops shells are often stranded in large numbers on muddy banks and sandy shores, particularly after a period of strong offshore winds. Scallop shells are easy to recognize, perhaps not to species, but certainly as a group. We have all seen the trademark sign with the familiar iconic shell announcing a Shell gas station ahead; that shell is a scallop. Scallop shells are fan shaped, usually strongly ribbed, and terminating in an eared or winged point. The shells are unequal: the lower shell is cupped and the upper shell is flatter.

The many species of scallops throughout the world are swimmers. They have a strong column of muscle connecting the upper and lower valves, which they use to quickly open and close their shells. This movement forcefully jets the water out of the shell and

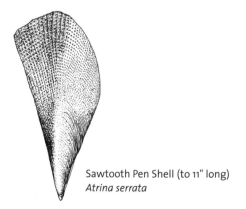

Sawtooth Pen Shell (to 11" long)
Atrina serrata

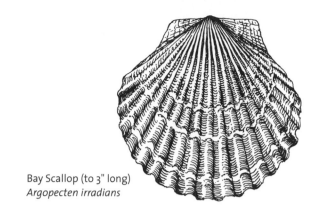

Bay Scallop (to 3" long)
Argopecten irradians

propels the scallop along the bottom in fits and starts. The strong muscle that connects the shells and enables scallops to be so active is the "scallop" that is a favorite of many seafood lovers.

Echinoderms

The common sand dollar, *Mellita isometra*, formerly *M. quinquiesperforata*, is the familiar sand dollar that beachcombers prize when they are fortunate to find an unbroken specimen. Sand dollars have flattened tests covered with a dense carpet of short spines. There are five lunules (slotlike holes) that pierce the test and five elongated, petal-shaped indentations that demark the ambulacral groove where the tube feet are located. The function of the lunules is not completely understood; some believe that they aid in food gathering, and others have suggested that they relieve excess water current pressures, which allows the sand dollar to maintain its position in high-energy zones. Sand dollars are selective deposit feeders; they pick up particles and crush them in a complex of skeletal elements, muscles, and teeth known as Aristotle's lantern. In some areas there may be large aggregations, as is the case with many echinoderms, with fifteen or more individuals in a tight group.

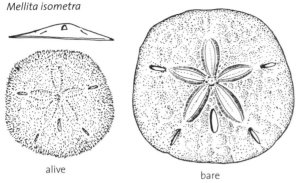

Common Sand Dollar (to 3" or more)
Mellita isometra

alive

bare

They are found in shallow-water sandy sediments all along the Inner Coast.

The green sea urchin, or variegated sea urchin, *Lytechinus variegatus*, is a short-spined urchin with an overall diameter of about 5 inches; the test is about 3 inches in diameter. Some individuals have greenish tests and green or whitish spines. A second form, *L. v. carolinus*, considered by some to be a subspecies rather than a variant, has a light red test and reddish spines.

Green sea urchins often selectively place debris on the upper surfaces of their tests, where it is held in place by their tube feet. Apparently the canopy of debris acts like a parasol to protect the urchins from strong light. Green sea urchins are sometimes very abundant in turtle grass and manatee grass beds. Florida Sea Grant reported that in August 1997 an infestation of green sea urchins in grass beds near Marathon in the Florida Keys swelled to immense aggregations, exceeding 200 individuals in a square yard. The onslaught of these "underwater locusts" resulted in the destruction of several square miles of grass beds; in some areas, the grass beds were reduced to barren sediments, and in other areas, only isolated patches remained. Green sea urchins range from Beaufort, North Carolina, and all along the Inner Coast where there are seagrass beds that grow in relatively calm waters with little turbidity.

The striped luidia, or gray luidia, *Luidia clathrata*, has a small disk with five flattened or strap-like arms. Each arm is marked with a dark gray or black stripe on the dorsal surface. This sea star can grow to 8 inches or more in diameter, but they are usually smaller. The arms are fringed with short, erect spines. The tube feet have pointed tips rather than the suckers that many sea stars' feet have. The pointed tube feet are adapted for digging through sand, but as is often the case, this specialized adaptation creates compromises. Because of the lack of suckers on its tube feet, the striped luidia cannot maintain a hold in high-energy waters. It is common in quiet, protected waters on sandy and muddy bottoms.

The marginal sea star, *Astropecten articulatus*, is a smooth-appearing sea star because of the fine, closely set granules covering the disk and arms. The arms are moderately long and tapering (about 3 1/2 inches long). The dorsal surface of the disk and the central portion of the arms are a striking deep blue

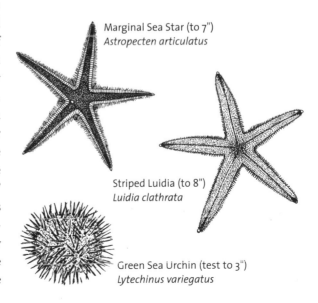

Marginal Sea Star (to 7")
Astropecten articulatus

Striped Luidia (to 8")
Luidia clathrata

Green Sea Urchin (test to 3")
Lytechinus variegatus

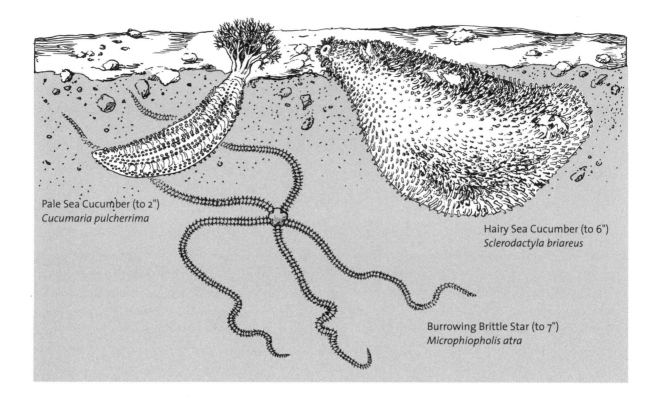

Pale Sea Cucumber (to 2")
Cucumaria pulcherrima

Hairy Sea Cucumber (to 6")
Sclerodactyla briareus

Burrowing Brittle Star (to 7")
Microphiopholis atra

or purple. The arms are outlined in white to orange, beadlike marginal plates. These are very common and sometimes locally abundant sea stars that live on soft, sandy bottoms. They are highly predacious and feed on a variety of snails and other mollusks, shrimps, small crabs, juvenile sand dollars, and small marginal sea stars. The marginal sea star ranges from lower Chesapeake Bay through North Carolina, where it is the most common sea star, and southward along the Inner Coast to the Florida Keys.

Brittle stars are five armed and prickly like their close relatives the sea stars. The arms of a sea star are not really appendages but are extensions of the central disk. In contrast, the arms of the brittle star are considered separate appendages, attached to a small, flat body disk. Brittle stars are so named be-

cause their arms are easily broken off; however, they have remarkable regenerative powers.

The burrowing brittle star, *Microphiopholis atra*, is a common, widely distributed species that lives in soft, muddy bottoms. It lies below the bottom surface in a burrow with two of its arms stretched upward. Water is circulated through the burrow, carrying with it microscopic food particles. The body disk is a mere 1/2 inch in diameter, but its long arms may be over 3 inches long, so the burrowing brittle star may have an overall diameter of 6–7 inches. The arms are jointed internally by interlocking plates that allow only a whipping, sideways movement.

Sea cucumbers are not vegetables, but are they animals? Of course they are animals, but they are notoriously sluggish; when they do move, they move slowly. Superficially, they have the appearance of sausages and really do not resemble sea urchins and sea stars at all. The bodies are cylindrical with a mouth at one end and an anus at the other. The mouths of sea cucumbers are surrounded by tentacles that are actually retractile, modified tube feet. In addition to these specialized tube feet, most sea cucumbers have tube feet that are scattered in various patterns over their bodies, depending on the species. Usually the tube feet are more numerous on the ventral surface of the sea cucumber. Internally, the body of a sea cucumber is equipped with circular and longitudinal muscles. The esophagus is supported by skeletal elements called ossicles that prevent the esophagus from collapsing on itself and also provide a place of attachment for the longitudinal muscles. The stomach and the intestine loop back and forth and then terminate at the anus.

Sea cucumbers may be the single most plentiful group of organisms in the ocean depths. They are very abundant in Australia, southeast Asia, and the Indian Ocean. They would seem to be prime targets for a bevy of predators, but as defenseless as sea cucumbers appear, they do have some means of protecting themselves. Some sea cucumbers have toxic substances within their bodies that repel fishes. Some sea cucumber species are able to expel masses of sticky tubules that are often toxic and can deter potential predators by fouling them with the obnoxiously adhesive mass. In addition, some sea cucumbers can thwart predators by ejecting almost their entire innards, including their intestines, respiratory organs, gonads, and guts.

The hairy sea cucumber, *Sclerodactyla briareus*, is a 5- to 6-inch-long, stout-bodied sea cucumber shaped like a sweet potato. Its round, rather fat body is studded with hairlike tube feet. These rotund sea cucumbers are usually green or brown and some-

times charcoal black. Hairy sea cucumbers may be found on muddy bottoms, particularly in eelgrass beds and seagrass meadows; they are rather tolerant of low salinities and consequently are widely distributed in estuaries throughout the East Coast. Hairy sea cucumbers are often washed up on beaches after coastal storms.

The pale sea cucumber, *Cucumaria pulcherrima*, is a very small sea cucumber. It is white to pale yellow and only about 2 inches long. Its tube feet are arranged in five distinct tracks along its body.

🌿
Birds of the Shallows

Birds, of course, are not bound to a particular habitat, unlike aquatic plants and clams. They are free to range in search of food at low tide in a high marsh or dabble over a riverine weed bed. They search for morsels of food around piers and rubble structures, and they roost in red mangrove canopies that overhang the shallows. The shallow-water habitat is an indefinable and varied region throughout the Inner Coast that encompasses diverse habitats and plentiful food for a variety of birds.

There are two little birds of the shallows that are most often seen feeding in vegetated areas: the green-winged teal and the ruddy duck. The green-winged teal, *Anas crecca*, is a very small dabbling duck that feeds over weed beds and seagrass meadows. They are predominantly dark grayish birds. The male has a russet head marked with a green patch that extends from the eyes to the back of the head. It also has a distinctive yellow rump. The female is brownish with a gray bill, and its head is marked with a dark line running through the eyes. Green-winged teals are named for the opalescent green speculum displayed by both sexes in flight. The male's call is a whistling

A male ruddy duck, Oxyura jamaicensis *(to 15"), swims on the surface to the left while his mate dives for food. On the right, a female green-winged teal,* Anas crecca *(to 14 1/2"), dabbles for food; her mate swims above.*

twitter; the female's is a quack. Green-winged teals are very swift and agile fliers resembling a flock of shorebirds as they explosively leap from the water, wheel away, and quickly vanish.

The ruddy duck, *Oxyura jamaicensis*, is also a very small duck but is a diver rather than a dabbler. Ruddy ducks are stubby birds with thick necks, large heads, and very wide, broad bills. In summer, the male has bold white cheek patches and a ruddy brown body and a blue bill; in winter, it has a grayish body and gray bill. The female, year-round, has a grayish brown body with whitish cheek patches that are tinged with grayish markings. Both have stiff, upturned tails. Ruddy ducks are excellent divers and swimmers, and when alarmed, they generally dive using their stiff tails as rudders. Look for these sassy little ducks to appear along the Inner Coast about mid-October.

The greater scaup, *Aythya marila*, and the lesser scaup, *Aythya affinis*, are also diving ducks. Scaups, often called bluebills by hunters, are typical divers that raft up, or flock, in great numbers on open wa-

Long-Tailed Duck (to 22')
Clangula hyemalis
female
male

Greater Scaup (to 18")
Aythya marila
female
male

Bufflehead (to 13 1/2")
Bucephala albeola
female
male

Common Goldeneye (to 18 1/2")
Bucephala clangula
male
female

ters. Adult male scaups, both greater and lesser, look essentially the same. Both species have blue bills and a blackish head. There are subtle differences, however: the lesser bluebill's head has a purplish sheen, and the greater bluebill's head is greenish. Their breasts and rumps are black, and their backs are gray with light gray or whitish sides. The females of both species are dark brown with slightly lighter flanks.

The differences in appearance between the two species of scaups are so subtle that it is difficult to distinguish one from the other, particularly when seen from a distance. The greater scaup has a larger bill with a wider black tip, but, of course, this is all relative. The head of the greater scaup is more rounded than the slightly peaked crown of the lesser scaup. The light wing stripe on the trailing edge of the wing is, perhaps, the most reliable field mark for separating the species. The light or whitish wing band of the greater scaup extends almost to the tip of the wing, as compared to that of the lesser scaup, which extends only about halfway to the tip of the wing. Of course, the birds must be flying for the

wing markings to be visible. Lesser scaups seem to prefer smaller bodies of fresher waters, in contrast to greater scaups, which are found in large numbers on saltier, more open bodies of water. But to roil the waters even more, their habitats often overlap, and both species often intermix. Because greater scaups prefer saltier water, during their winter stay, they hug the Inner Coast down to north Florida. Lesser scaups are much more wide ranging during the winter; they are found from the Atlantic coast westward and throughout the Inner Coast to the Florida Keys.

Scaups, both greater and lesser, feed on mollusks, insects, and crustaceans in saltier waters and on vegetation such as seeds, pondweeds, wild celery, and widgeon grass in fresher waters.

The canvasback, *Aythya valisineria*, is closely related to the scaups but is a larger and more robust diving duck with a distinctively shaped head. The head and bill of the canvasback merge into a long, sloping, unbroken line that leaves no doubt that it is a canvasback. The canvasback is the largest duck in the genus *Aythya*, which includes the greater and lesser scaups,

female

male

Canvasback (to 21")
Aythya valisineria

the ring-necked duck, and the redhead. Canvasbacks traditionally have been a favorite quarry of hunters because they are wary and challenging, they are large, and they taste good. Canvasbacks, typical of divers, have widespread legs set to the rear of their bodies, making them awkward walkers on land. The male's head and neck are chestnut colored, the breast is black, and the back and sides are grayish to almost white. The female has a light brown head and neck and a paler gray-brown back and sides. Both sexes have dark bills and the typical short wings of divers, yet they are very swift fliers. They range all along the Inner Coast in the winter.

The bufflehead, *Bucephala albeola*; the common goldeneye, *Bucephala clangula*; and the long-tailed duck, *Clangula hyemalis*, are diving ducks of the open waters.

The little bufflehead is an effervescent and energetic duck. These small, chunky butterballs are constantly moving—they scurry across the water's surface or bob underneath. The male is boldly marked with a white belly, a black back, and a glossy, greenish black head marked with a very visible wedge of white. The female is dark with lighter undersides and a white cheek patch behind each eye.

Most other diving ducks patter across the water and scramble for a takeoff. Not so with the bufflehead. It jumps out of the water and flies off just like a puddle duck. Buffleheads are abundant all along the Inner Coast to north Florida during the winter. They do not form huge flocks, but they are gregarious: where there is one bufflehead, there will be more. They prefer water depths of about 5 to 15 feet, where they feed on aquatic vegetation, seeds, mollusks, crustaceans, and small fishes.

The common goldeneye is a close relative of the smaller bufflehead. They both nest in Canada in trees near the water, in cavities that have been hollowed out by flickers and other woodpeckers. Seen at a distance, the mature male common goldeneye seems to have a mostly white body with a black back and head, but up closer, its dark, glossy green head with a characteristic white patch between the base of the bill and the eye becomes quite obvious. The female has a more subdued coloration, usually chestnut brown with a grayish back and a white neck collar. In some areas, common goldeneyes are known as whistlers for the piercing, humming sound of their wings as they pass overhead. Common goldeneyes winter along the Inner Coast to north Florida and are sporadically seen on the Florida peninsula.

The long-tailed duck, formerly known as old squaw, has a highly variable seasonal plumage; it does not always have a distinct pattern. Its plumage is usually colored a mixture of white, brown, black, and gray. Usually the sides are white or gray with a whitish head and neck. The male has a black breast and long, drawn-out tail feathers, which are the best field marks for identifying these ducks. The female's wings are dark and her sides and neck are whitish; she lacks the long tail feathers of the male. Long-tailed ducks are capable of deep diving and have been reported to dive as deep as 50 feet to forage for food. They use their wings and feet to fly through the water rather than using only their feet for propulsion; they feed on amphipods and other aquatic invertebrates, small fishes, and some vegetation.

Common Loon (to 32")
Gavia immer
winter
breeding

Long-tailed ducks generally do not associate with other ducks and are usually found in compact flocks or small aggregations within a large, loose, almost undefined gathering of several hundred birds. Long-tailed ducks are noisy, garrulous birds that constantly communicate by uttering clucking and yodeling calls. Their scientific name means "noisy" and "wintry"; they are certainly talkative, and they seem to be comfortable in bitterly cold, exposed conditions. These are constantly active ducks, quickly diving and bobbing up to the surface some distance away, and then, when some signal unknown to us passes through the flock, they are off on a short, careering flight, only to land nearby and resume their antics. They winter close to the coast down to about South Carolina or Georgia.

The common loon, *Gavia immer*, leaves the northern wilderness and begins arriving in Chesapeake Bay and North Carolina sounds in September, and by October there may be 10,000 or more loons between Maryland and North Carolina. The males and females arrive in their winter plumage, blackish gray above, paler below, with pale gray bills. The immature loons' plumage is similar to the adults' winter plumage. As the fall deepens into late October and November, the loons form large, loose flocks. They

are constantly peering, that is, swimming with their heads partially submerged as they visually hunt for fish. Loons are powerful swimmers and divers. When they sight their prey, they slip beneath the surface and, with the aid of their large, webbed feet, chase down their quarry. Frequently, small groups of loons cooperate in herding fish, often menhadens, into the shallows, where they glut themselves.

The common loon is a ducklike bird that somewhat resembles the double-crested cormorant, especially when swimming. They both ride low in the water, but loons usually hold their sharp-pointed bills horizontally, whereas cormorants point their long, hooked bills upward at an angle.

As winter approaches, common loons patter across the surface of the water, gain altitude, and, with their large feet extended beyond their tails and their long necks slightly bowed, with slow, deep wing beats, they head south to the Outer Banks of North Carolina. They go through a winter molt, which renders them flightless for a time in the Carolina sounds and just offshore in the Atlantic Ocean. Their insatiable feeding on oily menhadens and other fishes in the Chesapeake Bay tides them over until they are able to fly and feed once again. By that time, most of the adults have molted into their handsome breeding plumage: a black bill, a dark black head and neck marked with black and white necklace, and the unmistakable checkered black and white back. Again

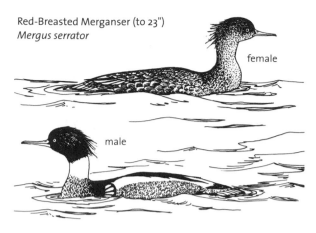

Red-Breasted Merganser (to 23")
Mergus serrator

female

male

the loons begin their heavy feeding on fish as they prepare for their flight north to their summer breeding grounds. Loons are generally silent on their wintering grounds, but occasionally on a quiet night, you can hear their primeval, tremulous yodel. Common loons are commonly seen in Inner Coast waters down to Florida.

The red-breasted merganser, *Mergus serrator*, is a winter visitor that feeds in the shallows teeming with shrimps and fishes. Mergansers are diving ducks, sometimes called saw bills because of the teethlike serrations on their slender bills, which enable them to grasp slippery, wriggling fish. The male red-breasted merganser has a lustrous head with a shaggy or wispy crest, a white collar, and a speckled black and brown breast. The female has a shorter crest and a reddish brown head and neck that merge into its lighter breast.

Red-breasted mergansers are very active swimmers, and they constantly patrol the shallows. It is a joy to watch them quickly dive and then pop up to the surface several yards away—never quite where you expect them. Mergansers usually hunt in mixed groups of males and females and, like loons, herd fish and feed on them underwater. They are common on

Inner Coast waters, particularly in brackish to high-salinity waters.

We have chosen to place the osprey, *Pandion haliaetus*, in the shallows, although it is also seen over deep waters, perched on tree limbs along verges of maritime and bay edge forests, and certainly on navigational structures all along the Inner Coast. The osprey is a fish hawk and is widely distributed throughout the world, on lakes, rivers, sounds, and estuaries.

The osprey belongs to a group of birds collectively referred to as raptors, which means "to seize"; the raptorial group includes eagles and hawks. Ospreys are large, hawklike birds, chocolate brown above, white below, and with a distinct dark eye stripe across their white heads. The dark wrist patches at the angles of the underwings are good identification marks as the osprey flies overhead. The breast feathers of the female are often tipped in brown, which gives the appearance of a ruffled necklace. The young look very much like the adults except that their feathers are edged in buff, giving them a speckled appearance, and their eyes are fiercely reddish orange rather than the penetrating yellow of the adults'.

The piercing, chirping call of adult birds is frequently heard, particularly when they wheel high in the sky in search of their next meal. Ospreys feed almost exclusively on medium-size fish about 6–10 inches long. Biologists estimate that it requires at least 3 pounds and, by some accounts, as much as 6 pounds of fish per day to feed the nesting female and three young. Ospreys hunt by soaring high over the water and searching for fish near the surface of the water. When an osprey sights its prey, it often hovers aloft by rapidly beating its wings to maintain position over the fish, and then suddenly it dives with folded wings and plunges talons-first into the water. Just as suddenly it seems to explode from the water.

Osprey and Young (to 23")
Pandion haliaetus

It vigorously shakes the water from its plumage, and with slow, labored, deep wing beats, the osprey heads for the nest, carrying the fish headfirst to streamline its flight. An osprey will also occasionally fly low over the water on a horizontal path, skim the water's surface, seize a fish in its talons, and head upwind for a controlled landing at the nest.

When ospreys fish in the upper parts of rivers, such as the Chowan and Alligator rivers and Currituck Sound, North Carolina, where the water is only slightly brackish and usually fresh, they very likely feed on catfish, golden shiners, and other freshwater species. In the higher-salinity waters in the sounds and bays of South Carolina, Georgia, and Florida, ospreys feed on menhadens and other herrings, mullets, silver and white perches, and other marine and estuarine fish species.

Most ospreys along the coast, except for those in southern Florida, migrate in the fall to Central and South America and some of the islands in the Caribbean. The male and female usually return to the same nesting site and either rebuild the existing nest, which has been buffeted by winter winds and rain, or construct a new one fashioned from branches snapped from trees. Cornstalks, shoreline debris, and even broken fishing rods are woven into their nests, which can be 5 feet in diameter, and sometimes larger. Ospreys build their nests on tree branches, on artificial nesting platforms erected by local landowners, on the tops of electric poles, and on navigation aids all along the Inner Coast. The eggs hatch in thirty-eight to forty days, and some fifty days later, the young are ready to try their wings.

In mid-September, as the days grow shorter, there are fewer and fewer ospreys circling overhead uttering their piercing "peep-peep" calls; the evenings become cooler, and tree leaves are beginning to change color—fall is in the air. Then, from far aloft, flying in long, V-shaped skeins, we hear the primal, two-note "honk-a-lonks" or "haronks" of Canada geese heralding the oncoming winter. The Canada goose, *Branta canadensis*, has a broad, round-tipped black bill, a long black neck, white cheeks, a gray-brown upper body, and light gray to buff underparts. Canada geese are plump birds with relatively short wings and widespread legs. They fly with deep, slow wing beats and can fly at speeds of 35 miles an hour over long distances. Canada geese are highly vocal: they honk

Canada Goose (25–45")
Branta canadensis

of increased agricultural production. In fact, many geese do not migrate back to their Arctic nesting grounds but rather remain year-round in the Inner Coast, where they nest and feed on grain and lush golf course grass. They usually breed in their third year and produce an average of four to seven goslings.

There are two species of swans that live in the shallows: the elegant but aggressive mute swan, *Cygnus olor*, and the tundra swan, *Cygnus columbianus*. The mute swan is a species from Europe that was introduced to North America in the 1800s and early 1900s to adorn private estates and zoos. Some of the mute swans managed to escape from private parks and estates along the Hudson River and in Chesapeake Bay and now have become firmly established and more widely distributed in many areas of the United States. These nonmigratory swans have increased in numbers and are now commonly seen in many shallow water areas throughout the year.

The tundra swan, formerly known as the whistling swan, nests in the Arctic tundra and migrates

when flying or when alarmed and continuously gabble and cackle when on the water. Geese and swans take off from the water by running across the surface of the water and flapping their wings to gain altitude, but Canada geese, when alarmed, can jump from the water like puddle or dabbling ducks and take wing.

Canada geese easily adapt to various types of habitats and are found in freshwater lakes, reservoirs, and estuaries. They feed in the shallows and the grassy uplands, where they thrive on corn and other grains. They have also become very accustomed to golf courses, residential areas, and parks, to the consternation of many. There well may be more Canada geese now than in colonial times, probably because

Mute Swan (to 60")
Cygnus olor

Tundra Swan (to 52")
Cygnus columbianus

in October and November to the mid-Atlantic and into the Carolinas. It is usually quite abundant in the Chesapeake Bay and in Lake Mattamuskeet near the shores of Pamlico Sound, North Carolina.

Both swans are entirely white. The mute swan is a more robust bird than the tundra swan, with a pinkish to orange bill and a black knob at the base of the bill; the tundra swan has a black bill with a dash of yellow in front of the eyes. The males of both species are slightly larger and heavier than the females. Tundra swans, although slightly smaller than mute swans, are still large birds, with a wing span of almost 6 feet. The immature tundra swans that arrive on our coast in the fall are as large as the adults. They molt from their light gray plumage to white by late winter or early spring.

Mute swans carry their long necks in a graceful S curve, and when they are in an aggressive posture, which can be quite frequent, they arch their wings over their bodies and pull their curved necks back. Mute swans often lift one black webbed foot out of the water and hold it alongside the body. Tundra swans can usually be distinguished from mute swans at a distance because they usually hold their slender necks straight rather than curved.

Mute swans are generally silent, but they do softly gabble and gurgle as they gather on the water, and when they are aroused or threatened, they utter an assortment of hisses and hoarse snorts. Tundra swans are much more vocal; they utter loonlike, liquid "who-who-whos" that softly echo across the water on quiet, cold winter nights.

Mute swans usually fly in small groups of twos or threes, with their wings making a loud whooshing sound as they pass overhead. Tundra swans tend to fly in larger flocks. Both species feed heavily on widgeon grass, redhead grasses, sago pondweed, and aquatic vegetation. They feed by extending their long necks down to reach the vegetation or, in deeper water, by tipping up like puddle ducks to reach the grasses, looking like marshmallow puffs on the water. They also feed on winter wheat and other grains, much to the displeasure of farmers. Tundra swans more commonly feed in grain fields than do mute swans. They often mix with flocks of snow geese on upland grain fields.

There are many that would like to control the reproductive capacity of the mute swan and even some that want to remove it from the wild because they believe that mute swans not only graze too heavily on valuable submerged aquatic plants but also harass the native tundra swans. Some state and federal wildlife agencies have actively addled (shaken) the swan eggs in the nest to prevent the eggs from hatching, and there has even been some sanctioned slaughtering of adult mute swans by wildlife agents. There has also been some discussion of permitting a hunting season on mute swans. But there are many people who enjoy seeing the graceful mute swans and who do not wish them to be harmed. Meanwhile, the mute swan continues to increase in numbers.

The American coot, *Fulica americana*, is a stocky, ducklike bird closely related to rails, gallinules, and moorhens. The coot is slate gray with a white bill shaped like a chicken's bill. The coot swims in a most peculiar way, bobbing its head back and forth as it

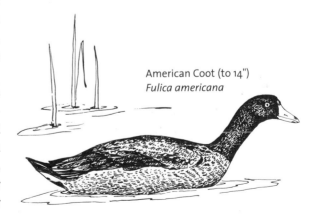

American Coot (to 14")
Fulica americana

swims like a windup toy. Coots have greenish or yellowish orange legs with large lobed feet set far back on the body. They are sometimes called spatterers because of their habit of skittering and scrambling across the water before they can gain altitude. They are excellent divers and swimmers and feed underwater in low-salinity areas on wild celery, redhead grass, sago pondweed, and small fishes and invertebrates. Even though they are strong divers and swimmers, they are not averse to pirating a choice morsel from other diving ducks. Coots are noisy birds and have a call, "kuk-kuk-kuk," similar to a rail's. They also communicate by arching and angling their white tails and swelling their forehead shields (the bulbous white patch at the base of the bill).

The American white pelican, *Pelecanus erythrorhynchos*, is one of the largest birds in North America. White pelicans have long, flat, yellow-orange bills, black flight feathers, and short orange legs and feet. In breeding season, a flat, disk-shaped plate grows on the middle of the upper bill that looks like the upside-down keel of a sailboat. White pelicans may appear clumsy and awkward on land, but once they are in the air, they are as graceful as their relatives the brown pelicans. White pelicans do not plunge-dive into the water to feed on their usual meal of fishes as do the brown pelicans; instead, they mill about in the water, usually in the company of other white pelicans, and dip their bills in the water to scoop up their meals.

Curiously, the American white pelican breeds in the freshwater lakes of the Great Plains and the Great Basin of the United States and the lakes of southern Canada. Huge flocks migrate to the Pacific, Gulf, and Atlantic coasts as winter approaches. American white pelicans are rather uncommon along the Atlantic coast; they are seen here and there along the Inner Coast, but their distribution is rather patchy. However, along the shores of the Saint Marys River, the boundary between southern Georgia and north Florida, there are often wintering colonies of these great white birds on the shell beaches that back up to the marshes along the river. They are usually in mixed flocks of great egrets, snowy egrets, and double-crested cormorants.

The pied-billed grebe, *Podilymbus podiceps*, is a shy, secretive, ducklike bird with a short, thick, black-ringed bill. The pied-billed grebe is not gregarious and is almost always solitary on marshy ponds, backwaters of meandering rivers, and open waters of

American White Pelican (to 62")
Pelecanus erythrorhynchus

estuaries, where they feed on a variety of aquatic organisms and some vegetation. They forage for their prey and avoid predators by diving and swimming underwater, but they hardly ever fly. These wary little birds can also lower their profile and slowly sink into the water until only their heads and necks are visible. Pied-billed grebes, similar to other grebes and loons as well as mute swans, often carry their little hatchlings on their backs. If they must dive to avoid a threat, the little ones cling to the mother's feathers until she bobs up some distance away from the disturbance. They are year-round residents of the Inner Coast.

The black skimmer, *Rynchops niger,* is a fascinating bird; it has a black back and a black-capped head with brilliant white underparts. But its long, compressed orangish red and black bill is the skimmer's most interesting feature; the lower mandible of its boldly marked bill is longer than its upper mandible. This remarkable bill separates the skimmers from all other birds.

Skimmers are very graceful and deliberate fliers that typically fly low over the water, particularly during the early morning and late afternoon, when

Black Skimmer (to 18")
Rynchops niger

the waters are often at their calmest. The skimmer's strong, long, pointed wings and broadly forked tail give it the buoyancy and control to skim the water with its long lower mandible, plowing an unseen furrow in the surface of the water. Skimmers are tactile hunters—they sense their prey by touch rather than sight—and so as they move along their chosen course, often in the company of other black skimmers, their unique bill immediately snaps shut on contact with a fish or shrimp.

Skimmers are often seen on sandbars, beaches, and shell banks along the coast. They have the look of large, somewhat blocky terns, and some ornithologists believe that they are closely related to terns. The skimmer's body has a long profile because of its prominent tail and large beak, but it also appears somewhat dumpy because of its very short, reddish legs.

❦ Subtropical Florida

Cape Canaveral, Florida, lies approximately 28 1/2 degrees north of the equator, or about 300 miles north of the Tropic of Cancer, which is considered

Pied-Billed Grebe (to 13")
Podilymbus podiceps

the northern boundary of the Tropics. The Cape juts eastward into the Atlantic between two biological provinces: the temperate Carolinian Province and the subtropical Caribbean Province. The Indian River Lagoon system, which includes Mosquito Lagoon and Banana River Lagoon as well as Indian River Lagoon, lies directly west of the Cape and extends about 125 miles along the Florida coast, from approximately New Smyrna Beach at the northern end to near Stuart at the southern end. There is a great diversity of species in the Indian River Lagoon system, indicative of the overlap between species that are characteristic of the temperate, or more northern, Carolinian Province and species that are typical of the subtropical Caribbean Province. The Indian River Lagoon forms the northern boundary of subtropical seagrass meadows, which includes seven species of seagrasses that flourish in those shallow waters. Salt marshes similar to those seen all along the Inner Coast to the Chesapeake Bay and beyond begin dwindling in the Indian River Lagoon system and give way to mangrove communities.

The faunal composition is highly diverse as well in the Indian River Lagoon. For example, in these waters, there are well over 200 known species of mollusks, 28 species of free-living and parasitic isopods, and about 400 species of fishes, as well as large concentrations of wading birds.

Farther down the coast, the plants and animals are decidedly more tropical in origin and are consequently less tolerant of wide shifts in temperatures.

Predatory Fishes

Schools of mackerels and marauding bluefishes unpredictably come in from offshore, deeper waters on occasional forays to feed on schools of baitfishes, including mullets, various species of herrings such as sardines and pilchards, anchovies, scads (spiny members of the jack family), ballyhoo, balao (halfbeaks), and even yard-long ladyfish. These toothy, pelagic fish may be driven into the shallow inshore waters by strong onshore winds, hunger, or the season of the year; they are not necessarily targeting seagrass beds or coral reefs, but they are after the abundant silvery fishes that school in the shallows over grasses, reefs, and mangrove flats. Spanish mackerels, and sometimes their larger relatives king mackerels, along with voracious bluefishes, churn the water with their frenzied feeding, and no snapper, grunt, blue tang, or parrotfish is safe when these fleet predators are on the scene.

Various sharks and rays, such as lemon and nurse sharks and spotted eagle rays, live in the "neighborhood" and move into seagrass meadows and other shallow-water habitats to feed on fishes and invertebrates with some regularity. There are a variety of other predators that move into the grass beds from nearby coral reefs and mangroves to feed during the night or day, depending on the species. Young barracudas gather in small schools, while the larger, solitary barracudas usually drift near the water's surface. Spotted sea trouts, blue runners, snappers, and grunts move into the seagrass beds from sandy shallows and from under the spreading canopies of mangrove prop roots to feed on fishes and shrimps and other invertebrates.

The nurse shark (no one is quite sure why it is called a nurse shark), *Ginglymostoma cirratum*, is a ponderous and sluggish shark that rests on bottoms, in crevices, and under ledges during the day. Nurse sharks are somewhat gregarious, and sometimes as many as three dozen sharks huddle up to each other, as one scientific wag has commented, "like pigs in a barnyard." They become quite active during the night, when they swim near the bottom in search of food. As sluggish as they may appear during the day, they are apparently speedy enough to suck in

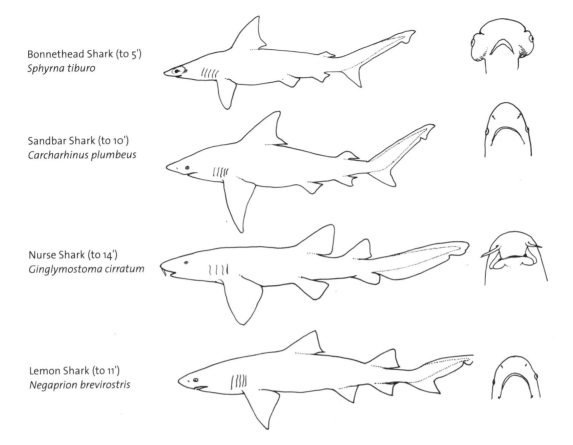

Bonnethead Shark (to 5')
Sphyrna tiburo

Sandbar Shark (to 10')
Carcharhinus plumbeus

Nurse Shark (to 14')
Ginglymostoma cirratum

Lemon Shark (to 11')
Negaprion brevirostris

stingrays, a favorite food, as well as other fishes, octopuses, squids, clams, and crustaceans.

The nurse shark is generally almost chocolate brown to black but is sometimes yellowish tan. It has a blunt, broad head; an inferior mouth, a mouth that is located on the underside of the head; and a pair of fleshy sensory barbels placed in front of the mouth, similar to catfishes and sturgeons. Its dorsal fins are large and rounded, although the second dorsal is smaller than the first and is positioned very close to the tail fin. The caudal or tail fin is quite unusual, as it is very large—it measures about 25 percent of the shark's length—and has no distinctive lower lobe. Young nurse sharks are marked with small black spots with lighter margins over the entire body. The females give birth to thirty to forty young in the late fall.

Nurse sharks and just a few other species of sharks do not need to constantly force water over their gills to breathe, as they have the ability to pump in water while lying motionless on the bottom.

Nurse sharks are not a threatening species; as a matter of fact, these lethargic fish are so sluggish that they are quite approachable as they rest on the bottom in the shallows, tempting scuba divers and snorkelers to pet them or tug on their fins—a definite no-no! Nurse sharks that are harassed can be provoked to bite, and they can inflict painful wounds with their raspy teeth.

The lemon shark, *Negaprion brevirostris*, is a pale

yellow to brownish, stocky shark with a short, broad snout; hence the species name, which is Latin for "short snout." The two widely separated dorsal fins are similar in size. Lemon sharks, similar to nurse sharks, can lie at rest on the sea bottom and pump water over their gills. Juvenile and adult lemon sharks tend to be gregarious, also like nurse sharks; 100 or so adults have been seen resting close together on the bottom. They mate in the spring, and the female carries the developing pups for approximately ten months. The newly born lemon sharks are about 2 feet long at birth. Lemon sharks usually inhabit shallow waters around coral reefs and mangroves, river mouths, and bays. They occasionally prowl the grass beds and feed on fishes such as jacks, stingrays, eagle rays, and slow-moving puffers and cowfishes.

Sharks have very large livers, and some shark species' livers produce copious quantities of oil. Scientists have puzzled over the extraordinary size of sharks' livers and the amount of oil, fats, and lipids they produce. Most experts reasoned that the oils were a ready source of energy, particularly when the sharks were not actively feeding. It wasn't until about thirty years ago that new research provided new insight and a more plausible explanation. Fishery scientists now believe that the major function of a shark's liver is to regulate the buoyancy of the shark, just as air bladders do for bony fishes. The rich oil reserves in the liver do also provide quick energy for the occasional burst of speed that a shark requires to pursue prey or to avoid becoming prey itself.

The spotted eagle ray, *Aetobatus narinari* (some call it a spotted duck-billed ray), is a large, graceful ray with a very long, slender tail. Spotted eagle rays can weigh as much as 500 pounds. They are related to cownose rays and have a similar body shape but a distinct head. The base of the spotted eagle ray's whiplike tail is equipped with two venomous spines. Its disc and pectoral wings are broader than long, and the wings are somewhat pointed. The upper surface is usually gray or brown and marked with white or yellowish spots. Spotted eagle rays are often seen in surface water or in the shallows, gliding or "flying" through the water. They feed on clams and crustaceans by rooting them out of the bottom with their shovel-like heads. They are usually solitary, but at times they gather in large schools of several hundred individuals. Spotted eagle rays make spectacular leaps from the water, particularly when they are spawning or evading sharks. They are commonly seen in Florida waters, but occasionally they stray as far north as the Chesapeake Bay.

The great barracuda, *Sphyraena barracuda*, is built for speed and predation. This streamlined, slender, silvery fish seems to be all head with a mouthful of razor-sharp teeth. Its body is almost round in cross section and is equipped with a pair of widely spaced dorsal fins and a forked tail. The lower jaw extends beyond the upper jaw, and the barracuda's large shearing teeth are often evident because of its habit of slowly opening and closing its mouth, especially when it is just drifting along and eyeing the

Spotted Eagle Ray (to 8' across wings)
Aetobatus narinari

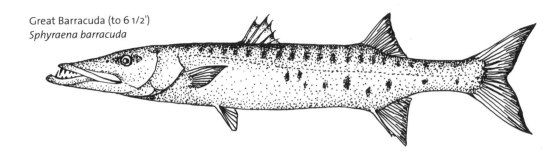

Great Barracuda (to 6 1/2')
Sphyraena barracuda

world, as barracudas constantly do. The great barracuda is silvery gray on its sides with a greenish tinge above and is marked with many small black spots along the sides.

Great barracudas are common in the shallows and can be seen lying motionless under a pier or near a bulkhead, usually near the surface. They are most common in seagrass meadows, on the edges of coral reefs, and among mangroves. Juvenile barracudas school together in the seagrasses and near mangroves; that is where their food is and where they can seek cover from predators. Adults are more solitary, although we have seen several large barracudas (4 to 6 feet) in the same vicinity, maintaining their space from one another. Barracudas are ever-watchful lurkers; they locate their prey by sight, and when they strike, it is, it seems, with the speed of a lightning bolt. They hit their prey with their large, gaping, fang-filled mouths. A medium-size or smaller fish will disappear down the gullet of the 'cuda; a larger fish—say, a 7- or 8-pound grouper or snapper—may have its head left behind. We have "shared" a fish with a barracuda just as we brought our catch to the surface. The 'cuda took the body of the yellowtail snapper, and we were left with a head on a hook.

The great barracuda is "great" because it is the largest of the twenty or so barracuda species throughout the world. Barracudas are curious fishes. They will trail snorkelers while keeping their distance; there

are always tales about barracuda attacks, but there have been few substantiated incidents of attacks on humans. There have been close calls between barracudas and spear fishermen who have impaled fishes on the ends of their spears, but those encounters are rare. The stories do, however, seem to grow and take on lives of their own.

The Spanish mackerel, *Scomberomorus maculatus*, is an elongated silvery fish with a greenish back that is well marked with oval yellow or bronze spots on its sides. The two dorsal fins are continuous. The first dorsal fin is black on the leading edge, and the second dorsal fin is scimitar shaped and followed by a series of finlets that continue to the deeply forked tail. Spanish mackerels are highly migratory schooling fish and do not spend a lot of time anywhere; they seem to always be on the move. They range as far north as New York in the summer and down through Florida from fall through spring. They are predacious fish that seem to target silvery baitfishes, especially sardines and anchovies that school over grass beds and shallow, sandy bottoms.

The blue runner, *Caranx crysos*, is an aggressive, schooling predator very much like the Spanish mackerel. It ranges from offshore around reefs and on grass beds to the inshore shallows around jetties and other structures. Blue runners are silvery gray on their flanks and are light olive to bluish green on their backs. Their snouts are slightly pointed, and their heads are dominated by large eyes. The spiny dorsal fin is continuous with a soft-rayed dorsal fin that extends to the tail. Blue runners, typical of the family members, have rigid, deeply forked tails and a row of thickened, modified scales called scutes on the posterior portion of the lateral line.

Blue runners often form very large schools, which explains why, when you catch one, you frequently catch many. They are relatively small fish; the maximum weight is about 7 pounds, but most blue runners weigh 1 pound or less. These small jacks are voracious feeders and, like mackerels and bluefishes, hunt for prey like fishy wolf packs. They swoop over grass beds and feed on squids, shrimps, and smaller fishes such as anchovies, silversides, and pilchards, and they will even take on larger prey in a joint effort, eating a larger fish one bite at a time.

Various species of snappers move in from deeper-water coral reefs, although some snappers and other fish species live in and around small coral patches embedded in the seagrass meadows and are actually permanent residents of the seagrass community. Snappers also move from inshore mangrove communities to feed on fishes and invertebrates in the seagrasses.

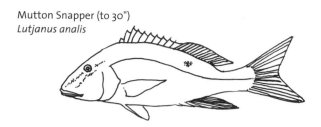

Mutton Snapper (to 30")
Lutjanus analis

The mutton snapper, *Lutjanus analis*, is a snapper that frequents grass beds and also is quite common around mangroves. It is a colorful fish whose sides, as well as the upper lobe of the tail fin, are olive green. It has a whitish belly with a rosy cast and a bright blue line below the eye. Resting mutton snappers usually have vertical dusky olive bars. Mutton snappers have a persistent dark spot just above the lateral line; the more colorful lane snapper and the somber gray snapper have a similar spot in the same location, which may cause some difficulty in identifying the fishes. The mutton snapper, however, is the only snapper with a black dot above the lateral line and with pointed dorsal and anal fins; the fins of the lane snapper and the gray snapper are rounded.

Mutton snappers seem to be homebodies when they become adults; they tend to stay within the same territory. Larval and juvenile mutton snappers feed on plankton and small invertebrates in the grass beds, and as they grow older and larger, they feed on shrimps, crabs, mollusks, and fishes during the day and the night. Mutton snappers are fairly large fish—10 pounders are not uncommon—and they are hard-fighting fish that are excellent to eat.

Fishes of Mangrove Swamps and Shallow Flats

The flats are grassy shallows that abound in the Indian River Lagoon, the Mosquito Lagoon, the Banana River, and farther south through Biscayne Bay, the Keys, and Florida Bay. Flats are seagrass mead-

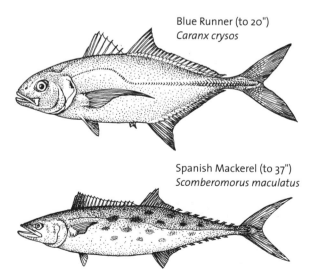

Blue Runner (to 20")
Caranx crysos

Spanish Mackerel (to 37")
Scomberomorus maculatus

ows, but they are very shallow. Although there is no precise technical definition of a flat, most fishing guides and avid anglers consider the flats to be 2–3 feet deep. Flats are punctuated with mangrove islets and winding channels that are usually scarred by outboard propellers. There are also coral patches, sponges, and seaweeds scattered throughout the flats. Local fishermen often refer to the "backcountry," the more remote area of Florida Bay, where there are thousands of acres of mangroves and grass flats. Almost all of Florida Bay is within the boundaries of Everglades National Park.

Many of the larger fishes that patrol the seagrass meadows in search of food also lurk around mangroves and over the shallow grass beds and flats in Florida. There are several species of sharks, including lemon, nurse, and bull sharks, as well as several members of the jack family. Barracudas, tarpons, cobias, red drums, and bonefishes are some of the major sport fishes that anglers spend a lot of time and money pursuing.

The bonnethead shark, *Sphyrna tiburo,* a member of the hammerhead family, is very common in the backcountry on the flats and in sounds and estuaries from North Carolina to Florida. Bonnetheads, however, are warm-water fish that move south as the waters cool. They are gregarious sharks that usually swim in small schools, but when they are migrating to warmer waters, they sometimes form vast schools of several hundred or more individuals. They are livebearers, as are most sharks, and give birth to a dozen or so 14-inch pups in shallow, inshore waters.

The bonnethead is the smallest of the hammerhead sharks; it grows to a maximum length of 5 feet. It is also the only shark in this family that has a semicircular head rather than a hammerhead. Its eyes are located on the rounded perimeter of its shovel-shaped head, which gives it wide-angle vision, and as it swims, it constantly sweeps its head from side to

side. Its teeth are small and are adapted to feeding on rock crabs and especially the ever-present blue crabs. Bonnetheads are opportunistic sharks and will dine on almost anything they find, including burrowing mantis shrimps, fishes, and even wary octopuses.

Tarpon, the "silver king," *Megalops atlanticus,* is considered one of the premier game fishes of the shallows. Once hooked, it makes towering leaps and scorching runs. It looks like a huge herring. It has a large, upturned mouth with a protruding lower jaw; a single, centrally placed dorsal fin, with the last ray of the fin drawn out into a long filament; and a deeply forked tail. Tarpons have very large, silvery scales that gleam like a thousand mirrors on their flanks and bellies, and their backs are metallic greenish blue. They have an unusual lower jaw

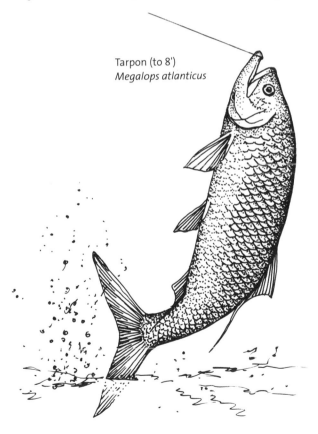

Tarpon (to 8')
Megalops atlanticus

structure called a gular plate, which is a bony plate overlying the throat. These big fish—some weigh over 200 pounds—have very small teeth. They feed nocturnally on fishes, crabs, and shrimps. They can live in waters that are low in oxygen, particularly around marshes and mangroves, because they have modified swim bladders that enable them to gulp in atmospheric air.

Tarpons have strange-looking larvae that resemble the larvae of eels. The larvae are transparent, compressed, and elongated creatures with a mouthful of fangs and a forked tail. The tarpon, ladyfish, bonefish, and eels are primitive fishes that all produce similar larvae, leptocephali, and are all closely related.

Tarpons sometimes swim in large schools in passes and channels between mangrove islands and near inlets. When they swim near the surface, they often roll in a way that can only mean tarpons are out there. Tarpons are at home in high-salinity ocean waters and in freshwater rivers as well. We have been startled more than once, when snorkeling over grass beds, by these large fish, which cruised by us and continued on until we could no longer see them. Tarpons are abundant around mangroves and over grassy bottoms in the Indian River Lagoon system and all through south Florida. Tarpons, however, are not confined to Florida; they are occasionally caught in Virginia during the summer, in the shallows behind the barrier islands and in the sounds of North Carolina and all along the Inner Coast.

The ladyfish, *Elops saurus*, also called tenpounder or chiro, is a close relative of the tarpon. The ladyfish is slender and elongated with a large, deeply forked tail, a very straight lateral line, and small, silvery scales. Ladyfishes are quite common in the shallows over grass beds and in the backcountry of Florida Bay, where they feed on fishes, crabs, and shrimps.

The ladyfish is not the premier game species that the tarpon and bonefish are, but it is fun to catch and release. Ladyfishes are wide ranging and are sometimes caught as far north as New England, but they are much more common and abundant in Florida.

The bonefish, *Albula vulpes*, whose scientific name translates as "white fox," is also called gray ghost. It is a superb game fish that is sought in the "skinny" waters of the Florida grass flats. It is almost venerated for its wariness and skittish behavior and, once hooked, its blazing speed, but certainly not for its bony flesh; it is almost always released.

The bonefish resembles the ladyfish except that the bonefish has a snout that protrudes over its small mouth, and the tip of the snout is marked with a dusky black patch. It is bluish green to gray above, with gleaming silver scales marked with linear black streaks on its sides. Bonefishes are so well camouflaged for their existence on the flats that it takes an experienced guide with polarized sun glasses to spot them. However, their feeding habits often give them away, because as they grub into the bottom, searching for crabs, shrimps, and small mollusks, their tails often stick out of the water, almost daring the angler to flip a lure their way. Bonefishes also have a leptocephalus larval form. Similar to tarpons, they are able to gulp air when the oxygen in the sometimes superheated waters is depleted.

Smaller bonefishes often form large schools in deeper waters and move into the shallows on rising tides. Larger, older bonefishes are generally solitary or in pairs when they feed on the flats.

Members of the jack family, including the crevalle jack, palometa, Florida pompano, and permit, are well represented on the flats and around mangroves.

The crevalle jack, *Caranx hippos*, is a deep-bodied fish with a sloping forehead, yellow fins, a yellowish belly, and a deeply forked tail. The base of the

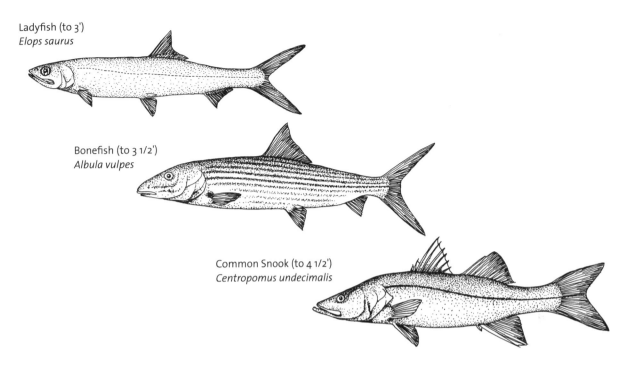

Ladyfish (to 3')
Elops saurus

Bonefish (to 3 1/2')
Albula vulpes

Common Snook (to 4 1/2')
Centropomus undecimalis

pectoral fin is marked with a black splotch and also with an elongated black mark on the trailing edge of its operculum. Crevalle jacks are voracious fish that scatter mullets and other baitfishes in a furious commotion of jumping prey, screeching gulls, and careering pelicans. Crevalle jacks are not considered good eating, but they are good catching; they readily take artificial bait, cut bait, and live bait. They are quite common around mangroves and flats, but they are also likely to be in brackish water around piers and in deeper, saltier water as well. Crevalle jacks of 1 to 4 pounds typically run in schools, but the larger jacks are usually solitary predators. And they do get large: the Florida record is 51 pounds.

The palometa, *Trachinotus goodei*; the permit, *Trachinotus falcatus*; and the Florida pompano, *Trachinotus carolinus*, are all quite similar. They are beautiful silvery fishes with compressed sides, deep bodies, and extended dorsal and anal fins. All three

species mainly feed on crabs, shrimps, mollusks, and small fishes.

Palometas are particularly beautiful and graceful fish when they are seen underwater. They often swim in small groups over sandy bottoms near beaches and are usually not alarmed by snorkelers. They have mirror-bright sides and are grayish blue-green across their backs and heads with a wash of yellow on their breasts. Their angular bodies that taper back to the tail, in combination with their elongated dorsal and anal fins, are perhaps their most defining characteristics and quickly separate them from permits and Florida pompanos. The front portions of the charcoal gray dorsal and anal fins are the deepest parts of a palometa's body, and from there the body tapers at a steep angle toward the tail.

The permit is the largest of the three species. Like the palometa, its body angles back to the tail beginning under the extended dorsal and anal fins. Permits

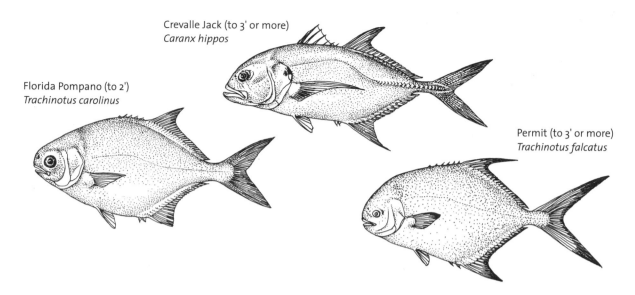

Florida Pompano (to 2')
Trachinotus carolinus

Crevalle Jack (to 3' or more)
Caranx hippos

Permit (to 3' or more)
Trachinotus falcatus

are silvery, deep-bodied fish with yellowish tints on their breasts. Their dorsal and anal fins are shorter than those of the palometa and may reach only to the base of the tail (the caudal peduncle). Permits are big and brawny fish that can weigh 40 pounds or more. They are part of the legendary threesome, the "Florida flats grand slam": bonefish, tarpon, and permit.

The Florida pompano is considered by many to be one of the most delicious of all the fishes. It is much smaller than the permit and usually weighs less than 3 pounds. It is not as deep bodied as the palometa or the permit, and its body is not as angular as the other two species. The Florida pompano is also silvery with a greenish gray back and gold to yellow throat and belly. The extended portions of the dorsal and anal fins are much shorter than those of the palometa and the permit. Florida pompano and palometa are often found along sandy beaches where the waves curl just before they spill on the beach, but they are also found over shallow flats and around mangroves and reefs.

The common snook, or robalo, *Centropomus undecimalis*, is an unmistakable fish with a sloping, concave head; strongly jutting lower jaw; high, an-

gular, separated dorsal fins; and a bold, dark slash of a lateral line that begins just over the gill plate and terminates in the soft rays of the tail fin. The common snook is another one of those prized trophy fishes that inhabit the mangroves, river mouths, and estuaries of Florida's east coast from the Indian River down to the Keys. Common snooks are subtropical fish that occasionally range as far north as Pamlico Sound in North Carolina. They can tolerate freshwater, brackish water, and high-salinity water, but they cannot endure water temperatures below 60°F. Juvenile snooks utilize river mouths and estuaries as nurseries where the food is plentiful in the warm, shallow waters and where mangroves and other shoreline vegetation give them places to hide from predators. Adult common snooks, some as large as 40 pounds, are common along mangrove-lined shores and occasionally appear on the flats; they also hover near structures such as piers and seawalls, and we have seen them from underwater lined up against the jetties in inlets.

Florida and Texas prohibit commercial fishing for snook because of the serious decline in the stocks,

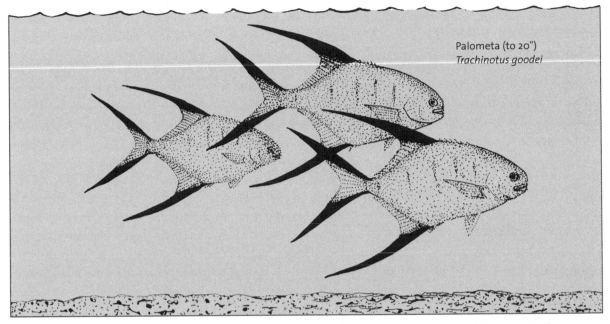

The long, dark fins immediately identify a school of palometas, Trachinotus goodei *(to 20"), cruising by in shallow waters, often close to shore.*

although some scientists believe that habitat degradation is more of a problem than overfishing. The Mote Marine Laboratory in Sarasota, Florida, has a very active research program on the biology, ecology, and aquaculture of the snook designed to enhance the wild stocks of common snook.

The goliath grouper, *Epinephelus itajara*, formerly known as jewfish, is truly a giant sea bass. It is the largest member of the sea bass family in the Atlantic, with a record 680-pound fish caught in Florida! The goliath grouper is brownish gray to olive with creamy yellow vertical bars and is generously sprinkled with small, dark spots over its head and fins. It has a barrel-shaped body, a typically large grouper mouth, and a rounded tail. Juveniles,

less than 4 feet long, live almost exclusively along fringing red mangrove shorelines in the Ten Thousand Islands area of Florida and in many red mangrove areas in the Keys. The adults, defined as more than 4 feet long, are solitary fish that favor rocky and coral reef ledges, isolated patch reefs, wrecks, and

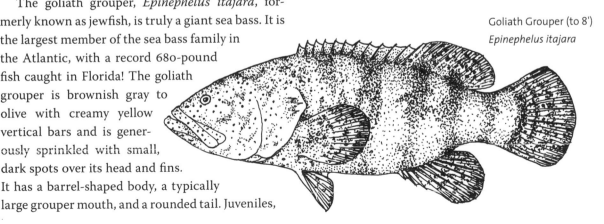

bridge pilings; they are very territorial and usually stay around their chosen locations. These reclusive giants range only far enough from their lairs to feed on spiny lobsters, apparently their favorite food, as well as on shrimps, crabs, and an assortment of fishes, including parrot fishes and stingrays. If there is an octopus or a young sea turtle available, the goliath grouper will seize it as well.

The popularity of the white meat fillets and steaks cut from these lumbering, slow-growing giants pushed the goliath grouper to near extinction. They are highly endangered and cannot be harvested commercially or caught by recreational anglers.

Subtropical Sand and Mud Bottoms

THE UPSIDE-DOWN JELLYFISH

Yes, an upside-down jellyfish! *Cassiopea xamachana* spends most of its life sprawling upside down on the muddy bottom rather than floating along on the surface propelled by wind and current, as is the lot of most other jellyfishes. Upside-down jellyfishes live in quiet backwaters, lagoons, and around red mangroves. They are usually brownish to olive or creamy yellow with white markings or, sometimes, greenish gray-blue. The medusal bell can measure 6 inches or more in diameter. Upside-down jellyfishes host thousands of symbiotic algae called zooxanthellae that are embedded in the mesogleas of the branched, frilly oral arms. These unusual jellyfishes usually lie upside down, sometimes by the hundreds, while absorbing the sunlight so that the zooxanthellae can photosynthesize and produce carbohydrates and oxygen that are utilized by the jellyfish. Apparently the symbiotic algae do not always provide enough nourishment for the jellyfish, as it is quite able to capture planktonic organisms and even small fishes with the aid of its lethal nematocysts. The upside-down jellyfish is even said to absorb nutrients directly from seawater as a secondary method of feeding.

view looking down into water

Upside-Down
Jellyfish (to 12")
Cassiopea xamachana

LUCINES

Lucines are almost always round with umbones that point forward and with a long, leathery ligament behind the umbones. The shells are usually yellowish, creamy, or white, and most species are sculpted with radial or concentric grooves. The many species of lucines found throughout the world dwell in muddy and sandy bottoms.

The tiger lucine, *Codakia orbicularis*, is one of the most common and abundant clam shells found along the south Florida shorelines. The thick, whitish shell is decorated with many close-set radial ribs crossed at right angles by narrow ridges that together form a beaded texture. The interior, particularly around the rim, is often tinged with pale purple, pink, or sometimes yellow.

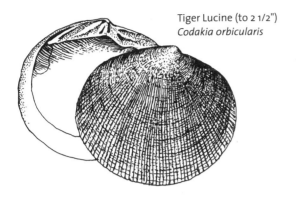

Tiger Lucine (to 2 1/2")
Codakia orbicularis

The common name of this clam, tiger lucine, is certainly a misnomer, because there is not a single stripe on its shell. Apparently this clam was confused at one time with another lucine, *Codakia tigerina*, known from Indo-Pacific waters; however, the mystery remains unsolved, as that species is also devoid of stripes.

SNAILS

The common sundial, *Architectonica nobilis*, has a beautiful creamy to tan-gold shell with splotches of red and brown on each whorl. The solid shells are 1–2 1/2 inches in diameter and have four or five beaded spiral whorls. The spire is low, which gives the shell the appearance of a coolie hat. Common sundials live in sandy areas, usually around clumps of soft corals.

The crown conch (pronounced "konk"), *Melongena corona*, has a solid, 2- to 4-inch, roughly pear-

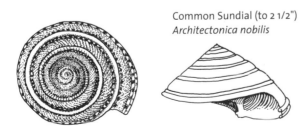

Common Sundial (to 2 1/2")
Architectonica nobilis

shaped shell with a conical spire and one to four rows of semitubular, or grooved, spines that usually point upward, but not always. It has a large, inflated body whorl with a wide aperture and a horny, dark brown operculum. The colors and patterns of this conch are quite variable, as are the length of the spines and the number and placement of the rows of spines. Crown conchs are usually cream with spiraling bands of purplish brown of various widths. However, it is difficult to determine the color and pattern of a live crown conch because they are usually covered with a film of mud and algae.

Crown conchs abound in muddy bottoms, particularly near mangroves, where they scavenge for food and prey on oysters. They also attach their tough, wafer-thin, paddlelike eggs to oyster shells and other hard objects; when the eggs hatch, the young conchs crawl out and begin feeding and growing.

The largest conch of all, the horse conch, *Pleuroploca gigantea*, is the state shell of Florida and is one of the largest shells in the sea; some reach a length of about 20 inches. Horse conchs are carnivorous and mostly prey on large whelks, other conchs, and pen shells. These very large conchs insert their proboscises into their victims' shells and then feed on their soft bodies. Horse conchs are heavy shelled and spindle shaped with orange-red apertures. Most shells are creamy-tan, but some are chalky-salmon, and small horse conch shells are usually a bright orange. Look for their cone- or vase-shaped egg capsules with five or six circular rings scattered on the sand bottom.

True tulip and banded tulip shells belong to the same carnivorous family of snails as does the huge horse conch, and like horse conchs, true tulips and banded tulips prey on other mollusks, such as oysters, small queen conchs, worms, barnacles, and each other. True tulips and banded tulips favor sandy- or

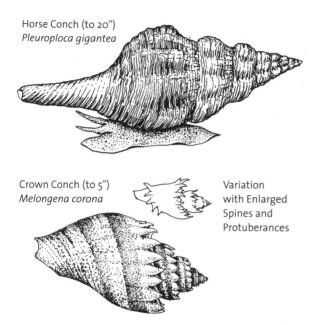

Horse Conch (to 20")
Pleuroploca gigantea

Crown Conch (to 5")
Melongena corona

Variation
with Enlarged
Spines and
Protuberances

muddy-bottomed turtle grass beds in relatively shallow and quiet waters.

The true tulip, *Fasciolaria tulipa*, is a graceful, spindle-shaped snail with a smooth and usually shiny surface with about eight body whorls that are separated by distinct lines called sutures. True tulips are large snails that reach a length of 8 inches. Some of the whorls are incised with spiral ridges. The aperture is broad, and the live snail is protected by a horny, brown operculum. The siphonal canal is long and somewhat twisted. True tulip shells come in a variety of colors: they may be golden tan, reddish brown, yellowish tinged with orange, bluish gray, or green. The body of this large snail is a startling red that contrasts with the charcoal gray, white-flecked muscular foot.

The banded tulip, *Fasciolaria lilium*, is a smaller, more delicate version of the true tulip. There are several subspecies of banded tulips (some specialists prefer to lump them as a single species) differentiated by overall size, body whorl shape, color, and geographical distribution. Banded tulips grow to 4–5

inches in length. They are typically spindle shaped and have thinner and lighter shells than does the true tulip. They are found in a variety of colors, but they are usually bluish gray and marked with spiraling bands of dark brown.

Both the true tulip and the banded tulip deposit egg capsules that are similar in shape to but smaller than those of the horse conch. The cone-shaped egg capsules of the true tulip and the banded tulip lack the circular ridges that are diagnostic of the horse conch's egg capsules. The egg capsules of both the true tulip and the banded tulip are smooth; however, the opening of the true tulip's vaselike capsule terminates in a frilly or crenulated band. The egg capsule of the banded tulip is similar except that it is not as coarsely fringed. Both species range from North Carolina southward, but they are much more common in Florida waters (see chapter 3).

The cameo helmet, *Cassis madagascariensis*, belongs to a family of about seventy species, including the Scotch bonnet. That family member grows to about 3 inches, whereas the largest species in this family, the massive cameo helmet, can grow to a length of 14 inches. Helmet shells historically

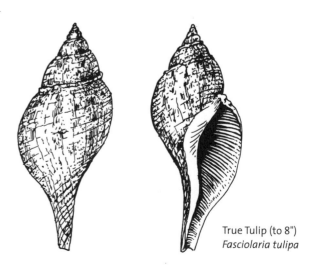

True Tulip (to 8")
Fasciolaria tulipa

Banded Tulip (to 5")
Fasciolaria lilium

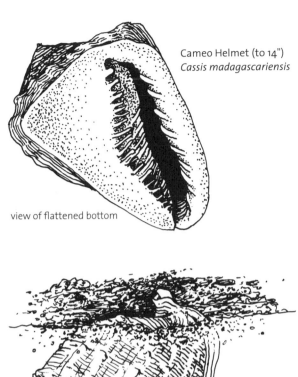

Cameo Helmet (to 14")
Cassis madagascariensis

view of flattened bottom

cameo helmet plowing
through bottom sands

were greatly valued by carvers who fashioned three-dimensional cameo jewelry from the thick shells (as some carvers still do). Cameo helmets are carnivorous snails that particularly savor the soft flesh of sea urchins, especially the long-spined black sea urchins that roam the sandy-bottomed seagrass meadows at night.

Cameo helmets are heavy and shaped like an ancient Roman soldier's helmet. They have practically no spire, and the single, inflated body whorl constitutes most of the shell. The shell of the cameo helmet is large and colorful and marked by a flaring cream to pinkish brown parietal shield, the expanded inner margin of the aperture. The brown aperture is lined with white folds, or teeth, separated by blackish brown streaks.

Cameo helmets seem to be gregarious at times and have been observed by the dozens apparently laying eggs on the sandy bottom. Usually they remain buried in the sand with only a small part of their shells exposed above the surface of the bottom. The shells are frequently covered with algal growth, making them almost indistinguishable from the scattered debris on the bottom. Cameo helmets range from North Carolina through the Florida Keys, where they are most abundant.

Cowrie shells are smooth, polished, elongated to oval shells that are a favorite to collect. About 200 species are found in warm waters throughout the world, with 5 species found off the coasts of the United States. Cowries have long, narrow, tooth- or riblet-lined apertures with canals at both ends. Similar to most mollusks that have porcelainlike or polished shells, the mantles of cowries partially or

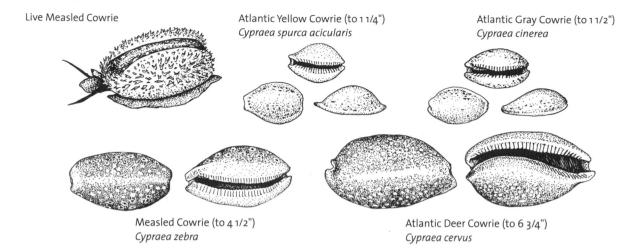

Live Measled Cowrie

Atlantic Yellow Cowrie (to 1 1/4")
Cypraea spurca acicularis

Atlantic Gray Cowrie (to 1 1/2")
Cypraea cinerea

Measled Cowrie (to 4 1/2")
Cypraea zebra

Atlantic Deer Cowrie (to 6 3/4")
Cypraea cervus

completely envelop the shell. Cowries are nocturnal feeders and move out of their hiding places under rocks and coral ledges to feed on algae and organic detritus. Cowries are favored shells of many cultures. They have been and still are used to decorate clothing and to string necklaces, and they were important as currency, much the way North American Indians used hard clam shells and tusk shells as wampum.

The Atlantic deer cowrie, *Cypraea cervus*, the Inner Coast's largest cowrie, grows to a length of 6 3/4 inches. Its lustrous shell is dark brown and decorated with white spots; it often has alternating light brown bands encircling the shell. Its mantle is charcoal gray to dark brown. The Atlantic deer cowrie shell is more bulbous than are the shells of other cowries. It has inward-rolling riblets or teeth that are alternately brown and white.

The measled cowrie, *Cypraea zebra*, is smaller and more streamlined than the Atlantic deer cowrie. The shell is also lighter in color; it is usually tan to light brown. The back is adorned with white spots, and the sides and edges of the shell are "eyed"—they have white spots with dark centers. The teeth of the measled cowrie are dark brown to reddish brown.

The Atlantic gray cowrie, *Cypraea cinerea*, is

about 1 1/2 inches long. The shell is swollen about the middle and is brownish gray to orange-brown or shading to lilac and frequently flecked with small dark spots. The base is creamy and the apertural teeth are small.

The Atlantic yellow cowrie, *Cypraea spurca acicularis*, is a small cowrie, only about 1 inch long. Its shell is ovate or somewhat inflated in the center and is colored orangish yellow and marked with many brown and white spots; the base is white. The mantle of the Atlantic yellow cowrie has branchlike appendages, and when it envelops the entire shell, the cowrie looks like a stone covered with seaweed.

Worm snails resemble certain worms that build sandy tubes that are cemented together to form large reef rocks. But worm snails are truly mollusks that construct calcareous spiral tubes to form "worm rocks," or reefs of tangled tubes. The typical worm snail begins life in a shell that has tightly coiled whorls and a sharp spire. As it grows, the tube becomes more loosely spiraled. Like most filter-feeding mollusks, worm snails pump water into the mantle cavity, where food particles are filtered out by the gill filaments and passed along to the mouth.

The variable worm snail, *Petaloconchus varians*,

Variable Worm Snail
(tubes to 1/8" long)
Petaloconchus varians

builds very narrow tubes, about 1/16 inch or less wide, and 8–12 inches long. Variable worm snails grow in tightly compacted entanglements with their scraggly orange, dark-gray, or purplish brown tubes in an upright position. A worm rock can contain thousands of individuals. Usually the empty tubes of worm snails that are cast up on shore are bleached white.

The West Indian worm snail, *Vermicularia spirata*, does not grow in compacted entanglements as do variable worm snails. It is a more solitary species, although occasionally a few West Indian worm snails do grow close together. These are true snails, although they certainly resemble worms growing

West Indian Worm Snail (tubes to 6" long)
Vermicularia spirata

in hard, shelly tubes. Their bodies are greatly elongated, but unlike typical worms, their heads bear molluskan tentacles, eyes, and radulae. The shell of a West Indian worm snail is a translucent amber to tan or yellowish color and can grow to 6 inches long or more. The shell is tightly coiled on itself from the spire for about a quarter of the length of the shell, and then the coils relax and the shell is loosely turned for the remainder of its length; the aperture is round and thin walled. West Indian worm snails are found only in southeastern Florida and particularly in the Keys, where they grow attached to rocks and other mollusks.

Cephalopods: Octopuses and Squids

Cephalopods, literally meaning "head feet," are active predators that have a well-developed head and a crown of strong, rubbery, sucker-bearing arms extending directly from the head. The arms, also called tentacles, surround a formidable mouth equipped with chitinous beaklike jaws. Cephalopods are soft-bodied animals, other than the nautilus, which is a cephalopod contained within a shell. Octopuses, in particular, have well-developed brains and complex nervous systems. Both squids and octopuses have large eyes and the ability to instantaneously change the texture, color, and pattern of their skin when the brain sends a message through the nervous system and then to the muscles, which stretch or contract the thousands of packets or sacs of pigment called chromatophores.

There are two important species of squids, longfin squid and northern shortfin squid, that are usually found in the deeper, open waters of the Atlantic Ocean. Both of these squid species feed voraciously on small shrimps, amphipods, butterfishes, and herrings, as well as other squids. In turn, they are favored food for a large number of carnivorous marine predators, such as dolphins, a number of species of whales, tunas, swordfishes, bluefishes, flounders, and silver hake, to mention only a few squid-loving fishes. These two species of squids are harvested in large numbers by commercial fishermen for the growing number of people who love to eat calamari; they are also landed for the very large bait industry.

There are four species of octopuses and squids that commonly live in Inner Coast waters: the common octopus, the Caribbean reef octopus, the Atlantic brief squid, and the Caribbean reef squid.

The common octopus, *Octopus vulgaris*, is normally a reddish brown, rather smooth-skinned animal. The common octopus is a widely distributed species and is found in most of the world's oceans except for polar seas. This species is usually a nocturnal hunter, although there are reports from fishermen and scientists that they do make hunting forays during daylight hours in some parts of the world. The common octopus is undoubtedly the best-studied octopus species of all because of its worldwide distribution and because of its importance as a commercial species; over 100,000 tons are harvested annually.

Octopuses are usually solitary, secretive, and territorial, and common octopuses are no exception. They lurk under rocky ledges or in crevices, and they can quickly burrow in the sand in seagrass meadows. They are always well hidden and are seldom seen by snorkelers or divers, but they are somewhat messy housekeepers, and this habit often reveals their hiding places. When the common octopus goes hunting, it typically takes it prey back to the lair. If it manages to catch a crab or a fish, there may not be a trace of their dinner, but if it brings home conchs or other thick-shelled mollusks, the empty shells will be strewn like so many dinner plates outside its den. This shell midden is a dead giveaway that there is an octopus secreted nearby.

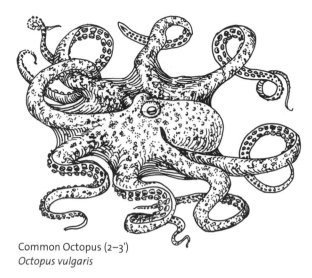

Common Octopus (2–3')
Octopus vulgaris

Octopuses have eight arms. The third right arm of the male is a specialized organ of reproduction known as a hectocotylus that has been adapted for moving sperm packets through a hollowed-out groove into the female's oviduct. The female stores the sperm sac along with others from previous matings, and when conditions are right, she produces eggs that are fertilized by the retained sperm. She lays thousands of eggs and glues them with her sticky secretions to a hard substrate. The female usually stops feeding as she broods her eggs and occupies her time by keeping her egg clutches clean of debris and guarding against intruders such as crabs and fishes. Shortly after the eggs hatch, the female and male die, and a new generation of octopuses that will last only twelve to fifteen months begins.

The Caribbean reef octopus, *Octopus briareus*, is smaller than the common octopus, with a length of about 18 inches, as compared to the 3-foot-long common octopus. The Caribbean reef octopus is a creature of warm waters; it is found in the semitropical and tropical waters of southern Florida, the Bahamas, the West Indies, and Central and South

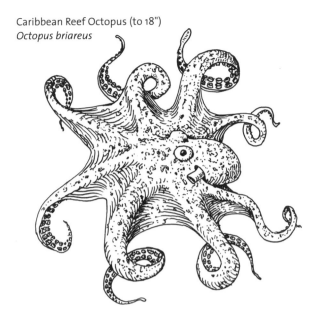

Caribbean Reef Octopus (to 18")
Octopus briareus

America. This species is a crepuscular hunter; that is, it usually leaves its den at dawn or dusk to hunt. It preys mostly on crabs and shrimps, but it also feeds on spiny lobsters and fishes when it can catch them. Octopuses stalk their prey in several ways. Sometimes they simply hunt by waiting close to the entrance of their den until a shrimp or crab wanders by. Other times they actively pursue a fish or shrimp from above by spreading their webbed arms to form a canopy and then dropping down and enveloping their meal. They also poke and grope into crevices with their incredibly sensitive arms and wrest their meal from its hiding place. Octopuses have a set of formidable tools for dispatching a thick-shelled mollusk or an armored crab or lobster. Octopuses are, of course, mollusks, and similar to many whelks and other snails, they have a radula, which they use to bore an access hole in the shell of a bivalve, after which they inject a paralytic toxin; the muscles of the bivalve relax, and the powerful arms of the octopus pry open the shells to reveal the soft-bodied tidbit within. When a crab or lobster is within the

grasp of an octopus, it usually takes only a bite with its parrotlike beak to overcome its prey.

Caribbean reef octopuses are usually blue-green and mottled with brown, but of course they can instantly change their colors and patterns when they are threatened or when they are in an amorous mood. This octopus usually produces less than 1,000 eggs, but the eggs are quite large. The eggs of the Caribbean reef octopus hatch into miniature copies of the adult and immediately begin their benthic existence. In contrast, the common octopus lays thousands of smaller eggs, which hatch into planktonic organisms, and as they develop in the water column, they are at a greater risk of being eaten than are their smaller cousins the Caribbean reef octopuses.

The Atlantic brief squid, *Lolliguncula brevis*, is a small squid, less than 5 inches long, that resembles the squid that is sold as bait or the larger squid that is sold in the marketplace as calamari. Atlantic brief squids have rounded fins and are not quite as streamlined as most offshore, pelagic squids are. Squids have a remnant of the molluskan shell, the pen, which they carry internally as a transparent, cellophanelike structure that gives support to their soft bodies. Atlantic brief squids, like other squid species, are agile and quick and swim in jet-propelled spurts, although they can slowly swim backward and forward when they are not threatened and trying to avoid being eaten. Water is drawn through the openings around the head and forcefully ejected through the tubular siphon. They spurt more rapidly to the rear, but they can move forward by directing the siphon to the rear. Squids have streamlined bodies with four pairs of arms and one pair of longer tentacles that surround the mouth; their eyes are large and almost humanlike. The pair of long, club-ended, sucker-equipped tentacles can whip out with lightning speed and snare a shrimp or a small fish in a blink of an eye. Atlantic brief squids can change

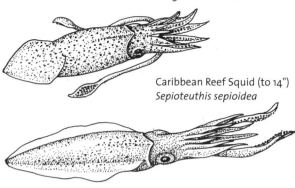

Atlantic Brief Squid (to 4 1/2")
Lolliguncula brevis

Caribbean Reef Squid (to 14")
Sepioteuthis sepioidea

their colors and patterns just as other squids and octopuses can. When it is alarmed, its typical dark-spotted pattern changes to hundreds of tiny, bright, blinking stars. Atlantic brief squids are quite common, but seldom seen, in brackish water back bays, sounds, and high-salinity inlets of the Inner Coast.

The Caribbean reef squid, *Sepioteuthis sepioidea*, is a spectacular jewel of the sea. These beautiful squids give the appearance of being somewhat wider than most squid species because the wide, rounded fins compose about 90 percent of the body length. Most squids, including the Atlantic brief squid, have small triangular or rounded lobes located near the posterior end of the body. The arms and tentacles of the Caribbean reef squid are short and rather thick.

The Caribbean reef squid is a tropical species often seen over coral reefs and coral patches and over seagrass meadows. These small squids, usually no longer than 14 inches, swim in small groups of twenty or so individuals and seem to be fascinated with snorkelers and divers. They hover a certain distance from swimmers by slowly undulating their fins, and if that uncertain boundary is violated, they spread their arms, dramatically change their color to the alarm mode, and jet away . . . but not too far,

for they are just as curious about us as we are about them.

These lovely creatures are social and gregarious and absolutely beautiful. It is difficult to describe the colors and patterns because they are forever changing, like liquid rainbows. They may be colored with hues of blue and green and highlights and speckles of pulsating opalescent pearl and gold, or they may flash false eyespots toward the rear of their bodies, and then again, if they see potential mates, they may flash an intense, black on white "zebra display." When Caribbean reef squids are alarmed by predators, they turn reddish brown, and if they are really alarmed, they eject a cloud of black ink and disappear.

Sea Turtles

There are seven species of sea turtles throughout the world, including the olive ridley, the smallest and most abundant sea turtle; the most enormous and swiftest swimmer, the leatherback turtle; and the least-known and most mysterious sea turtle, Australia's flatback sea turtle. The sea turtles most often seen along the Inner Coast and nearby coastal waters are the green, loggerhead, and hawksbill turtles.

All sea turtles are oviparous (egg layers). The soft, flexible, thin-shelled eggs feel like chamois skin or a slightly underinflated balloon. Turtles scoop nests from the sand with their hind flippers, deposit their 100 or so rubbery eggs into the chambers, cover the nests, and then laboriously crawl back to the sea. Most turtles return to their nesting beaches and lay second or third or even more clutches of eggs, depending on the species and the age and condition of the female. A loggerhead turtle, for example, may lay as many as 400 eggs in three or four separate clutches in one season. The eggs incubate in the warm sand nests and, depending on the temperature of the sand, hatch in as few as forty-five days or as many as seventy days. The temperature within the nest also controls the sex of the embryonic turtles. Cooler nest temperatures produce a preponderance of males, and warmer temperatures favor the production of females, with a mix of sexes produced between the temperature extremes.

As the time of hatching nears, excitement ripples through the turtle nest as first one and then another half-dollar-size hatchling breaks through its soft, pliant, two-month-old "home" with its sharp-pointed egg tooth. The hatchlings soon gather into groups and, crawling about with their flailing flippers, work themselves into what has been called a "hatching frenzy." The roof of sand begins raining down on the hatchlings, and the little turtles begin their first migration by moving upward and into a very hostile environment . . . the beach! The open nest carries a distinctive odor of residual yolk and bacteria that wafts out and, like a dinner bell, attracts a host of diners: raccoons, dogs, rodents, ghost crabs, and birds, particularly gulls, night herons, and black vultures.

Usually the hatchlings emerge by the dozens at night and scramble down the beach slope. With some luck, they are buoyed by a wave and carried seaward. Some hatchlings survive their first few days at sea, but many do not because of predation from below by many kinds of fishes and dolphins and from above by "aerial gleaners"—gulls, terns, frigate birds, and pelicans.

Those that manage to survive begin a new chapter in their young lives dubbed "the lost years" by the sea turtle scientist Archie Carr. The young turtles spend several years somewhere out to sea, carried by currents that eventually transport them to areas where there are endless meadows of floating gulfweeds, golden prairies that provide protection and a rich assortment of food. After some years, the much larger but still immature turtles instinctively make their way to coastal waters, where they feed, increase in size, and advance toward sexual maturity. Hormones begin surging through the males and females as they move along the age-old migratory routes and approach their ancestral nesting beaches, which are deeply imprinted within them. The powerful mating urge drives the males to search for receptive females—and sometimes not so receptive females, which results in a rough-and-tumble form of sexual mayhem replete with savage biting of flippers and necks between competing males. After mating, the females move toward the beach while the males remain at sea, never to return to land. The females eventually lumber up the beach where they originated fifteen or more years before to begin a new generation of sea turtles.

The green turtle, *Chelonia mydas*, is the Inner Coast's largest hard-shell sea turtle; the largest individuals may have a carapace length of about 4 feet and reach a maximum weight of 450 pounds, although most green turtles are smaller. Green turtles have relatively small, rounded heads and a smooth, oval-shaped carapace. The carapace is light to dark brown, sometimes tinged with olive, and marked with bold blotches of dark brown; the plastron is yellowish white.

Adult green turtles are mainly herbivores. They feed on seagrasses, particularly turtle grass and attached seaweeds, although occasionally they eat jellyfishes, crabs, and other invertebrates. The green color of their fat and muscles is derived from their diet of grasses. Juvenile green turtles are more predacious and feed on a variety of invertebrates.

As green turtles reach a size of 10 inches or so, they leave their high-seas pelagic feeding grounds and migrate to shallow coastal seagrass meadows in locations such as Florida Bay and the Indian River

Lagoon system. They often range northward to New England, but green turtles are more tropical in their habits and are much more abundant along the Florida coast and in the Caribbean Sea. Occasionally green turtles nest as far north as North Carolina, but their major nesting beaches are along the Florida coast.

The loggerhead turtle, *Caretta caretta*, has a massive head and strong crushing jaws and an elongated and somewhat heart-shaped carapace. The carapace of the loggerhead is frequently populated with a number of barnacles and algae, plus grazing organisms such as isopods and skeleton shrimps. These wide-ranging turtles are the most common and abundant sea turtles in the sounds, lagoons, and bays of the Inner Coast. Thousands of subadult loggerheads regularly spend their summers feeding on crabs and mollusks and jellyfishes in the Chesapeake Bay, Pamlico Sound, and estuaries in South Carolina and Georgia, and they can be very abundant in the Indian River Lagoon and southward into the Florida Keys and Florida Bay. They also occur throughout the world in temperate and tropical waters. Loggerhead turtles are the primary sea turtle nesters on the Atlantic coast beaches from North Carolina, and occasionally Virginia, southward to Florida, where the greatest nesting activity takes place.

The hawksbill turtle, *Eretmochelys imbricata*, is smaller than the green and loggerhead turtles; it usually weighs less than 200 pounds. But what it lacks in size it makes up in beauty, particularly because of its distinctive amber-colored carapace, adorned with splotches of brown and black known the world over as tortoiseshell. Over the ages the hawksbill has been sought for its beautiful shell to make tortoiseshell jewelry, boxes, combs, and valuable inlays for furniture. These turtles have strongly hooked beaks that resemble the beak of a hawk with which they graze on sponges. They are often seen swimming over coral patches searching for their favorite sponges in

Green Turtle (to 5' long)
Chelonia mydas

Loggerhead Turtle (carapace to 4')
Caretta caretta

Hawksbill Turtle (to 3')
Eretmochelys imbricata

the shallow waters of the Inner Coast. They nest on Caribbean and Gulf of Mexico beaches and, rarely, on Florida's beaches. These are warm-water sea turtles that are most often seen in Florida and Caribbean waters, but they do occasionally straggle north as far as New England.

The Magnificent Frigate Bird

There are a number of birds that fly over the flats and haunt the mangroves: herons, pelicans, white-

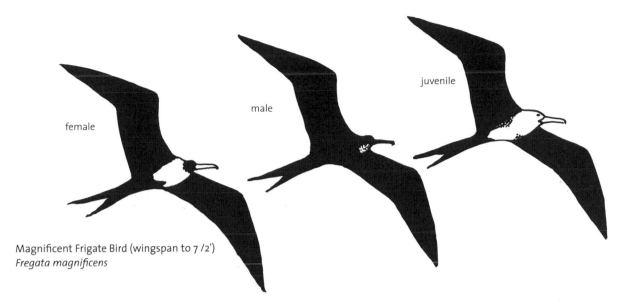

Magnificent Frigate Bird (wingspan to 7 /2')
Fregata magnificens

crowned pigeons, gulls, terns, and a graceful bird called the magnificent frigate bird.

When sailing aloft, the magnificent frigate bird, *Fregata magnificens*, cannot be mistaken for any other bird. A quick glance at the silhouette of a magnificent frigate bird is usually all you need to identify it. With a wingspan of 7 1/2 feet; sharply angular, long, pointed wings; and a long, deeply forked tail, the magnificent frigate bird is wonderfully adapted for effortlessly gliding at high altitudes. Its wingspan in proportion to its weight is the longest of all the birds. Magnificent frigate birds usually weigh less than 3 pounds because they have very light, hollow bones.

The male is a glossy black. In breeding season, it inflates its reddish orange throat pouch to the size of a balloon in hopes of catching the eye of a female, and if that isn't enough, it points its hooked bill skyward, shakes its raised wings, sways from side to side, and cackles. Occasionally a male can be seen on the wing with its pouch still inflated, but usually only a streak of hot pink is visible on the throat. The females have white breasts and sides, and immature birds have white necks and heads.

Magnificent frigate birds feed on the wing, and when they spot a meal on the surface of the sea, they dramatically dive from on high and swoop over the surface of the water to pluck it from the sea with their hooked bills. They will perish if they land in the water, because their extremely long wings cannot provide enough lift when wet. They feed on almost any type of fish if it is the right size—anchovies, flying fishes, sardines, mullets, and needlefishes—as well as on jellyfishes, squids, shrimps, and hatchling sea turtles. They also feed over land on carrion, eggs, and chicks by swooping and plucking without landing. And magnificent frigate birds are also "aerial pirates," often called man-o'-war birds, for their habit of harassing flying gulls and terns, forcing them to release their catch, which they then snatch on the wing.

These oceanic birds nest on isolated islands, where they build their stick nests on mangroves and shrubby trees. The only known nesting sites of magnificent frigate birds in the United States are on the Marquesas Keys and the Dry Tortugas west of Key West. Magnificent frigate birds sometimes range as

far north as North Carolina, but they are most common in south Florida, particularly in the Keys.

Dolphins

The Atlantic bottlenose dolphin, *Tursiops truncatus*, is a small, toothed whale. Some call these small whales dolphins, and others insist on calling them porpoises. There appears to be no clear preference or definition among scientists who study these wonderful marine mammals, although some make a distinction based on tooth shape. Many specialists consider marine mammals to be dolphins if they have conical or peglike teeth and porpoises if they have spade-shaped teeth. Atlantic bottlenose dolphins have beaklike snouts and slender, streamlined bodies, in contrast to the blunter snout and relatively stockier body shape of what some refer to as a porpoise. However, preference of "dolphin" or "porpoise" also seems to lie with common usage, which varies from region to region.

Bottlenose dolphins are very social animals and travel in schools or pods of sometimes 100 or more, but usually fewer; some groups tend to stay offshore, and others are found in the shallows off coastal beaches and in the mouths of rivers, lagoons, and well up estuaries. This species is the familiar dolphin that is seen performing in marine parks and aquariums.

Bottlenose dolphins can reach a length of about 12 feet and a weight of about 1,400 pounds. They are usually dark gray or slate gray on the back, lighter gray on the sides, and even lighter on the belly. Their teeth are used for grasping rather than shearing or biting. They make puffing and hissing sounds as they exhale moisture-laden air through a single blowhole located on the top of the head. They have been observed sleeping in calm waters just below the surface. With regular, almost imperceptible movements of their powerful tails, they periodically raise their heads just above the water's surface to breathe.

Bottlenose dolphins feed on many species of fishes, shrimps, and crabs. They often trail behind shrimp boats to feed on the fish discarded overboard. They also move into small leads or tributaries that wind through tidal salt marshes, especially in South Carolina and Georgia, herding fishes and shrimps in front of them. With a swipe of their powerful tails, they wash their prey up onto the slick, muddy banks, slide up to feed on the stranded fishes and shrimps, and then quickly return to the muddy waters.

Atlantic bottlenose dolphins are widely distributed from New England through Florida and into the Caribbean. From about Cape Hatteras southward, pods of bottlenose dolphins may associate with groups of Atlantic spotted dolphins during spring and summer as the Atlantic spotted dolphins move inshore. The two species can be differentiated based on size, color, pattern, and shape of the head and beak. The bottlenose dolphin ranges in length from 8 to 12 feet; the spotted dolphin is no longer than 8 feet. Bottlenose dolphins are not spotted, except for old females that may have spots on their bellies. Atlantic spotted dolphins have increasingly spotted bodies as they age, and they are a dark purplish gray on their backs, with gray sides and bellies. Bottlenose dolphins have broad heads and relatively short beaks, whereas spotted dolphins have slender heads and longer beaks.

❦ 7

Weed Beds and Seagrass Meadows

Beds of rooted aquatic plants often grow in profusion, particularly in the upper tributaries of rivers and estuaries, where the salinity of the water is quite brackish or almost fresh. A few species thrive as well in mid-estuarine waters. These aquatic plants are true vascular plants, similar to our familiar terrestrial plants, that bear green leaves and produce flower buds, fruits, and seeds and are firmly rooted in sandy and muddy bottoms. Their flower buds can often be seen just ruffling the surface of the water.

Aquatic plants grow intertidally out to depths limited only by the penetration of sunlight. Plant beds are often exposed for short periods of time during extreme low tides or when heavy winds drive the water from the shallows; however, they flourish only when they are submerged. The lack of sunlight limits their establishment and growth in the deeper waters of Inner Coast rivers, sounds, and estuaries.

Stands of aquatic vegetation create special habitats that are quite different from unvegetated shallows. The plants grow rapidly during the growing season and produce dense underwater gardens providing food and shelter for many animals. The roots of aquatic plants also stabilize the bottom sediments, and plant leaves dampen the surging waves, creating a more stable environment for benthic organisms.

Most organisms do not feed directly on aquatic plants; the plants serve as indirect food sources through the production of organic detritus as the leaves and stems die and decompose. In addition, the algal and bacteria growth, the slime, that coats the plants is fed on by many species. The detrital material is an important food source for snails, small fishes, amphipods, isopods, and planktonic grazers such as copepods and other microcrustaceans. Fishes and crabs and many other animals find food and protection among the aquatic plants. Submerged aquatic vegetation, sometimes referred to as SAV, is a principal source of food for many waterfowl and

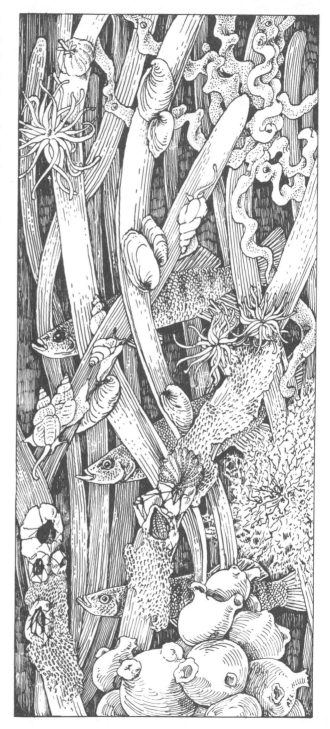

small mammals such as muskrats. Typically, the variety and number of organisms living within aquatic weed beds far outnumber those that live in adjoining unvegetated areas. Most of the species that live in weed beds can be found in unvegetated areas, but certain species are not generally found anywhere but in weed beds.

In the winter, most of the vegetation dies back except in the more southern areas of the Inner Coast. When the plants die back and the stems and leaves disappear, the weed bed habitat essentially disappears. Fishes and shrimps and other organisms move into deeper waters to spend the winter, and other organisms such as snails and worms bury into the mud. The once heavily vegetated weed bed becomes an unvegetated shallow water habitat. But then spring arrives, with warming temperatures and longer periods of sunlight, and the dormant roots and rhizomes respond and sprout stems, leaves, and seeds. Once again the aquatic weed beds become a flourishing garden for a host of animals.

🌿

Tidal Freshwater and Brackish Water Weed Beds

The diversity of underwater plants in freshwater and slightly brackish water is greater than in saltier waters, just as it is greater in tidal freshwater marshes than in tidal saltwater marshes. In the upper tidal rivers and brackish water sounds such as the lower Cape Fear River in North Carolina and the Saint Johns River in Florida, weed beds can be very thick and well populated with several species of plants.

Plants of the Weed Beds

Some of the more abundant and common species of plants are coontail, sago pondweed, redhead grass, horned pondweed, and widgeon grass.

Coontail, *Ceratophyllum demersum*, sometimes called hornwort, has alternately arranged floating leaves and oppositely arranged submerged leaves. This is a plant that can grow in great profusion, producing large masses in still and slow-moving waters. Long flower stalks arise from the axils of the floating leaves and bear very small white to pinkish flowers from spring to early fall.

Sago pondweed, *Stuckenia pectinata*, formerly *Potamogeton pectinatus*, has long, narrow, almost threadlike tapering leaves. The species name means "comblike," referring to the shape and arrangement of the leaves. The leaves characteristically spread out like a fan and float at the water's surface. The leaves are arranged alternately and grow in bushy clusters. Sago pondweed is a thin-leaved species and as such is notoriously difficult to separate from other thin-leaved species. Sago pondweeds produce a nutlike fruit called an achene that grows at the tips of long stalks. The fruits and almost all of the plants, including the starchy tubers, are consumed by many species of waterfowl. Sago pondweed is widespread, and it is one of those aquatic plant species that can grow so densely that it clogs irrigation canals and shallow channels.

Redhead grass, *Potamogeton perfoliatus*, probably was named for redhead ducks, which seemed to savor the plant. However, redhead ducks have seriously declined in past years, so perhaps the plant's other name, clasping-leaved pondweed, is more useful now. This plant's delicate, small, oval leaves do clasp the plant stem where they connect. The stems are slender and branch toward the upper part of the plant. Small flowers are borne at the end of a long spike. Redhead grass grows in tidal freshwater and brackish water ponds and in slow-moving rivers and streams throughout the Inner Coast.

Horned pondweed, *Zannichellia palustris*, is another one of those thin-leaved plant species that

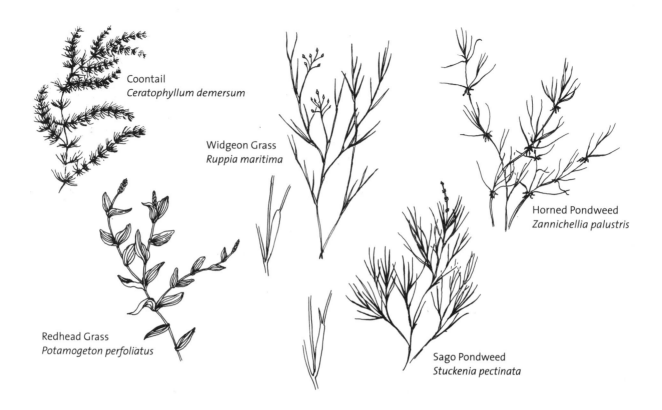

Coontail
Ceratophyllum demersum

Widgeon Grass
Ruppia maritima

Horned Pondweed
Zannichellia palustris

Redhead Grass
Potamogeton perfoliatus

Sago Pondweed
Stuckenia pectinata

are difficult to identify. The stems and leaves are very thin and fragile; its leaves are oppositely arranged and arise in pairs from each joint of the stem. Horned pondweed seems to have two growth spurts during the year, one in late spring and the other in late summer. It is quite common to observe floating mats of horned pondweed stems and leaves bobbing along on the surface of the water in the springtime. Sticklebacks, small fish, utilize the leaves of the horned pondweed to build nests under the floating mats of vegetation in the Chesapeake Bay and perhaps a little farther south in Inner Coast waters.

Widgeon grass, *Ruppia maritima*, is also a thin-leaved species with threadlike leaves that are alternately arranged along stems that can grow to 3 feet long. The stems are often branched, giving the plant a zigzag appearance. Widgeon grass can grow in freshwater, but it is usually found in brackish to rather high-salinity waters. This species can tolerate exposure during periods of very low tides, which are frequent in many areas.

Widgeon grass grows very thickly, particularly in mid-salinity areas, and is often the dominant species in weed beds. Waterfowl feed on the seeds and leaves, and small fishes and other organisms find cover and food among the densely growing plants. Widgeon grass is a wide-ranging plant throughout the Inner Coast.

Insects of the Weed Beds

On a calm day, particularly in the shallows, furiously active insects, sometimes by the hundreds, skitter and gyrate across the surface of the water, creating

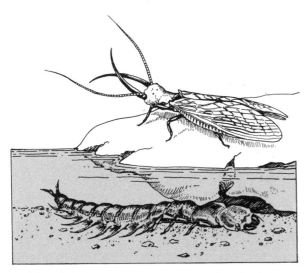

A dobsonfly hellgrammite rests on an overhanging ledge while a male dobsonfly, Corydalus cornutus *(to 1 5/8"), rests on an overhanging rock.*

tiny ripples as they dart and circle almost endlessly. There are many aquatic insects that spend all or part of their lives in the water. Some species, such as certain beetles and gnats, do so only as larvae; other species, such as the dobsonfly, are almost totally aquatic.

Some insects hatch from the egg and are small copies of the adult; entomologists call this process simple metamorphosis. Then there are those insect species that hatch from the egg into a soft-bodied wormlike stage called a larva. The larvae, variously called caterpillars, grubs, and maggots increase in size and complexity as they molt. After several molts, depending on the species, the larva transforms into a nonfeeding stage called a pupa, and finally into an adult. This process is called complete metamorphosis.

Some insects require freshwater to carry out their complete life cycle from egg to adult, and other insects, such as salt marsh mosquitoes, need brackish to fairly salty water to complete their life cycles.

Some species can tolerate a relatively swift current, and others inhabit only the quiet backwaters of rivers or nearby ponds. Certain species spend most of their time underwater, carrying their air supply in bubbles that adhere to hairs on their bodies, and other insects are surface dwellers and seldom spend time below the surface of the water.

The dobsonfly, *Corydalus cornutus*, is not a fly at all but a very large, winged insect that brandishes a pair of enormous and frightening tusklike jaws. These mandibles are especially threatening looking in the males. Dobsonflies belong to a group of insects called Megaloptera, which means "great winged." The irony is that these impressively winged creatures, some of which have a wingspread of over 4 inches, are weak fliers that can barely flutter through the air. The formidable tusklike mandibles are little used, as the nonfeeding adults are short-lived: after mating and depositing their eggs, they perish.

The female dobsonfly deposits eggs on branches that overhang freshwater or brackish water, on stones, or on the undersides of bridges and piers. The eggs hatch in a few days and the larvae drop into the water. These fierce-looking and predacious larvae, known to fishermen as hellgrammites, prey on almost any organism they can subdue. Hellgrammites have powerful jaws and paired lateral filaments that extend from each abdominal segment, with tufts of gills at the base of each filament. The hellgrammite is long-lived, sometimes existing in the larval form for three years. These voracious larvae live under stones and pebbles in swift-flowing waters, particularly around bridge abutments and other structures. Eventually the mature hellgrammite crawls out of the water and constructs a pupal chamber in the bank or in a rotting log, and a short time later, the fierce-looking but harmless adult dobsonfly emerges and prepares for the next generation.

Predacious diving beetles, *Dytiscus* spp., are also

fierce underwater denizens. The females lay individual eggs in plant stems, which may hatch in as little as five days or may be delayed for months, depending on temperatures. The larvae, aptly called water tigers, emerge and begin feeding by grasping prey in their sicklelike jaws. Like hellgrammites, they will eat anything that they can overwhelm, including fishes and tadpoles. Their sharp jaws have channels, and when they pierce their prey, they inject a toxic digestive juice that flows through the channels, which kills the organism and initiates digestion. The water tiger then sucks up its prey's tissues in its mandibles.

Diving beetle larvae cannot store oxygen or breathe underwater, so from time to time, they ascend to the surface, breaking the surface tension with their abdominal tips or terminal hairs and absorbing air through specialized pores, the spiracles. When the larvae are mature, they crawl from the water and construct a pupal chamber in a moist area. After several weeks, the adult predacious diving beetle emerges and enters the water, where it spends most of its time. However, this beetle is also attracted to lights and is often seen clinging to the sides of buildings and bridges.

Mature predacious diving beetles have specialized hind legs that they use like oars, rather than moving them alternately, as most swimming beetles do. The adult, like the larva, obtains a new supply of air by breaking the surface of the water or by tapping into bubbles formed on submerged aquatic plants.

In the shallow freshwaters of the upper rivers and creeks, there are insects that propel themselves across the surface of the water in various ways, scuttling here and whirling there. They are almost always gregarious. Some of these insects belong to the order Hemiptera, which means "half wing." Their first pair of wings is leathery at the base and membranous toward the tip; they also have sucking mouth parts,

An adult predacious diving beetle, Dytiscus *sp. (to 1 5/8"), swims under the water with its oarlike legs. Its ferocious larval stage, a water tiger (to 2 1/2"), comes to the surface to breathe through spiracle pores on its abdominal tip.*

usually in the form of a sharp beak. These insects are known as the "true bugs."

Water boatmen, *Corixa* spp., are one of the true bugs that can live in both freshwater and brackish water. They are elongated, oval bugs with heads and eyes as wide as their bodies. Their bodies are usually mottled grayish brown and marked with yellowish bands. Water boatmen's short forelegs are modified scoops that enable them to dip algae, plant particles, and tiny crustaceans from the water. Their middle and hind legs are flattened and fringed with hairs, a design that supports them on the water's surface as they scull about.

In the spring, the adult female water boatman attaches her eggs to various water plants and sticks. The eggs hatch in about two weeks, and after several

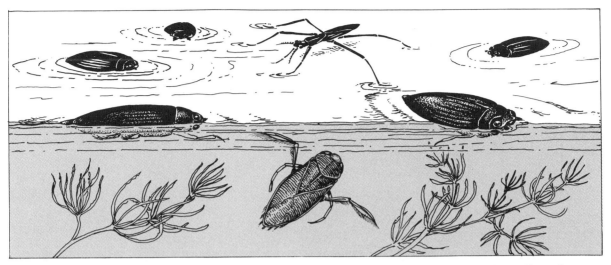

Common insects in the tidal freshwaters of the Inner Coast include the whirligig beetle, Gyrinus *sp. (to 3/4"), twirling on the surface; the water strider,* Gerris *sp. (to 3/4"), walking on the surface film; and the water boatman,* Corixa *sp. (to 1/2"), rising to the surface.*

intermediate stages, a new generation of water boatmen are propelling themselves around the surface of the water. The adults are able to fly and often end up swimming in pools and birdbaths. They are relatively defenseless and are often preyed on by more predacious insects and fishes. Water boatmen are also a favored food of birds, and their eggs are considered a delicacy by Mexicans, who gather them from lakes by the tons.

Water striders, *Gerris* spp., are true bugs also known as pond skaters. Some species of water striders prefer ponds and lakes or the quiet backwaters of streams; others inhabit swiftly flowing water; and one species lives on the surface of the open ocean. Water striders have long, spiderlike legs, which are adapted for supporting the water strider on the surface of the water without breaking through the surface film of water; the surface is bent or depressed but not pierced. These are very agile insects that dart about in large numbers, preying on all sorts of organisms, including members of their own species.

Female water striders cement their eggs in parallel rows to objects floating along the shore, and after several weeks and several stages, new adult water striders are ready to skate.

Whirligig beetles, *Gyrinus* spp., also known as waltzing beetles and scuttle bugs, are very active insects that whirl on the surface of the water. Their scientific family name, Gyrinidae, means "to whirl and turn about in a circle." Whirligigs are oval, shiny, black beetles with compound eyes that are divided into two parts, allowing them to see below and above the surface while swimming. Whirligig beetles congregate in large swarms or clusters with sometimes more than three species mixed together. They are commonly seen in freshwater and slightly brackish water and are generally quite active during the day.

The adults can dive readily and are strong fliers. Unlike water striders, whirligig beetles break through the surface film of the water, but they are supported on the surface by their bodies. When a whirligig beetle dives below the surface, it takes in

Eelgrass meadows are thriving habitats. Here small fishes like young spot move in to feed, blue crabs find protection for shedding, and a hogchoker waits for prey. The bottom supports a large variety of mollusks, algae, sponges, bryozoans, and many other organisms.

air and stores the quicksilverlike bubble under its wing covers, where the respiratory pore is located.

Female whirligig beetles lay eggs and attach them to submerged plants and sticks. Predacious larvae hatch from the eggs in one to three weeks and feed on other insect larvae, worms, and even fishes, which they kill by injecting a poison through a canal in their curved mandibles. The larvae have feathery gills attached to their abdominal segments, making them independent of surface air. The mature larva emerges from the water and ascends the stem of three-square sedge or cattail and constructs a pupal chamber in which it remains until it metamorphoses into an adult whirligig beetle.

Plants of Temperate Seagrass Meadows

Eelgrass, *Zostera marina*, is usually found in the mid-salinity or saltier zones of sounds and estuaries, where it often grows in thick and expansive stands that are frequently referred to as seagrass meadows. Eelgrass has long, narrow, ribbonlike leaves with rounded tips arising from nodes on creeping rhizomes. There seems to be a tendency for the leaves to be rather short and narrow in the shallows, where the sandy bottoms are scoured by waves. In deeper and muddy areas, the leaves tend to be longer and wider.

Two other species of submerged aquatic plants closely resemble eelgrass and often confound the casual observer. Eelgrass, shoalgrass, and wild celery all seem to be the same plant until you study the leaves. Shoalgrass has leaves that are usually less than half the width of eelgrass's leaves. The dead giveaway, however, is the shape of the leaf tips: shoalgrass leaves have two pointed tips separated by a crescentic indentation, known to botanists as bicuspidate, and eelgrass leaf tips are rounded. Wild celery leaves are indeed similar to eelgrass leaves, but the leaves of wild celery are relatively wider than the leaves of eelgrass, and wild celery has a pale green line down the center of each leaf, which eelgrass lacks. But perhaps the best way to separate the two species is to understand their habitat requirements: wild celery grows in tidal freshwater or very slightly brackish water, whereas eelgrass grows in higher-salinity waters.

In the early 1930s, a severe—some call it catastrophic—decline occurred in eelgrass populations on both sides of the Atlantic. The near extinction of eelgrass was attributed to "the wasting" caused by a fungus. Since that time eelgrass has recovered somewhat, but there have been smaller outbreaks

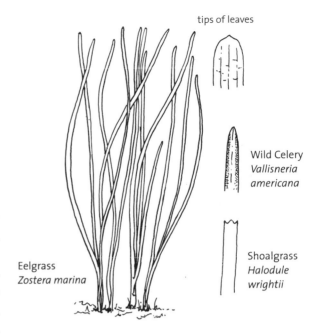

tips of leaves

Eelgrass
Zostera marina

Wild Celery
Vallisneria americana

Shoalgrass
Halodule wrightii

of the disease from time to time in various regions in Europe as well as in North America. Eelgrass is distributed from Nova Scotia to North Carolina and perhaps farther south, where it may grow in small patches. Eelgrass usually grows in pure stands, however it does coexist with widgeon grass and shoalgrass in some North Carolina sounds.

Shoalgrass, *Halodule wrightii*, is a species that moves into, or colonizes, disturbed areas, especially where boats have grounded or where anchors have been dragged. Shoalgrass is very abundant in extremely shallow water but also grows in deeper water. Its leaves are flat and about 1/8 inch wide; the tips of the leaves end in two or three points. Shoalgrass has a wide temperature tolerance, unlike the other seagrasses, and can be found in some North Carolina sounds, where it grows in association with eelgrass and widgeon grass, as well as in the warmer waters of Florida.

Wild celery, *Vallisneria americana*, is an SAV

that usually grows in freshwater and occasionally in slightly brackish water. It has long, linear leaves, each with a light-colored central stripe, that arise as basal leaves from the roots. Wild celery, also known as tape grass and freshwater eelgrass, provides cover for small fishes and is an important food source for a number of duck species.

Animal Life in the Weed Beds and Temperate Seagrass Meadows

Animals Attached to Plants

Aquatic plant leaves and stems provide firm places of attachment for many sessile invertebrates and plants. The attached life on widgeon grass leaves, for example, is, in a sense, the same as the life on a piling or jetty community; many of the same organisms that colonize underwater plants also live on rocks, pier pilings, oysters, and beer cans. The surfaces of the plants are first covered by a scum of microscopic algae and protozoans, and then seaweeds such as green hollow-tubed seaweed and sea lettuce float around the underwater entanglements or attach directly to the plants. Bay barnacles and sea squirts, which are abundant animals of the piling community, are frequently attached to eelgrass leaves. In fact, fouling organisms such as sea squirts can grow so thickly on eelgrass that the weight of the sea squirts kills the eelgrass and creates bare spots in the meadows. Feather hydroids attach to grass blades, as do crowded colonies of fragile convex slipper snails that are stacked one on another on leaves of eelgrass. In turn, the convex slipper snails may be completely enveloped by the creeping bryozoan, *Bowerbankia gracilis*, just barely visible as a soft, furry coating of minute, crowded, vase-shaped zooecia.

Grazers on Plants

The abundant supply of food attached to seagrasses and the protection that the plants offer attract a host of grazer organisms that wander over the surface of every leaf and stem.

WORMS

A wide and seemingly endless variety of errant, or wandering, worms slither about the plants and around their roots. Clamworms are here in large numbers, as are other worms that are so diminutive that they can be identified only with the aid of a microscope. Two very small ribbon worms are common inhabitants of seagrass meadows. These worms are only 3/4 inch to 1 1/2 inches long, and yet they avidly prowl the grass blades to prey on amphipods and isopods. Small flatworms also graze over the surfaces of plants, including the little, black oyster flatworm that grazes on barnacles and the yellowish gray slender flatworm that is less than 1/2 inch long.

ISOPODS AND AMPHIPODS

Isopods and amphipods are major predators and grazers of the seagrass community and can be easily seen as they scoot in and around the plants. The eelgrass pill bug, *Paracerceis caudata*, is abundant, particularly in high-salinity seagrass meadows. The female is about 1/2 inch long, and the male is only 1/4 inch long. The females have wide-set eyes at the corners of their heads. The males have elaborate arching processes projecting from the telson, the last body segment.

The elongated eelgrass isopod, *Erichsonella attenuata*, is a slender isopod with long antennae. As their common name implies, they prowl in eelgrass meadows southward to North Carolina.

The Baltic isopod, *Idotea baltica*, crawls over the

Eelgrass Pill Bug (male to 1/4",
female to 1/2")
Paracerceis caudata

Elongated Eelgrass Isopod (to 1/2")
Erichsonella attenuata

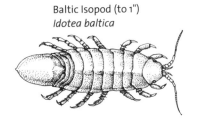

Baltic Isopod (to 1")
Idotea baltica

rooted plants looking for food, but it also catches rides on strands of passing algae and floating blades of seagrasses. This species, which may grow to a length of 1 inch, has highly variable patterns and colors even within a small population.

Tube-building amphipods and free-living, roaming amphipods abound in seagrass meadows. Some plant leaves, particularly the basal leaves, those at the bases of plants, are often covered with the soft mats of the slender tube-builder amphipod that are so common on pier pilings and rocks and anywhere

there are soft silts. There are other abundant tube-making amphipods in seagrasses as well; two closely related species are the long-antennaed tube-builder amphipod, *Ampithoe longimana*, and the wave-diver tube-builder amphipod, *Cymadusa compta*.

The long-antennaed amphipod builds weblike tube nests composed of plant material bound together with mucosal secretions. Long-antennaed amphipods move in and out of their tube nests to feed on algal scum coating the plant leaves. Long-antennaed tube-builder amphipods are less than 1/2 inch long. They have large black eyes and slender antennae almost as long as their bodies.

Wave-diver amphipods also live in tubes and wander out to feed on detrital matter, algae, and vascular plant tissue. Wave-divers are somewhat larger than their long-antennaed cousins; their antennae are shorter and their eyes are large and reddish. Wave-divers are also abundant on unvegetated bottoms.

There are many other species of amphipods found in seagrass meadows that are also found in a number of other habitats, such as spine-backed scuds, which are plentiful under seaweed wrack, on intertidal flats, and on upper beaches. Skeleton shrimps, those gangly amphipods found in piling communities, attach to hydroids growing on seagrass leaves.

The purple-eyed amphipod, *Batea catharinensis*, creeps among the lush epifaunal growth of hydroids, sponges, and bryozoans on the seagrass plants. This rather ordinary-looking amphipod that is only about

At the base of an eelgrass plant, a number of amphipods may cluster together. Two long-antennaed tube-builder amphipods, Ampithoe longimana *(to 2/5"), emerge from their weblike nests; two wave-diver tube-builder amphipods,* Cymadusa compta *(to 3/5"), move out of their tube nests; and small purple-eyed amphipods,* Batea catharinensis *(to 1/3"), creep over a sponge mat.*

An Atlantic oyster drill, at 2 inches, looms over other snails that are frequently found in eelgrass meadows. Two black-line triphoras feed on a sponge at left; a lunar dove snail glides over a blade at center; two grass ceriths, one covered with snail fur, graze on other blades; one impressed odostome attacks a convex slipper snail; and another impressed odostome attacks a sea squirt.

1/3 inch long has rather remarkable large, square-shaped, purplish brown eyes.

SNAILS

Hundreds of small snails, some no more than 1/4 inch long, crawl over the plants in the seagrass meadows. The most abundant species of snail in the seagrass meadows is the grass cerith, *Bittium varium.* This gregarious little snail may be found in dense concentrations gliding slowly over the grass blades and feeding on detritus and algae. The shell of the grass cerith is grayish brown and elongated and adorned with a crisscross pattern of ribs and whorls. The shells of some of the more mature grass ceriths may be completely covered by a hydroid, soft snail fur, *Stylactaria arge.* (Soft snail fur should not be confused with the very similar snail fur hydroid, *Hydractinia echinata,* that often grows over snail shells occupied by hermit crabs.)

The greedy dove snail, *Anachis avara,* is also a very abundant snail of eelgrass meadows. There are many species of dove snails distributed throughout the world; most are 1 inch high or less, and most live in the shallows. Dove snails typically cement a single, leathery egg capsule containing ten to twelve eggs to plants and rocks. Greedy dove snails are about 1/2 inch high with a thick shell and a sharply pointed spire. They are usually yellowish brown to dark gray when alive. The shells often show a faint pattern of white dots or brown speckles. The shell has six or seven whorls with about twelve ribs on each whorl. The greedy dove snail can be easily confused with its close relative the well-ribbed dove snail, as they are both found in seagrass meadows. The greedy dove snail has four weak teeth inside the inner lip; well-ribbed dove snails have about a dozen small teeth inside the inner lip. In addition, well-ribbed dove snails have about twice as many ribs (twelve to fourteen) on each whorl as greedy dove snails do.

The black-line triphora, *Triphora nigrocincta*; the lunar dove snail, *Mitrella lunata*; and the im-

Grass Cerith (to 1/8")
Bittium varium

Black-Line Triphora (to 1/4")
Triphora nigrocincta

Impressed Odostome (to 1/4")
Boonea impressa

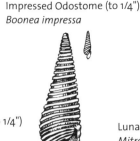

Lunar Dove Snail (to 1/4")
Mitrella lunata

Greedy Dove Snail (to 1/2")
Anachis avara

pressed odostome, *Boonea impressa*, are other small snails that frequent seagrass meadows. Black-line triphoras have slender, elongated, dark brown shells with a beaded surface and a dark band between the whorls of the shell. But the best clue for identification of this 1/4-inch snail is its left, or sinistral, aperture. Lunar dove snails have smooth and glossy shells that are beautifully marked with reddish brown or fawn-colored crescent-shaped, or lunate, markings. Impressed odostomes are ectoparasitic snails that prey on ceriths, slipper snails, oysters, and other mollusks, as well as sea squirts. They feed on their victims by inserting a long proboscis inside their shells and sucking out the flesh. Impressed odostomes have milky white elongated shells with flat, indented whorls.

A much larger carnivorous snail, the Atlantic oyster drill, *Urosalpinx cinerea* (see chapter 8), frequently moves into grassy areas from nearby oyster bars to prey on slipper snails, barnacles, tube worms, and bryozoans. Oyster drills range down to northeast Florida.

Seahorses and Pipefishes

The lined seahorse, *Hippocampus erectus*; the northern pipefish, *Syngnathus fuscus*; and the dusky pipefish, *Syngnathus floridae*, live almost exclusively in seagrass meadows. Most people are unaware that seahorses are quite common along the Inner Coast and are not confined to Florida and the tropics. Seahorses and pipefishes are closely related; a seahorse is, in a sense, a pipefish with a prehensile tail and a cocked head. Both seahorses and pipefishes have elongated, tubular snouts and small mouths with toothless jaws that limit the size of their food to minute organisms. Their bodies are encased in jointed, bony rings.

Both male seahorses and pipefishes have brood pouches in which the young are reared. It is quite a sight to see a male seahorse spurting out a cloud of tiny seahorses from his saclike brood pouch! The brood pouch of pipefish males is formed by elongated lateral folds on the underside of the belly, with the eggs lined up neatly in rows. The young of seahorses and pipefishes are well developed when they leave their brood pouches and quickly go about feeding in the vegetation.

Lined seahorses swim slowly with rapid movements of the pectoral and dorsal fins. They are rather weak swimmers and frequently pause to curl their tails around leaves and stems. Lined seahorses can be tan to olive or orange to yellowish and are marked with vertical dark lines.

Pipefishes are long and thin and often align themselves vertically with the long leaves of eelgrass and

Lined Seahorse (to 6")
Hippocampus erectus

specimens weighing upwards of 75 pounds of un-pleasantness have been recorded. Snappers have a fearsome reputation. They can strike and inflict a nasty wound, particularly when out of the water. They are distributed widely throughout North America, where they live in lakes, slow-moving rivers, and marshy estuarine rivers.

The snapper is easy to identify, with its large head, long, thick neck, and a tail as long as its keeled carapace. The tail has three rows of hard knobs down its length. The light yellow to cream-colored plastron is quite small. To complete the snapper's repertoire of characteristics, it can release a foul-smelling anal musk when alarmed.

Snapping turtles are mainly carnivorous in the spring, when they eat just about anything that moves: insects, crustaceans, amphibians, ducklings, and mammals. However, late in the spring and the summer, when aquatic vegetation appears, they depend more on plants for sustenance. Snapping turtles are highly aquatic and are not usually found out of the water, but they do bask on floating logs, usually some distance from the shore. If their pond is semipermanent and begins to dry up, snappers are capable of migrating substantial distances over land to reach another suitable body of water.

The female snapping turtle lays approximately thirty to fifty eggs during a protracted season that

gracefully sway to and fro, imitating the movements of the grasses. Northern pipefish and dusky pipefish are similar in appearance; both are about 6 to 8 inches long. They can be differentiated by the relative lengths of their snouts and dorsal fins: the northern pipefish has a shorter snout and longer dorsal fin than does the dusky pipefish. The northern pipefish usually has nineteen trunk rings, and the dusky pipefish has seventeen or eighteen trunk rings.

Freshwater Turtles

The common snapping turtle, *Chelydra serpentina*, is the largest freshwater turtle along the Inner Coast. This is a turtle short of temper and long of tail that usually attains a weight of about 35 pounds, although

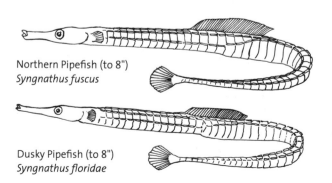

Northern Pipefish (to 8")
Syngnathus fuscus

Dusky Pipefish (to 8")
Syngnathus floridae

Common Snapping Turtle (carapace to 1')
Chelydra serpentina

Northern Diamondback Terrapin (carapace to 8")
Malaclemys terrapin terrapin

may extend from April through November, and she may lay two clutches of eggs per season. Depending on the seasonal temperatures, the eggs may hatch in eighty to ninety days; however, eggs laid in nests in late fall can survive winter temperatures and will hatch the following spring. Snapping turtles hibernate during the winter in muskrat houses, in burrows, and under logs. Their meat makes excellent soup, so there are small regional fisheries here and there to supply turtle meat to restaurants.

The Florida snapping turtle, *Chelydra serpentina osceola*, is similar in general appearance, but its knobs and other prominences are somewhat different in shape and position from those of the common snapping turtle, and their average weight is somewhat less. The Florida snapping turtle replaces the common snapping turtle in Florida.

The northern diamondback terrapin, *Malaclemys terrapin terrapin*, is a typical inhabitant of mid- and lower-salinity estuaries and is one of several subspecies of diamondback terrapins along the East Coast. The diamondback terrapin is a medium-size turtle: the female grows to about 8 inches, and the male is smaller. The carapace is sculpted with geometrical growth rings. The overall color of the carapace ranges from grayish green to almost black. The head and neck are light gray or brownish and are marked with fine black speckles. The plastron is yellow to greenish gray.

The female lays an average of ten to fifteen eggs in shallow nests dug in sandy areas along marshes and upper beach areas; the young hatch in about three months. The female may nest several times in one season and lay a total of thirty-five eggs or more. Diamondback terrapins feed on clams, worms, snails, crabs, carrion, and some vegetation. They are attracted to bait placed in the ever-present crab traps set in the Inner Coast, and many of them drown once they enter the traps. If they escape predation and crab traps, they can live to twenty-five years or older.

The Carolina diamondback terrapin is similar to the northern diamondback terrapin, but it has a slightly differently shaped carapace and plastron. This subspecies ranges from Cape Hatteras, North Carolina, to northern Florida. The Florida east coast diamondback terrapin has a darker carapace and lacks the concentric markings that are characteristic of the northern diamondback terrapin. The Florida east coast diamondback terrapin is distributed along the east coast of Florida. The mangrove diamondback terrapin has a boldly marked neck and some large hard bumps on the keel of the carapace. This subspecies lives in the Florida Keys in the mangroves.

Subtropical Seagrass Meadows

Shallow bays and sounds constantly change as you motor or sail along, especially when the water is gin-clear and the sun is brightly shining. White patches of sand with clumps of sponges loom ahead, and often a dark patch of coral with schools of small, silvery fishes in attendance comes into view. Then there are the acres and acres of sunlight-dappled bottom, with grasses waving in rhythm to the gentle surge of the waves. A closer look at these underwater gardens, called seagrass meadows, will reveal much more than grasses. There are fishes of various kinds: some are partially buried in the sand; others glide among the plants, occasionally excreting clouds of coral dust; and in the distance, a spotted eagle ray disappears into the infinite blue of deeper water. If you are in a boat or floating on an inflatable raft and have the good fortune to have a glass-bottom bucket or a dive mask aboard, you will be rewarded with a view of astonishingly beautiful underwater scenes if you only slow down and peer.

There are many places in south Florida to "swim with the grasses": There are seagrass meadows close to Key Biscayne, which is an island within sight of downtown Miami. There are other islands or keys that are more isolated in lower Biscayne Bay, such as Soldier Key and Elliott Key, but a boat is required to reach these lovely spots. There are also places off the highway in the Florida Keys where seagrass meadows are there for the looking. Swim off a small beach on the Florida Bay side of Islamorada or slip into the water at Bahia Honda State Park—all you need is dive mask, a pair of swim fins, and clear water.

Just what are these subtropical seagrass meadows that some call prairies of the sea? They are a unique association of rooted plants that form ecologically important habitats in the marine environment. They are rich, productive ecosystems that provide major food sources by producing prodigious amounts of the organic detritus that is necessary for a wide assortment of organisms; in addition, a few species feed on the plants themselves. Moreover, seagrasses are very important for providing shelter and bottom stabilization. Seagrass meadows provide shelter in the form of nursery grounds for a large number of commercially and recreationally valuable juvenile fishes and shellfishes, as well as uncountable species of worms, hydroids, and echinoderms, to mention just a few. Seagrasses also stabilize the bottom sediments by reducing underwater turbulence, which promotes retention of flocculent sediment particles. In addition, their robust roots and rhizomes form a stabilizing network, which binds the sediment and helps to reduce erosion along the coast.

Seagrasses

There are six important species of seagrasses that grow in these beautiful underwater meadows: turtle grass, *Thalassia testudinum*; manatee grass, *Syringodium filiforme*; shoalgrass, *Halodule wrightii*; star grass, *Halophila engelmanii*; paddle grass, *Halophila decipiens*; and Johnson's seagrass, *Halophila johnsonii*. There is also a seventh species, widgeon grass, which occasionally grows mixed in with shoalgrass, but widgeon grass is considered a brackish water species that can tolerate higher-salinity water.

Turtle grass is the largest and perhaps hardiest species of all the seagrasses. It has broad, flat, ribbonlike leaves with rounded tips; the leaves may grow to 1/4 to 1/2 inch wide. This plant arises from rhizomes that may grow as deep as 10 inches in the bottom. The plant produces pretty green flowers at the base of the plant in the spring.

Manatee grass has cylindrical leaves that can grow to a length of 20 inches, but they are highly

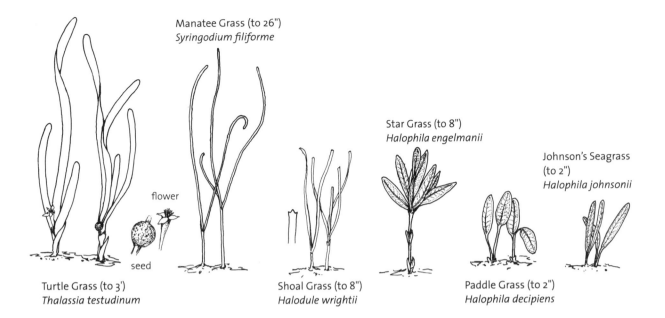

Manatee Grass (to 26")
Syringodium filiforme

Turtle Grass (to 3')
Thalassia testudinum

flower

seed

Shoal Grass (to 8")
Halodule wrightii

Star Grass (to 8")
Halophila engelmanii

Paddle Grass (to 2")
Halophila decipiens

Johnson's Seagrass (to 2")
Halophila johnsonii

variable in size. The individual plants are somewhat tall and spindly, but they grow in such profusion that they form soft, dense carpets. The rhizomes of this plant are more delicate than are the rhizomes of turtle grass, and they do not grow as deeply in the sediments. Manatee grass is a favorite food source for the manatee.

Shoalgrass is a species that moves into, or colonizes, disturbed areas where boats have grounded or where anchors have been dragged. Shoalgrass is very abundant in extremely shallow water but will also grow in deeper water. Its leaves are flat and about 1/8 inch wide; the tips of the leaves end in two or three points. Shoalgrass has a wide temperature tolerance; unlike the other seagrasses, it can be found in some North Carolina sounds, where it mixes with eelgrass and widgeon grass.

The three species of *Halophila* are small and fragile and are sparsely distributed from the Indian River Lagoon system to the Florida Keys. Star grass has elongated paired leaves up to about 1 inch long that arise directly from nodes on the rhizome. Paddle grass leaves are oblong and grow in whorls of four to eight 1-inch-long leaves on a stem that is less than 2 inches long. Paddle grass can grow with less light than can any other seagrass, and where the water is clear, it can grow in depths of over 100 feet deep. Johnson's seagrass is a comparatively newly determined species, originally described from the Indian River Lagoon near Sebastian, Florida. Johnson's seagrass is the smallest of the seagrasses. It lacks hairs on the surface of its leaves, and the leaf veins initiate from the midrib at a 45° angle. It can be confused with star grass, but star grass leaves emerge from the midrib at approximately a 60° angle.

Seaweeds

Many species of seaweeds, or more specifically macroalgae, grow in seagrass meadows. Some species have elaborate rhizome and stolon systems. Rhizomes are segmented horizontal runners that are usually below the surface of the bottom, and stolons are segmented horizontal runners that are usually aboveground. Both give rise to erect fronds or blades. Other species develop holdfasts in the bottom, and still others develop rhizoids, which are small hairs that usually intertwine in the bottom or attach to hard objects, such as pieces of coral rubble and shells.

Seaweeds, particularly those found in subtropical and tropical waters can be extremely varied in form as well as their community assemblages. Some species have been given fanciful, although usually quite descriptive common names such as mermaid's fan or petticoat algae. Several species grow as single individuals and some grow in large bushy entanglements.

The genus *Caulerpa* contains a number of species that are all quite varied in form and structure: some grow in feltlike mats; others have erect, feathery or quill-like blades; and still others produce sprawling clusters of green beads. Most of the species in this group have long, horizontal stolons, although they may be difficult to discern in some species. Some nonnative species of *Caulerpa* have been accidentally introduced and are quite invasive and crowd out native species.

Feather seaweed, *Caulerpa sertularioides*, is one of those distinctive species that is almost immediately recognizable. It has 10-inch-long upright blades or fronds that arise from a network of stolons. The blades have fine, cylindrical, oppositely arranged branchlets that are startlingly similar in appearance to feathers or quills. The light green blades are somewhat stiff, with the texture and feel of plastic. Feather seaweeds grow in sandy shallows interspersed in seagrass meadows, particularly with turtle grass, and they also may grow around red mangroves.

Green bead seaweed, *Caulerpa racemosa*, is another one of those seaweed species that, once identified, is quite easy to recognize again. Green bead sea-

weed grows in tangled mats that arise from creamy yellow stolons. The branches bear clusters of green to bluish green beads that can be highly variable in size and form. Green bead seaweed is a very common species. It will attach to rocks in high-energy swash zones and in seagrass meadows where there is frequent wave surge.

Fluff-headed seaweed, also known as tufted joint weed, *Cymopolia barbata*, has cylindrically segmented and strongly calcified branches that bear bright green filaments. The green filaments are so fine that the tufts appear to be fuzzy. This is a plant that attaches to rock and coral rubble in very shallow, quiet water.

Rip weed, *Rhipocephalus phoenix*, is a stalked, rather dull, dark green to whitish green plant that bears pinecone-shaped heads of tightly arranged, upturned platelets in a concentric arrangement. It is common in sandy seagrass meadows.

Mermaid's fan, *Udotea flabellum*, has broad, fan-shaped blades that have a leathery feeling; the blades may be pale green to dull green and are attached to a short stalk; the entire plant may be 8 inches high. Mermaid's fans accumulate calcium carbonate from seawater, and so they often have a whitish, powdery appearance. The rim of the blade may be crenulated or wavy. These plants are rooted in the sand by a bulb-like mass of rhizoids.

Soft fan seaweed, *Avrainvillea nigricans*, at first glance can be confused with mermaid's fan; it has a flattened or spatulate blade that grows on a short stalk and resembles the mermaid's fan. However, the blade of soft fan seaweed is just that: it is soft and feels like suede. The blade is much more flexible than that of the mermaid's fan because it is less calcified. The soft fan seaweed is a green alga although it is usually dull brown to black.

Smooth bubble seaweed, *Valonia ventricosa*, is an alga that produces thin-walled spherical bodies that

Mermaid's Fan (to 8" tall)
Udotea flabellum

Soft Fan Seaweed (to 8")
Avrainvillea nigricans

Rip Weed (to 1')
Rhipocephalus phoenix

Merman's Shaving
Brush (to 6")
Penicillus dumetosus

Feather Seaweed (to 8" tall)
Caulerpa sertularioides

Fluff-Headed
Seaweed (to 12")
Cymopolia barbata

Squirrel Tail (to 2 1/4")
Dasycladus vermicularis

Green Horsetail Algae
(to 4")
Batophora oerstedi

Papillated Red
Seaweed (to 6")
Laurencia papillosa

may measure over 2 inches in diameter; the spherical globes are single cells and are among the largest cells known to scientists. The round, shiny green globes look like glass marbles or small green balloons attached to corals and in turtle grass meadows by fine hairlike runners. Smooth bubble seaweeds usually grow as solitary plants, but sometimes a few plants are grouped together, particularly in coral crevices.

Merman's shaving brush, *Penicillus dumetosus*, has a blade, or more of a head, that looks like a dark green brush composed of coarse, tightly packed filaments that are somewhat calcified. The head blends into a short, stout stalk that is firmly connected to the substrate by a mesh of rhizoids.

Squirrel tail, also called worm alga or fuzzy fingers, *Dasycladus vermicularis*, has small, tightly packed whorls of branchlets wound around an axis that give the plant a velvety or spongy appearance. The small, clubby, olive green, fuzzy "sausages" attach to coral rubble, shells, and mangrove prop roots in the shallows.

Green horsetail, *Batophora oerstedi*, is similar in appearance to squirrel tail. Green horsetails grow in small, soft, feathery whorls 1–4 inches high. When they are fruiting, in the reproductive mode, they produce hundreds of bright greenish yellow spheres on the tips of their branchlets. Green horsetails are quite common in the low-salinity waters of Biscayne Bay, Card Sound, and Florida, where they grow on hard and soft muddy bottoms and on and around mangroves. They are apparently a preferred food of the beautiful queen conch.

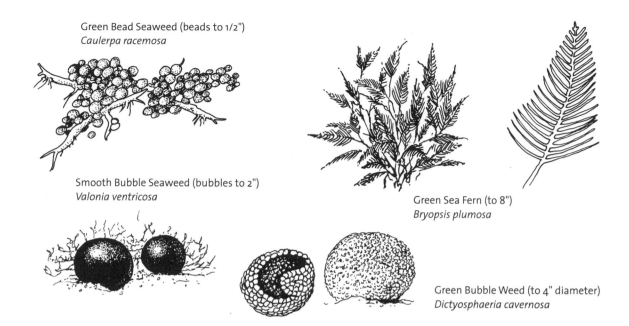

Green Bead Seaweed (beads to 1/2")
Caulerpa racemosa

Smooth Bubble Seaweed (bubbles to 2")
Valonia ventricosa

Green Sea Fern (to 8")
Bryopsis plumosa

Green Bubble Weed (to 4" diameter)
Dictyosphaeria cavernosa

Green sea fern, *Bryopsis plumosa*, is an erect, delicate, bushy seaweed that resembles bright green silky or feathery plumes. It grows to 8 inches tall. It lives in sheltered shallow waters attached to rocks and other hard substrates.

The red seaweeds, or red algae, are a diverse lot and are often difficult to identify. The genus *Laurencia* is distributed worldwide, and many species have yet to be classified and named. Species of *Laurencia* are often known as stiff-branched algae because the plants have a cartilaginous feel. There is a great deal of interest in these plants throughout the world because a number of their chemical constituents that have been isolated have promise for the formulation of pharmaceutical and industrial products.

The papillated red seaweed, *Laurencia papillosa*, is a common red seaweed found in the Florida Keys and the Caribbean. It has several erect, 5- to 6-inch-long branches that arise from a slender stem attached to a holdfast buried in the substrate. The blades, or the leaflike structures of the plant, are cylindrical and have the typical indentations at the ends that are characteristic of the genus. The tips are short and knobby and are usually olive green to greenish purple. Papillated red seaweeds usually grow on hard bottoms in shallow, moderately turbulent areas.

Sponges

There are many variations of sponges, even within species. For example, some sponges that typically grow in the form of tubes have also developed a fan-shaped form, particularly where the currents are strong. In addition, there may be several color variations within a species. Some sponges even resemble various corals and tunicates.

There are many sponges that grow in seagrass meadows, in coral patch communities, and on mangrove roots. Some sponges are quite small and drab and are often ignored as just "something" growing on a shell or a mangrove root, but there are also some rather spectacular sponges found in the shallows that grow in clusters of colorful tubes or look like large, round, leathery cakes.

Sponges, like most invertebrates, release their weak-swimming larvae into the water, and if they can avoid being eaten by fishes and find a place to settle before they are swept away by the currents, they will very likely produce a new sponge colony. Tube sponges expel their tiny larvae during the day, which is rather unusual, because they are very visible tidbits for hungry fishes. (In contrast, coral polyps, for example, release their larvae at night, which helps them avoid the onslaught of predacious fishes.) Some recent research on the behavior of tube sponge larvae has found that they are vulnerable to ultraviolet light, which causes them to move away from brightly lit areas toward shady and darker areas, where they suffer less mortality from both predation and UV light. They are further protected from predation because they contain a chemical that is distasteful to fishes.

The tube sponge, *Callyspongia vaginalis*, is a common species found in seagrass meadows and coral patches. Tube sponges look like clusters of colorful organ pipes. Often there are only a few, thin-walled tubes, but they can also grow in a profusion of twenty to thirty lavender tubes in a cluster, and when they reach a height of 2 feet or more, they add to the beauty of the underwater gardens. The tough tubes are open at their tops and covered with rubbery, conical projections. Tube sponges may be lavender, purple, greenish gray, or, sometimes, tan.

The stinker vase sponge, *Ircinia campana*, is a vase- or bell-shaped sponge with a deep interior cavity, which sometimes contains an accumulation of coral sediment. These are rather large red to brownish sponges that can grow to 2 feet wide and 3 feet high. The surface of this sponge is furrowed and coarse, and unlike the tube sponge, which is rubbery, a live vase sponge is . . . spongy.

The loggerhead sponge, *Spheciospongia vesparia* (which means "wasps' nest"), is also a very large sponge that can grow to more than 3 feet in diameter. It is usually flat topped and squatty, and it looks like a large cake with a central depression. Loggerhead sponges are blackish to brown, but their true colors are usually obscured by a coat of grayish coral sediment.

Most sponges play host to a variety of invertebrates and algae; some are free living and others are parasitic. The sponges that have large pores and coarsely wrinkled exteriors become living "hotels" for many guests. The mammoth loggerhead sponge may be the most successful "hotel" of all the sponges. Its convoluted surface is often populated with hundreds of organisms, particularly snapping shrimps and juvenile spiny lobsters.

Soft and Hard Corals

Sea fans are included in the subclass Octocorallia, which means that the polyp's mouth is surrounded by eight feathery tentacles. The polyps are embedded in soft tissues, which overlay a flexible, horny-calcareous skeleton sometimes referred to as gorgonin. Purple sea fans, typical of other corals, host symbiotic zooxanthellae (dinoflagellates), which provide the sea fan with carbon nutrients and oxygen. In turn, the host coral provides a substrate and access to sunlight required for photosynthesis.

The purple sea fan, *Gorgonia ventalina*, can be immediately recognized by its large, thinly compressed blade of latticelike branches. Purple sea fans are not always purple; they may be yellow or palest lavender. They are almost always found in areas of surg-

A typical turtle grass community is full of life. A large loggerhead sponge, Spheciospongia vesparia *(to 3' or more), nestles among turtle grass blades with petticoat algae and tufted joint seaweeds growing at their bases. Caribbean reef squids (to 14") arrive on the scene to join a scrawled cowfish,* Acanthostracion quadricornis. *Small tomtates,* Haemulon aurolineatum *(to 8"), with black spots at the bases of their caudal fins, and little spotfin mojarras,* Eucinostomus argenteus *(to 8"), swim among the blades. A cluster of tube sponges,* Callyspongia vaginalis *(to 3' tall), grow at the base of other turtle grass blades. In front are two merman's shaving brushes; a small growth of clubbed finger coral,* Porites porites *(colony to 4'); and an American star snail with umbrella algae growing on its shell. A great barracuda hovers in the background, and a gulf pipefish,* Syngnathus scovelli *(to 7"), is barely visible among the turtle grass blades.*

ing waves and strong currents. The wide fan, which may grow to 6 feet high and more than 3 feet wide, faces the oncoming waves so that the polyps, which are located within the reticulated mesh of branches, can feed on the tiny planktonic organisms brought to them by the surging sea. Waving branches of sea fans fed by the persistent energy of the ocean are living marine sculptures in motion. Purple sea fans are quite common in the Florida Keys around patch corals, in seagrass meadows, and on deeper, more extensive coral reefs.

The living animals, the polyps, of stony or hard

corals have six tentacles, or multiples of six tentacles, and to further complicate matters, the body cavity of a coral polyp is partitioned into six chambers. The outer layer of the polyp and the tentacles are called the ectoderm, or skin; the polyp contains the cnidoblasts, or stinging cells. The internal layer, the endoderm, forms the lining of the gastrovascular cavity, which is responsible for digestion. The gelatinlike material lying between the ectoderm and the endoderm is a noncellular layer termed the mesoglea. The ectoderm goes about the work of constructing a hard, continuously growing structure, in the case of most reef-building corals, which is composed of

In a shallow shoalgrass area, a bonefish roots through the bottom in search of a buried mollusk. A queen conch, Strombus gigas *(to 10"), and a banded tulip glide over the bottom in search of food. A rose coral,* Manicina areolata *(to 4" long), lies half buried in front, and a large stinker vase sponge,* Ircinia campana *(to 3' high), reaches almost to the surface. In the distance, two young permits cruise by.*

calcium carbonate; the process is complicated and beyond the scope of this book.

Clubbed finger coral, *Porites porites*, is not a massive reef-building species but does grow in small patches in seagrass meadows and more extensively within the coral reef community. Clubbed finger corals grow in clumps of stubby, irregular branches with swollen knobby ends. They are usually tan to yellowish brown and sometimes grayish purple. The polyps often actively feed during the day, which gives the colony a soft, fuzzy appearance. When you swim over shallow turtle grass beds, look closely for sinewy brittle stars and sea urchins lurking among the stubby branches of the clubbed finger coral.

Finger coral is considered by some as a subspecies of *Porites porites* and by others as simply a variant or form of clubbed finger coral. Finger coral lacks the knobby ends of clubbed finger coral and is more fragile. Finger coral sometimes grows in extensive stands in turtle grass beds.

Rose coral, *Manicina areolata*, varies in shape, seemingly dependent on the type of bottoms it lives on. Some individuals may be attached to the bottom by a short stalk, and others almost "float" on the underlying sediment. There are typically two shapes: a hemispheric or dome-shaped form and a roughly oblong form that tapers at both ends and has an undulating, furrowed margin. Young rose corals are usually weakly attached to the bottom by a short stalk that eventually breaks as the coral matures. Wave surge can turn over a rose coral colony, but it can actively right itself, usually within hours, by filling its tissues with water and rocking back and forth. Common rose corals are 3–4 inches long and vary in color from brown to golden or gray-green with whitish tentacles. They seem to be randomly distributed on turtle grass beds and also on the floor of coral reef communities. The dead coral "roses" are often washed up on shore.

Remains of Rose Coral Commonly Found on Beaches

Worms

The bearded fireworm, *Hermodice carunculata*, is a 10- to 12-inch-long, somewhat flattened worm with a greenish to brownish body highlighted by white, cottony tufts of bristles and red branched gills attached to the sides of each segment. These are stunningly beautiful creatures that are usually quite active during daylight hours as they slither and glide over coral rubble and through the turtle grass blades. Be aware! They are called fireworms because they can inflict a painful, burning irritation on your skin when their bristles break off and deliver a dose of venom. The bristles, or setae, are hollow and filled with a toxin, and when a fireworm is threatened, it often expands its bristles as a warning to stay away. The species name, *carunculata*, refers to the fleshy, pleated growth on the head (the caruncula) that serves as a sensory olfactory organ for searching out prey such as anemones and soft and stony corals. When a fireworm comes upon a likely meal, it everts its muscular pharynx and esophagus and secretes enzymes to break down the tissues of its victim before ingesting it. Bearded fireworms are abundant in turtle grass beds and coral reefs, and when they are not actively seeking out prey, they rest under stones and around seaweeds.

The sea wolf scale worm, *Polyodontes lupina*, is also known as a sea silk worm because of its ability to secrete silky, golden threads. These worms utilize the threads to fashion a tough, elastic tube to house their enormous bodies, which may be 2 feet long and

A Florida sea cucumber, Holothuria floridana *(to 10"), slides by a red heart urchin,* Meoma ventricosa *(to 8"). A cushion sea star,* Oreaster reticulatus *(to 20"), sits in front of a bearded fireworm,* Hermodice carunculata *(to 12"), crawling over a rock.*

1 inch wide. Unlike the highly active bearded fireworm, the sea wolf dwells in a tube that may protrude a few inches above the surface of the sandy bottom, where it waits for its prey to happen by. These very large worms are known as scale worms because of the brownish pearly scales called elytra that cover their backs. A tiny snail (less than 1/4 inch), *Conchiolepis parasiticus*, is sometimes found living in the worm tube, where it attaches to the elytra of the sea wolf scale worm.

Sea Wolf Scale Worm (to 2')
Polyodontes lupina

Echinoderms

The Florida sea cucumber, *Holothuria floridana*, is a gray to yellow-brown or reddish brown species that can grow to about 10 inches. These sea cucumbers are warty and tapered at both ends. Their color and pattern are highly variable; some are mottled with splotches of various colors on their dorsal surface, and others are a single, uniform color without markings. The tips of the tube feet on the ventral surface are yellow, and they may be marked with three longitudinal stripes along the entire ventral surface. The Florida sea cucumber is most often seen in turtle grass beds, sometimes hidden under a clump of seaweed, as well as in quiet waters under canopies of mangrove roots.

The spiny sea star, *Echinaster sentus*, has five rather stubby, slightly tapered arms with rounded ends. The entire dorsal surface of its body is covered with creamy pointed cone-shaped spines arranged

Spiny Sea Star (to 7")
Echinaster sentus

in longitudinal rows over a ground color that varies from dark red to reddish brown or sometimes purplish gray. Spiny sea stars are very common in seagrass beds, on shell hash bottoms, and in rocky areas along shores. These sea stars preferentially prey on sponges, particularly fire sponges, purple finger sponges, stinker vase sponges, and chicken liver sponges. Spiny sea stars range from North Carolina down through the Florida Keys, where they are most abundant.

The cushion sea star, *Oreaster reticulatus*, is easily the best known and most easily recognizable sea star in tropical waters. These are the large, inflated sea stars (infrequently as large as 20 inches in diameter) with heavy bodies and short, wide arms that have been so over-collected that they are now considered rare in much of their range. They vary in color from yellow or red to orange or brown. Their hard shells are made up of plates that bear raised, knobby spines arranged in a netlike or reticulated pattern.

Cushion sea stars usually feed on microorganisms and organic material in the sand bottom, and they also feed on seagrasses and algae. In addition, they feed on sponges and other echinoderms, such as sea eggs, sand dollars, and even smaller cushion sea stars, by everting their stomachs and digesting the tissues of their prey. Cushion sea stars range from North Carolina southward.

The sea egg, *Tripneustes ventricosus*, is an attractive sea urchin with a test that is dark brown or black and short whitish to purplish spines. Be careful when handling these urchins, as they produce a toxin to defend against predators. This toxin is injected by certain pedicellariae that are pincerlike organs used for defense and grooming. Sea eggs are herbivorous browsers, often associated with green sea urchins, that feed on seagrasses and algae. They roam grassy meadows and sandy bottoms, but they are also found on reefs and rocks, frequently in high-energy zones, where they tenaciously grip the substrate with their tube feet. Sea eggs are a tropical species and are found only in Florida and in other tropical areas.

The red heart urchin, also called the West Indian sea biscuit, *Meoma ventricosa*, is the most common heart urchin in the Florida Keys. The urchin's test resembles a biscuit because of its dome shape. The test is covered with short, reddish brown spines. Red heart urchins graze across the sand bottom or just under the surface, feeding on algal cells and organic detritus. They sometimes group in large aggregations when they feed. They generally burrow into the sand during the day, betrayed by only a slight hillock, and emerge during the night. Red heart urchins occupy a diversity of habitats; they may be found, sometimes in large numbers, in sandy patches near seagrass beds, on patch reefs, and even on silty sediments in deeper water. They are preyed on by loggerhead turtles, stingrays, and cameo helmets.

Mollusks

Several unusual snails live in the seagrass meadows. Some species are highly predacious, and others feed on organic detritus or scavenge on the flesh of dead

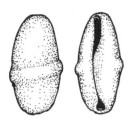

Flamingo Tongue (to 1 3/4")
Cyphoma gibbosum

American Starsnail (to 1 1/2")
Lithopoma americanum

Buttonsnail (to 1/2")
Modulus modulus

Striate Bubble (to 1")
Bulla striata

fishes. Many of the snail species that live in the seagrasses, such as common sundials, star snails, and flamingo tongues, are avidly sought by collectors because of their beautiful shapes and colors.

The button snail, *Modulus modulus*, is a knobby little shell that is only about 1/2 inch high. The conical grayish white shell has a low spire and a large body whorl with a nearly round aperture. There are also dashes of reddish brown spots or lines, especially on the spiral cords that wind around the body whorl. There are three or four whorls above the large body whorl that are sculpted with low, slanting ribs that thin out, or flatten, where they meet the spiral cords on the body whorl. Button snails feed on plants and organic deposits on the bottom. They lay their eggs in a series of gelatinous tubes and deposit them on seagrass plants.

The American star snail, *Lithopoma americanum*, is a high-spired, grayish white shell about 1 1/2 inches high and 3/4 inch wide. American star snails are frequently covered with a film of calcareous coralline algae. They have heavy, solid, conical shells with ribbed whorls that bulge somewhat between the sutures. The wavy ribs on the whorls terminate in knobs on the shoulders of the whorls. Look for these snails under rocks in turtle grass.

The striate bubble, *Bulla striata*, has an oblong, moderately heavy shell incised with fine, spiral grooves. Striate bubbles are nocturnal snails that are sometimes herbivorous and at other times may be predatory on other snails. The shells are whitish and mottled with dark brown, pink, or red; the aperture is longer than the body whorl, and the reflected lip is white.

The flamingo tongue, *Cyphoma gibbosum*, is undoubtedly one of the most beautiful snails when it is alive and gliding over a sea fan. The mantle, the thin tissue that secretes the material that forms the shell, envelops the entire shell; the mantle is creamy orange with black-ringed irregular rectangles that mimic the netlike structure of the sea fan. The shell itself is solid and glossy with an inflated or swollen ridge that occupies its center. The flamingo tongue is almost always found on sea fans and sea whips, usually in seagrass meadows.

The queen conch, or pink conch, *Strombus gigas*, is renowned for its size and beauty. These 8- to 10-inch-long snails have thick shells with relatively short, conical spires and a greatly flared outer lip, the hallmark of this snail that ranges in color from an opulent, porcelainlike rosy pink to hues of orange and yellow. The exterior of the shell is creamy to yellowish buff; live specimens, however, are usually covered with a layer of brown, almost papery periostracum, which is frequently laden with silt and algae.

The queen conch has a long, narrow foot that

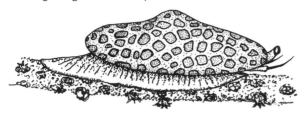

Flamingo Tongue on Sea Whip

bears two eyestalks with yellow eyes at the ends, an extensible proboscis, and two sensory tentacles. A small, horny, hook-shaped operculum is too small to close off the large aperture and protect the soft snail within, but it serves another purpose: it leverages the bulky shell by digging into the bottom and aids the conch in thrusting or leaping ahead with its muscular foot.

Female queen conchs, slightly larger than males, begin reproducing at around four years old. The female is internally fertilized by the male, and a few weeks later, she deposits very long, gelatinous strings containing thousands of eggs. After a few days, the eggs hatch, and larvae, called veligers, swim away and are distributed by currents to other areas, where they settle to the bottom, develop shells, and begin their journey to maturity. The young snails, called "rollers" in the Caribbean islands, lack the flaring lip of the adult. Their shells are fragile, and the spines around the whorls are pointed rather than knobby or blunt, as the adults' are.

Queen conchs tend to migrate offshore into deeper waters in the winter and then return to shallower summer habitats in the sandy seagrass meadows. Queen conchs are heavily harvested throughout the Caribbean and are greatly valued for their delicious meat, which is used in chowder and many other savory dishes, and for their gorgeous shells, but fishing for them is prohibited in Florida. There is justifiable concern about the overharvesting of queen conchs. To alleviate pressures on wild stocks, several aquaculture operations have been established in the Florida Keys, the Bahamas, and other locations in the Caribbean.

Fishes

There are fishes that visit seagrass meadows to feed and then return to deeper waters or offshore coral reefs. Other species lurk in the sand and coral rubble bottoms or move from the seagrass meadows to nearby mangrove habitats and back, whether in response to tides, prey availability, or diurnal rhythms.

SMALL FISHES

The gobies that live along the Inner Coast are usually quite small and are usually rather drab; however, there are some that grow to 15 inches or more and some that are very colorful, such as the peppermint goby and the neon goby that dwell on coral reefs.

The code goby, *Gobiosoma robustum*, is a common goby of vegetated shallows and high-salinity waters. The code goby's scaleless body is brindle brown and marked with irregular dark bands and pale spots.

The clown goby, *Microgobius gulosus*, is usually creamy tan and marked with irregular dark splotches. Clown gobies are slenderer than chunky code gobies. Both of these rather obscure gobies live in shallow seagrass habitats, where they feed on worms and other invertebrates. Scientists have been intrigued by the competitive interplay between the two similar species. They eat similar food items; they are approximately the same size; and they seem to prefer the cover of heavily vegetated areas. Recent studies in Florida Bay have shown that where the species overlap in a habitat, the clown goby gives way to the code goby: the code goby remains in its preferred high-salinity seagrass habitat, while the clown

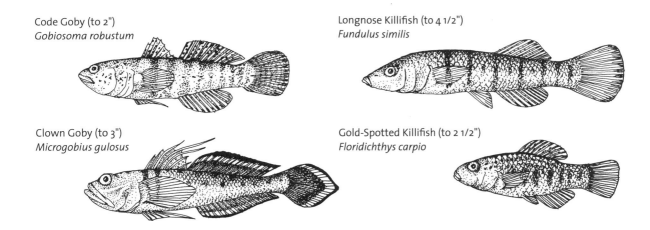

Code Goby (to 2")
Gobiosoma robustum

Clown Goby (to 3")
Microgobius gulosus

Longnose Killifish (to 4 1/2")
Fundulus similis

Gold-Spotted Killifish (to 2 1/2")
Floridichthys carpio

goby moves to unvegetated muddy bottoms in lower-salinity water. The center of abundance for both species is from the Indian River Lagoon to Florida Bay.

Killifishes, as we discussed in chapter 6, are a widespread group that inhabit freshwater, brackish water, and saltwater throughout the Inner Coast. The gold-spotted killifish, *Floridichthys carpio*, and the longnose killifish, *Fundulus similis*, are two species that are found only in south Florida.

The gold-spotted killifish is a stocky fish that resembles the sheepshead minnow, which is a close relative. Gold-spotted killifish have scooped-out or concave heads and upturned mouths. They have irregular, vertical bands on their sides, and their upper sides and back are marked with dark splotches and spots. Males during breeding season are brilliantly marked with orange and gold spots on the sides of their heads and bodies.

The longnose killifish closely resembles the striped killifish except that its snout is longer and more pronounced. Some experts believe that the longnose killifish is a subspecies of the striped killifish that is so common along the Inner Coast. The female striped killifish has vertical and longitudinal stripes; the female longnose killifish is marked only with vertical stripes.

PECULIAR FISHES

When snorkeling in the clear waters over south Florida seagrass meadows or simply wading through the shallows, you are likely to see some unusual fishes feeding among the grasses or perhaps darting into a crevice in a small reef patch, or in the distance you may see a fish drifting with its head down as it floats over a miniature forest of sea fans and sponges.

Triggerfishes and filefishes belong to a family of fishes known as leatherjackets. Most of the species in this group are deep bodied and laterally compressed, with pelvic fins that are highly reduced or completely absent. Triggerfishes are typically oval and compressed from side to side and are clothed in unusually large, diamond-shaped, platelike scales. They also have a prominent first dorsal spine, the "trigger," that is locked into position by the second dorsal spine.

Filefishes are as flat as pancakes, with keel-edged bellies, and high-set eyes, and shapes that are more variable than triggerfishes' shapes. Some species are oval and others are more elongated. Filefishes have very small scales, and their abrasive skin has been described as sandpapery or velvety in some species. Neither triggerfishes nor filefishes are particularly

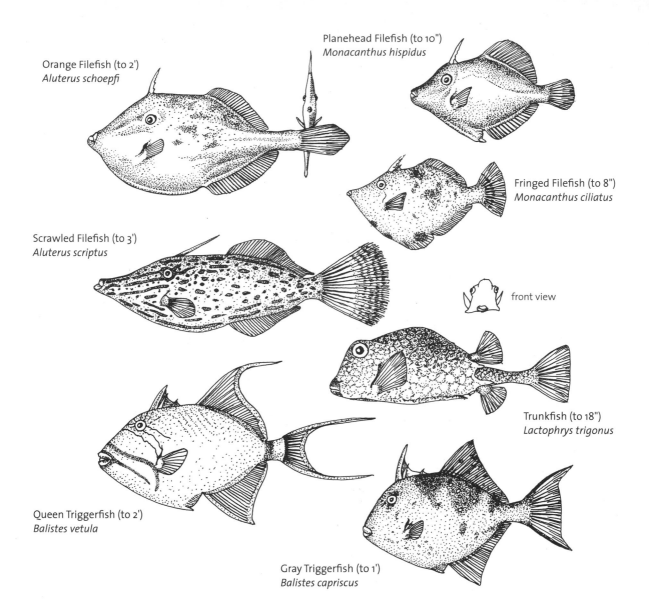

Orange Filefish (to 2')
Aluterus schoepfi

Planehead Filefish (to 10")
Monacanthus hispidus

Fringed Filefish (to 8")
Monacanthus ciliatus

Scrawled Filefish (to 3')
Aluterus scriptus

front view

Trunkfish (to 18")
Lactophrys trigonus

Queen Triggerfish (to 2')
Balistes vetula

Gray Triggerfish (to 1')
Balistes capriscus

powerful swimmers, as they only use their long, undulating dorsal and anal fins to slowly move them along. Both groups of fishes have small, terminal mouths with projecting incisor teeth.

The orange filefish, *Aluterus schoepfi*, is grayish with dusky blotches and is peppered with small dots of orange and yellow. These 2-feet fish can vary their color to match the background, but they retain their spots. Orange filefish and some other filefishes frequently are seen tilted at odd angles with their heads down, drifting slowly along with the current or weakly propelled by their dorsal and anal fins. This rather strange behavior has prompted some to call filefish "foolfish."

The planehead filefish, *Monacanthus hispidus*, is smaller and drabber than the orange filefish. Its large first dorsal spine is sharply serrated, in contrast to the smooth dorsal spine of the orange filefish. The planehead filefish's body is deep, and it has a strange bony keel, unique to this group of fishes, that slightly projects from the angle of the belly and is enclosed in a soft dewlap of flesh.

The scrawled filefish, *Aluterus scriptus*, is a colorful, elongated filefish that can grow to 3 feet. It has a grayish to olive brown or yellowish body decorated with electric blue lines and splotches, reddish orange eyes, a very long tail that often droops, and a long, pointed snout with an underslung jaw.

The fringed filefish, *Monacanthus ciliatus*, is a very strange-looking fish. It may be tan, brown, or green marked with dark longitudinal stripes. Its back is humped under the second dorsal fin. The curious thing about this filefish is its large, disproportionate dewlap, which looks like the keel of a sailboat. The fringed filefish feeds on algae and small crustaceans while tilting at odd angles in turtle grass beds.

Filefishes and triggerfishes have an ingenious way of eluding predators: they usually can't outswim other fishes intent on devouring them, as they are rather weak swimmers, but if they can find a crevice in a rock or a hole within a coral patch, they can lodge themselves in by erecting their first dorsal spine, the trigger, making it difficult for predators to dislodge them. Filefishes also have the ability to distend their bellies.

The queen triggerfish, *Balistes vetula*, is the most colorful of the triggerfishes; it has two bold, curving slashes of blue across its yellowish face and fine black lines that form a spidery, radiating pattern around its eyes. The body may be blue, purplish, turquoise, or greenish yellow and marked with a series of oblique lines across its sides with a patch of blue dots on its belly. But the colors and patterns of the queen trig-gerfish are highly variable, as it can readily change them. It also has streaming filamentous tips on its rear dorsal and tail fins, which set them apart from all other triggerfishes in the Inner Coast.

The gray triggerfish, *Balistes capriscus*, is a smaller and less colorful triggerfish than the queen triggerfish. The gray triggerfish varies in color from light gray to olive or yellowish brown. The upper portion of its body may be marked with bluish spots and a few blue lines. The gray triggerfish is fairly common all along the Inner Coast. These fish can be exasperating to anglers because they steal the bait off fishermen's hooks with their small, toothed mouths and come back again and again to do the same thing. Once in a while, a fisherman will hook a gray triggerfish, and despite their modest size—most of them are less than 1 foot from head to tail—they are hard fighters because they use their deep, wide bodies as leverage.

Both the queen triggerfish and the gray triggerfish feed on hard-shelled invertebrates such as sea urchins, barnacles, and mussels.

Boxfishes are unusual because they are enclosed in shells made up of modified scales. This cumbersome structure of bony armor, technically called a cuirass, restricts the movement of the fish's body: only the fins and the mouth and eyes, which project through openings in the bony box, are able to move. Boxfishes are slow-swimming bottom fishes that inhabit seagrass meadows and areas around rocks, coral reefs, and patch reefs.

The scrawled cowfish, *Acanthostracion quadricornis*, is a deep-bodied fish that is almost completely encased in very thick, hexagonal plates. It is called a cowfish because of the spinal processes or horns jutting out of its head in front of its eyes; it also has a pair of spines directed rearward on the lower corners of its armored box and directly in front of its anal fin. The scrawled cowfish, typical of boxfishes, has small, rounded dorsal and anal fins, no pelvic fins, and a long tail base and a rounded tail fin. Scrawled cowfish are well marked and easily identified; their bodies may be grayish brown to grayish green or gold to lemon yellow, and they are marked with bright blue or navy blue lines, scrawls, and irregular spots. Scrawled cowfish are quite common in seagrass meadows, where they feed on tunicates, sea fans, anemones, and small, slow-moving crabs.

The trunkfish, *Lactophrys trigonus*, is a close relative of the scrawled cowfish, and it is also enclosed in a bony cuirass. The trunkfish has a humped back and is greenish to tan and marked with small white spots and chainlike markings; however, trunkfish can change colors and patterns, and in some older and larger trunkfish, the chain pattern changes to a netlike pattern. Trunkfish feed on many different bottom invertebrates, including mollusks, crabs, and worms, as well as seagrasses.

There are a number of flatfishes in Florida, including flounders, soles, and tonguefishes. Most of them have a brownish pigmented side with spots or other markings and a whitish underside.

The most colorful flounder in the seagrass meadows is the left-eyed peacock flounder, *Bothus lunatus*. It is adorned with peacock blue rings over its body and accented by blue spots on its fins and head. These beautiful flounders are fairly common in the seagrass meadows. The colorful markings of the peacock flounder overlay a mottled brownish to tan background, but be forewarned: flounders, including the peacock flounder, are masters of disguise and can instantly change their vivid colors and markings to a pale, nondescript sand color. Peacock flounders have very long pectoral fins, the fins just behind the gills, and often hold them erect, so that even if the flounder is covered by sand, the pectoral fin sticking up out of the sand bottom is a dead giveaway.

Flounders, including the peacock flounder, are

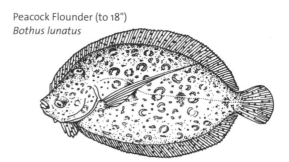

Peacock Flounder (to 18")
Bothus lunatus

Only the eyes, pectoral fin, and perhaps a bit of tail can be seen of a buried peacock flounder.

lurkers and lungers; they remain motionless in the sand until their quarry, a shrimp or a fish, comes within range, and then they explode out of the bottom, engulf their prey, swim off in an undulating movement, and then settle down once again in the sandy bottom.

The northern stargazer, *Astroscopus guttatus*, and its very close relative the southern stargazer, *Astroscopus y-graecum*, are shocking fish when you come upon one of them. For starters, they have upturned mouths that are almost vertical; their lips are draped with sand-filtering fringes; and their small eyes are perched on top of their very flat, wide heads. They look like English bulldogs with fins. The gaze of stargazers seems to be directed permanently skyward; no wonder that their scientific name is derived from the Greek meaning "one who stares at the stars." Stargazes have more than just "pretty faces." They have electric organs, modified from portions of their extraocular muscles, located behind their eyes, that are capable of delivering 50 volts of electricity. This fact has convinced both of the authors that it is

Northern Stargazer (to 22")
Astroscopus guttatus

not necessary to touch a stargazer, alive or recently dead, to admire it.

Stargazers are beautifully adapted to living under the sand; they use their shovel-like pectoral fins along with a side-to-side motion to bury in a matter of seconds. Their short-stalked eyes, fringed nostrils, and fringed mouth are all that remain above the sand. The fringes on the nostrils and the mouth keep the sand out, and even the gill slits are specially adapted to prevent sand from entering the gill chamber.

There is no end to the bag of tricks these fishes possess. When seawater exits the gill slits near the pectoral fins, the current of water stirs the sand, imitating the movement of some tasty creature, and as a curious fish comes closer to check on a possible dinner, the stargazer bolts out of the bottom, opens its capacious mouth, and sucks in its meal; then it settles back in its blanket of sand and awaits its next dinner. Apparently, stargazers do not use their electric organs to stun their prey, but the electrical discharge may confuse them. Some experts believe that they use their shocking ability as a defense mechanism.

Both the northern stargazer and the southern stargazer have club-shaped bodies and are similarly colored and patterned; they are an overall dull brown covered with white spots on the head and sides. Northern stargazers have three blackish brown stripes running horizontally across their tail fins; the middle stripe is longer and extends along the caudal peduncle and on to the rear part of its body. The middle stripe on the southern stargazer's tail fin does not extend beyond the tail.

The northern stargazer is found north of Cape Hatteras, North Carolina, and the southern stargazer ranges south of Cape Hatteras.

GRAZERS IN THE SEAGRASS MEADOWS

Some fishes are permanent residents of seagrass beds; they are usually rather small species that stay within relatively confined territories, with patterns and colors that usually match their backgrounds to make them even more obscure. Typical residential species include pipefishes, seahorses, gobies, the inshore lizardfish, and a few species of grass bed parrot fishes.

There are also seasonal resident fish species that come to the seagrass community to spawn and juvenile and subadult members of species that use this habitat as a nursery ground, where they feed and are somewhat sheltered from predation. Some of the species that occur on a seasonal basis are sea trouts, spots, several species of porgies, grunts, snappers, and mojarras.

A number of fish species move in from nearby coral reefs at night and then return to the reefs during the day. Secretive squirrelfishes that spend their day under coral ledges and crevices are nocturnal feeders, as evidenced by their very large eyes. Many species of grunts and snappers also make their appearance in the seagrasses at night.

There are also occasional visiting fishes, the top

A sand perch, Diplectrum formosum *(to 1"), hovers under a rock ledge while a grass porgy,* Calamus arctifrons *(to 10"), swims by and a bucktooth parrot fish,* Sparisoma radians *(to 8"), nibbles on an alga-covered blade. A chestnut turban grazes over the rock where a clump of feather seaweed and some green bubble weed have attached.*

carnivores or apex species, which migrate to the seagrass meadows from offshore deep water or adjacent coral reefs or from inshore mangrove communities. Spotted eagle rays and a variety of sharks, as well as tarpons, snooks, and voracious jacks are common but unpredictable predators on the grass beds.

Permanent Residents. Members of the porgy family are characterized by moderately compressed bodies, continuous dorsal fins, and forked tails. Their mouths are small, and most species have chisel-like front incisors. The grass porgy, *Calamus arctifron*, is a typical-looking porgy with a rather deep body and a large, sloping head with large eyes positioned well above its mouth, giving the grass porgy the usual "porgy vacant stare." Grass porgies are creamy tan to silvery on their sides, with dusky olive backs. Their sides are marked with a series of dusky blotches that give the appearance of vertical bars. They are often marked with a dark spot on the lateral line just behind the gill cover. Grass porgies feed on a variety of invertebrates that live in the grass beds. They are considered a good food fish and are fished for commercially in some areas.

The sea bass family includes the 7-inch, colorful butter hamlet and the enormous goliath grouper that can grow to several hundred pounds. It also includes groupers, hinds, hamlets, and creole fishes. Most of the species in this family are heavy bodied and elongated, although some look like perches. The dorsal fin is usually continuous with a shallow notch between the spiny- and soft-rayed portions of the dorsal fin. The gill cover usually has three flat spines near the posterior margin. Sea basses have complicated reproductive modes; they are hermaphroditic, and some females can become dominant males. In some species an individual will have both male and female sex organs that are functional at the same time.

The sand perch, *Diplectrum formosum*, is considered one of the "dwarf" sea basses. It is rather small, slender, and elongated, but it has a large mouth typical of groupers. The upper lobe of the tail fin is often extended into a filament. Sand perches are marked with a complex pattern of dark vertical bars against a lighter tan to bronze background and with alternating blue and orange streaky stripes running from head to tail. Sand perches have bright green eyes and a head that is marked with narrow blue lines.

The sand perch rests under rocks or in shallow burrows that it has excavated by fanning the sandy bottom with its fins or by vibrating its body to push the sand away. They can be very abundant in the grass beds and are very popular panfishes in spite of their rather small size.

Grunts are well represented in the seagrass meadows. There are populations of grunts in nearby coral reefs, and there are always grunts hovering over the coral patches in the grasses. Small grunts school in the mangrove shallows, suspended almost motionless, and then disperse as a predator cruises in to the flats. Many small grunts are permanent residents of seagrass communities, where they school in small aggregations or where individuals such as tomtates peck at the bottom and then disappear among the blades of grass.

Grunts are perchlike fishes with sloping heads and moderate-size mouths that are usually thick lipped. They have a continuous dorsal fin with the soft-rayed portion set rather close to the tail and with an anal fin that is armed with three strong spines. Most adults have very distinctive color patterns; however, the juveniles of some species are quite variable. Grunts characteristically grind their pharyngeal teeth, located on the pharynx situated between the mouth and the esophagus, producing the familiar rasping "grunts."

The tomtate, *Haemulon aurolineatum*, is a small, slender, very abundant grunt. It has a bright orange to red mouth lining (*Haemulon* is derived from the Greek for "bloody jaws" or "bloody cheeks"), a silvery body that is grayish to tan on the back, and a yellow-orange or bronze stripe running from the tip of the snout and through the eye to the brown or black spot at the base of the tail. However, the dark spot at the base of the tail is not always present, particularly in larger and older tomtates. These little grunts are quite common in the seagrass meadows, but they are also abundant around reefs and over hard, rubble bottoms as well. They are an important food for larger predators such as jacks, groupers, and mackerels. Fishermen in Florida often take the time to fish for tomtates to use as live bait for larger fishes.

The dwarf seahorse, *Hippocampus zosterae*, is a diminutive inhabitant of seagrass meadows and is probably the smallest seahorse in the stable. The dwarf seahorse is tan to greenish and has no conspicuous pattern. It has a rather large head with a short, tubular snout. Dwarf seahorses breed throughout most of the year except November through January. The male carries a maximum of about fifty eggs in its brood pouch for about ten days and then ejects the young and is ready to brood another generation in about two days. The young mature rapidly and are ready to reproduce about three months after leaving the male's brood pouch. Dwarf seahorses are common in the Indian River Lagoon system and in south Florida in seagrass meadows and around mangrove prop roots.

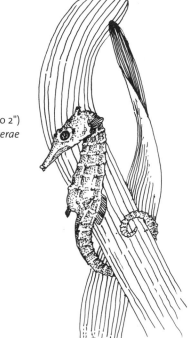

Dwarf Seahorse (to 2")
Hippocampus zosterae

The gulf pipefish, *Syngnathus scovelli*, may be the most common pipefish of the subtropical seagrass meadows. This pipefish occurs in freshwater and in saltwater seagrass habitats and also as part of the drift algae community. The gulf pipefish is a slender fish. The female has a deep, U-shaped belly, and the male is flat bellied; the female is usually a darker olive brown than the male. The number of trunk rings is a key characteristic in identifying the species of a pipefish; the gulf pipefish has approximately sixteen trunk rings. Typical of seahorses and pipefishes, the female produces the eggs and then deposits them into the male's brood pouch, where they are organized into two parallel rows where they develop for about two to three weeks.

Pipefishes and seahorses have similar tubular snouts that require them to slurp or suction their food items. Gulf pipefishes, according to some studies on their feeding behavior, feed on amphipods and barnacle larvae, and in some areas they also feed on microcrustaceans and immature shrimps.

Parrot fishes are entrancing and usually very colorful fishes. Most species have a pair of beaklike plates for teeth that resemble the beaks of parrots. They have continuous dorsal fins and oblong and moderately compressed heavy bodies covered with large, smooth scales. The tail fin in some species is rounded, but in other species it may be square, lobed, or crescent shaped. Parrot fishes come in a veritable rainbow of colors, with many species showing striking differences between the sexes. They are shallow-water fishes because they are mostly plant eaters and are therefore limited to the depths where plants grow, although some species bite off mouthfuls of coral to feed on the algae embedded in or growing on the corals.

The bucktooth parrot fish, *Sparisoma radians*, is a small, rather stubby parrot fish almost always found in the grass beds. Male bucktooth parrot fish are marked with a black edging on the tail and anal fin. Mature fish have a brilliant blue marking running from the eyes to the corners of the mouth. This species is able to change its colors and patterns readily. For example, it will change from a mottled gray to a greenish earth tone when moving off a sand bottom

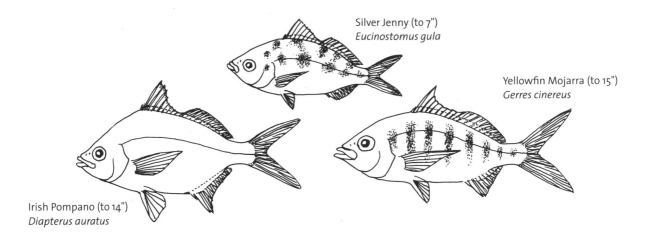

Silver Jenny (to 7")
Eucinostomus gula

Yellowfin Mojarra (to 15")
Gerres cinereus

Irish Pompano (to 14")
Diapterus auratus

onto turtle grass beds. When a bucktooth parrot fish is alarmed, it will often swim a distance away, squat near a clump of seaweed, and then blend in with the color and texture of the plant. These small parrot fish feed on blades of seagrasses and epiphytes (organisms that live on the seagrass plants) such as red algae and coralline algae and a number of epiphytic animals, such as tiny spiral-tube worms, snails, and hydroids. Bucktooth parrot fish and other species of parrot fishes that feed in the grass beds often leave telltale crescent-shaped bite marks on the blades of seagrass.

Mojarras are moderately deep-bodied fishes with large eyes, a continuous dorsal fin that may have a shallow notch between the spiny-rayed and soft-rayed dorsal fins, and a forked tail. Most species of mojarras have silvery bodies with glittering scales with faint or no markings. Mojarras are rather unremarkable fish except for their unique mouths. Their snouts are pointed and their mouths are very protrusible; that is, they can thrust out or project their mouths into almost tubular shapes. In addition, the area beneath the lower jaw is concave. Relatively little is known about this group of fishes.

The Irish pompano, *Diapterus auratus*, is a silvery mojarra with some olive shading on its back. The trailing edge of the first dorsal fin is edged in black, and the second dorsal spine is tall and strong. The Irish pompano inhabits seagrass meadows and areas around mangroves in lagoons and tidal creeks and is particularly abundant in the Indian River Lagoon system.

The spotfin mojarra, *Eucinostomus argenteus*, is somewhat more elongated than the Irish pompano. It has a gleaming silver body with a yellowish sheen and is marked with a dusky wash on the tip of its spiny dorsal fin and with a bold, black lateral line.

The silver jenny, *Eucinostomus gula*, also has an elongated body but is somewhat deeper bodied than the spotfin mojarra. The silver jenny, as its name implies, has a silvery body with mirrorlike bluish reflections on its back; its dorsal, anal, and caudal fins are dusky.

The yellowfin mojarra, *Gerres cinereus*, is moderately deep bodied. It has a large prominent eye and is marked with seven or eight indistinct, dark bluish or, sometimes, pinkish vertical bars on its silvery sides. Its pelvic and anal fins are tinged with yellow.

Many juvenile grunts utilize seagrass meadows to feed and mature into adults before they migrate to the nearby coral reefs. Young white grunts are representative of many grunt species that grow up in the grass beds. Juvenile white grunts sort themselves out into schools according to size and graze the seagrass meadows, feeding on copepods and smaller invertebrates. If you snorkel across the grass beds, pay particular attention to the small white grunts and other juvenile species that take shelter among the ominous spines of the long-spined black sea urchin.

Daily Migrants. The French grunt, *Haemulon flavolineatum* (the species name means "yellow lined"), is a deeper-bodied fish than the tomtate, with a body shape that is more typical of the grunts. French grunts have yellow to gold bodies and yellow fins. Their bodies are boldly marked with blue, black, or pale silvery stripes; the stripes run longitudinally above the lateral line and obliquely or diagonally below the lateral line. French grunts are very common and abundant over grass flats and reefs, where they often drift, almost hypnotically, back and forth with the swash of the waves.

The white grunt, *Haemulon plumieri*, has a similar shape to that of the French grunt. Its body is compressed and its back is arched; however its head is larger and its snout is more pointed than are those of the French grunt. White grunts have very large scales above the lateral line and smaller ones below the lateral line. They are silvery white to pearl gray; the head is bronze to yellow and marked with blue stripes. No other grunt has a combination of a blue-striped head and very large scales above the lateral line. White grunts can change their colors to match the background and can become quite pale over coral sands. They have red mouth linings typical of this genus.

White grunts are nocturnal feeders and migrate from the reefs at night to sandy, grassy bottoms where they feed on small crabs, shrimps, mollusks, sea urchins, and small fishes. The white grunt and other grunts are very good to eat and are marketed

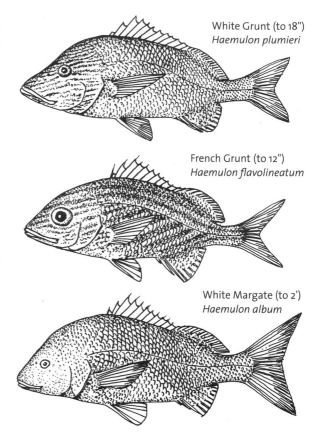

White Grunt (to 18")
Haemulon plumieri

French Grunt (to 12")
Haemulon flavolineatum

White Margate (to 2')
Haemulon album

fresh in Florida. We have always enjoyed using white grunts to make a local favorite, "grits and grunts."

The white margate, *Haemulon album*, is a robust, deep-bodied grunt with a sloping head and a large mouth. Margates are silvery gray with no distinctive markings; the dusky back is arched, and the soft portions of the fins are dusky gray. The white margate is the largest of the grunts and is mostly found singly or in small groups in seagrass beds and over sand flats.

Manatees

The West Indian manatee, familiarly known as the sea cow, *Trichechus manatus*, is a slow-moving, docile aquatic mammal, shaped like a large seal or a seagoing sausage, that may weigh 1,000 pounds or more.

Manatees have dull gray to dusky gray or even brown cylindrical bodies and small heads with squarish snouts. Their upper lips are deeply cleft, and the halves are capable of moving independently, which apparently aids them in feeding on vegetation. Their lips are peppered with stout bristles. Their eyes are small, and they lack external ears. The manatee's forelegs are modified rounded flippers, and its powerful, rounded tail is flattened horizontally and resembles a paddle. These gentle giants can grow to a length of about 15 feet. They swim by undulating the rear portion of their body and by steering and stabilizing themselves with their tail and flippers.

Manatees are herbivorous mammals that occasionally feed on insects, fishes, and other aquatic organisms. Their preferred food is submerged aquatic vegetation, such as hydrilla, wild celery, coontail, water-milfoil, widgeon grass, and shoalgrass, and in higher-salinity waters they feed on manatee grass and turtle grass. But they will also forage on emergent and floating vegetation. An adult manatee may eat 50 pounds or more of vegetation a day.

West Indian manatees are not particularly gregarious. They are usually solitary or swim and feed in small loose groups, except when they herd in warm-water springs or near the warm-water discharge from power plants during the colder times of the winter. Occasionally a manatee wanders up the coast and appears in Georgia or South Carolina and then reappears in one of the North Carolina sounds, only to be seen in Chesapeake Bay a week or two later. In August 2006 a manatee wandered as far north as Rhode Island.

Manatees have very few natural enemies. The greatest threat to a manatee is to be struck by a speeding boat; it can be killed by a crushing injury or severely injured by a propeller. Unfortunately manatees feed in the shallows and travel in channels where most of the Inner Coast boat traffic cruises. Manatees are now highly protected, and there are maximum speed zones posted in critical areas. It is difficult to obtain an accurate count of the West Indian manatee population. For several years the best estimates were of only about 1,000 to 1,500 manatees left, but there has been a steady increase in survival and reproduction in some subpopulations, and the best estimates now are that there are about 3,000 manatees swimming in Florida waters.

West Indian Manatee (to 15')
Trichechus manatus

Live Bottoms
Oyster Reefs, Patch Reefs, and Worm Rocks

Worms, corals, and oysters: what do they have in common? Some species within these disparate groups build living reefs that are relatively wave resistant and attract a variety of plants, invertebrates, and fishes to nearshore high-energy environments, intertidal estuarine habitats, and "islands" of corals in the seagrass meadows. These living reefs, often called live bottoms and sometimes hard-bottom communities, serve as places of attachment for many, many sessile species. They also attract grazers and predators and provide places for egg laying and hiding, just as piers and rubble structures do.

❧

Oyster Reefs

The eastern oyster, *Crassostrea virginica*, is the quintessential estuarine animal, sometimes called the American or Virginia oyster or, colloquially, just "the oyster." It tolerates wide ranges of salinities and temperatures and is very well adapted to live in the high-turbidity conditions that are typically found in mid-Atlantic Inner Coast estuaries. It is also widely distributed from about the latitude of the Gulf of Saint Lawrence in the Maritimes to south Florida. Oysters cluster together and spread in dense colonies over the surface of the bottom and other hard surfaces to create a special habitat, the oyster reef, also called an oyster bar, oyster rock, oyster bed, or oyster grounds. In areas where the tidal range or amplitude is 5 feet or less, such as Chesapeake Bay, Virginia, and most of North Carolina, eastern oysters grow subtidally; that is, they are almost always covered by water, except during periods of high pressure accompanied by strong winds that blow the water out of the sounds and estuaries. Farther south, in South Carolina and Georgia, where tides range from 6 feet to more than 12 feet, oyster reefs grow intertidally; that is, they are exposed twice a day, dur-ing ebb tides, and are covered by water during flood tides. These reefs are often extensive and contiguous in the Inner Coast waters of South Carolina and Georgia.

Eastern oysters have long been an important species to humans. They are without grace, beauty, or charm, but they were important to coastal Indians as food and for ceremonial and decorative purposes, and they have been scraped and plucked and raked from the bottom for centuries to satisfy humans' appetite for these succulent shellfish. An oyster fresh from the water and covered with muck is not an appetizing sight; one wonders who the first brave soul was to sup on an oyster. Subtidal oysters have always been superior to intertidal oysters. Oysters that grow intertidally have smaller and thinner shells, with smaller and lower-quality oyster meats within, making them more suitable as canned oysters than as the more valuable half shell oysters.

In addition, oyster shells were used for centuries to make tabby (a mixture of lime, water, sand, and oyster shells) for the construction of houses and walls in the South, as well as oyster shell roads. It is very common to see walls of tabby built around old cemeteries and churches. There is a good example of contemporary tabby construction along the waterfront park in Beaufort, South Carolina.

Regardless of the location of an oyster reef, the biology and ecology of the oysters are essentially the same. The sexes are separate in the eastern oyster, but over the course of a year, some members of the oyster population change sex from male to female. Usually there is a preponderance of males in the first year of an oyster's life, and as an oyster approaches its second year, many change from male to female. Spawning is usually triggered by a change in the water temperature. Most biologists agree that when water temperatures reach approximately 68°F, oysters begin spawning from about New York down to

Sea Anemone

Whip Mudworms

Oyster Spat

Hooked
Mussels

Barnacles

Skilletfish

Fan
Worms

Sea Grapes

Mud crab

Georgia, but there seems to be some indication that eastern oysters in warmer Florida waters are adapted to spawn at slightly warmer water temperatures.

When the threshold temperature is reached, the males emit clouds of sperm into the water, which stimulate the female oysters to release their eggs in what has been described by many oyster biologists as a chain reaction that sweeps dramatically over the local oyster population and turns the water white with the release of sperm and eggs. The eggs are fertilized in the water column by chance encounters with sperm, and then larval development quickly begins. The larvae develop into ciliated forms called trochophores, which become part of the zooplankton community that feed on small algal cells and are, in turn, fed on in copious amounts by larger plankton feeders. The trochophore continues to develop and secretes a pair of shells and a ring of cilia that functions for movement and for feeding; this first stage shelled larva is called a straight-hinge veliger.

As the oyster larva grows, its shell shape changes,

and an all-important foot and byssus gland are formed that will be used in a short time to attach the oyster forever to the substratum, which is usually another oyster shell. Oysters are gregarious creatures and respond to chemical cues called pheromones released by newly settled oysters as well as to proteins emanating from other oyster shells, enticing millions of larvae to continuously build and grow the oyster reef.

As the oysters cluster together and spread in dense colonies over the bottom, a special habitat is created: the oyster reef community. The dips and folds and crevices of the sprawling shells so closely wedged together over the bottom increase many times over the habitat available for sessile animals. The oyster reef then acts very much like a pier piling or a seagrass community: it provides a habitat where sessile organisms thrive and where mobile epifaunal worms, snails, and fishes come to feed and seek protection among the crevices.

Estuaries and associated tidal creeks that meander through the marshes provide the dominant habitat for oyster reefs along the southeast Atlantic coast. Because of the wide-ranging tidal amplitudes from the southern part of North Carolina through Georgia, the lagoons and marshes behind the barrier islands have been broken up into a complex and extensive network of tortuous channels flanked by muddy banks, bars, and spits—this is the environment of the intertidal oyster reef. The oyster reefs range in size from a few, scattered clumps to great, rolling, solid mounds of dead shells and live oysters. Most of the mature oysters are long and narrow and seem to grow upward and away from smothering sediment. Oysters that grow subtidally can tolerate a broad range of temperatures and salinities; oysters that grow intertidally in the Carolinas and Georgia generally are restricted to relatively high salinities.

Life in and among the Oysters

Oyster reefs are often heavily populated with little gray barnacles that grow near the high-tide line in the splash zone as well as ivory and bay barnacles that grow near the low-tide line and below. In addition, there are often thick growths of feathery hydroids, various kinds of bryozoans, jellylike anemones, and rubbery tunicates. All of these and many others that dwell within the oyster community produce eggs and larvae that are avidly fed on by many other organisms. Blue crabs prowl oyster bars and reefs to feed, as do many species of fishes, such as blennies, gobies, and pinfish.

Boring sponges, *Cliona* spp., are some of the most persistent pests of oysters, particularly on oysters that grow subtidally in oyster reefs; boring sponges are found only incidentally in the intertidal oyster reef community, probably because of mortality caused by exposure to the hot sun and drying wind.

Boring sponges riddle oyster shells with a bright

A live boring sponge, Cliona *sp., protrudes from the shell of a live oyster. An empty shell shows the characteristic scattering of small holes of an oyster infested with the sponge when alive.*

sulfur-yellow sponge material. As the sponge grows through the shell, it emerges in buttonlike mounds at numerous spots on the surface of the shell. An empty oyster shell covered with pockmarks is evidence of a former infestation by boring sponges. A shell that breaks easily when handled indicates the damage done by boring sponges when the oyster was alive. Boring sponges at times pierce through to the interior, and to combat this intrusion, a healthy oyster produces a thin coating of shell over each hole. At times, however, the sponge wins out over the oyster, and small dark spots can be seen on the mantle where the sponge has bored through the shell.

Worms are plentiful and varied in oyster communities. The oyster flatworm, *Stylochus ellipticus*, is a major predator of barnacles on oysters, pilings,

Oyster flatworms, Stylochus ellipticus *(to 1"), find refuge and food among the attached fauna on an oyster shell. Barnacles are favored prey. Here one can be seen within the gaping shell of a barnacle.*

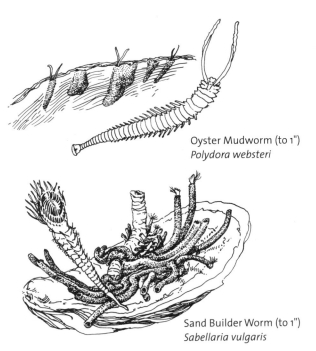

Oyster Mudworm (to 1")
Polydora websteri

Sand Builder Worm (to 1")
Sabellaria vulgaris

Sand-builder worms, *Sabellaria vulgaris*, are also tube-building worms that are sometimes quite abundant in the oyster community. They build thick mats of well-cemented sand grain tubes on the oyster shells. Sand-builder worms are small, conical worms, only about 1 inch long. Their bodies are pale, but their heads are adorned with two semicircular pads fringed with bright golden setae. A cluster of long, filamentous tentacles lies below the fringed pads.

In the higher-salinity regions of Inner Coast wa-

Worms in their tubes, often found in eelgrass beds, are also commonly attached to oysters. When the limy tube worm, Hydroides dianthus *(to 3"), emerges from its chalky white tube, the feathery red tentacles spread out. On retracting, the club-shaped operculum seals off the tube. Whip mudworms and fan worms,* Sabella microphthalma *(to 1 3/8"), form sand-encrusted tubes.*

and rocks. The flatworm slithers over to a feeding barnacle and quickly inserts its pharynx into the open valves of the barnacle. The barnacle, immediately disturbed, closes its valves, but it is too late; the pharynx of the worm remains within and begins to feed. Eventually the barnacle weakens and gapes, which allows the entire worm to slide in and continue its feast.

The oyster mudworm, *Polydora websteri*, is a tube-building worm that builds its tube on the inside edge of the shell. The oyster responds to the intrusion by secreting a thin shell coating over the worm tubes. Dark shell "blisters" on the inside edge of a freshly shucked oyster shell are signs of the worms that lived within. As the worm grows inward, it maintains contact with the outside world and its planktonic food source through the original entrance. The worms will not become an ingredient in your oyster stew, however, because they are walled off by the covering of shell nacre.

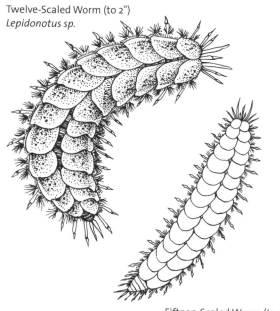

Twelve-Scaled Worm (to 2")
Lepidonotus sp.

Fifteen-Scaled Worm (to 3")
Harmothoe sp.

ters, eelgrass and oysters are often heavily populated with fan worms, *Sabella microphthalma*, and limy tube worms, *Hydroides dianthus*. Fan worms, or feather duster worms, live in flexible, mud-encrusted tubes attached to shells and plants. Limy tube worms, as their name implies, build hard, white, limy tubes, which may be twisted and entangled with other limy tube worms on eelgrass and on oyster shells and other hard surfaces.

Scale worms are unusual worms with overlapping scales that look like armor plating. They are usually found in high-salinity waters, especially around intertidal oyster reefs, where they crawl among barnacles, worm tubes, and other attached life on the reef. Twelve-scaled worms, *Lepidonotus* spp., are grayish green or brownish and covered with twelve pairs of oval scales. They are also found under rubble and rocks and sometimes in shells occupied by hermit crabs.

Fifteen-scaled worms, *Harmothoe* spp., are larger versions of twelve-scaled worms. They are longer and more robust, with fifteen pairs of scales. They are usually reddish to orange or tan. These worms crawl over oyster shells and rubble and around tunicates and other sessile organisms.

Crabs and Other Crustaceans

OYSTER PEA CRABS

Oyster pea crabs, *Pinnotheres ostreum*, are small crabs that live within oysters and sometimes in jingle shells, bay scallops, mussels, and even the tubes of parchment worms. For some it is quite a treat to discover these little round intruders served up with an oyster on the half shell or perhaps floating in a bowl of oyster stew. The spring-hatched young of these small commensal crabs are pelagic until late summer, when they enter an oyster by way of its incurrent siphon and take up residence within the mantle, where they attach to the gills. Females are slightly larger than males, about 1/2 inch wide, as compared to males, which are about 1/3 inch wide. The females become permanent residents, but the males soon depart on nuptial trips to other oysters in search of more females. These little crabs can cause some damage to the host oyster's gill tissue, and they also compete for food. Oyster pea crabs are more abun-

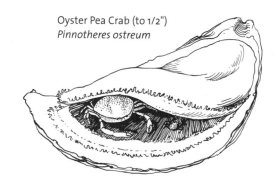

Oyster Pea Crab (to 1/2")
Pinnotheres ostreum

dant in saltier waters and particularly in subtidal oyster reefs, but they are relatively rare in intertidal oyster reefs. There are other species of these little commensal crabs known as pea crabs and squatter pea crabs that are found here and there in mussels, colonial tunicates, and worm tubes.

MUD CRABS

Small mud crabs are common and abundant members of oyster communities, where they live in crevices between oyster shells or secreted in empty oyster shells, usually referred to as "boxes." Mud crabs are common predators and grazers. Some species can crush the shells of small oysters, barnacles, and mussels and feed on their soft bodies; others are algal and detritus feeders and occasionally feed on amphipods. There are five common species of mud crabs found in the oyster communities, and all are similar in appearance.

The Harris mud crab, *Rhithropanopeus harrisii*, and the flatback mud crab, *Eurypanopeus depressus*, are the smallest of the mud crabs; they are only 3/4 inch wide or less. The Harris mud crab is the only species of mud crab with whitish- or pale-tipped claws; all the other mud crab species have black-tipped claws. The flatback mud crab has unequal-size claws and a flat, granular or sandpapery back. The flatback mud crab can be distinguished from other black-fingered mud crabs by the spooned-out inside edges of the fingers of its smaller claw. Both of these species are typical estuarine species found in moderate- to high-salinity waters.

The Atlantic mud crab, *Panopeus herbstii*, is the largest of the mud crabs, but it is still a small crab at only 1 1/2 inches wide. Its claws are unequal in size; the finger of the larger claw has a single large tooth visible when the claw is clamped shut. The Atlantic mud crab is tolerant of low-salinity water and can

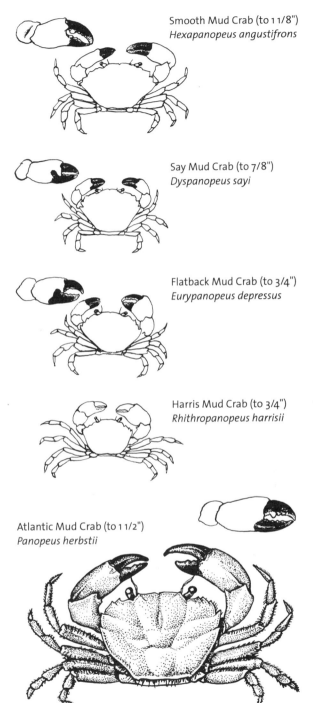

Smooth Mud Crab (to 1 1/8")
Hexapanopeus angustifrons

Say Mud Crab (to 7/8")
Dyspanopeus sayi

Flatback Mud Crab (to 3/4")
Eurypanopeus depressus

Harris Mud Crab (to 3/4")
Rhithropanopeus harrisii

Atlantic Mud Crab (to 1 1/2")
Panopeus herbstii

be found in oyster communities growing in brackish water.

The Say mud crab, *Dyspanopeus sayi*, is usually found in high-salinity water. It is small, about 1 inch wide, with claws of unequal size. Its back is smooth and decorated with reddish brown speckles. The inner margins of the somewhat smaller claw are chisel edged.

The smooth mud crab, *Hexapanopeus angustifrons*, is about 1 1/8 inches wide with a groove on the inside of the "wrist," the second joint, to which the claw is attached. It also has a large tooth on the finger of the major claw, as does the Atlantic mud crab, but the tooth of the smooth mud crab is hidden when the fingers are clamped. This species inhabits the high-salinity waters of lower estuaries.

The members of the mud crab family, which includes the highly prized stone crabs found in the warm waters of Georgia and Florida, are not limited to oyster reefs; they dwell in low-salinity waters and throughout saltier estuarine waters and can be found hiding under stones and crawling among tunicates, hydroids, and seaweeds on pilings and on the undersides of floating docks.

MOLLUSKS

Eastern oysters are, of course, the keystone species of oyster reefs, but there are many other mollusks in the oyster community. Some plow through the ooze, feeding on algae and other organic material; others prey on various organisms, including oysters; and still others, such as mussels, attach to other shells by their rubbery byssal threads and siphon in water laden with algal cells and other organic matter. Tiny impressed odostome snails prey on slipper snails, and nudibranchs glide over mud and shells to feed on encrusting bryozoans, sea nettle polyps, and small hydroids and sponges.

Jingle shells cling tenaciously to an oyster shell. Atlantic oyster drills and thick-lip oyster drills often attach their differently shaped egg cases to oysters.

Jingle Shell (to 2")
Anomia simplex

The hooked mussel, *Ischadium recurvum*, attaches to almost anything that is hard: pilings, rocks, or shells. Hooked mussels attach themselves firmly with their strong byssus, or beard. Mussels can actually move by pulling themselves forward on the somewhat elastic byssal threads and then releasing some and attaching others. This small mussel, generally only 1 to 2 inches long, has a dull-colored black or gray exterior, in contrast to its shiny, rosy brown to purple interior. The surface of its shell is distinctly ridged and curved.

The flat, circular valves of jingle shells, *Anomia simplex*, adhere tightly to the surfaces of oyster shells and are often mistaken for very young oysters, or oyster spat. Jingle shells are delicate little shells that are pearly and translucent. These lovely little shells often wash up on beaches in large numbers.

Oyster drills are serious predators of subtidal eastern oysters; however, there are fewer drills and other organisms on interdidal oyster reefs because they cannot endure the desiccation and severe swings in temperatures when they are exposed to the air. Drills rasp pinholes in oyster shells and then insert their proboscises to feed on the soft oyster meat within; they are particularly harmful to smaller oysters. They also attack barnacles and mussels. There are usually two species of oyster drills along the Inner Coast: the Atlantic oyster drill, *Urosalpinx cinerea*, and the thick-lip drill, *Eupleura caudata*.

The Atlantic oyster drill is a small, grayish snail, about 2 inches high, with a pointed spire and a knobby shell. The thick-lip drill is similar in size and varies in color from reddish brown to bluish white; however, its spire is lower than that of the Atlantic oyster drill, and it has a longer siphonal canal and a thick, flaring outer lip. Both drills lay distinctive, urn-shaped leathery egg cases, which are firmly anchored to the substrate by a pedestal-like stalk. The egg capsules are large enough to be easily seen; the Atlantic oyster drill egg case is spherical, and the thick-lip drill egg case is shaped like a spatula.

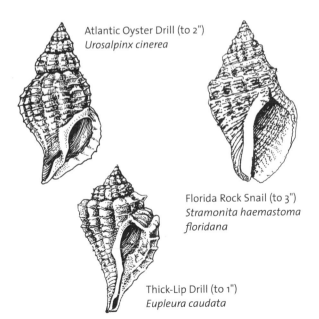

Atlantic Oyster Drill (to 2")
Urosalpinx cinerea

Florida Rock Snail (to 3")
Stramonita haemastoma floridana

Thick-Lip Drill (to 1")
Eupleura caudata

The Florida rock snail, also called the southern oyster drill, *Stramonita haemastoma floridana*, is about 3 inches long and is much larger and heavier than the Atlantic oyster drill and thick-lip drill. It is light gray to yellowish or brownish and flecked with reddish brown streaks. Florida rock snails are highly variable: some have blunt, knobby protrusions, while others are quite smooth. The body whorl is large, and the interior of the aperture is creamy to salmon pink. There is a series of ridges or crenulations marked with reddish brown along the flared outer lip of the aperture.

Florida rock snails live in the intertidal and subtidal zones on oyster reefs or under rocks. They are highly predacious on oysters and other bivalves, and they also feed on the reef-building tube worms that construct worm rocks along Florida's east coast. Florida rock snails lay clumps of tubular egg capsules.

Fishes

There are several fishes that are common inhabitants of oyster communities. They find cover and food there, and they deposit their eggs on the hard structure.

The oyster toadfish, *Opsanus tau*, may be the ugliest fish in Inner Coast waters; it has threatening, wide-gaping jaws; a slimy body embellished with warty nodules; and raggedy, fleshy flaps hanging from its lips and draped over its eyes. Toadfish are omnivores and will quickly take a baited hook, but beware of these pugnacious fish, which will instantly erect their sharp dorsal fin spines and snap aggressively with their powerful, toothed jaws. In addition to their formidable appearance, they are quite vocal and are capable of making at least two different calls. On a warm summer night aboard a moored or anchored boat, you may hear plaintive foghorn calls echoing

Oyster Toadfish (to 15") with Toadlets
Opsanus tau

through the hull; the foghorn or boat whistle, as it has been described, is emitted by an amorous male advertising for a mate. Females and nonspawning males do not make this call, but they are all capable of making grunting noises. The grunts express annoyance or fear—and when removed from the water, they grunt!

Oyster toadfish are not restricted to oyster reefs and are quite common in vegetated and unvegetated shallow bottoms. During the spring and summer breeding season, males can be found in tin cans, under boards, and in other dark, secretive places. Females attracted into the males' dens by the foghorn call turn upside down and attach their eggs to the top side of the nest and then leave it to the male to guard and brood the eggs and young. The males keep the nest clean by fanning their fins to clear out the silt and organic particles. Toadfish eggs are some of the largest fish eggs known, almost 1/4 inch in diameter. After the eggs hatch, the young tadpolelike

larvae remain attached to the huge, bulbous yolk until they have absorbed it, and they become little toadlets. As the young become free swimming, the male still guards his flock and is watchful over them as they swim in and out among his fins.

Gobies, blennies, and skilletfish are small fishes living in and among the shells of the oyster reef community. These small fishes are abundant but reclusive and solitary in habit, so they are not seen as frequently as are the more visible and gregarious schooling shore fishes, such as killifishes. Sometimes, with a bit of luck, you can pick up a pair of seemingly empty oyster shells from the shallows and discover one of these small fishes within; they also hide out in empty containers in the shallows. Gobies, blennies, and skilletfish are similar in size and behavior. They are about 1 or 2 inches long, and although they are closely associated with oysters, they are at times found in shallow flats and seagrass meadows. They are tactile little creatures; that is, they seem to need the feel of a shell, the inside of a can, or a rocky crevice. They lay their eggs on the inside of dead oyster shells—usually boxes, empty shells—that are still hinged together and gape only enough for a fish to enter. Typically, the males guard the eggs, which may be attached to the upper valve as well as the lower valve. The eggs of these species are usually small and amber-colored and are laid in clutches of a few hundred or more. The eggs of gobies are narrow and elliptical and attached by fibrous tufts; blennies lay spherical eggs, which are stuck to a flattened disk; and skilletfish deposit their closely packed oval eggs and attach them to oyster shells with a sticky mucus.

Gobies have large, prominent eyes set close together near the top of the head. They have two separate dorsal fins and pelvic fins that have been modified into a suctionlike disk that enables them to adhere to shells—or your finger if you catch one. Blennies are deeper-bodied fishes with large heads; a single, continuous dorsal fin; and small pelvic fins that have not been modified as suction disks. Most species of blennies are larger than gobies and skilletfish. Skilletfish are shaped like a skillet with a broad, flat head and a body that abruptly tapers down to the tail. They have small, widely spaced eyes and pelvic fins that are highly modified into a large suction disk.

The goby family is the largest family of marine fishes, with more than 1,500 species worldwide. They are primarily fishes of shallow tropical and subtropical waters, but many species have successfully adapted to freshwater as well as to depths well over 1,000 feet.

The naked goby, *Gobiosoma bosci*, is very abundant and wide ranging and occurs even into tidal freshwaters. Naked gobies are devoid of scales—thus their name. They are dark greenish brown on top and pale below and marked with eight or nine light vertical bars along their sides. Naked gobies range down to south Florida.

Seaboard gobies, *Gobiosoma ginsburgi*, are similar in appearance to naked gobies, with some subtle differences. They lack scales except for two on each side at the base of the tail fin. They are more irregularly marked, with fewer distinct bars, and their lateral line is usually defined by a line of dark spots. Seaboard gobies are found as far south as Georgia.

The other common goby found in oyster communities is the green goby, *Microgobius thalassinus*. The green goby has a longer second dorsal fin and anal fin than do the naked and seaboard gobies; it also has a long, pointed tail. Green gobies have scales on their backs but lack scales on their heads and bellies. They are very colorful fish. Male green gobies are greenish blue with an intense reddish hue on their spotted dorsal fin, a vivid orange to yellow pelvic fin, and a row of dark spots on the border of the white-edged anal fin. Females lack the row of spots along the edge of the anal fin, but they do have a large black spot on the rear of the dorsal fin. The sides of females are iridescent blue-green, and their heads are marked with gold and blue bands under the eyes. Green gobies are most often associated with redbeard sponges, which grow profusely on some subtidal oysters. Green gobies range from Chesapeake Bay to the Indian River Lagoon, Florida.

Most blennies are tropical species, but there are two species—the striped blenny, *Chasmodes bosquianus*, and the feather blenny, *Hypsoblennius hentz*—that are common and abundant inhabitants of oyster communities all along the Inner Coast and down into Florida.

Striped blennies are about 4 inches long and are rather colorful; the males are marked with bright blue horizontal lines that converge toward the tail. Their heads have an orange stripe that runs through the dorsal fin that is also marked with a brilliant blue

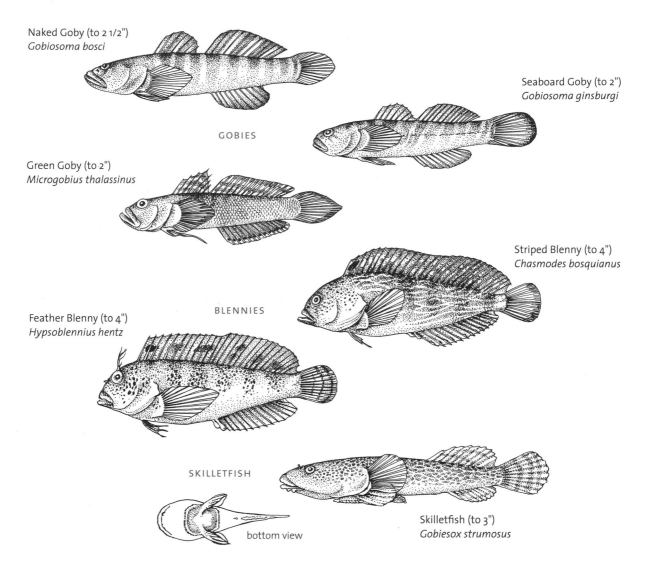

Naked Goby (to 2 1/2")
Gobiosoma bosci

GOBIES

Seaboard Goby (to 2")
Gobiosoma ginsburgi

Green Goby (to 2")
Microgobius thalassinus

Striped Blenny (to 4")
Chasmodes bosquianus

BLENNIES

Feather Blenny (to 4")
Hypsoblennius hentz

SKILLETFISH

bottom view

Skilletfish (to 3")
Gobiesox strumosus

spot near the anterior edge of the fin. Female striped blennies are a more subdued olive green and are marked with paler green lines.

Feather blennies are named for their two feathery protuberances, called cirri, which arise over the tops of their prominent eyes. They are about the same size as striped blennies, but they are not as colorful or as distinctly marked. The sides of their bodies are marked with brownish spots that form subtle verti-

cal bars, and the males also have a brilliant blue spot on the anterior edge of the dorsal fin.

The skilletfish, also known, aptly, as oyster cling-fish, *Gobiesox strumosus*, is not likely to be confused with either gobies or blennies because of its unique shape. Skilletfish are olive-brown, speckled, 3-inch fish that are well camouflaged against the muddy oysters and on muddy and sandy bottoms. Skilletfish spend most of their time clinging to the outsides of shells or lurking within empty shells, waiting to engulf a stray amphipod or isopod that passes by. They live throughout the Inner Coast around oysters, in grassy shallows, and in piling communities.

❧

Patch Reefs

There are some persistent oyster reef communities scattered along the Florida coast, but hard limestone bottoms and reef patches are the more dominant live-bottom habitats in south Florida. There are patch reefs here and there along the southeast coast of Florida, but they reach their zenith in the lagoon called Biscayne Bay, where there are 3,000 or more patch reefs extending from tiny Sand Key, just 4 miles from the southern tip of Key Biscayne, and around Elliott Key to the northern part of Key Largo. There are also many patch reefs farther south in the shallow waters around the Keys.

Patch reefs are small oases of coral reef communities usually surrounded by a band or halo of sand with seagrass meadows beyond. These amazing islets of intense beauty and activity arise from exposed rocky outcrops or fossil coral ridges and are initiated when coral larvae settle out of the plankton to begin their benthic and sessile existence. The hard bottoms of rock and fossil coral offer the coral larvae places to settle amid the shifting coral sands, and over hundreds of years, more coral larvae settle and develop coral colonies that reach for the sun and also spread laterally. Patch reefs are usually found rather close to shore, in waters about 10–20 feet deep. The primary corals that first develop in a patch reef are usually brain and star corals. Eventually, other hard and soft corals develop, followed by various sponges, worms, and mollusks. Crabs, shrimps, and spiny lobsters wander in and out of crevices while many resident colorful fishes flit in and out of their hiding places,

always wary of the larger predatory fishes that prowl around patch reefs. The herbivorous fishes and sea urchins that live on patch reefs feed on seagrasses and seaweeds close to where they live and hide. They make short excursions to feed on the nearby vegetation, where they feed so vigorously on the plants that they leave their signatures around the patch reef: sand halos.

We discuss only patch reefs in this book and exclude fringe reefs, offshore barrier reefs, and bank reefs because patch reefs are the only coral reef communities that live within Inner Coast waters. Fringe reefs occur in shallow waters close to shore and are common around the Caribbean islands and in the Bahamas but are not found along the Florida coastline.

Coral reefs, whether they are fringe reefs, offshore barrier reefs, bank reefs, or patch reefs, require certain environmental conditions. Corals are very sensitive to cold and are happiest in water temperatures of about 73°F to 80°F, which explains why coral reefs only thrive in a relatively narrow band around the world. In addition, coral reefs require ocean strength salinity of about 35 ppt, or a composition of 3.5 percent various salts in a given volume of water, which is one reason that coral reefs do not grow in estuaries where freshwater dilutes the seawater. Corals also cannot exist in very turbid estuarine environments because they require very clear water, so that sunlight will penetrate to the symbiotic zooxanthellae algae so necessary for the growth and health of corals. However, corals do require somewhat turbulent, high-energy seas to bring oxygen and planktonic food to the coral ecosystem and to remove deleterious silt that settles on the corals and other species in the community.

The formation of a coral reef starts with the settling of a ciliated coral larva, the planula, on the hard bottom, followed by many more coral larvae that di-

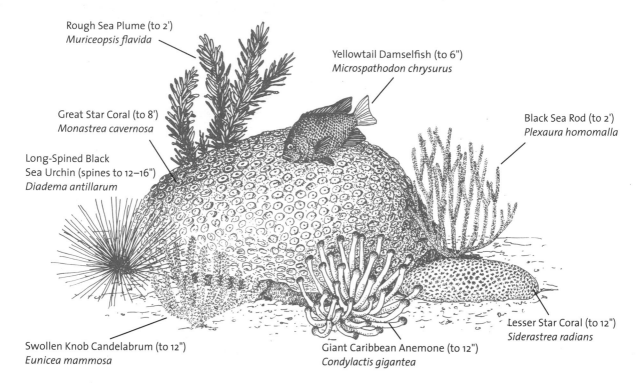

Rough Sea Plume (to 2')
Muriceopsis flavida

Yellowtail Damselfish (to 6")
Microspathodon chrysurus

Great Star Coral (to 8')
Monastrea cavernosa

Black Sea Rod (to 2')
Plexaura homomalla

Long-Spined Black
Sea Urchin (spines to 12–16")
Diadema antillarum

Swollen Knob Candelabrum (to 12")
Eunicea mammosa

Giant Caribbean Anemone (to 12")
Condylactis gigantea

Lesser Star Coral (to 12")
Siderastrea radians

vide and change into solitary polyps, the adult coral form, which set about the complex procedure of constructing a hard dwelling of calcium carbonate. As the colony prospers, the calcium carbonate fortress grows ever larger and takes on a certain characteristic shape, depending on the species. Each polyp builds a cylindrical structure called a calyx surrounded by a series of six buttresslike structures called septa, collectively called a corallite. As the polyp continues to grow, it lays down more septa and deposits additional calcium carbonate. As the calyx lengthens, it actually becomes too deep for the soft-bodied polyp to function. So these tiny blobs of protoplasm simply build calcareous floors to elevate their positions and, in doing so, seal off the floors below. As you snorkel above a patch reef and see a large coral boulder, you should be aware that the inner "apartments" have been abandoned as the polyps moved upward and

laterally, and the polyps exist only as a thin veneer on the periphery of the boulder.

A typical patch reef usually has some mounds of stony corals, sprawling brain corals, and perhaps some flat, leafy corals. There will quite likely be a few species of soft corals on the patch reef or nearby in the adjacent seagrasses, and there will probably be some fire corals encrusting the hard corals and the sea fans and other soft corals. Patch reefs do not all have the same cast of characters because the colonization of a hard bottom is dependent on several different circumstances. Populating a patch reef, as already stated, requires the settlement of larval corals that are recruited from reproducing corals some distance away. Some of these coral larvae originate from offshore barrier or bank reefs and others come from other nearby patch reefs, but the larvae all share a single characteristic: they are part of the plankton and are transported by the vagaries of the currents. Some larvae settle down and soon perish because of predation or incompatibility with the particular habitat. Some potential patch reefs are in high-energy areas where there is a great deal of surge. Some sites experience sediment deposition. Some sites may be in very shallow water, while others may be as deep as 20 feet. These seemingly subtle differences in patch reef sites along with happenstance settlement by coral larvae determine the species composition of patch reefs.

Hard Corals, Soft Corals, and Fire Corals

Our hypothetical patch reef might include a smooth star coral, *Solenastrea bournoni*, which often forms a bulky hemispherical cream or tan dome with a bumpy appearance. The corallite rims, about 1/4 inch in diameter, are outlined in conspicuous dark circles, and the polyp tentacles are long and are often extended into the water to feed during the day, rather than at night, as most corals do. This gives the colony a raggedy appearance apparent to any snorkeler. Smooth star corals are often found on patch reefs and can tolerate somewhat turbid environments.

The lesser star coral, *Siderastrea radians*, is a common solid coral that usually forms flat plates with sunken, dark-colored corallites; however, they are occasionally dome-shaped. These tan, brown, or grayish irregularly shaped colonies are usually 12–15 inches in diameter. Lesser star corals are somewhat tolerant of fluctuations in sedimentation, temperature, and salinity, which explains the dense populations of this species in Biscayne Bay, a marginal location for many other species of hard corals.

Occasionally, there are impressive growths of great star coral, *Monastrea cavernosa*, on patch reefs, but it usually grows in deeper-water bank reefs. It can form massive boulders, but it also grows as plates or sheets. Great star corals are quite variable in color and may be green, brown, gray, or orange. The shape of their corallites, however, is the clue to their identity, for they protrude like bulbous bug eyes, with diameters reaching as much as 1/2 inch.

Mustard hill coral, *Porites astreoides*, is generally an encrusting form on surging, shallow patch reefs, but in deeper waters, where the water currents and surging waves are diminished, mustard hill colonies more often form round or dome-shaped colonies. This yellow to yellow-green or even tan or gray coral is pebbly and lumpy and looks like an Osage orange. Finger coral, a close relative of mustard hill coral, and rose coral are common corals on patch reefs as well as in seagrass meadows.

As time goes by, some corals flourish and others perish. The growth and death processes slowly build patterns of relief: crevices and ledges appear; rubble fields, scattered bits and pieces of dead coral, are populated by bubble and disk seaweeds; and coralline algae in shades of red and pinkish gray overgrow the hard limestone substrates.

These beautiful underwater gardens are highlighted by swaying soft corals, lovely, plantlike corals that may be shaped like fans, feathery branched colonies, or singular, cylindrical rods. Some are purple, red, or yellow, and others are green, brown, or cream. Soft corals, also known as gorgonians or octocorals, lack the hard, stony calcium carbonate skeleton typical of reef-building corals. They sway back and forth in the restless seas because their skeletons are flexible. Their internal skeletons vary from group to group. Some consist of calcareous, needle-shaped rods called spicules that form a structural network. Other soft corals, such as sea fans, have an internal horny or woodlike skeleton. The horny material, gorgonin, is similar to collagen, the fibrous elastic material that makes up our connective tissues. Several

Smooth Star Coral (4–18")
Solenastrea bournoni

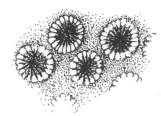

Lesser Star Coral (4–12")
Siderastrea radians

Corky Sea Fingers (to 2')
Briareum asbestinum

Rough Sea Plume (to 2')
Muriceopsis flavida

DETAILS OF HARD CORAL CORALLITES AND SOFT CORAL CALYCES

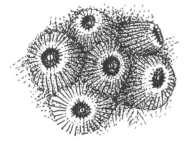

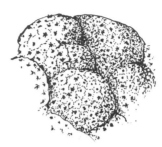

Great Star Coral (to 8')
Monastrea cavernosa

Mustard Hill Coral (to 2')
Porites astreoides

Black Sea Rod (to 2')
Plexaura homomalla

Swollen Knob
Candelabrum (to 1')
Eunicea mammosa

compounds have been isolated from soft corals that appear to have beneficial medicinal properties. Some soft corals also manufacture a chemical (terpene) that is unpalatable and may deter fish from preying on them.

Corky sea fingers, *Briareum asbestinum*, usually forms colonies of unbranched tubular or cylindrical rods that arise from an encrustation. The very large polyps are purplish brown to grayish brown, and when extended, they give the colony a bushy or hairy look. Corky sea fingers also grow as encrustations that sprawl over other soft corals.

Black sea rods, *Plexaura homomalla*, are very common, bushy, 2- to 3-feet-tall, flattened, plantlike soft corals that are often seen on patch reefs growing in clumps and also in adjacent seagrass meadows. The polyps are light brown to yellowish on brown to blackish stalks. There are two forms of this species: one grows in shallow waters, where patch reefs are located, and is rather thick branched; the other grows in deeper waters and is slenderer and taller.

Swollen knob candelabrum, *Eunicea mammosa*, is one of several species of rough-branched soft corals, most of which are difficult for anyone but experts to identify to species. Swollen knob candelabrum soft corals, however, are relatively easy to identify because of the color and shape of their polyp apertures (calyces). The calyces are swollen and protruding tubelike bumps that are tightly grouped along the stout stalks. The stalks typically branch off a main stem into a candelabrum-shaped growth form. The distinctive swollen knobs are yellowish green to golden brown.

The rough sea plume, *Muriceopsis flavida*, forms tall, feathery, bushy, purplish gray clusters. Small, round branchlets grow from all sides of the main branches, with the calyces randomly scattered over the branches and branchlets. The random growth

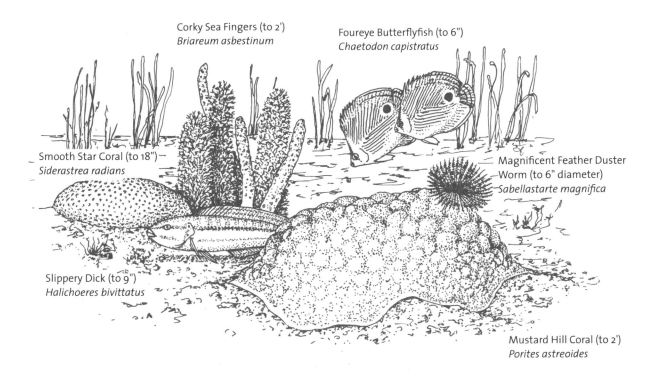

Corky Sea Fingers (to 2')
Briareum asbestinum

Foureye Butterflyfish (to 6")
Chaetodon capistratus

Smooth Star Coral (to 18")
Siderastrea radians

Magnificent Feather Duster
Worm (to 6" diameter)
Sabellastarte magnifica

Slippery Dick (to 9")
Halichoeres bivittatus

Mustard Hill Coral (to 2')
Porites astreoides

pattern of the rough sea plume's calyces easily distinguishes it from a similar-looking species, the purple sea plume, whose calyces are set in distinct rows or bands.

Fire corals are serious stingers and, similar to their relatives the dangerous Portuguese man-of-war, can instantaneously unleash a fiery barrage of nematocysts if one simply brushes against them. Their stings are uncomfortable but short-lived and, thankfully, no threat to life. Fire corals are not true corals but are actually hard, calcareous colonies of hydroids that are placed in the class Hydrozoa. Most fire corals are tan to mustard to golden brown with flattened blades, crenulations, or cylindrical branches and are usually tipped in white.

Fire corals build stony fortresses that grow over gorgonians and encrust coral rubble. There are two species that differ only in the shape of their solid skele-

tons. The first species, known simply as fire coral, *Millepora alcicornis*, forms fingerlike branches; the second species, bladed fire coral, *Millepora complanata*, constructs flattened, bladelike branches. There is some disagreement among experts about how many species of fire coral there are. Some scientists believe that there is only one species, with three forms or variations; others think that there are three species, including the massive box fire coral, *Millepora squarrosa*. However, recent research on fire corals strongly suggests that there are only two species, fire coral and bladed fire coral, and three forms.

The Giant Caribbean Anemone

Like hard corals and soft corals, anemones are in the class Anthozoa within the phylum Cnidaria.

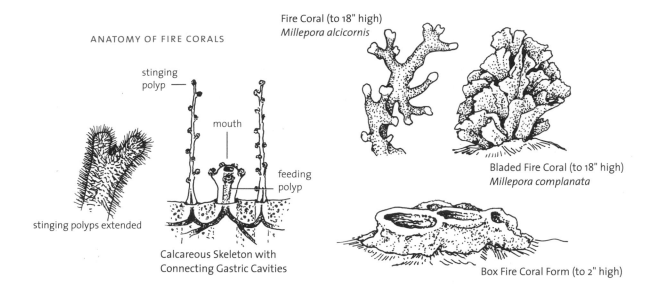

ANATOMY OF FIRE CORALS

stinging polyp

mouth

feeding polyp

stinging polyps extended

Calcareous Skeleton with
Connecting Gastric Cavities

Fire Coral (to 18" high)
Millepora alcicornis

Bladed Fire Coral (to 18" high)
Millepora complanata

Box Fire Coral Form (to 2" high)

The giant Caribbean anemone, *Condylactis gigantea*, is the most stunningly beautiful anemone in Inner Coast waters; it is also the largest. This is a common anemone that thrives in shallow seagrass meadows, on patch reefs, and on offshore coral reefs. However, they are not always apparent, as they tend to attach in crevices or take refuge under a shelf within the reef. As you snorkel over a patch reef, you may catch a glimpse of waving fingers gracefully streaming in the currents, seemingly beckoning you to take a closer look.

Giant Caribbean anemones are certainly worth a closer look, as they are the jewels within these sea gardens. There is considerable variation in the color of these giant anemones, but they are easily separated from other anemone species in the area. They may have as many as 100 6-inch tapering tentacles, each with a swollen, rounded tip. The tips of the tentacles seem to have been dipped in an artist's paint pot; they may be rose colored or lavender or green or yellow, or they may be the color of the tentacle, which is usually white or greenish white. Giant Caribbean

anemones are not permanently fixed to the hard substrate; in fact, they are quite mobile as they search for a more favorable position from which to hide or feed. When these anemones are threatened, they contract and withdraw their tentacles within their cavity, greatly reducing their size and presence. Of course, like all cnidarians, they are equipped with nematocysts; those toxic harpoons fend off predators as well as capture small animals for food.

Giant Caribbean anemones also bear close inspection because of the fishes and cleaner shrimps that set up shop in the tangles of their tentacles.

Worms

There are hordes of worms that crawl over coral communities, just as they do on oyster reefs, and many of them have been described in previous chapters. There are also some worms that are inhabitants of coral communities and are so very beautiful that they rival the alluring giant Caribbean anemone. These worms are separated into two groups: the family Serpulidae, whose members construct hard, calcareous tubes, and the family Sabellidae, whose members build tough, flexible, leathery, or parchmentlike tubes.

These worms are collectively called fan worms or feather duster worms because of their featherlike appendages, radioles, which act both as gills that extract oxygen from the water and as specialized tentacles that capture planktonic organisms. The radioles form a crown, which is extremely sensitive to the slightest changes in current movement and direction. In response to a sudden shadow, perhaps cast by a passing fish or a snorkeler, it will instantly vanish within its tube. The tube is than capped off by an operculum attached to a long stalk that originates within the tube.

Typical of most marine organisms, these beautiful feather duster worms start life out as tiny, feebly swimming larvae, which are carried by currents to a place where they can settle and develop into sedentary adult worms. Feather duster larvae of various species have particular, but little understood, preferences for certain species of corals. Regardless of the species of coral, the worm larvae settle down on the living tissue of the hard coral, and over time the coral polyps overgrow the worm tubes and incorporate them as permanent residents.

The star feather worm, or star horseshoe worm, *Pomatostegus stellatus*, a serpulid, has a folded horseshoe- or U-shaped crown that is usually about 1 to 1 1/2 inches high and a calcareous tube about 4 inches long. The operculum, which is attached to a thick stalk, has a spiny border that resembles a star. The radioles are often alternately banded with combinations of yellow and orange, dark gray and white, or maroon and white.

The Christmas tree worm, *Spirobranchus giganteus*, also a serpulid, has two spiral, cone-shaped crowns arising from its hard, limy tube. The brown, orange, maroon, or white crowns are about 1 to 1

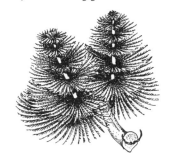

Christmas Tree Worm (crowns to 1 1/2" high)
Spirobranchus giganteus

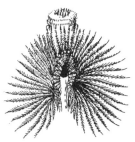

Star Feather Worm
(crown to 1 1/2" high)
Pomatostegus stellatus

1/2 inches high, and the tube is 4 inches long. A calcareous operculum is positioned between the twin radioles.

The magnificent feather duster worm, *Sabellastarte magnifica*, is the largest of the Florida and Caribbean feather duster worms. This worm belongs to the Sabellidae family and constructs a soft, leathery, 4- to 5-inch tube rather than a calcareous tube. Compared to those of the other feather duster worms of Florida, the crown of the magnificent feather duster worm is immense. It measures 3 to 6 inches in diameter and is arranged like two upside-down umbrellas, one above the other. The coronal head is banded in a variety of colors, ranging from brown and reddish brown to purplish, gold, tan, and white.

Echinoderms

Echinoderms, such as sea stars and sea urchins, are spiny animals on the prowl; they move slowly and deliberately, but move they do. Some species move in from deeper waters or nearby coral reefs to feed on sea grasses and mollusks; other species remain close to patch reefs and crawl over coral rubble and underneath ledges to find their food.

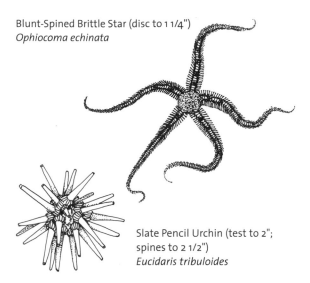

Blunt-Spined Brittle Star (disc to 1 1/4")
Ophiocoma echinata

Slate Pencil Urchin (test to 2";
spines to 2 1/2")
Eucidaris tribuloides

The blunt-spined brittle star, *Ophiocoma echinata*, is one of the larger brittle stars in Florida and Caribbean waters. Their arms, almost 6 inches long, are covered with numerous blunt spines. They are usually the same color as the granule-covered central disk, which may be mottled with black, brown, or gray; the five arms are usually marked with a light stripe running from the disk to the tip of each arm. These very abundant brittle stars, probably the most abundant in the region, usually remain sheltered under rubble, rocks, and ledges and even in the cavities of large sponges. They are common and abundant in turtle grass beds, under rubble on patch reefs, and in the quiet, shallow waters among red mangroves.

The slate pencil urchin, *Eucidaris tribuloides*, is an unmistakable urchin, with its few thick, blunt spines that give it the appearance of a World War II ocean mine. Its test is light to dark reddish brown, often marked with white flecks. The diameter of these urchins, including their spines, is about 5 inches. Their spines are often entangled with filamentous algae and encrusted with coralline algae and sponges. They forage for algae, bryozoans, small snails, and turtle grass on patch reefs and turtle grass beds.

The long-spined black sea urchin, *Diadema antillarum*, is as recognizable as the slate pencil urchin even though they are complete opposites. The long-spined black sea urchin has 12- to 16-inch, very thin, hollow, brittle spines with an overall diameter that may exceed 20 inches. Their spines are usually black, but some individuals have whitish or gray spines, and young long-spined sea urchins have black and white banded spines. The spines of these urchins are highly mobile and are attached to the test with a ball and socket–like arrangement. If a passing fish or swimmer casts a shadow over the long-spined urchin, it can immediately become menacing by waving its spines back and forth or by pointing its spines toward the threat. The sharply pointed, and barbed, spines can easily penetrate the skin of an unwary swimmer, and when they do, the spines break off, releasing a toxin that can cause a severe burning irritation that lasts for several hours. The spine tips will eventually be absorbed by the body with no further ill effects.

The long-spined black sea urchin is a very abundant and gregarious species. At night, these urchins emerge from their daytime hiding places and migrate across the grass flats to graze until dawn on algal turf and turtle grass, often creating the characteristic halos seen in seagrass meadows. Sometimes there are groups of these urchins clumped together in turtle grass beds and nearby patch reefs. Apparently they seek out patch reefs as places to hide from predators such as toadfishes, triggerfishes, grunts, and helmet shell snails. In turn, small fishes and shrimps seek shelter among the urchins' long, waving spines. It is quite common to see a cloud of small white mysid shrimps dancing up and down the long spines, along with young grunts, wrasses, and butterflyfishes. Those very abundant little mysid shrimps are collectively called krill and are a favorite food of baleen whales.

Long-spined black sea urchins are commonly seen in a number of habitats, including patch reefs and larger offshore coral reefs, seagrass beds, sandy flats, and mangroves.

Crustaceans

Patch reefs provide hiding places for lurking crabs, several species of cleaner shrimps and mysid shrimps, and spiny lobsters. Small mud crabs hide in empty shells, and nimble spray crabs, with carapaces of only 1 inch or so long, cling to the undersides of rocks and under long-spined black sea urchins. Occasionally a stone crab will scramble out of its muddy burrow in search of food. Menacing and agile blue crabs skulk along the bottom or swim over a patch reef, looking for a mate and always for food.

Patch reefs are favorite haunts of the Caribbean spiny lobster, *Panulirus argus*, also known as Florida spiny lobster and locally as crawfish or bugs. Spiny lobsters lack the massive claws of their Maine cousins, but they are more agile and are usually able to elude predators by snapping their muscular abdomens, or "tails," and rapidly swimming away to safety. Spiny lobsters are named for their forward-projecting, thornlike spines that protect them from predators. Typical of crustaceans, they have two pairs of antennae: the first pair is long and heavily spined, and the second pair, called antennules, is used to sense smells and movement. Spiny lobsters hide during daylight hours in crevices or under ledges on the patch reef, but their long antennae waving back and forth often give their hiding place away. Spiny lobsters are active feeders and emerge after dark to feed on a variety of mollusks, urchins, crabs, carrion, and seagrasses. Large fishes such as grouper, sharks, and moray eels prey on them.

These colorfully patterned lobsters are usually dark orange but can vary from whitish to greenish;

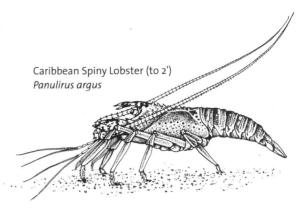

Caribbean Spiny Lobster (to 2')
Panulirus argus

their bodies are striped with brown and gray; and their abdomens are decorated with yellow or cream-colored spots. Spiny lobsters mate in late spring through summer; the female carries the cluster of fertilized eggs on the underside of her abdomen, and when they hatch, thousands of larvae called phyllosomes are carried by the currents to shallow seagrass and seaweed beds. A second-stage larva called a puerulus is a transitional stage between the phyllosome and the juvenile lobster. Spiny lobsters grow fairly rapidly and reach legal harvesting size in about two years.

Spiny lobsters make remarkable yearly mass migrations from the shallows to deeper waters when the water turns cool in autumn. They congregate by the dozens, line up in single formation, and maintain contact with one another with their antennules, much like a line of elephants marching along trunk to tail. Spiny lobsters are able to navigate with a highly developed internal magnetic compass, which allows them to establish their position and home to a specific location.

Caribbean spiny lobsters are an important commercial and sport species; there is a limited sport season in July and a commercial season from early August through March. The average annual recreational harvest exceeds 1 million pounds, and the commercial harvest of spiny lobsters is the most valuable fishery in Florida.

The yellowline arrow crab, *Stenorhynchus seticornis*, is a spindly, delicate crab that resembles a daddy longlegs. This elegant little crab is one of the smallest of the spider crabs. It has a golden brown or cream-colored body lined with brown, black, or iridescent blue markings and a carapace about 1/2 inch wide and 2 1/2 inches long. Its snout, really the rostrum, is drawn out into a pointed cone or arrow shape. Its tiny, elongated claws are often tinged with violet or blue. Its long, slender legs are more than three times the length of its body.

Yellowline arrow crabs are relatively abundant in many different habitats, but they are nocturnal feeders, so they are often not seen during daylight hours. They feed on bits of organic detritus and occasionally on small worms. These little crabs scramble over wharf pilings, on coral rubble and shell hash, and hide in patch reef crevices and in sponges, anemones, and sea fans. They range from North Carolina to Florida and the Caribbean.

Cleaner shrimps such as the peppermint shrimp (see chapter 5) are specialized little crustaceans that seem to have a symbiotic relationship with fishes that are "itching" to have their ectoparasites removed from their skin and even their mouths. Cleaner shrimps set up cleaning stations similar to those of some cleaner fishes, such as damsel-

Yellowline Arrow Crab (carapace to 2 1/4")
Stenorhynchus seticornis

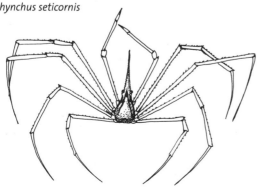

fishes and wrasses. Cleaner shrimps generally have extremely long, usually white, wispy antennae that they characteristically wave back and forth to advertise that they are open for business. They will pick off ectoparasites, dead skin, and other debris from passing fishes. Cleaner shrimps tend to be boldly colored and marked.

The banded coral shrimp, *Stenopus hispidus*, is an example of a boldly colored and marked cleaner shrimp. It has a red and white banded body and claws and two pairs of long, white antennae. The third pair of legs bears greatly enlarged claws. The banded coral shrimp, also called banded shrimp and barber-pole shrimp, is one of the largest cleaning shrimp known, although it is still rather small, only about 2 inches long. The banded coral shrimp usually sets up its cleaning station near a sponge or in a darkened recess on a patch reef, where it waits and waves for a customer. This species is widely distributed throughout the Pacific and Atlantic oceans.

The scarlet-striped cleaning shrimp, *Lysmata grabhami*, is a close relative of the peppermint shrimp, and, like the banded coral shrimp, it is very distinctive. This little shrimp, only about 2 inches long, boasts broad scarlet bands separated by a white stripe that extend to the tail with golden yellow to cream sides and belly. It also has very long, hairlike white antennae. This species is found only in South Florida and the Caribbean.

Fishes

Other than possibly damselfishes, squirrelfishes, snappers, grunts, and groupers, there are very few fishes that stay within large reefs and patch reefs. Most other species of fishes, such as barracudas and trumpetfishes, hover over the reefs; still other fishes cruise through the reefs foraging for food.

The water column over a patch reef is often popu-

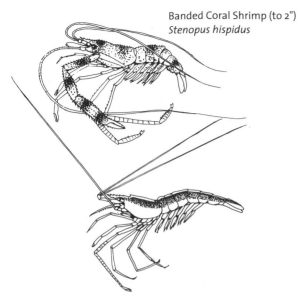

Banded Coral Shrimp (to 2")
Stenopus hispidus

Scarlet-Striped Cleaning Shrimp (to 2 1/2")
Lysmata grabhami

lated with a number of apex predators, such as great barracudas and the occasional blacktip shark or reef shark, but more often the water fairly sparkles with jewel-like blue tangs and ever-curious yellowtail snappers. Closer to the bottom, there are often small schools of French grunts, all pointing in the same direction and drifting with the roll of the sea. Little tomtates pick at small invertebrates and algae on the reef floor, and a chartreuse and blue striped queen triggerfish nearby is nose-down, searching for its favorite quarry, a sea urchin. Scrawled cowfish and the larger trunkfish slowly scull along the bottom with the aid of their whirring pectoral fins and pass over the vague form of a peacock flounder buried in the sand adjacent to the patch reef.

The trumpetfish, *Aulostomus maculatus*, has a long, thin, tubular body and a long, tubular, slightly upturned snout equipped with small jaws and minute teeth. Its unusual dorsal fins are made up of a series of unconnected conical spines just forward of

a triangle-shaped soft-rayed dorsal fin balanced by an anal fin of approximately the same shape and size. The trumpetfish is unmistakable in its appearance and behavior. It usually hovers, often among a group of soft coral, with its head down, drifting back and forth with the water's surge and seeming to be just another sea rod or sea whip. Trumpetfish are masters of camouflage because they can swiftly change their color from their usual brownish red to yellow or green or blue. They patiently stalk their prey, usually small fishes or shrimps, by lying in wait for them to come into range or by slowly, almost imperceptibly, gliding head-down until they near their meal and then suctioning in their unwary prey with a powerful vacuum formed by the tubular snout.

The blue tang, *Acanthurus coeruleus*, has a compressed, almost circular, deep blue to deep purplish body. It has a sharp yellow spine that fits into a groove at the base of the tail; the scientific name of this fish means "a blue fish with a thorny tail." The young of blue tangs are a brilliant yellow, and half-grown blue tangs are often seen with a blue body and a yellow tail. Blue tangs feed on filamentous algae growing on the rocks, but unlike their close relatives doctor and surgeon fishes, which have thick-walled, grinding stomachs, they usually avoid scraping algae off limestone because they cannot process quantities of sand and calcareous material with their thin-walled stomachs. At night, blue tangs find shelter from predators such as bar jacks, groupers, and mackerels in reef crevices and recesses. But during the day, they "fly" through the water, usually about halfway from the bottom. Blue tangs are very active fish that suddenly come into view and mill around, usually in loose aggregations of twenty or so, and then suddenly disappear. For some reason unknown to us, blue tangs frequently gather, it seems, by the hundreds and will head in one direction and then another, usually joined by a few doctor and surgeon

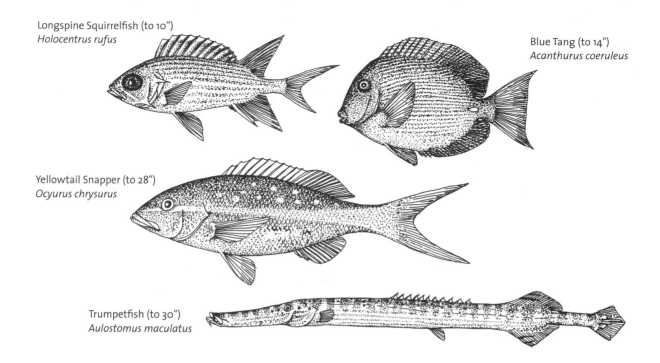

Longspine Squirrelfish (to 10")
Holocentrus rufus

Blue Tang (to 14")
Acanthurus coeruleus

Yellowtail Snapper (to 28")
Ocyurus chrysurus

Trumpetfish (to 30")
Aulostomus maculatus

fishes as well as trumpetfishes. They seem to be in a frenzy, but in an instant their high energy charge dissipates, and they break up into smaller groups and peacefully swim away to feed.

The yellowtail snapper, *Ocyurus chrysurus*, is another colorful fish of the midwater column that often loosely intermixes with blue tangs. Yellowtail snappers are streamlined fishes with deeply forked tails that do not resemble most other snappers, with their typical blocky bodies and square or only slightly forked tails. In addition, most other snapper species are solitary or swim in small schools near the bottom. Not so with the playful and curious yellowtail snapper. These elongated, silvery to bluish white fish with a yellow midline stripe marked with pale spots on the upper body and a yellow tail, mill about in midwater in small groups and are not shy about approaching a snorkeler. Yellowtail snappers are a pop-

ular game fish and commercial species and are excellent to eat. They feed on crabs and shrimps, squids, worms, and other fishes and in turn are preyed on by barracudas, sharks, jacks, and groupers.

Down closer to the floor of the patch reef, a bright reddish orange longspine squirrelfish, *Holocentrus rufus*, drifts in the shadow of a coral ledge overhang. This somewhat solitary fish has red and silvery stripes and white splotches along its slender, rather oblong body. The top of its head is bright red; the tips of its dorsal fin are marked with white; and its tail is deeply forked. Squirrelfish are primarily nocturnal, which accounts for their very large eyes. As light falls, longspine squirrelfish leave the safety of their hiding places along the edges of the patch reef and move out into adjoining seagrass beds and sandy areas, where they feed on shrimps and other invertebrates.

The foureye butterflyfish, *Chaetodon capistratus*, is a 6-inch-long, circular fish with characteristic black spots edged in white; the extra "eyes" are placed on the sides of its body, close to the base of its tail. The body is silver-gray with unusual lines that radiate diagonally from the midline toward the dorsal and ventral fins; a black, vertical bar also runs through its eyes. The combination of the black bar running through its eyes and the black spots near the tail, the false eyes, may serve to confuse predators into striking the wrong end. Young foureye butterflyfish have two pairs of spots near the tail. These little, enticing fish generally travel in pairs and actively glide among the coral and sponges and nearby grass beds during the day. Their small, projected mouths enable them to poke in small crevices and holes and feed on worms, tunicates, and other small invertebrates.

The yellowtail damselfish, *Microspathodon chrysurus*, is a small but chunky, dusky brown to dark grayish blue fish with a yellow to orangish tail. The juveniles, on the other hand, are jewel-like, with bright blue, almost iridescent spots sprinkled over a dark blue body; in fact they are often referred to as jewelfish. Adult yellowtail damselfish are often seen along the top of the reefs where they are rather territorial and make feeble efforts to protect their home turf while the young seek shelter among the blades of fire coral. Yellowtail damselfish feed on algae and organic detritus and occasionally on coral polyps and other invertebrates. The juveniles sometimes act as cleaner fish and pick parasites off larger fishes.

Wrasses are a group of fishes that live in many different habitats and environments, from temperate to tropical waters. There are approximately 600 species of wrasses, ranging in size from the 3-inch dwarf wrasse to the 300-pound humpback wrasse of the Indo-Pacific. Regardless of their size, wrasses share a number of characteristics: Most wrasses are carnivorous and have strong, projecting canine teeth and thick lips. Most species are active during the daytime, and they swim by flapping their short, stubby pectoral fins in a rowing fashion called labriform swimming. They also have long and continuous dorsal and anal fins and a wide tail base (the caudal peduncle). Some male wrasse species gather in great numbers to form communal courtship mating aggregations called leks. Reproduction and sexuality in wrasses and parrot fishes, their close relatives, can be quite complicated. For example, certain males within a species are neither particularly boldly colored nor very large and engage in leks, while other males within the same species become supermales that spawn in pairs and are much more colorful and larger than the males that engage in group spawning. Wrasses and parrot fishes sometimes also undergo sex reversal and change from females to supermales. Some wrasses, such as the slippery dick, bury in sand and coral rubble during certain times in the life cycle.

The slender, cigar-shaped fish with the improbable name of slippery dick, *Halichoeres bivittatus*, is one of the many wrasses. Slippery dicks are usually about 5–6 inches long, but they may occasionally grow to about 9 inches. They have several color phases and may be greenish along their backs and light greenish or even yellow or creamy white on their sides. They are marked with two narrow brown to purplish or black stripes. The top stripe runs from the snout through the eye to the base of the tail; the bottom stripe is usually paler and shorter. Slippery dicks are very common on reefs and in adjoining sandy areas of grass beds, where they feed on crabs, sea urchins, worms, and snails.

The stoplight parrot fish, *Sparisoma viride*, is one of those species of parrot fishes that, in spite of the various color phases displayed, is rather easy to iden-

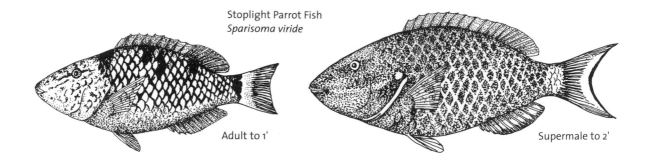

Stoplight Parrot Fish
Sparisoma viride

Adult to 1'

Supermale to 2'

tify because of its crescent-shaped tail marked with a band of white, cream, or yellow. Stoplight parrot fishes have three color phases and sizes: juveniles, young adults, and supermales.

The juveniles are not as large as the adults, which can grow to a length of 2 feet. They are marked with rows of prominent white spots on a dark brownish red body; the base of the tail is marked with a white band.

Young adults, the phase most often seen on the reef, are a swimming mosaic of black, white, and red. Some of the large scales along their flanks are black and some are white; their heads are grayish white marked with black, spidery streaks. Their bellies are brick red, and the trailing edges of their tails are marked with a curved, creamy-white band and a white bar across the base.

Supermales are aquamarine blue with some scales along their sides outlined in pinkish violet. The dorsal fin is violet; the top of the head has splotches of grayish violet; and a grayish violet stripe runs from the corner of the mouth to just beyond the eye. Supermales are also marked with a bright yellow spot on the edges of their gill covers, and, of course, the signature marking of the stoplight parrot fish is the yellow bar at the base of the tail and the yellow marking on the edge of the tail. Look for these abundant parrot fish nibbling on coral heads and scraping algae off plants and rocks.

Worm Rocks

Worm rocks, worm reefs, sabellariid worm rocks, and sand castle colonies are all names for unique reefs built by generations upon generations of colonial, barely 2-inch-high reef-building tube worms, *Phragmatopoma lapidosa*, also known as sand tube worms and honeycomb worms. Reef-building tube worms are members of the Sabellariidae family that construct thick-walled sand and shell fragment tubes, in contrast to the feather duster worms of the Sabellidae family, which construct tough, membranous tubes that sometimes have mud, sand, or shell fragments adhering to them. As noted above, there are also some worms of the family Serpulidae that construct hard, calcareous tubes in colonies that may be so large that they become economic pests by fouling the bottoms of boats or clogging intake pipes.

Reef-building tube worms are complex and highly organized polychaetes that have elongated, segmented, cylindrical bodies that are divided into four distinct parts: The head is equipped with a complicated opercular disk that serves as a trapdoor or stopper that seals the tube off when the worm retracts within. The operculum also has an array of specialized circular setae that manipulate sand grains cemented into the tube. The head also has two rows

of feeding tentacles, along with a horseshoe-shaped organ that secretes a proteinaceous adhesive for tube construction. The next section behind the head is the parathoracic region, which consists of three segments with branched, fleshy, lateral flaps and a pair of gills. The abdominal region is made up of about thirty-two segments, each bearing feetlike parapodia and numerous hooked setae that attach the body to the inner tube wall. The final section is the cylindrical caudal region, which includes the anus.

Reef-building tube worms have a peculiar method of feeding. They lie on their backs, the dorsum, and extend upward into their tubes. The specialized ciliated tentacles attached to the operculum reach out into the water, and the cilia begin their rhythmic beating, creating a current that draws suspended organic matter and planktonic organisms toward their mouths. Sand and bits of shell fragments are also drawn in, but rather than being ingested, the inorganic material is passed along to the building organ by clawlike setae, where it is mixed with a gooey protein that binds the particles into material used for building the millions of tubes that are incorporated into the worm rock.

Reef-building tube worms often build small lumps of tubes on pilings and other hard surfaces around inlets where the swirling waters bring in loads of silt and shell fragments necessary for the construction of their honeycombed homes. But it is in the swash zone of the subtropical waters along Florida's east coast, from Cape Canaveral to Biscayne Bay, that worm rocks reach their zenith. The roiling waters along the coast provide a constant source of building materials to reef-building tube worms, and in return, the worms build extensive ecosystems that play a major role in stabilizing beaches by trapping sediment and shell fragments. These large reefs—some are as wide as 1/2 mile and 2 or 3 miles long—are quite analogous to oyster reefs and patch reefs. The major players, oysters, coral polyps, and reef-building tube worms, perform a similar role: their larvae settle down and mature into adults while building stable live bottoms that attract a multitude of diverse organisms, from plants and invertebrates to a variety of vertebrates, ranging from sea turtles to a seemingly endless variety of fishes, dolphins, and even, in some instances, birds.

Worm rocks are usually seen in the intertidal zone and are frequently awash during low water, but they also occur subtidally in water depths of 6 feet or

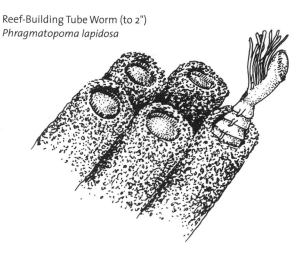

Reef-Building Tube Worm (to 2")
Phragmatopoma lapidosa

more. The distribution of reef-building tube worms is limited to about the latitude of Cape Canaveral, as the worms cannot survive in the cooler waters north of the Cape. The southern distribution of the worm is in the area of Key Biscayne in southern Dade County; the water temperatures are certainly adequate, but as the Florida coast curves to the southwest, the high-energy swash zone diminishes, and so do the reef-building tube worms.

The high-energy swash zone is a turbulent, highly unstable environment and accordingly is not usually highly populated with plants, invertebrates, or fishes. There are always a few wandering crabs and sometimes millions of colorful coquina clams and a few other mollusks and some species of fishes, such as pompanos, palometas, and several species of roving, rapacious jacks that suddenly appear and vanish just as quickly. However, when worm rocks are established in the shallows along the beach, many invertebrates as well as a few species of seaweeds take up residence in the crevices and ledges created by these small but abundant worms. Some invertebrates, such as ribbed barnacles and a number of different sponges, simply use the reef as a place of settlement.

Crustaceans

ISOPODS AND AMPHIPODS

There are two isopod species, *Paradella dianae* and *Sphaeroma walkeri*, that are quite abundant on worm rocks, where they apparently graze on bacteria film, algae, and organic detritus. There are no common names for these two species, so we have taken the liberty of naming them for simplicity's sake. We will call *Paradella dianae* Diane's paradella and *Sphaeroma walkeri* Walker's marine pill bug. Some members of this family (Sphaeromatidae) have been known to bore into wood pilings and destroy them (such as the gribble that is discussed in chapter 5), but most of the species in this family are grazers rather than borers. Most sphaeromatid isopods are similar in shape: they are rather wide bodied and flattened dorsally and ventrally. Many species can roll up into a tight, spiny ball, like their terrestrial cousins the pill bugs, and they are typically strong swimmers. Both species are considered invasive and have been introduced, probably by ships, to many parts of the world.

Diane's paradella is only about 1/5 inch long and is yellowish gray. The females brood their fertilized eggs in internal pouches on the undersides of their bodies, and when the young have reached a certain stage of growth, they are released to the surrounding water.

Walker's marine pill bug grows to almost 1/2 inch long. The females brood their embryos externally on modified swimmerets. Both Walker's marine pill bug and Diane's paradella are extremely abundant on worm rocks. They are also found within the fouling community on the prop roots of red mangroves.

There are also a number of amphipods that sprawl, dig, and busily forage for small bits of organic material and algae. Most of the amphipod species found in and around worm rocks are also found in many

Diane's Paradella (to 1/5")
Paradella dianae

Walker's Marine Pill Bug (to 1/2")
Sphaeroma walkeri

other habitats: among fouling organisms, under mats of algae and stones, and around rock jetties and pilings. There is some confusion among experts as to the correct identity of some of these amphipods, and so as not to exacerbate the taxonomic issues, we will not assign scientific names or describe individuals but simply make the reader aware that amphipods form a vital community within the worm rock environment.

SHRIMPS AND CRABS

Snapping shrimps, those curious little shrimps with one large claw, often compared to a boxing glove, and a body that is usually shorter than the length of your small finger, are some of the most numerous animals living in worm rocks, in coral reefs, and particularly in sponges. They are seldom seen, but the crackling clamor of their oversized claws can be easily heard when you snorkel over a reef. Scientists have long thought that snapping shrimps, sometimes called pistol shrimps, created their cacophonous reports by banging their armor-plated claws together, but that is not so. A team of researchers from the Netherlands reported in September 2000 on the noisemaking mechanics of these little shrimps because the clatter that they create can interfere with sonar signals that are important to underwater military and scientific

"listening posts." They discovered that the shrimps' large claw creates a bubble! When a snapping shrimp cocks its claw and snaps it shut, it violently squeezes out a bubble, called a cavitation bubble, which explodes when it is jetted out from the claw and stuns its prey. The din set up by these exploding bubbles is probably also used as a form of communication between these numerous, secretive shrimp.

The speckled snapping shrimp, *Synalpheus fritzmulleri*, has a creamy, almost colorless, 3/4-inch-long body marked with tiny red spots. It has two greenish claws: one large one, the "snapper," and a smaller claw. Speckled snapping shrimp are very abundant in worm rocks and in the canals of sponges. They are also found in dead mollusk shells, in coral rubble, and in pitted and eroded limestone rocks. They have even been found living under the overlapping scutes of hawksbill turtles. Speckled snapping shrimp range from North Carolina to Florida, along the rim of the Gulf of Mexico, and down the Atlantic coast of South America.

Several small species of crabs are closely associated with worm rocks, where they live in the crevices and cavelike holes. There are also larger crabs, such as the predacious and abundant blue crab and the mottled shore crab, that forage for food in and around the worm rocks.

The wormreef porcelain crab, *Pachycheles monilifer*, is a tiny crab that belongs to the family Porcellanidae, whose members are not considered true

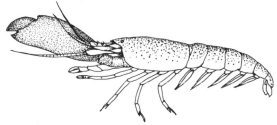

Speckled Snapping Shrimp (to 3/4")
Synalpheus fritzmulleri

crabs by carcinologists (crustacean experts). Crabs in this family superficially resemble true crabs, but there are some specific differences that separate them. True crabs have four pairs of walking legs and short antennae, whereas porcellanid crabs have long antennae and three pair of legs. Actually, they do have a fourth pair of legs, but they are greatly reduced in size and hidden under the carapace. Porcellanid crabs also have unusually large claws compared to the size of their bodies. These little crabs are usually no more than 1/4 inch wide and are flattened dorsoventrally, which allows them to slip into very narrow crevices and under rocks. Wormreef porcelain crabs feed on worms, sponges, small crustaceans, and algae.

There are three other small crabs that are closely associated with worm rocks. They belong to the mud crab family, Xanthidae, which is the group of crabs found so abundantly in oyster reefs.

Wormreef Porcelain Crab
(carapace to 1/4" wide)
Pachycheles monilifer

Short Spined Hairy Crab
(carapace to 1/2" wide)
Pilumnus dasypodus

Strongtooth Mud Crab
(carapace to 1/2" wide)
Panopeus bermudensis

The short-spined hairy crab, *Pilumnus dasypodus*, has a carapace that is sparsely covered with fine hairs. Its brownish red carapace is slightly wider than long and only about 1/2 inch wide. Its brownish red claws are heavy, with one claw larger than the other, and its four pairs of walking legs are hairy. Short-spined hairy crabs have essentially the same diet as wormreef porcelain crabs.

The strongtooth mud crab, *Panopeus bermudensis*, is a small crab with a brownish red carapace no wider than 1/2 inch. It has grayish claws with white fingertips. The four teeth along the anterior margin of the carapace are sharp and strong. Strongtooth mud crabs feed on worms, sponges, mollusks, crustaceans, seagrasses, and algae. They are also found in the mud around the prop roots of red mangroves.

The Cuban stone crab, *Menippe nodifrons*, is only about half the size of the famous and very delicious Florida stone crab and, therefore, has no commercial value. The diminutive Cuban stone crab has a rougher, redder carapace with narrower lateral lobes than its larger cousin. Cuban stone crabs also feed on other crustaceans, mollusks, sponges, worms, and a small amount of algae.

Fishes

Occasionally a sand or bull shark will meander through the shallows near the beach to pick up a delicacy or two, and the always unpredictable wolf packs of bluefish will sweep by and devour almost anything in sight, but mostly the fish in the swash zone near worm rocks are nibblers or sit-and-wait predators.

The hairy blenny, *Labrisomus nuchipinnis*, is an example of a carnivorous, bottom-dwelling, sit-and-wait predator. Typical of its family, it has an elongated, flexible body with long dorsal and anal fins. The hairy blenny can grow to a length of 9 inches, which makes it one of the largest blennies along the Florida coast and the Caribbean. It lives in a number of habitats, including worm rocks, rocky sand bottoms, and grass beds. It usually lurks in small holes and crevices in worm rocks, and when a small fish or shrimp happens by, the hairy blenny, with a fluid suddenness, engulfs its prey and settles down in its lair to sit and wait once again.

Male hairy blennies are usually unremarkably dark colored, with some mottling of various colors, but during their spawning season the males become highly visible; they turn yellowish green with red cheeks and bellies and are often marked with alternating gray and black bars on their sides. They can change their colors instantly and fade into the background when threatened.

There are a number of small to medium-size fishes that are not usually found in the high-energy swash zone, but worm rocks attract them. They are mostly nibblers, such as the sergeant major and porkfish, that eat a broad variety of plants and animals.

The spottail pinfish, *Diplodus holbrooki*, is a deep-bodied, silvery fish with a conspicuous black spot or saddle that almost encircles the base of its tail. Spottail pinfish may have faint, dusky gray bars on their sides at times. Similar to their close relative the pinfish, they have strong, protruding, incisor-like teeth, which they use to nip and crush. Young juveniles feed on the planktonic larvae of many species, but as they grow older, they feed on barnacles,

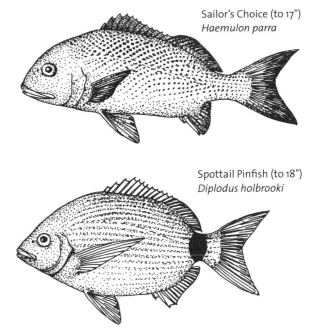

Sailor's Choice (to 17")
Haemulon parra

Spottail Pinfish (to 18")
Diplodus holbrooki

polychaetes, hydroids, shrimps, and crabs, as well as a substantial amount of plant material. Spottail pinfish are active fish that swim about in small schools, feeding on organisms that live on worm reefs and almost continuously nibbling on plants and foraging for food on pilings and around rock jetties.

The sailor's choice, *Haemulon parra*, is a very abundant small grunt that drifts in small schools. It is a somewhat deep-bodied, gray fish with brownish spots on its scales that form oblique, broken stripes. The interior of its mouth is scarlet red. Sailor's choice grunts are active feeders during the night around worm rocks and seagrass beds. The sailor's choice and spottail pinfish are very good to eat, and many people, young and old, fish for them.

To paraphrase an oft-quoted line from the 1989 movie *Field of Dreams*, "If there is a reef—be it oyster, coral, worm, or artificial—build it and they will come."

Hairy Blenny (to 9")
Labrisomus nuchipinnis

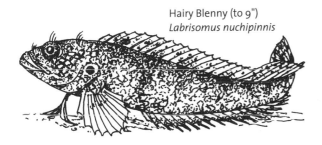

APPENDIX A. Plant and Animal Species List

SPECIES	REGION					SALINITY*			
	1	2	3	4	5	F	L	M	H
PLANTS									
Seaweeds									
Umbrella algae, *Acetabularia* spp.									
Tapered redweed, *Agardhiella tenera*									
Soft fan seaweed, *Avrainvillea nigricans*									
Green horsetail, *Batophora oerstedi*									
Green sea fern, *Bryopsis plumosa*									
Green bead seaweed, *Caulerpa racemosa*									
Feather seaweed, *Caulerpa sertularioides*									
Banded weeds, *Ceramium* spp.									
Pod weeds, *Chondria tenuissima*									
Tufted green algae, *Cladophora* spp.									
Green fleeces, *Codium* spp.									
Fluff-headed seaweed, *Cymopolia barbata*									
Squirrel tail, *Dasycladus vermicularis*									
Green bubble weed, *Dictyosphaeria cavernosa*									
Brown fuzz seaweeds, *Ectocarpus* spp.									
Hollow-tubed seaweeds, *Enteromorpha* spp.									
Graceful redweed, *Gracilaria foliifera*									
Calcified algae, *Halimeda* spp.									
Hooked redweed, *Hypnea musciformis*									
Papillated red seaweed, *Laurencia papillosa*									
Coralline red algae, *Lithothamnion* spp.									
Petticoat alga, *Padina gymnospora*									
Merman's shaving brush, *Penicillus dumetosus*									
Laver, *Porphyra* spp.									
Rip weeds, *Rhipocephalus* spp.									
Gulfweeds, *Sargassum* spp.									

* F = Tidal freshwaters
  L = Brackish waters, 1–10 ppt salinity
  M = Moderately salty waters, 11–18 ppt salinity
  H = High-salinity waters, 19–30+ ppt salinity

SPECIES	REGION					SALINITY*			
	1	2	3	4	5	F	L	M	H
Mermaid's fan, *Udotea flabellum*				▬	▬				▬
Sea lettuce, *Ulva lactuca*	▬	▬	▬	▬	▬			▬	▬
Smooth bubble seaweed, *Valonia ventricosa*				▬	▬				▬

Aquatic Weeds and Wetland Plants

SPECIES	REGION					SALINITY*			
	1	2	3	4	5	F	L	M	H
Sweet flag, *Acorus calamus*	▬	▬	▬	▬	▬	▬			
Alligator weed, *Alternanthera philoxeroides*	▬	▬	▬	▬	▬	▬	▬		
Water hemp, *Amaranthus cannabinus*	▬	▬	▬	▬	▬	▬	▬	▬	
Salt marsh asters, *Aster* spp.	▬	▬	▬	▬	▬	▬	▬	▬	
Marsh orach, *Atriplex patula*	▬	▬	▬	▬	▬	▬	▬	▬	
Saltwort, *Batis maritima*		▬	▬	▬	▬		▬	▬	
Sea oxeye, *Borrichia frutescens*	▬	▬	▬	▬	▬		▬	▬	▬
Sea rocket, *Cakile edentula*	▬	▬	▬	▬	▬		▬	▬	▬
Coontail, *Ceratophyllum demersum*	▬	▬	▬	▬	▬	▬			
Saw grass, *Cladium jamaicense*	▬	▬	▬	▬	▬	▬	▬		
Swamp lily, *Crinum americanum*	▬	▬	▬	▬		▬			
Titi, *Cyrilla racemiflora*	▬	▬	▬			▬			
Salt grass, *Distichlis spicata*	▬	▬	▬	▬	▬		▬	▬	▬
Water hyacinth, *Eichornia crassipes*	▬	▬	▬	▬	▬	▬			
Fire wheel, *Gaillardia pulchella*	▬	▬	▬	▬	▬	▬			
Shoalgrass, *Halodule wrightii*	▬	▬	▬	▬	▬			▬	▬
Paddle grass, *Halophila decipiens*				▬	▬			▬	▬
Star grass, *Halophila engelmanii*				▬	▬			▬	▬
Johnson's seagrass, *Halophila johnsonii*					▬			▬	▬
Seaside heliotrope, *Heliotropium curassavicum*	▬	▬	▬	▬	▬		▬	▬	
Marsh hibiscus, *Hibiscus moscheutos*	▬	▬	▬	▬	▬	▬	▬		
Spider lily, *Hymenocallis crassifolia*	▬	▬	▬	▬	▬	▬	▬		
Railroad vine, *Ipomoea pes-caprae*			▬	▬	▬			▬	▬
Salt marsh morning glory, *Ipomoea sagittata*		▬	▬	▬	▬		▬	▬	
Beach morning glory, *Ipomoea stolonifera*	▬	▬	▬	▬	▬			▬	▬
Coastal morning glory, *Ipomoea trichocarpa*	▬	▬	▬	▬				▬	▬
Slender blue flag, *Iris prismatica*	▬	▬	▬	▬	▬	▬			
Yellow flag, *Iris pseudacorus*	▬	▬	▬	▬	▬	▬			
Southern blue flag, *Iris virginica*	▬	▬	▬	▬	▬	▬	▬		
Black needlerush, *Juncus roemerianus*	▬	▬	▬	▬	▬		▬	▬	
Seashore mallow, *Kosteletzkya virginica*	▬	▬	▬	▬	▬	▬	▬		
Rice cut-grass, *Leersia oryzoides*	▬	▬	▬	▬	▬	▬			
Duckweeds, *Lemna* spp., *Spirodela* spp., *Wolfia* spp., *Wolfiella* spp.	▬	▬	▬	▬	▬	▬			

SPECIES	REGION					SALINITY*			
	1	2	3	4	5	F	L	M	H
Sea lavender, *Limonium carolinianum*	▬	▬	▬	▬	▬		▬	▬	
Sweet grass, *Muhlenbergia capillaris*	▬	▬	▬	▬	▬	▬	▬		
Spatterdock, *Nuphar lutea*	▬	▬	▬	▬	▬	▬			
White water lily, *Nymphaea odorata*	▬	▬	▬	▬	▬	▬			
Sundrop, *Oenothera fruticosa*	▬	▬	▬			▬			
Prickly pear cactus, *Opuntia humifusa*	▬	▬	▬	▬	▬	▬			
Golden club, *Orontium aquaticum*	▬	▬	▬	▬	▬	▬			
Cinnamon fern, *Osmunda cinnamomea*	▬	▬	▬	▬	▬	▬			
Royal fern, *Osmunda regalis*	▬	▬	▬	▬	▬	▬			
Switchgrass, *Panicum virgatum*	▬	▬	▬	▬	▬	▬	▬	▬	
Arrow arum, *Peltandra virginica*	▬	▬	▬	▬	▬	▬			
Common reed, *Phragmites australis*	▬	▬	▬	▬	▬	▬	▬		
Salt marsh fleabane, *Pluchea odoratus*	▬	▬	▬	▬	▬		▬	▬	
Halberd-leaf tearthumb, *Polygonum arifolium*	▬	▬	▬	▬	▬	▬	▬		
Water smartweed, *Polygonum punctatum*	▬	▬	▬	▬	▬	▬	▬		
Resurrection fern, *Polypodium polypodioides*	▬	▬	▬	▬	▬	▬			
Pickerelweed, *Pontederia cordata*	▬	▬	▬	▬	▬	▬			
Redhead grass, *Potamogeton perfoliatus*	▬	▬	▬	▬	▬	▬	▬		
Swamp rose, *Rosa palustris*	▬	▬	▬	▬	▬	▬			
Widgeon grass, *Ruppia maritima*	▬	▬	▬	▬	▬	▬	▬	▬	▬
Large salt marsh pink, *Sabatia dodecandra*	▬	▬	▬	▬	▬		▬	▬	
Common salt marsh pink, *Sabatia stellaris*	▬	▬	▬	▬	▬		▬	▬	
Big-leaved arrowhead, *Sagittaria latifolia*	▬	▬	▬	▬	▬	▬			
Lance-leaved arrowhead, *Sagittaria lancifolia*	▬	▬	▬	▬	▬	▬	▬		
Dwarf glasswort, *Salicornia bigelovii*	▬	▬	▬	▬	▬			▬	▬
Common glasswort, *Salicornia europaea*	▬	▬	▬	▬	▬			▬	▬
Russian thistle, *Salsola kali*	▬	▬	▬	▬	▬			▬	▬
Perennial glasswort, *Sarcocornia perennis*	▬	▬	▬	▬	▬			▬	▬
Chairmaker's rush, *Schoenoplectus americanus*	▬	▬	▬	▬	▬	▬	▬		
Common three-square, *Schoenoplectus pungens*	▬	▬	▬	▬	▬	▬	▬		
Salt marsh bulrush, *Schoenoplectus robustus*	▬	▬	▬	▬	▬		▬	▬	
Sea purslane, *Sesuvium portulacastrum*		▬	▬	▬	▬			▬	▬
Seaside goldenrod, *Solidago sempervirens*	▬	▬	▬	▬	▬		▬	▬	▬
Salt marsh cordgrass, *Spartina alterniflora*	▬	▬	▬	▬	▬			▬	▬
Big cordgrass, *Spartina cynosuroides*	▬	▬	▬	▬	▬		▬	▬	
Salt meadow hay, *Spartina patens*	▬	▬	▬	▬	▬	▬	▬	▬	
Sago pondweed, *Stuckenia pectinata*	▬	▬	▬	▬	▬	▬	▬		
Sea blite, *Suaeda linearis*	▬	▬	▬	▬	▬		▬	▬	
Manatee grass, *Syringodium filiforme*	▬	▬	▬	▬	▬			▬	▬

SPECIES	REGION					SALINITY*			
	1	2	3	4	5	F	L	M	H
Turtle grass, *Thalassia testudinum*				▬	▬				▬
Marsh fern, *Thelypteris thelypteroides*	▬	▬	▬	▬	▬	▬			
Spanish moss, *Tillandsia usneoides*	▬	▬	▬	▬	▬	▬			
Narrow-leaved cattail, *Typha angustifolia*	▬	▬	▬	▬	▬	▬	▬		
Southern cattail, *Typha domingensis*	▬	▬	▬	▬	▬	▬	▬		
Broad-leaved cattail, *Typha latifolia*	▬	▬	▬	▬	▬	▬	▬		
Sea oat, *Uniola paniculata*		▬	▬	▬	▬				
Common bladderwort, *Utricularia macrorhiza*	▬	▬	▬	▬	▬	▬			
Wild celery, *Vallisneria americana*	▬	▬	▬	▬	▬	▬			
Summer grape, *Vitis aestivalis*	▬	▬	▬	▬	▬	▬			
Fox grape, *Vitis labrusca*	▬	▬	▬	▬	▬	▬			
Muscadine grape, *Vitis rotundifolia*	▬	▬	▬	▬	▬	▬			
Horned pondweed, *Zannichellia palustris*	▬	▬	▬	▬	▬	▬	▬		
Wild rice, *Zizania aquatica*	▬	▬	▬	▬		▬			
Giant cut-grass, *Zizaniopsis millacea*	▬	▬	▬	▬		▬			
Eelgrass, *Zostera marina*					▬			▬	▬

Trees and Shrubs

SPECIES	REGION					SALINITY*			
	1	2	3	4	5	F	L	M	H
Red maple, *Acer rubrum*	▬	▬	▬	▬	▬	▬			
Devil's walking stick, *Aralia spinosa*	▬	▬	▬	▬	▬	▬			
Black mangrove, *Avicennia germinans*				▬	▬			▬	▬
Groundsel tree, *Baccharis halimifolia*	▬	▬	▬	▬	▬	▬	▬	▬	
River birch, *Betula nigra*	▬	▬	▬	▬		▬			
Australian pine, *Casuarina equisetifolia*			▬	▬	▬				
Atlantic white cedar, *Chamaecyparis thyoides*	▬	▬	▬	▬		▬			
Sea grape, *Coccoloba uvifera*				▬	▬			▬	▬
Buttonwood, *Conocarpus erectus*				▬	▬			▬	▬
Loblolly bay, *Gordonia lasianthus*		▬	▬	▬	▬	▬			
Sea hibiscus, *Hibiscus tiliaceus*					▬	▬	▬	▬	
American holly, *Ilex opaca*	▬	▬	▬	▬	▬	▬			
Yaupon holly, *Ilex vomitoria*	▬	▬	▬	▬	▬	▬	▬		
Winterberry, *Ilex verticillata*	▬	▬	▬	▬	▬	▬			
Marsh elder, *Iva frutescens*	▬	▬	▬	▬	▬				
Seashore elder, *Iva imbricata*	▬	▬	▬	▬	▬		▬	▬	
White mangrove, *Laguncularia racemosa*				▬	▬		▬	▬	
Sweet gum, *Liquidambar styraciflua*	▬	▬	▬	▬	▬	▬			
Southern magnolia, *Magnolia grandiflora*	▬	▬	▬	▬		▬			
Sweet bay, *Magnolia virginiana*	▬	▬	▬	▬	▬	▬			
Melaleuca tree, *Melaleuca quinquenervia*				▬	▬	▬			

SPECIES	REGION					SALINITY*			
	1	2	3	4	5	F	L	M	H
Wax myrtle, *Myrica cerifera*	▬	▬				▬			
Northern bayberry, *Myrica pensylvanica*	▬	▬	▬	▬		▬			
Water tupelo, *Nyssa aquatica*	▬	▬	▬			▬			
Black gum, *Nyssa sylvatica*	▬	▬	▬			▬			
Red bay, *Persea borbonia*		▬	▬	▬		▬			
Swamp bay, *Persea palustris*		▬	▬	▬		▬			
Longleaf pine, *Pinus palustris*	▬	▬	▬						
Pond pine, *Pinus serotina*	▬	▬	▬						
Loblolly pine, *Pinus taeda*	▬	▬	▬	▬					
American sycamore, *Platanus occidentalis*	▬	▬	▬			▬			
Water oak, *Quercus nigra*	▬	▬	▬	▬		▬	▬		
Live oak, *Quercus virginiana*	▬	▬	▬	▬	▬	▬	▬		
Red mangrove, *Rhizophora mangle*				▬	▬		▬	▬	▬
Dwarf palmetto, *Sabal minor*			▬	▬			▬	▬	
Cabbage palmetto, *Sabal palmetto*		▬	▬	▬	▬		▬	▬	
Brazilian pepper, *Schinus terebinthifolius*				▬	▬		▬		
Saw palmetto, *Serenoa repens*		▬	▬	▬	▬				
Bay cedar, *Suriana maritima*				▬	▬				
Bald cypress, *Taxodium distichum*	▬	▬	▬	▬		▬			
Pond cypress, *Taxodium ascendens*	▬	▬	▬			▬			
Seaside mahoe, *Thespesia populnea*				▬	▬				
Spanish bayonet, *Yucca aloifolia*		▬	▬	▬	▬		▬		

INVERTEBRATE ANIMALS

Phylum Porifera: Sponges

SPECIES	1	2	3	4	5	F	L	M	H
Yellow tube sponge, *Aplysina fistularia*				▬	▬				▬
Tube sponge, *Callyspongia vaginalis*				▬	▬				▬
Chicken liver sponge, *Chondrilla nucula*				▬	▬			▬	▬
Boring sponges, *Cliona* spp.	▬	▬	▬	▬	▬		▬	▬	▬
Crumb-of-bread sponge, *Halichondria bowerbanki*	▬	▬	▬	▬	▬			▬	▬
Eroded sponges, *Haliclona* spp.	▬	▬	▬	▬	▬		▬		▬
Finger sponge, *Haliclona oculata*				▬	▬				▬
Pink tube sponge, *Haliclona tubifera*				▬	▬				▬
Sun sponge, *Hymeniacidon heliophila*				▬	▬		▬		▬
Stinker vase sponge, *Ircinia campana*			▬	▬	▬			▬	▬
Redbeard sponge, *Microciona prolifera*	▬	▬	▬	▬	▬		▬	▬	▬
Loggerhead sponge, *Spheciospongia vesparia*	▬	▬	▬	▬	▬		▬	▬	▬

SPECIES	REGION					SALINITY*			
	1	2	3	4	5	F	L	M	H

Phylum Cnidaria: Hydroids, Jellyfishes, Sea Anemones, and Corals

Hydroids

SPECIES	1	2	3	4	5	F	L	M	H
Gulfweed hydroid, *Aglaophenia latecarinata*	X	X	X	X	X				X
Bushy hydroids, *Bougainvillia* spp.	X	X	X	X	X	X	X	X	X
Pink-mouth hydroid, *Ectopleura crocea*	X	X	X	X	X				X
Tube hydroid, *Ectopleura dumortieri*	X	X	X	X	X		X		
Red stick hydroid, *Eudendrium carneum*	X	X	X	X	X			X	X
Pink stick hydroid, *Eudendrium ramosum*	X	X	X	X	X			X	X
Feather hydroid, *Halocordyle disticha*	X	X	X	X	X				X
Snail fur hydroid, *Hydractinia echinata*	X	X	X	X	X			X	X
Bushy wineglass hydroid, *Obelia dichotoma*	X	X	X	X	X		X	X	
Garland hydroid, *Sertularia cupressina*	X	X	X						X
Soft snail fur, *Stylactaria arge*	X								X

Jellyfishes

SPECIES	1	2	3	4	5	F	L	M	H
Moon jellyfish, *Aurelia aurita*	X	X	X	X	X			X	
Upside-down jellyfish, *Cassiopea xamachana*				X	X				X
Sea nettle, *Chrysaora quinquecirrha*	X	X	X	X	X	X	X	X	
Lion's mane jellyfish, *Cyanea capillata*	X	X	X	X	X		X	X	X
Portuguese man-of-war, *Physalia physalis*	X	X	X	X	X				X
Mushroom cap jellyfish, *Rhopilema verrilli*	X	X	X	X	X				X
Cannonball jellyfish, *Stomolophus meleagris*		X	X	X	X				X

Sea Anemones

SPECIES	1	2	3	4	5	F	L	M	H
Gulfweed anemone, *Anemonia sargassensis*	X	X	X	X	X				X
American warty anemone, *Bunodosoma cavernata*	X	X	X	X	X				X
Tricolor anemone, *Calliactus tricolor*	X	X	X	X					X
Giant Caribbean anemone, *Condylactis gigantea*				X	X				X
Ghost anemone, *Diadumene leucolena*	X	X	X	X				X	X
Elegant burrowing anemone, *Edwardsia elegans*	X	X	X	X	X		X		
Striped anemone, *Haliplanella luciae*	X	X	X	X	X			X	X
Sea onion, *Paranthus rapiformis*	X	X	X	X	X				X

Fire Corals, Soft Corals, and Hard Corals

SPECIES	1	2	3	4	5	F	L	M	H
Corky sea fingers, *Briareum asbestinum*				X	X				X
Swollen knob candelabrum, *Eunicea mammosa*				X	X				X
Purple sea fan, *Gorgonia ventalina*				X	X				X
Sea whip, *Leptogorgia virgulata*	X	X	X	X	X				X

SPECIES	REGION					SALINITY*			
	1	2	3	4	5	F	L	M	H
Rose coral, *Manicina areolata*					X				X
Fire coral, *Millepora alcicornis*					X				X
Bladed fire coral, *Millepora complanata*					X				X
Box fire coral, *Millepora squarrosa*					X				X
Black sea rod, *Plexaura homomalla*					X				X
Mustard hill coral, *Porites astreoides*					X				X
Clubbed finger coral, *Porites porites*					X				X
Lesser star coral, *Siderastrea radians*					X				X
Smooth star coral, *Solenastrea bournoni*					X				X
Great star coral, *Monastrea cavernosa*					X				X
Rough sea plume, *Muriceopsis flavida*					X				X

Phylum Ctenophora: Comb Jellies

SPECIES	REGION					SALINITY*			
Pink comb jelly, *Beroe ovata*	X	X	X	X	X			X	X
Sea walnut, *Mnemiopsis leidyi*	X	X	X	X	X		X	X	

Phylum Platyhelminthes: Flatworms

SPECIES	REGION					SALINITY*			
Oyster flatworm, *Stylochus ellipticus*	X	X	X	X	X			X	

Phylum Rhynchocoela: Ribbon Worms

SPECIES	REGION					SALINITY*			
Milky ribbon worm, *Cerebratulus lacteus*	X	X	X	X	X				

Phylum Bryozoa: Bryozoans

SPECIES	REGION					SALINITY*			
Dead man's fingers, *Alcyonidium hauffi*	X	X	X	X	X				X
Spiral bryozoans, *Amathia* spp.	X	X	X	X	X			X	X
Hair, *Anguinella palmata*	X	X	X	X	X			X	X
Bushy bryozoan, *Bugula neritina*	X	X	X	X	X				X
Lacy crust bryozoan, *Conopeum tenuissimum*	X	X	X	X	X				X
Coffin box bryozoan, *Membranipora tenuis*	X	X	X	X	X				X
Lettuce bryozoan, *Thalamoporella floridana*		X	X	X	X				X
Cushion moss bryozoan, *Victorella pavida*	X	X	X	X	X		X		

Phylum Annelida: Polychaete Worms

SPECIES	REGION					SALINITY*			
Ornate worm, *Amphitrite ornata*	X	X	X	X	X			X	X
Opal worm, *Arabella iricolor*	X	X	X	X	X			X	X
Lugworm, *Arenicola cristata*	X	X	X	X	X			X	X
Parchment worm, *Chaetopterus variopedatus*	X	X	X	X	X			X	X
Bamboo worm, *Clymenella torquata*	X	X	X					X	X

SPECIES	REGION					SALINITY*			
	1	2	3	4	5	F	L	M	H
Plumed worm, *Diopatra cuprea*	X	X	X	X					X
Bloodworm, *Glycera dibranchiata*	X	X	X	X	X			X	X
Fifteen-scaled worms, *Harmothoe* spp.	X	X	X	X	X				X
Bearded fireworm, *Hermodice carunculata*	X	X	X	X	X				X
Limy tube worm, *Hydroides dianthus*	X	X	X	X	X			X	X
Twelve-scaled worms, *Lepidonotus* spp.	X	X	X	X	X				X
Red-gilled marphysa, *Marphysa sanguinea*	X	X	X	X	X				X
Common clamworm, *Neanthes succinea*	X	X	X	X	X		X	X	X
Trumpet worm, *Pectinaria gouldii*	X	X	X	X	X			X	X
Reef-building tube worm, *Phragmatopoma lapidosa*				X	X				X
Sea wolf scale worm, *Polyodontes lupina*			X	X				X	
Whip mudworm, *Polydora cornuta*	X	X	X	X	X	X	X	X	X
Oyster mudworm, *Polydora websteri*	X	X	X	X	X		X	X	
Star feather worm, *Pomatostegus stellatus*				X	X				X
Fan worm, *Sabella microphthalma*	X	X	X	X	X			X	X
Sand-builder worm, *Sabellaria vulgaris*	X	X	X	X					X
Magnificent feather duster worm, *Sabellastarte magnifica*				X	X				X
Christmas tree worm, *Spirobranchus giganteus*					X				X

Phylum Mollusca: Mollusks

Gastropods
Greedy dove snail, *Anachis avara*	X	X	X	X				X	
Common sundial, *Architectonica nobilis*		X	X	X				X	X
West Indian false cerith, *Batillaria minima*	X	X	X					X	X
Grass cerith, *Bittium varium*	X	X	X	X				X	X
Impressed odostome, *Boonea impressa*	X	X	X	X	X			X	
Striate bubble, *Bulla striata*		X	X	X				X	X
Knobbed whelk, *Busycon carica*	X	X	X					X	X
Lightning whelk, *Busycon sinistrum*		X	X	X				X	X
Channeled whelk, *Busycotypus canaliculatus*	X	X	X					X	X
Cameo helmet, *Cassis madagascariensis*					X				X
Ladder horn snail, *Cerithidea scalariformis*			X	X				X	
Ivory cerith, *Cerithium eburneum*				X	X				X
Convex slipper snail, *Crepidula convexa*	X	X	X	X				X	X
Atlantic slipper snail, *Crepidula fornicata*	X	X	X	X				X	X
White slipper snail, *Crepidula plana*	X	X	X	X	X			X	X
Flamingo tongue, *Cyphoma gibbosum*		X	X	X	X				X

SPECIES	REGION					SALINITY*			
	1	2	3	4	5	F	L	M	H
Atlantic deer cowrie, *Cypraea cervus*				X	X				X
Atlantic gray cowrie, *Cypraea cinerea*		X	X	X	X				X
Atlantic yellow cowrie, *Cypraea spurca acicularis*		X	X	X	X				X
Measled cowrie, *Cypraea zebra*				X					X
Cayenne keyhole limpet, *Diodora cayenensis*	X	X	X	X	X			X	X
Angulate wentletrap, *Epitonium angulatum*	X	X	X	X	X				X
Thick-lip drill, *Eupleura caudata*	X	X	X	X	X			X	
Banded tulip, *Fasciolaria lilium*		X	X	X	X				X
True tulip, *Fasciolaria tulipa*		X	X	X	X				X
Eastern mud snail, *Ilyanassa obsoleta*	X	X	X	X	X		X	X	
American star snail, *Lithopoma americanum*					X				X
Mangrove periwinkle, *Littoraria angulifera*				X	X			X	
Marsh periwinkle, *Littoraria irrorata*	X	X	X	X	X			X	
Common Atlantic marginella, *Marginella apicina*				X	X				X
Eastern melampus, *Melampus bidentatus*	X	X	X	X	X		X		
Crown conch, *Melengena corona*			X	X	X		X	X	
Lunar dove snail, *Mitrella lunata*	X	X	X	X	X		X	X	
Button snail, *Modulus modulus*		X	X	X	X				X
Bruised nassa, *Nassarius vibex*	X	X	X	X	X			X	X
Bleeding tooth, *Nerita peloronta*				X	X				X
Checkered nerite, *Nerita tessellata*				X	X				X
Four-tooth nerite, *Nerita versicolor*				X	X			X	
Olive nerite, *Neritina reclivata*	X	X	X	X	X	X	X		
Shark eye snail, *Neverita duplicata*	X	X	X	X	X				X
Zebra periwinkle, *Nodilittorina ziczac*				X	X				X
Lettered olive, *Oliva sayana*	X	X	X	X	X				X
Variable worm snail, *Petaloconchus varians*		X	X	X					X
Scotch bonnet, *Phalium granulatum*	X	X	X	X	X				X
Apple murex, *Phyllonotus pomum*		X	X	X	X				X
Horse conch, *Pleuroploca gigantea*				X	X				X
Zebra nerite, *Puperita pupa*				X	X				X
One-tooth simnia, *Simnialena uniplicata*	X	X	X	X	X				X
White baby ear, *Sinum perspectivum*	X	X	X	X	X				X
Striped false limpet, *Siphonaria pectinata*			X	X	X				X
Florida rock snail, *Stramonita haemastoma floridana*	X	X	X	X	X			X	X
Queen conch, *Strombus gigas*					X				X
Beaded periwinkle, *Tectarius muricatus*				X	X				X
Eastern auger snail, *Terebra dislocata*	X	X	X	X	X				X

SPECIES	REGION					SALINITY*			
	1	2	3	4	5	F	L	M	H
Black-line triphora, *Triphora nigrocincta*	■	■	■	■	■			■	■
Chestnut turban, *Turbo castanea*		■	■	■	■				■
Atlantic oyster drill, *Urosalpinx cinerea*	■	■	■	■	■			■	■
West Indian worm snail, *Vermicularia spirata*				■	■				■
Scaphopods									
Ivory tusk shell, *Graptacme eborea*			■	■	■				■
Bivalves									
Atlantic strawberry cockle, *Americardia media*		■	■	■	■				■
Blood ark, *Anadara ovalis*	■	■	■	■	■				■
Transverse ark, *Anadara transversa*	■	■	■	■	■				■
Buttercup lucine, *Anodontia alba*	■	■	■	■	■				■
Jingle shell, *Anomia simplex*	■	■	■	■	■			■	■
Turkey wing, *Arca zebra*	■	■	■	■	■				■
Bay scallop, *Argopecten irradians*	■	■	■	■	■				■
Stiff pen shell, *Atrina rigida*	■	■	■	■	■				■
Sawtooth pen shell, *Atrina serrata*	■	■	■	■	■				■
Gould's shipworm, *Bankia gouldi*	■	■	■	■	■			■	■
Atlantic mud-piddock, *Barnea truncata*	■	■	■	■	■				■
Scorched mussel, *Brachidontes exustus*	■	■	■	■	■				■
Leafy jewel box, *Chama macrophylla*		■	■	■	■				■
Cross-barred venus, *Chione cancellata*		■	■	■	■				■
Tiger lucine, *Codakia orbicularis*				■	■				■
Eastern oyster, *Crassostrea virginica*	■	■	■	■	■		■	■	
Angelwing, *Cyrtopleura costata*	■	■	■	■	■			■	■
Frond oyster, *Dendostrea frons*				■	■				■
Atlantic giant cockle, *Dinocardium robustum*	■	■	■	■					■
Cross-hatched lucine, *Divaricella quadrisulcata*	■	■	■	■	■				■
Coquina, *Donax variabilis*	■	■	■	■	■				■
Disk dosinia, *Dosinia discus*	■	■	■	■	■				■
Elegant dosinia, *Dosinia elegans*	■	■	■	■	■				■
Atlantic jackknife clam, *Ensis directus*	■	■	■	■	■			■	■
Minor jackknife clam, *Ensis minor*	■	■	■	■	■			■	■
Ribbed mussel, *Geukensia demissa*	■	■	■	■	■		■	■	
Hooked mussel, *Ischadium recurvum*	■	■	■	■	■		■	■	
Flat tree oyster, *Isognomon alatus*				■	■				■
Lister purse oyster, *Isognomon radiatus*				■	■				■
Egg cockle, *Laevicardium laevigatum*	■	■	■	■	■				■
Morton egg cockle, *Laevicardium mortoni*	■	■	■	■	■				■

SPECIES	REGION					SALINITY*			
	1	2	3	4	5	F	L	M	H
Baltic macoma, *Macoma balthica*	●	●	●				●	●	
Sunray venus, *Macrocallista nimbosa*		●	●	●	●			●	●
Hard clam, *Mercenaria mercenaria*	●	●	●	●	●			●	●
Dwarf surf clam, *Mulinia lateralis*	●	●	●	●	●			●	●
Dark false mussel, *Mytilopsis leucophaeata*	●	●	●			●	●		
Ponderous ark, *Noetia ponderosa*	●	●	●	●	●				●
False angelwing, *Petricola pholadiformis*	●	●	●	●	●			●	●
Atlantic kitten paw, *Plicatula gibbosa*		●	●	●	●				●
Carolina marsh clam, *Polymesoda caroliniana*	●	●	●			●	●	●	
Channeled duck clam, *Raeta plicatella*	●	●	●	●				●	●
Atlantic rangia, *Rangia cuneata*	●	●	●			●	●	●	
Atlantic semele, *Semele proficua*		●	●	●	●				●
Atlantic awning clam, *Solemya velum*			●					●	●
Green jackknife clam, *Solen viridis*	●	●	●	●	●		●	●	●
Purplish tagelus, *Tagelus divisus*	●	●	●	●	●		●	●	●
Stout tagelus, *Tagelus plebius*	●	●	●	●	●		●	●	●
Alternate tellin, *Tellina alternata*		●	●					●	●
Rose-petal tellin, *Tellina lineata*		●	●	●				●	●
Florida prickly cockle, *Trachycardium egmontianum*		●	●	●	●				●
Yellow prickly cockle, *Trachycardium muricatum*		●	●	●	●				●
Chitons									
Fuzzy chiton, *Acanthopleura granulata*				●	●				●
Eastern surf chiton, *Ceratozona squalida*			●	●	●				●
Eastern beaded chiton, *Chaetopleura apiculata*	●	●	●	●	●			●	●
Cephalopods									
Caribbean reef octopus, *Octopus briareus*			●	●	●				●
Common octopus, *Octopus vulgaris*	●	●	●	●	●			●	●
Atlantic brief squid, *Lolliguncula brevis*	●	●	●	●	●		●	●	●
Caribbean reef squid, *Sepioteuthis sepioidea*			●	●	●				●
Phylum Arthropoda: Jointed-Legged Animals									
Barnacles									
Striped barnacle, *Balanus amphitrite*	●	●	●	●	●			●	
Ivory barnacle, *Balanus eburneus*	●	●	●	●	●	●	●	●	●
Bay barnacle, *Balanus improvisus*	●	●	●	●	●	●	●	●	●
White barnacle, *Balanus subalbidus*	●	●	●	●	●	●	●	●	●
Little gray barnacle, *Chthalamus fragilis*	●	●	●	●	●			●	●

SPECIES	REGION					SALINITY*			
	1	2	3	4	5	F	L	M	H
Star barnacle, *Chthalamus stellatus*			▬	▬	▬			▬	▬
Sea whip barnacle, *Conopea galeata*			▬	▬	▬				▬
Goose barnacle, *Lepas anatifera*	▬	▬	▬	▬	▬				▬
Scaled goose barnacle, *Lepas pectinata*	▬	▬	▬	▬	▬				▬
Volcano barnacle, *Tetraclita stalactifera*			▬	▬	▬				▬
Isopods									
Slender isopod, *Cyathura polita*	▬	▬	▬	▬	▬		▬	▬	
Elongated eelgrass isopod, *Erichsonella attenuata*	▬	▬						▬	▬
Baltic isopod, *Idotea baltica*	▬	▬	▬	▬	▬			▬	▬
Sea roach, *Ligia exotica*	▬	▬	▬	▬	▬			▬	▬
Gribble, *Limnoria tripunctata*			▬	▬	▬			▬	▬
Fish-gill isopod, *Lironeca ovalis*	▬	▬	▬	▬	▬		▬	▬	▬
Fish-mouth isopod, *Olencira praegustator*	▬	▬	▬	▬	▬		▬	▬	
Eelgrass pill bug, *Paracerceis caudata*	▬	▬	▬	▬	▬			▬	▬
Diane's paradella, *Paradella dianae*	▬	▬	▬	▬	▬			▬	▬
Parasitic shrimp isopod, *Probopyrus pandalicola*	▬	▬	▬	▬	▬		▬		
Sea pill bug, *Sphaeroma quadridentatum*	▬	▬	▬	▬	▬		▬	▬	▬
Walker's marine pill bug, *Sphaeroma walkeri*	▬	▬	▬	▬	▬			▬	▬
Amphipods									
Long-antennaed tube-builder amphipod, *Ampithoe longimana*	▬	▬	▬	▬	▬			▬	
Purpled-eyed amphipod, *Batea catharinensis*	▬	▬	▬	▬	▬			▬	▬
Skeleton shrimps, *Caprella* spp.	▬	▬	▬	▬	▬			▬	▬
Tube-builder amphipods, *Corophium* spp.	▬	▬	▬	▬	▬		▬	▬	
Wave-diver tube-builder amphipod, *Cymadusa compta*	▬	▬	▬	▬	▬			▬	
Sand-digger amphipod, *Neohaustorius schmitzi*	▬	▬	▬	▬	▬		▬	▬	
Beach flea, *Orchestia platensis*	▬	▬	▬	▬	▬			▬	
Beach hopper, *Talorchestia longicornis*	▬	▬						▬	
Shrimps									
Big-claw snapping shrimp, *Alpheus heterochaelis*	▬	▬	▬	▬	▬			▬	▬
Seven-spine bay shrimp, *Crangon septemspinosa*	▬	▬	▬	▬			▬	▬	
Brown shrimp, *Farfantepenaeus aztecus*	▬	▬	▬	▬	▬			▬	▬
Pink shrimp, *Farfantepenaeus duorarum*	▬	▬	▬	▬	▬			▬	▬
Short-browed mud shrimp, *Gilvossius setimanus*	▬	▬	▬	▬	▬			▬	
White shrimp, *Litopenaeus setiferus*	▬	▬	▬	▬	▬			▬	
Scarlet-striped cleaning shrimp, *Lysmata grabhami*			▬	▬	▬				▬

SPECIES	REGION					SALINITY*			
	1	2	3	4	5	F	L	M	H
Peppermint shrimp, *Lysmata wurdemanni*	■	■	■	■	■				■
Daggerblade grass shrimp, *Palaemonetes pugio*	■	■	■	■	■		■	■	
Mantis shrimp, *Squilla empusa*	■	■	■	■	■			■	
Banded coral shrimp, *Stenopus hispidus*		■	■	■	■				■
Speckled snapping shrimp, *Synalpheus fritzmulleri*		■	■	■	■				■
Coastal mud shrimp, *Upogebia affinis*	■	■	■	■	■			■	
Crabs and Lobsters									
Mangrove tree crab, *Aratus pisonii*				■	■	■	■	■	■
Blue crab, *Callinectes sapidus*	■	■	■	■	■	■	■	■	■
Blue land crab, *Cardisoma guanhumi*				■	■	■			
Tricolor hermit crab, *Clibanarius tricolor*				■					■
Thin-stripe hermit crab, *Clibanarius vittatus*		■	■	■	■		■	■	■
Say mud crab, *Dyspanopeus sayi*	■	■	■	■	■		■	■	■
Mole crab, *Emerita talpoida*	■	■	■	■	■				■
Flatback mud crab, *Eurypanopeus depressus*	■	■	■	■	■		■	■	■
Sally lightfoot crab, *Grapsus grapsus*				■					■
Smooth mud crab, *Hexapanopeus angustifrons*	■	■	■	■	■		■	■	■
Longnose spider crab, *Libinia dubia*	■	■	■	■	■			■	■
Portly spider crab, *Libinia emarginata*	■	■	■	■	■			■	■
Spongy decorator crab, *Macrocoeloma trispinosum*		■	■	■	■				■
Florida stone crab, *Menippe mercenaria*		■	■	■	■			■	■
Cuban stone crab, *Menippe nodifrons*		■	■	■	■				■
Atlantic ghost crab, *Ocypode quadrata*	■	■	■	■	■				■
Lady crab, *Ovalipes ocellatus*	■	■	■	■	■			■	■
Wormreef porcelain crab, *Pachycheles monilifer*			■	■	■				■
Mottled shore crab, *Pachygrapsus transversus*		■	■	■	■				■
Banded hermit crab, *Pagurus annulipes*	■	■	■	■					■
Long-wrist hermit crab, *Pagurus longicarpus*	■	■	■	■				■	■
Flat-claw hermit crab, *Pagurus pollicaris*	■	■	■	■	■				■
Strongtooth mud crab, *Panopeus bermudensis*				■	■				■
Atlantic mud crab, *Panopeus herbstii*	■	■	■	■	■		■	■	■
Caribbean spiny lobster, *Panulirus argus*				■	■				■
Cryptic teardrop crab, *Pelia mutica*	■	■	■	■	■				■
Short-spined hairy crab, *Pilumnus dasypodus*		■	■	■	■				■
Nimble spray crab, *Percnon gibbesi*		■	■	■	■				■
Parchment worm crab, *Pinnixa chaetopterana*	■	■	■	■	■			■	
Oyster pea crab, *Pinnotheres ostreum*	■	■	■	■	■				■

SPECIES	REGION					SALINITY*			
	1	2	3	4	5	F	L	M	H
Harris mud crab, *Rhithropanopeus harrisii*	●	●	●	●	●		●	●	●
Square-back marsh crab, *Sesarma cinereum*	●	●	●	●	●			●	●
Mangrove marsh crab, *Sesarma curacaoense*				●	●				●
Heavy marsh crab, *Sesarma reticulatum*	●	●	●	●				●	●
Humic marsh crab, *Sesarma ricordi*		●	●	●					●
Yellowline arrow crab, *Stenorhynchus seticornis*		●	●	●	●				●
Red-jointed fiddler crab, *Uca minax*	●	●	●	●			●	●	
Atlantic sand fiddler crab, *Uca pugilator*	●	●	●	●				●	●
Atlantic marsh fiddler crab, *Uca pugnax*	●	●	●	●				●	●
Mudflat fiddler crab, *Uca rapax*					●				●
Swamp ghost crab, *Ucides cordatus*				●					●

Insects

Springtails

SPECIES	REGION					SALINITY*			
Seashore springtail, *Anurida maritima*	●	●	●	●	●			●	

Beetles

SPECIES	REGION					SALINITY*			
Northeastern beach tiger beetle, *Cicindela dorsalis*	●	●	●	●					
Predacious diving beetles, *Dytiscus* spp.	●	●	●	●	●	●			
Water boatmen, *Corixa* spp.	●	●	●	●	●	●			
Water striders, *Gerris* spp.	●	●	●	●	●	●			
Whirligig beetles, *Gyrinus* spp.	●	●	●	●	●	●			

Flies and Mosquitoes

SPECIES	REGION					SALINITY*			
Salt marsh mosquito, *Aedes solicitans*	●	●	●	●	●			●	●
Common house mosquito, *Culex pipiens*	●	●	●	●	●	●	●		

Dobsonfly

SPECIES	REGION					SALINITY*			
Dobsonfly, *Corydalus cornutus*	●	●	●	●	●	●			

Dragonflies and Damselflies

SPECIES	REGION					SALINITY*			
Green darner, *Anax junius*	●	●	●	●	●	●	●		
Dancers, *Argia* spp.	●	●	●	●	●	●	●		
Doubleday's bluet, *Enallagma doubledayii*	●	●	●	●	●	●	●		
Seaside dragonlet, *Erythrodiplax berenice*	●	●	●	●	●			●	●
Twelve-spotted skimmer, *Libellula pulchella*	●	●	●	●	●	●	●		

Butterflies and Moths

SPECIES	REGION					SALINITY*			
Mangrove buckeye, *Junonia evarete*	●	●	●						
Mangrove skipper, *Phocides pigmalion*			●	●					

Phylum Echinodermata: Spiny-Skinned Animals

SPECIES	REGION					SALINITY*			
	1	2	3	4	5	F	L	M	H
Sea Stars									
Common sea star, *Asterias forbesi*	X	X	X						X
Marginal sea star, *Astropecten articulatus*	X	X	X	X	X				X
Spiny sea star, *Echinaster sentus*					X				X
Striped luidia, *Luidia clathrata*	X	X	X	X	X				X
Cushion sea star, *Oreaster reticulatus*		X	X	X	X				X
Brittle Stars									
Burrowing brittle star, *Microphiopholis atra*	X	X	X				X		X
Blunt-spined brittle star, *Ophiocoma echinata*				X	X				X
Spiny brittle star, *Ophiothrix angulata*	X	X	X	X	X			X	X
Sea Urchins									
Purple sea urchin, *Arbacia punctulata*	X	X	X	X	X				X
Long-spined black sea urchin, *Diadema antillarum*			X	X	X				X
Slate pencil urchin, *Eucidaris tribuloides*		X	X	X	X				X
Green sea urchin, *Lytechinus variegatus*		X	X	X	X				X
Red heart urchin, *Meoma ventricosa*				X	X				X
Sea egg, *Tripneustes ventricosus*					X				X
Sand Dollars									
Common sand dollar, *Mellita isometra*	X	X	X	X	X				X
Sea Cucumbers									
Pale sea cucumber, *Cucumaria pulcherrima*	X	X	X	X					X
Florida sea cucumber, *Holothuria floridana*			X	X	X				X
Hairy sea cucumber, *Sclerodactyla briareus*	X	X	X	X	X				X

Phylum Chordata: Nerve Chord Animals

SPECIES	REGION					SALINITY*			
	1	2	3	4	5	F	L	M	H
Subphylum Hemichordata: Acorn Worms									
Golden acorn worm, *Balanoglossus aurantiacus*		X	X	X	X				X
Kowalevski's worm, *Saccoglossus kowalevskii*		X	X						X
Subphylum Urochordata: Tunicates									
Sea pork, *Aplidium stellatum*	X	X	X	X	X				X
Interrupted tunicate, *Ascidia interrupta*		X	X	X	X				X
Black tunicate, *Ascidia nigra*				X	X				X

SPECIES	REGION					SALINITY*			
	1	2	3	4	5	F	L	M	H
Star tunicate, *Botryllus schlosseri*	X	X							X
Lightbulb tunicate, *Clavelina oblonga*			X	X	X				X
Painted tunicate, *Clavelina picta*				X	X				X
Bermuda tunicate, *Distaplia bermudensis*		X	X	X	X				X
Mangrove tunicate, *Ecteinascidia turbinata*				X	X				X
Sandy lobed tunicate, *Eudistoma carolinense*		X	X	X	X				X
Sea liver, *Eudistoma hepaticum*		X	X	X	X				X
Sea grape, *Molgula manhattensis*	X	X						X	X
Striped tunicate, *Styela plicata*		X	X	X	X			X	X
Red encrusting tunicate, *Symplegma rubra*		X	X	X	X				X
Green encrusting tunicate, *Symplegma viride*				X	X				X

VERTEBRATES

Fishes

Sharks, Rays, and Skates

SPECIES	REGION					SALINITY*			
	1	2	3	4	5	F	L	M	H
Spotted eagle ray, *Aetobatus narinari*		X	X	X	X				X
Bull shark, *Carcharhinus leucas*	X	X	X	X	X	X	X	X	X
Sandbar shark, *Carcharhinus plumbeus*	X	X	X	X	X				X
Nurse shark, *Ginglymostoma cirratum*	X	X	X	X	X			X	X
Lemon shark, *Negaprion brevirostris*	X	X	X	X	X				X
Bonnethead shark, *Sphyrna tiburo*	X	X	X	X	X				X
Southern stingray, *Dasyatis americana*	X	X	X	X	X				X
Atlantic stingray, *Dasyatis sabina*	X	X	X	X	X		X	X	X
Bluntnose stingray, *Dasyatis say*	X	X	X	X	X			X	X
Smooth butterfly ray, *Gymnura micrura*	X	X	X	X	X		X	X	X
Cownose ray, *Rhinoptera bonasus*	X	X	X	X	X			X	X
Clearnose skate, *Raja eglanteria*	X	X	X	X	X				X

Sturgeons

SPECIES	REGION					SALINITY*			
	1	2	3	4	5	F	L	M	H
Atlantic sturgeon, *Acipenser oxyrhynchus*	X	X	X	X	X	X	X	X	X

Tarpons

SPECIES	REGION					SALINITY*			
	1	2	3	4	5	F	L	M	H
Ladyfish, *Elops saurus*	X	X	X	X	X	X	X	X	X
Tarpon, *Megalops atlanticus*	X	X	X	X	X		X	X	X

Bonefishes

SPECIES	REGION					SALINITY*			
	1	2	3	4	5	F	L	M	H
Bonefish, *Albula vulpes*			X	X	X				X

SPECIES	REGION					SALINITY*			
	1	2	3	4	5	F	L	M	H
Freshwater Eels									
American eel, *Anguilla rostrata*	█	█	█	█	█	█	█	█	█
Conger Eels									
Conger eel, *Conger oceanicus*	█	█	█	█					█
Herrings									
Blueback herring, *Alosa aestivalis*	█	█	█			█	█		
Hickory shad, *Alosa mediocris*	█	█	█			█	█		
Alewife, *Alosa pseudoharengus*	█	█	█			█	█		
American shad, *Alosa sapidissima*	█	█	█			█	█		
Atlantic menhaden, *Brevoortia tyrannus*	█	█	█	█			█	█	█
Gizzard shad, *Dorosoma cepedianum*	█	█	█			█	█		
Threadfin shad, *Dorosoma petenense*	█	█	█			█	█		
Anchovies									
Striped anchovy, *Anchoa hepsetus*	█	█	█	█	█			█	█
Bay anchovy, *Anchoa mitchilli*	█	█	█	█	█			█	█
Bullheads and Catfishes									
White catfish, *Ameiurus catus*	█	█	█			█	█		
Yellow bullhead, *Ameiurus natalis*	█	█				█	█		
Brown bullhead, *Ameiurus nebulosus*	█	█				█	█		
Channel catfish, *Ictalurus punctatus*	█	█	█			█	█		
Sea Catfishes									
Hardhead catfish, *Arius felis*		█	█	█	█	█	█	█	█
Gafftopsail catfish, *Bagre marinus*			█	█	█			█	█
Lizardfishes									
Inshore lizardfish, *Synodus foetens*	█	█	█	█	█			█	█
Toadfishes									
Oyster toadfish, *Opsanus tau*	█	█	█	█				█	█
Clingfishes									
Skilletfish, *Gobiesox strumosus*	█	█	█				█	█	█
Needlefishes									
Atlantic needlefish, *Strongylura marina*	█	█	█	█	█		█	█	█

SPECIES	REGION					SALINITY*			
	1	2	3	4	5	F	L	M	H
Killifishes									
Sheepshead minnow, *Cyprinodon variegatus*	●	●	●	●			●	●	
Gold-spotted killifish, *Floridichthys carpio*				●	●			●	
Banded killifish, *Fundulus diaphanus*	●	●	●	●		●	●		
Mummichog, *Fundulus heteroclitus*	●	●	●	●			●	●	
Striped killifish, *Fundulus majalis*	●	●	●	●			●	●	
Longnose killifish, *Fundulus similis*			●	●				●	
Livebearers									
Eastern mosquitofish, *Gambusia holbrooki*	●	●	●	●		●			
Sailfin molly, *Poecilia latipinna*		●	●	●		●	●		
Silversides									
Rough silverside, *Membras martinica*	●	●	●	●				●	
Inland silverside, *Menidia beryllina*	●	●	●	●	●	●	●	●	
Atlantic silverside, *Menidia menidia*	●	●	●	●	●			●	
Squirrelfishes									
Longspine squirrelfish, *Holocentrus rufus*				●					●
Trumpetfishes									
Trumpetfish, *Aulostomus maculatus*				●	●				●
Pipefishes and Seahorses									
Dusky pipefish, *Syngnathus floridae*	●	●	●	●				●	●
Northern pipefish, *Syngnathus fuscus*	●	●	●	●		●	●	●	●
Gulf pipefish, *Syngnathus scovelli*				●		●	●	●	●
Lined seahorse, *Hippocampus erectus*	●	●	●	●	●		●	●	●
Dwarf seahorse, *Hippocampus zosterae*				●	●			●	●
Snooks									
Common snook, *Centropomus undecimalis*			●	●	●	●	●	●	●
Temperate Basses									
White perch, *Morone americana*	●	●	●	●		●	●		
Striped bass, *Morone saxatilis*	●	●	●	●		●	●	●	●
Sea Basses									
Black sea bass, *Centropristis striata*	●	●	●	●	●				●
Sand perch, *Diplectrum formosum*		●	●	●	●				●
Goliath grouper, *Epinephelus itajara*				●	●				●

SPECIES	REGION					SALINITY*			
	1	2	3	4	5	F	L	M	H
Sunfishes									
Pumpkinseed, *Lepomis gibbosus*	■	■	■			■	■		
Bluegill, *Lepomis macrochirus*	■	■	■	■		■	■		
Largemouth bass, *Micropterus salmoides*	■	■	■	■		■	■	■	
White crappie, *Pomoxis annularis*	■	■	■			■			
Black crappie, *Pomoxis nigromaculatus*	■	■	■	■		■			
Perches									
Yellow perch, *Perca flavescens*	■	■	■			■	■		
Bluefishes									
Bluefish, *Pomatomus saltatrix*	■	■	■	■	■			■	■
Cobias									
Cobia, *Rachycentron canadum*	■	■	■	■	■			■	■
Jacks									
Blue runner, *Caranx crysos*	■	■	■	■	■				■
Crevalle jack, *Caranx hippos*	■	■	■	■	■				■
Lookdown, *Selene vomer*	■	■	■	■	■				■
Florida pompano, *Trachinotus carolinus*	■	■	■	■	■			■	■
Permit, *Trachinotus falcatus*	■	■	■	■	■				■
Palometa, *Trachinotus goodei*	■	■	■	■	■				■
Snappers									
Mutton snapper, *Lutjanus analis*	■	■	■	■	■				■
Schoolmaster snapper, *Lutjanus apodus*	■	■	■	■	■			■	■
Gray snapper, *Lutjanus griseus*	■	■	■	■	■		■	■	■
Lane snapper, *Lutjanus synagris*		■	■	■	■		■	■	■
Yellowtail snapper, *Ocyurus chrysurus*	■	■	■	■	■				■
Mojarras									
Irish pompano, *Diapterus auratus*		■	■	■					■
Spotfin mojarra, *Eucinostomus argenteus*	■	■	■	■	■				■
Silver jenny, *Eucinostomus gula*	■	■	■	■	■	■	■	■	■
Yellowfin mojarra, *Gerres cinereus*				■	■	■	■	■	■
Grunts									
Porkfish, *Anisotremus virginicus*				■	■				■
White margate, *Haemulon album*				■	■				■
Tomtate, *Haemulon aurolineatum*					■				■

SPECIES	REGION					SALINITY*			
	1	2	3	4	5	F	L	M	H
French grunt, *Haemulon flavolineatum*				▬	▬				▬
Sailor's choice, *Haemulon parra*				▬	▬				▬
White grunt, *Haemulon plumieri*	▬	▬	▬	▬	▬				▬
Pigfish, *Orthopristis chrysoptera*	▬	▬	▬	▬	▬				▬
Porgies									
Sheepshead, *Archosargus probatocephalus*	▬	▬	▬	▬	▬			▬	▬
Grass porgy, *Calamus arctifrons*					▬				▬
Spottail pinfish, *Diplodus holbrooki*		▬	▬	▬	▬				▬
Pinfish, *Lagodon rhomboides*	▬	▬	▬	▬	▬				▬
Scup, *Stenotomus chrysops*	▬	▬	▬	▬	▬				▬
Drums									
Silver perch, *Bairdiella chrysura*	▬	▬	▬	▬	▬			▬	▬
Spotted sea trout, *Cynoscion nebulosus*	▬	▬	▬	▬	▬		▬	▬	▬
Weakfish, *Cynoscion regalis*	▬	▬	▬	▬	▬				▬
Spot, *Leiostomus xanthurus*	▬	▬	▬	▬	▬		▬	▬	▬
Atlantic croaker, *Micropogonias undulatus*	▬	▬	▬	▬	▬		▬	▬	▬
Black drum, *Pogonias cromis*	▬	▬	▬	▬	▬				▬
Red drum, *Sciaenops ocellatus*	▬	▬	▬	▬	▬			▬	▬
Spadefishes									
Atlantic spadefish, *Chaetodipterus faber*	▬	▬	▬	▬	▬			▬	▬
Butterflyfishes									
Foureye butterflyfish, *Chaetodon capistratus*	▬	▬	▬	▬	▬				▬
Damselfishes									
Sergeant major, *Abudefduf saxatilis*		▬	▬	▬	▬				▬
Yellowtail damselfish, *Microspathodon chrysurus*				▬	▬				▬
Mullets									
Striped mullet, *Mugil cephalus*	▬	▬	▬	▬	▬	▬	▬	▬	▬
White mullet, *Mugil curema*	▬	▬	▬	▬	▬	▬	▬	▬	▬
Barracudas									
Great barracuda, *Sphyraena barracuda*	▬	▬	▬	▬	▬			▬	▬
Wrasses									
Slippery dick, *Halichoeres bivittatus*		▬	▬	▬	▬				▬
Tautog, *Tautoga onitis*	▬	▬	▬						▬

SPECIES	REGION					SALINITY*			
	1	2	3	4	5	F	L	M	H
Parrot Fishes									
Bucktooth parrot fish, *Sparisoma radians*				▬	▬				▬
Stoplight parrot fish, *Sparisoma viride*				▬	▬				▬
Sand Stargazers									
Northern stargazer, *Astroscopus guttatus*	▬	▬						▬	▬
Southern stargazer, *Astroscopus y-graecum*			▬					▬	▬
Blennies									
Striped blenny, *Chasmodes bosquianus*	▬	▬	▬	▬				▬	▬
Feather blenny, *Hypsoblennius hentz*	▬	▬	▬	▬				▬	▬
Hairy blenny, *Labrisomus nuchipinnis*				▬					▬
Gobies									
Naked goby, *Gobiosoma bosci*	▬	▬	▬	▬			▬	▬	▬
Seaboard goby, *Gobiosoma ginsburgi*	▬	▬	▬					▬	▬
Code goby, *Gobiosoma robustum*				▬				▬	▬
Clown goby, *Microgobius gulosus*	▬	▬	▬	▬		▬	▬	▬	▬
Green goby, *Microgobius thalassinus*	▬	▬	▬					▬	▬
Surgeonfishes									
Blue tang, *Acanthurus coeruleus*				▬					▬
Snake Mackerels									
Atlantic cutlassfish, *Trichiurus lepturus*	▬	▬	▬	▬				▬	▬
Mackerels									
Spanish mackerel, *Scomberomorus maculatus*	▬	▬	▬	▬				▬	▬
Butterfishes									
Harvestfish, *Peprilus alepidotus*	▬	▬	▬	▬			▬	▬	▬
Butterfish, *Peprilus tricanthus*	▬	▬	▬	▬	▬			▬	▬
Left-Eyed Flounders									
Peacock flounder, *Bothus lunatus*				▬					▬
Summer flounder, *Paralichthys dentatus*	▬								▬
Windowpane flounder, *Scopthalmus aquosus*	▬	▬	▬	▬					▬
Right-Eyed Flounders									
Winter flounder, *Pleuronectes americanus*	▬	▬	▬						

SPECIES	REGION					SALINITY*			
	1	2	3	4	5	F	L	M	H
Soles									
Blackcheek tonguefish, *Symphurus plagiusa*	X	X	X	X	X			X	X
Hogchoker, *Trinectes maculatus*	X	X	X	X	X		X	X	X
Leatherjackets									
Orange filefish, *Aluterus schoepfi*	X	X	X	X	X				X
Scrawled filefish, *Aluterus scriptus*			X	X	X				X
Gray triggerfish, *Balistes capriscus*	X	X	X	X	X				X
Queen triggerfish, *Balistes vetula*	X	X	X	X	X				X
Fringed filefish, *Monacanthus ciliatus*	X	X	X	X	X				X
Planehead filefish, *Monacanthus hispidus*		X	X	X	X				X
Boxfishes									
Scrawled cowfish, *Acanthostracion quadricornis*	X	X	X	X	X				X
Trunkfish, *Lactophrys trigonus*	X	X	X	X	X				X
Puffers									
Striped burrfish, *Chilomycterus schoepfi*	X	X	X	X	X				X
Northern puffer, *Sphoeroides maculatus*	X	X	X	X			X	X	X
Amphibians and Reptiles									
Amphibians									
Southern leopard frog, *Rana sphenocephala*	X	X	X	X	X	X	X		
Turtles									
Loggerhead turtle, *Caretta caretta*	X	X	X	X	X				X
Green turtle, *Chelonia mydas*	X	X	X	X	X				X
Common snapping turtle, *Chelydra serpentina*	X	X	X	X	X	X	X		
Florida snapping turtle, *Chelydra serpentina osceola*	X	X	X			X			
Chicken turtle, *Deirochelys reticularia*		X	X	X	X	X	X		
Florida chicken turtle, *Deirochelys reticularia chrysea*			X	X		X	X		
Hawksbill turtle, *Eretmochelys imbricata*	X	X	X						X
Eastern mud turtle, *Kinosternum subrubrum*	X	X				X	X		
Northern diamondback terrapin, *Malaclemys terrapin terrapin*	X	X	X				X	X	
Florida cooter, *Pseudemys floridana*	X	X	X			X			
River cooter, *Pseudemys concinna*	X	X	X	X		X			
Yellow-bellied slider, *Trachemys scripta*	X	X	X	X		X			
Common musk turtle, *Sternotherus odoratus*	X	X	X	X	X	X			

SPECIES	REGION					SALINITY*			
	1	2	3	4	5	F	L	M	H
Snakes									
Eastern diamondback rattlesnake, *Crotalus adamenteus*		■	■	■	■	▬	▬	▬	▬
Eastern cottonmouth, *Agkistrodon piscivorus*		■	■	■	■	▬			
Southern copperhead, *Agkistrodon contortrix*	■	■	■			▬			
Alligators and Crocodiles									
American alligator, *Alligator mississippiensis*	■	■	■	■	■	▬	▬		
American crocodile, *Crocodylus acutus*					■	▬	▬	▬	▬
Mammals									
Marsupials (Pouched Mammals)									
Opossum, *Didelphus virginiana*	■	■	■	■	■				
Bats									
Seminole bat, *Lasiurus seminolus*	■	■	■	■					
Eastern pipistrelle, *Pipistrellus subflavus*	■	■	■	■					
Armadillos									
Nine-banded armadillo, *Dasypus novemcinctus*			■	■	■	▬	▬	▬	▬
Rabbits									
Marsh rabbit, *Sylvilagus palustris*	■	■	■	■	■	▬	▬	▬	▬
Rodents									
Beaver, *Castor canadensis*	■	■	■			▬	▬		
Nutria, *Myocastor coypus*	■	■	■			▬			
Muskrat, *Ondatra zibethicus*	■	■	■			▬	▬		
Marsh rice rat, *Oryzomys palustris*	■	■	■	■		▬	▬	▬	
Cotton mouse, *Peromyscus gossypinus*	■	■	■	■					
Key Largo cotton mouse, *Peromyscus gossypinus allapaticola*					■				
Carnivores									
Raccoon, *Procyon lotor*	■	■	■	■	■	▬	▬	▬	
River otter, *Lutra canadensis*	■	■	■	■		▬	▬	▬	▬
Atlantic bottlenose dolphin, *Tursiops truncatus*	■	■	■	■	■			▬	▬
Manatees									
West Indian manatee, *Trichechus manatus*	▬	▬	▬	▬	▬				

APPENDIX B. Bird Species List

Common loon *Gavia immer*

Pied-billed grebe *Podilymbus podiceps*

*Magnificent frigate bird *Fregata magnificens*

American white pelican *Pelecanus erythrorhynchos*

Brown pelican *Pelecanus occidentalis*

Anhinga *Anhinga anhinga*

Double-crested cormorant *Phalacrocorax auritus*

Least bittern *Ixobrychus exilis*

American bittern *Botaurus lentiginosus*

Black-crowned night-heron *Nycticorax nycticorax*

Yellow-crowned night-heron *Nyctanassa violacea*

Green heron *Butorides virescens*

Tricolored heron *Egretta tricolor*

Little blue heron *Egretta caerulea*

*Reddish egret *Egretta rufescens*

Snowy egret *Egretta thula*

Great egret *Casmerodius albus*

Cattle egret *Bubulcus ibis*

Great blue heron *Ardea herodias*

Wood stork *Mycteria americana*

Glossy ibis *Plegadis falcinellus*

White ibis *Eudocimus albus*

*Roseate spoonbill *Ajaia ajaja*

Tundra swan *Cygnus columbianus*

Mute swan *Cygnus olor*

Snow goose *Chen caerulescens*

Canada goose *Branta canadensis*

Mallard *Anas platyrhynchos*

American black duck *Anas rubripes*

Gadwall *Anas strepera*

Green-winged teal *Anas crecca*

American wigeon *Anas americana*

Northern pintail *Anas acuta*

Northern shoveler *Anas clypeata*

Blue-winged teal *Anas discors*

Ruddy duck *Oxyura jamaicensis*

Wood duck *Aix sponsa*

Canvasback *Aythya valisineria*

Greater scaup *Aythya marila*

Lesser scaup *Aythya affinis*

Long-tailed duck *Clangula hyemalis*

Common goldeneye *Bucephala clangula*

Bufflehead *Bucephala albeola*

Red-breasted merganser *Mergus serrator*

Hooded merganser *Lophodytes cucullatus*

*Limpkin *Aramus guarauna*

King rail *Rallus elegans*

Clapper rail *Rallus longirostris*

Virginia rail *Rallus limicola*

Purple gallinule *Porphyrula martinica*

Common moorhen *Gallinula chloropus*

American coot *Fulica americana*

American oystercatcher *Haematopus palliatus*

American avocet *Recurvirostra americana*

Black-necked stilt *Himantopus mexicanus*

Wilson's plover *Charadrius wilsonia*

Semipalmated plover *Charadrius semipalmatus*

Black-bellied plover *Pluvialis squatarola*

Marbled godwit *Limosa fedoa*

Whimbrel *Numenius phaeopus*

Willet *Catoptrophorus semipalmatus*

Greater yellowlegs *Tringa melanoleuca*

*Primarily a Florida species that may infrequently stray northward.

Solitary sandpiper *Tringa solitaria*
Lesser yellowlegs *Tringa flavipes*
Short-billed dowitcher *Limnodromus griseus*
Long-billed dowitcher *Limnodromus scolopaceus*
Ruddy turnstone *Arenaria interpres*
Spotted sandpiper *Actitis macularia*
Sanderling *Calidris alba*
Dunlin *Calidris alpina*
Western sandpiper *Calidris mauri*
Least sandpiper *Calidris minutilla*
Laughing gull *Larus atricilla*
Bonaparte's gull *Larus philadelphia*
Ring-billed gull *Larus delawarensis*
Herring gull *Larus argentatus*
Great black-backed gull *Larus marinus*
Common tern *Sterna hirundo*
Forster's tern *Sterna forsteri*
Least tern *Sterna antillarum*

Royal tern *Sterna maxima*
Caspian tern *Sterna caspia*
Black skimmer *Rynchops niger*
Turkey vulture *Cathartes aura*
Black vulture *Coragyps atratus*
Bald eagle *Haliaeetus leucocephalus*
Northern harrier *Circus cyaneus*
Red-tailed hawk *Buteo jamaicensis*
Osprey *Pandion haliaetus*
*White-crowned pigeon *Columba leucocephala*
Belted kingfisher *Ceryle alcyon*
Tree swallow *Tachycineta bicolor*
Barn swallow *Hirundo rustica*
Fish crow *Corvus ossifragus*
Prothonotary warbler *Protonotaria citrea*
Red-winged blackbird *Agelaius phoeniceus*
Boat-tailed grackle *Quiscalus major*

Glossary

Adipose fin: A fleshy, lobe-like fin without supporting rays, situated on the back, behind the dorsal fin, on some fishes, particularly salmons and catfishes.

Alternate arrangement: Leaves or buds that are positioned alternately along a stem.

Ambulacral groove: The furrow on the ventral side, or underside, of sea star arms, where the tube feet are positioned.

Amphipod: A small crustacean, usually with a laterally compressed body, belonging to the phylum Arthropoda.

Anadromous: Fishes, such as herrings, that migrate from the ocean to freshwater to spawn.

Aperture: In gastropods, the opening of the shell out of which the head and foot protrude.

Apex: The narrow, usually pointed end of a snail's shell.

Axial ribs: Ribs or raised ridges, usually parallel to the lengthwise axis of the shell, from the apex to the base.

Axil: The angle between a leaf or branch and the stem.

Axillaries: The feathers that line the wings in the armpit region of birds.

Barbels: Fleshy, elongated, tactile whiskers, usually located on the lower jaw or in the corners of the mouth, in some fishes.

Basal disk: The bottom end of sea anemones and certain jellyfish polyps that is attached to a substrate.

Beak: A rounded swelling, also called the umbo, near the hinge in clams, mussels, and other bivalves; the bill of birds and the mouth part of some cephalopods, turtles, and whales and porpoises.

Benthos: Aquatic plants and animals that live in or on the bottom.

Body whorl: The largest and final coil of a snail shell.

Byssus: A bundle of rubbery fibers created by mussels and some other mollusks that anchors the mollusk to a substrate; the beard of a mussel.

Carapace: The hard exoskeleton covering a crustacean's head and thorax; the upper shell of a turtle.

Cardinal teeth: Ridges, protuberances, or grooves on the inner shell surface near the ligament and beak that serve to hold the shell in alignment.

Catadromous: Pertaining to fishes, such as the American eel, that migrate from freshwater to the ocean to spawn.

Catkin: A scaly spike of small, usually inconspicuous flowers.

Caudal peduncle: The narrow part of the fish that connects the body to the tail fin.

Chondrophore: A spoon-shaped indentation in the hinge that serves as a place of attachment for the ligament.

Colonial animals: An association of individual organisms that are interconnected, such as bryozoans and corals, or an association of single or related species, such as barnacles, that settle down in close proximity, or various species of herons and egrets that come together to nest.

Columella: The axis around which the shell coils in a snail shell.

Compound leaf: A leaf that is separated into two or more parts (leaflets).

Cypris: The second stage, free-swimming larva, of a barnacle, which metamorphoses into the adult.

Deciduous: Leaves that shed and are not persistent.

Dextral: In snails, having the aperture to the right side of the shell axis when the shell is held with the apex pointing upward and the aperture facing the viewer.

Drupe: A fleshy fruit surrounding a pit or stone.

Elytra: A modified horny forewing common in beetles and true bugs.

Entire: Referring to leaves with smooth or wavy margins and without teeth.

Epibenthos: Plants and animals that live on the surface of the bottom.

Epifauna: Animals that inhabit or move over the substrate in aquatic habitats.

Epiphyte: A plant that grows on another plant, such as a resurrection fern growing on a live oak.

Euryhaline: Pertaining to organisms that are physiologically adapted to a broad range of salinities.

Fouling organisms: Organisms, such as barnacles and mussels, that settle on boat hulls and pilings and other hard surfaces.

Girdle: The muscular portion of the mantle that borders the eight shell plates or valves.

Gorgonin: A complex of fibrous protein that forms the internal skeleton of gorgonian soft corals, such as sea whips and sea fans.

Hectocotylus: In cephalopods, a modified arm for the transfer of a spermatophore into the mantle cavity of the female.

Herbaceous: Fleshy or nonwoody plant.

Heteronereis: Highly modified breeding form of certain species of polychaete worms adapted for spawning in the water column.

Hinge: The dorsal margin of clams and other bivalves that functions to open and close the valves (shells).

Hinge teeth: Toothlike projections on the inner shell surface of bivalves that prevent slippage of the valves.

Hydroid: The polyp form of hydrozoans (phylum Cnidaria): a complicated colonial form often composed of highly specialized feeding and reproductive individuals.

Hydromedusa: The sexually reproductive jellyfish stage of hydrozoans.

Infauna: Benthic animals that live within the soft bottom, usually in tubes or burrows.

Inner lip: See *parietal wall*.

Isopod: A small crustacean belonging to phylum Arthropoda, usually dorsally and ventrally flattened.

Larva: The immature form of some animals, usually invertebrates and fishes.

Ligament: In bivalves, the strong, elastic, usually dark band that joins the two valves and provides leverage against the adductor muscle.

Madreporite: The sieve plate that is linked to the water vascular system in echinoderms and is particularly visible on sea stars on the aboral or dorsal surface.

Mantle: The back of a bird, including the upper surface of its wings; a fleshy tissue surrounding a mollusk's body that secretes the shell.

Marsupium: A specialized pouch in various species for brooding eggs and young.

Medusa: The sexually reproductive stage of certain cnidarians; the jellyfish stage usually characterized by a gelatinous, saucer-shaped bell and trailing tentacles.

Megalopa: The large-eyed, second-stage larval form of crabs that metamorphoses into a juvenile crab.

Mesoglea: The jellylike layer between the external and internal tissues of a cnidarian.

Nacre: The shiny, pearly lining on the inside of some mollusk shells; also known as mother-of-pearl.

Naiad: The aquatic larva of certain insects, such as dragonflies.

Nape: The back of the neck.

Nauplius: The first larva in some crustaceans, such as copepods and barnacles; usually abundant in the plankton.

Nekton: Pelagic animals capable of swimming with a directed velocity.

Nematocyst: Stinging cell of jellyfishes, anemones, and other cnidarians for injecting toxins and capturing prey.

Nymph: Larva of terrestrial insects that undergo simple metamorphosis.

Operculum: The leathery or horny plate attached to the foot in some snails that seals off the aperture when the animal withdraws into its shell.

Opposite arrangement: Leaves or buds positioned oppositely along a stem.

Osculum: The large, excurrent pore on the surface of a sponge.

Outer lip: In snails, the edge or external margin of the body whorl.

Oviparous: A reproductive stage in which eggs are released to the environment.

Ovoviviparous: A reproductive stage in which the eggs are brooded internally and released as larvae.

Panicle: A highly branched, flowering structure of some grasses.

Parapodia: In Polychaete worms, paddlelike appendages extending from the body segments for locomotion and respiration.

Parietal wall: In gastropods, the wall or region of the body whorl opposite the outer lip.

Pedicellariae: Pincerlike organs on the bodies of sea stars and sea urchins that are used for defense and grooming.

Pelagic: Pertaining to the open waters of seas and other bodies of water or to the organism suspended or swimming in those waters.

Periderm: The thin exoskeleton of certain hydroids.

Periostracum: The thin, horny, organic layer of mollusk shells.

Phytoplankton: Free-floating or weakly motile groups of microscopic aquatic plants that drift with the currents.

Plankton: The entire community of floating and weak-swimming plants and animals transported by currents and tides.

Plastron: The bottom shell of a turtle.

Pneumatophore: Specialized roots of certain mangroves that emerge above the waterlogged soil to allow the exchange of gases.

Primaries: The outermost and longest flight feathers on a bird's wing.

Pupa: The inactive form of an insect between the larval stage and the adult.

Radula: The chitinous rasping teeth of gastropods.

Rhizome: An underground horizontal or ascending stem.

Rostrum: In Crustacea, an anterior extension of the carapace projecting between the eye stalks.

Salinity: The combined weight of certain salts dissolved in one kilogram of seawater and usually expressed as parts of salt per thousand parts of water (ppt).

Scute: A large scale or plate covering a turtle's shell.

Sepal: An individual segment, usually green, surrounding a flower.

Shrub: A woody bush, usually 20 feet tall or shorter, and often multistemmed.

Sinistral: In snails, having the aperture to the left side of the shell axis when the shell is held with the apex pointing upward and the aperture facing the viewer.

Spat: Newly attached juvenile oysters.

Speculum: Iridescent or brightly colored feathers on the trailing edge of a duck's wing.

Spiral coils: The turns or whorls of a snail shell.

Stamen: The male reproductive organ of a flower.

Stolon: A horizontal stem or runner that forms new plants at nodes or at its end.

Suture: The juncture or groove between individual whorls of a snail shell.

Swamp: A wetland containing water-loving trees and shrubs.

Telson: The terminal abdominal segment of crustaceans.

Test: The body shell of a sea urchin.

Thorax: The intermediate section of an insect's body bearing the wings and legs.

Trochophore: The first larval stage of polychaete worms and mollusks.

Tuber: A fleshy, enlarged portion of an underground stem.

Tunic: The outer covering of a tunicate.

Uropod: The tail fan of some crustaceans.

Veliger: A free-swimming larva of mollusks.

Viviparous: The reproductive stage in which the embryos develop within the mother and the young are live.

Zoea: The tiny, planktonic, larval stage of crabs.

Zooecium: In bryozoans, the individual covering or chamber in which each animal dwells.

Zooid: One of the individual animals of hydroid or bryozoan colonies.

Zooplankton: Groups of floating or weak-swimming animals that are transported by currents and tides.

Selected References

REGIONAL

Brown, Alexander Crosby. *Juniper Waterway, a History of the Albemarle and Chesapeake Canal.* Charlottesville: University Press of Virginia, 1981.

Fisher, Allan C., Jr. *America's Inland Waterway: Exploring the Atlantic Seaboard.* Washington, D.C.: National Geographic Society, 1973.

Kirk, Paul W., Jr., ed. *The Great Dismal Swamp.* Charlottesville: University Press of Virginia, 1979.

Lane, Carl D. *Go South Inside: Cruising the Inland Waterway.* Camden: International Marine, 1977.

Simpson, Bland. *The Great Dismal: A Carolinian's Swamp Memory.* Chapel Hill: University of North Carolina Press, 1990.

Stick, David. *The Outer Banks of North Carolina: 1584–1958.* Chapel Hill: University of North Carolina Press, 1958.

NATURAL HISTORY

Amos, William H., and Stephen H. Amos. *Atlantic and Gulf Coasts.* Audubon Society Nature Guides. New York: Knopf, 1985.

Colin, Patrick L. *Marine Invertebrates and Plants of the Living Reef.* Neptune City, N.J.: TFH, 1978.

Fotheringham, Nick, and Susan Lee Brunenmeister. *Common Marine Invertebrates of the Northwestern Gulf Coast.* Houston: Gulf, 1975.

Frankenberg, Dirk. *The Nature of North Carolina's Southern Coast: Barrier Islands, Coastal Waters, and Wetlands.* Chapel Hill: University of North Carolina Press, 1997.

George, Jean Craighead. *Everglades Wildguide: The Natural History of Everglades National Park, Florida.* Washington, D.C.: U.S. Department of the Interior, 1988.

Gosner, Kenneth L. *A Field Guide to the Atlantic Seashore: Invertebrates and Seaweeds of the Atlantic Coast from the Bay of Fundy to Cape Hatteras.* Peterson Field Guide Series. Boston: Houghton Mifflin, 1978.

Kaplan, Eugene H. *A Field Guide to Coral Reefs of the Caribbean and Florida.* Peterson Field Guide Series. Boston: Houghton Mifflin, 1982.

———. *A Field Guide to Southeastern and Caribbean Seashores: Cape Hatteras to the Gulf Coast, Florida, and the Caribbean.* Peterson Field Guide Series. Boston: Houghton Mifflin, 1988.

Keatts, Henry. *Beachcomber's Guide from Cape Cod to Cape Hatteras.* Houston, Tex.: Gulf, 1995.

Langley, Lynne. *Nature Watch in the Carolina Lowcountry.* Charleston, S.C.: News and Courier, 1987.

Larson, Ron. *Swamp Song: A Natural History of Florida's Swamps.* Gainesville: University Press of Florida, 1995.

Lazell, James D., Jr. *Wildlife of the Florida Keys: A Natural History.* Washington, D.C.: Island Press, 1989.

Lippson, Alice Jane, and Robert L. Lippson. *Life in the Chesapeake Bay: An Illustrated Guide to the Fishes, Invertebrates, Plants, Birds and Other Animals of Bays and Inlets from Cape Cod to Cape Hatteras.* 3rd ed. Baltimore: Johns Hopkins University Press, 2006.

Meyer, Peter. *Nature Guide to the Carolina Coast: Common Birds, Crabs, Shells, Fish and Other Entities of the Coastal Environment.* Wilmington, N.C.: Avian-Cetacean Press, 1991.

Niering, William A. *Wetlands.* Audubon Society Nature Guides. New York: Knopf, 1985.

Spitsbergen, Judith M. *Seacoast Life: An Ecological*

Guide to Natural Seashore Communities in North Carolina. Chapel Hill: University of North Carolina Press, 1980.

Voss, Gilbert L. *Seashore Life of Florida and the Caribbean.* Miami: Banyan Books, 1976.

Waller, Geoffrey, ed. *SeaLife: A Complete Guide to the Marine Environment.* Washington, D.C.: Smithsonian Institution Press, 1996.

Wernert, Susan J., ed. *Reader's Digest North American Wildlife.* Pleasantville, N.Y.: Reader's Digest Association, 1996.

Zim, Herbert S., and Lester Ingle. *Seashores: A Guide to Shells, Sea Plants, Shore Birds, and Other Natural Features of American Coasts.* Golden Nature Guide. New York: Simon and Schuster, 1955.

SEAWEEDS

Dawson, E. Yale, and Isabella A. Abbott. *How to Know the Seaweeds.* 2nd ed. Pictured Key Nature Series. Dubuque, Iowa: Brown, 1978.

Kingsbury, John M. *Seaweeds of Cape Cod and the Islands.* Chatham, Mass.: Chatham Press, 1969.

Littler, Diane Scullion, Mark M. Littler, Katina E. Bucher, and James N. Norris. *Marine Plants of the Caribbean: A Field Guide from Florida to Brazil.* Washington, D.C.: Smithsonian Institution Press, 1989.

Taylor, William Randolph. *Marine Algae of the Northeastern Coast of North America.* Ann Arbor: University of Michigan Press, 1957.

OTHER PLANTS

Austin, Daniel. *Coastal Dune Plants: A Pocket Guide to the Common Wildflowers, Trees, Shrubs and Vines of Southeast Florida's Ocean-side Communities.* Palm Beach, Fla.: Gumbo Limbo Nature Center, 1991.

Bell, C. Ritchie, and Bryan J. Taylor. *Florida Wildflowers and Roadside Plants.* Chapel Hill, N.C.: Laurel Hill Press, 1982.

Duncan, Wilbur H., and Marion B. Duncan. *The Smithsonian Guide to Seaside Plants of the Gulf and Atlantic Coasts from Louisiana to Massachusetts,* *Exclusive of Lower Peninsular Florida.* Washington, D.C.: Smithsonian Institution Press, 1987.

———. *Trees of the Southeastern United States.* Athens: University of Georgia Press, 1988.

———. *Wildflowers of the Eastern United States.* Athens: University of Georgia Press, 1999.

Eastman, John. *The Book of Swamp and Bog: Trees, Shrubs, and Wildflowers of Eastern Freshwater Wetlands.* Mechanicsburg, Penn.: Stackpole Books, 1995.

Elias, Thomas S. *The Complete Trees of North America: Field Guide and Natural History.* New York: Outdoor Life/Nature Books, 1980.

Forey, Pamela. *American Nature Guides: Wild Flowers.* Surrey: Dragon's World, 1990.

Harrar, Ellwood S., and J. George Harrar. *Guide to Southern Trees.* New York: Dover, 1962.

Justice, William S., and C. Ritchie Bell. *Wild Flowers of North Carolina: Also Covering Virginia, South Carolina, and Areas of Georgia, Tennessee, Kentucky, West Virginia, Maryland, and Delaware.* Chapel Hill: University of North Carolina Press, 1968.

Kingsbury, John M. *200 Conspicuous, Unusual, or Economically Important Tropical Plants of the Caribbean.* Ithaca, N.Y.: Bullbrier Press, 1988.

Lötschert, Wilhelm, and Gerhard Beese. *Collins Guide to Tropical Plants.* London: Collins, 1983.

Nelson, Gil. *The Shrubs and Woody Vines of Florida: A Reference and Field Guide.* Sarasota: Pineapple Press, 1996.

———. *The Trees of Florida: A Reference and Field Guide.* Sarasota, Fla.: Pineapple Press, 1994.

Niering, William A., and Nancy C. Olmstead. *National Audubon Society Field Guide to North American Wildflowers: Eastern Region.* New York: Knopf, 1998.

Petry, Loren C. *A Beachcomber's Botany.* Chatham, Mass.: Chatham Conservation Foundation, 1963.

Porcher, Richard D. *Wildflowers of the Carolina Lowcountry and Lower Pee Dee.* Columbia: University of South Carolina Press, 1995.

Silberhorn, G. M. *Common Plants of the Mid-Atlantic Coast: A Field Guide.* Rev. ed. Baltimore: Johns Hopkins University Press, 1999.

Stuckey, Irene H., and Lisa Lofland Gould. *Coastal Plants from Cape Cod to Cape Canaveral*. Chapel Hill: University of North Carolina Press, 2000.

Taylor, Walter Kingsley. *The Guide to Florida Wildflowers*. Dallas: Taylor, 1992.

Tiner, Ralph W. *Field Guide to Coastal Wetland Plants of the Southeastern United States*. Amherst: University of Massachusetts Press, 1993.

INVERTEBRATES

Abbott, R. Tucker. *American Seashells*. Princeton, N.J.: Van Nostrand, 1954.

———. *A Guide to Field Identification: Seashells of North America*. New York: Golden Press, 1968.

Andrews, Jean. *A Field Guide to Shells of the Florida Coast*. Nature Field Guide Series. Houston, Tex.: Gulf, 1994.

Borradaile, L. A., and F. A. Potts. *The Invertebrata: A Manual for the Use of Students*. London: Cambridge University Press, 1961.

Borror, Donald J., and Richard E. White. *A Field Guide to Insects: America North of Mexico*. Peterson Field Guide Series. Boston: Houghton Mifflin, 1970.

Brusca, Richard C., and Gary J. Brusca. *Invertebrates*. Sunderland: Sinauer Associates, 1990.

Dunkle, Sidney W. *Dragonflies through Binoculars: A Field Guide to Dragonflies of North America*. Oxford: Oxford University Press, 2000.

Gosner, Kenneth L. *Guide to Identification of Marine and Estuarine Invertebrates: Cape Hatteras to the Bay of Fundy*. New York: Wiley-Interscience, 1971.

Hendler, Gordon, John E. Miller, David L. Pawson, and Porter M. Kier. *Sea Stars, Sea Urchins, and Allies: Echinoderms of Florida and the Caribbean*. Washington, D.C.: Smithsonian Institution Press, 1995.

Humann, Paul. *Reef Coral Identification: Florida, Caribbean and the Bahamas; Including Marine Plants*. Jacksonville, Fla.: New World, 1993.

———. *Reef Creature Identification: Florida, Caribbean and Bahamas*. Jacksonville, Fla.: New World, 1992.

Johnson, William S., and Dennis M. Allen. *Zooplankton of the Atlantic and Gulf Coasts: A Guide to Their Identification and Ecology*. Baltimore: Johns Hopkins University Press, 2005.

Meinkoth, Norman A. *The Audubon Society Field Guide to North American Seashore Creatures*. New York: Knopf, 1981.

Milne, Lorus, and Margery Milne. *The Audubon Field Guide to North American Insects and Spiders*. New York: Knopf, 1980.

Morris, Percy A. *A Field Guide to Shells of the Atlantic and Gulf Coasts and the West Indies*. 3rd ed. Peterson Field Guide Series. Boston: Houghton Mifflin, 1975.

Porter, Hugh J., and Jim Tyler. *Sea Shells Common to North Carolina*. Raleigh: North Carolina Department of Natural and Economic Resources, Division of Commercial and Sports Fisheries, 1971.

Rehder, Harald A. *The Audubon Society Field Guide to North American Seashells*. New York: Knopf, 1981.

Robin, B. *Living Corals*. Singapore: Times Editions, 1980.

Roessler, Carl. *Coral Kingdoms*. New York: Abrams, 1990.

Ruppert, Edward, and Richard Fox. *Seashore Animals of the Southeast: A Guide to Common Shallow-Water Invertebrates of the Southeastern Atlantic Coasts*. Columbia: University of South Carolina Press, 1988.

Schultz, George A. *How to Know the Marine Isopods*. Dubuque, Iowa: Brown, 1969.

Williams, Austin B. *Shrimps, Lobsters, and Crabs of the Atlantic Coast of the Eastern United States, Maine to Florida*. Washington, D.C.: Smithsonian Institution Press, 1984.

Williams, Winston. *Florida's Fabulous Seashells and Other Seashore Life*. Tampa, Fla.: World, 1988

Zeiller, Warren. *Tropical Marine Invertebrates of Southern Florida and the Bahama Islands*. New York: Wiley, 1974.

FISHES

Allen, Thomas B. *The Shark Almanac: A Fully Illustrated Natural History of Sharks, Skates, and Rays*. New York: Lyons Press, 1999.

Böhlke, James E., and Charles C. G. Chaplin. *Fishes of the Bahamas and Adjacent Tropical Waters.* Wynnewood, Penn.: Livingston, 1968.

Boschung, Herbert T., Jr., James D. Williams, Daniel W. Gotshall, David K. Caldwell, and Melba C. Caldwell. *The Audubon Society Field Guide to North American Fishes, Whales, and Dolphins.* New York: Knopf, 1983.

Fischer, W., ed. *FAO Species Identification Sheets for Fishery Purposes: Western Central Atlantic.* Vols. 1–6. Rome: Food and Agricultural Organization of the United Nations, 1978.

Hildebrand, Samuel F., and William C. Schroeder. *Fishes of Chesapeake Bay.* Bulletin of the U.S. Bureau of Fisheries 43 (1928). Reprint, Washington, D.C.: U.S. Government Printing Office, 1995.

Humann, Paul. *Reef Fish Identification: Florida, Caribbean and Bahamas.* Jacksonville, Fla.: New World, 1994.

La Monte, Francesca. *North American Game Fishes.* Garden City, N.Y.: Doubleday, Doran, 1945.

Manooch, Charles S., III. *Fisherman's Guide: Fishes of the Southeastern United States.* Raleigh: North Carolina State Museum of Natural History, 1984.

Moore, Charles J., and Charles H. Farmer III. *An Angler's Guide to South Carolina Sharks.* Charleston: South Carolina Wildlife and Marine Resources Department.

Moore, Charles J., Donald L. Hammond, and Elizabeth C. Roland. *A Guide to Saltwater Recreational Fisheries in South Carolina.* Charleston: South Carolina Wildlife and Marine Resources Department.

Murdy, Edward O., Ray S. Birdsong, and John A. Musick. *Fishes of Chesapeake Bay.* Washington, D.C.: Smithsonian Institution Press, 1997.

Page, Lawrence M., and Brooks M. Burr. *A Field Guide to Freshwater Fishes: North America, North of Mexico.* Peterson Field Guide Series. Boston: Houghton Mifflin, 1991.

Robbins, C. Richard, and G. Carleton Ray. *A Field Guide to Atlantic Coast Fishes of North America.* Peterson Field Guide Series. Boston: Houghton Mifflin, 1986.

Rohde, Fred C., Rudolf G. Arndt, David G. Lindquist, and James F. Parnell. *Freshwater Fishes of the Carolinas, Virginia, Maryland, and Delaware.* Chapel Hill: University of North Carolina Press, 1994.

Sale, Peter F., ed. *The Ecology of Fishes on Coral Reefs.* San Diego: Academic Press, 1991.

Schwartz, Frank J., and Jim Tyler. *Marine Fishes Common to North Carolina.* Raleigh: North Carolina Department of Conservation and Development, 1970.

Smith, C. Lavett. *National Audubon Society Field Guide to Tropical Marine Fishes of the Caribbean, the Gulf of Mexico, the Bahamas, and Bermuda.* New York: Knopf, 1997.

Wheeler, Alwyne. *Fishes of the World: An Illustrated Dictionary.* New York: Macmillan, 1975.

AMPHIBIANS AND REPTILES

Ashton, Ray E., Jr., and Patricia Sawyer Ashton. *Handbook of Reptiles and Amphibians of Florida.* 2 vols. 2nd ed. Miami, Fla.: Windward, 1988–91.

Behler, John L., and F. Wayne King. *The Audubon Society Field Guide to North American Reptiles and Amphibians.* New York: Knopf, 1979.

Carmichael, Pete, and Winston Williams. *Florida's Fabulous Reptiles and Amphibians.* Tampa, Fla.: World, 1991.

Carr, Archie. *The Sea Turtle: So Excellent a Fishe.* Austin: University of Texas Press, 1986.

Conant, Roger, and Joseph T. Collins. *Reptiles and Amphibians: Eastern Central North America.* Peterson Field Guide Series. Boston: Houghton Mifflin, 1991.

Duellman, William E., and Linda Trueb. *Biology of Amphibians.* Baltimore: Johns Hopkins University Press, 1994.

Martof, Bernard S., William M. Palmer, Joseph R. Bailey, and Julian R. Harrison III. *Amphibians and Reptiles of the Carolinas and Virginia.* Chapel Hill: University of North Carolina Press, 1980.

Spotila, James R. *Sea Turtles: A Complete Guide to Their Biology, Behavior, and Conservation.* Baltimore: Johns Hopkins University Press, 2004.

BIRDS

Bull, John, and John Farrand Jr. *The Audubon Society Field Guide to North American Birds: Eastern Region.* New York: Knopf, 1977.

Burton, Phillip, Trevor Boyar, Malcolm Ellis, and David Thelwell. *Birds of Prey: American Nature Guides.* New York: Gallery Books, 1991.

Cameron, Ad, and Christopher Perrins. *Birds: Their Life, Their Ways, Their World.* New York: Abrams, 1976.

Ehrlich, Paul R., David S. Dobkin, and Darryl Wheye. *The Birder's Handbook: A Field Guide to the Natural History of North American Birds.* New York: Simon and Schuster, 1988.

Forbush, Edward Howe, and John Richard May. *Natural History of the Birds of Eastern and Central North America.* Boston: Houghton Mifflin, 1939.

Fussell, John O., III. *A Birder's Guide to Coastal North Carolina.* Chapel Hill: University of North Carolina Press, 1994.

Hancock, James, and James Kushlan. *The Herons Handbook.* New York: Harper and Row, 1984.

Harrison, Peter. *Seabirds: An Identification Guide.* Boston: Houghton Mifflin, 1983.

Hayman, Peter, John Marchant, and Tony Prater. *Shorebirds: An Identification Guide to the Waders of the World.* Boston: Houghton Mifflin, 1986.

Kaufman, Kenn. *Lives of North American Birds.* Peterson Natural History Companions. Boston: Houghton Mifflin, 1996.

Peterson, Roger Tory. *A Field Guide to the Birds: East of the Rockies.* 4th ed. Peterson Field Guide Series. Boston: Houghton Mifflin, 1980.

Potter, Eloise F., James F. Parnell, and Robert P. Teulings. *Birds of the Carolinas.* Chapel Hill: University of North Carolina Press, 1980.

Richards, Alan. *Shorebirds: A Complete Guide to Their Behavior and Migration.* New York: Gallery Books, 1988.

Sibley, David Allen. *National Audubon Society: The Sibley Guide to Birds.* New York: Knopf, 2000.

Stokes, Donald, and Lillian Stokes. *Stokes Field Guide to Birds: Eastern Region.* Boston: Little, Brown, 1996.

Terres, John K. *The Audubon Society Encyclopedia of North American Birds.* New York: Wings Books, 1980.

Tinbergen, Niko. *The Herring Gull's World: A Study of the Social Behaviour of Birds.* New York: Basic Books, 1961.

Williams, Winston. *Florida's Fabulous Birds.* Tampa, Fla.: World, 1987.

MAMMALS

Brown, Larry N. *Mammals of Florida.* Miami, Fla.: Windward, 1997.

Burt, William H., and Richard P. Grossenheider. *A Field Guide to the Mammals: North America North of Mexico.* Peterson Field Guide Series. Boston: Houghton Mifflin, 1980.

Leatherwood, Stephen, David K. Caldwell, and Howard E. Winn. *Whales, Dolphins, and Porpoises of the Western North Atlantic: A Guide to Their Identification.* Seattle: U.S. Dept. of Commerce, National Oceanic and Atmospheric Administration, National Marine Fisheries Service, 1976.

Nowak, Ronald M. *Walker's Bats of the World.* Baltimore: Johns Hopkins University Press, 1994.

Nowak, Ronald M., and John L. Paradiso. *Walker's Mammals of the World.* Vols. 1–2. Baltimore: Johns Hopkins University Press, 1983.

Whitaker, James O., Jr. *The Audubon Society Field Guide to North American Mammals.* New York: Knopf, 1980.

SPECIAL AND TECHNICAL PUBLICATIONS

Bahr, Leonard M., and William P. Lanier. *The Ecology of Intertidal Oyster Reefs of the South Atlantic Coast: A Community Profile.* Washington, D.C.: National Coastal Ecosystems Team, Office of Biological

Services, U.S. Fish and Wildlife Service, U.S. Department of the Interior, 1981.

Cairns, Stephen D., et al. *Common and Scientific Names of Aquatic Invertebrates from the United States and Canada: Cnidaria and Ctenophora*. Bethesda, Md.: American Fisheries Society, 1991.

Nelson, David M., Mark E. Monaco, Elizabeth A. Irlandi, Lawrence R. Settle, and Linda Coston-Clements. *Distribution and Abundance of Fishes and Invertebrates in Southeast Estuaries*. Estuarine Living Marine Resources report no. 9. Rockville, Md.: Strategic Environmental Assessments Division, National Oceanic and Atmospheric Administration/National Ocean Service, 1991.

Odum, William C., Carole C. McIvor, and Thomas J. Smith III. *The Ecology of the Mangroves of South Florida: A Community Profile*. Washington, D.C.: National Coastal Ecosystems Team, U.S. Fish and Wildlife Service, U.S. Department of the Interior, 1982.

Ogden, John C., and Robert C. Carpenter. *Species Profiles: Life Histories and Environmental Requirements of Coastal Fishes and Invertebrates (South Florida); Long-Spined Black Sea Urchin*. Biological Report 82 (11.77). Washington, D.C.: U.S. Fish and Wildlife Service, U.S. Department of the Interior, 1987.

Peterson, Charles H., and Nancy M. Peterson. *The Ecology of Intertidal Flats of North Carolina: A Community Profile*. Slidell, La.: National Coastal Ecosystems Team, U.S. Fish and Wildlife Service, 1979.

Richards, W. J., ed. "Indian River Lagoon Biodiversity Conference." *Bulletin of Marine Science* 57, no. 1 (1995).

Robins, C. Richard, et al. 1991. *Common and Scientific Names of Fishes from the United States and Canada*. 5th ed. Bethesda, Md.: American Fisheries Society, 1991.

Sverdrup, H. U., Martin W. Johnson, and Richard H. Fleming. *The Oceans: Their Physics, Chemistry, and General Biology*. Englewood Cliffs, N.J.: Prentice-Hall, 1942.

Thayer, Gordon W., W. Judson Kenworthy, and Mark S. Fonseca. *The Ecology of Eelgrass Meadows of the Atlantic Coast: A Community Profile*. Washington, D.C.: U.S. Fish and Wildlife Service, U.S. Department of the Interior, 1984.

Turgeon, Donna D., et al. *Common and Scientific Names of Aquatic Invertebrates from the United States and Canada: Mollusks*. Bethesda, Md.: American Fisheries Society, 1988.

U.S. Department of Commerce. *United States Coast Pilot 4, Atlantic Coast: Cape Henry to Key West*. Washington, D.C.: U.S. Government Printing Office, 1985.

Williams, Austin B., et al. *Common and Scientific Names of Aquatic Invertebrates from the United States and Canada: Decapod Crustaceans*. Bethesda, Md.: American Fisheries Society, 1989.

Zale, Alexander V., and Susan G. Merrifield. *Species Profiles: Life Histories and Environmental Requirements of Coastal Fishes and Invertebrates (South Florida); Reef-Building Tubeworm*. Biological Report 82 (11.115). Washington, D.C.: U.S. Fish and Wildlife Service, U.S. Department of the Interior, 1989.

Zieman, Joseph C. *The Ecology of the Seagrasses of South Florida: A Community Profile*. Washington, D.C.: National Coastal Ecosystems Team, Office of Biological Services, U.S. Fish and Wildlife Service, U.S. Department of the Interior, 1982.

Index

Note: Page numbers in italics refer to illustrations.